PENGUIN BOOKS

CHARLES DICKENS:
HIS TRAGEDY AND TRIUMPH

Born in New York City in 1901, Edgar Johnson was graduated from Columbia University in 1922. His first books were the novels *Unweave a Rainbow* and *The Praying Mantis*. These were followed by *One Mighty Torrent: The Drama of Biography* and by two critical anthologies, *A Treasury of Biography* and *A Treasury of Satire*. His other works include *The Dickens Theatrical Reader* (with Eleanor Johnson) and *The Heart of Charles Dickens: His Letters to Angela Burdett Courtts*. In 1953 the two-volume edition of *Charles Dickens: His Tragedy and Triumph* appeared to great critical acclaim, and in 1970 Edgar Johnson published another much-praised two-volume study, *Sir Walter Scott: The Great Unknown* (which won the American Heritage Biography Prize). He has contributed to numerous journals and periodicals. Professor Johnson has served on the faculties of Columbia University, Washington University, and Hunter College; been a visiting professor at Princeton University, the University of Chicago, Vanderbilt University, the University of Hawaii, and Vassar College; and lectured at Harvard University, Yale University, Cambridge University, Edinburgh University, and the Sorbonne. Presently a Distinguished Professor Emeritus of the City University of New York, he lives in Manhattan and is at work on another biographical study.

DICKENS AT TWENTY-FIVE

From the Drawing by
Samuel Laurence, 1837

Edgar Johnson

Charles Dickens

HIS TRAGEDY AND TRIUMPH

Revised and Abridged

PENGUIN BOOKS

Penguin Books Ltd, Harmondsworth,
Middlesex, England
Penguin Books, 625 Madison Avenue,
New York, New York 10022, U.S.A.
Penguin Books Australia Ltd, Ringwood,
Victoria, Australia
Penguin Books Canada Limited, 2801 John Street,
Markham, Ontario, Canada L3R 1B4
Penguin Books (N.Z.) Ltd, 182–190 Wairau Road,
Auckland 10, New Zealand

First published in the United States of America and
Great Britain in two volumes 1952
This revised and abridged edition first published in the United States
of America by The Viking Press (A Seaver Book) 1977
This revised and abridged edition first published
in Great Britain by Allen Lane 1977
Published in Penguin Books 1979

LIBRARY OF CONGRESS CATALOGING IN PUBLICATION DATA
Johnson, Edgar.
Charles Dickens, his tragedy and triumph.
Includes index.
1. Dickens, Charles, 1812–1870—Biography.
2. Novelists, English—19th century—Bio-
graphy. I. Title.
PR4581.J6 1979 823'.8 [B] 78-20982
ISBN 0 14 00.4895 2

Printed in the United States of America by
Offset Paperback Mfrs., Inc., Dallas, Pennsylvania
Set in Monotype Baskerville and Linotype Electra

Appreciation is expressed to the following for their courtesy in granting
permission to reproduce various pictures from their collections in the
photographic sections of this book:

New York Public Library Picture Collection: 3, 4, 15, 16, 17, 18, 19, 21, 22,
23, 27, 44, 47, 52, 57, 60, 62, 63, 64, 65, 66, 67, 68, 79, 80, 85
Dickens House, Doughty Street, London: 11, 20, 25, 43, 53, 59
National Portrait Gallery, London: 24
Major Philip Dickens and Dickens House, Doughty Street, London: 30
Leigh B. Block: 31
Leslie C. Staples: 37
Carlyle House, Cheyne Row, Chelsea, London: 40, 41
Central Office of Information, London: 72
William M. Elkins Collection, Philadelphia: 84

The following are from a rare portfolio in the possession of the author, F.
J. Kitton's *Charles Dickens by Pen and Pencil:*

Frontispiece, 1, 2, 5, 6, 7, 8, 9, 10, 12, 13, 14, 26, 28, 29, 32, 33, 34, 35, 36, 38,
39, 42, 45, 46, 48, 49, 50, 51, 54, 55, 56, 58, 61, 69, 70, 71, 73, 74, 75, 76, 77,
78, 81, 82, 83, 86

For my grandchildren
Miranda, Mark, Lisa, Alison, Galen, and Laura

Contents

5

CONTENTS

Illustrations follow pages 112 and 382

Preface

Charles Dickens belongs to all the world. He is a titan of literature, and his own moving life story, with its radiances of laughter, its conquests of genius, and its dark and fateful course, even in the midst of universal acclaim, epitomizes hardly less powerfully than his works the interwoven comedy and tragedy of the human struggle. This book is addressed to all who find compelling the colour and richness and travail of life itself.

Dickens was himself a Dickens character, bursting with inordinate and fantastic vitality. His everyday world was identical with the world of his novels, brilliant in hue, violent in movement, crammed with people all furiously alive and places as alive as the people. He found his own friends as funny as Mr Micawber, Mr Toots, and Flora Finching, and felt their joys and sorrows as deeply as he did those of the characters in his fictions. His own adventures were as hilarious and painful as those of Mr Pickwick or David Copperfield or Pip. In his prodigal exuberance he poured out through his letters a wealth of psychological observation and comic episode and a vividness of language that might have enlivened a dozen more novels.

But Dickens is significant for more than the sheer intensity with which he reflects experience. His is a penetrating vision of modern life. The unifying thread of his entire career was a critical analysis of nineteenth-century society unsurpassed by any novelist in grasp or scope.

This biography is based on the thousands of letters in the *Nonesuch Edition*, those in the three volumes that have so far appeared of the great new *Pilgrim Edition*, and on thousands more still unpublished, as well as on many other primary and secondary sources. I have also made copious use of Dickens's letters to newspapers and his articles in magazines, and – since he printed nothing with which he did not agree – used also the many pages of *Household Words* and *All the Year Round*, the two weeklies over which he exercised a rigid control for twenty years.

1 December 1976   Edgar Johnson

PART ONE

The Anvil and the Iron
1812–1833

[1]

Birth and Background

On the highest strip of ground in the main road from Gravesend to Rochester stands a brick Georgian dwelling with bow windows and a small white bell turret. More than a century and a half ago a rather sickly small boy used to cross Rochester Bridge with his father and ascend the two-mile slope to stare with admiration at its rose-and-madder façade and draw a low breath of longing and incredulity when his father told him that if he were to work very hard he might come to live there some day. The house was called Gad's Hill Place and the little boy was Charles Dickens. The dream came true: he lived there for the last twelve years of his life, and there he died.

His way to Gad's Hill had descended into shabby-genteel suburbs and urban slums; his family's sinking fortunes had jailed the father in the Marshalsea for debt and condemned the despairing child to drudgery and tears in a blacking warehouse. But the child became an office boy, a shorthand writer, a reporter, an author. With *Pickwick Papers*, at the age of twenty-four, he stepped into instant fame, and from then on he marched from triumph to triumph. It would be difficult to name any novelist of our own time who has so commanded the respect of serious criticism and at the same time reached so widespread an audience. In the end, this writer who was the son of a perennially improvident father became the most celebrated literary figure of his time and left an estate of £93,000, a sum then worth far more than it would be a century later.

Seen thus, the career of Charles Dickens is one of the most glittering success stories. But it has darker and profounder depths. Beneath the blare of applause there is the heartbreak of his father's imprisonment, the terror of butcher and baker raising angry voices, of insufficient meals choked down with tears, of rooms pawned bare of household goods. Beneath the later fame there is the weeping of a child taken out of school and delivered to toil, all his early ambition of growing up to be a learned and distinguished man crushed within his breast. And, after the first exhilaration of fame, despite a gusto and a sense of the comic that look like happiness, Dickens was not happy in his good fortune. Sheer vitality and the stimulation of companionship could key him to an electric flow of high spirits. But this only masked an underlying "vague unhappy loss or want of something" which he lamented in the very height of his achievement, and which goaded him to perpetual restlessness and dissatisfaction with himself and the world. There were hidden wounds in his home life, secret burdens and disappointed hopes, which pride and reserve led him to fight with vigorous activity and with a determined and infectious display of social vivacity. The genial human contact he had always enjoyed became – like his titanic literary labours and the lethal excitement of his public readings – a part of his desperate endeavour to escape a crushing sense of hollowness and futility.

But this personal unhappiness helped deepen his insight and sharpened his criticism, spurred him to a continued intellectual and artistic growth that turned him from humour and romantic pathos and the lashing of isolated wrongs to the indictment of an entire society. The later Dickens becomes a social critic and a social prophet whose amazing imaginative comprehension of his environment illumines the problems of our contemporary world. His early boundless confidence that good will and common sense could conquer all the abuses of society yields to a disillusioned analysis of the endlessly interlinked evils piled up in an economic system dominated by industrialism and material greed. There is a steady line of growth from the glorious humour of *Pickwick* to the penetrating social analysis of *Little Dorrit* and *Our Mutual Friend* – an analysis that encompasses the dominant forces of the world we live in today.

On one level, then, Dickens was painfully vanquished by the challenges existence posed for him. On another and loftier level he magnificently surmounted them. In this tension between his splendid public success and his deep-rooted dissatisfaction with the world that heaped rewards upon him lies the drama and the pity of his life. Its tragedy grows out of the way in which the powers that enabled him to overcome the obstacles before him contained also the seeds of his unhappiness. Its triumph is that his inward misery stimulated his powers to that culminating achievement of his work.

*

The baby who was to be named Charles Dickens was born in a little house at 387 Mile End Terrace, Landport, Portsea, on 7 February 1812. The building was one of a row of attached brick dwellings. A minute square of garden lay between each house and the street, and another square of green behind. John Dickens had exuberantly taken the house when he was married, almost three years before. But now, although it was but a modest house and his income had risen to £176 a year, he was finding it too dear for him. On 24 June, before their baby son was five months old, the Dickens family moved to a cheaper house at 18 Hawke Street.

John Dickens was at this time a lively, talkative, energetic young man of around twenty-six. He worked faithfully at his post, that of clerk in the Navy Pay Office; and he talked vividly and entertainingly, even if somewhat magniloquently. He was generous, kindly, warm-hearted; he loved to play host to his friends over a bottle of wine or a steaming bowl of punch; his manner was ornately genteel. No one would have guessed that his father, William Dickens, had been steward at Crewe Hall or his mother before her marriage a servant in the house of the Marquess of Blandford, in Grosvenor Square; and that even now his mother was housekeeper at Crewe.

William Dickens had died in 1785, leaving his wife with two children, William and the baby, John. John Crewe (later Lord Crewe), for whom the young child may have been named, had been Member of Parliament for Chester, and was a warm friend of George Canning, then Treasurer of the Navy. When John Dickens was about nineteen years of age he was appointed by Canning, probably through Crewe's influence, to a clerical post in the Navy Pay Office at Somerset House. The date of the appointment was 15 April 1805, and the beginning salary was five shillings a day – not quite £80 a year. The bright young fellow must have given satisfaction: a little more than two years later he was made fifteenth assistant clerk at £70 a year plus two shillings extra for every day of actual attendance – a probable total of £100 a year. He had broken away from the menial background of his parents and become a government functionary. In later years there were family legends of being a branch of the ancient Dickens family of Staffordshire, and Charles Dickens assumed its crest, which he referred to as "my father's crest: a lion couchant, bearing in his dexter paw a Maltese cross."

At the same time that John Dickens received his appointment another young man was nominated to a clerkship in the same office. This was Thomas Culliford Barrow, whose father, Charles Barrow, had the responsible post of Chief Conductor of Moneys in Town with a suite of rooms in Somerset House. At this time a man of fifty, Charles Barrow was originally a native of Bristol who had made his way to London, where in 1788 he had married Mary Culliford, a daughter of a musical instrument maker. A few years later Barrow became a partner in the business with his father-in-law, Thomas Culliford, and a man named William Rolfe. In 1797 Charles Barrow and his father-in-law retired. Barrow taught music and ran a circulating library, and then, at the close of 1801, was appointed an extra clerk in the Navy Pay Office.

Suddenly, in little more than a year, this man with no previous experience was jumped to the important position he had since occupied, with an annual salary rising from £330 to £350. The Barrows were of markedly higher pretensions than John Dickens, the steward's and housekeeper's son. But John Dickens and young Thomas Culliford Barrow became friends. John was soon asked to Barrow's home, and met his sister Elizabeth. She was a small, pretty girl of about sixteen, with bright hazel eyes, an inordinate sense of the ludicrous, and remarkable powers of comic mimicry, cheerful, sweet-tempered, and well educated.

In the course of the next two years she and her brother's friend fell in love with each other. They were married at St Mary-le-Strand, opposite Somerset House, on 13 June 1809. Not long afterwards, the young couple proceeded by stagecoach to Landport, where John Dickens was assigned to the paying off of ships at Portsmouth Dockyard. To the young husband his marriage must have seemed yet another step in his rise into gentility.

Part of Charles Barrow's work was to send money both for salaries and incidental expenses under armed guard to Plymouth, Portsmouth, Sheerness, and Chatham. He was entitled to obtain money for these purposes by signing bills of £900 each on his own authority. But about six months after his daughter's marriage, the authorities began to be suspicious of this trusted official and started quietly investigating him. In February 1810 it transpired that he had been systematically stating false balances since 1803. The deficiency by now was £5,689 3s. 3d.

Summoned before the Treasurer, Barrow confessed his guilt, pleading as excuse the burden of a family of ten children and the expenses of constant illness. He appealed for time to see if a brother in Bristol would not make good the money. A few days later he resigned, still begging not to be sent to jail. But the Treasurer started criminal proceedings, and Barrow absconded to the Continent, from which he never returned to England. (Thirteen years later he turned up in the Isle of Man, outside the jurisdiction of the British law, where he died in 1826.) His household furniture was seized and sold by the Sheriff of Middlesex. It realized

£499 9s. The rest of the money that Charles Barrow had embezzled was never recovered.

This shaming business was a severe shock to the family pride of the Barrows. Thomas Barrow, however, did not lose his post in the Navy Pay Office; ultimately, indeed, he rose to be head of its Prize Branch and retired on a pension of £710 a year. For John Dickens the blow may have been more palpable. Any help his father-in-law might have given towards paying his £35 a year house rent would have to be found elsewhere now. And already John Dickens was revealing the weakness that was to dog him all his life. He was not lazy, he was a good father and a good husband. He neither gambled nor drank to excess, though he did like a convivial glass. But he simply could not live within his income. He loved the orotund gesture and the display of hospitality: both of them easier for a bachelor than for a married man with children. Friends about the festal board, a glowing hearth, songs and toasts; later in the evening devilled mutton grilled over the fire, and a nightcap of punch downed with oratorical sentiments, all these were irresistible to his expansive nature.

Down at Crewe old Mrs Dickens used to fascinate the Crewe children in the housekeeper's room with fairy tales and stories from history, and sometimes with personal reminiscences. She would grumble to them about "that lazy fellow John, who used to come hanging around the house," adding "and many a sound cuff on the ear I've given him." But he received cash as well as cuffs, although she was too shrewd to give him much. Her will bequeathed £500 to William and £450 to John, explaining that he was entitled to no more because he had already received "several sums of money some years ago." Thomas Barrow and his brother John Henry Barrow, a barrister-at-law, received appeals for aid so often that at last they lost all patience and refused to communicate with him.

There was no shadow of these future events, however, in the small upstairs bedroom when Charles was born. Although her time was near, his mother had put on a dance frock and attended a ball in Rope Walk. Returning in the small hours, she bore her son before dawn. The child was baptized, as his little sister Fanny had been before him, at St Mary's, Kingston, the parish church for Portsea. In the register for 4 March 1812, his full name is entered as Charles John Huffham Dickens, although "Huffham" is a clerical error for Huffam. Charles was for his maternal grandfather, the absconded Conductor of Moneys; John for his father; and Huffam for his godfather, Christopher Huffam, a prosperous naval rigger whom John Dickens had met while he was at Somerset House.

Shortly after, when Charles was still not five months old, the family's straitened circumstances forced its move to Hawke Street. There was no front garden, the cramped sitting-room was up two tiny wooden steps from the street, and a bay window overhung the very paving stones. But baby Charles and his sister played about the little back garden happily, while a maid kept an eye on them through the kitchen area window. He enjoyed, too, being carried to see the soldiers drill at Portsmouth, and a quarter of a century later recognized the exact shape of the military parade as he had seen it when an infant.

Portsea was fun for a small child. It was a fortified town with six gates. Through the Lion Gate on the direct road to London the stage-coach came dashing, to wind up in the yard of the George, the town's principal inn. There were pretty lanes in the surrounding country, and there was a ferry to Gosport, Portsmouth – a penny in fine weather and thruppence in foul. In these times of the war with the United States and the last battles of the Napoleonic struggle, it was full of sailors and dockyard craftsmen, and of the lively bustle of the military and naval conflict.

Suddenly, after Christmas 1814, John Dickens was summoned back to London. He established his family in lodgings at 10 Norfolk Street, near the Middlesex Hospital. There was now another infant, named Alfred, who had been born in 1813, but who died in childhood. Charles had just a faint memory of having come away from Portsea in the winter, but he retained no separate recollections of this first stay in London. Perhaps its impressions were absorbed in the sharper and more painful ones that came to him there later. No one knows exactly how long the family remained in Norfolk Street, or even whether the next three years while Charles was growing from a toddler of two to a child of five were entirely spent in the metropolis. At the beginning of 1817, however, John Dickens was ordered to the large government dockyard at Chatham, a shipbuilding town that even then melted almost imperceptibly into the cathedral city of Rochester.

2

The Happy Time

The family was larger now, but it was more prosperous. Five-year-old Charles had a baby sister, Letitia, born in 1816. His mother's eldest sister, Mary, whom the children called Aunt Fanny, had come to live with them when her husband, a naval lieutenant, was drowned at Rio de Janeiro. John Dickens, who had been given another increase in salary in 1815, was earning almost £300 a year.

Consequently he rented a three-storey brick house at 2 Ordnance Terrace. This was a row of attached houses having an airy hilltop position looking down towards the River Medway. There were small front and back gardens, two lovely hawthorn trees, and, across the way, a hay field bright with daisies and buttercups.

Here in Chatham the Dickens family had two servants, Jane Bonny and a young girl named Mary Weller who looked after the children. Charles could remember her putting him to bed and humming the evening hymn to him, while he cried on the pillow, "either with the remorseful consciousness of having kicked Somebody else, or because still Somebody else had hurt my feelings in the course of the day." She may have been the "very sympathetic nurse" who took the child visiting with her when she went to see friends. "At one little green-grocer's shop," he recalled, there had been a lady "who had had four children (I am afraid to write five) at a birth"; and he saw "how the four (five) deceased young people lay, side by side, on a clean cloth on a chest of drawers," reminding the little boy by their complexion "of pigs' feet as they are usually displayed at a neat tripe-shop."

Mary Weller took his imagination on even more horrifying journeys that afflicted him at night, telling him stories of bloody vengeance and supernatural hauntings. One of these gory narratives concerned a certain Captain Murderer who slaughtered his successive wives, baked them in meat pies, ate them, and picked the bones. Ultimately this sinister character met his just fate through a poison injected into the pie crust by a suspicious victim, which caused him to swell up and turn blue and scream until he filled the room from floor to ceiling and finally burst. Still another dismal tale was about a shipwright named Chips who sold himself to the Devil for an iron pot, a bushel of nails, half a ton of copper, and a rat that could speak. Thereafter he found himself haunted by rats, nestling in his pockets, curled up in his hat, dripping from his sleeves, and running up his trouser legs. And worse, he knew what the rats were doing, wherever they were, so that he would sometimes cry aloud, "There's two of them smelling the baby in the garret!" In the end, the rats gnawed away the oak of his ship, and what was left of Chips floated ashore with a great rat sitting on him, laughing. Little Charles would lie in bed rigid with terror at such horrors projecting themselves before him in the dark.

"He was a very little and a very sickly boy," his friend and first biographer John Forster wrote, "subject to attacks of violent spasm which disabled him for any active exertion. He was never a good little cricket-player; he was never a first-rate hand at marbles, or peg-top, or prisoners' base; but he had great pleasures in watching the other boys, officers' sons for the most part, at these games, reading while they played . . ."

It was his mother who taught him to read, and later even a little Latin. The alphabet Charles learned in thin books "with deliciously smooth covers of bright red or green. What fat black letters to begin with! 'A was an archer, and shot at a frog.' Of course he was. He was an apple-pie also, and there he is! He was a good many things in his time, was A, and so were most of his friends, except X, who had so little versatility that I never knew him to get beyond Xerxes or Xantippe – like Y, who was always confined to a Yacht or a Yew Tree; and Z condemned for ever to be a Zebra or a Zany." He speedily became, as his nurse put it, "a terrible boy to read," sitting with his book in his left hand, holding his wrist with his right hand, and constantly sliding it up and down while he sucked his tongue.

Charles and Fanny were sent to a dame school upstairs over a dyer's shop in Rome Lane. There was a puppy pug-dog in the long and narrow entry who terrified him by snapping at his undefended legs, and who belonged, as he wrote later, "to some female, chiefly inhabiting a back parlour, whose life appeared to us to have been consumed in sniffing, and in wearing a brown beaver bonnet." The woman who kept the school was a grim old creature upon whom he later partly modelled Mrs Pipchin and the gloomy establishment at Brighton where little Paul Dombey was one of the inmates. When Charles was puzzled she poked his head with a hard knuckle "by way of adjusting the confusion of ideas in which he was generally involved."

Next door in Ordnance Terrace were two children, George and Lucy Stroughill. Charles was invited to Lucy's birthday party. She was "a peach-faced creature in a blue sash," with whom he fell in love, and the two small people sat blissfully "in a shady bower – under a table" consuming sweet foods and liquids, while he imagined this glorified young person to lead a life consisting entirely of birthdays and to be reared exclusively on seedcake, sweet wine, and shining presents.

Although he was still small for his age, outdoor air and sunlight in Chatham were making him stronger. "Here, in the haymaking time," he remembered, "had I been delivered from the dungeons of Seringapatam, an immense pile (of haycock), by my countrymen, the victorious British (boy next door and his two cousins), and had been recognized with ecstasy by my affianced one" (Lucy), "who had come all the way from England (second house in the terrace) to ransom me, and marry me."

When they played indoors, Charles would rush downstairs and say authoritatively, "Now, Mary, clear the kitchen, we're going to have such a game." Then in would come George Stroughill with his magic lantern, and there would be a spirited acting out of plays. Fanny was learning the piano, and they would sing comic songs together, such as "The Cat's Meat Man," with its recurrent chorus of

> *Down in the street cries the cat's meat man,*
> *Fango dango, with his barrow and can.*

This small talent for comic singing gave the sociable John Dickens such delight that he often hoisted Charles up on a table to entertain the guests in his clear, unshy treble, or strolled down into the lower part of the town with the youngster to show him off there. The Dickenses were on visiting terms with the Tribes, who owned the Mitre Inn and Clarence Hotel, a fine old place with beautiful grounds and trees. Mounted on one of the dining tables, Charles sang sea duets with Fanny. He would begin:

> *Long time I've courted you, miss,*
> *And now I've come from sea;*
> *We'll make no more ado, miss,*
> *But quickly married be.*

Then they would join in a "Sing fol de rol" chorus, she would take the
next stanza, and the two would continue alternately:

> I ne'er will wed a tar, sir,
>   Deceitful as yourself;
> 'Tis very plain you are, sir,
>   A good for nothing elf. (Sing fol de rol)

> I ne'er deceived you yet, miss,
>   Though like a shrew you rave;
> But prithee, scold and fret, miss –
>   A storm I well can brave. (Sing fol de rol)

And so on through long cheerily tuneful sessions, though Dickens in
later years told Forster that the memory of his shrill little voice tingled in
his ears and made him redden to think what a nuisance he must have
been to unoffending grown-ups called upon to admire him.

It was an innocent and happy time for the children. If their family
felt any of the economic distresses that followed the end of the Napoleonic wars, they knew nothing of it. But it is probable that John
Dickens, on an undiminished government salary, was benefited by
falling prices that were bankrupting businesses, making ruined farmers
hang themselves, and pauperizing farm labourers and factory hands by
the scores of thousands. The radical press was fought with savage prose-
cutions, *habeas corpus* was suspended, and starving rioters were tried for
treason.

The fat and corseted Prince Regent, that deplorable and disgraceful
old rake who represented the Crown, was more violently despised and
execrated even than before. But the only echo of all these events that
came to seven-year-old Charles was his being told in confidence "of
the existence of terrible banditti, called 'The Radicals,' whose principles
were, that nobody had a right to any salary, and that the army and navy
ought to be put down – horrors at which I trembled in my bed, after
supplicating that the Radicals might be speedily taken and hanged."

It was not until 1821 that John Dickens's incurable financial carelessness caught up with him again. He had, to be sure, two more
children now, Harriet, born in the autumn of 1819, and Frederick, born
in the summer of 1820, so that there were five children in the house at
Ordnance Terrace, ranging from ten-year-old Fanny down to the baby.
Although he had received a final salary increase in 1820 to £350 a year,

he was again living beyond his means. On Lady Day (25 March) 1821, he found himself forced to give up their pleasant quarters at Ordnance Terrace and move to 18 St Mary's Place, called "The Brook."

The move was both literally and figuratively downhill. The new home was a small tenement with a front of whitewashed plaster. From the window of Charles's attic room it was possible to see the spire of St Mary's Church and the surrounding churchyard with its graves, but there were no such open spaces as the meadow across the way from Ordnance Terrace and no longer any youthful parties. The Brook was much nearer the Dockyard, in the crowded poorer quarter of Chatham. John Dickens had to put a curb upon his generosity.

But Charles, although he was nine by this time, hardly noticed these changes. Trotting along by his father's side when he went to his office in the Dockyard, Charles was wide-eyed for everything – the street posts of cannon and ornaments of shells, and the handsome houses of the leading officials. He watched the ropemakers and sniffed the smell of tarred rope, heard the anchor-smiths clanging away, saw the block-makers surrounded by oak chips and wooden shavings, and stood under the huge wooden walls of vessels rising in the slips. On St Clement's Day the artificers had a pageant in which they wore masks and flowing wigs, made doggerel speeches, and paraded "Old Clem" in a chair of state through the town.

Sometimes Charles sailed up the Medway with his father as far as Sheerness and the Thames on the *Chatham*, the Navy Pay Yacht. Entranced, the boy would pass all the ships floating out in the Medway and in the larger stream, bringing with the sight their far visions of the sea. Returning, they would see the Yard from a distance, "snug under hill-sides of corn-fields, hop-gardens, and orchards; its great chimneys smoking with a quiet – almost a lazy – air, like giants smoking tobacco."

They would have passed a black convict hulk lying out in the stream "like a wicked Noah's ark," all cribbed and barred and moored by rusty chains, seeming in the eyes of its childish observer "to be ironed like the prisoners" themselves. And back in the Dockyard once more, amid the canvas, and the clanging, and the booming, and the smell of oakum, the boy would stare spellbound at long files of convict labourers carrying planks of heavy lumber, two tall men sometimes bearing all the weight, and a little man in between happily bearing none.

Now that he was older, Charles could venture farther afield. On the hill above the town were the Chatham Lines, where the gay bright regiments were always parading and firing; and between Chatham and Rochester, he could revisit Fort Pitt with its endless succession of sham sieges and defences. Behind Fort Pitt fields, half a mile out of town was a house erected by a recluse named Tom Clarke who lived alone there for twenty-five years, whence it received the name Tom-all-Alone's. Other houses had been built around it, but when the land was needed for a prison the soldiers destroyed them with mines, and Charles saw the explosions and the crashing walls.

On the High Street, below the Fort, was Simpson's coach office, which ran a coach to London, mellifluously entitled the Blue-Eyed Maid. The office window displayed an oval transparency representing the Maid bowling past a milestone with a full consignment of stylish passengers, all enjoying themselves tremendously. The High Street, meandering along until Chatham merged into Rochester, seemed to boyish eyes "as wide as Regent Street, London, or the Italian Boulevard, Paris." The Guild Hall was "so glorious a structure" that he set it up in his mind "as the model on which the Genie of the Lamp built the palace for Aladdin."

Farther along loomed College Yard Gate, a cavernous portico with a room above reached by a tiny winding stair in the thickness of the wall. Thence one came into the precinct of the old Cathedral and its shady trees, greensward, and worn gravestones. A side entrance gave on to the choir transept, and then the shady Norman columns of the nave stretched out to the right, the porch, with its ancient carvings, the ruins of the monks' cloisters, and the grey rook-haunted tower soaring over all. Up the slope extended the quaint houses of Minor Canon Row and the King's School, and over the brow of the hill the great square pile of Rochester Castle, gaunt and ruinous, with bare holes of windows like the empty eyes of a skull contemplating the river far below.

Across the stream there were rural pilgrimages that Charles took with his father, John Dickens orating all the way. At Cobham were the square Gothic-arched porch and tower of St Mary Magdalene, and the Leather Bottle, with its long, low-roofed room and fantastic high-backed leather chairs. Past Cobham Hall, then, its octagonal corner towers and innumerable chimneys bristling above a long façade of square-bayed windows and mellow Elizabethan brickwork, they could pass into the shady depths of Cobham Wood and come out by Gad's Hill, where Falstaff robbed the travellers. Here the boy would gaze across the road at the ivied front and white portico of Gad's Hill Place. And here, while his father informed him again that if he were to work very, very hard he might someday come to live there, the boy would heave a deep low sigh of incredulity and longing. Then down the Dover Road and so back across Rochester Bridge, and home.

The minister of the Zion Baptist Chapel in Chatham during the time the Dickenses lived in St Mary's Place was the Reverend William Giles. The Dickens family were Church of England, though not at all devout or interested in matters of doctrine. They had no objection, however, to hearing their neighbour preach occasionally, and Charles suffered bitterly from his or some other preacher's long-winded two-hour sermons.

Sitting there uncomfortably on a Sunday, he felt as if his mind were being steamed out of him, hating the minister's "big round face" and loathing "his lumbering jocularity." Haled out of the chapel, the boy would find himself "catechized respecting" the minister's "fifthly, his sixthly, and his seventhly," until he "regarded that reverend person in the light of a most dismal and oppressive Charade." These experiences laid the foundations for his lifelong hatred of Nonconformity and his revulsion from formal religious affiliation.

But Mr Giles had a son, also named William Giles, who had established a school in Clover Lane around 1817. To his school, about the time they moved to the Brook, Fanny and Charles were sent. Giles was a young man of twenty-three, an Oxford graduate of more than average ability and cultivation. He speedily recognized in the handsome child with long, light, curly hair a boy of unusual promise. Charles took to his studies with delight and made rapid progress.

Outside school, too, he now enjoyed himself with the other boys. Among these schoolmates there were romps in Fort Pitt fields, rowing and skating, the colour and excitement of Guy Fawkes celebrations around the glowing bonfires, and Twelfth-Night festivities, with Twelfth-cakes and dancing till midnight.

But these everyday boyish enjoyments did not supersede the fanciful play of earlier childhood. He had loved reading since his mother had taught him to distinguish "the easy good nature of O and Q and S" from each other. Jack and the Bean Stalk, Red Riding Hood, Valentine and Orson, Robin Hood, the Yellow Dwarf: with what brilliant colours they glowed before his mind's eye! John Dickens owned a cheap series of novels which were

in a little room upstairs to which I had access (for it adjoined my own) . . . From that blessed little room *Roderick Random, Peregrine*

Pickle, Humphry Clinker, Tom Jones, The Vicar of Wakefield, Don Quixote, Gil Blas, and Robinson Crusoe came out a glorious host, to keep me company. . . .

It is curious to me how I could ever have consoled myself under my small troubles (which were great troubles to me), by impersonating my favourite characters in them – as I did . . . I have been Tom Jones (a child's Tom Jones, a harmless creature) for a week together. I have sustained my own idea of Roderick Random for a month at a stretch, I verily believe. I had a greedy relish for a few volumes of Voyages and Travels – I forget what, now – that were on those shelves; and for days and days I can remember to have gone about my region of our house, armed with the centrepiece out of an old set of boot-trees – the perfect realization of Captain Somebody, of the Royal British Navy, in danger of being beset by savages, and resolved to sell his life at a great price. . . .

When I think of it, the picture always arises in my mind of a summer evening, the boys at play in the churchyard, and I sitting on my bed, reading as if for life. Every barn in the neighbourhood, every stone in the church, and every foot of the churchyard, had some association of its own, in my mind, connected with these books, and stood for some locality made famous in them. I have seen Tom Pipes go climbing up the church steeple; I have watched Strap, with the knapsack on his back, stopping to rest himself upon the wicket-gate; and I know that Commodore Trunnion held that club with Mr Pickle in the parlour of our little village alehouse.

Besides this noble company, there were the *Arabian Nights*, the *Tatler* and *Spectator* papers, Johnson's *Idler*, Goldsmith's *Citizen of the World*, and Mrs Inchbald's *Collection* of *Farces*. It is impossible to calculate the entire extent of their effect upon Dickens, but the nature and direction of their stimulus is unmistakable. No writer so intimately fuses the familiar and the strange as he does. His physical world is an utterly everyday one of the most prosaic places: Goswell Street, the drab suburbs of Camden Town and Somers Town, Covent Garden Market, the Golden Cross, the poor streets of the Borough – all noted in the sharpest detail. And yet they are transfigured by an inward vision that bathes Bob Cratchit's fireside in glowing warmth and Fagin's thieves' cellar in sordid romance. The clear daylight sanity of *Tom Jones* and the brutal realism of *Roderick Random* are mingled in the works of Dickens with the fantasy of Ali Baba's cave and Sinbad's valley of diamonds.

In later years Dickens remembered how, as a boy, "sitting in by-places near Rochester Castle," he had heard of the Yorkshire schools: some boy had come home with a suppurated abscess, "his Yorkshire Guide, Philosopher, and friend having ripped it open with an inky penknife." Dickens's childish imagination had been haunted by a vision of the dirty schoolroom as a hideous dungeon and the Schoolmaster as an ogre torturing little boys. The strange ambivalence that endows Wackford Squeers and Dotheboys Hall in *Nicholas Nickleby* with a comic nightmare realism is identical with that which bursts out in the image of the M'Choakumchilds of *Hard Times* as utilitarian Morgianas striving to fill their little vessels brimful of boiling fact and slay the robber Fancy lurking within. The small boy who found the unpretentious Guild Hall of an ordinary provincial town a palace built by the Genie of the Lamp is father to the creator of Quilp and Mr Jingle, Sairey Gamp, Captain Cuttle, poor mad little Miss Flite, our eminently practical friend Gradgrind, the Circumlocution Office, and Boffin's Dust Heaps.

In his childhood, too, his imagination received another powerful stimulus, and one which all his life exerted over him the strongest fascination – the theatre. At the age of seven he had been taken up to London to behold the splendour of Christmas pantomimes, had delighted in the beautiful complexions of the clowns and their appetite for sausages, exulted in Harlequin and Pantaloon, and "thought that to marry a Columbine would be to attain the highest pitch of all human felicity!" At fair time once, a pantomime had come lumbering to Chatham, and he had thrilled to the glorious smell of sawdust and orange peel and the confounding of the crafty magician who had been holding the young lady in bondage.

Despite his father's continuing financial struggles, Charles enjoyed exciting tastes of such theatrical fare as Rochester and Chatham could provide. In the little Theatre Royal, with its two-columned portico and wrought-iron lantern, Edmund Kean and Charles Mathews had sometimes played, and here little Charles, when he was eight, had precociously clapped his hands for the great Joe Grimaldi, nonpareil of clowns. Later he was occasionally taken to some of the melodramas, farces, and tragedies that held its boards, and was inspired to compose a tragedy entitled *Misnar, the Sultan of India* (founded on one of the *Tales of the Genii*), which won him fame in his childish circle.

His mother's widowed sister, the children's Aunt Fanny, had become acquainted with a Dr Matthew Lamert, an army surgeon quartered at

Chatham. The bustling middle-aged man with an abrupt odd way of talking was the figure that later suggested Dr Slammer, in *Pickwick*. Soon it was understood that he and Aunt Fanny were to be married. Dr Lamert had a taste for the drama, and sometimes good-naturedly took his prospective wife's bright young nephew to the Rochester theatre. A son by a former marriage, James Lamert, shared his father's theatrical enthusiasm, and got up private performances in the almost uninhabited rambling Ordnance Hospital. These the eager-eyed Charles was allowed to see, drinking in also the wonders of rehearsals and stage business and grease paint and costumes.

When Dr and Mrs Lamert left for Ireland, James Lamert remained behind as a lodger at the Brook, and became Charles's admired patron and elder friend. He continued taking the boy to the Theatre Royal. Here Charles learned, "as from a page of English history, how the wicked king Richard III slept in war-time on a sofa much too short for him, and how fearfully his conscience troubled his boots." And he recalled how that monarch "made my heart leap with terror by backing up against the stage-box in which I was posted, while struggling for life against the virtuous Richmond."

There, too, had I first seen the funny countryman, but countryman of noble principles, in a flowered waistcoat, crunch up his little hat and throw it on the ground, and pull off his coat, saying, "Dom thee, squire, coom on with thy fistes then!" At which the lovely young woman who kept company with him . . . was so frightened for his sake, that she fainted away.

But for Charles the bright sunlight days were fast drawing to a close. Some time around the autumn of 1822 John Dickens was transferred back to London. His financial position was now very bad, and before the family's removal there was a sale of the household goods. Their parlour chairs were purchased by the former servant, Mary Weller, who had married a dockyard worker and been replaced by a little orphan from the Chatham Workhouse.

It is believed that Charles did not go with the rest of the family to London, but was allowed to stay on in Chatham until Christmas to finish his school term with Mr Giles. If so, the other Dickens youngsters were all piled into the coach, and Charles saw them off. The departure of the Micawber family for Plymouth, in *David Copperfield*, hints a memory of this separation:

26

I think, as Mrs Micawber sat at the back of the coach with the children, and I stood in the road looking wistfully at them, a mist cleared from her eyes, and she saw what a little creature I really was. I think so, because she beckoned me to climb up, with quite a new and motherly expression in her face, and put her arms around my neck, and gave me just such a kiss as she might have given to her own boy.

On the night before he came away, his kind schoolmaster, Mr Giles, "came flitting among the packing-cases," Dickens remembered, "to give me Goldsmith's *Bee* as a keepsake. Which I kept for his sake, and its own a long while afterwards." This might seem rather precocious reading for a boy in his eleventh year. But William Giles evidently knew his pupil; Goldsmith's graceful humour and gentle charm captivated the boy. The gift was the beginning for Dickens of an enduring affection for Goldsmith and a lifelong fascination with the periodical miscellany.

The happy time was over. It was farewell to the daisied hay field, the tales of poisoned murderers and satanic talking rats, to peach-faced Lucy and the magic lantern, to Fort Pitt and Chatham Lines and the red-coated regiments, to the clanging Dockyard, the bright river, and the ships with their far visions of the sea. It was farewell to the arcaded Guild Hall, the dim Cathedral and the hoary Castle, the shady verdure of Cobham Woods and the sunlight warming the rosy bricks of Gad's Hill Place. Like the Palace of Aladdin spirited away by the African magician, all were about to vanish.

In a gloomy drizzle the next morning Charles was stowed away in Simpson's Blue-Eyed Maid, and said good-bye to Chatham. He never forgot, David Copperfield tells us, "the smell of the damp straw in which I was packed – like game – and forwarded carriage-paid, to the Cross Keys, Wood Street, Cheapside. There was no other inside passenger, and I consumed my sandwiches in solitude and dreariness, and it rained hard all the way, and I thought that life was sloppier than I had expected to find it."

3

The Challenge of Despair

The new home at 16 Bayham Street, Camden Town, was a further decline in the Dickens fortunes. In the early 1820s, to be sure, Camden Town was not the slum it later became. Separated from London by open fields, with the dome of St Paul's looming in the distance through the smoke of the City, it had pleasant walks through the meadows to Copenhagen House. Bayham Street was a row of about forty houses with grassy fields at the back. Next door to the Dickens dwelling lived a washerwoman, and across the way a Bow Street runner. Number 16 itself was a four-room house with a basement and garret, renting for £22 a year. Into this cramped box fitted John and Elizabeth Dickens, the six Dickens children, James Lamert – who was still living with them – and "the Orfling," the small maid-of-all-work from Chatham Workhouse.

Charles had left Mr Giles expecting that his parents would continue his schooling, but they took no such course. There were no boys near by, and he sank into a loneliness and neglect that bewildered and upset him. It stabbed him to the heart that his sister Fanny was given a scholarship in April as a pupil-boarder at the Royal Academy of Music on Tenterden Street, and went away, with the tearful good wishes of everybody in the house. "As I thought in the little back garret in Bayham Street, of all I had lost in losing Chatham," he said bitterly in later years to Forster, "what would I have given, if I had had anything to give, to have been sent back to any other school, to have been taught something anywhere!"

I know my father [he went on] to be as kindhearted and generous a man as ever lived . . . Everything that I can remember of his conduct to his wife, or children, or friends, in sickness or affliction, is beyond all praise. By me, as a sick child, he has watched night and day, unweariedly and patiently . . . He never undertook any business, charge or trust, that he did not zealously, conscientiously, punctually, honourably discharge . . . He was proud of me, in his way, and had a great admiration of the comic singing. But, in the ease of his temper, and the straitness of his means, he appeared to have utterly lost at this time the idea of educating me at all . . . So I degenerated into cleaning his boots of a morning . . . and going on such poor errands as arose out of our poor way of living.

Charles was eleven now – old enough to feel those changes of atmosphere that afflict a worried household. He heard of a mysterious and ominous something called "The Deed," which he tremblingly confounded with one of those satanic compacts in the tales that had terrified him or with the dark deeds of the witches in *Macbeth*. What dreadful thing had his kind father done? What awful fate was about to descend upon them?

In reality the Deed was a composition with John Dickens's tradesmen and other creditors. Did the Barrows come to the aid of their brother-in-law in this emergency? Did John Dickens beg money from his mother, who was now living on the interest from her savings and a pension from Lord Crewe? No one knows; but certainly the meagre accommodations of Bayham Street were part of the retrenchments intended to help meet the payments demanded by the Deed.

Meanwhile Charles solaced his small heart as best he could. James Lamert took pity on his solitude, and made and painted a toy theatre for him. Sometimes he was taken to see his uncle, Thomas Barrow, who was laid up at his lodgings in Soho with a broken leg. Here the landlady, widow of a bookseller, used to lend the bright-looking lad books, among them Jane Porter's *Scottish Chiefs*, Holbein's *Dance of Death*, and George Colman's *Broad Grins*. The description of Covent Garden in the last of these impressed him so greatly that he stole down to the market and sniffed up "the flavour of the faded cabbage-leaves as if it were the very breath of comic fiction."

There were also longer excursions across London to the handsome residence of Christopher Huffam, at 12 Church Row, Limehouse. His godfather would show off Charles's comic singing to his friends, one of whom, a boatbuilder, was so tickled that he pronounced the boy to be a "prodigy." The return trips through the night sights of London – the Strand, Covent Garden, the sinister regions of St Giles – were deliriously exciting to him. Seven Dials exerted a macabre fascination over his fancy. "Good Heaven!" he would exclaim in later years, "what wild visions of prodigies of wickedness, want, and beggary arose in my mind out of that place!"

But these visits were interrupted by one of the attacks of mysterious spasm and fever that still prostrated him. Throughout this later part of his childhood, indeed, his troubled state was marked by a recurrence of the illnesses that had seemed less frequent in the happy Chatham days. When his fever had subsided, the Deed had redoubled the distresses in Bayham Street. At this stage his mother was struck by an inspiration. The time had arrived, she announced, for her to exert herself; she "must do something." She would start a school and they would all grow rich! "Perhaps," thought the sickly lad, "even I might go to school myself."

Energetically Mrs Dickens rushed about, found a good-sized house at 4 Gower Street North, and took it from Michaelmas 1823, at a rental of £50 a year. A large brass plate was ordered, inscribed "MRS DICKENS'S ESTABLISHMENT," and fastened to the door. What a brainstorm, born of desperation, was this scheme, that, when they had no money and John Dickens was on the verge of arrest for debt, they should take an expensive house at more than twice what they had been paying; and that Mrs Dickens, who had no experience in either teaching or administering a school, and who had a family of six small children to take care of, should undertake it! The end of the endeavour is summarized in Dickens's own words: "Nobody ever came to the school, nor do I recollect that anybody ever proposed to come, or that the least preparation was made to receive anybody."

Meanwhile things drifted steadily into a more hopeless state. "I know that we got on very badly with the butcher and the baker, and that very often we had not too much for dinner." Gradually the distracted parents began selling or pawning their remaining household goods. First to go were the books they had brought from Chatham, *Peregrine Pickle, Roderick Random, Tom Jones, Humphry Clinker*, and the rest. Charles sadly carried them off to a tipsy bookseller in Hampstead Road. More than once the boy found him still in bed, with a cut forehead or a black eye; and the man would try with shaking hand to find the needed shillings from the pockets of his clothes, which lay strewn upon the floor, while his wife, in down-at-heel shoes and with a baby in her arms, berated him shrilly. If the boy was not going to school, he was acquiring an education in the seamier side of human affairs.

But events were soon to stab him with a sharper and more personal anguish. It came, ironically enough, through the kindly intentions of James Lamert. He became manager for a cousin in a rival to "Warren's Blacking, 30, Strand," at that time very famous. "One Jonathan

Warren (the famous one was Robert), living at 30, Hungerford Stairs, or Market, Strand . . . claimed to have been the original proprietor of the boot-blacking recipe, and to have been deposed and ill-used by his renowned relation. At last he sold his recipe, and his name, and his 30, Hungerford Stairs, Strand (30, STRAND, very large, and the intermediate direction very small) for an annuity." "In an evil hour for me," Dickens felt, James Lamert now proposed that Charles should make himself useful in the warehouse where the blacking was made. His salary would be six shillings a week.

His father and mother accepted the offer very willingly, and on a Monday morning only two days after his twelfth birthday Charles started to work. The event left him stunned, sick with despair.

It is wonderful to me how I could have been so easily cast away at such an age. It is wonderful to me, that, even after my descent into the poor little drudge I had been since we came to London, no one had compassion enough on me – a child of singular abilities, quick, eager, delicate, and soon hurt, bodily or mentally – to suggest that something might have been spared, as certainly it might have been, to place me at any common school. Our friends, I take it, were tired out. No one made any sign. My father and mother were quite satisfied. They could hardly have been more so, if I had been twenty years of age, distinguished at a grammar-school, and going to Cambridge.

It is the shock and bitterness of a hurt child that speaks in these words – a child so deeply wounded that the hurt is still there, a quarter of a century later, when they were spoken. But if the patience of the family's friends was exhausted, it was hardly to be expected that they should single out one of the Dickens children and offer to be responsible for him. No doubt his harassed parents were thankful enough for James Lamert's well-meant offer, but they were hardly apt to look upon it or any other aspect of their plight with complacency. Their income was entirely devoured in the endeavour to deal with their debts. Nor was there anything unusual, even much later in the nineteenth century, in a boy going to work at twelve. Six shillings a week was no bad wage for a boy and the hours at the warehouse were not more prolonged than usual. They began at 8 a.m. and ended at 8 p.m., with a lapse of one hour for dinner and half an hour for tea. And despite the comic singing and the admiration of the boatbuilder at Limehouse Hole, neither John Dickens nor his wife suspected that their bright, small-bodied youngster would turn out to be a prodigy.

But in the self-absorbed grief of childhood, Charles hardly realized how frantic his parents were or what a relief even this provision for one of their children must be. He had an extraordinary desire to learn and distinguish himself, and to him this was the end of all his hopes. Furthermore, John Dickens's pretensions had led his son to regard himself as a young gentleman, to whom this descent into drudging among common boys with uncouth manners was unspeakably humiliating. One of them, named Bob Fagin, wore a ragged apron and a paper cap, and lived with his brother-in-law, a waterman. Another, whose name was Paul Green, "but who was currently believed to have been christened Poll," was son of a fireman employed at Drury Lane Theatre. It was with these boys that Charles generally worked side by side.

At first, to be sure, James Lamert tried to dissociate him from the others. The blacking warehouse was a crazy tumble-down old place abutting on the river at Hungerford Stairs. Dirty and decayed, its wainscoted rooms and rotten floors and staircase resounded with the squeaking and shuffling of the old grey rats swarming down in the cellars. Charles sat and worked by himself in a recess of the counting-house. His task was "to cover the pots of paste-blacking; first with a piece of oilpaper, and then with a bit of blue paper; to tie them round with a string; and then to clip the paper close and neat, all round, until it looked as smart as a pot of ointment from an apothecary's shop." On each, finally, he pasted a printed label.

But the separate working place was inconvenient and his small work table was moved downstairs to the common workroom. He was not so young as not to know that he would be slighted and despised if he could not work as well as the others, so despite his unhappiness he soon made himself quick and skilful. But there was a difference of manners between him and the boys that resulted in his being called, perhaps not quite reverentially, "the young gentleman." "Poll Green uprose once, and rebelled against the 'young gentleman' usage; but Bob Fagin settled him speedily."

No words can express the secret agony of my soul [the autobiography goes on], as I sunk into this companionship; compared these every day associates with those of my happier childhood; and felt my early hopes of growing up to be a learned and distinguished man, crushed in my breast. The deep remembrance of the sense I had of being utterly neglected and hopeless; of the shame I felt in my position; of the misery it was to my young heart to believe that, day

32

by day, what I had learned, and thought, and delighted in, and raised my fancy and my emulation up by, was passing away from me, never to be brought back any more; cannot be written. My whole nature was so penetrated with the grief and humiliation of such considerations, that even now, famous and caressed and happy, I often forget in my dreams that I have a dear wife and children; even that I am a man; and wander desolately back to that time of my life.

But in his pride Charles bottled all his despair within his breast. "I never said, to man or boy, how it was that I came to be there, or gave the least indication of being sorry that I was there. That I suffered in secret, and that I suffered exquisitely, no one ever knew but I."

Just eleven days after the Monday when Charles began his forlorn labours, his father was arrested for debt. The first three nights of his detention he lodged in the sponging house maintained by the bailiff, while he tried to raise money and avoid being formally committed to prison. Charles, his eyes swollen with tears, spent the weekend running errands and carrying messages for the weeping prisoner. But all efforts were in vain: on Friday, 20 February, John Dickens was taken to the Marshalsea. His last words to the sorrowing lad as he entered the gates were that the sun had set upon him forever. "I really believed at the time that they had broken my heart."

The fragment of autobiography continues with reminiscences of later visits to the prison:

My father was waiting for me in the lodge, and we went up to his room (on the top storey but one), and cried very much. And he told me . . . to take warning by the Marshalsea, and to observe that if a man had twenty pounds a year, and spent nineteen pounds nineteen shillings and sixpence, he would be happy; but that a shilling spent the other way would make him wretched.

Presently it was dinnertime, and Charles was sent upstairs to "Captain Porter," one of the prisoners there, to beg the loan of a knife and fork. "There was a very dirty lady in his little room; and two wan girls, his daughters, with shock heads of hair. I thought I should not have liked to borrow Captain Porter's comb." Even at such a time of anguish as this the observant boy was always taking things in. He noted the Captain's untrimmed whiskers, and his bed rolled up in a corner; and, despite the few minutes that he stood timidly wondering on the threshold, he says, "I knew (God knows how) that the two girls with the shock heads were Captain Porter's natural children, and that the dirty lady was not married to Captain P."

Even in a debtors' prison John Dickens could not lose his natural ornateness of utterance, but he was dreadfully shaken. He became tremulously tragic; it may have been at this time that his son observed in his father that fluttering and frightened motion of the fingers about the lips that he later attributed to William Dorrit in the same misfortune.

And there was reason enough to be frightened. There was no way in which John Dickens could pay his debts; he must either remain in prison or take advantage of the Insolvent Debtors' Act. He had been in the Navy Pay Office nineteen years, but a man who incurred the disgrace of insolvency could hardly expect to be retained there. Income, pension possibilities, all hope, would vanish.

Something might be salvaged from his years of faithful labour by applying for immediate retirement, and getting his pension before he was legally declared insolvent. So, on 2 March, John Dickens obtained from Dr John Pool, surgeon, of Dover Street, Piccadilly, a certificate stating that he had a chronic affection of the urinary organs that incapacitated him for public duty. In due course, Treasurer of the Navy Huskisson recommended that he be retired on an annual pension of £145 16s. 8d. (five twelfths of his salary). But long before the matter progressed any further, John Dickens's efforts to avoid insolvency failed.

Meanwhile Charles crept every hopeless day from Gower Street to the drudgery of Hungerford Stairs, and his distracted mother tried to keep things going and the whimpering children fed by pawning brooches and spoons and gradually stripping the rooms bare of furniture. At last there was nothing left in Gower Street but a few chairs, a kitchen table, and some beds; and the family camped out in the two parlours of the emptied house.

It was too far to go home from the blacking warehouse within the dinner hour, so Charles usually carried his meal with him or bought it at some near-by shop out of his six-shilling wage. Sometimes he got

a saveloy and a penny loaf; sometimes, a plate of beef from a cook's shop; sometimes, a plate of bread and cheese, and a glass of beer, from a miserable old public-house over the way . . . Once, I remember tucking my own bread (which I had brought from home in the morning) under my arm, wrapped up in a piece of paper like a book, and going into the best dining-room in Johnson's alamode beef-house in Clare court, Drury Lane, and magnificently ordering a small plate of alamode beef to eat with it. What the waiter thought of such a strange little apparition, coming in all alone, I don't know; but I can see him now, staring at me as I ate my dinner, and bringing up the other waiter to look. I gave him a half-penny, and I wish, now, that he hadn't taken it.

Saturday night was the boy's great weekly triumph. He would walk home feeling the grandeur of having six shillings in his pocket, looking in shop windows, and thinking what it would buy, if only he could afford to spend it. Often he could not resist the extravagance of buying *The Portfolio of Entertaining and Instructive Varieties in History, Science, Literature, and Fine Arts, etc.*, a two-penny magazine which contained burlesques of plays and outrageous poetic parodies.

John Dickens's creditors had refused to listen to any proposal of executing a new "Deed," and there was now no recourse but to insolvency proceedings. The law provided that the clothing and personal effects of the debtor and his dependents must not exceed £20 in value. The clothes that Charles wore therefore had to be inspected by the appraiser. He had a half holiday to call on this official and was terrified lest his grandfather's fat old silver watch, given him by old Mrs Dickens and now ticking loudly in his pocket, might bring him over the £20. But the man came out, glanced at the boy's poor white hat, little jacket, and corduroy trousers, and said "it was all right." "So I was greatly relieved, and made him a bow of acknowledgment as I went out."

At Lady Day the encampment at Gower Street broke up and Mrs Dickens and the younger children went to live in the Marshalsea. Though they were rather crowded, with four small children in the same little room with their parents, it was cheaper than paying for outside quarters. The debtors could not leave the prison but their families could go in and out freely until the gates were locked at night. And if no one could leave until morning, they were no longer subject to angry siege from their creditors. The Dickens family did not lack for bodily comforts there; John Dickens's income from the Navy Pay Office was still going on. The move, however, meant redoubled loneliness for Charles, who did not go with them. "I (small Cain that I was, except that I had never done harm to any one) was handed over as a lodger to a reduced old lady," Mrs Elizabeth Roylance, "who took children in to board, and had once done so at Brighton; and who, with a few alterations and embellishments, unconsciously began to sit for Mrs Pipchin in *Dombey* when she took me in."

His lodging was paid by his father; but now Charles had to pay, not only for his noonday dinner, but for his breakfast of bread and milk and his supper of bread and cheese out of his own money from the blacking warehouse.

They made a hole in the six or seven shillings, I know well; and I was out at the blacking-warehouse all day, and had to support myself upon that money all the week . . . I certainly had no other assistance whatever . . . from Monday morning until Saturday night. No advice, no counsel, no encouragement, no consolation, no support, from any one that I can call to mind, so help me God.

I was so young and childish, and so little qualified – how could I be otherwise? – to undertake the whole charge of my own existence, that in going to Hungerford Stairs of a morning, I could not resist the stale pastry put out at half-price on trays at the confectioners' doors in Tottenham Court Road; and I often spent in that, the money I should have kept for my dinner. Then I went without my dinner, or bought a roll, or a slice of pudding.

We had half-an-hour, I think, for tea. When I had money enough, I used to go to a coffee-shop, and have half-a-pint of coffee, and a slice of bread and butter. When I had no money, I took a turn in Covent Garden Market, and stared at the pineapples.

One coffee-shop in St Martin's Lane stood near the church and had in the door

an oval glass-plate, with COFFEE-ROOM painted on it, addressed towards the street. If I ever find myself in a very different kind of coffee-room now, but where there is such an inscription on glass, and read it backward on the wrong side MOOR-EEFFOC (as I often used to do then, in a dismal reverie), a shock goes through my blood.

I know I do not exaggerate, unconsciously and unintentionally, the scantiness of my resources and the difficulties of my life. I know that if a shilling or so were given me by anyone, I spent it in a dinner or a tea. I know that I worked, from morning to night, with common men and boys, a shabby child. . . . I know that I lounged about the streets, insufficiently and unsatisfactorily fed. I know that, but for the mercy of God, I might easily have been, for any care that was taken of me, a little robber or a little vagabond.

Sundays at nine in the morning he called for Fanny at the Academy of Music and the two walked on across Westminster Bridge to the

Borough and spent the day at the prison. Charles considered his rescue from the blacking warehouse quite hopeless, but felt his solitude so keenly that one Sunday night he broke down and wept before his father. Apparently John Dickens had not thought about it before, but now his kind nature was touched. A back attic was found for the child in Lant Street, not far from the Marshalsea. When Charles took possession of his new abode, he thought it was Paradise.

Now he could breakfast "at home" – in the Marshalsea – going there as early as the gates were open in the morning. He also had supper in the prison, and generally returned to Lant Street at nine o'clock. His landlord there was a fat, lame old gentleman with a quiet old wife and an innocent grown-up son who was also lame – a trio who were to become the Garlands in *The Old Curiosity Shop*.

Despite the nearness of his new lodgings to the prison, he was separated from his family for most of every day, and he continued to feel very lonely. Now and then he played on the coal barges with Poll Green and Bob Fagin during the dinner hour, but mostly he was by himself, strolling about the back streets of the Adelphi. Coming home over Blackfriars Bridge and along Blackfriars Road on Saturday nights, he would sometimes be seduced into going into a show van at a corner to see the fat pig, the wild Indian, and the Little-lady. Even in these small diversions, though, he was alone.

He was still so far from looking the twelve years he had attained that when he went into a bar for a glass of ale or porter to wash down the saveloy and loaf he had eaten in the street, they didn't like to give it to him. One evening he stopped at a public house in Parliament Street,

and said to the landlord behind the bar, "What is your very best – the VERY *best* ale – a glass?" For, the occasion was a festive one, for some reason: I forget why . . . "Twopence," says he. "Then," says I, "just draw me a glass of that, if you please, with a good head to it." The landlord looked at me, in return, over the bar, from head to foot, with a strange smile on his face; and instead of drawing the beer, looked round the screen and said something to his wife, who came out from behind it, with her work in her hand, and joined him in surveying me. . . . They served me with the ale, though I suspect it was not the strongest on the premises; and the landlord's wife, opening the little half-door and bending down, gave me a kiss that was half-admiring and half-compassionate, but all womanly and good, I am sure.

During the spring Charles was present with some of the family in
Tenterden Street to see his sister Fanny receive one of the prizes
awarded to pupils at the Royal Academy of Music. He loved Fanny,
and he was proud of her, but the gala occasion reminded him bitterly of
the opportunities he himself was deprived of. "I could not bear to think
of myself – beyond the reach of all such honourable emulation and
success. The tears ran down my face. I prayed, when I went to bed that
night, to be lifted out of the humiliation and neglect in which I was."

Seizures of his old illness came back to him repeatedly in these days of
misery. Agonizing in their constriction of the kidneys, they were doubtless the protests of his small body at the unhappiness in his heart. One of
them occurred at the warehouse:

> Bob Fagin was very good to me on the occasion of a bad attack of
> my old disorder. I suffered such excruciating pain that time, that they
> made a temporary bed of straw in my old recess in the counting-
> house, and I rolled about on the floor, and Bob filled empty blacking-
> bottles with hot water, and applied relays of them to my side, half the
> day. . . . Bob (who was much bigger and older than I) did not like the
> idea of my going home alone, and took me under his protection. I
> was too proud to let him know about the prison; and after making
> several efforts to get rid of him . . . shook hands with him on the
> steps of a house near Southwark Bridge on the Surrey side, making
> believe that I lived there. As a finishing piece of reality in case of his
> looking back, I knocked at the door, I recollect, and asked, when the
> woman opened it, if that was Mr Robert Fagin's house.

In the Marshalsea, after his first outburst of despair, John Dickens had
recovered his usual bounce. The other debtors made him chairman of
the committee to regulate the internal workings of the prison, to provide
coal, hot water, the means of cooking, and to maintain order in the alehouse common room. The new chairman flung himself energetically into
his duties. With his consistent talent for managing everything except his
own affairs, he did an excellent job and soon was on lordly terms with
everyone from the turnkeys to the humblest inmate. Once, when the
prisoners made a petition for a royal bounty to enable them to drink the
King's health on his forthcoming birthday in August, Charles begged
to be allowed to see them affix their signatures to the document. It had
been drawn up by John Dickens and was stretched out on a great
ironing board. The door was flung open, and a long file of debtors began
to come in, each signing it in turn. To anyone who "weakly showed the

least disposition to hear it," Captain Porter read every word in a loud sonorous voice, giving a roll to such orotund words as "gracious Majesty," "your gracious Majesty's unfortunate subjects," "your Majesty's well-known munificence": "my poor father meanwhile [so his son recalled] listening with a little of an author's vanity, and contemplating (not severely) the spikes on the opposite wall."

On 26 April 1824, John Dickens's mother died. Though she left him £450, the bequest did not overcome his financial difficulties. On 28 May, well before the will could be proved, he had been declared insolvent; and in any event, whatever money he came into had to be applied to his debts. On 2 November of the following year, and a year later still, on 13 November, his creditors received two dividends. But at least now John Dickens was free of the Marshalsea. He had been there just a few days over three months.

The family returned to Camden Town and lodged temporarily with Mrs Roylance. But by June Mrs Dickens had taken a small house at 29 Johnson Street, an even poorer locality than Bayham Street. John Dickens hopefully resumed work at the Navy Pay Office, although his petition for retirement had stated that his health incapacitated him for duty. Perhaps the authorities would overlook the fact that he had been declared insolvent, and let him stay on at his post. In the family, though, not a word was said about taking Charles from the blacking warehouse.

He waited, but nothing happened. Evidently his father's release from prison meant no end of slavery for him. The blacking warehouse had moved from Hungerford Stairs to Chandos Street, Covent Garden. Here Charles trudged from Somers Town daily, with some cold hotchpotch for his dinner in a small basin tied up in a handkerchief. "I had the same wanderings about the streets as I used to have, and was just as solitary and self-dependent as before; but I had not the same difficulty in merely living. I never however heard a word of being taken away, or of being otherwise than quite provided for."

The new establishment was larger than the old, with several windows on the street. At one of these, for light, Charles worked with Bob Fagin. The two boys had become so dexterous in tying up pots that they could turn out a great many in five minutes; sometimes a little crowd of people gathered to watch them. "I saw my father coming in the door one day when we were very busy, and I wondered how he could bear it."

Perhaps, when John Dickens saw him in the window, the public exhibition of the boy, engaged in menial toil, did strike some chord of pride or of paternal pity in him. For shortly afterwards he quarrelled with James Lamert, who may well have thought it absurdly pretentious that an improvident man for whom so many favours had been done should cavil about whether his son worked by a public window or did the same work in private. He told the boy he was very much insulted. "I cried very much, partly because it was so sudden, and partly because in his anger he was violent about my father, though gentle to me. . . . With a relief so strange that it was like oppression, I went home."

His mother was appalled. Probably John Dickens's tangled affairs were not yet straightened out. There may already have been reason to suspect that he would not be kept on in the Navy Pay Office. In that event, what would they do? How could they afford to throw away even the seven shillings a week Charles had now been earning? She set herself the next day to accommodate the quarrel, and softened James Lamert. "She brought home a request for me to return next morning, and a high character of me, which I am very sure I deserved."

But John Dickens had taken a stand. Charles, he said, should go back to the blacking warehouse no more, but should go to school. On the boy their divergent positions made a deep impression. He summarized it,

> I do not write resentfully or angrily for I know how all these things have worked together to make me what I am: but I never afterwards forgot, I never shall forget, I never can forget, that my mother was warm for my being sent back.
>
> From that hour until this at which I write, no word of that part of my childhood . . . has passed my lips . . . I have no idea how long it lasted; whether for a year, or much more, or less. From that hour, until this, my father and mother have been stricken dumb upon it. I have never heard the least allusion to it, however far off and remote, from either of them. I have never, until I now impart it to this paper, in any burst of confidence with any one, my own wife not excepted, raised the curtain I then dropped, thank God.

Indeed, his wife and children never learned of the blacking warehouse during his lifetime. They heard of it first in his friend Forster's biography after his death. And even Forster learned it, he says, only by the chance of mentioning to Dickens that Charles Wentworth Dilke thought he had once seen him as a child in a warehouse near the Strand. He had gone in there with the elder Dickens, given the child a half crown, and received in return a very low bow. Dickens listened to the anecdote in silence, and then spoke on another subject. "I felt," Forster says, "that I had unintentionally touched a painful place in his memory." It was not until some time later that Dickens told him the story, and placed the written narrative of those days in his hands.

Actually, the time spent in the blacking warehouse can have been little over four months. But that had nothing to do with what it seemed to the child, or with the lasting impression it made upon the man. In his secret agony, the hours and weeks prolonged themselves into an eternity. As he remembered them, and projected them, both in the fragment of autobiography he wrote in 1845 or 1846 and in their fictional guise in *David Copperfield*, their hapless victim was a poor little mite of only ten, and their protraction an endless sentence of torment.

No emphasis can overstate the depth and intensity with which these experiences ate into his childish soul. For years afterwards, he could not go near Hungerford Stairs. For years, when he drew near Robert Warren's in the Strand, he crossed to the other side of the way, to avoid smelling the cement of the blacking corks. "It was a very long time before I liked to go up Chandos Street. My old way home by the Borough made me cry, after my eldest child could speak."

But it is more than a mere unavailing ache in the heart, however poignant, and however prolonged into manhood, that gives the Marshalsea and Warren's Blacking their significance in Dickens's life. They were formative. Somewhere deep down inside, he made the decision that never again was he going to be so victimized. He would fall prey to none of the financial imprudence that had been his father's undoing. He would subject himself to a steel discipline. No obstacle should stand between him and ambition; no grief or frustration interfere with his strivings. In one sense, the grieving child in the blacking warehouse might be said to have died, to be succeeded by a man of deadly determination, of insuperable resolve, hard and aggressive. In another, that child never died, but was continually reborn in a host of children suffering or dying young and other innocents undergoing injustice and pain; from Oliver and Smike and poor Jo to all the victims of a stony-hearted and archaic social system who throng Dickens's later books. In a final sense, the great and successful effort of his career was to assimilate and understand the blacking warehouse and the Marshalsea, and the kind of world in which such things could be.

4

Ambition's Ladder

In May 1827, a brisk new office boy started working for Ellis and Blackmore, attorneys, of 5 Holborn Court, Gray's Inn. He was just a quarter past his fifteenth birthday, and had dropped out of school only that spring. His parents had been finding it hard to meet the fees; that March they had been evicted from their house at 29 Johnson Street for failure to pay their rent, and in the course of the year had acquired another mouth to feed, when their last child, Augustus, was born. They were now living at 17 The Polygon, but only as "lodgers."

During the previous two and a half years Charles had been at Wellington House Academy, where he had risen to be one of the senior boys. The child whose eyes had filled with tears of gratitude on hearing his father's determination to send him back to school had become a romping curly-head given to pranks and wild explosions of laughter. He bore no visible shadow of the blacking warehouse. No more is heard of bouts of fever or attacks of spasm. But no one could have imagined, from the bright unclouded face, how fatefully that past lay within him, or how piercing was his ambition to get ahead.

John Dickens had acted quickly on his decision. Within a few days the youngster had been sent to Wellington House Academy nearby to ask for a card of terms. And at seven o'clock one morning, very soon afterwards, before the end of June 1824, he started as a day pupil.

This third schooltime was a buoyant period of recovering from the anguish of the blacking warehouse. He never spoke of his experiences to his schoolmates, but he well knew what set him off from them. It was not the things they knew and he had forgotten; he relearned them quickly enough. It was the things he knew and could never forget, which they did not know. "What would they say, who made so light of money," David Copperfield asks, "if they could know how I had scraped my halfpence together for the purchase of my daily saveloy and beer, or my slices of pudding? How could it affect them, who were so innocent of London life and London streets, to discover how knowing I was (and ashamed to be) in the meanest phases of both?"

But all his companions saw was a rather short, plump, fresh-coloured youngster, jolly-looking, and given to immoderate laughter. He dressed with extreme neatness and wore a turn-down collar instead of a frill, so that he looked less youthful than he was. His head he carried with extraordinary erectness. Nobody would have recognized in this well-turned-out lad with the proud head and the uncontrollable laughter the shabby labouring hind he was trying to forget.

Wellington House Academy had a certain local celebrity, because its Welsh owner, Mr William Jones, though no great scholar himself, had the judgement to employ competent masters. "The master was supposed among us," Dickens says in "Our School," "to know nothing, and one of the ushers was supposed to know everything." The teacher believed to know everything was Mr Taylor, the writing, mathematics, and English master, who shared the younger boys with the Latin master. Mr Manville, or Mandeville, the Latin master, took pains with the boys who showed ability and a desire to learn and ignored the lazy or stupid. There were also the junior master, Mr Shiers, a fat little dancing master who taught the hornpipe, and a sharp little French master.

Mr Jones, the headmaster, was a sadist, forever smiting the palms of offenders with "a bloated mahogany ruler," "or viciously drawing a pair of pantaloons tight with one of his large hands, and caning the wearer with the other." The pupil-boarders were constantly smarting from his ferocity, especially any of those who appealed to his tastes by a pleasing plumpness. But Charles and the other day boys, who might bear tales home, heard the swish of his cane less often.

The schoolroom was a timber structure in the large playground behind Mr Jones's residence. Here the boys kept redpolls, linnets, and canaries, and trained white mice, "better than the masters trained the boys." One white mouse, who lived in the cover of a Latin dictionary, "ran up ladders, drew Roman chariots, shouldered muskets, turned wheels, and even made a very creditable appearance on the stage as the Dog of Montargis."

The Dog of Montargis was one of the plays that Charles and the other boys amused themselves by staging in toy theatres with gorgeous scenery. They also did *Cherry and Fair Star*, a dramatic version of Mme d'Aulnoy's *La Princesse Belle-Étoile et le Prince Chéri*, and Pocock's exciting melodrama, *The Miller and His Men*, a lurid story of robbers innocently disguised as millers by day. The mill was so constructed that it could be made at the end to tumble to pieces by means of firecrackers.

All the other things that schoolboys usually do, Charles did. He devoured successive numbers of a penny weekly entitled *The Terrific Register*, "making myself unspeakably miserable, and frightening the very wits out of my head" with tales "in which there was always a pool of blood, and at least one body." He wrote stories for a school paper that also contained such items as "*Lost.* – By a boy with a long nose, and green eyes, a very bad temper. Whoever has found the same may keep it, as the owner is better off without it." With the other boys Charles chattered about the streets, talking a lingo that they hoped would lead to their being mistaken for foreigners, and playing pranks on old ladies. In Drummond Street once, Charles led his companions in pretending to be beggars, staggering the old ladies by the impudence with which he asked for charity, and then exploding with laughter and taking to his heels.

During his first year at the Academy, in December 1825, his father's elder brother William unexpectedly died at the age of forty-three, leaving an estate of some £1,300. Of this, £300 was left to his widow outright, and she was to receive the interest on the remaining £1,000 – which was invested in consols – as long as she lived and remained unmarried. But on her death, or in the event that she remarried, these invested funds, after a few other minor bequests, were to be shared in equal parts among his brother's children.

The next year and a half passed swiftly. Apart from learning to be something like a cheerful everyday boy again, it is not certain what Charles learned during this last brief schooling. One thing he did *not* learn, his schoolfellow John Bowden said, was to play the piano; the music master declared it would be robbing his parents. Another fellow pupil, Henry Danson, thought in later years that Charles had not taken Latin, but, in fact, he won a Latin Prize, having been coached by the junior master, Richard Shiers, to whom in gratitude he gave an inscribed copy of the works of Horace.

Dickens shows few signs, however, of having been influenced by Roman literature. One can only imagine what the periods of Cicero and the polished elegances of Horace meant to the boy who had gone hungry beneath the Adelphi arches and wept in the spiked shadow of the Marshalsea. Certainly they made no such impression on his boyhood as the eighteenth-century novelists and the glowing worlds of fairy-tale romance had made upon his childhood.

The classics of the silver age may well have seemed to him very remote from anything he had known or dreamed. Long before he returned to declining *mensa* and *dominus* the roots of his inspiration were already sunk in a far different soil.

The days when he would leave school had not drawn near without his mother's having taken thought about his future. She had an aunt, Mrs C. W. Charlton, who kept a lodging-house at 16 Berners Street. On visits to this aunt she had often met one of the lodgers, Mr Edward Blackmore, a partner in the law firm of Ellis and Blackmore. He considered Charles a clever, good-looking youth, and consented at Mrs Dickens's earnest request to take him on as an office boy.

When Charles reported for duty to Ellis and Blackmore on that May morning of 1827, he was still rather undersized and appeared younger than his age, but he made up for it by the aggressive bearing with which he wore his blue jacket and the military-looking cap perched jauntily on one side of his head. It promptly earned him a black eye, which George Lear, a fellow clerk, commented on. "Yes," Charles replied, "a big blackguard fellow knocked my cap off as I was crossing over Chancery Lane from Lincoln's Inn gateway. He said 'Halloa, sojer!' which I could not stand, so I at once struck him and he then hit me in the eye."

Shortly after Charles's start with the firm, it moved to 1 Raymond Buildings, where the clerks had a second-floor office overlooking Holborn. In the intervals of carving his name on his desk and keeping an account book for his employers in which his own salary rose slowly from ten shillings to thirteen and six and then to fifteen shillings, he also had a keen eye for his surroundings. Mr Ellis, the senior partner, by his inveterate snuff-taking probably later suggested Mr Perker in *Pickwick;* and Charles was delighted by queer characters among the clients, one of whom later emerged as Newman Noggs.

But the work itself he found dull: getting wills registered, serving processes, carrying documents to and from counsel's offices and courts of law. It was, to be sure, the apprenticeship of a responsible and dignified profession; one might become a prosperous solicitor or a K.C. in silk terrifying witnesses with his sarcasms, or even a learned judge. Nevertheless, Charles found the law slow and irksome. He wanted some more exciting – above all, some speedier – way of rising to prosperity.

His mind turned towards journalism, in which during the last two years his father had been engaged. For, as John Dickens had feared, the Navy Pay Office would have none of a man who had been declared insolvent. He had, therefore, tremulously renewed his petition for retirement. Ultimately, on compassionate grounds, and in consideration of his almost twenty years of service and his six children, the Treasurer of the Navy had recommended that he be granted a retirement allowance of £145 a year. In March 1825, John Dickens, by then forty-one, found himself obliged to meet his loss of income by discovering a new means of earning a living.

Save for his careless ways with money, however, and his flowers of speech, John Dickens was no Micawber. With enormous vigour and industry he tackled the difficulties of learning shorthand, to such effect that little over a year later he was one of the Parliamentary corps of the *British Press*. Its members were a group of crack reporters who during the time Parliament was in session earned a princely salary of almost fifteen guineas a week. To John Dickens's son the prospect of rising from fifteen shillings to fifteen guineas within a few years looked sufficiently splendid. More enticing still, many men distinguished in other walks of life, Charles learned, had begun their careers by reporting Parliamentary debates. Let him get his foot on the beginning round of that ladder, and he'd climb far enough!

While he was still at Wellington House Academy, he would sometimes take in to the *British Press* what was called "penny-a-line stuff"; notices of accidents, fires, or police reports that had escaped the regular reporters. A knowledge of shorthand was almost indispensable for a career in journalism, and he had been told that a perfect command of its mysteries was about equal in difficulty to mastering six languages. But with a tenacity of purpose beyond his years, he set himself to the task.

He laid out half a guinea on a copy of Gurney's textbook, *Brachygraphy, or an Easy and Compendious System of Shorthand*, then the most celebrated manual of the subject. Possibly with some help from his father and from one of his uncles, John Henry Barrow, who was a reporter on *The Times*, he gritted his will to master its intricacies. As the months crept on at Ellis and Blackmore's, though he often groaned over the toil, he kept at it relentlessly.

The changes that were wrung upon dots, which in such a position meant such a thing, and in such another position something else entirely different; the wonderful vagaries that were played by circles; the unaccountable consequences that resulted from marks like flies' legs; the tremendous effect of a curve in the wrong place; not only troubled my waking hours, but reappeared before me in my sleep. When I had groped my way, blindly, through these difficulties, and had mastered the alphabet, there then appeared a procession of new horrors, called arbitrary characters; the most despotic characters I had ever known; who insisted, for instance, that a thing like the beginning of a cobweb meant expectation; and that a pen-and-ink sky-rocket stood for disadvantageous. When I had fixed these wretches in my mind, I found that they had driven everything else out of it; then, beginning again, I forgot them; while I was picking them up, I dropped the other fragments of the system; in short, it was almost heart-breaking.

However, life was not all toil. Fanny had been graduated from the Royal Academy of Music in January 1827, after having studied there under the well-known composer Ignaz Moscheles. She had blossomed into a charming and talented girl with a musical career opening before her. Through her fellow pupils at the Academy she had friends who joined each other in evenings of piano music and song. Although Charles had been pronounced hopeless at the piano himself, he had not lost his relish for such comic songs as "The Dandy Dog's Meat Man," or escaped the taste for romantic ballads, and often joined his sister at these melodious gatherings.

He was also busy exploring the life of London. He roamed over all the crowded City, from Tower Hill and Aldgate Pump to Temple Bar and the Strand. He knew Palace Yard, Whitehall, the Horse Guards, St James's Park, the Golden Cross, Piccadilly, Pall Mall, and Regent Street. He was familiar with Vauxhall Gardens, Knightsbridge, Bond Street, Lincoln's Inn Fields. He ranged as far as from distant Hampton Court and Richmond to Greenwich, and from the Old Kent Road to Hampstead Heath and Islington. He had seen the drunken revellers staggering home at early dawn and women bringing in baskets of fruit to Covent Garden Market, and, long past midnight, watched the baked-potato men and kidney-pie vendors closing their stalls in the neighbourhood around Marsh Gate and the Royal Coburg Theatre. "I thought I knew something of the town," said George Lear, remembering their days together at Ellis and Blackmore's, "but after a little talk with Dickens I found that I knew nothing. He knew it all from Bow to Brentford."

He knew more than the streets; he knew their people. "He could imitate, in a manner that I never heard equalled," Lear testified, "the low population of the streets of London in all their varieties, whether mere loafers or sellers of fruit, vegetables, or anything else," and, besides these, all the leading actors and popular singers of the day, comic or patriotic.

This knowledge of the theatre and its performers Charles was gaining with another fellow clerk, Thomas Potter. Charles had suddenly shot up into a young man and, in a new brown suit, of which the coat was cut like a dress coat, and a high felt hat, entertained "a befitting contempt for boys at day-schools." These two youngsters – Charles was just past sixteen – dined in low-priced restaurants on chops and kidneys with a draught of stout, roamed the town together, and were beginning to experiment in mild Havana cigars and whiskey and water.

After dinner there was the theatre. Admission to the galleries was only one shilling, and half-price at nine o'clock, leaving a good part of the mixed bill to be still enjoyed. The only theatres licensed for spoken drama were the so-called "major" theatres at Covent Garden, Drury Lane, and the Haymarket. Besides these, however, there were a good many "minor" theatres ostensibly devoted to musical performances, but mostly these evaded the rules by disguising their offerings with a few songs and calling them "burlettas." And across Westminster Bridge in Surrey, in the East End, and to the north and west, there were other theatres which gave a wide range of performances. Astley's was a circus that also did plays about savage chiefs and tyrannical Eastern monarchs; the Surrey had nautical melodramas with pirates and gallant tars; the Pavilion dealt in bloodcurdling criminals; the Grecian Saloon was a sort of cabaret, with a Moorish band and liquid refreshments served in its gardens.

Finally, in Wilson Street, Gray's Inn Lane, Catharine Street, Strand, and other places, there were "private" theatres. In these, which were even cheaper, stage-struck amateurs were allowed for a fee to play Shylock, Captain Absolute, Charles Surface, or Macbeth. For £2 anyone could be Richard, Duke of Gloucester, and stab King Henry, make love to the Lady Ann, shout "Orf with his ed!" and then, slow and sneeringly, "So much for Bu-u-u-uck-ingham!" and clash blades in the excitement of the end.

But these minor dissipations were not making Charles lose sight of his goal. He continued to grind away without ceasing at Gurney's shorthand. He had left Ellis and Blackmore, where his salary obstinately remained at fifteen shillings a week, and taken a post with Charles Molloy, a solicitor with offices at 6 Symonds Inn. Here one of his fellow clerks may have been Thomas Mitton, who had gone to school with his brother Frederick, and who in the course of the next few years became one of Charles's friends.

The position with Molloy, however, seemed little more promising. By November 1828, Charles had resolved upon and taken a bold step. He was still too young for the reporters' gallery, but it would be better to take his own way and do something that would prepare him for it. His great-aunt's husband, Mr C. W. Charlton, had a younger relation, Thomas Charlton, Jr, who was a freelance reporter in the Consistory Court of Doctors' Commons. There he sat in a rented box waiting until one of the proctors engaged him to take down a case. This box Charles could share. He felt confident of his command of shorthand, and was sure he would earn more than fifteen shillings a week. Before the end of November he quit his job with Molloy. He still lacked two months of being seventeen.

Doctors' Commons no longer exists today. But in 1828 it lay between St Paul's and the river. An archway from Paul's Chain opened on a stone-paved court of old red brick houses. The inside of the Court was a black-wainscoted and columned room looking like a chapel, Dickens thought. Doctors in red gowns and grey wigs surrounded a platform; upon it others in black gowns with white fur sat at a green table "like a billiard table without the cushions." Above them, blinking like an owl, sat the presiding judge.

Doctors' Commons included the Admiralty Court; the Prerogative Office, where wills were registered and filed; the Prerogative Court, which dealt with testamentary matters in the dioceses; the Court of Arches, which was the provincial court of the Archbishop of Canterbury; and the Consistory Court, which was the diocesan court of the Bishop of London. The last of these was the one in which Dickens mainly worked. None of them raised in any way his estimate of the law. They were crabbed, archaic, muddled, expensive of time and money, and obstructive of justice. Watching these "monkish attorneys," he felt himself being wrought to a fine mood of scorn and impatience.

Of his first year as a shorthand writer little is known. In the beginning, waiting for a proctor to engage his services, he had plenty of time on his hands. As soon as he was eighteen (the very earliest age allowed), on 7 February 1830, he applied for a reader's ticket at the British Museum. During the next three or four years he read with eager industry. His self-directed explorations into Addison, Shakespeare, and his *Life* by Symonds, Goldsmith's *History of England*, Berges's *Short Account of the Roman Senate*, were an enormously valuable addition to his brief formal education. In later years he would refer to them as the most useful that he had ever made.

During this time he continued to be a visitor in the homes of his Barrow uncles. One of them, Edward Barrow, had married Janet Ross, a talented miniaturist who did a portrait of Charles when he was eighteen. It is his earliest known portrait, and shows a surprised young face stiffly perched at the top of an enormously high black stock.

In Doctors' Commons he had found it helpful to have a place in which to transcribe his notes, and had taken an office, of which he shared the expense with a proctor named Charles Edward Fenton. But Dickens found law reporting wearisome, and his income wearily uncertain; outside of term times, of course, his fees dwindled away almost entirely. Even the addition of practising in the Metropolitan Police Courts as well as in Doctors' Commons did not swell his earnings enough.

He was unhappy at this monotonous work; and he had other reasons now for being desperately anxious to increase his income. For he had fallen violently in love with the bright eyes and bewitching curls of a little beauty named Maria Beadnell who had taken him into a delirious captivity. And even through the luminous mists of love he knew well enough that her father, who was a banker, would not be much impressed by the pretensions of an impecunious youth making a precarious living as a shorthand reporter.

He had to achieve more brilliant prospects, and that speedily. He could not wait forever, hoping for a chance of Parliamentary reporting that never came. Spurred by this necessity, his mind turned to other means of livelihood. He knew he sang a comic song well. Perhaps experience in the private theatres had suggested to him that he had more ability as an actor than most aspirants to such a career. He resolved to make an attack upon the stage. Apparently, he did not stop to ask whether Mr Beadnell would be more impressed by an actor than by a law reporter.

If it were not for the intensity and efficiency with which Dickens went about everything he did, this determination of his might sound not unlike Mrs Dickens's notion of establishing a school. But with characteristic energy he began a business-like campaign. He had been going to the theatre almost every night for the preceding three years. He had been especially devoted to Charles Mathews, and had sat in the pit whenever that actor played. He now started practising industriously, "often four, five, six hours a day: shut up in my own room, or walking about in the fields. I prescribed to myself, too, a sort of Hamiltonian system for learning parts; and learnt a great number." Besides this self-training, he took a series of lessons from the well-known actor Robert Keeley.

Inspired by dreams of Maria Beadnell, who had been sent to Paris "to complete her education," he worked away to perfect his acting technique. After weeks of drill, he thought himself sufficiently adept. From his little office in Bell Yard he wrote to Bartley, the stage manager for Mathews at the Lyceum. He stated his age and what he thought he could do, adding that he believed he had "a strong perception of character and oddity, and a natural power of reproducing" what he observed.

Bartley wrote to me almost immediately to say that they were busy getting up the Hunchback (so they were), but that they would communicate with me again, in a fortnight. Punctual to the time another letter came, with an appointment to do anything of Mathews's I pleased, before him and Charles Kemble, on a certain day at the theatre. My sister Fanny was in the secret, and was to go with me to play the songs. I was laid up when the day came, with a terrible bad cold and an inflammation of the face . . . I wrote to say so, and added that I would resume my application next season.

But the application was never renewed. At the very moment he was wavering in his original hopes of Parliamentary reporting, the opportunity came. His uncle John Henry Barrow had in 1828 started a new venture called the *Mirror of Parliament*. It was a sort of Hansard, devoted to a verbally exact and well-printed transcript of Parliamentary proceedings. John Dickens was one of its reporters in the Gallery. The Barrows had begun to realize that their young nephew had ability as well as ambition. Somewhere early in 1832 he was taken on by his uncle's paper. Not only this, but in the spring of the year a new sevenpenny evening newspaper, the *True Sun*, was inaugurated and Dickens became a member of the reporting staff of this paper from its first day of publication, 5 March 1832.

For the *True Sun* he did general reporting; for the *Mirror of Parliament*, besides whatever assistance he may have given in its offices, he was specifically a Parliamentary reporter. It is not clear which engagement preceded the other, but for a time he certainly worked concurrently on both publications. If he first entered the Gallery for his uncle's paper, he was, as his friend Forster claims, still only nineteen years of age; if not, less than a month past his twentieth birthday.

Once in the Gallery, he strode rapidly to a position of distinction – in his own words, "made a great splash." Among the eighty or ninety reporters there, James Grant of the *Morning Advertiser* declared, he "occupied the very highest rank, not merely for accuracy in reporting, but for marvellous quickness in transcript." And at Westminster, as it was before the fire of 1834, reporting was not made easy. Reporters had to squeeze through the narrow door of the crowded Strangers' Gallery, and shift as best they could in the back row with five or six rows of seats in front of them. "I have worn my knees," Dickens said, "by writing on them in the old gallery of the old House of Commons; and I have worn my feet by standing to write in a preposterous pen in the old House of Lords, where we used to be huddled together like so many sheep – kept in waiting, say, until the woolsack might want restuffing." Under these circumstances, and against no inconsiderable competition from a body of veterans, this youth in his early twenties achieved pre-eminence. "There never *was* such a shorthand writer!" said one of them.

The young reporter's mind had travelled a long way since he had trembled in childhood at the radicals as terrible banditti who deserved to be hanged. Now he was an ardent reformer. And he reached the Gallery just in time to witness the final stages of the struggle over the Reform Bill of 1832. Bad trade and economic misery had united the nation in a sense of its political wrongs. There was rick-burning in the south, and workmen drilling in preparation for social war in the industrial north. The middle classes feared revolution from below as much as they desired to wrest political power from the aristocracy. Wellington was defeated in Parliament and Lord Grey's ministry formed explicitly on the issue of reform.

The Reform Bill the new Government brought in was a shock to the Tories. Rotten boroughs that had sent 140 representatives to Parliament were either to be abolished outright or to lose half their members. All £10 householders were to be admitted to the borough franchise, and the seats obtained by disfranchisement redistributed among the large centres of population. The opposition had so little expected anything so drastic that they were stunned and had no plan ready. Within three weeks the Bill passed its second reading by a majority of just one vote.

Further manoeuvres forced the election of a new Parliament, in which the Bill had a majority of 136. But when it had passed the House of Commons, the Lords threw it out by a majority of forty-one. Popular indignation exploded. There were outrages against bishops and peers.

In the south ricks were burning night after night. Unemployment, starvation, and cholera added to the terrors of the winter of 1831–2.

The last stages of the Parliamentary struggle Dickens witnessed from the Gallery. A new Bill was introduced, modified in some details, but not weakened. When it reached the Lords again, the month of May saw a determined attempt to amend it out of recognition. But the country was equally determined; Lord Grey knew it and resigned. The King was obliged to come to terms and Grey consented to return only on securing a written promise to create any number of peers necessary to carry the Bill. The threat proved enough, and, to a flying of flags and ringing of bells, the Bill became law.

The reformed Parliament was a hard-working group of men far superior in ability to the usual mediocrity of such legislative bodies. It achieved a remarkable legislative record, recasting municipal institutions, passing the first effective Factory Act, and abolishing Negro slavery. It contained such outstanding veterans of debate as Lord Grey, Lord John Russell, and Edward Stanley, later fourteenth Earl of Derby, as well as the Irish leader O'Connell; among the brilliant more recent arrivals were Cobbett, Gladstone, Macaulay, Grote, and the successful novelist Edward Lytton Bulwer.

But although Dickens had a settled antagonism to the Conservatives, who were outnumbered three to one in this Parliament, he was not impressed by the body or by what it accomplished. He saw the House as a place of protracted talk, dominated by a mania for archaic rules and precedents and red tape and sealing-wax, and even after its reform hardly less the defender of privileged interests than before. He saw its members, with few exceptions, as a mob of brainless windbags, place-warmers, and agents of chicanery and corruption. Even when he knew them to be honest and able, he was apt to dislike them simply for being the kind of men Parliament moulded its members into being. He could not bear Lord Grey's "style of speaking, his fishy coldness, his uncongenial and unsympathetic politeness, his insufferable though most gentlemanly artificiality."

During the midnight debates of the new Parliament, however, Dickens was working overtime, making as much as twenty to twenty-five guineas a week. And sometimes, for all the ennui generated by dull speakers, there could be moments of intense dramatic excitement. When O'Connell was speaking against the Bill for the Suppression of Disturbances in Ireland, he drew such an affecting picture of a widow seeking her only son among the peasants killed by soldiers in an anti-tithe riot that the young reporter, abandoning his pencil, was obliged to lay his head on his arms and weep. After sessions such as this, he and his fellow reporters would repair to a little tavern in the Palace Yard. Here, in an upstairs room, they could write out their copy and compare doubtful passages with colleagues who had sharper ears.

Only one of these associates, however, was a personal friend. This was Thomas Beard, a reporter for the *Morning Herald*, whom Dickens knew well enough to invite to a party his parents gave on his twentieth birthday. Towards all the rest of his fellow journalists his manner was described as courteous but exceedingly reserved. Leaving them after a late session of the House, he would make his way up Whitehall and the Strand to the lodgings in Cecil Street that he had recently taken in order to be near his work.

All week long his professional duties kept him busy so late that he often had to sleep throughout the morning. There were still visits to the theatre when he was not on duty, and sometimes on Saturdays convivial evenings with other young men, when they would "knock up a chaunt or two" over punch and cigars. Among these were Beard and perhaps his brother, Francis Carr Beard, who was a young medical student, and Henry Kolle, a bank clerk who was also acquainted with Maria Beadnell's family.

Dickens did not remain long in his lodgings in the Strand. "The Cecil Street people," he explained to Kolle, "put too much water in their hash, lost a nutmeg grater, attended on me most miserably, dirted the table cloth, &c., &c.,; and so (detesting petty miseries) I gave them warning and have not yet fixed upon a 'local habitation and a name.'" Soon he was living with his parents again, this time at 13 Fitzroy Street.

Dickens had resigned from the *True Sun* towards the end of July. His position with the *Mirror of Parliament* was now high indeed. Often he was invited to spend the weekend at the home of his uncle John Henry Barrow in Norwood, and his responsibilities were coming to embrace much more than reporting. By early December he was writing to an applicant for a position, "I shall be happy to avail myself of your assistance when the session commences; and as soon as our arrangements at the *Mirror of Parliament* are completed, I shall write to you." Within the course of the year, it is plain, he had become a sort of subeditor, entrusted with hiring other members of the staff.

He was still so boyish-looking, however, that it was often hard for mature men to believe how completely he had made himself the master of his profession. During the legislative consideration of the Irish

Coercion Bill, the Chief Secretary, Edward Stanley, in moving the second reading had spoken at great and eloquent length on the condition of Ireland. His address was so long that the eight *Mirror* reporters, working in three-quarters-of-an-hour shifts, were obliged to put Dickens in to cover the end of the speech as well as the beginning. When it appeared in print, Stanley found all except the first and last parts full of errors. He therefore asked the editor of the *Mirror of Parliament* if he would not send the reporter who had taken down those two parts to do the entire speech.

John Dickens, all aglow with pride, was dispatched to fetch his son back from a Sunday in the country. Dickens was shown into a room with newspaper-strewn tables, and told to wait. Mr Stanley strode in, glanced at the young man suspiciously, and said, "I beg pardon, but I had hoped to see the gentleman who had reported part of my speech." Reddening, Dickens answered, "I am that gentleman." "Oh, indeed," returned Stanley, looking down to hide a faint smile. Dickens was accommodated with a seat in the middle of the room. When the ordeal was over, Stanley's secretary, Richard Earle, congratulated Dickens in the hall; and after receiving the young man's transcript of his speech, Stanley wrote a letter of gratitude and compliment.

How far behind now was the ten-years-past misery of the warehouse and the prison! With all the desperate intensity of his nature, he had worked and beaten and hammered away, in a resolution, Dickens said, that "excluded every other idea from my mind for four years, at a time of life when four years are equal to four times four"; and "went at it with a determination to overcome all the difficulties which fairly lifted me up into that newspaper life, and floated me away over a hundred men's heads." As he entered his twenty-first year he might well have felt proud of himself. But Maria Beadnell had returned from Paris, his love affair was going with heartbreaking badness, and he was miserable.

5

First Love

They had first met in 1829, when he was seventeen. Maria's father, George Beadnell, was connected with Smith, Payne, and Smith's banking establishment and later became its manager. He and his family lived next door at 2 Lombard Street. There were three lovely daughters. Margaret, the eldest, was already engaged. Anne, the second, had auburn curls and a tender heart. Maria, the youngest, was a year older than Charles, and a diminutive siren with dark ringlets, the brightest of eyes, and eyebrows that drew together when she pretended to frown. He thought her "prettily pettish manner" adorable, and her an angel. By the following spring he was abjectly and rapturously enslaved.

Maria was well aware of her own charms and not at all averse to a flirtation with a good-looking boy. And there was something about him, too, beneath the shining high spirits and buoyant flow of words, that made him more interesting than the other boys whom she knew. Mr and Mrs Beadnell hardly noticed him at first; to them he was no different from any of the other young men who were always about the house.

During 1830, when he was reading at the British Museum and listening to the drone of voices in Doctors' Commons, Charles passed ecstatic hours in Lombard Street. Anne played the lute and gently sympathized with his infatuation; Maria was ravishing as her fingers wove in and out among the trembling strings of the harp. Seeing her in a raspberry-coloured dress with black velvet trimming at the top, he felt his heart pinned like a captured butterfly.

He was not her only worshipper. Among the other young men who clustered around her was one named Henry Austin. He did a pretty painting of her and her little brother George in gouache as Dido and Ascanius for her album, and Charles wrote a feeble but infatuated poem for the opposite page. Another tinted sketch that Austin made of Maria, as a milkmaid with dangling sunbonnet and pail, he gave as a present to Dickens.

Everything connected with Maria, Charles found distinctive and admirable. Mr Beadnell, her father, was an excellent man, so hospitable, friendly, and kind, and of such liberal opinions. Her mother was flawless. (Though, to be sure, she never got his name right, but always called him "Mr Dickin.") Her sister Margaret sang ballads in a tender voice, Anne was very well read, and both were witty and sweet-tempered. Charles even loved Daphne, Maria's little white and liver-coloured dog.

Meanwhile Mr and Mrs Beadnell were beginning to notice him. His family and position were not striking. His prospects as a mere shorthand reporter in the law courts were not impressive. For a young man who earned so little, Maria's parents may have thought, to waste so much of it in the theatre showed no very solid character. In any case, the thought of anything between him and Maria was absurd; he was not yet even nineteen years of age. But they took no immediate action. Charles continued to be enchained by Maria's fascinating little ways, and to indulge in blissful visions of marrying and loving her forever.

Of course he wanted to marry her. He would work even harder than he had, and accomplish wonderful things. Meanwhile Doctors' Commons (still his only regular source of income at this time) seemed deader and dustier than ever. It was strange to realize that those dim old judges and doctors "wouldn't have gone out of their senses with rapture at the thought of marriage" to Maria; that she might have sung and played her harp until she led *him* to the verge of madness, "yet not have tempted one of those slow-goers an inch out of his road!"

The only discordant element in the enchantment that bathed Lombard Street was Maria's closest friend, Marianne Leigh. She was keen to spy out the secrets of every flirtation, and her tongue was spiced with small bits of scandal. With Charles she assumed a teasing, insinuating manner that he found half pleasing, half tormenting. She provoked a steady series of Beatrice–Benedick verbal sparring matches between them. Charles hardly knew whether he was attracted to her or detested her. But he would have preferred to be alone with Maria in a mist of love and beauty.

He was not altogether sure, now, that Mr and Mrs Beadnell greeted him as warmly as they had once done. The marriage of Margaret Beadnell to David Lloyd, which was to take place on 20 March 1831, was fast approaching, and all the Beadnell ladies were very busy. When Dickens was not occupied in Doctors' Commons, he walked the streets where the best shops were in the hope of seeing Maria. Once he came upon the three girls with their mother on Cornhill. The girls were all wearing green merino cloaks; Maria looked bewitching. They were bound for a dressmaker's at St Mary Axe. He gallantly escorted them to the dressmaker's door, where Mrs Beadnell, evidently seized with an apprehension that he might even come in, said emphatically, "And now, Mr Dickin, we'll wish *you* good morning."

In May, not long after the wedding, the Beadnells gave a dinner party in Lombard Street. Charles was present, and recited a metrical composition he had written for the occasion, a parody of Goldsmith's "Retaliation," entitled "The Bill of Fare." The verses begin by describing the participants of the feast under the metaphor of items in the banquet, and progress, rather confusedly, to a series of epitaphs upon the same persons, all catastrophically dead after having partaken of it. The Beadnells are given nothing but praise. The host is "a good fine sirloin of beef": and his wife "an excellent *Rib* of the same"; the Misses Beadnell "two nice little Ducks; and very well dressed"; the recently married Lloyds a side dish "Of Honey and sweets in the form of a Moon."

Though Dickens allows himself to insinuate Anne's interest in the young bank clerk, Henry Kolle, by a feeble pun that her favourite reading is "*Colley* Cibber," he remains discreet about Maria. He does confess, however, that the departure from this world of one so beautiful and good would leave him with no desire but for death. There are light hits at some of the other young men: Francis M'Namara, with his bright yellow gloves and other fripperies, is a dish of "gooseberry-fool"; William Moule "of a Trifle, a trifling dish"; Joe Moule, with his mania for swords and red uniforms, a victim of "*scarlet fever*." The sharpest epithets are reserved for the Leighs. Marianne's father, a corn chandler residing at Lea Bridge Road, Clapton, is portrayed as a good-natured drunkard, and Mrs Leigh as a stupid woman with a tongue dipped in gall; Marianne herself is summed up as a flirt, a pryer into secrets and retailer of scandal. Himself Dickens describes as

> . . . *a young Summer Cabbage, without any heart; Not that he's* heartless, *but because, as folks say, He lost his a twelve month ago, from last May.*

Doubtless he received polite compliments upon this *jeu d'esprit*, which is neither better nor worse than hundreds of such doggerel compositions by clever young men. Emotionally the verses are significant chiefly for suggesting how Dickens's feelings for Maria made him regard the Beadnells and their guests.

And what were Maria's feelings for him? Was she a teaser and tormentor using her delightful little voice, her gay little laugh only to play with his devotion? Was she a rattle-brained little creature displaying her charms as thoughtlessly as a butterfly, or was she an artful siren entrapping him to feed her vanity? Had she gradually found herself really and troublingly in love with this handsome and sensitive boy, whose high spirits were a wine in the veins, but who had about him, too, a touch of something unintelligibly and frighteningly strange? There is no direct evidence, though years later she seems to have told Dickens that she had loved him in these youthful days.

Certainly, however, she and Charles had some kind of secret understanding. They exchanged letters and little gifts, and he believed her words meant that she loved him too, and he treasured every keepsake from her. It was a time for him of ardour and shining dreams and wretched happiness.

But at last Mr and Mrs Beadnell made up their minds about Charles. (Somehow Mr Beadnell had also discovered that John Dickens had been in the Marshalsea.) This sparkling but ineligible young man was growing dangerous; Maria had better be got out of his way. Suddenly Charles felt his existence " entirely uprooted and my whole being blighted by the Angel of my soul being sent" to Paris "to finish her education." Just when this separation took place is not clearly established. Probably, however, it was towards the latter part of 1831, when Dickens was growing discouraged over his prospects of ever becoming a newspaperman, and formed his extraordinary plan of achieving fame and winning Maria's hand by becoming an actor.

The Maria who returned from abroad, some time in the following year, was strangely altered. Now there were coldnesses, quarrels, caprices, reproaches. And, though Charles still visited at Lombard Street, Mr Beadnell was always about, and there never seemed to be the means of setting things straight. Charles was bewildered and sick and desolate. He tried to appeal to Maria by letters. One of the Beadnell servants named Sarah would come to meet him at Finsbury Place with a face of good-humoured compassion, and carry his letter away and leave him forlorn. But presently something cut off this channel of communication too. Maria's father was more vigilant than ever; her unhappy lover was unable to be alone with her long enough to melt the mysterious barrier between them.

In his desperation he appealed to young Henry Kolle, now a declared suitor to Anne Beadnell, to place a letter in Maria's hands. Kolle took pity on him and delivered the note. Maria replied, asking Charles to send a response by Kolle again. From then on he was continually picking up or leaving notes at Kolle's home. But Maria did not grow kinder and Charles's burden of misery did not grow lighter. Working away in the *Mirror of Parliament* offices, he ended the year 1832 in an agony of uncertainty and foreboding.

His family had moved from Fitzroy Street to 18 Bentinck Street, and his twenty-first birthday was celebrated there, a few days after it actually took place, on 11 February. The party was a beautiful one, with music and quadrilles, and, if a sketch in *The Uncommercial Traveller* has an autobiographic foundation, hired waiters to serve the refreshments. Late in the festivities, as Dickens describes them, "in the crumby part of the night, when the wine glasses were to be found in unexpected spots," he managed to get his beloved alone behind a door. She called him "a boy," and went away soon afterwards. With that "short and dreadful word" scorching his brain, he sought oblivion and found a dreadful headache. He woke to the throbbing light of the next day's noon, all his wretchedness more bitter than ever in his heart. So passed away the happy occasion of his coming of age.

He had no idea of how the early brightness had faded from the air. Painfully, patiently, humbly, he tried to elicit some explanation from Maria. But whatever she said or wouldn't say made it no clearer to him. In his low-spirited bewilderment, he appealed to her sister Anne to tell him what was wrong. But all she could find to reply was "My dear Charles, I really cannot understand Maria, or venture to take the responsibility of saying what the state of her affections is."

His confusion was redoubled by Marianne Leigh, who revealed so thorough an acquaintance with facts he thought known only to Maria and himself that he was forced to believe her statement that she had learned them from Maria. But she added so many malicious distortions that he hardly knew whether to think that she had invented them or that Maria had falsified her account of their relations. Whatever the truth, he distrusted Marianne's professions of sympathy and doubted her reports of Maria's feelings. So he stumbled on from day to day in an increasing state of complex misery and fruitless devotion.

Marianne Leigh's conduct, in fact, cannot be explained with any certainty. She may have been only a spiteful mischief-maker, delighting in what misunderstandings she could bring about. She may have been helping Maria terminate a flirtation of which she was tired. Possibly what followed was a conspiracy between the two girls, in which he was to be badgered into a state of bewilderment; confused by accusations of faithlessness, or betrayals of confidence, or want of faith and proper loyalty; and finally jilted upon plausible but fictitious grounds. Whatever Marianne's role, she made herself the main instrument in deepening the breach between her friend and Charles.

By the middle of March, the strain upon his emotions was more than he could bear. He decided that it would be better to break with Maria altogether. On the 18th, he wrote to tell her so. "Our meetings of late have been little more than so many displays of heartless indifference on the one hand; while on the other they have never failed to prove a fertile source of wretchedness and misery." He would not want to hurt her feelings by anything he said, but would feel it "mean and contemptible of me to keep by me one gift of yours or to preserve one single line or word of remembrance or affection from you. I therefore return them, and I only wish that I could as easily forget that I ever received them."

His wounded pride could not resist a few words to show that he knew he had been ill treated. He had ever "acted fairly, intelligibly, and honourably, under kindness and encouragement one day and a total change of conduct the next." "I have never held out encouragement which I knew I never meant; I have never indirectly sanctioned hopes which I knew well I did not intend to fulfill. I have never made a mock confidante to whom to entrust a garbled story for my own purposes . . ." In conclusion, he hoped that she, his first and last love, would be happy and have every blessing the world can afford.

He tried to prevent himself from brooding, during the hours he was not busied in the Gallery or in Abington Street, by throwing himself vigorously into the preparation of some amateur theatricals that were to be presented in Bentinck Street by members of his family and some friends. It was not the last time he was to deal with unhappiness by violent activity. The main piece was *Clari, the Maid of Milan*. On the same bill were "the favourite Interlude of *The Married Bachelor*," and, as a finale, the farce of *Amateurs and Actors*. Dickens made himself producer, director, and stage manager, designed scenery, worried with the stage carpenter about how to produce moonlight, played an accordion in the band, wrote the prologue to the performance, rehearsed the actors – everything. All the Beadnells had already been invited: there was no avowed sign that her parents knew how things were with him and Maria; they – and she! – would see what he could do!

Maria had returned his letter to him – not without keeping a copy – and sent with it a reply that raised his hopes into a renewed blaze. He wrote her another note breathing unaltered devotion. She sent it back by hand, "wrapped in a small loose piece of paper." Deep within, he knew that he should adhere to his resolution of going his way and seeing her no more. By now, for that matter, he hardly ever caught more than the most occasional glimpses of her. And many a night he came from the House of Commons at two or three o'clock, walked almost three miles to the corner of Lombard Street, only to wander past the place where she slept.

Henry Kolle, who was now engaged to Anne, was playing a Nobleman in two scenes of *Clari*. They were to be married on 22 May. Dickens offered his "heartfelt congratulations . . . because you are, or at all events will be, what I never can, happy and contented." "Now turning from feeling and making oneself miserable," he added, could Kolle spare one evening to rehearse his part: Thursday was to be a rehearsal with the band, Friday week the dress rehearsal, and the performance on Saturday, 27 April.

The evening came. Among the other players were Henry Austin and Thomas Mitton, John Dickens, Fanny and Letitia, and their uncle Edward Barrow. Dickens played Rolamo, and three other roles, and the accordion as well. Maria was in the audience, but there was none of the sweetness of having her peep backstage, eager and anxious for his success. She remained in the audience, cold and remote. And when the performance was over, and they went upstairs, Marianne Leigh threw herself in his way all the rest of the evening.

Sixteen days later Maria saw Charles, and evidently explained her coldness by reproaching him with having discussed their relations with Marianne. He vehemently denied it at once. He was even more distressed that Maria could believe him so indelicate and dishonourable. As if, remembering how they once had been, and "the happy hopes the loss of which have made me the miserable reckless wretch I am," he could ever "breathe the slightest hint to any creature living of one single circumstance that ever passed between us" – and least of all to Marianne Leigh!

Maria's reply interpreted his indignation at the thought that *he* could have confided in Marianne as a criticism of *her* having done so. It also pettishly implied that he had been seen so often immersed in such intimate conversation with Marianne that he could hardly have the aversion for her that he stated. He granted that Marianne had thrown herself in his way of late, but denied that he had had, then or ever, any pleasure in speaking to her. "Kind words and winning looks" for her – he quoted Maria's phrases – he had never sought or been moved by. "*Unkind* words and cold looks" from Maria he had suffered again and again, as her pleasure changed. "I have borne more from you than I do believe any living creature breathing ever bore from a woman before." The very last time he had seen Maria, he had heard, even among her own friends, "remarks on your own conduct and pity – pity, Good God! for my situation."

A few days later Kolle's brother gave a farewell bachelor dinner for him. Innumerable bottles of hock were opened. It was a Friday night; Dickens would have no Parliamentary duties again till the following week. There had been no further sign from Maria. As he looked across the board at Kolle and reflected that he was soon to marry Maria's sister, it is easy to imagine what thoughts and emotions filled him at the memory of those months of wasted tenderness and undeserved humiliation. The end of the evening for him was such that he was still recovering two days later and wrote to Kolle, "Yesterday I felt like a maniac, today my interior resembles a lime basket."

But he had made a final resolution. He was no longer even received in Lombard Street. With Kolle's marriage and Anne's departure from her parents' home, he would lose his only means of communication with Maria. He would make one last effort. He begged Kolle to deliver an appeal which he now penned: "Sans Pride, Sans Reserve, Sans everything but an evident wish to be reconciled."

In his letter to Maria he earnestly pleaded his hope that they might try again.

I will allow no feeling of pride, no haughty dislike to making a reconciliation to prevent my expressing it without reserve. I will advert to nothing that has passed, I will not again seek to excuse any part I have acted or to justify it by any course you have ever pursued; I will revert to nothing that has ever passed between us – I will only openly and at once say that there is nothing I have more at heart, nothing I more sincerely and earnestly desire, than to be reconciled to you. . . . I have no guide by which to ascertain your present feelings and I have, God knows, no means of influencing them in my favour. I have never loved and I can never love any human creature breathing but yourself. We have had many differences, and we have lately been entirely separated. Absence, however, has not altered my feelings in the slightest degree, and the Love I now tender you is as pure and as lasting as at any period of our former correspondence. . . . I could entreat a favourable consideration on my own behalf but I purposely abstain from doing so because it would be only a repetition of an oft told tale and because I am sure nothing I could say would have the effect of influencing your decision in any degree whatever.

When Maria's answer came, it was cold and reproachful. His clear statement of a refusal to engage in any more accusations or excusings, and his fair suggestion of wiping the slate clean, she utterly ignored. Dickens realized that all his serious endeavours had brought him back to exactly where he was before. To go on would mean no more than a renewal of the old round of neglect and fleeting favour, of self-abasement for him and caprice from her. He understood it at last, and went his way.

*

Years later they were to meet again, when she would no longer be the tyrannous little beauty who had tormented a loving boy. Dickens, too, would be altered out of all recognition from the hurt and puzzled and adoring young man who finally mustered courage to forgo a hopeless pursuit instead of waiting for her to dismiss him when she had wearied of playing with his heart. But the imprint of his youthful sufferings would be neither forgotten nor eradicated, and their second encounter was to have for him consequences no less fateful than their earlier relationship.

What these four years of loving Maria Beadnell had done for Dickens and done to him, he himself came partly to understand. All the imagination, romance, passion, and aspiration of his nature she had brought into flower and she would never be separated from. Not, of course, that he would never have had these qualities save for her, but she vitally influenced the form they assumed. His intense capacity for suffering, and for feeling with suffering – which the suppressed but unforgotten misery of the Marshalsea and the blacking warehouse had ground into his being – his misery over her made still more sharply a part of him. It revived and re-emphasized those shapes of suffering that he remembered so well: the suffering of helplessness and of undeserved humiliation.

The wounds his defeat left him to heal as best he could deepened two ways of sublimating his self-pity until they formed a characteristic psychological pattern. A grief or an annoyance, he had found, could be exorcized by being magnified to such grotesque proportions that it exploded into the comic and was lost in laughter. And, alternatively, the private emotion could be transcended by being used as a means of understanding and sympathizing with other living creatures, with whose joys and griefs one merged one's own. Both these forms of sublimation he displays again and again, both in his personal life and in his artistic career.

His love and his unhappiness hardened Dickens's determination to cut through all material obstacles. He well knew how much his shabby background and his mediocre prospects had to do with his ineligibility as a suitor – for though he fought against admitting the cogency of all these objections to him, he saw and recognized their existence as clearly as the Beadnells did. Neither they nor his hard-hearted little mistress, perhaps, would have been so obdurate if his financial position had been different. In desperate earnest and animated by the one absorbing hope, the vision of desire, he had set himself to fight his way out of poverty and obscurity. The loss of that hope came just as his efforts were beginning to be rewarded with recognition. The experience focused into burning clarity his realization of the importance of financial status and his impassioned resolve never again to be a victim of indigence. He always remained warm-heartedly generous, and with prosperity he became lavish in expenditure, but in business he was to grow relentlessly set on obtaining the last fraction of what he regarded as his due. And no less in other directions, when his will was pitted against the will of others, he was to become adamantine in the determination that not he but they must always give way.

Linked with this overbearing and domineering tendency was an excessive vulnerability to psychological pain. In society it rendered him, on some occasions, shrinking and oversensitive; and, on others, truculently assertive of his independence. In his writing it accounts for the difficulty he exhibits until almost the close of his career in delineating love between men and women as anything other than idealized unreality or a kind of comic pathos. He can think of David Copperfield adoring an etherealized child-bride or poor Mr Toots painfully and hilariously infatuated with Florence Dombey: it took him a lifetime to be able to deal with a Bradley Headstone so desperate in his thwarted passion for Lizzie Hexam that he must beat his hand bloody against a cemetery wall. But it would be a shallow reading of human character that failed to see Bradley Headstone latent in the youthful Charles Dickens so caught and ground between hurt pride and anguished passion.

All the rest of his life he lay under the shadow of this lost love, which in its darkest places merges with the shadow cast by the spiked wall of the Marshalsea and the imprisoning shades of the blacking warehouse. He tried to write it down when he attempted his autobiography, but that part of his story he could not bear to show even to his closest friend, could not bear even to have anyone read after he was dead; he lost courage and burned it. The most eager craving for affection and sympathy he therefore almost habitually armoured in a stern isolation and reserve that were no less real for all the bright mask of exuberance he presented to the world. He locked his own most intimate griefs in his heart, revealing them only to a few, and to those few only in part. The wasted tenderness of his youthful love for Maria Beadnell, he said years afterwards, "made so deep an impression on me that I refer to it a habit of suppression which now belongs to me, which I know is no part of my original nature, but which makes me chary of showing my affections, even to my children, except when they are very young."

If there were a Fate that had deliberately aimed at forming the young man who now stood upon the threshold of his career, it could hardly have gone about its task more effectively than circumstances had done. Follow the sensitive, imaginative child living in a bright-coloured world of happiness; the drop into an abyss of absolute despair; the rescue just in time to spare his nature from being coarsened or his courage from being broken, and the healing reprieve after that agonizing experience of cosmic injustice. But had there been only one such experience, it might have come in the course of time to seem an accident, and the lines drawn by the Marshalsea and Warren's Blacking might have been gradually obliterated. The exaltation, the wretched happiness, the ultimate and inexorable misery of his love for Maria Beadnell bit in those lines with so bitter an acid that they could never again be blurred, not even by the lifetime of triumph now beginning to dawn.

PART TWO

Climb to Fame
1833–1837

6

The Career Takes Shape

Dickens did not allow his heartache to impair the efficiency with which he did his work for the *Mirror of Parliament*. From the dark rear row of the Strangers' Gallery, with the members of the House sprawling about, coughing, oh-ing, groaning, Parliament was a spectacle of noise and confusion worse, Dickens said, than Smithfield on market day. But there he sat at his task day after day and night after night, his pencil indefatigably jotting down its curves and dots and skyrockets and flies' legs. No grief or hopelessness could shake the performance of his duties.

No sooner had the Irish Coercion Bill become law than Edward Stanley had at once framed the Bill for the Abolition of Slavery in the Colonies. Dickens recorded the debates on this measure, saw young Mr Gladstone leap up to deny (in an indignant maiden speech) that the administrator of his family estates in Demerara was a "murderer of slaves," heard Bulwer's address about keeping faith with the Negro and O'Connell's valedictory "There is nothing to add; the House must divide!" as he tore up the notes for his own speech. Dickens was in the Gallery during Macaulay's notable contributions to the passing of the Act that remade the East India Company into a corporation charged solely with the ruling of Hindustan. It is probable that in the previous year he witnessed the defeat of Sadler's Ten Hours Bill and the rejection of Lord Ashley's Bill to limit the working hours of adults; during 1833 he certainly heard the legislators debating the labouring conditions in the factories and the operations of the Poor Law. Out of these debates emerged Lord Althorp's Factory Act of 1834, the first effective act of factory regulation, and the new Poor Law, which Dickens was to attack so violently in *Oliver Twist*.

It would be misleading to say that he was indifferent to the results of these legislative proceedings, but he grew steadily more sceptical of their being attended by any real benefits. Though he certainly did not desire to see the Conservatives returned to power, he could not help noting that in the Whig House, where they were a negligible minority, there was a determined effort to defeat or emasculate the very measures for which he felt most sympathy: those designed to ameliorate the lives of the poor and their children. Whatever hopes he might have entertained that the Reform Bill would change the nature of Parliament evaporated before this demonstration that the privileges of landowners and industrialists still took precedence over the welfare of the people.

The truth was that Dickens was intolerant of the very way in which legislative bodies act. Nothing in his past experiences had given him any very high respect for the wisdom of his elders or any reverence for flagrant respectability. Those solid members of the community he had observed filled him with impatience for conventional viewpoints. And while he could be affectionately amused at his father's elaborate turns of phrase, he had no filial affection for Parliament. Some few members excepted, that body seemed to him merely a device for obstructing the passage of proper legislation.

But as he sat in the Gallery or pushed his way through its narrow two-foot door at the end of a session, he kept these thoughts to himself. He continued to perform his duties with assiduity and dispatch. After the unsatisfactory Cecil Street lodgings where they had put water in the hashes, he had temporarily taken a room on the top floor at 15 Buckingham Street, but during most of this time he was still living with his family on Bentinck Street.

Young Henry Austin and Thomas Beard, from the Gallery, were often there, as well as Thomas Mitton, who had by now given up his clerkship and was starting out as a solicitor himself. Fanny Dickens had returned to the Academy of Music in 1832 for further study, and the next year there entered a young composer named John Hullah who became a friend to both Fanny and Charles. There were more amateur theatricals in the Dickens home, for which Charles wrote a burlesque extravaganza entitled *O'Thello*, with John Dickens in a role suggestively named "The Great Unpaid." Dickens continued to be intimate with Henry Kolle and his wife, the gentle-hearted Anne, and to go out to see them in their home at Newington.

The *Mirror of Parliament* could pay its staff well during Parliamentary sessions, but at other times Dickens still had to fall back upon his old work at Doctors' Commons or other occasional employment as a stenographer. John Henry Barrow, by this time strongly impressed with his nephew's abilities, made efforts to get him a post on one of the dailies. There were no vacancies on the staff of *The Times*, with which

Barrow was connected. Dickens himself wanted to get on the *Morning Chronicle*, a strongly liberal paper with whose views he sympathized. A former *Times* man, John Payne Collier, had become sub-editor in charge of Parliamentary reporting for that paper. Barrow praised Dickens to Collier, and asked him to recommend the young man.

Collier, however, was cautious. The *Chronicle* was on the verge of being taken over by new proprietors, of whom the moving force was John Easthope, a stockholder who had been in Parliament. He was an irascible man, who became known to his subordinates as "Blasthope"; Collier had no desire to risk his neck for an unknown youth. Where was the young man educated? What were his qualifications? The first inquiry Barrow rather evaded, saying only that Dickens was the son of a former clerk in the naval department at Portsmouth; to the second he replied enthusiastically that his nephew was extremely clever, wrote shorthand well, and had worked for the *True Sun*. How old was he, Collier demanded, and where had he been employed before being on the *True Sun*? Once again Barrow was somewhat vague: his father's financial difficulties had driven him to earn a living in any way he could; "at one time he had assisted Warren, the blacking-man, in the conduct of his extensive business."

Collier felt he should meet Dickens before committing himself. Barrow suggested that he come out to Norwood for dinner and make the acquaintance of the young man. Accordingly, on 27 July 1833, Collier dined with Barrow, Dickens, and a few others. He was surprised by a youthfulness so extreme as to show no trace of beard or whisker. But it was not long before he decided that Barrow had by no means exaggerated his smooth-cheeked nephew's cleverness. Dickens sang a couple of comic songs, one of them of his own invention, about a milkmaid with enticing eyes named "Sweet Betsey Ogle," and her amorous adventures with a barber. "We were all very merry," Collier wrote in his Diary, "if not very wise." At the end he hesitated no longer about writing the recommendation. But it proved ineffective; Dickens received no offer of a post on the *Morning Chronicle*.

He had begun to write small fictional sketches based on types of London life he had observed and people with whom he had come in contact. In one of these he used Marianne Leigh's loud and red-faced father, the corn chandler of Clapton. Disguised under the name of Octavius Budden of Poplar Walk, he is shown crudely trying to curry favour with a cousin in Somerset House who has £10,000 in the funds. The cousin, Mr Augustus Minns, is a prim and middle-aged bachelor

with a horror of dogs and children, upon whom Mr Budden's coarse
insensibility, large white dog, and revolting small son produce the
reverse of the impression aimed at. It is not a superlatively brilliant
story, but there are some amusing scenes of Mr Minns agonizing while
the dog devours a bit of toast butter-side-down on his carpet.

"With fear and trembling" one twilight evening towards winter
Dickens stealthily dropped this sketch "into a dark letter-box in a
dark office up a dark court in Fleet Street." This was the office of the
Monthly Magazine, subtitled "The British Register of Literature,
Sciences, and Belles Lettres." Just that October it had been sold to a
Captain Holland who had fought with Bolivar in South America and
who was now editing the magazine to voice his own ardent liberalism.
Holland had no money to pay contributors, but he gave fledgling
authors a chance to appear in print.

On a December evening, just before closing time, Dickens stepped
into a bookshop on the Strand and asked for the new number of the
Monthly Magazine. Would his piece be there? A little birdlike shopman
gave him a copy from the counter; Dickens turned aside to glance
hastily and nervously through the pages. There it was! – "A Dinner at
Poplar Walk" – "in all the glory of print." So agitated that he wished
only to be alone, he turned out of the crowded Strand and strode down
the pavement of Whitehall to take refuge in Westminster Hall from the
eyes of pedestrians. There for half an hour he paced the stone floor
"my eyes so dimmed with pride and joy that they could not bear the
street, and were not fit to be seen."

More exciting news was to follow. Captain Holland liked the story
so well that he sent "a polite and flattering communication" to its
author "requesting more papers." A week after its appearance, it was
pirated in the *London Weekly Magazine*. Not without a certain pleased
vanity, Dickens passed this news on to the Kolles, and added that he
was "in treaty" with the *Monthly* and planning his next paper, "Private
Theatricals." He suggested that when their expected child was born he
would like to be godfather if it "could afford to have one poor godfather."

His contributions to the *Monthly* continued apace. In January 1833,
appeared "Mrs Joseph Porter Over the Way," a sketch based on Mrs
Leigh's malicious tongue and the amateur performance of *Clari*. Three
more followed in rapid succession: "Horatio Sparkins" in February;
"The Bloomsbury Christening" in April; the two parts of a longer
story called "The Boarding House" in May and August. The earlier

sketches had borne no author's name; with the August contribution came the first use of the signature "Boz." This had arisen out of Dickens's jesting nickname for his seven-year-old brother, Augustus, "whom in honour of the *Vicar of Wakefield* he had dubbed Moses." The child's nasal mispronunciation of Moses as "Boses" was facetiously adopted and shortened to "Bose," and finally became "Boz" by the time Dickens borrowed it for his own pseudonym. "Boz was a very familiar household word to me, long before I was an author."

In the same month that Boz was thus born, Dickens achieved his ambition of becoming a regular Parliamentary reporter on a daily newspaper. Though the *Morning Chronicle* had had no opening the year before, now it was strengthening its staff to give more bellicose competition to *The Times* and to provide the Whigs with a vigorous party organ. Joseph Parkes, the Parliamentary agent of the Whigs and a powerful figure behind the political scenes, was helping in the reorganization. Parkes engaged Thomas Beard as a reporter, and asked him to recommend a colleague. Beard had no hesitation in naming Dickens as "the fastest and most accurate man in the Gallery." He was engaged at the "Fleet Street minimum" (paid by all papers except *The Times*) of five guineas a week. This was less than he had been earning on the *Mirror of Parliament*, but it continued all year round instead of ceasing when Parliament was not in session.

Never since the shabbiness of his blacking warehouse days had Dickens allowed himself to be other than neat and well turned out. But now he celebrated his prosperity by blossoming into something of a dandy. Payne Collier mentions meeting him in

a new hat and a very handsome blue cloak with velvet facings, the corner of which he threw over his shoulder *à l'Espagnol*. . . . I overtook him in the Adelphi, and we walked together through Hungerford Market, where we followed a coal-heaver, who carried his little rosy but grimy child looking over his shoulder; and C. D. bought a half-penny worth of cherries, and . . . gave them one by one to the little fellow without the knowledge of the father.

Under John Black, the *Morning Chronicle* had had a long and honourable record of liberal journalism. A blunt, thickset farmer-like Scotsman, Black was also a scholar and book-lover whose 50,000 volumes in Greek, Latin, English, French, and Italian crammed even the halls and pantries of the apartment he occupied over the *Chronicle* offices at 322 Strand. He was a philosophical radical, a close friend of James Mill, and a disciple of Bentham, but no slavish follower of any man. He could not be stampeded by popular excitement; he poured indignation on the Peterloo Massacre but was unable to regard the divorce proceedings against Queen Caroline in 1820 as the persecution of a saint and martyr.

Black's influence during the decade preceding the Reform Bill had been no slight one. He was, John Stuart Mill said,

> the first journalist who carried criticism and the Spirit of Reform into the details of English institutions. Those who are not old enough to remember those times can hardly believe what the state of public discussion then was. People now and then attacked the constitution and the borough-mongers, but no one thought of censuring the law or the courts of justice; and to say a word against the unpaid magistrate was a sort of blasphemy. Black was the writer who carried the warfare into those subjects, and by doing so he broke the spell.

This was the editor under whom Dickens was to work on the *Chronicle*. Easthope, its leading spirit, was an irritable superior, but he was not afraid to spend money to get results. With his vigorous though often quarrelsome support, Black was able within a few years to bring the circulation up from 1,000 to 6,000. This placed it well ahead of every other London newspaper except *The Times*.

Dickens speedily found himself leading a life of varied and exciting movement. What was probably his maiden assignment was that of covering the reception for Earl Grey at Edinburgh in September 1834. With Beard Dickens made the trip to Leith by sea. He was in intense high spirits, and unspeakably delighted to notice a sandy-haired commercial traveller on board reading "The Bloomsbury Christening" in the April number of the *Monthly* with roars of laughter.

From Edinburgh Dickens sent in to the *Chronicle* for 17 September an account of the preparations being made to dine 1,500 guests in a special banquet pavilion on Calton Hill above the city. The following day the paper had eleven closely printed columns covering the reception and the ceremonial dinner that took place that evening. This story, describing the glittering chandeliers, the painted ceiling, and the crimson pillars, and giving the speeches in full, was probably the joint work of Dickens and Beard.

One passage, however, is indubitably pure Dickens. The guest of honour and the principal visitors, as usual, were late, and one gentleman, the account says, overcome by the cold fowls, roast beef, lobster, and other tempting delicacies . . . appeared to think that the best thing he could possibly do, would be to eat his dinner, while there was anything to eat. He accordingly laid about him with right good-will, the example was contagious, and the clatter of knives and forks became general. Hereupon, several gentlemen, who were not hungry, cried out "Shame!" and looked very indignant; and several gentlemen who were hungry cried "Shame!" too, eating, nevertheless, all the while, as fast as they possibly could. In this dilemma, one of the stewards mounted a bench . . . imploring them for decency's sake, to defer the process of mastication until the arrival of Earl Grey. This address was loudly cheered, but totally unheeded; and this is, perhaps, one of the few instances on record of a dinner having been virtually concluded before it began.

Irreverently frisky, this, in dealing with a solemn feast! How unbelievable it would have seemed to the flippant young reporter as he looked at Lord Grey that only seven years later fame would raise him to that same eminence as Edinburgh's guest of honour receiving the freedom of the city! Not that even so grandiose a vision would have changed his sentiments. About politics and politicians Dickens was simply unable to feel worshipful. At another public dinner, when the Earl of Lincoln floundered through a few halting words and resumed his seat in confusion, Dickens reported: "Lord Lincoln broke down, and sat down."

When the Houses of Parliament burned to the ground in October, Dickens sympathized with the popular feeling on their destruction. To him the origin of the fire symbolized the results of a social system cumbered by useless tradition. Accounts had formerly been kept on splints of notched elm called "tallies." The revolutionary suggestion was made that they be disposed of; but instead of letting the poor have them for firewood, they were stuffed into a stove in the House of Lords, where they set fire to the panelling and started a conflagration that destroyed the entire building. It demonstrated, Dickens liked to say later, how "all obstinate adherence to rubbish which the time has long outlived is certain to have in the soul of it more or less what is pernicious and destructive, and will one day set fire to something or other."

Back in London after the Grey dinner, Dickens had the first of four London *Street Sketches* in the *Morning Chronicle* on 26 September, and another contribution, "The Steam Excursion," in the October _Monthly._ By this time John Black, now in on the secret of the identity of Boz, was repeatedly predicting that Dickens would go far. It was not usual for periodicals to comment on the articles published by other periodicals, but the _Weekly Dispatch_ singled out for praise no fewer than three of his pieces as they appeared in the _Monthly._ The popular dramatists, too, began to pay him the compliment of stealing from him. In mid-October the _Chronicle_ sent him to review a new farce by J. B. Buckstone at the Adelphi, which turned out to be derived from his own "Bloomsbury Christening." Dickens noted the plagiarism good-naturedly enough in his review, but he wrote to the editor of the _Monthly_ protesting against "the kidnapping" of his offspring.

In the course of 1834, the fact that Dickens was Boz became an open secret. Visiting the _Chronicle_ offices in the Strand, William Harrison Ainsworth noticed the young reporter's flashing face and was told his identity. Ainsworth quickly made his acquaintance. He was seven years Dickens's senior, his historical novel _Rookwood_ had recently scored a sensational success, he was a spectacular figure in the literary world. Small, handsome, dressed to the height of dandyism, he glittered in the best-known intellectual salons, and whatever he wrote was sure of eager readers. Dickens was soon imitating his style of waistcoat, and Ainsworth was to introduce Dickens to his first publisher, John Macrone.

Meanwhile, though Dickens now had an income of £275 a year, he was still shadowed by financial difficulties. John Dickens was either falling into old ways again or had never mended them. He was no longer on the _Mirror of Parliament_; John Henry Barrow and Thomas Culliford Barrow had lost all patience and disowned him. Though he had managed to find employment as a reporter on the _Morning Herald_, whatever his earnings there may have been, he was unable to live within them. By November 1834 his affairs had reached a state of crisis. A creditor named Burr refused to wait any longer. This time the son took charge. He stripped himself of all the cash he had on hand to stave off disaster, and appealed to Mitton for a loan of "what you can possibly spare till Saturday."

But of course John Dickens was found to have still other creditors. He went out to obtain some money, and when his efforts were unsuccessful simply failed to return home. In Bentinck Street the family were in great tribulation. Dickens was not as much worried as the others; his father had developed the habit of disappearing when there were troubles of this kind. Waking next morning, Dickens learned that his father "had just been arrested" and was in Sloman's sponging house.

Undaunted, Dickens set himself to straighten out the tangle. His loyalty would not allow him to stand by and see them all suffer from his father's imprudence. He was fond of his prodigal father, too, despite all his improvident ways with money. And so he took the first step in a course that was to saddle him throughout his life with helpless or idle dependants. As soon as his day's work was finished, he visited his father and found out the extent of his embarrassments. He provided for his temporary needs by asking Mitton to cash an order for £5. He arranged for his mother, the girls, and the younger children to take cheaper lodgings, and took chambers for himself and his brother Frederick at Furnival's Inn. He persuaded a bill broker to renew a note for two months, got Edward Barrow (evidently more amenable than his brothers) to lend his signature to some accommodation, and mortgaged his own salary for two weeks to pay the removal expenses.

By the middle of December Dickens had worked out a solution of the family's problems. "We have much more cause for cheerfulness than despondency after all," he resiliently told his friend Beard. The £35 he had had to pay in advance for his three back rooms at 13 Furnival's Inn, together with the other sums he had had to lay out, had exhausted his resources, but he faced the end of the year in good spirits.

Early in January Dickens reported the elections at Ipswich and Sudbury, in Suffolk. No sooner had he returned to London than he was ordered to Essex to cover further elections there. "I wish to God you could have seen me," he reported to Beard, "tooling in and out of the banners, drums, conservative emblems, horsemen, and gocarts with which every little green was filled . . ."

On 31 January 1835, the proprietors of the *Morning Chronicle* inaugurated an evening paper under the name of the *Evening Chronicle*. George Hogarth, their music critic, was made editor and asked Dickens to write for its first number a sketch similar to the four *Street Sketches* that had appeared between September and November. Dickens at once agreed. Then it occurred to him to suggest that he might do a series of such articles. If he did, would they think he "had any claim to *some* additional remuneration (of course, of no great amount)"? The proposal was approved, and his salary was increased from five to seven guineas a week. Not yet quite twenty-three, he was already earning more than his father's official salary had ever been in the Navy Pay Office.

Hogarth had been a Writer to the Signet in Edinburgh, one of a privileged class of legal practitioners before the Court of Session. He had been a friend of Sir Walter Scott and one of the trusted advisers whom he consulted after his ruin in the financial crash of 1826. Hogarth's sister had married James Ballantyne, the elder of the two brothers running the printing business in which Scott was a silent partner. Hogarth himself married one of the daughters of George Thomson, "the friend of Burns." He had joined the staff of the *Morning Chronicle* less than three months before Dickens was taken on.

The older man – Hogarth was already fifty – rapidly developed a friendly interest in his young colleague and invited him to his home off the Fulham Road. The eldest daughter, Catherine, who was nineteen at this time, was a pretty girl with a rosy complexion, heavy-lidded blue eyes, and a slightly retroussé nose; among her sisters the next in age was a sweet, grave-looking child named Mary, who was only fourteen.

During the next seven months Hogarth printed twenty of Dickens's sketches in the *Evening Chronicle*. They ranged from word pictures of street scenes, pawnshops, glaring gin palaces, Astley's Circus, and the poor amusing themselves at Greenwich Fair, to short vignettes of character or miniature narratives based on people or events he remembered from the Ordnance Terrace days in Chatham. Now that he had a remunerative outlet, he notified the *Monthly Magazine* that he would write no more unpaid stories and his contributions to that periodical ended with the publication in January and February of "A Passage in the Life of Mr Watkins Tottle."

The new vitality of the *Morning Chronicle* was sharpening the antagonism between that paper and *The Times*. Through a new system of "extraordinary expenses" *The Times* had managed at a cost of £290 to print the speeches at the Edinburgh banquet for Lord Grey the very next morning, and jeered at the *Chronicle*, whose report appeared a day later. When Lord John Russell offered himself for re-election in South Devon, Dickens and Beard therefore made careful preparations to beat *The Times*. They set out for Exeter in a pelting rain that never stopped, and on 1 May in the midst of a downpour in the castle yard Dickens recorded Lord John's speech while two good-natured colleagues "held a pocket-handkerchief over my note-book."

He and *The Times* men raced back to London neck and neck; in the end Dickens got there before they did, with a longer and more accurate account than any other paper. *The Times* had no better resources than to vent its spleen on its rival by calling it "that squirt of filthy water" and describing it as a "licentious" feeder "on falsehood and lies," to which the *Chronicle* retorted that "the poor old *Times*, in its imbecilic ravings, resembles those unfortunate wretches whose degraded prostitution is fast approaching neglect and disgust." *The Times* thundering from Printing-House Square and Black bellowing in return from the Strand make it easy to see where Dickens found Pott and Slurk, the rival editors in *Pickwick*.

After the exciting dash to Exeter, Dickens was in London most of the time until November. In the course of the last six months he and Catherine Hogarth had fallen in love with each other, and Dickens had taken a room in Selwood Place, to be near her as often as his duties allowed. But he had not yet cleared off the debts he had contracted at the time of his father's arrest, so they were deferring their marriage until his financial position was brighter.

No sooner had the series of sketches Dickens was contributing to the *Evening Chronicle* drawn to a close than he was undertaking a new series for *Bell's Life in London*. These were signed "Tibbs," a pseudonym probably derived from the character of Beau Tibbs, in Goldsmith's essays. There were a dozen of them, running from 27 September 1835, to 17 January of the following year, under the general title of *Scenes and Characters*. Like the pieces in the *Evening Chronicle*, these sketches varied from clear-cut pictures of streets and places to lightly satirical portrayals of character with touches of pathos.

Dickens's acquaintance with Harrison Ainsworth, which had begun in the previous year, had warmed into friendship. Ainsworth had taken a pleasant dwelling named Kensal Lodge on the Harrow Road. At his dinner table could be found Father Prout keeping the company in a roar with classical witticisms, the brilliant young artist Daniel Maclise, the famous George Cruikshank taking more wine than anyone else and presently roaring a street ballad or dancing the hornpipe, Disraeli in his gold-flowered waistcoat and Edward Bulwer extravagantly loaded with jewels, Samuel Laman Blanchard, the editor of the *True Sun*, William Jerdan, the editor of the *Literary Gazette*, the scholarly Alexander Dyce, and many others Dickens presently came to know.

One evening, leaving Kensal Lodge with Ainsworth's publisher, Macrone, to walk back to Holborn, Dickens was delighted to learn that his companion was also going to Furnival's Inn. The publisher told him that his *Sketches* were "capital value" and should be collected into a volume for publication. Macrone added the suggestion that they might be illustrated by Cruikshank. This was an exhilarating thought, for the cartoonist had long been famous and his pre-eminence was so unchallenged that his name alone ensured a large sale.

Macrone and the young author soon reached an agreement. Dickens would write a sufficient number of additional sketches to make the contents fill two volumes; Macrone would pay him £150 for the copyright of the first edition and publish it early in 1836. Dickens was filled with excitement. Albany Fonblanque, the editor of the *Examiner*, liked his sketches; so did Samuel Carter Hall, of the *New Monthly Magazine*; William Jerdan of the *Literary Gazette*, whose approval was enough to make the reputation of any author, had praised them. Dickens saw a new realm of achievement opening before him.

He already stood, he knew, in the topmost rank among the reporters of the Gallery. But what was it to be a mere journalist in comparison with being a man of letters published in book form! His brain was seething with ideas for dozens of additional sketches: "The Cook's Shop – Bedlam – The Prisoner's Van – The Streets – Noon and Night – Banking-Houses – Fancy Lounges – Covent Garden – Hospitals and Lodging Houses." Once he began, the future was illimitable!

7

Boz Is Born

Enthusiastically, Dickens had committed himself to a task that involved prodigal expenditures of energy. John Black, to be sure, thought so highly of his talents that he spared him a great deal of the mere drudgery of a reporter's life. "Any fool," he said, "can pass judgement, more or less just or unjust, on a book or a play, but 'Boz' can do better things; he can create works for other people to criticize . . . Keep 'Boz' in reserve for great occasions. He will *aye* be ready for them."

Nevertheless, Dickens knew he would be obliged to go to Bristol early in November to cover the Stroud by-election in which Lord John Russell was the Government candidate, so he wished before he left to settle as many details concerning his book as possible. He rushed about collecting proof slips of the articles that had appeared in the *Evening Chronicle*, planned additional sketches, and discussed possible titles for the book with Macrone. "What do you think," he asked Macrone, "of

Sketches by Boz
and
Cuts by Cruikshank

– – – – – – – –

Etchings by Boz
and
Woodcuts by Cruikshank."

The order to Bristol came on 7 November 1835. Dickens and Beard were again a team. They arranged that as soon as Lord John Russell had finished speaking, one of them would dash to Marlborough in a chaise, transcribing his notes as he rode. At Marlborough a horse express would be waiting to rush the report to London.

Making preparations at the George and Pelican in Newbury, Dickens was surrounded by a confusion of road maps, roadbooks, ostlers, and postboys. After a cold journey, he and Beard arrived at the Bush Inn, Bristol, and after the speech got the report to Marlborough.

The next night they reported a dinner at Bath, twelve miles away; after staying up all night long, they snatched a little sleep and returned to London. The Russell dinner had made the next morning's edition with three and a quarter columns on page three, and was concluded in another three columns the day after: a great triumph.

In town Dickens had a hundred things to attend to. He conferred with Cruikshank on the sixteen illustrations that were to go with the two volumes. Soon he was indignant at Cruikshank's taking his desire for speed rather coolly, and saying that he would "have 'a' plate next week, and 'two' the week afterwards" – until he remembered that Cruikshank had also said each plate would contain four subjects. But at the end of a fortnight, he was hot again at Cruikshank for being slow. In between these activities he was completing the additional sketches to fill the two volumes.

The middle of December took Dickens to Kettering to watch the by-election there. Party feeling in Northamptonshire was running so high that Dickens expected violence. The polling was riotous with "bells ringing, candidates speaking, drums sounding, a band of *eight* trombones," and "the blue swine" of conservative voters fighting, "drinking and guzzling and howling and roaring." Dickens and his fellow reporters retired to his room over the stable yard, locked the door, and ordered a dinner of "cod and oyster sauce, roast beef, and a pair of ducks, plum pudding, and mince pies." "Damn the Tories," he exclaimed, "– They'll win here I am afraid."

In the midst of this hum of activity, he had still other irons in the fire. The young composer John Hullah was planning an operetta with a Venetian background, to be called *The Gondoliers*, and asked Dickens to supply the libretto. With the assurance that was becoming characteristic of him, he took charge of Hullah's idea, had him drop the Venetian setting, and transformed it into a bucolic drama of would-be seducers, rustic maidens, and upstanding farmers. He could work, he argued, with effect on a play where the characters behaved like people he saw and heard every day; and it would not require the costly and elaborate décor of an Italian scene. Hullah yielded, in part no doubt to the impact of Dickens's arguments, but in part, too, to the force of his personality. It was not the last time Dickens was to seize another man's notion and transform it beyond recognition. Hogarth introduced Dickens to John Braham, the famous tenor, who was opening the new and splendid St James's Theatre in the middle of December, and it was arranged that the operetta should be submitted to him.

By Christmas Dickens had almost finished the dramatic portion, though the lyrics were still to do. In January he sent out announcements of his *Sketches* to magazine and newspaper editors and worked out with Macrone the wording of the advertisement for the press. He expected at any moment, he wrote Macrone, to hear from Cruikshank that his work was finished; they would then go together to spend an evening with the artist and see the plates. He would arrange with the printer at the *Chronicle* that the advertisement should be placed at the head of a column.

His other activities, of course, could not slacken in the midst of these personal excitements. He reported the procession and ceremony on the occasion of Lord Melbourne's opening the Licensed Victuallers' School at Kennington. He also led a successful strike of reporters on the *Morning Chronicle* against being required to sign an agreement the management desired to impose upon them. Easthope had no wish to lose the services of his two star reporters and the best part of his reporting staff, and gave way. Dickens gained considerable fame on Fleet Street at having conducted the case so triumphantly.

Sketches by Boz was published on 7 February 1836, its author's twenty-fourth birthday. Volumes were dispatched to Catherine's Edinburgh relatives, and complimentary copies inscribed to Easthope and John Black. Dickens also presented an inscribed copy to Edward Stanley, by then become Lord Stanley, who had so highly praised his accuracy at the time of the Irish Disturbances Bill. Still another copy went to the generous and amiable Thomas Noon Talfourd, formerly a law reporter for *The Times*, a Serjeant-at-Law, and since 1835 a member of Parliament for the town of Reading. Copies were also sent to the *Sun*, the *Spectator*, the *Athenaeum*, the *Literary Gazette*, the *Court Journal*, and other periodicals.

A paragraph in the *Morning Chronicle* heralded the book's appearance at the end of the week, and two days before its publication there had been a review by Hogarth which praised its style as like Washington Irving's "in his happiest hours," and likened "A Visit to Newgate" to Victor Hugo's "Dernier Jour d'un Condamné." Its author, Hogarth said, was "a close observer of human nature. He has the power, too, of producing tears as well as laughter."

Provokingly, copies did not reach the Sunday papers in time to receive immediate attention, but Dickens was deeply moved by "Hogarth's beautiful notice." Other favourable reviews began to appear. The *Literary Gazette* for 15 February spoke of his "talent" and "fidelity" and was struck by the "genuine acquaintance with his subjects" revealed in these scenes of common life "cleverly and amazingly described." The *Satirist*, the same week, found the two volumes "in their way inimitable" and their author "a man of unquestionable talent and of great and correct observation." John Forster reviewed it favourably in the *Examiner*, the *Athenaeum* praised it, and so did the *Sun*, the *Sunday Times*, and the *Sunday Herald*. The *Morning Post*'s review in March, Dickens joyfully reported, was "as good as Hogarth's." In August there was a second edition, and in 1837 there were two more.

It was no coincidence that the reviews all emphasized Dickens's knowledge of his subjects and his closeness of observation. The subtitle of the *Sketches* proclaimed them "Illustrative of Everyday Life and Everyday People," and more than half the contents strictly deserved that description. But the *Sketches by Boz* are no mere exercise in smooth journalistic objectivity, however vivid. The personality of their author lights a hundred perspectives and sharpens a thousand epithets. Dickens had suffered enough from the mistakes and inadequacies of his elders to have no reverence for age and experience. He can sympathize with the underpaid milliners' and staymakers' apprentices, and pity the scantily clad ballad singer with the wailing child whose only reward from the passing crowd is "a brutal laugh at her weak voice." Such sights, he says, "will make your heart ache – always supposing," he bitterly adds, "that you are neither a philosopher nor a political economist." Well bred ladies and gentlemen might do something more generous and useful than recoil from the sixteen-year-old streetwalker whose features are already branded with depravity "as legibly as if a red-hot iron had seared them" and whose later career "in crime will be as rapid as the flight of a pestilence . . . in its baneful influence and wide-spreading infection." In such comments we already hear the clarion-tongued crusader who will make the world ring with the evils of political and industrial exploitation.

If the interests suggested by Dickens's first published volumes thus anticipate the social themes of his novels, their style and characters no less clearly foreshadow his astonishing literary achievement. At this stage, to be sure, he is often crude and clumsy, falling sometimes into a polysyllabic turgidness that shows little of the startling verbal felicity he came to command. He indulges in a showy and cocksure jibing full of the fierce vanity and hardness of youth. Though *Sketches by Boz* has many of the flaws and shortcomings that disclose it to be the work of an apprentice, it is also bursting with something more than promise: of a kind of not entirely ripe fulfilment. Apprentice work of an apprentice so enormously gifted and even here so precociously skilled might well banish all surprise if its author, in his very next effort, leaped into the circle of the masters.

Dickens's own confidence in his prospects had been raised to a state of effervescence. For hot upon the publication of the *Sketches* he had received a proposal to write a serial work in twenty instalments. Although it would mean turning out 12,000 words a month in addition to all his regular newspaper duties, it would pay nine guineas a sheet and add a clear £14 monthly to his income. With this he felt he and Catherine might venture to marry. "The work," he wrote her, "will be no joke, but the emolument is too tempting to resist."

Out of this new undertaking *Pickwick Papers* came into being. It is curious to reflect how easily Mr Pickwick, Sam Weller, Jingle, and all the rest of that extraordinary company might have remained in the realms of the unborn; for the proposition came to Dickens almost by chance and only at the end of an involved chain of coincidences. A young publishing firm named Chapman and Hall was just starting a monthly Library of Fiction, edited by Charles Whitehead, and Dickens had written for it "The Tuggses at Ramsgate," which was to appear at the end of March with an illustration by the popular comic artist Robert Seymour. The latter had conceived the idea of a series of plates depicting the mishaps of a "Nimrod Club" of cockney sportsmen. He tried to get several people to do the accompanying humorous text, but all these efforts fell through. Eventually he broached his notion to Chapman and Hall.

Chapman had been impressed by Dickens's early sketches in the *Monthly Magazine*. Boz's *Sketches*, just off the press, were obtained and looked through; it was decided that he would do. To Furnival's Inn, therefore, on the morning of 10 February, repaired little Mr William Hall, the junior partner, to lay the proposal before Mr Charles Dickens. The young man who threw open the door was just three days past his twenty-fourth birthday, but, with his smooth face and his luxuriant brown hair waving down over his shoulders, he looked much younger.

As Dickens took in the brisk, birdlike little figure of his visitor, he broke into a shout of recognition. This was the very man who had sold him the copy of the *Monthly Magazine* containing his first story to appear in print! The transaction had been charged with no such inner excitement for Hall, of course, as it had been for his youthful customer, and he did not remember it. But the two agreed to hail the incident "as a good omen, and so fell to business." Hall had the proposition all cut and dried. The members of Seymour's Nimrod Club were to go out shooting, fishing, and so on, and involve themselves in difficulties through their lack of dexterity. The writing was only a hack job to go with the plates. But to Dickens, earning seven guineas a week on the *Morning Chronicle* and picking up small sums by irregular contributions to other periodicals, a dependable addition of fourteen guineas a month to his income was tempting. He knew at once that he would accept the offer – but only on his own terms.

With swift conclusiveness he marshalled his conditions before the publisher. Though born and bred partly in the country, he himself was not much of a sportsman except for walking. The idea of sporting misadventures was not novel. Having thus disposed of Seymour's idea, Dickens added that it would be infinitely better for the plates to arise out of the text, and that he should like to take his own way through a free range of English scenes and people. All this amounted to the cavalier suggestion that instead of *his* illustrating Seymour, Seymour should illustrate *him*.

What William Hall thought of his host's audacity can only be conjectured. One thing is clear: he was impressed. This was a writer they must certainly obtain! Hall assured Dickens that there ought to be no trouble in meeting his views, and went into details about the manner of publication.

He suggested that the book be brought out in monthly parts of about 12,000 words each, totalling twenty issues selling at a shilling apiece. There was an element of novelty in this scheme, although it had previously been used for Pierce Egan's *Tom and Jerry*. Generally, it had been standard practice to issue original works of fiction in three volumes selling at one and a half guineas. But there was no reason why the serial form of publication should not be applied to new works of all kinds. Many people would find it easier to pay a shilling once a month than twenty times that amount all at once, and even the sum total was one third cheaper than the standard price. The interview ended with Dickens and Hall in thorough accord.

The junior partner hurried back to the Strand and urged that Dickens be given his way. Edward Chapman concurred. But to Seymour the new turn in the plan came with a painful jolt. He was an excitable and touchy person, given to fits of gloom, and it was almost more than he could bear to see *his* pet scheme being wrested away from him and twisted completely out of shape. Worse still, it was all too clear that he would be playing second fiddle to the hack originally called in merely to concoct a story around his plates. But Chapman and Hall seemed determined to do things in the mangled way suggested by this young upstart or not to do them at all. Seymour swallowed his spleen and grudgingly consented.

It was understood that the story was to be entertaining and humorous, but not a single character, scene, or situation had been so much as mentioned in their discussions, or even conceived in Dickens's mind. At once he imagined his central character. He tells of this event in one of those bare little sentences that history makes famous when time has invested their flatness with pregnancy. "I thought," he said simply, "of Mr Pickwick."

Within a week of Hall's first visit, Dickens was writing the opening number. He announced to Chapman and Hall, "Pickwick is begun in all his might and glory." Another three days, and he had "Pickwick and his friends on the Rochester coach," "going on swimmingly" with Alfred Jingle, who, Dickens felt sure, would "make a decided hit." The name of Pickwick he borrowed from that of the well-known coach proprietor of Bath, Moses Pickwick. Dickens had retained the apparatus of the Pickwick Club as a relic of Seymour's original scheme, and good-humouredly thrown in Mr Winkle, with his terror of horses and his ignorance of guns, as a special concession to the artist's love of boastful but incompetent sportsmen.

But Seymour did not feel mollified, and had trouble producing illustrations to the publishers' liking. His first sketch of Pickwick was a tall, thin man. Edward Chapman at once protested. Pickwick must be fat; "good humour and flesh had always gone together since the days of Falstaff." For Seymour's benefit he described a friend of his own at Richmond, "a fat old beau who would wear, in spite of the ladies' protests, drab tights and black gaiters." Still filled with memories of his own plan, Seymour drew for the cover page of the monthly parts a cockney blazing away at an unconcerned little dickybird on a near-by branch and a plump Mr Pickwick dozing over a fishing line in a punt, although in the story Mr Winkle never manages to aim so straight and Mr Pickwick never goes fishing at all.

Meanwhile preparations were being made for Dickens's marriage to Catherine Hogarth. He had agreed on a three-year tenancy of his larger and sunnier chambers at Furnival's Inn before there had been any such prospect as Chapman and Hall's offer, and he could not afford to lose the £50 a year he paid in rent, so the young couple decided to start housekeeping there. Kitchen equipment and additional furniture now had to be obtained, and Catherine frequently came in from Chelsea with her younger sister Mary and stayed overnight in the Dickens family home at 34 Edwards Street, Portman Square. In high fettle, Dickens went about acquiring all sorts of objects: "a pair of quart decanters, and a pair of pints, a chrystal jug, and three brown dittoes with plated tops, for beer and hot water, a pair of lustres, and two *magnificent* china jars" – all great bargains.

Writing the second number of *Pickwick* went more slowly than he had imagined it would. "The sheets," he confessed to Catherine, "are a weary length – I had no idea there was so much in them." He was obliged to write in intervals between his other work; on Sunday, 20 March, he told her he would have to be at his desk till one or two that night. The impatience with which he was looking forward to their wedding day two weeks hence may have made application difficult. "Here's another day off the fortnight," he exclaimed the next afternoon. "Hurrah!"

Everything was in readiness for the two great events. On 26 March Chapman and Hall announced, through a large advertisement in *The Times* and an entire page in the *Athenaeum*, of which the upper half was devoted to *The Pickwick Papers*, the forthcoming publication of its first number for 31 March 1836. Next day there were shorter advertisements in *Bell's Life in London*, the *Observer*, *John Bull*, the *Weekly Dispatch*, the *Satirist*, the *News and Sunday Herald*, and *The Times*. Dickens looked forward to the success of the enterprise and his approaching marital happiness in as high spirits as ever Mr Pickwick and his friends bowled along on top of the Commodore while it rolled to Rochester.

[8]

Catherine

There seemed little resemblance between Catherine and the love whom Dickens had ceased to see three years before. Maria Beadnell was a tiny and teasing charmer with enchanting ringlets; Catherine a full-bosomed lass with long, dark hair and a sleepy voluptuousness more suggestive of the south than of the Scottish north. Her blue eyes were large and heavy-lidded. She had little of Maria's light-headed chatter, though when in spirits she would burst into bright laughter. But she was not seldom in low spirits, with feelings of vague crossness or causeless melancholy. These moods sometimes impelled her to display towards her lover a mingling of petulance and capriciousness that sounds like an echo of her predecessor's "prettily pettish" ways.

Dickens was determined, though, that he would not again be slavishly subservient under ill-treatment. He would be neither the plaything of high spirits nor the whipping boy of low spirits. His letters to Catherine during the period of their engagement are tender and devoted, and there is no doubt that he was in love with her. But even in the lovers' quarrels sometimes mirrored there, he reveals none of the wild misery of worship that trembled through his letters to Maria and none of the desolate and hurt endeavour to regain his own dignity in the midst of humiliation. He speedily reduced Catherine to the position of pleading to be forgiven for her exhibitions of ill-humour.

The realization that Catherine was subject to these fits of moodiness and spleen did not come to him, to be sure, until after they became engaged. In his earliest visits to the Hogarths the attraction had not even been Catherine but her father, who was Dickens's superior on the papers for which they both worked. George Hogarth was an unassuming man of gentlemanlike manners, and although he was self-educated he had made himself a person of considerable cultural attainments. He had mingled with literary society in Edinburgh and was even mentioned in Christopher North's *Noctes Ambrosianae*. He was the editor of an anthology of poetry and prose called *The White Rose of*

York, and his *Musical History, Biography, and Criticism* was published early in 1835. The ambitious young writer not merely liked him for himself but fundamentally had far more esteem for the kind of attainment Hogarth represented than he had for a mere successful businessman like George Beadnell.

Little by little the rural Chelsea home had become a pleasant refuge from his bachelor chambers at Furnival's Inn and the cramped family quarters of Edwards Street. Catherine, with her buxom figure and rose-petal complexion, and her younger sister Mary, whose admiration for Dickens was unbounded, listened eagerly to his adventures as a reporter, and doubtless giggled at his account of the Grey banquet being gobbled down before it began. Gradually Dickens fell under the spell of Catherine's somnolent charm.

With the Hogarths he was on a very different footing than he had been with the Beadnells, who even now might not have been much impressed by his magazine stories or by his rise in what had not yet become a recognized profession. But Hogarth himself was a journalist and saw in Dickens a writer of extraordinary promise. There was no question of his hearty approval when Dickens and Catherine became engaged in the spring of 1835. Everyone was pleased.

It was not long, though, before he had a taste of Catherine's sulkier moods. In an early letter to her, written in May, soon after their engagement, he reproached her for the "sudden and uncalled for coldness with which you treated me just before I left last night." This was the second time she had indulged recently in such a display, and he owed a duty to himself as well as to her. He "could not have believed that such sullen and inflexible obstinacy could exist in the breast of any girl in whose heart love had found a place."

"If a *hasty* temper produces this strange behaviour, acknowledge it when I give you the opportunity – not once or twice, but again and again. If a feeling of you know not what – a capricious restlessness of you can't tell what, and a desire to tease, you don't know why, give rise to it – overcome it; it will never make you more amiable, I more fond, or either of us more happy." If she is already tired of him, let her say so – "I shall not forget you lightly, but you will need no second warning." She may depend upon it that what she does not take the trouble to control for a lover, she will not for a husband.

He knew as well as if he were by her side, he concluded, that her impulse on reading this note would be "one of anger – pride perhaps, or to use a word more current with your sex – 'spirit.' " But she must realize that he had written thus only because he "cannot turn coolly away and forget a slight" from her as he might "from any other girl" to whom he was not deeply attached.

A remarkable, even an alarming, letter for a young woman to receive from a fiancé of three weeks' standing! One more experienced than Catherine, or even more endowed with cunning, might have felt that whether the upbraiding were justified or unjustified, this was a tone too lofty to promise well for her comfort. Though Dickens disavowed any claim to be her superior, he was unmistakably monitorial.

But Catherine had no guile and was no fighter. She knew she had in fact behaved peevishly. She sent Dickens a frightened and remorseful note asking his forgiveness and begging him to love her "once more." Dickens was magnanimous. It was unnecessary, he said, for her to ask him to love her again: "*I have never ceased to love you for one moment, since I knew you; nor shall I.*"

Catherine tried to control her moods, and during the summer Dickens came to his lodgings in Selwood Place, just around the corner from her father's house, to be near her whenever his work for the *Chronicle* or his sketches would allow. Writing away industriously, even when the same sketch needed revision for the fifteenth time, he was still in the most joyous of spirits. Once, when the Hogarths were all quietly sitting in the family drawing-room, "a young man dressed as a sailor jumped in at the window, danced a hornpipe, whistling the tune, jumped out again, and a few minutes later Charles Dickens walked gravely in at the door, as if nothing had happened, shook hands all round, and then, at the sight of their puzzled faces, burst into a roar of laughter."

Often his "dearest Kate" came tapping at his door with her sister Mary to share his breakfast with him. Once he asked Catherine to indulge his "childish wish" of having her make his breakfast for him: "It will give me pleasure," and it will be excellent practice for her "against Christmas next." Sometimes, worn out with work, and with an aching head, he facetiously complained of "furteeg," or at three o'clock in the morning lamented that he had not seen her since seven o'clock of the previous evening, a deprivation that "seems an age."

That October Catherine and her mother both came down with scarlet fever. He was in great anxiety for them, and somewhat worried, too, lest he get it himself. He sent his brother, Fred, with blackcurrant jam to ease Catherine's throat, went again and again to see how she was, and wrote, "Should you not be well, I *must* see you, and *will not be prevented.*"

His letters abounded in little endearments. She was his "ever dearest Katie" and his "dearest love" and "Dearest darling Pig" and "My Dearest Life." "God bless you my dearest Girl," he would write, and add "990000000000000000000000000000000000000000 kisses." By October he had to be back in Furnival's Inn again, working furiously to gather together his *Sketches* for publication by Macrone, writing the supplementary ones despite a cold so severe that he tottered on his legs and could hardly see for dizziness, and trying to meet Cruikshank for a conference about the illustrations. His cold grew so much worse that he felt obliged to stay at home, and sent Kate a copy of Ainsworth's *Rookwood* to aid her "in getting through the day."

Kate, however, began to feel neglected and aggrieved. She complained of being in "low" spirits and tried to make him sorry for her by saying with a childish pout that she was "coss," reiterating that he could come to her if he would and that he took pleasure in being away. Dickens patiently reasoned with her. However strongly disposed to be "coss" she was, surely she must see that he had no alternative but to set to work as best he could? "You may be disappointed: – I would rather you would – at not seeing me; but you cannot feel vexed at my doing my best with the stake I have to play for – you and a home for both of us."

But all that Kate seemed to have been able to learn from their conflicts was to substitute a feeble plaintiveness for sullen coldness or angry reproach. With these disturbances, and the pitch at which he was working, Dickens had a recurrence of his old attacks of spasm more severe than any he had suffered since he was a child. "It still continues exceedingly painful," he told Kate, "and my head is aching so from pain and want of rest that I can hardly hold it up."

It is not surprising, therefore, if he sometimes lost patience and spoke with a certain asperity. Shortly after his return from reporting the dinner to Lord Russell at Bristol, he wrote that he hoped she had "no new complaints either *bodily* or *mental*: indeed I feel full confidence after last night that you will not have a renewal of the latter." Finally he attained a kind of philosophic resignation on the subject. Working on the first instalment of *Pickwick*, he told her that though he liked the *matter* of what he had written that day, "the quantity is not sufficient to justify my coming out tonight. If the representations I have so often made to you, about my working as a duty, and not as a pleasure, be not sufficient to keep you in the good humour, which you, of all people in the world should preserve – why then, my dear, you must be out of temper, and there is no help for it."

Despite these cloud-shadows, however, the year of their engagement was a time of happiness and hope. Dickens was constantly in and out of the house in York Place, and Kate and Mary occasionally came in to London escorted by Fred. Sometimes, on a sunny day, Dickens would walk out along Piccadilly, crossing the road at Hyde Park Corner and continuing until he met the two girls coming along Brompton Road to meet him. There was theatre-going, too, at Covent Garden, Drury Lane, the Adelphi, and probably the Olympic, where the beautiful, brilliant, and naughty Mme Vestris staged extravaganzas with remarkable imaginative delicacy and grace. The introduction to Braham, and the great tenor's receptivity to the operetta Dickens was doing with Hullah, also brought tickets to the red-and-gold magnificence of the St James's Theatre, just opened on King Street on 14 December.

Meanwhile John Pritt Harley, who had become Braham's stage manager, had asked Dickens to write a one-act farce with an amusing part in which Harley himself could appear, and Dickens began to turn his story "The Great Winglebury Duel" into a play under the title of *The Strange Gentleman*. These two theatrical enterprises he carried on simultaneously with all his other work. The first scene of the operetta, which he and Hullah had agreed to call *The Village Coquettes*, was finished by the middle of November. Early in December Dickens was submitting the book of the songs to Hogarth's criticism and in January he was beginning the second act. Near the end of December he wrote, "I am finishing my Duel"; in February he asked Chapman and Hall if they would care to publish *The Strange Gentleman*. But then there is no further mention of the operetta until late spring or of the farce until the autumn.

As the day of the wedding drew near, he worked more furiously than ever in order to clear his desk for the honeymoon. His letters to Kate were full of rueful little explanations for delays in seeing her, and tender rallyings to keep in spirit: "Is it my fault that I cannot get out tonight? I must work at the opera." "If you are unjust enough to be cross, I will not deprecate your anger, or ill humour." And he adds other cajoleries and pet names: "Dearest Titmouse," "Darling Tatie," "My dearest Wig," "an unlimited number of kisses."

On the last day of March Dickens wrote his uncle, Thomas Culliford Barrow, announcing his approaching marriage. He felt proud of the favourable reception given *Sketches by Boz*, he said, and confident about his future. He was not a little pleased, too, with the merits of the match he had made, describing Kate as "the daughter of a gentleman who has recently distinguished himself by a celebrated work on music, who was the most intimate friend and companion of Sir Walter Scott, and one of the most eminent of the literati of Edinburgh."

Since Kate was still some six weeks short of being of age, a special licence was necessary, officially stating that she married with her father's consent. Dickens obtained the proper authorization in the name of the Archbishop of Canterbury. Four days later, on 2 April 1836, he and Catherine were married quietly at St Luke's Church, Chelsea, and there was an unpretentious wedding breakfast at Mr Hogarth's home in York Place.

The ceremony and the wedding breakfast were so simple that Thomas Beard, who served as best man, was able in later years to remember nothing about it save that he and Macrone were the only guests outside the members of the Dickens and Hogarth families. Henry Burnett, who was now engaged to marry Dickens's sister Fanny, described the event long afterwards: "I can see him now helping his young wife out of the carriage after the wedding . . . A few common, pleasant things were said, healths were drunk with a very few words . . . and all seemed happy, not the least so Dickens and his young girlish wife."

That evening the couple arrived at Mrs Nash's little slatted cottage on the north side of the Gravesend Road in the tiny village of Chalk. Here they spent the one-week honeymoon that was all the time Dickens had before his work compelled him to return to town. He and Kate went back to London and his chambers at Furnival's Inn, where a newly purchased sideboard and all Dickens's bargains, from the brown beer jugs to the pair of lustres, were arranged within the three rooms.

With them in these modest quarters would be staying Kate's sixteen-year-old sister Mary. She was dazzled by the genius and fascination of her brother-in-law, and he found it impossible to speak too highly in her praise: her intelligence, her virtues, and her beauty were constantly on his lips. Soon Mary was a part of their home. She made her way more deeply and intimately into Dickens's heart even than either of his own sisters. She became, he said of her, "the grace and life of our home"; "so perfect a creature," he believed, "never breathed."

So, Dickens began his married life. He had an ideal picture in his imagination of what marriage should be like. There would be no more of "the moping solitude of chambers," but always the warm companionship of their own fireside, where he would tell Catherine "rationally what I have been doing" throughout a day whose pursuits and labours would all have for their mainspring her "advancement and happiness."

It was a dream no more unreal or egotistic than many people form and no more ignorant of the adjustments each would have to make if their life together was to run smooth. Not the least of the ways in which Dickens is extraordinary is that he actually did learn from experience, and refused to be with Kate the servant of whim or caprice that he knew he had been with Maria Beadnell. Although it would not be true to say he did not love Kate, it must be said that there were reservations in his love and that he regarded her from a certain judicial if affectionate elevation.

These aspects of their relationship are implicit in the entire tone of his correspondence with her. He denied feeling himself her superior, but one does not deny what there is no danger of anyone thinking. Her displays of coldness and temper drew from him neither the grief nor the anger of the desperate lover, only the assurance that he had been "hurt" and the calm "advice" to overcome her defects. Undoubtedly Kate had moods of sulky ill-humour and was unreasonable in her inability to see that he could not neglect his work. When he wrote that if she could not refrain from being sullen and obstinate she should say so and he would take himself off, that ultimatum fixed their relative positions once and for all.

But though Dickens could force Kate to surrender, he did not see her character more clearly than many lovers are apt to do. He thought her tendency to pout and feel "coss" and complain would melt away in the sweetness of intimacy. He did not observe that she understood no better than she had at the beginning the claims of the imaginative labours that chained him to his desk. He did not realize that the incapacity to resist which made her go down before his will also made her an easy prey to the mistrust and passive self-pity he told her to overcome. If Kate could not fight him, neither could she master a weakness that rendered her more immovable to change than if she had met him with the strength of hot defiance.

His own nature and its springs Dickens understood little better than he did Kate's. With his boundless confidence in the power of the will – which had already made him so different from the sickly and heart-broken little boy of only twelve years ago – it was impossible for him to believe that the will has limits. He could not imagine that there were elements in his own character as well as in his wife's beyond the ability of the will to alter. And therefore he could not conceive that Kate might not change at all or that he might grow less patient and gentle than he had been in his criticism during the period of their courtship.

Already deeply grained in Dickens was a quality whose existence he himself did not come to realize clearly until long after, when he referred it to the wound Maria Beadnell had given his heart. But even before that, so far as his deeper emotions were concerned, he had become intensely reserved, and his unhappiness over Maria had only sharpened a tendency already there. His companions in the blacking warehouse had never received from him any sign of his secret grief, and his school-fellows had never known that hidden shame of his life. He had told Maria Beadnell all his heart; it would be only with the greatest difficulty that he could so let himself become defenceless again.

He did not do so with Kate. He could be playfully tender with her, but some last surrender, some inner heart of his heart he did not yield, and could not yield to anyone. He probably could not and did not conceal from her his father's continuing misadventures, but the fact that he never told her of the blacking warehouse is curiously symbolic. Surely she would have pitied him for his sufferings? Yes, but though he pitied himself he could not bear to be pitied. He yearned for tenderness and yet trembled away from it as a net in which he might be entangled. There were depths in his being that he shrank from exposing to the gentlest touch.

With these obstacles to complete intimacy between them, it was probably unfortunate that Dickens and Kate began their married life with a third person in their household. Kate loved her sister deeply, and Dickens enveloped her in an imaginative idealization, but for a young married couple to have anyone else in their home is an inevitable restraint. Neither husband nor wife can be so singly impelled to explore each other's resources as a companion. Whatever problems there may be between them are more apt to be suppressed in the interests of seeming harmony than solved by the attainment of real harmony.

The existence of an almost permanent guest in the household is fraught with other dangers. If Mary Hogarth had been troublesome and tactless, Dickens would certainly have resented her presence as an imposition. In fact she bathed Dickens in an admiration that probably had its share in generating his praise of her. When the third member of the family is a beautiful and adoring young girl who admires her sister's husband beyond measure, it is easy for him to believe that any flaws in the serenity of his home are no fault of his, and easy for him, too, without quite realizing that he is doing so, to exalt the younger sister at the expense of the other. Dickens's eulogies of Mary Hogarth were indubitably innocent in all conscious feeling, and there is no evidence for assuming that Kate ever resented them or felt any twinge of jealousy or diminished love for her sister. But there is still the possibility that the entire lives of Charles Dickens and his wife might have been different if when they had set up housekeeping in Furnival's Inn they had been alone.

Could a sufficiently prescient observer, connecting all the facts about them, have forecast the course they were to travel? The unbelievable success of *The Pickwick Papers* – the amazing trajectory of Dickens's career from that point on – and its impact on his character and outlook, were beyond the powers of the wildest imagination to foresee. Catherine might well have lived happily enough if Dickens had been a busy journalist and minor literary man with a home in some leafy London suburb. But how would she do as the wife of an enormously ambitious, volatile, and determined genius who would soon be moving as a conqueror among the great of his time?

Pickwick Triumphant

A modest 400 copies were printed of the first number of *Pickwick*. Nevertheless, Chapman and Hall evidently had strong hopes for the new publication, and made unusually vigorous efforts to obtain as much newspaper publicity as possible. Their first full-page spread in the *Athenaeum*, and a corresponding announcement in *The Times*, had been followed up by a whole cluster of smaller advertisements in all the more important weeklies.

But at first the critical reception was chilly in comparison with the praise that had greeted *Sketches by Boz*. The opening chapter of *Pickwick*, with its crude satire on learned societies and Parliamentary manners, struck the *Atlas* as representing a vein of "exhausted comicality." The Bath *Herald* found Dickens's humour "enigmatic" but "harmless."

Nor were sales other than discouraging. After the first number, Chapman and Hall sent out 1,500 copies of each number to the provinces "on sale or return," but for the first five numbers an average of 1,450 of these came back. The London sales gave no reason to increase the quantity of their printings.

Relations with Seymour were uneasy. The touchy artist had not been mollified by the retention of his club idea or by the invention of Mr Winkle as the boastful and blundering sportsman. The whole second number seemed to exasperate him. His indignation boiled over at the tragic melodrama of "The Stroller's Tale" and its dying clown. This interpolated story Seymour angrily took as a deliberate violation of the tone of broad comedy he felt he excelled in. He couldn't even ignore it; the story was so prominent a part of the number that it would clearly have to supply the subject for an engraving.

Inwardly seething, Seymour forced himself to the distasteful task. When the drawing was done, Chapman and Hall didn't like it; neither did Dickens. The publishers adroitly passed on to Dickens the problem of dealing with the fretful artist by suggesting that the young author and the older man had better meet face to face; Dickens was delighted to do so. On 14 April, he wrote Seymour that he was asking Chapman and Hall in for "a glass of grog" the following Sunday evening and hoped the artist would be able to come too.

In his opening paragraph he tactfully praised Seymour's rendering of "our mutual friend Mr Pickwick," and added that he was happy to be able to congratulate the artist, the publishers, and himself on the success of their enterprise. Although more favourable reviews had by this time appeared, the feeble sales might have excused Seymour if his irritation went up another few degrees at this remark and if he thought the "success" might have been more pronounced had they kept to *his* scheme. But worse was to follow.

He had seen Seymour's sketch for "The Stroller's Tale," Dickens continued, and thought it "extremely good; but still, it is not quite my idea." The woman should be younger, the "dismal man" less miserable and more solicitous, the sick man emaciated but not repulsive. "The furniture of the room," he concluded, "you have depicted *admirably*." Seymour must have been gratified to have it conceded that he could draw a bed and three-cornered table, and that it was merely the people he had got all wrong.

On the appointed evening, Sunday, the 17th, Seymour arrived at Furnival's Inn. Their interview, Dickens said, was "short," and Seymour "certainly offered no suggestion whatsoever." In fact Seymour had no ideas except his sense of grievance at having been supplanted.

Against Dickens he had no chance. Very courteous, very handsome, very happy, seemingly calm but seething with excitement within, Dickens takes his stand. The future course of *Pickwick* will be determined entirely by himself, and he must reserve the right from time to time to issue such instructions about the illustrations as he deems necessary. Whatever the exact course of the meeting, Seymour went away committed to illustrating whatever Dickens wrote. They parted with an appearance of cordiality, but inwardly Seymour was sick with the humiliation of defeat.

Next day he set to work on "The Dying Clown" again, but in his perturbed emotion he spoiled the plate. All the following day he worked hard at the re-engraving. Wednesday morning young Frederick Dickens came knocking on his brother's door at Furnival's Inn with startling news. Seymour had gone into the summerhouse in his garden at Islington, placed the muzzle of a fowling piece in his mouth, and blown out his brains.

Dickens received the news with consternation. Just how much he knew of Seymour's kickings and rebellions with Chapman and Hall cannot be determined. But he could not have failed to guess that the unhappy artist's suicide had been precipitated by his failure to control the project he had initiated. And yet it could hardly be said that Dickens was to blame. He had not been obliged to accept an offer from Chapman and Hall in a form uncongenial to him, and there was no reason why he should not propose any changes in that offer that he pleased. Seymour had not been forced to yield to Dickens's ultimatum of the night before, nor could Dickens have anticipated that the artist would blow his brains out because he had been asked to redo one of the illustrations. Dickens had not been deliberately cruel; his genius had merely annihilated the weaker man.

That Chapman and Hall, in fact, decided to go on appears little less than a magic of personal magnetism. But in the same way that this extremely confident young man had persuaded them to follow his proposals rather than Seymour's original plan, so he had managed to infect them with something of his own enthusiasm. He did more. Chapman and Hall not only went on with *Pickwick*; they agreed that a new artist should take Seymour's place, and that Dickens should have the final voice in choosing him and superintending his work.

Rapid action had to be taken. Chapman and Hall published an announcement dated 25 April: "Arrangements are in progress which will enable us to present the ensuing number of the *Pickwick Papers* on an improved plan which, we trust, will give entire satisfaction to our numerous readers." The second number appeared with the three engravings that were all Seymour had finished. Meanwhile they conferred with Dickens on the "improved plan," and cast about for a man to illustrate the third number.

George Cruikshank might have seemed the natural choice, but he was booked up with as much work as he could handle. (Some three months after Seymour's death, Cruikshank sent them a youthful artist named John Leech, whom he thought promising. By that time, of course, a choice had been made.) Dickens saw several other applicants in Furnival's Inn. Among them came a young Anglo-Indian giant with a broken nose, one William Makepeace Thackeray, who showed him two or three sketchy line drawings completely different in style from Seymour's elaborate etchings. Dickens found the drawings quite unsuitable. Time pressed, and still no one had been chosen.

An engraver who worked for Chapman and Hall then suggested that they approach Robert William Buss, who had supplied an illustration for Dickens's "A Little Talk about Spring and the Sweeps." Buss was a well-known artist; he had exhibited subject pictures at the Royal Academy: *Watt's First Experiment with Steam, The Introduction of Tobacco by Sir Walter Raleigh.* He had begun work on another painting for the Academy, but obligingly he set this aside and concentrated on the illustrations for the third number.

Fortunately, there were now only two to be made. For the "improved plan" turned out to be that Dickens should supply eight more pages of story each month and that the number of engravings should be reduced from four to two! Dickens seized the occasion to suggest that, since he was to increase his contribution, they increase his *rate* of remuneration from nine to ten guineas a sheet. The new plan of more text and fewer illustrations was accordingly announced to the public as one that "entails upon the publishers a considerable expense, which nothing but a large circulation would justify them in incurring."

Buss knew nothing, unfortunately, about etching. He dropped everything else and worked night and day in the two or three weeks he had before the plates must be handed in, but he could not make himself even passably competent in so brief a time. His two unsatisfactory plates had to be placed in the printer's hands, "abominably bad" though Buss confessed them to be.

Chapman and Hall were almost desperate. They had laid out considerable sums in advertising; the artist whose name would have been a powerful selling point was dead, the man who had followed him was a failure; sales were still lagging, and they might have to foot a heavy loss. Dickens had convinced them that the book ought to go well, but illustrations were then regarded as essential to a book's success.

Happily, another suggestion presented itself: a young man named Hablôt Knight Browne who was still a few months short of twenty-one but had already scored notable successes in his work. At the age of seventeen he had earned the medal of the Society of Arts for the best representation of a historical subject, and had just won a prize offered by the Society with a laughable etching of *John Gilpin*. Browne was shy and extremely nervous, but Dickens took to him at once. Better still, the young artist immediately hit the mark with his etching of Mr Pickwick and Sam Weller in the yard of the White Hart. His first few plates were signed "Nemo," but then came the famous pseudonym of "Phiz," which marked the long years of his artistic collaboration with "Boz." Chapman and Hall sent a curt note to R. W. Buss dispensing with his services.

Buss was thunderstruck. He had dropped work on his Academy painting at a time that rendered it impossible for him to make that year's date of entry any longer, and he had believed himself definitely engaged for the entire course of the work. But Chapman and Hall claimed that he had only been on trial and felt they could afford no further risks. Whether or not Hall had misled him, the firm certainly repaid the favour Buss did them by dismissing him with brusque ingratitude.

Though the illustrating problem had now been overcome, sales still lingered in the doldrums. In February Dickens had effervescently announced that Pickwick was "begun in all his might and glory"; but three months later that worthy's circulation was so poor that Dickens agreed to let his own remuneration be reduced to ten guineas a number. When Macrone offered him £200, early in May, for a three-volume novel to be entitled *Gabriel Vardon, the Locksmith of London*, he was glad to accept it. This new work of fiction he rashly calculated, despite his newspaper work, he might be able to complete by the end of November or soon thereafter.

Meanwhile he did not allow himself to be discouraged. *The Village Coquettes* needed to be completed and put in Braham's hands. Some of the lyrics had to be altered to accord with Hullah's music, there was a dramatic duet to be worked out, and the "Finale" to be composed; Hullah's part of the work dragged. "When, oh *when*," Dickens pleaded desperately, "will this music be ready?"

Finally, book and music were finished and submitted to Braham. His answer, when it came, was enthusiastic. Talking with Hogarth, he was full of Dickens's "works and 'fame,'" and added that he intended to produce the opera within a month after he opened the season at Michaelmas.

During these same weeks, despite all these preoccupations and his work on *Pickwick*, Dickens made the time to indite an angry pamphlet significant of his entire viewpoint at this period. Towards the end of April he had listened indignantly to the reintroduction in Parliament of a Bill offered by Sir Andrew Agnew that would have prohibited not merely all work but all recreation on Sunday. Agnew had been repeatedly bringing up or supporting measures of this stamp since 1832.

Dickens felt infuriated by the persistence with which this repressive and puritanical measure was introduced. But he was even more infuriated by its discriminatory character, as a Bill that would bear down on the pleasures of the poor, forbidding them the few harmless enjoyments available to them at the same time that it left the well-off complacently untouched. Writing in a hot rage, he tore off a molten political pamphlet called *Sunday Under Three Heads: As it is; As Sabbath Bills would make it; As it might be made.* By working at top speed, he got it in print by June, signed with the pseudonym "Timothy Sparks."

It was dedicated caustically to Dr Blomfield, the Bishop of London, who had raised pious hands of horror over the viciousness of Sunday excursions among the lower classes. It irritated Dickens to hear the upper-class cant about the poor not knowing their stations in life because the workman bought his wife a ribbon for her dress and his child a feather for her bonnet, and the entire family sallied forth for one day's outing after six devoted to toil. Only a gloomy fanaticism would insist on closing the shops for people who work so late that they have no other time to buy their Sunday's supplies with their Saturday night's wages.

The enthusiasts for whom Sir Andrew spoke, professing to be horrified about the desecrating of the Sabbath, wanted to shut the bakeshops and deprive poor folk of their weekly hot dinner of mutton and browned potatoes. The iron-hearted man who would rob them of their only pleasures, Dickens points out, would be doing his best to drive the respectable poor into the filth, disease, fornication, and drunken squalor that characterized the wretched slum dwellers of St Giles and Drury Lane. They had no amusement for the mind, no means of exercising the body. Consequently they flocked to the gin shop as their only resource, and then, when they lay wallowing in the gutter, "your saintly law-givers lift up their hands to heaven, and exclaim for a law which shall convert the day intended for rest and cheerfulness, into one of universal gloom, bigotry, and persecution."

But hardly less objectionable than its oppressiveness to the poor was the "deliberate cruelty and crafty injustice" with which Sir Andrew's Bill exempted the rich from its provisions. They might continue to have their servants cook their Sunday dinners and to travel in their escutcheoned carriages. Nothing forbade the fashionable promenade, the Sunday feast, the private oratorio. But the poor man who saved his money to enjoy some little luxury on a Sunday must not have it; for he usually did not, and therefore it *was not* "necessary" to *him.*

It is customary [Dickens wrote] to affect a deference for the motives of those who advocate these measures, and a respect for the feeling by which they are actuated. They do not deserve it. If they legislate in ignorance, they are criminal and dishonest; if they do so with their eyes open, they commit wilful injustice; in either case, they bring religion into contempt. But they do NOT legislate in ignorance. Public prints, and public men, have pointed out to them again and again, the consequences of their proceedings.

Instead of making Sunday into a day of lassitude and dejection, Dickens insisted, it should be made into one of rational enjoyment. Let people play outdoor games, go on walks, take excursions by boat or coach. Let the British Museum, the National Gallery, and the Gallery of Practical Science be open on the one day working men could go to these places instead of closed at that very time. Let the fields neighbouring London resound to the stroke of the bat, the ring of the quoit, and the sound of laughing voices – and vice would be weakened, true religion strengthened.

Sir Andrew's Bill was thrown out on its second reading on 18 May by a majority of thirty-two votes. Dickens's blast had nothing to do with this defeat, however, since it was not printed until June. The greatest significance of *Sunday Under Three Heads* lies in its indication that Dickens had already attained a defined social attitude. It clearly displays the stand he was taking towards rich and poor, and reveals the broad sympathy with which he surveys the duties and enjoyments of existence. Its satire upon the intolerance and narrowness of the dissenting clergy, too, strikes a characteristic and prophetic note. The Nonconformist preacher of the pamphlet, with his frantic thumping of the pulpit, and the groaning enthusiasm of his congregation, did not precede by many months the red-nosed and hypocritical Stiggins in *Pickwick*. Flagrant rectitude was always to make Dickens see red.

Meanwhile, on the *Chronicle* he continued to be assigned to all the most important news events. On 22 June he covered the Melbourne–Norton trial. The defendant in this notorious case was no less a personage than the Prime Minister, Lord Melbourne, and there was supposed to be scandalous evidence that the beautiful and charming Caroline Norton had been his mistress.

The Court of Common Pleas at Westminster was jammed. The case turned out to rest on nothing but the spiteful tattle of discharged servants. The supposedly incriminating letters between the lady and her alleged lover were so empty of illicit implications as to suggest Dickens's parody of them in Bardell vs. Pickwick: "Dear Mrs B. – Chops and Tomato sauce. Yours, Pickwick." "I shall not be at home tomorrow. Slow coach. Don't trouble yourself about the warming-pan." The jury acquitted Lord Melbourne at half-past eleven that night, without leaving the court. Dickens, exhausted with his prolonged labours, fell into bed and stayed there all the following day.

Since the publication of *Sketches by Boz* he had agreed with Macrone on a second series, also to be illustrated by Cruikshank, and was hard at work visiting Bedlam and gathering material in other places for additional sketches. Macrone suggested that he take fifteen-year-old Fred into his accounting house. "I have deliberated a long time," Dickens told Macrone, "about the propriety of keeping him at his present study, but I am convinced that at his present period of life, it is really only so much waste time." Fred would sit himself upon a stool to be initiated into business habits forthwith.

By the latter part of July, the revisions in *The Village Coquettes* were completed. Braham, when the new version was placed in his hands, spoke of it in the highest terms. "Depend upon it," he said, "there has been no such music since the days of Sheil, and no such piece since the Duenna."

And, to top all these glittering prospects, *Pickwick* at last turned the corner. The sales were still going but languidly as Dickens finished the fourth number, in which Mr Pickwick comes upon Sam Weller cleaning shoes in the White Hart Yard and determines to take Sam into his own employ. The editor of the *Gazette*, William Jerdan, reading this fourth number, found Sam Weller irresistible. Mr Pickwick's discovery of Sam in fact marked the crucial point in *Pickwick*'s fortunes. During July, sales began to swell, all at once it was a flood. By the end of the month Dickens was writing in excited capitals at the close of a letter to Macrone: "PICKWICK TRIUMPHANT." In August, Chapman and Hall suggested that from November they pay him £25 a month. Before the end of its course *Pickwick* was selling 40,000 copies of every number.

Some of the highly charged activity and glory of these weeks radiates from a letter Dickens wrote to Catherine's grandfather, George Thomson, at the end of July. His exultation fairly crackles: "I am at present engaged in revising the proof sheets of the second Edition of the Sketches which will shortly appear; I am preparing another series which must be published before Christmas, I have just finished an opera which will be produced at Braham's Theatre in October, I have to get Mr Pickwick's lucubrations ready, every month . . ."

The skyrocketing sales of *Pickwick* brought Dickens offers of further work, which he accepted with gay abandon. The editor of the *Carlton Chronicle*, just started that June, wanted a series of fortnightly sketches at liberal rates. Thomas Tegg, the publisher of cheap reprints, offered £100 for a children's book to be called *Solomon Bell the Raree Showman*, which Dickens agreed to finish by Christmas. All this was in addition to the regular instalments of *Pickwick*, the three-volume novel promised to Macrone, and his newspaper work on the *Morning Chronicle*, not to mention that both his farce and the operetta would soon be going into rehearsal.

Now that the popularity of *Pickwick* was established, however, almost every week brought even more golden opportunities. The preceding March Dickens had met Richard Bentley, the New Burlington Street publisher. A short, pink-faced man with bristling hair and huge whiskers, he was a fluent talker who exuded a warm bonhomie. Bentley was on the alert for new talent. He was a clever and daring businessman who did things in a grandiose way; within two months of their meeting he decided that Dickens was a rising figure. He therefore proposed that Dickens write a novel for him, but was disappointed to discover that Macrone had forestalled him, apparently by a matter of weeks.

Dickens must also have been sorry, for in the course of the next three months he secured or believed he secured from Macrone a release from the engagement to write *Gabriel Vardon*. He also succeeded in cancelling his arrangement about a children's book with Thomas Tegg. Around the middle of August, Dickens told Bentley he was now free to consider a contract. Bentley promptly offered to buy the entire copyright of two novels of undetermined titles and subject matter and with no time limit specified for their delivery, for the sum of £400 each.

Dickens was shrewdly aware not merely of his soaring market value but of his swelling literary prestige. Confidential friends advised him, he wrote Bentley on 17 August, that he should demand £500. "Recollect," he said, "that you are dealing with an author not quite unknown but who, so far as he has gone, has been most successful." Bentley accepted the amendment, and Dickens signed a contract for both books on 22 August. This leap to £500 and the extremely flexible conditions show how Dickens's prestige had risen skyward in the amazing six months since William Hall had gone to Furnival's Inn looking for a hack writer.

After these breathless developments, Dickens and Kate relaxed for some weeks in a little cottage they rented at Petersham. But even so

Dickens was constantly shuttling back and forth, between its rural sports and the business activities of London – now demanding why he hadn't seen Browne's designs for the next number of *Pickwick*, now getting proofs of his own manuscript, now dropping in to see how things were going at the St James's Theatre, where Braham had decided to put on *The Strange Gentleman* before *The Village Coquettes*.

Near the end of September Dickens and Kate returned to town for the opening of *The Strange Gentleman* on the 29th. It is a conventional farce of cross-purposes and confused identities, but its elaborate mis-understandings, though mechanically arranged, are ingenious, and it is easy to see that they would be ludicrous enough in the hands of skilled actors. Mme Sala, one of the leading actresses of the day, scored a resounding success as the portly Julia Dobbs, relentlessly bent on marrying anyone she could capture, whether it was a weak-witted young nobleman or a complete stranger. Dickens's friend Harley was a riot as the "Strange gentleman" fleeing from a duel and terrified to believe himself surrounded by an inn full of lunatics. The piece ran for almost sixty nights and was put on again after the new year – no inconsiderable success. It gave still wider currency to the name and fame of Boz.

Dickens's contributions to the *Carlton Chronicle* lapsed after the publication of two sketches, that publication – together with *Bell's Life in London* – apparently finding it simpler and cheaper to pirate his articles as they appeared concurrently in the *Morning Chronicle* and the *Evening Chronicle*.

In October the printers were to set to work on the second series of *Sketches by Boz*. He was quite certain, though, Dickens told Macrone, that he could not get out the second volume before Christmas; the time was too short. "I cannot do more than one pair of hands and a solitary head can execute," he desperately wrote, "and am really so hard pressed just now that I must have breathing time." In the end, he found it impossible to supply the material for a second volume at all, and at last, in December 1836, the second series appeared in one volume.

The Village Coquettes opened at the St James's Theatre, with *The Strange Gentleman* on the same bill, on 6 December. Braham himself played the wicked Squire Norton in a hunting coat of scarlet velvet, and John Parry was Young Benson in rustic garb and a preposterous wig with long ringlets that wobbled over his brow. At the end of the performance the audience screamed for Boz, who "appeared, and bowed, and smiled, and disappeared," the critic of the *Examiner* wrote, "and left the audience in perfect consternation that he neither resembled the portraits of Pickwick, Snodgrass, Winkle, or Tupman. Some critics in the gallery were said to have expected Sam Weller. The disappointment was general and deeply felt."

Backstage, Mme Sala's son Augustus, a small boy of ten, was a witness to all the excitement of the occasion. He was patted on the head by Braham, chucked under the chin by Parry, and saw a "very young gentleman with long brown hair falling in silky masses over his temples," "dressed up to the very height of the existing fashion," but with eyes "full of power and strong will." Throughout the engagement, in fact, Dickens was constantly in the wings and the greenroom, drinking in the intoxication of the experience.

Hullah's music was well received, but most of the reviewers did not think much of the play. "Have you seen the Examiner?" Dickens wrote Hullah. "It is *rather* depreciatory of the opera, but like all their critiques against Braham, so well done that I cannot help laughing at it, for the life and soul of me. I have seen the Sunday Times, the Dispatch, and the Satirist, all of which blow their little trumpets against unhappy me, most lustily." The play pretty well deserved what the reviewers said of it, but Hullah's music was charming and the eighteenth-century costumes were pretty. It ran, however, only nineteen nights, though it was revived intermittently in 1837.

Many of the reviewers were affronted by the endeavour to exploit the literary prestige of Boz. It was not customary then for dramatic authors to appear in theatres and take curtain calls, and many of the papers clearly thought that the cries for Boz came from a claque. The *News* thought Dickens "extremely ill-advised to come forward to receive the congratulations of a *packed* house." Even Jerdan's well-disposed *Literary Gazette* commented unfavourably on the innovation: "When will this ridiculous nonsense end? Will they have Bulwer on the Covent Garden stage next Wednesday at the close of 'La Vallière'?"

For that matter, Dickens had friends who disapproved of his letting Chapman and Hall bring out *Pickwick* in monthly parts, and spoke of it slightingly as "a low, cheap form of publication" that would ruin his rising hopes. The only style suitable to the dignity of a man of letters, they felt, was the three-volume novel selling for a guinea and a half, not this scrabbling for the shillings of the impecunious. But Dickens had no such delicate notions of dignity, and no desire to limit his audience to an élite. From the beginning he had a keen awareness of the value of publicity and considerable adroitness in seizing and using it. And there could be no doubt now of the victorious course the *Pickwick Papers* was running.

The reviews and newspapers were almost a unanimous chorus of praise. Appreciation in the press ranged from *John Bull*'s declaration that "Smollett never did anything better," to the *Metropolitan Magazine* comparing Mr Pickwick and Sam Weller to Don Quixote and Sancho Panza. But more than this, readers in every class of society became Mr Pickwick's devoted admirers and followed his adventures from month to month with roars of loving laughter. "Judges on the bench and boys in the street," wrote Forster, "gravity and folly, the young and the old, those who were entering life and those who were quitting it, alike found it to be irresistible."

Out in the country Mary Russell Mitford, the author of *Our Village*, was amazed that her friend Miss Jephson hadn't heard of *Pickwick*, and bore testimony to Dickens's triumph: "I did not think there had been a place where English was spoken to which 'Boz' had not penetrated. All the boys and girls talk his fun – the boys in the streets; and yet they who are of the highest taste like it the most. Sir Benjamin Brodie takes it to read in his carriage between patient and patient; and Lord Denman studies *Pickwick* on the bench whilst the jury are deliberating." And to Elizabeth Barrett she writes that she holds Dickens "to be the next great benefactor of the age to Sir Walter Scott."

The glory to which all readers succumbed was the glory of a triumphant laughter that is the spirit of comedy. For great comedy does not close its eyes to the existence of suffering and evil, but is as true a victory over them as the exalted acceptance of tragedy. Without ever denying or falsifying the dark realities, comedy rises above them in a glorious flood of transcendence. Evil is neither subdued nor destroyed, and is nevertheless conquered by the sheer ringing affirmation of the human spirit.

Again and again Mr Pickwick's adventures achieve this victory. He is tricked by Jingle and Trotter, plucked by Dodson and Fogg, routed by Serjeant Buzfuz. Chicanery wins the battle, innocence is ludicrously defeated. And yet never has the comedy slackened. Mr Pickwick retains our sympathy, and, indeed, rises in our respect, but his mishaps arouse our inextinguishable merriment. The sniggering scoundrelism of his foes has been exposed in a gleaming rain of ridicule. Trickery and stupidity combine to defeat the right, but above their ascendency a triumphant derision soars to an annihilating vision of their moral meanness. Here, in truth, Dickens is one of the great humourists, freeing our imaginations from the bondage of respect for the sordid manipulators with a laughter of ringing delight.

What Dickens has done has been to create a new literary form, a kind of fairy tale that is at once humorous, heroic, and realistic. Mr Pickwick's world is bursting with hundreds of people as grotesque as those to be found in any street: the hypocritical Stiggins soaking up pineapple brandy and extolling tea and temperance, the magistrate Nupkins browbeating court officials and prisoners with an impartial ignorance of the law, the learned members of the legal profession twisting truth for their own profit, the rival newspaper editors Pott and Slurk exchanging scurrilities, the Parliamentary candidates Fizkin and Slumkey slinging violent political abuse. It is a world seen with no endeavour to deny the reality of ignorance, prejudice, malice, rascality, suffering, vice, and evil.

But it is also a world in which, as in the world of the fairy tale, its innocently guileless hero can experience no irretrievable loss and meet no imperishable sorrow. He can be temporarily victimized by the plots of designing men, but he bears a charmed life. He is a beaming fairy godfather to almost all the world, forever rescuing maidens and bestowing them on their true loves, succouring the oppressed, shaming even the cheats and petty tricksters with his kindness. His very existence and personality represent a kind of magic; if not that of the ugly duckling turned into a swan, a very foolish goose transformed into an angel in gaiters.

Before the last number of *Pickwick* had appeared in its green paper covers, its plump and amiable little hero with his gaiters and benevolently glittering spectacles, together with Sam Weller and his other friends, had become more than national figures – they had become a mania. Nothing like it had ever happened before. There were Pickwick chintzes, Pickwick cigars, Pickwick hats, Pickwick canes with tassels, Pickwick coats; and there were Weller corduroys and Boz cabs. There were innumerable plagiarisms, parodies, and sequels – a *Pickwick Abroad*, by G. W. M. Reynolds; a *Posthumous Papers of the Cadger Club*; a *Posthumous Notes of the Pickwickian Club*, by a hack who impudently called himself Bos; and a *Penny Pickwick* – not to mention all the stage piracies and adaptations. People named their cats and dogs "Sam," "Jingle," "Mrs Bardell," and "Job Trotter." It is doubtful if any other single work of letters before or since has ever aroused such wild and widespread enthusiasm. Barely past the age of twenty-five, Charles Dickens had become world-famous, beaten upon by a fierce limelight which never left him for the remainder of his life.

While this process was no more than beginning, Dickens himself felt an intimation that he was achieving something even greater than he had aimed at. "If I were to live a hundred years," he wrote Chapman and Hall on 1 November 1836, "and write three novels in each, I should never be so proud of any of them as I am of Pickwick, feeling as I do, that it has made its own way, and hoping, as I must own I do hope, that long after my hand is withered as the pens it held, Pickwick will be found on many a dusty shelf with many a better work." Dickens could hardly have dreamed how fully the years would realize his proudly humble wish. Wonder still lingers in the words.

[1] JOHN DICKENS, a portrait by John W. Gilbert

[2] ELIZABETH DICKENS, a portrait by John W. Gilbert

DICKENS'S FATHER AND MOTHER

[3] 387 MILE END TERRACE, LAND-PORT, PORTSEA, Dickens's birthplace, 1812. Photograph by F. J. Mortimer

[4] 2 ORDNANCE TERRACE, CHATHAM, Dickens's home between the ages of five and nine, 1817-1821

[5] NAVE OF ROCHESTER CATHEDRAL, a childhood haunt. Pen-and-ink sketch by Donald Maxwell

[6] *Above,* 16 BAYHAM STREET, CAMDEN TOWN, the Dickens home as financial desperation deepened, 1824. Sketch by F. G. Kitton

[7] *Right,* THE MARSHALSEA, scene of John Dickens's imprisonment for debt, 1824. Pen-and-ink drawing by Arthur Moreland

[8] DICKENS AT EIGHTEEN. Miniature by his aunt, Janet Barrow, 1830

[10] DICKENS AT TWENTY-THREE, by Rose Drummond, 1835. He gave this miniature to his fiancée, Catherine Hogarth, as an engagement present

[9] *Below*, MARIA BEADNELL, Dickens's first love, the original of David Copperfield's Dora. From *The Sphere*, February 20, 1909

[11] *Above*, MARY HOGARTH, his wife's sister, dead at seventeen, who inspired the creation of "Little Nell." Portrait by Hablôt Knight Browne

[12] 48 DOUGHTY STREET, LONDON. Dickens's home, 1837-1839, where he wrote *Pickwick*, *Oliver Twist*, and *Nicholas Nickleby*. Photograph by T. W. Tyrrell

[13] *Below*, THE FLEET PRISON, where Mr. Pickwick was incarcerated. After Rowlandson and Pugin

[14] JOHN FORSTER at twenty-eight, Dickens's most intimate friend. Sketch, May 22, 1840, by Daniel Maclise, R. A.

[15] WILLIAM HARRISON AINSWORTH, popular novelist, who introduced Dickens to his first publisher. Sketch by Daniel Maclise

[16] Left, HABLÔT KNIGHT BROWNE, "Phiz," illustrator of most of Dickens's books. Drawing by his son, Walter Browne

[17] THOMAS NOON TALFOURD, Serjeant-at-Law, to whom Dickens dedicated *Pickwick Papers*, the original of Tommy Traddles in *David Copperfield*

[18] GEORGE CRUIKSHANK, illustrator of *Sketches by Boz* and *Oliver Twist*. Sketch by Daniel Maclise

[19] *Right*, WILLIAM CHARLES MACREADY, famous actor, a lifelong friend

[20] BROADSTAIRS in the 1830's, a favorite Dickens summer resort. Drawing by George Shepherd

[21] SAMUEL ROGERS, sharp-tongued host of the famous "Literary Breakfasts." Sketch by Daniel Maclise, R. A.

[22] LEIGH HUNT, friend of Keats and Shelley, and the original of Harold Skimpole in *Bleak House*. Sketch by Daniel Maclise, R. A.

[23] FRANCIS, LORD JEFFREY, famous Scottish critic, one of those who wept for Little Nell. Portrait by G. Hayter

[24] WALTER SAVAGE LANDOR, the leonine original of Boythorn in *Bleak House*. Portrait by William Fisher

[25] DANIEL MACLISE, "Mac," the painter of the "Nickleby Portrait"

[26] OLD BAILEY AND NEWGATE, scene of the Courvoisier hanging, 1840.
(see p. 177) Before such a crowd Fagin would have been hanged

[27] 1 DEVONSHIRE TERRACE, YORK GATE, REGENT'S PARK, LONDON,
Dickens's home, 1839-1851, where he wrote *The Old Curiosity Shop, Barnaby Rudge, A Christmas Carol, Martin Chuzzlewit,* and *David Copperfield*

[28] DICKENS in 1839, from the "Nickleby Portrait," painted by Daniel Maclise, R. A.

[29] CATHERINE DICKENS, 1842, Dickens's wife, from the portrait by Daniel Maclise, R. A.

[30] DICKENS'S CHILDREN IN 1841. Charley, Mamey, Katey, and Walter, with the raven, in Devonshire Terrace. Water-color by Daniel Maclise, R. A.

[31] DICKENS, 1840. Pastel portrait by unknown artist

[32] CATHERINE DICKENS, 1846 Portrait by Daniel Maclise, R. A.

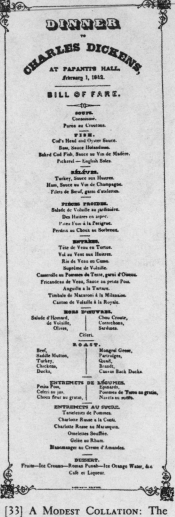

[33] A MODEST COLLATION: The Hartford dinner menu listed seventy dishes

[34] DICKENS IN AMERICA, lionized by Boston, 1842. Portrait by Francis Alexander

[35] HENRY WADSWORTH LONG-FELLOW, age thirty-three, 1840. Portrait by Cephas G. Thompson

[36] STEAMER "MESSENGER" on which Dickens traveled down the Ohio from Pittsburgh to Cincinnati

[37] SALON, PALAZZO PESCHIERE, the Dickens home in Genoa, 1844

[38] WHERE DICKENS READ *The Chimes* to a circle of friends, December 3, 1844; also the scene of Mr. Tulkinghorn's murder in *Bleak House*. Pen-and-ink drawing by Arthur Moreland

[39] READING *The Chimes*. From left to right the audience includes Forster, Jerrold, Blanchard, Carlyle, Frederick Dickens, Maclise, Fox, Stanfield, Dyce and Harness. Sketch by Daniel Maclise, R. A.

[40] THOMAS CARLYLE, 1868. From a photograph

[41] JANE WELSH CARLYLE, 1850 Portrait by Karl Hartmann

[42] DICKENS AS CAPTAIN BOBADIL in *Every Man in His Humour*. Painting by Charles R. Leslie, R. A.

[43] GEORGINA HOGARTH, 1850, the sister-in-law who lived in Dickens's home from 1842 until his death. By Augustus Egg, R. A.

[44] ANGELA BURDETT COUTTS, philanthropist, with whom Dickens collaborated in many charitable activities. Portrait by J. R. Swinton

PART THREE

Troubles and Triumphs
1837–1839

10

Metamorphosis of a Journalist

Even before *Pickwick* began its spectacular rise, Dickens had been eager to give up his post on the *Morning Chronicle*. He was tired of having his bones bruised in wild nocturnal gallops over the byroads of England, tired of trying to fit his writing into the uncertain hours left over from reporting, above all he was tired of the House of Commons. In the autumn of 1836 he seized an opportunity to drop reporting forever.

Richard Bentley was planning to establish a new magazine, to be called *Bentley's Miscellany*, and asked Dickens to assume its editorship. He offered liberal terms – £20 a month for his editorial duties, another twenty guineas for contributing sixteen pages of his own writing to each month's issue, the copyright of which was to belong to Bentley. This was at a rate more than 75 per cent higher than Chapman and Hall were paying for *Pickwick*. The new agreement was unconnected with the novel contract between Bentley and Dickens except for the provision that at the conclusion of *Pickwick* Dickens might write one more novel for Chapman and Hall, instead of being pledged to give his very next two to Bentley. Signed 4 November 1836, the agreement was for one year, renewable at Bentley's option for another three. With the £300 a year he was beginning to receive from *Pickwick*, Dickens would have a dependable income of almost £800.

As soon as these arrangements were concluded, Dickens wrote a letter of resignation from the *Morning Chronicle*. To Easthope personally, he expressed his "warmest and most sincere thanks for all the courtesies and kindnesses" received at his hands. But Easthope, irritated at losing a valuable employee, dispatched a furious blast.

Dickens began a temperate response. Easthope's letter, he wrote, might have been expected when a servant gave warning and took himself elsewhere. But *he* had expected some written acknowledgement of his work in their behalf.

I may say now, that on many occasions at a sacrifice of health, rest, and personal comfort, I have again and again, on important expresses in my zeal for the interests of the paper, done what was always before considered impossible, and what in all probability will never be accomplished again. During the whole period of my engagement wherever there was difficult and harassing duty to be performed – travelling at a few hours' notice hundreds of miles in the depth of winter – leaving hot and crowded rooms to write, the whole night through, in a close damp chaise . . . under every possible circumstance of disadvantage and difficulty – for that duty I have been selected. . . .

Depend upon it, Sir [Dickens concluded scathingly], that if you would stimulate those about you to any exertions beyond their ordinary routine of duty, and gather round you competent successors of the young men whom you will constantly find quitting a most arduous and thankless profession, as other prospects dawn upon them, this is not the way to do it.

With these words Dickens turned his back on his reporting days. In later years, however, when he looked back on his newspaper experiences, he remembered them with more affection. "I went into the gallery of the House of Commons," he said at a Newspaper Press Fund dinner in 1865,

when I was a boy not eighteen, and I left it – I can hardly believe the inexorable truth – nigh thirty years ago . . . I have been, in my time, belated on miry bye-roads, towards the small hours, forty or fifty miles from London, in a wheelless carriage, with exhausted horses and drunken postboys, and have got back in time for publication, to be received with never-forgotten compliments by the late Mr Black, coming in the broadest of Scotch from the broadest of hearts I ever knew.

And in time, even towards the proprietors of the *Chronicle* he came to feel more amicable. "What gentlemen they were to serve," he wrote Forster in 1845.

I have had to charge for half-a-dozen breakdowns in half-a-dozen times as many miles. I have had to charge for the damage of a great-coat from the drippings of a blazing wax-candle, in writing through the smallest hours of the night in a swift-flying carriage and pair. . . . I have charged for broken hats, broken luggage, broken chaises, broken harness – everything but a broken head, which is the only thing they would have grumbled to pay for.

But now, his ties with the *Morning Chronicle* severed, Dickens flung himself into the task of lining up potential contributors for *Bentley's Miscellany*. He wrote Douglas Jerrold, author of the popular comedy *Black-eyed Susan*, proposing to call on him and obtain the promise of a paper for the first number. He asked Macrone for the address of the Reverend Francis Mahony, who wrote witty mystifications in verse under the pseudonym of Father Prout. For the opening number, he himself wrote "The Public Life of Mr Tulrumble" and sent it to Cruikshank, who was doing most of the magazine's illustrations.

With Macrone, Dickens continued to be on the best of terms. All through the autumn he dropped in at Macrone's place of business in St James's Square about the publication of the second series of *Sketches by Boz*. In Macrone's office, which was adorned with busts of distinguished men, he met the sculptor responsible for some of them, the sweet-tempered Angus Fletcher, whom Dickens affectionately nicknamed "Kindheart."

But suddenly these amicable relations with Macrone were shattered. As Dickens described it two years later, "A dispute arose between myself and Mr Macrone, whether an agreement for a novel, which we had together, was not understood to be cancelled between us." With the news of *Bentley's Miscellany*, Macrone flew into a rage. He wrote Dickens an intemperate letter of complaint and angry accusation. Dickens's reply was unsatisfactory. Macrone, in his agitation, asked Ainsworth for his advice.

It is impossible, on the known evidence, to determine the rights of the case. Perhaps Macrone, early in July, had casually said he would be willing to cancel their agreement and then later when *Pickwick* soared into success regretted it, while Dickens, upon this oral assurance, had gone ahead in his arrangement with Bentley for the two novels. Dickens's behaviour during the entire dispute is that of a man indignantly resentful of a piece of chicanery. Certainly, Macrone, however, had neither returned the letter of agreement nor destroyed it, but still had the document.

Macrone's appeal put Ainsworth in an equivocal position. He and Dickens were on the friendliest terms, and the younger novelist was a frequent guest at Ainsworth's home. But Ainsworth had also introduced Dickens to Macrone, and felt that the publisher was entitled to fulfilment of his contract. He told Macrone that he had blundered in losing his temper and vilifying Bentley. Nevertheless he condoled with Macrone on the loss of Dickens as a serious misfortune. Even Bentley's terms, Ainsworth considered, were inadequate; Dickens ought to have received £800 for a novel, and Macrone's £200 were preposterously small. "I am exceedingly sorry for your loss. You will not easily repair it."

Macrone protested the assumption that Dickens was lost. Did he not have Dickens's letter of agreement? Doubtless, the friendliest course for Ainsworth to have followed would have been, not to advise Macrone secretly, but to ask permission to discuss the subject with Dickens. This, however, he did not do. He felt uncomfortable, he insisted that he must not be quoted, but agreed that Dickens was bound.

Much to Dickens's irritation, Macrone continued to advertise *Gabriel Vardon* as a forthcoming publication. Their relations became so strained that they ceased to communicate with each other directly. When Macrone offered on 1 December to buy the entire copyrights of the first and second series of *Sketches by Boz* – he had previously bought only the copyrights of their first editions – Dickens asked £50 more than the £200 Macrone offered for both copyrights, and demanded that Macrone cease advertising a novel by him and return his letter of agreement. His irritation was sharpened by the fact that on that very day Macrone had sent an advertisement of *Gabriel Vardon* for inclusion in the next number of *Pickwick*, which Chapman and Hall rejected at Dickens's request. Still chafing, Dickens sent around to Bentley's the next morning asking them to refuse any similar advertisement for the *Miscellany*.

But, as Ainsworth had seen, Macrone had Dickens at a disadvantage. Whether Macrone could have enjoined his writing for any other publisher, is very doubtful. But Dickens feared these possibilities and worried lest publicity on his breach of contract gravely injure his reputation.

Consequently, whatever the good faith in which Dickens had believed himself released, Macrone's unyielding position forced him to a compromise. On 5 January 1837, after six weeks of acrimony, he accepted only £100, instead of the £250 he had at first insisted upon, for the entire copyright of both series of *Sketches*, but with this sum he received the agreement he had believed cancelled. "First and last by these books," he told Mitton bitterly, "I had some £400, Macrone had some £4,000 . . ."

But meanwhile he seemed to be free of Macrone, and he had already thrown himself full force into his new pursuits. Bentley inaugurated a series of literary dinners in the "red room" of his offices in New Burlington Street. Here Dickens met for the first time many of their contributors who were friends of Bentley's, and deepened his acquaintance with others. Bentley was delighted with his new editor, and insisted on Dickens being proposed for membership in the Garrick Club, to which he was elected early in January.

Success also smiled on his playwriting. Despite its poor reception by the dramatic critics, *The Village Coquettes* was doing fairly well on the stage, and was published by Bentley in December. At the same time Chapman and Hall brought out *The Strange Gentleman*. Harley was so pleased with his success in the title role that he begged Dickens to write another farce for production in the spring.

The year ended, despite the necessity of completing the next instalment of *Pickwick*, in a round of social activities. From one party Dickens arrived home at one in the morning "dead drunk, and was put to bed by my loving missis." There was a holiday turkey sent by Mitton's partner, Charles Smithson, of which Beard and Mitton were invited to partake. And on Christmas Day, at Kensal Lodge, Harrison Ainsworth initiated the longest and most deeply intimate friendship in Dickens's life by introducing him to the literary and dramatic critic of the *Examiner*, John Forster.

It was strange that they had not met before. Forster had come up to University College in 1828 and then entered the Inner Temple. He had speedily made his way into journalistic and literary circles, become a friend of Charles Lamb and Leigh Hunt, joined the staff of the *Examiner* when he was no more than twenty years of age in 1832, and been dramatic critic on the *True Sun* throughout a period overlapping Dickens's employment on that paper. Albany Fonblanque, the editor of the *Examiner*, had the saltiest appreciation of the *Sketches by Boz* and was always praising them to his young coadjutor. And Forster had written a laudatory review of *Pickwick* in the *Examiner* and a depreciatory but not unfriendly comment on *The Village Coquettes*.

Voluble, opinionated, overbearing, and quarrelsome, Forster was also sincere, deeply interested in literature, and selflessly faithful to his friends. Untiring in his endeavours to serve authors whose work he admired, he was even now trying to prod Ainsworth into finding a publisher for Browning's *Sordello* and pressing Macready to stage his *Strafford*. Although he was to attach himself with special devotion to Dickens, many other writers, Landor, Tennyson, and Carlyle among them, came to be grateful for his generous helpfulness. Thackeray declared of him, "Whenever anybody is in a scrape we all fly to him for refuge – he is omniscient and works miracles."

The person whom Dickens beheld when they met at Kensal Lodge was a serious young man with a mane of dark hair, a firm chin, sensuous lips, and dark intense eyes. Two months the novelist's junior, he wore a self-assured sobriety contrasting oddly with Dickens's boyish effervescence that made him seem considerably older. He carried himself in a way that satirical observers said was modelled upon Macready's stage presence, stalking into a room hand on heart, intoning in his loud voice some such formula as "It is with infinite regret" or "Believe me I feel it sensibly." "A most noisy man," Carlyle said, "but really rather a good fellow . . . and with some substance in his tumultuary brains." He and Dickens – opposites in many ways – warmed to each other at once. Dickens was all fire and charm; Forster thorny but solidly dependable. Although they often quarrelled – Forster fought with everybody – the friendship then begun survived all shocks and lasted until Dickens's death thirty-four years later.

The young man Forster saw at that first meeting looked amazingly youthful, with a marked expression of openness and candour. His face revealed no more beard than a girl's, and his head, covered with rich brown hair in luxurious abundance, was carried in a manner extremely spirited. But above all his face had that in it, Forster summarized, "which no time could change . . . Light and motion flashed from every part of it." Though the two young men were strongly attracted, they were prevented from meeting again for almost two months by Kate's approaching confinement and Dickens's search for larger living quarters than the three rooms at Furnival's Inn.

On the morning of 6 January Kate's labour began. Dickens's mother and Mrs Hogarth both arrived to help. Dickens and Mary went out to buy a little table for Kate's bedroom, dispatched on the errand, perhaps, by the two mothers to get them out of the way. They wandered up and down Holborn and the neighbouring streets for hours, going from one dealer to another. The baby, a boy, was born at quarter past six that evening, and was thus a Twelfth-Night child. He was named Charles after his father. "I shall never be so happy again," Dickens said in his diary a year later, "as in those chambers three storeys high – never if I roll in wealth and fame."

The first issue of *Bentley's Miscellany* made its appearance in the world only a few days before the birth of Dickens's child. It made an immediate success: the second number sold 6,000 copies; at the end of six months Bentley was "fairly inundated with *orders*." It was a cheerful magazine of humorous tales and articles, lively and sometimes melodramatic biographical sketches, ghost and adventure stories, light verse, facetiae, and even an occasional brief dramatic farce. Its contributors came to include Dickens's father-in-law Hogarth, William Jerdan, Father Prout, Captain Medwin, Dr Maginn, Samuel Lover, James Morier, author of *Hajji Baba of Ispahan*, James Fenimore Cooper, Thomas Love Peacock, Bentley's close friend Barham, and of course Dickens himself.

He tackled his editorial duties with determination and energy. Even the "Answers to Correspondents" showed his tremendous attention to detail. They overflowed with bold high-spiritedness, and revealed the young editor's almost boisterous determination to do and say exactly what he pleased. Rejected articles were accompanied by individual letters of tactful explanation, and promising contributors received detailed criticisms brightened by friendly praise. He recommended Phiz, "my Pickwick artist," to Bentley, and passed upon all illustrations with an eagle eye. Into his own new story, *Oliver Twist*, beginning in the February number, "I have thrown my whole heart and soul," he wrote, ". . . and most confidently believe he will make a feature in the work . . ."

Oliver Twist was a bold departure from the genial tone of *Pickwick Papers*. Instead of safely echoing the humour and hilarity that had set all England roaring with affectionate laughter, Dickens embarked on a scathing denunciation of the new Poor Law and moved on to a lurid and sombre portrayal of London's criminal slums. The comedy had a bite he had seldom previously attempted even in painting the Fleet or describing Dodson and Fogg. Bumble, the workhouse beadle, is comic, but the laughter has an acid quality and Bumble is slowly subjected to a kind of vindictive ferocity.

The very language of the opening pages is steeped in a boiling sarcasm. At the end of the first chapter, describing Oliver's birth, "Oliver cried lustily," Dickens wrote. "If he could have known that he was an orphan, left to the tender mercies of church-wardens and overseers, perhaps he would have cried the louder." In the following chapter Dickens spoke of the orphans in the baby farm as "juvenile offenders against the poor-laws" who "perversely" "sickened from want and cold, or fell into the fire from neglect, or got half smothered by accident," or were sometimes "overlooked in turning up a bedstead or inadvertently scalded to death when there happened to be a washing – though the latter accident was very scarce, anything approaching to a washing being of rare occurrence."

It took courage to risk alienating his readers by stirring in this second novel emotions so different from what they were expecting. But Dickens was building a career, not merely consolidating a sudden popularity. He would consider anxiously how to make his readers receptive to what he wanted to say; he would not consider saying only what they wanted to hear. All his sympathy with the warm feeling of the life that politicians and economists forgot was simmering in his heart and demanding that he make himself its spokesman.

His fusion of bravery and instinct justified itself. Masses of readers hated Bumble and laughed at him with an angry laughter; they loathed Fagin and shuddered at Sikes. The pathos and the horror of Dickens were as triumphant as his humour had been. It proved that *Pickwick* was no flash-in-the-pan. Rendered gloriously self-confident by *Oliver's* reception, Dickens definitely determined to give up his rooms in Furnival's Inn. His lease there still had until Christmas 1838, to run, but he could afford the loss now. In good earnest he began looking for a house suitable to an established author.

While agents were searching in their behalf, Dickens, Kate, and Mary went down for a few weeks to the cottage at Chalk where he and Kate had spent their honeymoon. There he finished revising the farce he was writing for Harley, "a comic burletta in one Act," called *Is She His Wife?* It is an ineffective piece with an elaborate comic intrigue based on a series of misunderstandings among all the characters and including a somewhat strained scene between a bored husband and a nagging wife only recently married. Although Braham paid £100 for this piece, and produced it at the St James's on 6 March 1837, Harley did not score anything like the success with it that he had with *The Strange Gentleman*, and it enjoyed only a short run.

In March Dickens found a pleasant twelve-room dwelling of pink brick, with a white-arched entrance door on the street level, and a small private garden in the rear. It was located just north of Gray's Inn at 48 Doughty Street, a genteel private street with a lodge at each end and gates that were closed at night by a porter in a gold-laced hat and a mulberry-coloured coat. Dickens leased it for three years beginning Lady Day (25 March) at £80 a year.

The Doughty Street home was soon full of lively doings. In addition to Mary, young Frederick Dickens – by this time sixteen – was now a member of the household, and added to its high spirits. A full-lipped, snub-nosed youth, with raised eyebrows and an amusingly oily laugh, he had a ludicrous gift for comic imitations in which Dickens abetted him. The bright first-floor sitting-room often resounded with Kate's and Mary's laughter.

During his mornings Dickens did editorial work for the *Miscellany* and wrote *Oliver Twist* and *Pickwick* in his upstairs study overlooking the garden. In the afternoons he took long walks or went horseback riding with Ainsworth. As fast as he turned out *Oliver* he sent the manuscript to Cruikshank for illustration.

The little family circle was often joined in the evenings by his younger sister Letitia, who had become engaged in January to Henry Austin, with whom Dickens had so many times listened to Maria Beadnell's harp in Lombard Street. The young man whom Fanny was soon to marry, Henry Burnett, was a singer like herself. He often visited the family when Dickens was working, as he sometimes did, in the evening. Burnett recalled one such occasion:

> One night in Doughty Street, Mrs Charles Dickens, my wife and myself were sitting round the fire cosily enjoying a chat, when Dickens, for some purpose, came suddenly into the room. "What, you here!" he exclaimed; "I'll bring down my work." It was his monthly portion of "Oliver Twist" for Bentley's. In a few minutes he returned, manuscript in hand, and while he was pleasantly discoursing he employed himself in carrying to a corner of the room a little table, at which he seated himself and recommenced his writing. We, at his bidding, went on talking our "little nothings," – he, every now and then (the feather of his pen still moving rapidly from side to side), put in a cheerful interlude. It was interesting to watch, upon the sly, the mind and the muscles working (or, if you please, *playing*), in company, as new thoughts were being dropped upon the paper. And to note the working brow, the set of mouth, with the tongue tightly pressed against the closed lips, as was his habit.

On 31 March came the anniversary of the first instalment of *Pickwick*. In celebration Chapman and Hall sent Dickens, in addition to the sums that had been agreed on, a cheque for £500 and gave a dinner in honour of the anniversary. On the last day of April Dickens celebrated his editorial dignity by inviting his new publisher Bentley to dinner. Portly John Dickens was there, and George Hogarth, Mary, and one of the younger Hogarth sisters. The fun was unceasing and so were the successive glasses of the brandy punch. Not until almost midnight did Bentley think of leaving, and then Dickens pressed him to a final glass, which, by that time, he would gladly have avoided.

Dickens begged his lovely young sister-in-law Mary to add her persuasions, and Bentley yielded. "At the hands of this Hebe," he wrote, "I did not decline it."

Never had a writer's position more splendidly and amazingly changed than Dickens's during these twelve months. At its beginning he was merely a successful journalist with the foreshadowings of a literary reputation, glad to take on a job of hack-writing in order to afford to get married. Now he was a family man living on an income more than doubled in a comfortable house with a pretty wife, an infant son, and an adoring and deeply loved sister-in-law. He was the editor of a magazine impressively prosperous from its inception. He was already more than halfway through one incredibly popular novel and had started another that bade fair to be hardly less so. Mr Pickwick, bursting out of his green covers, had beamingly played the fairy godfather in actual fact, and magically transfigured the life of his own creator.

[11]

Lost Love

But soon there were shadows on the brightness. Early in May, a few weeks after they had so happily settled themselves at Doughty Street, Dickens experienced his first and possibly his greatest loss. The week after the dinner for Bentley, Mary went to Brompton to spend two days with her mother. She returned in time to accompany Dickens and Kate to see his farce *Is She His Wife?* at the St James's Theatre on Saturday night. They reached home in the highest spirits, and after good nights were said and lights put out downstairs, Mary "went upstairs to bed at about one o'clock in perfect health and her usual delightful spirits." But she had hardly closed her door when Dickens heard her utter a strange choking cry.

Rushing into her room, he saw that she was severely ill. Kate joined him; Frederick ran for a doctor. During the night and the next morning she grew worse. Although no danger was "apprehended until nearly the very last," Dickens wrote, "she sank under the attack and died – died in such a calm and gentle sleep, that although I had held her in my arms for some time before, when she was certainly living (for she swallowed a little brandy from my hand) I continued to support her lifeless form, long after her soul had fled to Heaven." In an agony of grief Dickens slipped a ring from her pale hand and slid it on his own finger. It remained there until his death.

Her loss shook the family, and in Dickens left scars as deep as those of his youthful love for Maria. But where Maria had brought him bitter disillusion, Mary set in motion in the springs of his imagination a vision of ideal womanhood that was never realized for him again. How far Mary was all he thought her, we cannot know. Her light shone briefly on his life. But her memory never faded from his mind, nor his love for her from his heart.

Almost from the beginning, when as a girl of sixteen Mary had come to stay with the young couple shortly after their honeymoon, she had won a unique place in Dickens's love. Now, as he reflected on her sweet and gentle spirit and recalled her joyful vitality, he ached with wretchedness. "You cannot conceive," he wrote the day after her death, "the misery in which this dreadful event has plunged us. Since our marriage she has been the peace and life of our home . . . she has been to us what we can never replace, and has left a blank which no one who ever knew her can have the faintest hope of seeing supplied."

The burial was in Kensal Green Cemetery on the Harrow Road. Dickens himself composed the inscription on the tombstone:

MARY SCOTT HOGARTH
DIED 7TH MAY 1837
YOUNG, BEAUTIFUL, AND GOOD,
GOD IN HIS MERCY
NUMBERED HER WITH HIS ANGELS
AT THE EARLY AGE OF
SEVENTEEN

For years it was Dickens's hope to be buried in that same grave.

When all was over, he was so prostrated that he felt unable to go on with his writing. Never before or again were his habits of industry so shaken that he was totally unable to work. He took Kate off with him to a small farm in rural Hampstead. "I have been so much unnerved and hurt," he wrote Ainsworth, "by the loss of the dear girl whom I loved, after my wife, more deeply and fervently than anyone on earth, that I have been compelled for once to give up all idea of my monthly work and to try a fortnight's rest and quiet."

There was no number of *Pickwick Papers* for the end of May, and in the June issue of *Bentley's Miscellany*, no instalment of *Oliver Twist*. The most fantastic rumours broke out. All literary London knew by this time who Boz really was, but there were persons who none the less gravely maintained that *Pickwick* was the work of an association that had disbanded, that Boz was a prisoner who had been many years in King's Bench, that he was a youth of eighteen so shattered in health by his literary labours "that there was not the slightest chance of his ever publishing another number."

The brief two weeks' rest after the funeral passed quietly in the little secluded cottage. Kate, too, had been dreadfully shaken by their ordeal, but in the country solitude she slowly attained some peace, though shortly before or after their return to London she suffered a miscarriage. The bond between herself and Mary had been so close, Dickens recorded, that "she has nothing to remember but a long course of affection and attachment, perhaps never exceeded. Not one cross word or angry look on either side even as children rests in judgment against her . . ."

But for Dickens the anguish was not easily softened. Writing to Beard while at Collins's Farm, he poured out his heart: "Thank God she died in my arms, and the very last words she whispered were of me. . . . The first burst of grief has passed, and I can think and speak of her calmly and dispassionately. I solemnly believe that so perfect a creature never breathed. I knew her inmost heart, and her real worth and value. She had not a fault."

When he revisited the cemetery a month after her death he felt her loss as painfully as ever.

I saw her grave but a few days ago and the grass around it was as green and the flowers as bright, as if nothing of the earth in which they grew could ever wither or fade. Beneath my feet there lay a silent but solemn witness that all health and beauty are but things of the hour . . . as none loved her better living, so none laments her more constantly and deeply in death . . .

As the months went by he thought of Mary with ever-increasing love. In the fall, thanking Mrs Hogarth for a lock of Mary's hair, he wrote, "I have never had her ring off my finger by day or night, except for an instant at a time, to wash my hands, since she died. I have never had her sweetness and excellence absent from my mind so long. I can solemnly say that, waking or sleeping, I have never lost the recollection of our hard trial and sorrow, and I feel that I never shall. . . ."

During her lifetime there had been natural boundaries to the development of Dickens's feelings for his adoring sister-in-law. And if he had idealized her then into the unattainable of perfection, it was no doubt partly because she was in fact unattainable. But her early death not only eased the barriers; it made that perfection permanent and unassailable, forever safe from the hazards of time. If he had, before her death, idealized her partly because he loved her, from then on he loved her even more because he could idealize her forever.

But the image of her death he could not fully conquer. When he was drawing near the end of *Oliver Twist*, he found himself unable to carry out his original intention of having Rose Maylie die. He could not bear to describe the fair young creature breathing her last amid the blossoms of May. Two years later, Mary dominated his imagination again, throughout the whole story of Little Nell, in *The Old Curiosity Shop*. He felt such anguish at the approaching death he had planned for his child heroine that he spun out the narrative to delay the moment when he must face the ending. Nobody, he said, would miss Nell as he would. "It is such a very painful thing to me, that I really cannot express my sorrow. Old wounds bleed afresh when I only think of the way of doing it: what the actual doing it will be, God knows. . . . Dear Mary died yesterday, when I think of this sad story."

Towards the end of October 1841, Mary's grandmother died, and suddenly, a few days later, her brother George, at the age of twenty. Dickens yielded his hoped-for place near Mary to the bereaved family. But although to Mrs Hogarth he generously minimized the sacrifice, he could not suppress a desperate outcry to Forster: "It is a great trial to me to give up Mary's grave; greater than I can possibly express. . . . The desire to be buried next her is as strong upon me now, as it was five years ago; and I *know* (for I don't think there ever was love like that I bear her) that it will never diminish." And in a letter to Forster in 1848 he was still marking the anniversary of her loss: "This day 11 years poor dear Mary died."

Indeed, out of his imagination she never died. Throughout almost his entire literary career his novels continue to reveal glimpses of now one and now another aspect of her shining image. Mary's gaiety and tenderness animate loving, laughing Ruth Pinch in *Martin Chuzzlewit*. His vision of her nobler qualities recurs again and again, in Florence Dombey's devotion to her brother and father, in David Copperfield's serene and perhaps too perfect Agnes, in the sacrificial spirit of Little Dorrit. The very sentimentality that we sometimes find in their delineation is only a further index to the transcendent goodness with which he endowed Mary in his heart.

The memory of her death, too, deepened the pathos with which Dickens was always to contemplate youth or innocence condemned to die. As it was agonizingly present to him in the last hours of Little Nell, six years later it suffused with tenderness the death of Paul Dombey. It lends a dignity to the fading away of David Copperfield's foolish, frivolous child wife Dora. Even in the last book he completed, *Our Mutual Friend*, echoes of Mary's loss are still lingering in the death of Betty Higden's grandchild, little Johnny.

It is impossible to exaggerate the significance of this early love and early sorrow for Dickens. His devotion to Mary was an emotion unique in his entire life, not only enduring and unchanging, but one that touched his being in a way no other did. Unlike Maria Beadnell, who tortured his heart and his pride and taught him to be forever on his guard, unlike Kate, whose slow-minded and pedestrian goodness he ultimately found impossible to mould into the shining pearl of perfection, Mary alone remained elevated by her death to her high altar. Her gradual enshrinement in Dickens's memory subjected Kate to comparisons that she could not possibly equal – that perhaps no living person could have done – and had its share in the slow growth of the catastrophe that years later overtook the married life of Dickens and Kate.

12

Ascent of the Rocket

At the Prince of Wales Tavern on 18 November a banquet was held to celebrate the completion of England's most popular contemporary work of fiction. Just before "*the* toast of the evening," "the head waiter . . . entered, and placed a glittering temple of confectionery on the table, beneath the canopy of which stood a little figure of the illustrious Mr Pickwick." For, after nineteen months of steadily mounting success, *Pickwick* had at last come to its triumphant close. It was a merry company and a merry occasion.

In welcoming Dickens as their guest of honour, Chapman and Hall put in his hands a cheque for £750. Above the sums they had contracted to pay him, they had presented him with what Forster later estimated as another £2,000 and Edward Chapman remembered as £2,500. They could well afford this generosity, for they had made about £14,000 from their investment in the unknown young man whom Hall had sought out to do a piece of literary hack work. Promptly on the Monday following, Dickens opened an account in Coutts's bank with an initial deposit of £500.

In contrast to the frictions that were already developing between him and Richard Bentley, Dickens had for Chapman and Hall the warmest of feelings. With generous bonuses and gifts, they had created a human bond between themselves and an author sensitively responsive to friendly ties. Now, he was much moved by the affection of his friends and the excitement of the occasion. Besides the two publishers, those present included Hogarth and the beaming John Dickens, Talfourd, the dignified and stately actor William Charles Macready, Ainsworth with his gusty laugh, the witty and epigrammatic Jerdan, editor of the *Literary Gazette*.

Jerdan recalled that at the table "the pleasant and uncommon fact was stated . . . that there never had been a line of written agreement, but that the author, printer, artist, and publisher had all proceeded on simple verbal assurances, and that there never had arisen a word to interrupt the complete satisfaction of everyone." It was true that there had been no formal contract, although there had been exchanges of letters agreeing on terms. In the course of the evening Dickens received from his publishers a set of silver "Apostle" spoons with characters from *Pickwick* instead of the Twelve Apostles on the handles.

By this time, after the first shock and suffering over Mary's death, Dickens's life was settling into a pattern prophetic of the future. His days hummed with the electric energy of a dynamo. Before *Oliver Twist* was more than half finished he began his third novel. His circle of friends grew constantly larger. And, only eight months after the *Pickwick* dinner, he received what almost amounted to official recognition as one of England's celebrities, election to the Athenaeum Club.

The intimacy between Dickens and Forster grew at a rapid pace, once the initial obstacles to their seeing each other had been passed. Dickens sent him the parts of *Oliver* already published, and was delighted with his enthusiasm. Forster in turn sent Dickens one of the biographies of the *Statesmen of the Commonwealth* that he was contributing to Dionysius Lardner's *Cabinet Cyclopaedia*. "I don't know what to say," Dickens told him, "about your beautiful present . . . Conclude that I am like the parrot who was doubly valuable for not speaking, because he thought a great deal more."

Richard Bentley, however, did not take as enthusiastically to Forster as Dickens did. They met on a river excursion to Blackwall, where Bentley was giving a dinner. He had invited Forster at Dickens's request and was introduced to him on the steamer going down the Thames. "This ill-mannered man broke up the pleasure of the party," Bentley declared, "by some rude remarks at several of my guests; so markedly rude as almost to precipitate personal violence."

Although Dickens had already been having differences with Bentley over the *Miscellany*, their dispute still simmered below the boiling point. But with Macrone there was a renewal of trouble, which now brought Forster actively into Dickens's affairs and started him on his lifelong role of unofficial business manager. Dickens learned that Macrone planned to reissue the *Sketches* in monthly parts got up in green covers exactly imitative of *Pickwick*. Already irritated at hearing that Macrone was "making thousands" from the copyright he had hastily sold, he felt that three simultaneous publications "must prove seriously prejudicial to my reputation," and might even damage the sale of *Pickwick*. He asked Forster to try to dissuade Macrone by reminding him how cheaply he had purchased the *Sketches* and that when he obtained their copyright he had not even hinted at publishing them in this form. If he still persevered in his scheme he was to be warned that Dickens would advertise everywhere that the reprint was against his wishes and brought him no profit.

But Macrone was unfrightened. The *Sketches*, he insisted to Forster, were now his absolute property. If Dickens had chosen to surrender the copyrights to get out of writing the novel he had promised, that did not alter Macrone's right to make as much from them as he could. Macrone's position, in fact, was sound. The only part of it that smacked of sharp practice was the proposal to reap an advantage from the *Pickwick* harvest by a misleading duplication of its green covers.

Forster saw that he must alter his attack. He knew from Dickens that Chapman and Hall would advance the money to repurchase the copyrights, and asked what Macrone would take for them. The £2,000 Macrone demanded "opened so wide a mouth," Forster considered, that he advised Dickens to "keep quiet for a time." But that was just what Dickens could not do. He was too vexed and impatient. He himself pressed Macrone who "peremptorily refused," Dickens wrote Forster, "to take one farthing less than the two thousand pounds . . ."

Meanwhile, Chapman and Hall had reflected that if the *Sketches* were *going* to appear in monthly numbers, they and the author might as well profit. They might attain a far larger sale than Macrone could and own the book at the same time. They therefore suggested putting up the money to buy the copyrights jointly, deducting Dickens's share from the profits.

Perplexed about what to do, Dickens sought further advice from Forster. But he was not at home, and Macrone refused to wait. In desperation Dickens consented. Macrone received £2,250, a sum that may have allowed for expenses already incurred in the projected reprint. "Was I right?" Dickens asked Forster. "I think you will say yes." "I could not say no," Forster comments, "though I was glad to have been no party to a price so exorbitant. . . ."

From this time forward there was hardly any of Dickens's work that Forster did not see and comment upon in manuscript. Regularly he took off Dickens's hands the burden of correcting proofs, beginning with the fifteenth number of *Pickwick*. With the sixteenth, Dickens wrote Forster that he could not go for an intended ride that day: "Here I am slippered and jacketted . . . and can't get out.

"I am getting on, thank Heaven, 'like a house o' fire,' and the next Pickwick will bang all the others. I shall expect you at 1."

Forster became also his constant companion in the long walks and rides by which Dickens rested from his mental labours. Always just one jump ahead of the printer, he nevertheless managed on many a day to clear his writing table by eleven. He ought to dine in Bloomsbury Square today, Dickens would tell Forster, but he would rather ride. "So engage the osses." Or, "Where shall it be – oh where – Hampstead, Greenwich, Windsor? WHERE????? While the day is bright, not when it has dwindled away to nothing! For who can be of any use whatsomdever such a day as this, excepting out of doors?"

Walking, he put in seven or eight miles at a fast pace. "Is it possible that you can't, oughtn't, shouldn't, mustn't, *won't* be tempted, this gorgeous day!" "You don't feel disposed, do you, to muffle yourself up and start off with me for a good brisk walk over Hampstead Heath? I knows a good 'ous there where we can have a red-hot chop for dinner, and a glass of good wine" – an invitation that led to their first experience of Jack Straw's Castle. Occasionally Ainsworth and Talfourd joined them on their rides, sometimes going through the vale of Middlesex and home by Stanmore and Harrow, at others crossing Old Oak Common and stopping at Berrymead Priory to greet Edward Lytton Bulwer.

Dickens and Bulwer did not become intimate for a number of years, but they were already on a friendly footing. Bulwer's rapid literary success, with *Paul Clifford*, *Eugene Aram*, *The Last Days of Pompeii*, and *Rienzi*, his luxurious scale of living, and perhaps his consciousness of his distinguished social position, evoked among many of his fellow writers a good deal of spiteful resentment. "A thoroughly *satin* character," one of them remarked, "but then it is the *richest* satin." Bulwer, however, was magnanimously quick to recognize the merits of others. Although the rising star of Dickens threatened to eclipse his own, he gave to *Pickwick*, from its earliest numbers, the warmest praise.

In the middle of June Forster took Dickens round to Covent Garden to present him to Macready. With the great actor Forster was on terms of warm friendship, despite the trials he inflicted on Macready's furious temper by tactless contradiction. Macready was forty-four and famous in Shakespearean roles; Forster was only twenty-five, but he would arrogantly attempt "to dictate how a Shakespearean sentence should be emphasized." For all Forster's bumptiousness, though, Macready valued his good qualities, and received his visitors cordially in his dressing-room.

In the course of these warming companionships, Dickens and Kate, with Hablôt Browne, took a week's holiday across the Channel in

July, dashing from Calais to Ghent, Brussels, and Antwerp. "We went this afternoon," Dickens wrote Forster, "in a barouche to some gardens where the people dance, and where they were footing it most heartily – especially the women, who in their short petticoats and light caps look uncommonly agreeable."

Part of August and September Dickens spent with Kate and eight-months-old Charley at Broadstairs, a picturesque Kentish seaside resort where the Macreadys often went for summer bathing. Hardly more than a fishing village at the time, it zigzagged in three crooked old streets to the edge of the white chalk cliffs. From its perch there, surrounded by fields of rippling corn, it looked down on the blue water of a toy semicircular bay. At low tide the fishing boats lay on their sides like exhausted fish and the "brown litter of tangled sea-weed and fallen cliff" looked "as if a family of giants had been making tea" and untidily thrown "their tea-leaves on the shore."

> I have walked upon the sands at low-water, from this place to Ramsgate [Dickens reported to Forster] and sat upon the same at high-ditto till I have been flayed with cold. I have seen ladies and gentlemen walking upon the earth in slippers of buff, and pickling themselves in the sea in complete suits of the same. I have seen stout gentlemen looking at nothing through powerful telescopes for hours, and when at last they saw a cloud of smoke, fancying a steamer behind it, and going home comfortable and happy. I have found out that our next neighbour, has a wife and something else under the same roof with the rest of his furniture – the wife deaf and blind, and the something else given to drinking.

Back in London in the autumn, Dickens superintended the appearance of the final double number of *Pickwick*, and dedicated its first edition in book form to Talfourd in friendship and recognition of his efforts to get through Parliament a copyright Bill extending an author's rights for sixty years. At that time, not merely did they expire with the writer's death, but even during his life he had no protection against piracy in the form of abridgement or alteration. There was, of course, no international copyright, and publishers of all countries appropriated the works of foreign authors. Dickens had made detailed suggestions on the provisions of Talfourd's Bill, and was disappointed when its defeat left no recourse except to begin over again.

About the innumerable dramatic piracies of his own work, however, he was still able to feel reasonably calm. Later on, he was to be less philosophic about piracy and plagiarism. Even at this time, however, he was careful not to countenance any liberties with his work. To a firm of American publishers who offered him £50 in acknowledgement of the profits from their own edition of *Pickwick*, he replied that "under the circumstances" he should not feel "quite at ease" in drawing upon them for the proffered sum. He would, however, be happy to enter into arrangements with them for transmitting early proofs of *Oliver Twist*. Though polite and willing to do business, he would not in any way imply his acquiescence in his work having been used without his permission.

The reckless energy with which Dickens kept both these novels running concurrently, sometimes barely a week ahead of the printer, was already arousing amazed doubts of his ability to keep it up. Abraham Hayward in an otherwise highly laudatory critique in the October *Quarterly Review* remarked that "Mr Dickens writes too often and too fast," and warned that if he persisted in this course his fate was certain: "he has risen like a rocket, and he will come down like the stick." Dickens, already oversensitive to all but the most lavish praise, chose to give this a personal motive. "I think Hayward has *rather* visited upon me, his recollection of my declining his intimate acquaintance . . ."

But, although swift in resentment, Dickens melted readily to forgiveness. Bitter as he had been against Macrone, when he learned that the publisher had suddenly died in September, leaving his widow and children destitute, he joined with Ainsworth in a benefit volume. Cruikshank donated illustrations and Dickens, in addition to his other work, contributed a story and attended to all the details of getting the book into print.

Meanwhile, during the first week in November, Dickens and Kate spent a few days at Brighton. It was their first visit there, and the weather was stormy.

> It blew a perfect hurricane [Dickens wrote Forster], breaking windows, knocking down shutters, carrying people off their legs, blowing the fires out, and causing universal consternation. The air was for some hours darkened with a shower of black hats (second hand) which are supposed to have been blown off the heads of unwary passengers in remote parts of the town, and have been industriously picked up by the fishermen.

Returning from this holiday, Dickens sat to Samuel Laurence for a portrait which the artist insisted on presenting to him. It shows a young man whose assured face and firm jaw reveal the will that vitalized his imaginative powers. Dickens evidently liked it, for he had Laurence do a portrait of Kate too. A somewhat different view of him appears in a slightly earlier pencil sketch by Cruikshank, portraying Dickens as a dandified D'Orsay figure in frock coat, tight trousers, and enormous silken cravat, with a delicate face and curling hair.

It was in the midst of the sittings to Laurence that the banquet for *Pickwick* occurred. At the same time Chapman and Hall revised their arrangements with Dickens. For, although they were on the best of terms, Dickens had no share in the copyright, and Forster had been pressing emphatically for his having a legal part of the profits. Forster had established himself by now as a literary adviser and arbiter to Chapman and Hall, swinging into their offices at 186 Strand as though the whole place belonged to him and telling everyone exactly what must be done. Under his influence, they agreed to give Dickens a one-third share in the copyright of *Pickwick* after five years, in consideration of a contract signed on that very day, 18 November 1837, for a new periodical work of undecided title. Dickens was to receive £150 for each of its twenty numbers, and the publishers were to have the copyright for five years, after which it also reverted to Dickens in its entirety.

Saturday, 9 December 1837, saw the baby's christening, delayed from June by Kate's miscarriage after Mary's death. "We christen the living wonder," Dickens wrote Beard, "on Saturday, at 12, at New Pancridge" – an anticipation of the way in which Mrs Gamp might have described New St Pancras Church. The boy was to be named Charles Culliford, but when the clergyman asked what the child's names were, John Dickens excitedly cried out "Boz!" in consequence of which the full name that appeared on the register was Charles Culliford Boz Dickens.

Young Charles was to have a kind patron in Angela Burdett Coutts, to whom Dickens was introduced by Edward Marjoribanks, one of the partners in Coutts and Company, probably in the course of the following year. She was already dazzling society as the heiress to two enormous fortunes. The youngest daughter of Sir Francis Burdett, himself a radical reformer, she was resolved to use her wealth to help those less fortunate. Between the 26-year-old author and the earnest 24-year-old heiress, from their very first meeting, there was a deep sympathy and understanding that made them lifelong friends. To

Kate and the growing Dickens family Angela Burdett Coutts became a kind and generous friend. But even more than these personal ties was the fact that Charles Dickens became the guiding conscience of her philanthropic career and she the power through which Dickens would bring about many a social and educational programme in which the world did not even suspect his hidden hand.

But these joint enterprises were still several years to come. Meanwhile the year 1838 brought an endless round of demands on Dickens's time. Cruikshank had to be set straight about the illustrations for *Oliver*: "I have described a small kettle," Dickens pointed out, "for one on the fire – a *small* black teapot on the table with a little tray and so forth – and a two ounce tin tea cannister. Also a shawl hanging up – and the cat and kittens before the fire." In a further effort for Fred, he succeeded in getting Lord Stanley to appoint his brother to the Secretary's Office in the Custom House.

Dickens was also busy on plans to collaborate with Ainsworth on a book to be entitled *The Lions of London*. But the pressure on his energies grew crushing; "my month's work," he complained, "has been dreadful – Grimaldi [an editing job for Bentley], the anonymous book for Chapman and Hall [the *Sketches of Young Gentlemen*], Oliver, and the Miscellany. They are all done, thank God, and I start on my pilgrimage to the cheap schools of Yorkshire (a mighty secret of course) next Monday Morning." In fact, with his next novel, *Nicholas Nickleby*, already bursting its bonds to get started, he was far too busy to take on this enterprise with Ainsworth and it was later abandoned.

The theme of *Nicholas Nickleby* had been vaguely shaping itself in his mind around the abuses in the Yorkshire schools that had made such a deep impression on him in his childhood days in Chatham. Purporting to give an education and board their pupils for the cheapest of fees, the Yorkshire schools were notorious for negligence, cruelty, and pedagogical incompetence. William Shaw, who kept an academy at Bowes, near Greta Bridge, was sued by the parents of two children who became totally blind there through the lack of medical treatment for an infection. Shaw was convicted and paid damages of £500 but continued to conduct his school. The small churchyard at Bowes has the graves of twenty-five boys from seven to eighteen who died there between 1810 and 1834.

There were similar schools in other parts of Yorkshire, largely used, of course, as a means of getting rid of illegitimate and other unwanted children. They advertised "no extra charges" and "no vacations," and took their pupils entirely off the hands of those responsible for them for as little as twenty guineas a year. But they also victimized a considerable number of impecunious but well-intentioned parents.

With his strong journalist's feeling for documentation, Dickens decided on a trip to Yorkshire for direct observation of his material. On 30 January, a blustery cold morning, he set off in the Mail from the Saracen's Head. "Phiz" went along to note the pictorial background. After travelling through howling snowstorms they reached, about midnight of the second day, "a bare place with a house standing alone in the midst of a dreary moor." This was the George and New Inn, at Greta Bridge. They warmed themselves before a "rousing fire halfway up the chimney," and in the morning they went for a look at Bowes Academy.

To avoid suspicion, Dickens travelled under an assumed name, pretending to be in search of a school for the son of a widowed friend. But William Shaw, the one-eyed master of the Academy, was mistrustful and let them see very little. From Greta Bridge the investigators took a post chaise for Barnard Castle. An attorney there gave them two introductions to local schoolmasters, but himself avoided all talk on the subject of schools. That night, however, he turned up at their inn, and after some embarrassed hesitation explained that their search had been weighing on his mind all day. Then, with a sudden rush, his feelings burst through his legal caution: "Ar wouldn't mak' ill words amang ma neeburs, and ar speak tiv'ee quiet loike. But I'm dom'd if ar can gang to bed and not tell 'ee, for weedur's sak', to keep the lattle boy for a' sike scoondrels while there's a harse to hoold in a' Lunnon, or a goother to lie asleep in!"

On their return trip, Dickens and Browne stopped off and attended services in York Minster, where they saw the grisaille window called the "Five Sisters" and heard the fifteenth-century legend of its origin that Dickens soon inserted in the second number of *Nicholas Nickleby*. After a week's absence he was back in Doughty Street and attacked the new book at once. "I *have* begun!" he announced to Forster on 7 February – his twenty-sixth birthday. "I wrote four slips last night, so you see the beginning is made. And what is more I can go on: so I hope the book is in training at last." Two days later he told Forster triumphantly, "The first chapter of Nicholas is done."

When Mary, their second child, was born early on 6 March 1838, Dickens asked Forster to help him ride off his excitement, declaring, "I can do nothing this morning." On the way home they dined at the

Red Lion in Barnet, after going fifteen miles out on the Great North Road. Three days later he wrote Forster, "I was thinking about Oliver till dinner-time yesterday, and just as I had fallen upon him tooth and nail, was called away to sit with Kate. I did eight slips however, and hope to make them fifteen this morning."

By the end of the month Kate was well enough to go with Dickens to Richmond. Having been out of London when *Pickwick* first appeared, he was mildly superstitious about being away when *Nickleby*'s first number came out on 1 April. But he couldn't resist riding into town to learn how it had gone. He sent Forster an imperious summons. "Meet me at the Shakespeare on Saturday night at eight; order your horse at midnight, and ride back with me." The next evening, at the Star and Garter, Forster, Dickens, and Kate marked a triple celebration. It was their second wedding anniversary, and Forster's twenty-sixth birthday, and *Nickleby* on its first day had sold almost 50,000 copies!

For June and July Dickens rented a cottage at Twickenham and had a stream of summer visitors and week-end guests. Forster, of course, was always on the scene, and had been "elected president of a balloon club . . . on condition of supplying all the balloons," for the children, whom Dickens had nicknamed "the Snodgering Blee" and "Popem Jee."

New faces, too, turned up in this Twickenham summer, and later at Broadstairs, where they spent August and September. Among these was the playwright Douglas Jerrold, soon to be editor of *Punch* – a little man, almost deformed, but "bright-eyed, quick, and eager in spirit." And since the time when Thackeray had applied to do the *Pickwick* illustrations, Dickens had grown better acquainted with him at the Garrick Club and published a story of his, "The Professor," in the September 1837 *Miscellany*. The towering, squash-nosed young man was now a frequent dinner guest, as was also the Scottish-Irish painter Daniel Maclise, whom Dickens had met through Ainsworth.

Another new friend in the living flesh, though an old one on the printed page, was Leigh Hunt. He was a poet of considerable grace and charm, and, as a critic and essayist who interpolated descriptions of familiar scenes and people, had been one of the formative influences of Dickens's own youth. After a life of trials he was now, at fifty-four, still as slim and brisk as a boy, animated, sweet-tempered, full of whimsical and gay-hearted fancy.

Another old friend was Dickens's kind Chatham schoolmaster, William Giles, who sent him a silver snuffbox inscribed to "the inimitable Boz," a signature Dickens had been using exuberantly in the *Miscellany*'s "Answers to Correspondents." Warmly acknowledging the gift, Dickens sent Giles copies of his published books, and promised to send a set of *Oliver* when it appeared in book form.

Around this time Dickens met Dr John Elliotson and first became interested in mesmerism. Professor of the Practice of Medicine at London University, Elliotson was one of the founders of University College Hospital. He was a daring innovator in unorthodox realms of knowledge and, as the first president of the Phrenological Society, one of the pioneers in experimenting with the use of mesmerism to relieve pain. Dickens saw Elliotson magnetize sufferers, totally unable to sleep, into mesmeric slumber and witnessed some remarkable feats performed by a Belgian boy. Under mesmerism and blindfolded, the boy read the name of the maker of Kate's Geneva watch when it was held behind his head and also gave correctly the number inside its case.

Oliver Twist was now almost finished and poured itself out of Dickens in a fever of creation. He often wrote till late at night, something he never did in later years. "Hard at work still, Nancy is no more," Forster learned one October night. Dickens had shown the pages describing Nancy's death to Kate, "who was in an unspeakable '*state*'" at those sickening thuds that beat out the girl's life, "from which and my own impression, I augur well. When I have sent Sikes to the devil, I must have yours."

There remained only to sum up the rest and put an end to the merry and black-hearted old Fagin, "who is such an out and outer that I don't know what to make of him." Talfourd had been pleading on behalf of Charley Bates, and even of the Artful Dodger, as earnestly "as ever at the bar for any client." Dickens discussed with Forster what should be their fate.

For all the lurid melodrama of *Oliver Twist* there can be no doubt of its literary success. It was based upon a fundamental truth, that treating poverty and pauperism as crimes brought forth a dreadful harvest of criminality and vice. If Oliver himself illustrates the fact that sometimes there are survivors who are not corrupted by even the harshest environment, the jeering Dodger, the ferocious Sikes, and the crafty and sinister Fagin make clear the corroding effect of foul surroundings on callous and insensible natures. The deaths of Sikes and Fagin at the end of the novel achieve a hideous intensity: the burly thief on the roof above the waving torches of Folly Ditch and the rope running taut; the villainous old fence struggling with his jailers in a mad fury of rage and terror.

Oliver Twist was the first of Dickens's books to be published under his own name. Forster gave Bentley directions that the title page should read:

Oliver Twist
in 3 Vols.
By Charles Dickens author
Of the "Pickwick Papers."

From then on, in public comment, his name and Boz were used interchangeably.

No sooner was *Oliver Twist* out of the way than Dickens, in spite of the fact that he was finding *Nicholas* hard going, promised Macready a new farce for Covent Garden. He wrote a feeble and laborious concoction entitled *The Lamplighter*, of which Macready wrote in his diary, "Manifest disappointment. It went flatly, a few ready laughs . . . broken in upon by the horse-laugh of Forster, the most indiscreet friend that ever allied himself to any person. . . . I cannot sufficiently condemn the officious folly of this marplot, Forster, who embroils his friends in difficulties and distress in this most determined manner."

Forster, however, changed his mind about *The Lamplighter*, and agreed that it should be vetoed. Macready, somewhat nervous about Dickens's reaction, tried to soften its rejection and warmly thanked him for his effort. Dickens replied that his only disappointment was in not having been able to be of some use to Macready. "An answer which is an honour to him," Macready commented. "Dickens and Bulwer have been certainly to me noble specimens of human nature . . ."

Although Macready told Dickens that *Oliver Twist* was utterly impractical for the stage, the usual crew of piratical adapters had seized upon it long before it had run its course in the *Miscellany*. One version at the Surrey Theatre was so excruciatingly bad that in the middle of the first scene the agonized novelist lay down on the floor of his box and never rose until the curtain fell. Nevertheless, Dickens hankered to make a dramatic version himself, and suggested it to Frederick Yates. Although less than half the numbers of *Nicholas Nickleby* had appeared in print, the actor was already scoring an enormous success at the Adelphi with his own dramatization of the story. Despite his general resentment of the liberties taken with his work, Dickens was delighted with Yates's performance: "*that glorious Mantalini,*" he wrote, "*is beyond all praise.*" Nothing came of Dickens's plan to dramatize *Oliver Twist* himself, but he saw and applauded later productions both of that book and of *The Old Curiosity Shop*, in which Yates played Fagin and Quilp.

At the end of October Dickens had gone up, again accompanied by Browne, to the Midlands and North Wales to see the cotton mills. The industrial north made an impression of lurid horror on Dickens's imagination, "miles of cinder-paths and blazing furnaces and roaring steam-engines" coming through fog and smoke and clamorous glares, "such a mass of dirt gloom and misery," he wrote Kate, "as I never before witnessed."

From Shrewsbury they made a rapid tour of North Wales and thence to Liverpool. Here Forster joined them and the three went on to Manchester. Ainsworth had given Dickens letters of introduction to some friends in his native city, the bulky James Crossley and Gilbert Winter and Hugh Beaver. Over the dinner table at Winter's home on Cheetham Hill Dickens dined with the brothers William and Daniel Grant, merchants and manufacturers, of Cheeryble House, upon whom he was shortly to model the Cheeryble brothers in *Nicholas Nickleby*.

On his return to London, Dickens wrote Edward Fitzgerald, an Irish journalist, "I went, some weeks ago, to Manchester, and saw the *worst* cotton mill. And then I saw the *best. Ex uno disce omnes.* There was no great difference between them." Lord Ashley – later the seventh Earl of Shaftesbury – who had been fighting the horrors of factory conditions since 1833, had offered, through Fitzgerald, to have Dickens shown what the mills were like, and in asking Fitzgerald to convey his gratitude Dickens wrote feelingly, "So far as seeing goes, I have seen enough for my purpose, and what I have seen has disgusted me and astonished me beyond all measure. I mean to strike the heaviest blow in my power for these unfortunate creatures, but whether I shall do so in the 'Nickleby,' or wait some other opportunity, I have not yet determined."

But although horror and indignation sank deep in his heart, Dickens did not feel himself ready to deal with things still so strange to his imagination as those dust-laden mills and their thunderous machines. The sodden misery of nineteenth-century industrialism spreading like a slow sore through the factory towns and the potteries and the iron foundries was to elude his pen for years to come. Not until a decade and a half later, in *Hard Times*, the fiercest and bitterest of his books, would he strike that "heaviest blow" against those dark satanic mills and the greed that imprisoned helpless human beings in their dismal shades.

Dickens made a second trip to Manchester in the middle of January, combining further investigation with a public dinner for Ainsworth and himself. The day after the banquet James Crossley had them to dinner at his house, and astonished them mightily by the sight of his triangular table with his portly form wedged between its apex and the wall. It was probably on this visit also that Beaver found Dickens reading an adverse review of his work that said, "What is good is not original, and what is original is not good," and remembered Dickens stamping up and down the room, greatly upset, and swearing, "They shall eat their words!"

But he need hardly have exercised himself. Only a few weeks earlier, he had heard the pleasant news from Edinburgh that the powerful critic Lord Jeffrey was giving *Oliver Twist* the highest praise. "It has done wonders here in the way of sale," Dickens wrote, "and as to Nickleby, I don't know when he is going to stop." With these triumphs, not only the doors of London's literary and artistic circles but those of the great world were opening ever wider before him.

The young man who wore a shabby coat in a three-pair rear in Holborn now issued brilliantly waistcoated and magnificent of neck-cloth from his own doorway to visit mansions in Curzon Street and St James's Place. The patchily educated shorthand writer, who had doggedly bent over books in the British Museum to repair the gaps in his education, now met men who came from public schools and universities, who had travelled in France and Italy, and spoke the languages of those countries. How would Dickens adapt himself to the leonine Walter Savage Landor, with his classical learning and alarming temper, the cosmopolitan dandy Count D'Orsay, the icily sardonic Samuel Rogers, the steep-nosed social gorgon Lady Holland, the witty Lady Blessington?

Anyone less superbly self-assured than Dickens might have been intimidated. But mingled with a resolution to make his way everywhere, there was a proud though veiled resentment at the insolence of privilege, and a consciousness of his own gifts, which made him determined to hold his own and not allow himself to be patronized. He had quickly experienced, of course, some of that odd upper-class snobbery that regarded a writer as a strange animal to be made to go through its tricks, and patted on the head if it were docile. His feelings may be divined from a description of Mr Lillyvick in *Nicholas Nickleby*: "if he had been an author, who knew his place, he couldn't have been more humble." But Dickens felt the glamour of power and prestige, too, and though no one could more sharply repel any attempted condescension, he was pleased by his new importance. With his vivid perception of the colour of any group, and the mimetic talent that had made him at one time think of becoming an actor, he rapidly acquired the tone and manner of his surroundings.

In 1836 Talfourd had introduced Dickens to Count D'Orsay, a dilettante man-about-town whose ornate and startling dress inspired some of Dickens's later extravagances. In his white greatcoat, blue-satin cravat, skin-tight primrose-coloured gloves scented with jasmine, and hair precisely curled, D'Orsay might have seemed effeminate were it not for his polished ease and six-feet-four of height. He lived at Gore House with his wife's stepmother, the widowed Countess of Blessington, in relations of which the world felt deeply suspicious.

In consequence, although Lady Blessington was beautiful, witty, and charming, few women frequented her famous literary salon. But hardly a well-known man in London failed to appear in her mirrored drawing-room and long, magnificently arched and columned library with its white-and-gold furniture. Wellington would be grimly amused by the talking crow she had saucily taught to repeat his own "Up, Guards, and at 'em!" That brilliant clergyman, Sydney Smith, scattered sparkling showers of harmless wit. Disraeli might talk of Beckford's fantastic spire at Fonthill Abbey. Landor could be heard talking in his vehement and impassioned manner or giving a roar of laughter, throwing back his noble head with its mane of hair. And sometimes, leaden-eyed and silent in a corner, sat Prince Louis Napoleon.

If Gore House was luxuriously Bohemian and cosmopolitan, Samuel Rogers's classic little mansion at 22 St James's Place represented the severely literary. A banker and poet whose *Italy* and *Pleasures of Memory* had a bloodless elegance, Rogers made a triumphant career of the cautious but smoothly firm determination to enjoy a place in the sun. For all his wealth, he spent only £2,000 a year. Stumping out on foot to parties in stately salons, he walked home even on the rainiest nights, and entertained everyone of note at small economical breakfasts where the guests were expected to be brilliantly entertaining on topics chosen by their host. Now in his seventies, he looked on the world with a pale head, white, bare, and cold as snow, through large blue eyes, cruel and disillusioned as the frigid epigrams that fell from lips tight above a sardonic shelf of chin. With him, said Thomas Moore, one walked on roses, but with a constant apprehension of the thorns among them.

But Rogers could be gracious too. Whereas most of the great world hardly troubled to conceal its feeling that Dickens's wife was rather negligible, Samuel Rogers was always gentle to her and affable when he visited at the Dickens home. Although ladies were not excluded from the famous literary breakfasts, Kate was never one of those present. She had no conversation, and Rogers, for all his kindness, would not endanger the sparkle of his table by a dead weight.

While these morning feasts were frugal, their setting, though small, dripped opulence. The Titians, the Raphael Madonna, the little St George that Rogers believed to be a Giorgione, hung gold-framed against walls of crimson damask. Among other treasures were Milton's receipt for *Paradise Lost*, framed upon a door. The mantelpieces were by Flaxman; luxuriously bound volumes and rare editions were shelved in bookcases painted by Stothard with scenes from Boccaccio, Chaucer, and Shakespeare. "Sam lives very comfortably," Sydney Smith liked to say.

Holland House, one of the great Whig strongholds, gave huge crushes that Rogers's miniature drawing-rooms could never have accommodated. The old Jacobean mansion had a stately entrance hall, liveried footmen who led one up the grand staircase to a lofty dining-room with gilded wainscoting and a long library containing, Macaulay said, all the books in the world that one ever wished to read. The guests were less literary, more political and diplomatic than those at Gore House, and their arrogant hostess disciplined them like a drill sergeant. Those who could provide her table with game, venison, cheeses, or foreign delicacies were ruthlessly forced to pay up for the privilege of being bullied, interrupted, or silenced at the will of their hostess.

"Lay down that screen, Lord Russell," Lady Holland would say brusquely. "You will spoil it." Or to Rogers, whom she liked, "Your poetry is bad enough, so pray be sparing of your prose." She once interrupted Macaulay, who was being long-winded about the Christian Fathers, by bursting in with "Pray, Macaulay, what was the origin of the doll?" She ordered her guests to draw the curtains, close the window, ring the bell; only Sydney Smith ventured impertinently to ask if he should also dust the room.

Not until 1838 did Dickens meet this fearsome apparition. Lady Holland rather grandiosely asked Bulwer, "if Boz were presentable, and became the condescending with a man of genius, a thing not to be forgiven," wrote Bulwer in his journal; "so I growled and snapped."

Taking these noises as sufficient testimonial, Lady Holland commanded Talfourd to present his "little friend."

Some time that summer Dickens successfully passed through the ordeal of presentation. Lady Holland's sister found him intolerably dandified, but thought his face "beautiful, because blended with his intelligence there is such an expression of goodness." Lady Holland was also impressed by him, and Dickens, with the instinct he often had about people, felt the kindness that she concealed behind that harsh façade.

Another event of the year 1838 indicates how absolute now was Dickens's conquest of the cultivated world: his introduction to a pair of little old ladies, the Misses Mary and Agnes Berry. Both now around seventy-five, for several decades they had made their town house at Curzon Street a centre of the most exclusive circles of the literary and fashionable world. Their associations went back not merely to the days of Chesterfield and Garrick, but to those of Swift and Pope, and well-nigh to those of Addison and Congreve. They had been young girls when Horace Walpole was in his seventies and the witty old worldling had fallen in love with Mary. They had been intimate with Georgianna, the renowned Duchess of Devonshire, and known the Duchess of Queensbury, a youthful beauty at the Court of Queen Anne. For Thackeray they symbolized all the glamour of the English past.

But Dickens had no such reverence for tradition. When the two mittened and gentle old creatures called on the Dickenses during the summer at Twickenham to ask them to dinner, Dickens excused himself on the ground that he was working frantically on the next instalment of his new book. But the world had decided that this remarkable young man had really arrived; eager and desperate, they invoked the aid of Sydney Smith.

"The Miss Berrys," he wrote Dickens, "live only to become acquainted with you," and he conveyed a second invitation, for "Friday 29th or Monday July 1st." "The Miss Berrys and Lady Charlotte Lindsay," he wheedled enticingly, "have not the smallest objection to be put into a Number, but on the contrary would be proud of the distinction: and Lady Charlotte, in particular, you may marry to Newman Noggs. Pray come, it is as much as my place is worth to send them a refusal." Dinner with the Misses Berry Dickens consequently had, and evidently found the experience agreeable, for he dined with them again on a number of later occasions.

But the high point of the year was Dickens's election to the Athenaeum Club. Founded in 1824, it was primarily a cultural rather than a political or social institution, designed as a gathering place for England's men of achievement. Its membership included the leading scholars, men of letters, artists, scientists, and statesmen.

The Athenaeum is still housed in the majestic building on Waterloo Place designed by Decimus Burton and erected in 1830. Its Roman–Doric portico of six columns has a frieze with triglyphs carved in Bath stone. The hall is modelled on the Temple of the Winds at Athens. Pillars of primrose marble with gilded capitals support a wagon-vaulted ceiling, and the great staircase rises, under a central lantern fifty-four feet above the floor, to the statue of Pallas presiding over the landing. On the left of the entrance a Pompeian dining-room with five tall windows overlooks the garden. Running the entire width of the building on the floor above, the drawing-room rears its twelve columns and sixteen pilasters between red damask walls with three carved marble fireplaces.

Such was the grandiose institution of which Dickens became a member in June of 1838. Among the forty persons eminent in art, literature, and science who were brought in at the same time were Macready, Grote, the classical scholar and historian, and Charles Darwin. Thackeray had to wait until he was forty before he was granted the freedom of those august portals, and Browning until he was fifty-six. Dickens, at the time he achieved the same honour, had written only two published books, and had two others appearing in serial form. Within a brief career of two years and by the age of twenty-six, he had attained not merely the widest popular success, the highest literary acclaim, and admission to the most famous salons, but one of England's most coveted distinctions.

13

War to the Knife

During the two years of Dickens's rocketing fame, his relations with the flamboyant, pink-faced owner of the *Miscellany* grew less and less amicable. When Dickens had to buy off Macrone from imitating *Pickwick* by publishing *Sketches by Boz* in similar green covers, Bentley had suggested to Macrone that he might purchase the *Sketches* himself. Dickens felt that Bentley had exacerbated the already deteriorating negotiations and stiffened Macrone's demands.

In addition, they disagreed about editorial control. Bentley had the right to veto any article, but aside from this Dickens was supposed to be in complete charge. Initially, Dickens's inexperience and limited literary acquaintance had led Bentley to solicit contributions from his own friends, and the two men would settle the magazine's contents in informal discussion at the New Burlington Street offices. Nevertheless, Dickens did not regard this procedure as in any way surrendering his own editorial powers.

Differences first arose over financial arrangements. As early as March 1837, just two months after the first issue appeared, the *Miscellany*'s popularity led to a renegotiation of the original agreement. Bentley wanted to retain Dickens as editor for five years instead of three and the option of another five. He also wanted the exclusive use of Dickens's periodical writings, aside from the as yet untitled successor (*Nicholas Nickleby*) to *Pickwick* that Dickens was to write for Chapman and Hall. In addition, Bentley offered Dickens an extra £10 monthly for every 1,000 increase in the magazine's circulation over 6,000.

To Dickens these terms did not compensate for his abstention from any other periodical writing. He proposed that the second five-year option be omitted, that he be given £250 or twelve months' notice if the magazine were discontinued, and that his salary be increased on the publication of the sixth, twelfth, twenty-fourth, and thirty-sixth numbers. After consultations with Forster, he accepted a compromise. Bentley was to have both options on his services. Dickens was to have the notice or £250, but half of this was to be a set-off against the novels. And his increases would be £10 for the first additional thousand of monthly circulation and £5 for each further five hundred. "I have the most unfeigned pleasure in saying that the arrangement . . . is alike highly satisfactory to me and highly creditable to yourself," Dickens wrote Bentley.

However, the terms on which Bentley was to have Dickens's next two novels were not affected. And soon Forster came to suspect that they had been disposed of too hastily. Dickens concurred. "It is a very extraordinary fact . . . that I have NEVER HAD from him a copy of the agreement . . . I fear he has my second novel on the same terms as the first. This is a bad look-out but n'importe we will try and mend it."

But the situation had a bright side. For Bentley had often expressed his earnest desire to be liberal. Surely when Dickens's growing popularity was considered, Bentley would concede the justice of changes. Dickens proposed that Bentley increase to £600 the sum for permission to publish 3,000 copies (instead of the entire copyright) of *Barnaby Rudge*, the first of the two novels. He further proposed that Bentley pay £700 for permission to publish the same number of *Oliver Twist*, which he now referred to as the second novel, deducting from the sum whatever was paid for its magazine appearance. Dickens asserted that if Bentley invoked his "power to hold me to the old agreement," he would abide by its strict letter "and arrange my future plans . . . accordingly."

Behind this implied threat may have lurked a realization that Bentley would hardly consider his proposal "a fair and very reasonable one." For *Oliver Twist* was not the second novel Dickens had agreed to write for Bentley; it was part of his monthly sixteen-page contribution to the *Miscellany*, the entire copyright of which already belonged to Bentley. In essence, Dickens was now trying to make one literary work fulfil two separate agreements.

Bentley countered that their agreement was mutually binding but declared that, although *he* could have obtained no reduction had Dickens's popularity declined, he was willing to *present* Dickens with the additional sums. For this, however, he insisted on the entire copyrights, as already agreed. Moreover, he refused to consider *Oliver Twist* as the second novel; it had now been running through five numbers of the *Miscellany* and the copyright of those published parts belonged to him.

Dickens was furious. With *Oliver* only half finished, he threatened to stop writing it altogether. Bentley held firm. Dickens then suggested that

Serjeant Talfourd arbitrate. Bentley objected that Talfourd was a friend of Dickens, and proposed a co-referee, to which Dickens consented.

Instead of approaching Talfourd, Dickens appealed to his old friend Thomas Beard. Only to gain time, he said, Bentley wished "a friend of mine to meet a friend of his" for discussion. But the "friend" Beard met in New Burlington Street was Bentley's solicitor, John Gregory. Beard feared he might injure Dickens if he tried to match wits with a professional.

At his report Dickens blew up. As "the disinterested, unprejudiced, private friend whom you were to select with so much care – was no other than your own Solicitor," he wrote Bentley, there would be no further meetings between them. He requested that his remuneration and all correspondence about the *Miscellany* be sent to him.

Bentley became concerned lest Dickens was neglecting the magazine. Stopping in at the printer's he learned that Dickens had ordered numerous papers set up in type. Bentley confirmed the selection of almost all, but vetoed two or three, as he had the right to do, and directed that the usual place on the first sheet be kept open for Dickens's instalment. But, to be certain of something for the lead, he set in reserve a story they had agreed to use.

To avoid recourse to law, Bentley accepted an offer from Cruikshank to mediate. "Cruikshank has been here," Dickens wrote Forster after the first of several visits, "– deputed by Bentley to say nothing." Cruikshank reported that Dickens rigidly refused to entertain any proposition that did not recognize *Oliver Twist* as the second novel. For Bentley the struggle with Dickens was proving more difficult than he had anticipated. Suppose he won a court case, what good would that do? A sullen editor and a reluctant novelist were worse than none. Meanwhile, *Pickwick Papers* grew more deliriously popular every day, and *Oliver* was a drawing card the *Miscellany* could ill afford to lose. After further stubborn contentions, he decided that he must yield. He empowered Cruikshank to offer Dickens a larger sum for the two novels and even to consent that *Oliver Twist* be regarded as the second novel.

But hard upon this concession came an angry letter from Dickens. He was bitterly indignant at changes Bentley had made in the October issue. His whole arrangement had been altered, articles inserted that he had never even seen. "By these proceedings I have been actually superseded in my office as Editor . . ." He therefore declined any further connection with the *Miscellany* beyond "this month – no longer."

Now it was Bentley's temper that was aroused. He had exercised great self-control. Only the day before, learning that Dickens objected to a piece he had ordered set up in type, he had withdrawn it. He had "no alternative but that of consulting my legal advisers," he wrote Dickens, and holding him to all his agreements.

Dickens replied curtly: "Mr Molloy . . . is my solicitor." And to Cruikshank Dickens wrote that there would be no *Oliver Twist* that month. To fill the gap he sent in a laboured satire on learned societies, "Full Report of the First Meeting of the Mudfog Association for the Advancement of Everything."

A fruitless interview now took place between Bentley, Gregory, and Molloy. Gregory became convinced Dickens's real grievance was that other editors were more highly paid, and advised Bentley either to insist on the agreement and proceed against Dickens, or accept a pecuniary loss as the cost of retaining him. Certainly, Gregory did not understand the young writer-editor. Dickens did say the remuneration originally agreed upon for the novels was inadequate; he would not have hesitated to say the same about his editorial salary. But so far he had never mentioned such an inadequacy.

Furthermore, Gregory was in error in imagining that Dickens was using Bentley's editorial interferences only as a trick to drive a better bargain. From the beginning Dickens had complained, with some asperity, on these points. "I must beg you once again," he wrote in one letter, "not to allow anybody but myself to interfere with the Miscellany." He had rigid ideas of his own dignity and authority and resisted their infringement even at the hands – one might say especially at the hands – of his employer.

This does not mean that his financial dissatisfaction had no connection with his resentment of editorial interferences. Nor does his desire for a more equitable return for his work justify his actions. He was not entitled to repudiate his agreements because he now saw that publisher would gain more than author, or because he could now get more elsewhere, or because he had undoubtedly been victimized by his inexperience. But it was understandable that he chafed at "the consciousness that my books are enriching everybody connected with them but myself," and that he should struggle to amend the discrepancy. Less defensible are the weapons he used.

But they won this round of the duel. In September Bentley surrendered, conceding practically all he had refused in August. He offered to acquiesce in Dickens's demand that *Oliver Twist* be considered the second novel and would pay £600 and £700 respectively for the first 3,000 copies of *Oliver* and of *Barnaby Rudge*, the first novel; after which they should be published on joint account with author and publisher sharing equally. Although Bentley would retain the copyright on all Dickens's other *Miscellany* contributions, he would agree that should any of these be separately reprinted, they would also be on joint account. Finally, he offered to raise Dickens's salary as editor to a straight forty guineas a month independent of circulation and retroactive from the beginning of Dickens's editorship.

These adjustments, however, did not salve Dickens's wounded editor .l dignity. There must be no more interferences. But Bentley also had his dignity to maintain. He would not be a nonentity on his own magazine. He must have more than the mere right of veto. Dickens had promised some contributors exaggeratedly high sums; Bentley must not be thus committed without his approval.

In a conference to reach a compromise, Forster represented Dickens and Gregory's partner Follett represented Bentley. Struggling almost all day over a draft, they settled point after point in Dickens's favour. Finally the agreement, dated 28 September 1837, provided that he would edit the *Miscellany* for three years from December 1837, dropping both the previous five-year options. His salary would be £30 a month, plus £10 additional when sales exceeded 6,000 copies and £5 for each additional 500. Bentley retained his right to veto, could originate three articles in every number, and made all arrangements about payments. *Oliver Twist* would continue in the *Miscellany* till midsummer 1838; meanwhile Dickens would furnish the remainder of the copy by 1 May, when he would receive £500. Concurrently with its final instalment, the novel would be published in book form. Bentley was to have a three-year copyright, after which half the copyright would revert to Dickens. *Barnaby Rudge*, in three volumes, was to be delivered on similar terms before or during October 1838, for £700.

Dickens thus scored an almost complete victory – in some respects, indeed, considerably more than he had originally contended for. Their respective editorial powers were clarified; he would receive £100 more for *Barnaby* than he had first asked; for *Oliver* he would receive only £500, but no deductions would be made for its periodical appearance; and most important, he won his main point that *Oliver* was to be regarded as the second novel.

But the peace that now ensued was only an uneasy lull. Bentley resented the extortion he had been subjected to. Dickens burned at his struggle to obtain a reasonable sum for the novels and at what he considered the infringement of his editorial powers. Beneath the surface cordiality, there smouldered bitter resentments. Bentley, however, endeavoured to be conciliatory; and agreed to defer *Barnaby* until the end of October 1838.

He had acquired a life of the famous clown Grimaldi, long-windedly arranged by Thomas Egerton Wilks from autobiographical notes. He proposed that Dickens revise it. Dickens stipulated that his name should appear only as editor, not as author, and demanded a minimum of £300 and a half share of the profits. He was to do no original writing, except for an introductory and possibly a concluding chapter. The book's reception surprised Dickens, who thought little of it. "Seventeen hundred Grimaldis have already been sold," he wrote Forster during the first week of publication, "and the demand increases daily!!!!!!!!!!!!!! !!!!!!!!!!!!!!!"

The armistice did not long endure. Although their new agreement gave Bentley the right to initiate three articles in each issue, the two men continued to differ repeatedly about editorial authority. Some of Bentley's friends were not only appearing solely at his desire, but in addition they wished to extort Dickens's approval. "I will not bind myself," he wrote Bentley, "to any man, either to commend Mr Wilks, or Mr Hughes, or Mr Richard Hughes or Mr Alfred Brown or anybody else." And again, "I do not choose Captain Marryat to suppose that *I* pillage his articles from American papers, and advertize his name as a contributor to the Miscellany. . . . I cannot and will not bear the perpetual ill will and heart-burnings and callings and writings consequent upon my accepting papers which are never inserted." Clearly, by this time Dickens's editorial powers were almost entirely annulled. "Order the Miscellany just as you please," he told Bentley wearily. "I have no wish or care about the matter."

Presently Dickens discovered petty deductions when his monthly contributions were short by a page or half-page of his sixteen pages. As he had often cut them for lack of space after he and Bentley had laid out the magazine, it is difficult to acquit Bentley of tactlessness at the best. If he really desired friendly relations, he might better have forgotten such cheese-paring economies – they totalled some sixteen guineas for the entire year. Dickens reacted to these annoyances as if stung. Did Bentley think it liberal, he asked "to your editor and principal contributor to deduct his half pages and count him down by the line"? Did he "consider that such treatment . . . is likely to make me wish for a very long continuance of our business connection?"

Their relations, however, staggered on into 1838. In February, as Dickens struggled to finish *Oliver Twist* for the printers, he realized that it would be impossible to have *Barnaby Rudge* ready by the end of October. Consequently he wanted Bentley to make the same change for this novel that had been wrested from him for *Oliver*. Would it not be more to Bentley's interest, as well as within the scope of Dickens's ability, if *Barnaby* succeeded *Oliver* in the *Miscellany* and were published afterwards in three volumes? This way Dickens "could do the best for you as well as for myself."

But Bentley did not at all agree. He insisted on keeping *Barnaby Rudge* and Dickens's contributions to the *Miscellany* two distinct matters. And if it was unrealistic for Dickens to have undertaken them in the first place, it must be remembered he was still a newcomer to his profession. To have allowed him to undertake them was certainly no less unrealistic of Bentley, who was a publisher of long standing. Dickens can hardly be cleared, however, of recklessness and, even, of disingenuousness when he undertook still another work for Chapman and Hall less than a fortnight after protesting to Bentley that it was impossible for him to write what he had already agreed to.

The two antagonists wrangled over *Barnaby Rudge* for the next six months, while the writing of *Oliver Twist* was drawing to its close and the shining sun of *Nicholas Nickleby* was rising upon the world. At last, in September 1838, after further contentions, Bentley agreed to Dickens's demand that *Barnaby Rudge* first be published in the *Miscellany*, instead of his writing another series to follow *Oliver*, which would conclude in April 1839.

But by January their uneasy peace broke down again. Editorial interferences still exasperated Dickens. In addition he found Bentley's premature notices of *Barnaby* irritating. As far back as November, Forster had asked Bentley, "Is it exactly prudent to use the expression 'forthwith' respecting the appearance of *Barnaby* in the Miscellany?"

All these sources of friction, together with the labour on *Barnaby* so exacerbated Dickens that Forster had much trouble to restrain him. "The immense profits which Oliver has realized for its publisher and is still realizing," Dickens complained; "the paltry, wretched, miserable sum it brought me . . . and the consciousness that my books are enriching everybody connected with them but myself, and that I, with such a popularity as I have acquired, am struggling in old toils, and wasting my energies in the very height and freshness of my fame, and the best part of my life, to fill the pockets of others . . . all this puts me out of heart and spirits: and I cannot – cannot and will not – under such circumstances that keep me down with an iron hand, distress myself by beginning this tale until I have had some time to breathe; and until the intervention of summer, and some cheerful days in the country, shall have restored me to a more genial and composed state of feeling."

With this outburst Dickens enclosed a letter to Bentley demanding a six-month postponement in the starting date of *Barnaby*'s appearance in the *Miscellany*. But for Forster, he said, he would repudiate the agreement altogether. "For I do most solemnly declare that morally, before God and man, I hold myself released from such hard bargains . . . This net that has been wound about me, so chafes me, so exasperates and irritates my mind, that to break it at whatever cost – *that* I should care nothing for – is my constant impulse. But I have not yielded to it. I merely declare that I must have a postponement very common in all literary agreements . . ."

An eloquent and heartfelt utterance. But the facts are coloured in personal emotion. For Bentley had neither entangled Dickens in a net nor forced him into slavery. From the beginning it was Dickens's terms that had prevailed, and Bentley had repeatedly further modified them in Dickens's favour.

Indubitably, however, Bentley was profiting to an enormously greater degree than Dickens. And he resisted every concession until it was wrung from him by the fear that these golden fruits might vanish. Chapman and Hall had also gained more from *Pickwick* than Dickens had, but it is significant that he did not resent them as he did Bentley. Nor was Dickens the only person with whom Bentley had difficulties. He had differences with Forster, with Ainsworth, and with Cruikshank. He even tried to pare down the sums paid his old college friend Richard Barham, who promptly obtained twice as much from his rival, Colburn.

Clearly, if Dickens was a man of growing determination, Bentley bristled with thorny traits. And, although Dickens was unscrupulous in threatening a literary strike if Bentley insisted on what was "nominated in the bond," Dickens's revisions represented a commonsense view of fairness even if they were not embodied in contractual law. Much of their trouble arose from a practice then common – the outright sale of a copyright for a lump sum. This might work fairly for a writer of established position, but it would naturally be unsatisfactory to Dickens, whose popularity continually outstripped every attempted readjustment.

An equal irritant was that, despite all his surface bonhomie and cordiality, Bentley had strong authoritarian impulses – to which Dickens would never submit. As a successful publisher, Bentley considered his literary judgement better than that of the editor he had put in what he regarded as nominal, but Dickens insisted must be real, charge of the *Miscellany*. Dickens, too, was proud and determined. In the end, Bentley's every way of doing things rasped him: the small deductions for half-page shortages, the delays in running pieces long accepted, the petty assertions of his rights that Bentley could not resist making even in the very act of yielding.

The last of these tendencies appeared in his reply to Dickens's demand for the delay in *Barnaby Rudge*. Ostentatiously, Bentley underlined his own flexibility. Although he could find no clause in their agreement that entitled Dickens – and he now quoted Dickens's own words – " 'to require a postponement of six months,' " he would raise no objection. Only *he* required that Dickens suspend all work except *Nicholas Nickleby*. But this Dickens could not promise. He had already agreed to edit the benefit volume for Macrone's widow. He had not yet given up, although he had done no work on, the comic book for Chapman and Hall.

At Bentley's new stipulation Dickens exploded with anger. Within two days he repudiated any further connection with the *Miscellany*. In vain Bentley tried to shake this determination. He even offered to acquiesce in Dickens's writing the Chapman and Hall book, if Dickens would only remain nominal editor of the *Miscellany* and agree not to conduct any other periodical. And for this mere use of his name Bentley now offered £40 a month. But Dickens was adamant, and suggested that his friend Harrison Ainsworth become the editor. Then, and then only, although still withdrawing, would he express himself as friendly towards the magazine.

Furious but desperate, Bentley was bitter at what he stigmatized as Dickens's dishonourable conduct and resisted having Ainsworth forced upon him. Dickens refused to budge. He would, he conceded, write a paper for the *Miscellany* of February 1839, announcing his resignation and expressing his friendship for the new editor. He would also write gratuitously two further papers within the next six months. He would give Ainsworth *personally* any information that might help in conducting the magazine, and would regard it as a point of honour not to edit, conduct, originate, or write for any other magazine whatever until the end of the year.

Reluctantly Bentley had to agree. He realized the futility of a chancery suit; at enormous expense he might ruin Dickens but would still be as far as ever from furthering his own ends. Nor would a rancorous court battle aid the *Miscellany* or enhance its standing with other authors. There remained only to settle the disposition of *Barnaby Rudge*, on which Bentley still had claims.

The draft agreement, dated 27 February 1839, provided that *Barnaby Rudge* was to be delivered to Bentley on 1 January 1840, for publication in three volumes, an extension three months longer than Dickens had been demanding. He was to undertake, until then, no other work except *Nicholas Nickleby*, the comic book, and the benefit volume for Mrs Macrone. For *Barnaby Rudge*, Bentley agreed to pay £2,000 outright, another £1,000 if the sale exceeded 10,000, and still another £1,000 if the sale came to 15,000; a possible total of £4,000 for the entire copyright of the book which, two years before, Dickens had agreed to write for only £500.

It was a bitter pill for Bentley to swallow. Dickens was triumphant. In the February *Miscellany* he withdrew in a "Familiar Epistle from a Parent to a Child, Aged Two Years and Two Months." The infant for whom he had cared since birth, he said, he handed over to his good friend Mr Ainsworth with his best wishes and without gain or profit to himself, for it had "always been literally 'Bentley's' Miscellany, and never mine."

But it was not until eight months later, in October 1839, that Dickens had even made a start in writing *Barnaby*. By December when its delivery date was only a month away, he had written just two chapters. He was finding it hard going. And his repeated delays reinforce the suspicion that, by now, he didn't feel like writing *Barnaby* and was labouring against the grain. For although he complained of the strain of *Nicholas Nickleby*, it had not taken all his time. He had dropped the comic book but had written instead an anonymous potboiler that Chapman and Hall published in January 1840, under the title of *Sketches of Young Couples*. For this he received only £200, and there can be no doubt that *Barnaby Rudge* would have brought in the full £4,000 agreed to by Bentley. (At that time *Nicholas Nickleby* was selling around 50,000 copies a month.) Mercenary reasons were not the cause of his delay, nor does it seem possible that, for all his prodigious energy, Dickens could have expected to finish a three-volume novel in the three months between October and January.

The book's stormy history may well have built up within him an insuperable resistance. He had had trouble about it with Macrone, before its title was changed from *Gabriel Vardon, the Locksmith of London*. It had been a bone of contention through all the bitter hostilities marking his two years on the *Miscellany*. Deep within him he wished to be free of Bentley altogether. Whether or not he consciously put it off, he certainly pounced, shortly before the delivery date, upon two excuses he conceived Bentley's conduct to give him.

"Mr Bentley in his advertisements and hired puffs of other books with which I never had . . . any possible connection," Dickens wrote his attorneys, "has repeatedly used my name and the names of some of my writings in an unwarrantable manner . . . calculated to do me serious prejudice." Second, he disapproved of Bentley's bringing out a three-volume novel for twenty-five shillings and then, while the book-sellers' shelves still groaned with unsold copies, republishing it in fifteen weekly parts for a shilling each.

As to the first accusation, it was true that Bentley had advertised Ainsworth's *Jack Sheppard* as "uniform in style and price with *Oliver Twist*." But Ainsworth was one of the most popular authors of the day, so that it is hard to see how this could do Dickens any "serious prejudice." To the second accusation there is somewhat more substance; Bentley had published Ainsworth's novel in October and then begun reissuing it in serial parts only two months later. There was no use, Dickens insisted, in Bentley's advertising that *Barnaby* was "preparing for publication." He was working on something else, and the manuscript would not be ready on 1 January.

Gregory reminded Dickens's attorneys that Bentley had already granted several postponements, that this one would be "provably of pecuniary loss"; what compensation did Dickens propose? Meanwhile, Bentley went on advertising *Barnaby Rudge*, and Dickens announced a new publication by Chapman and Hall. Gregory noted that, whereas Dickens's solicitors had merely said the manuscript would not be ready on time, Dickens was proposing to violate the agreement. It was, Dickens exclaimed in fierce exultation, "War to the knife . . . with the Burlington Street Brigand."

For another week all was quiet. Macready offered to mediate. But in the privacy of his diary, he considered Dickens quite wrong. "He makes a contract which he considers advantageous at the time, but subsequently finding his talents more lucrative than he had supposed, he refuses to fulfil the contract."

Dickens, however, no less convinced that he was entirely right, refused Macready's offer with grateful thanks. "The law, bad as it is, is more true and more to be trusted than such a hound as *he*, and unless he gives me the opening for a negociation, I must . . . submit to its vexations with what philosophy I can."

The hysterical sincerity of this letter reveals Dickens's almost obsessional hatred. Threatened with a chancery suit, he belligerently retorted that no court in England should compel him to write the novel.

From this high moment of defiance, the dispute slowly simmered down. Bentley was advised that he could not obtain an injunction restraining Dickens from the publication of any new work until the delivery of *Barnaby*. His only recourse would be to a court of law for damages.

After another protracted series of negotiations between Forster and the editor of the *Literary Gazette*, William Jerdan, representing Bentley, they at last – though not until June 1840 – arranged a settlement that both antagonists accepted. Dickens was to pay Bentley £1,500 for the assignment to him of Bentley's interest in *Oliver Twist* and the relinquishment of all further claims upon Dickens's writings. In addition, Dickens also purchased the Cruikshank plates for *Oliver Twist* and its remaining stock for £750. Chapman and Hall agreed to finance Dickens and to deduct the sum from £3,000 for their six-month copyright of *Barnaby Rudge*. Thus Dickens concentrated the publication of all his books in one firm, his "trusty friends" Chapman and Hall, whom he proclaimed "the best of booksellers, past, present, and to come." It was a daring prediction, but at last Dickens was happy and satisfied.

With Bentley, who thereby lost the most remunerative author of his time, it is impossible not to sympathize. For at every stage he had had the law on his side. It was his misfortune that his legal remedies were so expensive and uncertain that they were feeble weapons. Against his clear claims was only Dickens's burning sense of injustice and ruthless determination not to yield.

But the imponderables are more difficult to assess. For if Dickens had no case, he did have a grievance. It was true that the talent which had achieved so tremendous a popularity profited much less than the hands which distributed its work. The heart of their breach, however, was a clash of radically opposed temperaments. Although Bentley spoke of his desire to be generous, he disputed every guinea. And every concession – he did make six of them! – was extorted from a reluctance that resisted long enough to destroy any grace in its final yielding. Nor were matters helped by his subsequent petty economies on the enormously profitable *Miscellany* and his wrangles about editorial authority. In the end Dickens found that he had to fight for everything he got.

From their three-year duel Dickens emerged not only victorious but with a will forged into a weapon of steel. Strong from the days of his delicate and unhappy boyhood that will had always been, but it had operated with diffidence and almost as an invisible force in his struggles to surmount obstacles. His imperiousness and his indignation had flared on only a few previous occasions. Never before had it tempered itself to a prolonged conflict with an individual foe. Always clever in shaping the facts of a dispute to his advantage, Dickens became a brilliant controversialist, highlighting every weakness in the position of his adversary. And never, from the time of his struggle with Bentley, did Dickens surrender in the smallest point to any antagonist. Once opposed, whether by his publishers, his friends, members of his family, or the entire American press, he hardened into a relentless determination that was to sweep fatefully through all the successes and sorrows of his life.

PART FOUR

Deeper Cast
1839–1841

[14]

The Will in Command

Around the wine-red mahogany table in Doughty Street friends raised their glasses to toast Dickens on his twenty-seventh birthday. Ainsworth and Forster were there, and Tom Mitton, Browne, Dickens's mother and father, the latter bursting with pride and conviviality, Fanny and her husband Henry Burnett, Laman Blanchard, who had been editor of the *True Sun* in Dickens's days there, and Leigh Hunt, with his gentle grace and luminous eyes. Hunt found Dickens "as pleasant as some of the best things in his books," and exclaimed, "What a face is his to meet in a drawing-room! It has the life and soul in it of fifty human beings."

It had been, Dickens felt, "a most prosperous and happy year." For its feverish contentions with Bentley had never really dampened his spirits or poisoned the enormous excitement with which he dashed at experience; indeed, even in disputation he laid about him with the fierce enjoyment of one glorying in giant combat. Although the final settlement was still to come, his freedom from editorial subjection to a man he found unendurable was a triumph that cast its light backward over all the past excitement of the struggle. And what radiant prospects lay ahead!

The immediate future, to be sure, brought Dickens a problem. For his father had again become a source of embarrassment. His financial irresponsibility had not diminished with middle age. But this time Dickens was to deal with his father's infirmities far more sternly than he had five years before. The status he had achieved gave him a sense of his own importance and power and made him resentful of such shabby doings. Further, in the past two years he had learned to enforce his will by taking a stand and insisting that everyone else must yield.

For some time now, unknown to Dickens, his father had been up to his old ways. No sooner was *Pickwick* a success than he was on Chapman and Hall's doorstep for a £4 loan to tide him over some trifling trouble. Little Mr Hall, pacing up and down the room, murmured "something that sounded like, 'Well, it's not business, you know'; while Mr Chapman, with a mild, meditative smile, rejoined: 'Oh, but we *must*; we can't refuse him so small a sum as that!' "

Then, in February 1837, before this sum was repaid, John Dickens had another "moment of some difficulty," and advanced an ingenious proposition. Would the publishers deduct the amount already due, plus interest, from the enclosed promissory note for £20 and send him the balance? Their failure would "be productive of fatal consequences." By July he needed another £15 to pay the rent. "Mind," he wrote, "the subject is one of settlement by 2 o'clock, and unless I so arrange it, I am lost." A little later a document marked "Confidential" bore witness to another loan. He now owed Chapman and Hall £55 5s., but had to have £50 at once to save him "from perdition," so he proposed insuring his life in their favour for £100 for three years. The money must be had "by one o'clock tomorrow" to avert "the most awful consequences." At the end of 1837 he apologized for not paying them and thanked them for not telling Charles about these matters. Early in the next year he begged a further renewal.

His affairs grew constantly more tangled. And his other victims were less discreetly complaisant than Chapman and Hall. Although he had even been selling sheets of manuscript and autographs to scrape together cash, his involvements were too great. He received a notice of eviction from his house; he was liable to arrest on behalf of innumerable tradesmen. At last, towards the end of February 1839, shortly after the buoyant birthday dinner, his piled-up debts could no longer be concealed from his son.

Dickens acted with authoritative, with dictatorial, speed. He would find a house for his father and mother and Augustus in the country – in Exeter, remote from London. He would pay the rent they owed and contrive some temporary living arrangement for Frederick. Alfred had already been put to studying engineering in Yorkshire. To the tradesmen "let them say nothing," Dickens ordered. "The best hope I have of making any composition short of paying in full is founded on their being previously non est inventus." His father would have to get out of town at once and could reach Exeter in a week.

Dickens took his place in the coach for Exeter and the next morning, strolling along the Plymouth high road, exactly a mile out at Alphington he came upon a little white cottage with a For Rent sign. It had a vegetable and flower garden, an orchard, and a splendid view with a glimpse of the cathedral towers. Within, it was "bright as a new pin," freshly painted and papered, with an excellent parlour, a beautiful drawing-room, and two or three bedrooms, all for £20 a year.

He quickly signed an agreement with the landlady, a fat and fresh-faced old widow in the cottage next door. He bought some tables and imitation rosewood chairs, a couch, secondhand red curtains for the sitting-rooms, two secondhand carpets, a tester bedstead and white-dimity furniture for the best bedroom, glass, crockery, garden tools, and coal.

In high spirits, he wrote Forster that he was sure his mother and father would be happy there, and sent Kate directions for his mother to take the coach from its starting place at the Black Bear, Piccadilly. To Mile End Cottage consequently came Mrs Dickens, and, on Saturday, John Dickens, Augustus, and the dog Dash. There was no resisting the relentless whirlwind of Dickens's will. But before going off into exile, John Dickens rather plaintively asked Chapman and Hall what he would do in a little place like Alphington. He was only fifty-three, and despite his unreliability with money he had always been industrious.

But Dickens was confident that he had "the governor" settled for life. And, indeed, at first John and Elizabeth Dickens seemed pleased with the pretty rural retreat that was so different from the faded London lodgings they had known for years. But at the end of a month there was an "unsatisfactory epistle from Mother"; by June both parents were writing "hateful, sneering letters." "I do swear," Dickens groaned, "I am sick at heart with both her and father too."

Gradually, however, his "prodigal parent" and his mother grew reconciled. By July of the following year Dickens found them apparently "perfectly contented and happy" and the "little doll's house" beautifully kept. Chastened by the drastic fate that had overtaken him, perhaps a little afraid of his son, John Dickens did make some improvement in his ways. But he never reformed entirely; in 1841 and 1844 Dickens again had to pay some of his debts. Little by little, though, his banishment became less absolute. In August of 1841 John Dickens and his wife stayed at Broadstairs with Dickens, and his spirits were bounding with an exuberantly wild scheme to "proceed to Paris to consolidate Augustus's French." By the end of 1842 he would be allowed to return to London again.

No sooner had his father's troubles been straightened out than Dickens was obliged to "buckle-to again and endeavour to get the steam up" on *Nicholas Nickleby*. "If this were to go on long," he told Forster, "I should 'bust' the boiler. I think Mrs Nickleby's love-scene will come out rather unique." He also had ready for the printer the benefit volume for Mrs Macrone, now entitled *The Pic-Nic Papers*.

By this time Dickens had removed for the summer to Elm Cottage, Petersham. Here there were the same generous hospitalities and lively pastimes as in the preceding summer at Twickenham. Though in childhood Dickens had been sickly and unskilled in games, he was now ardent at quoits and bowls, pursued battledore and bagatelle with relentless activity, and even leaped the bar against such vigorous athletes as Beard and Maclise. He also attended the Petersham races almost daily, and worked himself far harder than the horses.

Maclise was at Petersham a good deal this June, for Chapman and Hall had commissioned him to paint a portrait of Dickens that was to be used as the frontispiece to *Nicholas Nickleby* in its three-volume form that autumn. He was a laborious craftsman and throughout the bright summer days studied Dickens in countless sketches which he destroyed in dissatisfaction. "Maclise has made another face of me," Dickens reported at the end of the month, "which all people say is astonishing." Out of this grew the brilliant "Nickleby" portrait, alive and gleaming as if reflected in a mirror, of which Thackeray said that it was the real "inward Boz."

George Cruikshank also came down to Elm Cottage, bursting with enthusiasm over a cockney variant he had recently heard of the ancient ballads of Lord Bateman. With this discovery he had regaled a dinner of the Antiquarian Society, and was now drawing illustrations for it. Dickens wrote a burlesque introduction and notes, altered lines, and substituted a new last verse. Cruikshank published "The Loving Ballad of Lord Bateman" with plates that Dickens considered a triumph of comic draughtsmanship: "You never," he assured him, "did anything like those etchings – never."

During the course of the summer, as Dickens got into the home stretch of *Nicholas Nickleby*, he began to think a good deal about his future relations with Chapman and Hall. He had received offers, he wrote Forster, to publish anything he wrote at a percentage of the profits but he felt well disposed towards his present connection and if they behaved with liberality he would not leave them. But they must be primed to "do something handsome, even handsomer perhaps than they dreamt of doing." Knowing all this, and knowing that when *Barnaby Rudge* was written Dickens would be clear of all engagements, Forster should put before them "the glories of our new project" and make them realize "that if they wish to secure me and perpetuate our connection, now is the time for them to step gallantly forward . . ."

Edward Chapman and William Hall were majestically summoned to Forster's chambers to hear this ultimatum. They presented themselves there in amenable mood. No doubt anything that Mr Dickens desired would be entirely satisfactory. Might they not, however, be given a few details about "the glories of our new project"? They would also like to have some intimation of what Mr Dickens would consider a proper financial arrangement. The answer to both these humble inquiries came promptly. In a letter crackling with vitality, Dickens outlined a scheme with enough ideas for three enterprises.

The new project was a weekly periodical to be sold for threepence a copy, modelled somewhat upon Addison and Steele's *Tatler* and *Spectator*, or Goldsmith's *Bee*, only far more popular. Mr Pickwick and Sam would reappear; there would be "amusing essays on the various foibles of the day"; there would be a set of Arabian Nights tales by Gog and Magog, the Giants in the Guildhall; there would be a series of Savage Chronicles, satirizing British magistrates by portraying "the administration of justice in some country that never existed." Dickens might even pledge himself to go to Ireland or America, and write a series of descriptive sketches and traditional legends after the plan of Washington Irving's *Alhambra*.

The financial terms he demanded showed that he had not forgotten a single detail of his protracted struggle with Bentley. He must be a proprietor of the paper with a share in its profits. He must be guaranteed a weekly minimum sum for his own contributions. He must choose any other collaborators *he* saw fit, who were to be paid by the publishers on his order according to an agreed scale. Or they might pay him for the whole of each number, and he would make whatever arrangements *he* chose for other contributions. None of these payments, however, were deductible from his share of the profits. Finally, if he went abroad, there must be additional provision about his travelling expenses.

Dickens was ready to start publication on 31 March 1840. In the course of July calculations were made, proposals offered and rejected, modifications accepted. For the opening numbers at least of the new publication (which was to turn into *Master Humphrey's Clock*) it was agreed that Dickens was to be the sole contributor and that, whatever might be the success of the shorter papers he wrote, he would also provide some continuing story. Phiz would be joined by George Cattermole in doing the illustrations.

The financial part of the agreement Dickens and Forster subjected to exacting scrutiny. Unknown to Chapman and Hall, Dickens rigidly checked all their estimates with printers and papermakers, who pronounced them perfectly accurate. The arrangement that was hammered out represented not merely another startling increase in Dickens's remuneration but a significant alteration in the very nature of his relationship to his publishers.

First, Chapman and Hall gave him an additional £1,500 on *Nicholas Nickleby*. Second, they paid him £50 a week for the new work, which even with a liberal allowance for assistance would net him £38. They paid all expenses of advertising, printing, and illustrating. Third, they paid Dickens half the realized profits on each number, but bore all the loss on an individual number if there were any. "If the work went on for two years and were to sell 50,000 . . . my profits would be between ten and eleven thousand pounds, and theirs five thousand," over and above the £50 per week guaranteed.

Clearly Dickens had proved no inept pupil in the school of business experience. Only four years before he had diffidently asked if his employers on the *Chronicle* would not perhaps think him entitled to *some* additional remuneration for the additional contribution of his sketches – and had been happy to receive an increase of two guineas a week. Now, with Forster's aid and advice, he made a bargain not merely shrewd but stringent and, as Forster put it, one in which he would rightfully not only always be the gainer but always the greatest gainer. Henceforth he would see to it, and his would be the "iron hand," that he had full control of his work. His earnings would be proportional to his sales, his would be the major share of the profits, and he would have no losses at all.

While these matters were being settled, Dickens went into London to attend a farewell banquet for Macready. Despite Dickens's usual touchiness to adverse criticism, his friendship for the great actor had not been impaired by his discouragement of Dickens's ambitions as a dramatist. He had been most enthusiastic about the whole course of Macready's management of Covent Garden. The actor's magnificent Shakespearean revivals had won ovations. He had encouraged current drama by producing the works of such living dramatists as Bulwer, Miss Mitford, Browning, and Talfourd. But his period at Covent Garden had been financially disastrous and he had announced his approaching abdication that March.

A few days after the last performance under Macready's management, at the farewell dinner on 20 July, Dickens proposed the toast to the late

Covent Garden Company. During the summer Macready was his guest at Petersham; in August Dickens visited the Macreadys at Elstree and served as godfather to their son Henry. In return he asked Macready to be godfather to the child he was innocently expecting to be "the last and final branch of a genteel small family of three which I am told may be looked for in that auspicious month when Lord Mayors are born and guys prevail."

At the end of August, Dickens took his family down to Broadstairs again, where he rented for a month a little house with a beautiful view of the sea. Here he worked hard at winding up *Nicholas Nickleby*. Chapman and Hall brought some of Browne's sketches for *Nickleby* and imparted "intentions as to a Nicklebeian fete," he wrote Forster, "which will make you laugh heartily." "I have had pretty stiff work," he told Forster, ". . . and I have taken great pains. The discovery is made, Ralph is dead, and the loves have come all right, Tim Linkinwater has proposed, and I have now only to break up Dotheboys and the book together." At two o'clock in the afternoon of 20 September he wrote the last lines of *Nickleby*, and rushed off immediately with Kate and Fred to Ramsgate to dispatch the copy to the printers.

Nicholas Nickleby mingles the sunlight of *Pickwick Papers* with the darkness of *Oliver Twist*. Rascality and thievery are forever forcing themselves into its jubilant high spirits: the dissolute Sir Mulberry Hawk and his toadies, Squeers and the bleak schoolroom dungeon of Dotheboys Hall, Ralph Nickleby fleecing his victims amid the glittering mirrors of his ornate drawing room. But in contrast to these scenes there is a wide range of laughter little less glorious than that of *Pickwick*: Mr Mantalini cajoling his wife with improbable endearments, Mrs Nickleby gabbling about the Prince Regent's legs and Miss Biffin's toes, Vincent Crummles and his company of actors. Though on the whole the story is a picaresque improvisation, it rises to heights of grotesque hilarity in its details. What would be mere rococo embellishment in another novel becomes the very *raison d'être* of *Nicholas Nickleby*. We never tire of Crummles saying farewell with a stage embrace, laying his chin on Nicholas's shoulder and looking over it, or of Mantalini praising his wife's "graceful outline" and depreciating the society ladies he has fascinated: "The two countesses had no outlines at all, and the dowager's was a demd outline."

The "Nicklebeian fete" came off on Saturday, 5 October at the Albion in Aldersgate Street. Macready was chairman, and besides Chapman and Hall, and the printers Bradbury and Evans, the guests included

Jerdan, Forster, Talfourd, Beard, Maclise, George Cattermole, Harley, the marine and landscape painter Clarkson Stanfield, who also painted scenery at Drury Lane, the well-known artist Sir David Wilkie, and Hablôt Browne, nervously timid, lurking in a corner or trying to hide behind a curtain.

The banquet provided by the hosts on this occasion, Macready thought, was even "*too* splendid." Chapman and Hall, following the tradition of Constable's presentation to Scott of his portrait, made a personal and at the same time magnificent occasion out of formally presenting to Dickens the portrait by Maclise. In the casual conversation that followed the speeches, Macready asked Dickens about his handsome young brother-in-law, Burnett, from whom Browne had drawn the physical type of Nicholas Nickleby. Was it really true that he intended to quit the stage? Dickens, surprised, said he had heard nothing of it. After making inquiries, he wrote Macready a few days later that on the contrary Burnett was painfully anxious for an engagement. Macready bestirred himself in Burnett's behalf, and Dickens thanked him when, shortly afterwards, he sent Macready a presentation copy of *Nickleby* handsomely gilt and bound in crimson.

The last week in October Dickens spent awaiting the birth of the new baby. "I go to bed every night," he wrote, "to horrid nightmares, concerning a nurse who is not to be found, a doctor with a night-bell that can't wake him, and a cab with a motionless horse and wheels that go round without moving onward." But on the 29th of the month Dickens's third child, Kate Macready, arrived without mishap.

Beneath the surface, Dickens's home life had not been perfectly serene during the last year and a half. From the time of Mary's birth rifts had appeared that were known only to his closest friend. "What is now befalling me," Dickens sadly reminded Forster almost twenty years years later, "I have seen steadily coming, ever since the days you re-member when Mary was born . . ." In *Oliver Twist* and *Nicholas Nickleby* Mrs. Corney and Miss Petowker hint the possibility of wives turning out very different from what they had seemed before marriage. And although these are drawn entirely from lower-class life and handled as farce, the comedy has an acid edge and the theme is a recurrent one in the later novels.

Towards Kate herself, Dickens's letters now begin to reveal a trace of something that only half disguises itself in jest. Remarking to Forster on her garbling someone's name, "By a happy touch of Kate's accustomed cleverness," he writes, "I find now that the name is Mullrainy." And towards her family, too, his attitude is shifting. "The Loving Ballad of Lord Bateman" has a note on critical mothers-in-law: "During the whole of her daughter's courtship, the good old lady had scarcely spoken, save by expressive smiles and looks of approval. But now that her object is gained, and her daughter fast married (as she thinks), she suddenly assumes quite a new tone . . ." "This is an exquisite touch of nature," Dickens adds, "which most married men, whether of noble or plebeian blood, will quickly recognize." Great weight cannot, of course, fairly be given to such stock situations of farce. But, in the light of his later feelings about Mrs Hogarth, his exploitation of them even at this time is not without significance.

These changes in his attitude certainly reflect also the rising distinction of Dickens's own social contacts. And as they widened there were more and more of them in which Kate did not share. It was not merely that many of them, like the Shakespeare Society, were almost exclusively masculine gatherings, or that Kate was often obliged by pregnancy to remain at home. It was not only that the social position of Lady Blessington and Lady Holland was such that conventional ladies did not go to Gore House and Holland House. Kate was not invited to Rogers's breakfasts or to great fashionable gatherings of the distinguished because she could not sustain a role in society. She could look wholesome, even pretty, and behave with good breeding, but she hardly sparkled. Even acidulous Jane Carlyle, for all her cleverness, often sat at home while her husband stalked off like a black-coated Isaiah to some elegant feast at Lady Ashburton's. The wives of famous authors had no social position as such in London's upper circles, nor had they the privilege sometimes granted ladies of the nobility of being received despite an insignificance of personal distinction.

Towards other women in society, especially if they were young and charming, Dickens could not resist a tone of gallant roguish raillery. Of an unknown lady, he admits to Forster, "Yes – I wrote to that effect to the beautiful Mrs F, whose eyelashes are in my memory. Would you know this hand? Oh, Evins, how misty I am." It was all harmless enough, a kind of high-spirited play-acting, but of dubious reassurance to the wife of a husband whose "magnificent eyes" lingered in other women's memories.

In the autumn of 1839 Dickens went back to London determined, at last, to get a start on the much-put-off *Barnaby Rudge*, which at this stage he was still supposed to write for Bentley. Now he would dash it off, and clear the way for his new project. "Thank God, all goes famously," he announced. "I have worked at Barnaby all day, and moreover, seen a beautiful (and reasonable) house in Kent Terrace, where Macready once lived, but larger than his." For with his three children, his redoubled prosperity, and the luxurious scale of living that he had seen in Rogers's little mansion on the Green Park, Dickens had decided that he needed a larger and more impressive residence than the house in Doughty Street.

In November, just south of the Regent's Park, he found so exactly what he desired that he was on tenterhooks. "A house of great promise (and great premium), 'undeniable' situation and excessive splendour, is in view," he wrote Forster. This was No. 1 Devonshire Terrace, a handsome structure with a large brick-walled garden between it and the New Road.

The entrance, set back a little from the street, had a portico of brick and stone, and curving into the garden were two semi-circular bow windows. Within, a spacious square hall opened on a library to the right with steps descending into the garden, and beyond the library, splendid with ornamental columns, a dining-room that also overlooked the garden and the coach house in the rear. On the floors above were a drawing-room and bedrooms and nursery.

By the middle of November Dickens was "in agonies of house-letting, house-taking, title proving and disproving, premium paying, fixture valueing, and other ills too numerous to mention." But he obtained the house on a twelve-year lease, and promptly entered upon a series of extensive improvements. John Chapman, "a genius in houses," was called in to suggest elaborate installations of water closets. With the image of Rogers's luxury in his mind, Dickens replaced deal doors with panelled mahogany, and wooden mantels with carved marble. For the reception rooms and chief bedrooms entire new suites were ordered, white spring roller blinds were made to measure for the dining-room windows, curtains festooned, deep-piled carpets laid, shining mirrors set in the walls.

The library was very different from the little back room in which Dickens had written at Doughty Street. When George Lewes, the friend of George Eliot, had visited Dickens there in 1838, that scholarly book-lover had seen "nothing but three-volume novels and books of travel, all obviously presentation copies from authors or publishers." But the fitted shelves at Devonshire Terrace displayed fine bindings, books of plates, pamphlets, and a representation of the great writers that had been conspicuously absent before.

A library was among the visible signs of the place one had achieved in the world. Only in his childhood, and in the days of his youthful striving for self-improvement, had Dickens been a voracious reader; and his childhood reading had all been dreaming romance, his later efforts an unsystematic plunging in random directions. Not that they had failed to be of the greatest value; if Dickens was no assiduous scholar, he tore through those books that were valuable to him, almost fiercely soaking up their riches. The comments Dickens made on those books he found time to read in his busy later career – more numerous and more varied than he is sometimes given credit for – are always vividly alive, and often sharply penetrating. But it is doubtful that the well-stocked shelves of Devonshire Terrace ever meant to him what that little upstairs room in Chatham had, whence came forth Tom Jones, Dr Primrose, Don Quixote, and Robinson Crusoe in a glorious host.

One part of that Devonshire Terrace library, however, is more richly significant – the table by the garden windows where Quilp and Dick Swiveller, Barnaby and his raven, Pecksniff, Sairey Gamp, Scrooge, Micawber, Peggotty, Betsey Trotwood, and Mr Dick were magically to rise into life from his pen. There, in a deep, mysterious inner world Dickens lived with his imagination.

Seeing the carriages of the great and famous sweep up to the portico of that splendid embodiment of ambition, hearing Dickens devising noisy fun in the garden for his happy children, who would have suspected that the cheerful house was haunted by a sickly small boy dreaming in a corner of Rochester Castle, by an unhappy child-waif creeping from Bayham Street to the blacking warehouse?

15

Master Humphrey's Clock
Strikes One

I am utterly lost in misery, and can do nothing [Dickens wrote
Forster]. I saw the Responsibilities this morning, and burst into
tears. The presence of my wife aggravates me. I loathe my parents.
I detest my house. I begin to have thoughts of the Serpentine, of the
Regent's Canal, of the razors upstairs, of the chemist's down the
street, of poisoning myself . . . or murdering Chapman and Hall
and becoming great in story (SHE must hear something of me then
– perhaps sign the warrant: or is that a fable?), of turning Chartist,
of heading some bloody assault upon the palace and saving Her by
my single hand . . .

It was just two days after Queen Victoria's marriage to Prince Albert.
And Dickens was infectiously carrying Forster and Maclise along with
him in a wild fantasy of all three being madly in love with their young
Sovereign. Dickens had been told that the Queen was fond of his books.
But what was that to a lover wearing a marriage medal near his heart
and weeping over her portrait!
   The jest reflects the high spirits of these rushing days when he was
getting settled in his splendid new home and making preparations for
the "great new project" – the weekly periodical he was to start in the
spring. For Dickens played with the same prodigious vitality that he
brought to his work, and that produced the staggering total of over a
million words in the four short years since the beginning of *Pickwick*.
From a positive fury of industry at his writing table he turned to a no
less furious energy in diversion – extravagant pranks like this one about
the Queen, rides through country lanes, prowls through London slums,
playgoing, dining at the tables of the great.
   Mingled with his pretence of love-insanity were jokes about a pet
raven, a talkative and rambunctious bird named Grip, who alarmed the

children and lady visitors by pecking at their ankles. The bird served as the model for his namesake in *Barnaby Rudge* and when he died Dickens wrote his friends characteristic descriptions of its demise. A bird fancier was first called in to administer a powerful dose of castor oil. The next morning, much better, Grip "so far recovered his spirits as to be enabled to bite the groom severely." But he had a relapse, in which he talked to himself incoherently. "On the clock striking twelve he appeared slightly agitated, but he soon recovered, walked twice or thrice along the coach-house, stopped to bark, staggered, exclaimed Halloa old girl (his favourite expression), and died."

Master Humphrey's Clock was the title Dickens had finally decided on for his new weekly periodical, now fast taking definite shape. He told Forster,

> I have a notion of this old file in the queer house, opening the book by an account of himself, and, among his other peculiarities, of his affection for an old quaint queer-cased clock ... Then I mean to tell how that he has kept odd manuscripts in the old, deep, dark, silent closet where the weights are; and taken from thence to read ... And thus I shall call the book either Old Humphrey's Clock, or Master Humphrey's Clock.

By the middle of January he had finished the first number and brought the Guildhall Giants on the scene.

Confident as Dickens was of his own popularity, he still did not fully realize the intensity of the appetite for his works that he had created. He imagined that he must find some novelty to give his public if he was not to wear out his success. Consequently he conceived his Arabian Nights – Mr Spectator salmagundi of Master Humphrey and Mr Pickwick sitting beside the old clock and Gog and Magog telling various unconnected tales of old times in the shadowy Guildhall. He was completely unprepared for the discovery he would soon unhappily make that his readers did not want sketches, tales, essays, squibs on current absurdities; and that they refused to be satisfied with anything less than another full-scale novel from his pen.

But meanwhile, with his head full of visions of the contents of that "dark, silent closet," he went off to Bath with Forster at the end of February on an overnight visit to Landor. In Landor's lodgings in St James's Square, with Italian paintings crowded over all the walls and even the doors, there was a glorious evening of luminous conversation over the wine. Dickens treated the older man with just the right measure of respect, but "allowed his wit to play about him, bright and harmless as Summer lightning," and the Olympian Landor was in turns grave, violent, tender, and thunderous with tremendous laughter. During this evening Dickens sketched out to his two companions an imaginative fancy that had seized his mind. With further reflection it grew into a tale of gentle pathos. It could fill several numbers of *Master Humphrey's Clock*. Should it be called, he asked Forster, *The Old Curiosity Dealer and the Child* or simply *The Old Curiosity Shop*?

The first number of *Master Humphrey* went on sale on Saturday, 4 April, and Dickens again observed his custom of leaving town on the eve of publication. On Friday he and Kate went to Birmingham; there Forster hastened to them with the exciting news that almost 70,000 copies of the *Clock* had been sold.

"The clock goes gloriously indeed," Dickens wrote when he had returned to town. His exultation, however, proved short-lived. The public had flocked to *Master Humphrey* under the impression that it was another Dickens novel. With the second number the sales fell off alarmingly; by the third their decline was disastrous. There was a hasty editorial conference at Chapman and Hall's offices in the Strand. Dickens flung himself at once into the breach with a new plan to enlarge *The Old Curiosity Shop* into a full-length narrative. Meantime Mr Pickwick and Sam Weller would stem the tide while he was elaborating the story. In part this expansion of the tale was a result of the increasing hold it took upon Dickens's feelings. But even more it was a consequence of his ability to adapt himself to adverse circumstances, and there can be no doubt that it saved him from what might have proved a grave setback.

Once started, Dickens progressed with dispatch and enthusiasm, though he felt rushed by the short intervals between numbers; his sudden change had given him no time to get ahead. He also felt harassed by the necessary brevity of weekly instalments. Nevertheless his enjoyment of the tale grew steadily. Dick Swiveller's "behaviour in the matter of Miss Wackles," he wrote Forster, "will, I hope, give you satisfaction. I cannot yet discover that his aunt has any belief in him, or is in the least degree likely to send him a remittance . . ." At the end of May, resolved on getting on with his pressing task, Dickens decided to spend June at Broadstairs, dashed down there, and rented 37 Albion Street for the month.

Within hours of his arrival he had, as he invariably did, neatly rearranged the furniture in all the rooms, set out his writing table, and installed a good array of bottles labelled "Gin," "Brandy," and

"Hollands," together with wine, in the dining-room closet. Two weeks later the entire family were "as brown as berries," and Dickens was beginning No. 15. "There is a description of getting gradually out of town, and passing through neighbourhoods of distinct and various characters, with which, if I had read it as anybody else's writing, I think I should have been very much struck. The child and the old man are on their journey, of course, and the subject is a very pretty one." In the following chapter the two wanderers meet the travelling showmen Codlin and Short, and the morose Thomas Codlin tries to ingratiate himself with Nell at the expense of his partner: "Codlin's the friend, not Short. Short's very well as far as he goes, but the friend is Codlin – not Short."

Back in London in July, a sudden impulse took Dickens to see the hanging of the murderer Courvoisier. Before the prison barriers crowds waited for the spectacle. The mob stretched beyond St Sepulchre's Church, jammed so tight that the pickpockets who were everywhere had no room to operate, and women who fainted from the pressure remained upright though unconscious. From this packed mass came a constant tumult of men and women bawling slang obscenities. At last the wretched murderer appeared, "feeble and agonized . . . with wringing hands – uplifted though fettered – and moving lips as if in prayer." The blood thirsty mob remained to the very end, and only then, after "a ghastly night in Hades with demons," did Dickens get away.

The experience sharpened Dickens's horror of making a public show out of executions. Granting that the public safety required murderers to be exterminated – and even this he considered debatable – there was no excuse for disposing of them in such barbarous fashion and with such evil effects upon the witnesses.

The remainder of July and August passed in less lurid diversions. Dining with Dr Elliotson, Dickens made the acquaintance of the Reverend Chauncey Hare Townshend. He shared Dickens's interest in mesmerism and was to become a close friend. And towards the end of August, Dickens invited Harley and a number of other friends to be present at the christening of baby Kate Macready on the 25th, when a fatted calf would be served in celebration. "It (the calf, not the baby) is to be taken off the spit at 6."

Although Dickens found time for these social distractions, he felt harried by the perpetual effort to keep at least one jump ahead of the printer. Made tense possibly by weariness and work, he gave way to exasperation one August night in Devonshire Terrace when Forster was more tactlessly domineering than usual. The only other guests were

Maclise and Macready. "Forster got on to one of his headlong streams of talk (which he thinks argument)," Macready wrote, "and waxed warm . . ." Dickens broke in; Forster endeavoured to carry things off with a high hand. Losing his temper, Dickens burst out that this was his house and he should be glad if Forster would leave it. Forster started to stamp out, but Macready stopped him, pleading that they should not let one angry instant destroy a friendship valuable to both. Dickens, regaining self-control first, admitted "that he had spoken in passion, and would not have said what he said, could he have reflected." But, he added, given the same offence, he would do just the same again.

It was a painful scene. Forster, distressed at the thought of wrecking their friendship, no longer wished to walk out, but neither could he be satisfied with the expressions of regret that Dickens now repeated. And so he remained feebly vacillating, neither going nor letting the subject drop, but, as Macready put it, "skimbling-skambling a parcel of unmeaning words." Only after protracting the uncomfortable situation, did he at last make "a sort of speech, accepting what he had before declined."

Dickens was very much grieved about the episode, he wrote Macready the next day. And yet, reason with himself as he would, he could not be penitent. With all the regard he had for Forster, he could not close his eyes to the fact that he did not quarrel thus with other men. "I declare to you solemnly, that when I think of his manner (far worse than his matter) I turn burning hot and am ashamed and in a manner degraded to have been the subject of it." Nevertheless, they resumed their friendship, as they were always to do through many other similar trials.

In September Dickens was once more at Broadstairs, this time in Lawn House, a small villa with a cornfield between it and the sea. "Come down for a week, come down for a fortnight, come down for three weeks, come down for a month," he begged Maclise. Fletcher was there, he added, sketching beggars and idiots, committing all manner of absurdities, as usual. The first time he went bathing, he fell into the water, letting out a howl like a wolf at its coldness. "You never heard anything so horrible."

Nothing, however, was allowed to distract Dickens from his writing table and *The Old Curiosity Shop*, every morning from eight-thirty until one. He pressed steadily onwards all through September and into the first week of October, despite an attack of facial rheumatism that tortured him desperately. "I am as bad as Miss Squeers – screaming out loud all the time I write."

Although the end of the story was not yet written, when Dickens returned to London he helped Frederick Yates with a dramatization of it at the Adelphi and "made a great many improvements . . . with divers pieces of bye-play" at the rehearsals. But he had no faith in its merits and didn't have the heart to be at the first night; Kate and Fred went without him. Only in Yates as Quilp did he have any confidence.

His misgivings over the stage version were sharpened by the emotional tension of nerving himself for Nell's death. "All night," he wrote, "I have been pursued by the child; and this morning I am unrefreshed and miserable." He was "inundated with imploring letters recommending poor little Nell to mercy." Writing George Cattermole a description of Nell lying dead upon her couch to aid him in illustrating the scene, he burst out, "I am breaking my heart over this story . . ." As he remembered the bitterness of death that he had known, Nell's features seemed to reveal transparently the image of the dead face he had loved and his old wounds bled again.

Dickens's readers were drowned in a wave of grief no less overwhelming than his own. When Macready, returning home from the theatre, saw the print of the child lying dead by the window with strips of holly on her breast, a chill ran through his blood. Thomas Carlyle, previously inclined to be a bit patronizing about Dickens, was utterly overcome. Waiting crowds at a New York pier shouted to an incoming vessel, "Is Little Nell dead?" Lord Jeffrey was found by a friend in his library with his head bowed upon the table; he raised it and she saw that his eyes were bathed in tears. "I had no idea that you had any bad news or cause of grief," she said, "or I would not have come. Is anyone dead?" "Yes, indeed," he replied, "I'm a great goose to have given way so, but I couldn't help it. You'll be sorry to hear that little Nelly, Boz's little Nelly, is dead."

Many later readers have felt the death of Nell overdone in its sentimental pathos, and it is true that Dickens is too indulgent to his own emotion and unduly prolongs the narrative of her slow decline. But the emotion itself is neither excessive nor inappropriate. The early death of innocence makes *The Old Curiosity Shop* a sad Hans Christian Andersen fairy tale of a snow princess slowly melting away. "All the good fairies," writes G. K. Chesterton, "and all the kind magicians, all the just kings . . . go after one little child who had strayed into a wood, and find her dead."

But the story is more than a fairy tale, it is a kind of fable. The old grandfather's crazed belief that he can gamble himself into a fortune and make his grandchild a lady is a fantasy upon the nineteenth-century dream of speculative wealth derived from the stock exchange as both gaming table and Golconda pouring forth gold. The dark analogy surrounds Nell and her grandfather with hands of greed and evil, from the bold and grotesque villainy of Quilp and the sneaking villainy of Sampson Brass to the sharp acquisitiveness of race-track touts and strolling gypsies and the hectoring voice of Miss Monflathers reproving poverty and misfortune as moral stigmas. Dickens "is embodying in his people and scenes," as Rex Warner notes, "the cruelties and delusions which he observes in wider society."

The misfortunes of Nell and her unhappy grandfather, with the interwoven lives of the Nubbles family, Quilp, Sampson and Sally Brass, Dick Swiveller, and the Marchioness, were the turning point in the fortunes of *Master Humphrey's Clock*. Before its end as many as 100,000 copies of each number were being purchased. Dickens had saved himself from what might have been a most disastrous reversal in the ever-swelling tide of his hold upon his readers.

Unlike *Pickwick Papers*, this had been achieved by no stroke of lucky appeal, but by deliberate design. Dickens knew that his position depended on his readers, who could not be argued or battered into liking what they did not like. Though he was not afraid to assert views to which they might be opposed, he worked assiduously to provide a kind of writing that they would enjoy. And so, when the public response to the first few numbers of *Master Humphrey's Clock* warned him that it might break down at any minute, he had quickly altered its scheme. The public desired from him long continued stories; henceforth that was what he should give them.

He had saved *Master Humphrey's Clock* from failure by reverting to his primary role as a writer of fiction. Consequently the close of the one story in its pages was followed immediately by the beginning of another. Of the original *Clock* machinery he revived Master Humphrey and his friends for only the few pages necessary to bridge the gap between *The Old Curiosity Shop* and *Barnaby Rudge*, that often postponed task for which he had at last found a potent motivating force.

16

Emergence of a Radical

The writing of *Barnaby Rudge* was a time of enormous development for Dickens, although it continued to give him almost as much trouble as when he was struggling to do it for Bentley. "I didn't stir out yesterday," he wrote Forster, "but sat and *thought* all day; not writing a line; not so much as the cross of a t or the dot of an i." "Last night I was unutterably and impossible-to-form-an-idea-of-ably miserable," but the next morning he managed to go to work "in good twig."

Preparations for the appearance of *Barnaby* considerably antedated its first instalment on 13 February 1841. To represent the Maypole, Cattermole had drawn an inordinately ornate and many-gabled inn, with which Dickens was greatly pleased, and the artist was soon doing Gabriel Varden's house and The Warren. From his studio at Clapham Rise, with its dark nooks and tapestried walls, came almost three dozen of the illustrations used in *Master Humphrey's Clock*, and his home saw many dinners with Dickens and his friends as the guests.

Here, after sitting over their port at dinner, or in Cattermole's cavernous drawing-room with its heavy carved furniture, would assemble a group calling themselves "the Portwiners" – Dickens, Forster, Thackeray, Bulwer, Charles and Edwin Landseer, Macready, Mark Lemon, Maclise. While a great log of ship timber blazed on the hearth and fumes rose from the cigars, conversation glowed with anecdote and wit. Thackeray buttonholed Forster over one of Cattermole's drawings of a waterfall to express his wonder that anyone could get such an effect "with only a bit of charcoal." "*And brains,*" added Forster with Johnsonian decision through a cloud from his cigar. Meanwhile the kettle boiled, and Dickens, wildly squirting lemon juice into his eyes and over his floreate waistcoat, brewed the punch.

During the latter part of January, Kate was expecting the birth of their fourth child, an event that delayed itself from the 23rd until more than two weeks later. Throughout the entire time, Kate was extremely unwell. Finally, on 8 February, the child was born, "a jolly boy" who was to be named Walter Landor Dickens.

In early March Dickens found himself again obliged to deal with his father's debts. This time they had assumed so embarrassing a form that he had Mitton insert in the newspapers a notice the deliberate vagueness of which does not disguise what John Dickens had been doing: "Certain persons having or purporting to have the surname of our said client have put into circulation, with a view of more readily obtaining credit thereon, certain acceptances made payable at his private residence or at the offices of his business agents"; and it went on to give warning that for the future Dickens would pay no debts except those contracted by himself or his wife.

Despite the unrelenting pace of his work, he wrote generously detailed letters to would-be authors who were constantly sending him their work. Though he praised what he could, he was severe on fancy writing. How, he asked, did one "spell a tiger from all thoughts of harm," "clasp blood springs with tendril fingers," or "fold love's banner o'er a lady's brow"? It was foolish and wrong, Dickens told the same young writer in a further letter, to plead the absence of needful revision. The question was not only the merit of the author's thought but his power of expressing that thought.

Another of these literary neophytes came to Dickens's attention just as he was leaving the *Miscellany*. A carpenter named John Overs had sent in some songs for the different months of the year, stating that he had written them in his spare time. Dickens would gladly have published them but would ask no favours of Bentley. He learned that Overs was self-educated, had a wife and family of small children, and earned thirty shillings a week as foreman in a factory of medicine chests. Dickens felt uneasy about the risks of a literary career for such a man, but Overs explained that his aspirations were modest, that he thought these pursuits as harmless as the alehouse or the skittle ground, and that he did not neglect his daily work. Touched by "arguments so unpretentious and so true," Dickens made no further efforts at dissuasion and tried to advance the carpenter's literary career.

He gave one of Overs's compositions to Ainsworth when he took over the editorship of the *Miscellany*. He had Overs send the songs, with his comment on them, to *Tait's Magazine* at Edinburgh, where they were published. During the following year, Dickens made time in his busy schedule to help Overs with revisions. On a story about Wat Tyler's rebellion, he made a comment that significantly foreshadows his approach to the climactic riots of *Barnaby Rudge*: "I object on principle to making Wat such a thorough-paced villain, because a rebel on such grounds has a certain claim to one's sympathy, and I feel that if I had lived at his time I should have been very likely to have knocked out the collector's brains myself . . ."

Not many writers would take time from so busy a career to comment in detail on the compositions of unknown young men or to spend hours revising their work. In addition, he was also struggling to shorten the delays in publishing *The Pic-Nic Papers* for the benefit of Mrs Macrone. Just when all the contributions that had been donated for it were ready, Colburn, the publisher, aroused Dickens's indignation by rudely deleting Landor's offering. Resenting the insult offered by "this sneaking vagabond" to a distinguished writer, Dickens at first refused to send in his own piece. But in pity for the unhappy widow he gave way. When the book was published later that summer of 1841 he was able to put £300 into the widow's hands.

From Washington Irving in America came a letter of gratifying praise for *The Old Curiosity Shop*. Dickens replied,

> I wish I could find in your welcome letter some hint of an intention to visit England. I can't. I have held it at arm's length, and taken a bird's-eye view of it, after reading it a great many times, but there is no greater encouragement in it this way than on a microscopic inspection. I should love to go with you – as I have gone, God knows how often – into Little Britain, and Eastcheap, and Green Arbour Court, and Westminster Abbey. I should like to travel with you outside the last of the coaches down to Bracebridge Hall.

Barnaby Rudge was now driving on to the fury of the Gordon Riots. As his imagination plunged into the surging tumult of the riots themselves, Dickens's emotions boiled up in strange turmoil. Fear and horror of the ferocities of mob violence struggled with his fierce sympathy for the wrongs of the oppressed rising like fiends to avenge themselves in destruction. He obviously shared with the rioters an orgiastic joy in the flaming demolition of Newgate amid clamour and smoke. He shuddered and at the same time he exulted in this overthrow of authority. "I have just burnt into Newgate," he wrote Forster excitedly, "and am going in the next number to tear the prisoners out by the hair of their heads."

These pages – the most powerfully written in the book – are deeply coloured both by his own past experience and by the public strife taking place almost as these very scenes were being written. The jail was the dark symbol of suffering and imprisonment that had indelibly branded his memories of childhood, the cruel bond that united him with all the suffering and exploited. The actual riots of 1780, to be sure, around which his story centred, had supposedly sprung from anti-Catholic fury, and though Dickens himself strongly disliked the Catholic Church, as a good liberal he deplored persecutions of any faith. The events of that uprising, however – churches and homes burnt wholesale, the prisons of London broken open, the Bank of England attacked – suggest deeper discontents than feeling only against the Roman Catholics, and strongly resemble the storming of the Bastille and the lootings in Paris that were the first signs of revolutionary violence in 1789.

Dickens certainly read mutterings of this deeper rebellion in the disturbances that were his theme. The years immediately preceding 1840 had been years of industrial depression. The Chartist agitation for universal suffrage and labouring-class representation in Parliament had collapsed in 1839 into rioting among the South Wales miners. In Manchester during the following year the cotton mills stood empty and threatening jobless men filled the streets; the whole north of England went out on one gigantic general strike that the authorities were able to put down only by firing into the crowds. These were the events that Dickens and the readers of *Barnaby Rudge* had before their eyes as they responded to the excitement of its smoking pages.

Dickens had never thought of himself as one of " the people " – even in the blacking warehouse he had always been "the young gentleman," and painfully humiliated by the common associations to which he had been reduced. And yet he felt at the same time an obscure inward identification not only with the poor but even with the bloody rebellion that he described in such fascinated horror.

His sympathies were reflected not solely in the ambiguous overtones of *Barnaby Rudge*, but were increasingly coming to the surface in his feelings and actions. When Dr Southwood Smith, the Chief Commissioner, put the report of the Children's Employment Commission in his hands, Dickens read with anger and horror of the ruthless ways in which even small children were worked in the mines. He found no less cause for fury in a later report on conditions in the factories and iron foundries. The two reports painted hideous pictures of dark tunnels through which seven-year-old children dragged loaded carts to which they were chained; of girls clad only in ragged trousers working in the dark, often up to their knees in water and carrying heavy loads of coal up steep ladders a distance exceeding the height of St Paul's Cathedral; of dreadful accidents constantly occurring; of deformed and stunted boys toiling fourteen hours a day, fed on offal, struck with bars, burned by showers of sparks from red-hot irons, pulled by the ears till the blood ran down.

About these revelations Dickens arranged to write for the *Edinburgh Review* an article of burning comment. He also contributed to the *Examiner* during the summer of 1841 a series of angry rhymed squibs on the Tories and other opponents of factory regulation.

The bitterest of these lampoons was a new version of "The Fine Old English Gentlemen," "to be said or sung at all Conservative Dinners":

> *I'll sing you a new ballad, and I'll warrant it first-rate,*
> *Of the days of that old gentleman who had that old estate;*
> *When they spent the public money at a bountiful old rate*
> *On ev'ry mistress, pimp, and scamp, at ev'ry noble gate,*
> > *In the fine old English Tory times;*
> > *Soon may they come again!*

> *The good old laws were garnished well with gibbets, whips, and chains,*
> *With fine old English penalties, and fine old English pains,*
> *With rebel heads, and seas of blood once hot in rebel veins;*
> *For all these things were requisite to guard the rich old gains*
> > *Of the fine old English Tory times;*
> > *Soon may they come again!*

> . . . . . .

> *The bright old day now dawns again; the cry runs through the land,*
> *In England there shall be – dear bread! in Ireland – sword and brand!*
> *And poverty, and ignorance, shall swell the rich and grand,*
> *So, rally round the rulers with the gentle iron hand,*
> > *Of the fine old English Tory days;*
> > *Hail to the coming time!*

Everywhere Dickens looked, and in every direction his mind ran, he saw conditions to arouse indignation. Walking at his vigorous pace through the crowded areas of Houndsditch, Whitechapel, or Seven Dials, observing the filth, the congestion, remembering the inadequate water supply, and knowing what consequences in disease and crime they all engendered, he swore to himself that he would strike blow after blow against these evils. Hearing the shrill voices of children, with no place to play but the refuse heaps of the streets and without sufficient schooling, Dickens saw how hoodlumism and corruption inevitably sprouted from the very cobblestones. Only changes in society's treatment of these problems could smite to the root of the evil.

He had been sympathetic to the Chartist programme of universal manhood suffrage, vote by ballot, annual Parliaments, abolition of property qualifications for election to Parliament, payment of members, and division of the country into equal electoral districts. He agreed with Carlyle's declaration in a thick pamphlet entitled *Chartism* that the movement voiced a just protest against a social organization dominated by privilege and wealth. Parliamentary reform had not accomplished much that Dickens regarded as valuable, nor would it, he was convinced, so long as Parliament was controlled by the aristocracy, the industrialists, and the rich merchants.

Consequently, although Dickens reveals no trace of Carlyle's doctrine of leaders divinely born to command and a populace endowed only with the right to obey, he shared Carlyle's scorn for a Parliament that represented only a sham aristocracy. All Dickens's writings from *Oliver Twist* to *Our Mutual Friend*, make it clear that he was not advocating tyrannic authority, however kindly in intention. Carlyle's searing contempt for Parliament seemed to Dickens to voice only his own unbelief in a government that did not represent the people.

The two men had met in February 1840, at a dinner.

Know [Carlyle wrote], Pickwick was of the same dinner party, though they did not seem to heed him much. He is a fine little fellow – Boz, I think: clear blue intelligent eyes that he arches amazingly, large protrusive, rather loose mouth, a face of the most extreme *mobility*, which he shuttles about – eyebrows, eyes, mouth and all – in a very singular manner while speaking. Surmount them with a loose coil of common coloured hair, and set it on a small compact figure very small and dressed à la D'Orsay rather than well – this is Pickwick. For the rest, a quiet, shrewd-looking little fellow, who seems to guess pretty well what he is and what others are.

Carlyle's disdain of the law-makers at Westminster, furthermore, strongly confirmed Dickens's disillusioning experience, sitting in the Reporter's Gallery, seeing good men like Lord Ashley and Lord John Russell being defeated in the most necessary reforms by callous political obstruction. Nevertheless, when Dickens was offered the opportunity in 1841 to forward social reform from a seat in the House of Commons, he hesitated for a few days. In May Lord Melbourne's Government fell, and a group of citizens from Reading asked Dickens to stand as their second candidate with his friend Talfourd. Dickens refused on the ground that he could not afford the expense of a contested election. When a few days later they suggested that the Government might support his candidacy even to the extent of paying the entire cost of the contest, he again refused. He could not compromise his independence by putting himself under any such obligations.

This concern with public welfare that paradoxically kept him from accepting a seat in Parliament was, from the very beginning, an animating force in Dickens's work. *Sketches by Boz* had its flickering flame-tongues of wrath for the miseries of milliners' apprentices and the hopelessness that drove the slum-dweller to the gin palace; and *Pickwick* clearly makes its points against hypocritical temperance reformers, corrupt borough elections, the inequities of Chancery, and the abuses of prison administration. But, as he swept into the full stride of his career, his most striking growth was in the scope and penetration of his criticism. He moved towards an understanding of the intricate network that bound all the abuses he hated into a linked system dominating every major institution of society.

The time would come when he no longer struck merely at the isolated cruelties of the workhouse and the foundling asylum, the ignorance and brutality of the cheap schools, the enslavement of human beings in mines and factories, the hideous evils of slums where crime simmered and proliferated, the injustices of the law, and the cynical corruption of the law-makers. His comprehensive vision would perceive them all as no more than vicious symptoms of the great evil permeating every field of human endeavour: the entire structure of exploitation on which the social order was founded. And the fiercest of his attacks he would direct against that golden-faced idol with a heart of iron and bowels of brass.

Fanfare in Scotland and
the Eve of a New Departure

Lord Jeffrey had been earnestly pressing Dickens to visit Scotland. All Edinburgh, he wrote Dickens, was eager to welcome him. Dickens had been thinking of going to Ireland, but now, in 1841, his mind began to run instead on Rob Roy's country, Arthur's Seat, and the lochs and glens of the Highlands. He determined that on 21 June he would take the road to Scotland. He asked his friend Angus Fletcher "to bespeak the needful accommodations" at an Edinburgh hotel and perhaps keep them company later. As for a dinner Dickens had heard they were planning to offer him in Edinburgh, he told Fletcher he "would not for the world" reject their cordiality.

Dickens and Kate left London two days earlier than originally planned, and on the evening of the 22nd took up quarters at Edinburgh's Royal Hotel. He wrote Forster,

> The hotel is perfectly besieged, and I have been forced to take refuge in a sequestered apartment at the end of a long passage, wherein I write this letter. They talk of 300 at the dinner. We are very well off in point of rooms, having a handsome sitting-room, another next it for Clock purposes, a spacious bedroom, and large dressing-room adjoining. The castle is in front of the windows, and the view noble.

The ceremonies of lionization began immediately. Judges, the Solicitor-General, the Lord-Advocate, and other dignitaries all came to call. In the Hall of the Courts of Law, Dickens was introduced to "the renowned Peter Robertson," "a large, portly, full-faced man, with a merry eye, and a queer way of looking under his spectacles." Here, too, striding up and down at a slashing pace, was John Wilson, Professor of Moral Philosophy at the University, the "Christopher North" of *Blackwood's Magazine*, who was to preside as chairman of the dinner in place of Jeffrey, who was ill.

On Friday, 25 June, the public dinner took place. Besides some 270 diners cramming the room to the throat there were almost 200 feminine spectators. As the guest of honour made his appearance the band struck deliriously into "Charlie Is My Darling," and cheers rang through the room.

How different was Dickens's position now from that of seven years ago, when he had been an obscure reporter gazing across the sea of faces to the high table where Lord Grey had been the guest of honour. Now the music and the clamour and the speeches were for him. Robertson convulsed the company with laughter by an imaginary interview between Squeers and Scott's Dominie Sampson, culminating in the latter worthy schoolmaster's "Pro-di-gi-ous!" As Dickens rose to reply he was interested to realize that, "notwithstanding the enthoosemoosy, which was startling," he was "as cool as a cucumber." How remarkable it was, though, "to see such a number of grey-headed men gathered about my brown flowing locks!"

The parallel between his own reception and that tendered Earl Grey was made complete four days later. The Lord Provost, Council, and Magistrates voted him by acclamation the freedom of the city of Edinburgh. What a triumph for a young writer of twenty-nine, to be accorded a recognition not bestowed upon the veteran statesman until his seventieth year!

During the week-end he had visited Jeffrey at Craigcrook. The following week was a rush of breakfasting, lunching, and dining. He made a public appearance at the theatre, attended an evening party given by the Treasurer of the Town Council, had supper with the artists of Edinburgh. At last, at seven-thirty in the morning on Sunday, 4 July, he took the stage for Stirling and a brief tour of the Highlands, somewhat wearied by his tumultuous honours.

With Fletcher as their guide, Dickens and Kate made their way through the Trossachs to Loch Katrine, trudged in a pouring rain through a rocky pass to see the island of the Lady of the Lake, and drove on, wet to their skins, another twenty-four miles to Loch-Earn-Head. When they arrived at their inn, they found the fires in their rooms not yet lighted, and Fletcher ran back and forth between the sitting-room and the bedrooms wielding "a great pair of bellows, with which he distractedly blew each of the fires out in turn." They dined on a meal of oatcake, mutton, hotchpotch, trout from the loch, small beer bottled, marmalade, and whisky.

Dickens was able to dispatch the next instalment of *Barnaby Rudge* before they proceeded on through the pass of Glencoe. The approach lay through "the most desolate part of Scotland, where the hill-tops are still covered with great patches of snow: and the moors and mountains sprinkled with huge rocks." "Glencoe itself is perfectly *terrible*. The pass is an awful place. It is shut in on each side by enormous rocks from which great torrents come rushing down in all directions." Among the rocks were "scores of glens, high up, which form such haunts as you might imagine yourself wandering in, in the very height and madness of a fever."

Bad weather made it impossible for them to ferry across an arm of the sea to Oban, and forced their return in a drenching rain through Glencoe in order to reach Inveraray. At one place they had to cross a foaming stream by foot on a tiny bridge of slippery planks with only a trembling rail on one side between them and the broken rocks below. The carriage, plunging into the swollen ford farther downstream, sank so deep that only the horses' heads and the postboy's body were visible amid the turmoil of the rushing water.

It made me quite sick to think how I should have felt if Kate had been inside. The carriage went round and round like a great stone, the boy was as pale as death, the horses were struggling and splashing and snorting like sea-animals, and we were all roaring to the driver to throw himself off and let them and the coach go to the devil, when suddenly it all came right (having got into shallow water) and, all tumbling and dripping and jogging from side to side, climbed up on the dry land.

Returning to London in the middle of July, Dickens cleared up a few matters of business before going on to Broadstairs for August and September. There he worked at concluding *Barnaby Rudge*. Cattermole had drawn the mob at the Maypole smashing bottles and drinking out of the best punch bowls while John Willet, fallen back in his chair, regarded them with stupid horror. "The rioters went, sir, from John Willet's bar," Dickens now wrote him, " (where you saw them to such good purpose) straight to the Warren, which house they plundered, sacked, pulled down as much of as they could, and greatly damaged and destroyed. They are supposed to have left it about half an hour. It is night, and the ruins are here and there flaming and smoking." Throughout the next month Dickens dispatched Cattermole a series of vignette descriptions for the scenes he desired to have depicted.

With the end of *Barnaby Rudge* it had been decided that Dickens would discontinue *Master Humphrey's Clock* and revert to publication in monthly parts. Despite its enormous sales while it was running *The Old Curiosity Shop*, the *Clock*'s circulation had trembled and fallen since, and was now around 30,000. In addition, the strain of meeting a weekly deadline was becoming too exhausting for Dickens to carry on alone. It had therefore been tentatively decided to go back to the tried green format of *Pickwick* with a new serial beginning next March. Dickens went up to town on 20 August to discuss this matter. Walking about Lincoln's Inn the next day, he revolved the subject in his mind.

Was it really judicious for him to follow one story by another without any interval? "I remembered that Scott failed in the sale of his very best works, and never recovered his old circulation (though he wrote fifty times better than at first) *because he never left off*." Would he himself not do better, with a view to his future fame, to stop now, to publish not another word for a year, and then come out with a complete novel in three volumes and "put the town in a blaze again"?

These ideas sorted out in his head, Dickens put them before Forster. Would Forster lay the case before Chapman and Hall after dinner that day? Let them stop the *Clock* on 27 November as planned, but advertise, instead of the new serial in March, a novel in three volumes to come out a year from that date. That agreed, the question to be put to Chapman and Hall was, what would they give him for one half the copyright of that book, over and above the sum of £2,000 in quarterly instalments that he would require for his living expenses during this year of retirement?

At dinner the two publishers were sanguine and cheerful. William Hall toasted "Success to our new undertaking." At this, Forster announced that he was going to startle them by something Dickens had mentioned to him just half an hour before. He then stated with great force Dickens's argument. Little Hall and big Chapman were as if knocked down by a thunderbolt. Chapman recovered first. Looking forward, he said, for twenty years, not for two, he believed that Dickens was right. Then little Hall chimed in that "He thought so too." The publishers had only to consider what terms they could offer. Assured of more than half a year's rest from novel writing, Dickens returned triumphantly to Broadstairs.

During this London visit he had seen John Overs, who had depressing news. He had recently been told that his lungs were infected, and that he could not possibly live very long if he continued to work as a cabinetmaker. Dickens promptly sent him for a more expert diagnosis to Dr Elliotson, who confirmed the opinion.

Dickens gently passed this information on to Overs, saying emphatically that Dr Elliotson had cured several such cases. To these encouragements Dickens added that Elliotson had sent a £5 note to help Overs meet his immediate needs, to which he himself was adding another five. He also wrote describing the case to Macready. As a result mid-October saw Overs installed in a minor post at the theatre.

Meanwhile, the August and September days at Broadstairs were bright and vigorous. With *Barnaby Rudge* rapidly progressing to its last page and the prospect of a respite, after some six years of steady writing, Dickens's spirits soared like a balloon. He would emerge from his morning's work eager to whip everyone else up to a pitch of exhilaration matching his own. Broadstairs was now full of friends and members of his family: Maclise, Fletcher, Mitton, the Macreadys, John Dickens and his wife on a visit from Alphington, Fanny and Henry Burnett, Fred Dickens taking off a few days from his post in the Treasury, a little later Henry Austin and Letitia.

Dickens's contagious gaiety bubbled among them like flowing champagne. Fred, with his weary expression and raised eyebrows, made ludicrous remarks and outrageous puns that Dickens capped with even more absurd ones, though he pretended to be disgusted when Kate too joined the game. Kate would perpetrate her small, harmless attempts, "turning up her eyes in affected terror of his wrath and terminating in a pretty little *moue*," while Dickens went through a pantomime of tearing his hair and writhing in attitudes of anguish.

When Fred and Dickens went sailing, they would keep the sailors in a broad grin by roaring out a series of nautical commands with the greatest gravity and earnestness: "Now then, a reef in your taffrail," "Sheepshank your mizzen," "Abaft there! brail up your capstan-bar," "Haul up your main-top-gallant-sprits-sail-boom!"

In the evenings there were cards, guessing games, dancing, and strolls down to the pier or the Tivoli Gardens. Dickens was brilliant in routing everybody at "Animal, Vegetable, or Mineral," although he himself failed to guess a vegetable object mentioned in "mythological history" and belonging to a queen, and was chagrined to have it identified as the tarts made by the Queen of Hearts.

Among other visitors were two ladies, one of them named Millie, and the other her considerably younger friend Eleanor Picken. The latter had met the Dickenses in London the year before, and was thrilled at the renewal of the acquaintance. After her first terror of Dickens had subsided, she was riveted by the marvellous power of his eyes, lighting into such luminous depths that for the moment she could see nothing else. But his style of dress disappointed her, with its loud expanse of waistcoat and the finicking patent-leather-toed shoes.

With this young lady and her more mature friend Dickens pretended to be in love. Rhapsodically he called them, in turn, "My charmer," "Beloved of my soul," "Fair enslaver," and "Queen of my heart." He entreated them to dance: "Wilt tread a measure with me, sweet ladye? Fain would I thread the mazes of this saraband with thee"; and then went through a stately burlesque of the dance with a deportment mingling the airs of Turveydrop with those of Malvolio. "'Tis my lady! 'Tis my love!" he exclaimed dramatically, hand on heart. "Oh, that I were a glove upon that hand, that I might touch that cheek!" "Which of us do you intend to be Juliet to your Romeo?" Millie inquired. Whereupon, with a swift upset, "Whichever you choose, my little dears," Dickens replied, and strolled off. Eleanor was horribly frightened of him and at the same time half bewitched.

She came to feel that she was not the only one who was afraid of Dickens. His whole family, she noted, held him in awe and were appreciably subdued in his presence, as if they feared to arouse his wrath. His mother, in the face of his displeasure, hardly dared indulge her love of dancing and "that old buck, her husband," for all his corklike optimism and orotund phraseology, also kept a sharp eye on Dickens's moods. Their young observer probably did not know, of course, that only the preceding June the father had again bobbed up out of debt only by the help of his son.

In general, though, Dickens was in tearing high spirits that September. Discussing Byron's *Childe Harold*, he criticized the words "Dazzled and drunk with beauty" and "The heart *reels* with its fulness" as less suggestive of Venus than of gin-and-water, then without warning slapped his brow, tossed his waving hair, and exclaimed, "Stand back! I am suddenly seized with the divine afflatus!" Taking up a pencil, he looked wildly around for paper, and finding none, stalked to the window and wrote on the white-painted shutter:

LINES TO E. P———. AFTER BYRON
O maiden of the amber-dropping hair
May I, Byronically, thy praises utter?
Drunk with thy beauty, tell me, may I dare
To sing thy paeans borne upon a shutter?

From the scene of these unrestrained high jinks, Dickens sent Chapman a burlesque warning against his approaching marriage. He should reflect, before it was too late. "To see a fellow creature – and one who has so long withstood – still if – will *nothing* warn you." Following these broken phrases came a succession of postscripts:

P.S. – Pause.
　Put it off.
P.P.S. – Emigrate.
P.P.P.S. – and leave me the business – I mean the
　　　　Strand one.

During the preceding two weeks Dickens had occasionally been running up to London to discuss the details of his new understanding with Chapman and Hall. On 7 September an agreement was signed. Dickens was to have his rest from writing, but Hall's counsel had prevailed against publication in three volumes, and the new work was to appear in monthly numbers beginning November 1842. During its publication Dickens was to receive £200 a month, calculated as one of the expenses, and, in addition, three quarters of all the profits. Six months after the novel's completion, upon paying Dickens a quarter of the value of all existing stock, Chapman and Hall were to have half the future earnings. During the fourteen months before publication started, Dickens was to draw £150 a month as an advance against his three quarters of the profits. "M[acready] was quite aghast last night," Dickens wrote exultantly on 9 September, "at the brilliancy of the C. and H. arrangement . . ."

Hardly had these matters been settled before Dickens impulsively dashed in a new direction. In the early plans for *Master Humphrey's Clock* thoughts of a visit to Ireland and even to America had been in his mind. The desire to see the New World now took violent possession of him. "Washington Irving writes me that if I went, it would be a triumph for me from one end of the States to the other, as was never known in any nation." His reception in Edinburgh would pale beside it.

The United States symbolized for Dickens the goal of liberty and democracy towards which he hoped that England might be moving. It was the glowing promise of a future in which the worn-out snobberies, aristocratic privileges, and corruptions of the Old World melted away and men were valued according to their character and accomplishment. "I am still haunted," he wrote Forster, "by visions of America . . . Kate cries dismally if I mention the subject. But, God willing, I think it *must* be managed somehow!"

PART FIVE

The New World
1842

[18]

The American Dream

With Dickens, to form a desire was to be overwhelmed with hot haste for its realization. At once he began to devise reasons why he should set out for the United States without delay. Mrs Trollope's *Domestic Manners of the Americans* had given a caustic picture of the new country, and Harriet Martineau's *Society in America* had also found much to criticize. Dickens was convinced that, with his concern for the advancement of the common people, he could understand a democratic kingless country freed from the shackles of class rule.

What, then, if he "ran over to America" for four or five months, and returned with a one-volume book that would redress the balance of the tone of depreciation almost universal among earlier travellers? "In going to a New World," he prescribed, "one must utterly forget, and put out of sight the Old one and bring none of its customs or observations into comparison"; or, at the very least, remember how much brutality there was in England. These judicious reflections he was to find easier to preach than to practise. He did not realize how deeply he was permeated by European attitudes, or how much that was alien he would find in the United States. Chapman and Hall leaped at his proposal of an American notebook and speedily regarded the idea of the American visit as quite settled.

"Now to astonish you," Dickens announced to Forster. "After balancing, considering, and weighing the matter in every point of view, I HAVE MADE UP MY MIND (WITH GOD'S LEAVE) TO GO TO AMERICA — AND TO START AS SOON AFTER CHRISTMAS AS IT WILL BE SAFE TO GO." Kate was in tears whenever the project was even mentioned. How could they travel with four small children, she wept, little Charley not yet five, Mamey and Katey younger still, and the baby less than a year old? Her lamentations were so grievous that Dickens asked Macready's advice and help. Ought he to take the children or leave them at home?

Macready decidedly recommended that the children remain behind and generously offered to care for them in his own home. He would not use so selfish an argument, Macready wrote, as the delight of seeing "that grand country." But it was Kate's duty to go with her husband and "*must be a source of happiness to her*." She should view the matter in its proper light, and make it happier by putting a smiling face upon it. Kate gave way. Instead of accepting the Macreadys' offer for the entire six months, it was decided that Fred should take charge of the children during the earlier part of it. Kate felt comforted by this arrangement, for all the children were fond of Fred. Thus consoled, and reassured by the fact that her highly capable maid Anne would be with her to lighten the rigours of the journey, she even began to talk gaily of the trip.

Accommodations were taken on the steam packet *Britannia*, sailing from Liverpool on 4 January for Boston. By 26 September Dickens was writing to Washington Irving and Lewis Gaylord Clark, the editor of the *Knickerbocker Magazine*, announcing his arrival in the third week of the new year. Coming back to London from Broadstairs at the end of September, Dickens was suddenly stricken ill with a fistula. It would have to be removed by an operation rendered unspeakably painful by the fact that surgery had not yet developed the use of anaesthetics. The ordeal took place on 8 October, and left Dickens so weak that he was obliged to lie on the sofa every day while Kate wrote his letters to his dictation. Within ten days, however, he was able to go out on short visits and take a daily airing in his carriage, and had regained his usual spirits.

His friends were assiduous in obtaining for him letters of introduction to outstanding people in the United States. To be sure, Dickens already felt as if he were well acquainted in New York. He had corresponded with Lewis Gaylord Clark; and in the four or five letters he had exchanged with Washington Irving he and the distinguished American writer were already warm friends. At Macready's on several occasions he had met one of the actor's great friends David Cadwallader Colden, of New York, whose wife was a sister-in-law of Lord Jeffrey. Through Landor's friend John Kenyon he secured letters to George Ticknor, the historian of Spanish literature, Charles Sumner, and other leading citizens of Boston. For presentation in Philadelphia he had a letter to Lucretia Mott, the well-known Quaker anti-slavery advocate, and another from Charles Leslie, the painter, to his brother-in-law Henry C. Carey, the publisher.

Entire new wardrobes must be ordered. Kate rustled in and out of a rainbow profusion of pretty new frocks, travelling dresses, gowns suitable for whatever glamour of Embassy balls and White House dinners. Dickens must have the most elegant of coats and trousers, a sheen of velvet and satin waistcoats, gold chains and tie-pins and rings. All the details of the journey Dickens worked out with Forster, aided by advice from Macready based on his own travel experience in America. Edward Marjoribanks, of Coutts and Company, arranged for a letter of credit for £800. An American journalist who called at Devonshire Terrace on the eve of the departure found Dickens's study piled high "with Marryat's, Trollope's, Fidler's, Hall's, and other travels and descriptions of America," and blazing "with highly-coloured maps of the United States." Dickens chatted in happy excitement, volatile with anticipation.

December was feverish with eleventh-hour activities. Letters of welcome from America were arriving and demanding to be answered, and letters of farewell needed to be written. A Boston portrait painter, Francis Alexander, asked Dickens to sit for him. Not all his friends approved the approaching visit. "Aren't there disagreeable enough people to describe in Blackburn and Leeds?" Albany Fonblanque asked. Lady Holland tried to dissuade him from going at all, saying plaintively, "Why cannot you go down to Bristol and see some of the third and fourth class people there and they'll do just as well?"

On New Year's Day Devonshire Terrace was in readiness to turn over to General Sir John Wilson, who had rented it for the six months of Dickens's absence. The next day, a Sunday, good-byes were said to Fred and the children, and Forster accompanied Dickens and Kate to Liverpool, whence they were to sail on Tuesday the 4th. The day before, they took their luggage on board in the cold bright sunlight, with a thin crust of morning ice crackling under their heels. In the preposterous box that was their stateroom they were hilarious about its minute areas, into which they could no more force their two portmanteaus, Dickens said, "than a giraffe could be got into a flowerpot." By nearly closing the door, he demonstrated, twining in like serpents, and counting the washing slab as standing room, very nearly four people could be insinuated into it at one time.

Back at the Adelphi Hotel that evening there was a magnificent dinner that included turtle, cold punch, hock, champagne, and claret. The next afternoon Dickens, Kate, and Forster crowded up the gangway, under the huge red funnel pouring out smoke, and the tangle of masts and spars for the auxiliary sails, amid a confusion of roaming stewards and swarming luggage. Forster presented Dickens with a pocket Shakespeare as a farewell gift.

The eighteen-day passage across the Atlantic was one of the stormiest in years. Dickens was sick for the first five days; Kate for six and in the utmost terror throughout the entire voyage. The ship tossed so heavily that when the travellers played whist they stuffed the tricks into their pockets to keep them from disappearing: "five or six times in the course of every rubber we are all flung from our seats, roll out at different doors, and keep on rolling until we are picked up by stewards." "Four dozen plates were broken at dinner. One steward fell down the cabin-stairs with a round of beef, and injured his foot severely. Another steward fell down after him and cut his eye open. . . . Twelve dozen of bottled porter has got loose upon deck, and the bottles are rolling about distractedly, overhead."

Ten days out so violent a gale struck that the smoke-stack had to be lashed with chains to prevent its being blown over and setting fire to the decks and cabins. Next noon, while the sea ran mountainously high, smashed lifeboats hung from their davits in a faggot of crazy boards, and the planking of the paddle-boxes had been torn away so that the wheels dashed spray over the decks. Kate moaned in her berth, and in the ship's cabin Dickens found only four out of the eighty-six passengers rubbing their hands with the cold. Throughout these wild experiences Dickens tried to spread cheer by borrowing an accordion and regaling the ladies' cabin with his performances.

On the fourteenth day the sea grew comparatively smooth. Two nights later they were piloted into Halifax Harbor with a light wind and a bright moon. By nine-thirty the next morning they were gliding along a broad stream, the sun shining brilliantly on the white wooden houses, flags flying, and crowds shouting on the quays. The wharf to which they were heading was paved with upturned faces, the gangway thrust out almost before they were made fast. Arm in arm with the ship's doctor, Dickens immediately went ashore for some oysters.

Then, sir, comes a breathless man . . . shouting my name as he tears along. . . . The breathless man introduces himself as the Speaker of the House of Assembly; *will* drag me away to his house; and *will* have a carriage and his wife sent down for Kate, who is laid up with a hideously swoln face.

Then he drags me up to the Governor's house (Lord Falkland is Governor), and then Heaven knows where; concluding with both houses of parliament, which happen to meet for the session that very day, and are opened by a mock speech from the throne delivered by the governor . . . I wish you could have seen judges, law-officers, bishops, and law-makers welcoming the Inimitable. I wish you could have seen the Inimitable shown to a great elbow-chair by the Speaker's throne . . .

The *Britannia* lay over for seven hours at Halifax and then stood off for Boston. Two days later, on the afternoon of 22 January, Dickens stood on deck watching New England rise from the green sea. Soon they were in Boston Harbor, but long before the boat was moored "a dozen men came leaping on board at the peril of their lives, with great bundles of newspapers under their arms . . . 'Aha!' says I, 'this is like our London Bridge': believing of course that these visitors were news-boys. But what do you think of their being EDITORS? And what do you think of their tearing violently up to me and beginning to shake hands like madmen?" (Dickens was mistaken in his identification the second time as well as the first; they were reporters.) "If you could have seen how I wrung their wrists! And if you could but know how I hated one man in very dirty gaiters, and with very protruding teeth, who said to all comers after him, 'So you've been introduced to our friend Dickens – eh?'" Another of these reporters, however, after learning that Dickens had made no advance arrangements for hotel accommodation, raced ahead to the Tremont House and ordered rooms and dinner.

The Charles Dickens whom the Americans saw was a young man of middle size, wearing a shaggy greatcoat of bear or buffalo skin that might have been envied by a Kentucky woodsman. Soon he was shaking hands with T. Colley Grattan, the British Consul, and with Francis Alexander, the artist. Accompanied by the young Earl of Mulgrave, a lively fellow passenger with whom Dickens had struck up a friendship, the entire party went ashore. Alexander took them in his carriage from the waterfront to the Tremont House, a four-storey hotel with a Grecian portico.

Dickens bounded into the lobby, his face aglow, shouting "Here we are!" as the lights burst upon his party. By this time it was already dark, and, after presenting Kate with a bouquet of flowers, Alexander left them to sit down with Lord Mulgrave to a handsome dinner. Invitations began to pour in from the moment it was known where they were staying. Hardly was dinner over before a delegation including the

22-year-old James Russell Lowell arrived from the "Young Men of Boston" to invite him to a banquet in his honour. Dickens willingly accepted, and the first day of February was named for the occasion.

Despite the fatigue of their arrival, Dickens's vitality was not exhausted, and about midnight he and Lord Mulgrave sallied out for a look at the city. Boston was then a town of 125,000, with shade trees lining the well-paved streets and porticoed houses whose grass plots were enclosed by iron railings. Dickens was in the most elated of spirits. It was a stinging night, but in the light of the full moon everything stood out sharp and glittering. Muffled in his fur coat, he ran over the shining snow, keeping up a continual shout of uproarious laughter.

Sunday morning, walking down to the Custom House with Lord Mulgrave, Dickens was impressed by the brightness of the signs with their gilded letters, the redness of the brick, the whiteness of the stone, the greenness of shutters, the polish of the doorknobs and plates, all shining with the prim neatness of a child's new toy. In the afternoon he and Kate unpacked; later he was sketched by Pierre Morand in the hotel parlour, and interviewed for the *Transcript*. At tea with Lord Mulgrave and Grattan, it was decided that Dickens would have to hold a daily reception to accommodate the throngs eager to see him, but he was still blissfully unaware of the flood that was about to descend upon him.

When George Ticknor called next morning he found Dickens sitting to Henry Dexter, the sculptor, and tossing off autographs in response to the hundreds of requests that had come in the mail. In the afternoon he was led through cheering crowds and presented to John P. Bigelow, the Secretary of the Commonwealth, and Josiah Quincy, the President of the Senate. Rushing back to his hotel for supper, he then pushed his way across the street through a surging mob to the Tremont Theatre, where he was escorted into a gaily decorated box, and had to bow and smile while the orchestra played the Boz Waltzes especially composed for the occasion and the audience cheered. The bill consisted of *Charles O'Malley*, a dramatization of *Nicholas Nickleby* written and acted by the comedian Joe Field, and an entertainment devised by the same versatile gentleman, entitled *Boz: A Masque Phrenologic*.

With Dickens's first sitting to Alexander his lionization began to swell to embarrassing proportions. Ladies pressed into the studio to stare at him until Dickens bolted for the door, only to be mobbed there and forced to retreat and lock himself within. When hunger obliged him to emerge for lunch they were still besieging the doorway, and surged about him instantly again, clinging to him while they furtively snipped bits of fur from his coat to treasure as souvenirs, and filling the passage with a soprano clamour of adulation. "Really, it is too bad," commented an onlooker, "that he should get such an idea of the ill-breeding of our people."

Social engagements continued in ever-mounting proportions. Cornelius Felton, "heartiest of Greek professors," the younger Richard Henry Dana, Charles Sumner, and Henry Wadsworth Longfellow were among the callers. There were dinners with William Hickling Prescott, the historian, dinners with other prominent citizens. There was a sumptuous ball at Papanti's Dancing Academy, with its great French mirrors and its ornate prismatic chandeliers imported from Paris. Escorted by Charles Sumner, Dickens was received, in the midst of a terrific jam, by Mayor Jonathan Chapman, introduced to countless pretty young ladies, and regaled on oysters, ices, charlotte russe, and champagne.

In the course of the week that followed Dickens and Kate found themselves obliged by sheer fatigue to break several engagements. Instead of dining with George Hillard, a prominent lawyer, they sent word that both were ill, and dined in their suite. But even at his hotel he was not left alone. One man, in spite of repeated refusals to receive him, forced his way into the parlour, where Dickens was stretched on a sofa, and remained an hour. Dickens, pleading illness, went to his room, and threw himself on his bed, but in spite of this the man brought up his wife and passed another hour with Kate. "This is one of the million things I could tell you," wrote Mrs Motley, the wife of the historian, "which make me feel sometimes as if I could cry with mortification."

Within three days of his arrival Dickens was snowed under by letters and decided he must have a secretary. Francis Alexander recommended for the post a young pupil of his, George W. Putnam, who was hired at ten dollars a month and his board. Putnam speedily settled down to a routine. Arriving at nine o'clock, he would start working at a side table while Dickens and Kate had breakfast. Dickens autographed small cards while he ate. No request for an autograph was refused, but he drew the line at gratifying the numerous young ladies who wanted locks of his hair. In one corner of the breakfast room Alexander made sketches of Dickens's head for the portrait he was painting in his studio; in another Henry Dexter worked on the moist clay of the bust.

Forster could have no idea, Dickens wrote him, of all the communications he received, "copies of verses, letters of congratulations, welcomes of all kinds." "Authorities from nearly all the states have written to me. I have heard from the universities, congress, senate, and bodies, public and private, of every sort and kind." There were also more eccentric epistles. One requested an original epitaph for the tombstone of an infant, another an autograph copy of Mrs Leo Hunter's "Ode to an Expiring Frog." A New Jersey lady had family records of 100 years, interesting and tragic, which she would allow Dickens to rewrite and publish for a half share of the profits.

"I can give you no conception of my welcome here," Dickens wrote to Mitton. "There never was a king or emperor upon the earth so cheered and followed by crowds, and entertained in public at splendid balls and dinners . . ." And to Forster: "I have had deputations from the Far West, who have come more than two thousand miles distance: from the lakes, the rivers, the backwoods, the log-houses, the cities, factories, villages, and towns . . . 'It is no nonsense, and no common feeling,' wrote Dr Channing to me yesterday. 'It is all heart. There never was, and never will be such a triumph.' "

Some of those who saw Dickens, however, were less than carried away. In restrained Boston, where gentlemen invariably wore black-satin waistcoats in the evening, his velvet waistcoats in vivid green and brilliant crimson were looked on as startling and even vulgar. Nor did his personal appearance and manner please everyone. The first response of young Dana, author of *Two Years Before the Mast*, was one of disappointment. Dickens had, Dana said, "a dissipated looking mouth with a vulgar draw to it, a muddy olive complexion, stubby fingers, and a hand by no means patrician."

Nevertheless, Dana admitted a fascination, and later, seeing Dickens with Prescott, Sparks, and Ticknor, revised his estimate. "The gentlemen all talking their best, but Dickens perfectly natural and unpretending. He couldn't have behaved better. He did not say a single word for display." And finally, won over completely, "He is full of life," Dana wrote William Cullen Bryant. "And with him life does not appear to be according to the Brunonian theory – a forced state – but a truly *natural* one. I never saw a face fuller of light."

Everyone noticed this flashing animation. "Dickens himself is frank and hearty," William Wetmore Story wrote, "and with a considerable touch of rowdyism in his manner. But his eyes are fine, and the whole muscular action of the mouth and lower part of the face beautifully free and vibratory. People eat him here! . . . Lafayette was nothing to it."

There were continued criticisms, however, of Dickens's breeding. At one great family mansion, observing in a mirror that his hair was disarranged, he calmly combed it at the dinner table. In the Prescotts' quaint old family residence in Bedford Street, during a discussion about whether the Duchess of Sunderland or Mrs Caroline Norton were the more beautiful, Dickens dropped a social bombshell among the staid Bostonians. "Mrs Norton is perhaps the most beautiful," he nonchalantly remarked, "but the Duchess, to my mind, is the more kissable."

Not all cultivated Boston even admired Dickens as a writer. Mrs Andrews Norton would grant no more than that his books "were well, some of them *very well*." The enthusiastic Felton, however, replied that they were much more than that. "I had been convinced since the first number of Pickwick, that one of the greatest minds of the age was coming out and . . . that Dickens was the most original and inventive genius since Shakespeare!"

In spite of the mauling and mobbing to which he was subjected, Dickens's enthusiasm for America was high. The women were beautiful, the behaviour neither stiff nor forward, the good nature universal. "If you ask the way to a place – of some common waterside man, who don't know you from Adam – he turns and goes with you." "The American poor, the American factories, the institutions of all kinds – I have a book, already. There is no man in this town, or in this State of New England, who has not a blazing fire and a meat dinner every day of his life. A flaming sword in the air would not attract so much attention as a beggar in the streets."

As Dickens penned these words to Forster, nothing seemed clearer to him than that *his* book on America would be keyed to a very much more laudatory note than those of his predecessors. At the Perkins Institute for the Blind he had warmed to the happy faces of the children, and been pleased by the fact that the inmates of this charity school wore no ugly uniforms but followed their own tastes. He was deeply moved by the loving success with which Dr Samuel Gridley Howe and his helpers taught blind, deaf, and dumb children to communicate with their fellows and develop into intelligent and cheerful human beings. He was strongly impressed by the use of kindness and of occupational therapy in the State Hospital for the Insane. He remembered potted plants on the window-sills of the paupers, and observed that it was not assumed that these unfortunates were there because of their inherent viciousness.

When he visited the factories and mills of Lowell, he was equally delighted. The town was trim and cheerful with its red brick buildings and brisk young river. There was little child labour, and that regulated by state law. The girls wore neat dresses and worked in bright rooms with green plants. They had accounts in the Lowell Savings Bank, shared the use of a piano in their boarding-houses, belonged to circulating libraries, and published a periodical called the *Lowell Offering* written by themselves.

Many people might exclaim, "How very preposterous!" Dickens remarks, and say, "These things are above their station." To which he responds, what is their station? "It is their station to work. And they do work. They labour in these mills, upon an average, twelve hours a day, which is unquestionably work, and pretty tight work too." And if these young ladies of Lowell even buy parasols and silk stockings, he concludes, he is not aware of any evil consequences.

For "the University of Cambridge," as Dickens called Harvard, he expressed warm admiration. The American universities, he said, "disseminate no prejudices; rear no bigots; dig up the buried ashes of no old superstitions; . . . exclude no man because of his religious opinions; above all, in their whole course of study and instruction, recognize a world, and a broad one too, lying beyond the college walls." "The professors of the Cambridge university, Longfellow, Felton, Jared Sparks, are noble fellows," he wrote Forster. "So is Kenyon's friend, Ticknor. Bancroft is a famous man; a straightforward, manly, earnest heart; and talks much of you, which is a great comfort."

With Longfellow, Dickens swiftly headed towards a sympathetic intimacy. "Gay, free and easy," Longfellow found him, "fine bright face; blue eyes, long black hair, and with a slight dash of the Dick Swiveller about him." Four days after their first meeting, Longfellow joined with Sumner to take Dickens off for a long Sunday walk around Boston. They visited the waterfront and the wharves where the Boston Tea Party had taken place, Paul Revere's house, and the Bunker Hill Monument. At the end of their jaunt, the three men parted the warmest of friends, and Longfellow invited Dickens to breakfast with him at Craigie House on the following Friday.

The great dinner of Tuesday, 1 February, held at Papanti's, was the public climax of Dickens's reception at Boston. The fifteen dollars a head charged for the tickets gave great dissatisfaction to many. For that sum, however, a choice of more than forty dishes was provided. By five in the afternoon a full band was playing in the balcony, and the invited guests were beginning to assemble in front of the black marble fireplace in the second-floor reception room. The most prominent were Josiah Quincy, Sr, the President of Harvard, Washington Allston, the poet and artist, George Bancroft, the historian, and Richard Henry Dana, Jr. The band played "Washington's March" as the 150 subscribers made their way into the hall, then it struck up "God Save the Queen," when Dickens, the other guests, and the officers of the banquet were shown to their seats.

The speaking began with an eloquent introduction by Josiah Quincy, Jr. Quoting Falstaff, he said, " 'If the rascal have not given me medicines to make me love him, I'll be hanged: it could not be else – I have drunk medicines.' " Had they not all investigated with Mr Pickwick the theory of tittlebats? Had they not all played cribbage with the Marchioness and quaffed "the rosy" with Dick Swiveller? How then could anyone think of Boz as a stranger!

Dickens expressed heartfelt gratitude for the cordial welcome they had rained down on his head. Moved by a secret sympathy for the ideals of America, he had "dreamed by day and night, for years, of setting foot upon this shore, and breathing this pure air." As to his work, he said, it was not easy for an author to speak of it. But his purposes were plain and simple. "I believe that virtue shows quite as well in rags and patches as she does in purple and fine linen. . . . I believe that she goes barefoot as well as shod. I believe that she dwells rather oftener in alleys and by-ways than she does in courts and palaces . . ." and that the rejected and forgotten and misused of the world "are moulded in the same form and made of the same clay" as their more fortunate fellow creatures.

Before he sat down, there was one more topic on which he desired to lay stress. There were great writers in America, who were already "as familiar to our lips as household words."

I hope the time is not far distant when they, in America, will receive of right some substantial profit and return in England from their labours; and when we, in England, shall receive some substantial profit and return in America from ours. Pray do not misunderstand me. . . . I would rather have the affectionate regard of my fellowmen than I would have heaps and mines of gold.

But the two were not incompatible, for nothing good was incompatible with justice. He concluded by giving the toast: "*America and England –* and may they never have any division but the Atlantic between them!"

The applause that followed was tumultuous. No later speaker that night, however, left the safe regions of eloquent platitude by referring to the subject of international copyright. The next day newspapers screamed that Dickens had been guilty of bad taste, and charged that he had "created huge dissonance where all else was triumphant unison."

The enormous furore ultimately created on this theme, and Dickens's refusal to be silenced, either by abusive anonymous letters or by vituperation in the press, make it one of the excited controversies of his visit. Much of the anger was no doubt whipped up by the news-papers, who were themselves often among the worst offenders against the rights of authors – which was much as if a burglar should object to the ill-breeding of a reference to housebreaking. But Dickens did not ask whether his claim was selfish, but whether it was just. If they thought "that he, of all men, ought not to speak" because he was interested, he thought that he, of all men, ought to speak because he was wronged. And there were many who felt that he had right on his side and that there was nothing objectionable in either his manner or his matter. James T. Fields, sitting at the foot of one of the tables, among the youngest of the young men, remembered no flaws in the occasion:

It was a glorious episode in all our lives . . . We younger members of the dinner-party sat in the seventh heaven of happiness and were translated to other spheres. . . . And when Dickens stood up at last to answer for himself, so fresh and so handsome with his beautiful eyes moist with feeling and his whole frame aglow with excitement, how we did hurrah, we young fellows. Trust me it was a great night, and we must have made a great noise at our end of the table, for I remember frequent messages came down to us from the "Chair" begging that we hold up a little and moderate if possible the rapture of our applause.

19

Conquest – with Undertones

Four days later Dickens left Boston. The breakfast at Longfellow's, on the day before his departure, took place in the beautiful old colonial house with its yellow clapboards and classical pilasters, where Washington had made his headquarters during the first year of the Revolution.

At the round table they sat down to "a bright little breakfast, at which Felton's mirthfulness helped, and Andrews Norton's gravity did not in the least hinder, the exuberant liveliness of the author of Pickwick." Afterwards Dickens was shown about the College and the Library and was introduced to other Cambridge worthies. Then he returned to the Tremont House, where Anne had been packing steadily in preparation for the departure the following day.

The leave-taking was a grand turmoil. Dickens's party descended the marble staircase for the last time. Crowds shouted in the streets as they drove to the Railroad Station. Governor Davis, with whom the Dickenses were to stay in Worcester, arrived with his party and they boarded the three o'clock train. Felton accompanied them, his gold spectacles glittering and his face beaming. "Wherever the cars stopped," he said, "heads were incontinently thrust in bawling out, 'Is Mr Dickens here?'"

Dickens liked the New England towns and villages, with their white frame houses and crisp green blinds. That night Governor Davis introduced him to his "general friends," a term that seemed to mean practically everybody, and Dickens made a speech from his chamber window to the throng overflowing the snow-covered lawn. Sunday he met the Governor's "particular friends." Later he joked about the parsimonious hospitality of his hostess's table. "She is too good a housekeeper and has a hungry eye," he wrote Charles Sumner. And William Prescott told his wife that Dickens "laughed about the short commons at the Governor's, where I believe they got tea and roast apples."

Monday morning, Dickens and Kate went on by rail to Springfield, and then by a shallow-bottomed steamboat down through the crunching ice of the Connecticut River to Hartford. Here he visited the Institute for the Deaf and Blind, the Insane Asylum, and the State House. Late one evening, after they had retired for the night, they were serenaded outside their door by a nephew of John Quincy Adams and a friend. How "ridiculous and commonplace," Dickens suddenly thought, his boots must look at their door in the dead of night while the earnest young men sentimentally strummed on their guitars! He had to pull the covers over his face to stifle his shouts of hilarity.

At Hartford there was another dinner, of seventy persons, and the bill of fare outdid that of the Boston dinner by listing over seventy dishes. Dickens, determined to be bullied by no newspaper outcry, spoke again on the subject of international copyright. As if to emphasize the fact that *he* could not be gagged or frightened, he amplified the mild remarks he had made at Boston. He had made a compact with himself, he told his audience, that while he was in America he would omit no opportunity of referring to the subject.

If Scott had been aided in his labours by the existence of such a law, he "might not have sunk beneath the mighty pressure on his brain." And Dickens reminded his listeners of that touching scene when the great man was dying, listening on his couch through the open window to the rippling of the Tweed that he had loved. Think of the shame and the sorrow that even as he lay crushed by financial struggle the phantoms of his imagination – Jeanie Deans, Rob Roy, Caleb Balderstone, Dominie Sampson – should have brought him not even "one grateful dollar-piece . . ."

It is nothing [Dickens wrote Forster], that of all men living I am the greatest loser . . . The wonder is that a breathing man can be found with temerity enough to suggest to the Americans the possibility of their having done wrong. I wish you could have seen the faces that I saw, down both sides of the table at Hartford, when I began to speak about Scott. I wish you could have heard how I gave it out. My blood so boiled as I thought of the monstrous injustice that I felt as if I were twelve feet high when I thrust it down their throats.

But the faces of his audience gave Dickens no intimation of what was to follow this speech. The howl in the press began immediately. The Hartford *Times* said, "It happens that we want no advice on the subject and it will be better for Mr Dickens if he refrains from introducing the subject hereafter . . ." Other newspapers asserted that he was no gentleman, that he was a mercenary scoundrel, that he was abusing the hospitality of the United States by uttering any such criticism of his hosts, that he had malignantly come to the country with that low purpose. Anonymous letters echoed these attacks in every key of scurrility. Dickens burned with scorn and indignation. But he did not give way. What had happened, he wrote to Jonathan Chapman in Boston, had "had the one good effect of making me iron upon this theme, and iron I will be here and at home, by word of mouth and in writing as long as I can articulate a syllable or hold a pen."

Opposition had had its usual effect of making Dickens more adamantine in his determination than before. But it had, this time, other and more sweeping results as well. The anonymous insults and the yelpings of the yellow press altered the visionary image he had entertained of America as a land of freedom and changed the attitude he brought to all the later experiences of his visit.

I believe that there is no country, on the face of the earth [he wrote Forster], where there is less freedom of opinion on any subject in reference to which there is a broad difference of opinion than in this. . . . There! I write the words with reluctance, disappointment, and sorrow; but I believe it from the bottom of my soul. . . . I tremble for a radical coming here, unless he is a radical on principle, by reason and reflection, and from the sense of right. I fear that if he were anything else, he would return home a tory. . . . I do fear that the heaviest blow ever dealt at liberty will be dealt by this country, in the failure of its example to the earth.

It was not merely that the great dream of America as the shining citadel of liberty had burst as if it were an iridescent bubble. It left behind a disillusion like an ugly smear colouring the scene. Dickens granted that "the respectable newspapers and reviews" took up "the cudgel as strongly in my favour, as the others have done against me," but the ruffian outcries seemed to him to drown the voices of decency and justice.

The general crudity and the ill-breeding of the intrusions that at first he had regarded as an amusing excess of lionization came to rasp him more and more.

I can do nothing that I want to do [he said], go nowhere where I want to go, and see nothing that I want to see. If I turn into the

street, I am followed by a multitude. If I stay at home, the house
becomes, with callers, like a fair. . . . I go to a party in the evening,
and am so enclosed and hedged about by people . . . that I am exhausted for want of air. I go to church for quiet, and there is a
violent rush to the neighbourhood of the pew I sit in, and the clergyman preaches at *me*. I take my seat in a railroad car, and the very
conductor won't leave me alone. I get out at a station, and can't
drink a glass of water, without having a hundred people looking
down my throat . . .

Consequently Dickens determined that, apart from two invitations
in New York, to a ball and to a dinner, which he had already accepted,
he would accept no further public entertainments during his stay in the
United States. As for the copyright controversy, he would *not* let it drop.
He asked Forster to obtain a short letter from the principal English
authors, supporting his position; its publication in the best American
journals would unquestionably do great good. Henry Clay had written
from Washington "to declare his strong interest in the matter, his
cordial approval of the 'manly' course I have held in reference to it,
and his desire to stir in it if possible." It would be "a thousand pities if
we did not strike as hard as we can, now that the iron is so hot."

Meanwhile Dickens had moved on from Hartford, and taken the
boat down Long Island Sound. At New Haven he was serenaded by
the Yale students, and the crowd assembled to see him at the Tontine
Hotel was so numerous that the landlord placed two stout porters to
lock their hands across the main staircase to the reception room and
keep the throng at bay. It was nearly midnight before Dickens could
retire to his room. One citizen, in a letter to the press, commented that
he must despise such adulation as the behaviour of a nation of silly
parasites, and satirically asked why "some shrewd enterprising Yankee"
did not "put him in a cage, and take him about the country for a
show?"

Continuing down the Sound Dickens had a rest from these turmoils.
Felton was "unaffected, hearty, genial, jolly," and the two "drank all
the porter on board, ate all the cold pork and cheese, and were very
merry indeed." Presently they were passing through Hell Gate. Soon
he was driving up Broadway, noting the ladies in rainbow silks and
satins, the beaux in Byronic collars and tasselled cloaks, the great
blocks of ice being carried into shops and bars, and the "gentlemanly
pigs" rooting in the gutters. New York then had a population of

around 300,000, mostly concentrated on the lower tip of Manhattan Island. Fifth Avenue at Tenth Street was uptown, Bloomingdale and even Murray Hill were summer resorts, and so was Hoboken, with its sweeping views of the Hudson.

At the Carlton House, Dickens was accommodated with "a very splendid suite of rooms" which he feared was also "(as at Boston) *enormously* dear." David Colden, who was a member of the New York committees for both the ball and the banquet, joined Dickens and Kate at dinner. Colden had no sooner departed than Washington Irving's card was brought in. Dickens dashed into the reception room, napkin still in hand, and the two met with open arms. Dragging his guest into the room where they were still at the dinner table, "What will you have to drink," he went on enthusiastically, "a mint julep or a gin-cocktail?"

The following evening the Boz Ball took place at the Park Theatre. The interior was decorated in an amazing manner, the dome covered by festoons hanging from a golden rosette, the galleries and tiers of boxes draped in white muslin trimmed with gold, all serving as a background for the arms of the states under a trophy of English and American flags, medallions representing Dickens's works and, in the centre, a portrait of Dickens brooded over by a golden eagle with a crown of laurel in its beak. All these splendours were illumined by a blaze of 500 lights, from two chandeliers suspended by golden ropes, from lamps and candelabra on golden columns, and from six astral lamps hanging from the proscenium pillars. The stage, which was to be the scene of a series of twelve *tableaux vivants*, had been widened to sixty feet to permit the erection of "a large and magnificent chamber of carved and gilded oak, with deep Gothic windows on each side, and a lofty, fretted ceiling."

The doors of the theatre were thrown open at seven-thirty, and within half an hour the building was densely crowded. Three thousand people who had tickets that 5,000 more had been unable to obtain at any price milled around and trod on each other's toes. When the curtain went up on one of the *tableaux* and revealed a silly-looking short gentleman in a green velvet suit, someone screamed, "There he is! There's Boz!" and the audience shrieked with laughter.

Finally, a little after nine, the band burst into "See the Conquering Hero Comes," and Dickens made his appearance escorted by General George Morris in full-dress military uniform, and followed by Kate under the escort of David Colden. The house rang with cheers, and handkerchiefs waved from the floor to all the boxes and tiers. The Mayor made a speech that nobody heard, the committee gave Kate a huge bouquet, Dickens "breathed heavily, and cast one look up at the house, partly curious, partly bewildered, partly satiric, and a good deal humorous." Then came the Grand March, twice around the enormous ballroom. Dickens escorted the Mayoress, the Mayor escorted Kate, and two thirds of the crowd shouted that they couldn't see him. Between more *tableaux* there were quadrilles and waltzes. "It was like dancing in a canebrake," wrote one spectator, "the poor girls clinging to their partners to avoid being swept beyond their power to protect them."

Following this exhausting affair Dickens was both amused and exasperated by the newspaper reports of his activities, which mingled "all manner of lies" with an occasional truth "so twisted and distorted that it has as much resemblance to the real facts as Quilp's leg to Taglioni's."

> Another paper . . . hugs itself and its readers upon all that Dickens saw; and winds up by gravely expressing its conviction that Dickens was never in such society in England as he has seen in New York, and that its high and striking tone cannot fail to make an indelible impression on his mind! For the same reason I am always represented, whenever I appear in public, as being "very pale"; "apparently thunderstruck"; and utterly confounded by all I see.

Hard upon the Boz Ball came the grand Dickens Dinner on Friday, the 18th. Washington Irving, who was to preside, dreaded the dire necessity of making a speech, and lamented in half-ludicrous, half-melancholy tones, "I shall certainly break down!" The dinner committee were dismayed by the hornets' nest Dickens had stirred up over copyright, and besought him "not to pursue the subject, *although they every one agreed with me*." But Dickens was unmoved. "I answered that I would. That nothing should deter me." Accordingly, putting the best face they could upon it, the committee resolved to support him by having Irving propose the sentiment "International Copyright" and Cornelius Mathews, the Editor of the *Arcturus*, reply with a speech defending it.

At the City Hotel, where the dinner was held, an unusual feature was the presence of a small coterie of ladies, Mrs Colden, her sister Miss Wilkes, Kate, and others, in a room adjoining the banquet hall. Gradually they edged their way into the main room and, by the time the speechmaking began, had taken possession of the stage behind the speakers' table. Irving began in his pleasant voice with two or three sentences comparing the other more able speakers, waiting their turns, to mounted knights eager for the tournament, and then went on to speak of this enthusiastic welcome to Dickens as representing a national homage to intellect. At this point one of his listeners broke in with a loud "Admirable! excellent!" which so threw Irving off his balance that he lost what he was going to say, stumbled, and gave up, concluding only with the words, "*Charles Dickens*, the literary guest of the nation." "There!" he said, as he fell back into his seat, "there! I told you I should break down, and I've done it."

Dickens, completely cool, made only a brief and mild allusion to the theme that had so worried the committee. Then he went on to speak in the warmest terms of Washington Irving. "Why, gentlemen, I don't go upstairs to bed two nights out of seven . . . without taking Washington Irving under my arm." Was there an English farm, an English city, or an English country seat where Knickerbocker and Geoffrey Crayon had not been? "Go farther still – go to the Moorish fountains, sparkling full in the moonlight," and would it not be found that he had "peopled the Alhambra, and made eloquent its shadows?" What pen but his had made Rip Van Winkle, playing at ninepins, a part of the Catskill Mountains? Dickens ended the speech with a graceful reference to Irving's having just been appointed Minister to Spain. America well knew, he said, "how to do honour to her own literature, and that of other lands," when she chose "Washington Irving for her representative in the country of Cervantes."

Cornelius Mathews, in his copyright speech, argued primarily for the welfare of American literature and American authors. That the profits on pirated books were stolen was too miserably obvious to need demonstration. But what was the effect on native letters, he asked, when unscrupulous publishers could snatch the writings of Ainsworth, Bulwer, Lever, and Dickens without the payment of a single penny? The "enormous fraud practised upon their British brethren" was also a blight upon a national literature.

This support for Dickens went almost entirely ignored in the New York newspapers. An exception was Horace Greeley's New York *Tribune*. On the very day of the Boz Ball, Greeley had come to Dickens's defence in a vigorous editorial. Who should protest against robbery if not those robbed? Did America look well offering Dickens "toasts, compliments, and other syllabub, while we refuse him naked justice?" Let the American people put their names to a petition for an international copyright law, and then they could honestly take Dickens's hand, instead of trying to bribe him from criticism with "acres of inflated compliments soaked in hogsheads of champagne."

On the Monday following the dinner, the *Tribune* not only printed Mathews's speech in full but supported it in a further editorial. The author had the same rights in his books, the *Tribune* declared, as the farmer in his wheat, the blacksmith in his axes, or the grazier in his ox. The robbery of foreign authors also meant the indigence of American authors. The agitation Dickens had started progressed to such effect that before he left New York he had in his portmanteau "a petition for an international copyright law, signed by all the best American writers with Washington Irving at their head." "So 'Hoo-roar for the principle, as the money-lender said, ven he vouldn't renoo the bill.' "

Dickens spent a total of three weeks in New York. Irving was an almost daily caller, and took him on a visit to Sunnyside, his picturesque home in Tarrytown. On another occasion Irving came to breakfast, together with Bryant and Halleck. "Good Heaven!" exclaimed the clerk at the Carlton, "to think what the four walls of that room now contain! Washington Irving, William Cullen Bryant, Fitz-Greene Halleck, and Charles Dickens!"

The devoted Felton, who had not been able to tear himself away, was still in New York. The two were together "daily and almost hourly," wrote Felton's friend Sam Ward, in a letter to Longfellow; "they have walked, laughed, talked, eaten Oysters and drunk Champagne together until they have almost grown together – in fact nothing but the interference of Madame D prevented their being attached to each other like the Siamese Twins, *a volume of Pickwick serving as connecting membrane.*"

These dissipations with Felton had not prevented Dickens from continuing his observation of American institutions. He was not as favourably impressed by those in New York as he had been by those in New England. The Lunatic Asylum was dirty, listless, bleak, and horribly overcrowded; the Alms House badly ventilated, badly lighted, and not too clean; the Island Jail, which he saw on a rainy day when the convicts could not work in the stone quarries, was filled with an odour like that of "a thousand old mildewed umbrellas wet through, and a thousand dirty clothes-bags, musty, moist, and fusty."

Escorted by two police officers, Dickens also made a night visit to the Five Points and its haunts of drunkenness, poverty, and vice. He noted rotten beams, broken windows, leprous houses sometimes attainable only by crazy outside steps, sometimes with pitch-dark stairs of trembling boards. There were other rooms suffocating with the stench of clothes and human flesh; alleys knee-deep in mud; dens where sailors and their girls, even as they drank and danced, rubbed shoulders with robbery and murder.

The Tombs prison, with its bastard Egyptian architecture, affected Dickens even more painfully than the slums. The noisome vapours and foul smell of the underground cells where drunkards were thrown overnight, the iron doors within which there was not even a drop of water, filled him with a disgust he found it impossible to repress. In a cell no larger than the wine cellar at Devonshire Terrace there were often, the night policeman told him, as many as twenty-six young women locked up together. In one cell Dickens saw a miserable-looking boy of ten or twelve. "What's *he* been doing?" he asked. "Nothing," said his guide. "Nothing!" said Dickens. "No," replied the officer. "He's here for safe keeping. He saw his father kill his mother, and is detained to give evidence." "But that's rather hard treatment for a witness, isn't it?" – "Well! I don't know. It ain't a very rowdy life, and *that's* a fact." Dickens had heard American prison discipline lauded in England, but if what he had now seen in New York was characteristic he felt that his homeland had little to learn about prison reform from America.

The glories of the New World Dickens had come to see were beginning to seem like those legendary inns mentioned by earlier travellers in America, "where they undercharge literary people for the love the landlords bear them." Dickens's own experience was one of monstrous overcharge. American hotels and hospitality, American enlightenment in public institutions, American freedom of opinion – none were quite so admirable upon further knowledge as they had seemed to the eye of buoyant enthusiasm. America had shown Dickens her most glowing face during the triumphant first two weeks at Boston. Slowly the shining dream was darkening into shapes of prison cruelty, slums as foul as Seven Dials at home, rude mobs, vulgar intruders, malignant newspaper abuse, and intolerance of criticism.

20

Not the Republic of
My Imagination

Dickens was delayed in leaving New York for Philadelphia until 8 March. By this time Kate was miserably homesick. Her only comfort was the portrait of the children, which was set up on a table or mantel-piece wherever they stayed. Her despondency was deepened by not having had any news of them. The *Caledonia*, on which they expected letters, had been twenty-four days at sea. Dickens was less distressed than Kate, but he too longed for word from England and shared her fears that the ship had gone down.

The trip to Philadelphia took six hours by train and involved two changes to ferries. It was Dickens's first considerable experience of American railway travel. He thought it neither as safe nor as comfort-able as in England. The unguarded tracks drove right through the main street of a large town "with pigs burrowing, and boys flying kites and playing marbles, and men smoking, and women talking, and children crawling, close to the very rails." Inside the coaches, Dickens noted, the windows were "usually all closed," and "a hot, close, most intolerable charcoal stove in a red-hot glow" rendered the heat so insupportable that he had a violent headache.

Spitting was revoltingly universal all over America.

> In the courts of law, the judge has his spittoon on the bench, the counsel have theirs, the witness has his, the prisoner his, and the crier his. The jury are accommodated at the rate of three men to a spittoon . . . I have twice seen gentlemen at evening parties in New York, turn aside when they were not engaged in conversation, and spit upon the drawing-room carpet. And in every bar-room and hotel passage the stone floor looks as if it were paved with open oysters – from the quantity of this kind of deposit which tesselates it all over.

Philadelphia Dickens found more provincial than either Boston or

New York. He made his usual survey of public institutions and attended an evening party given by the publisher Henry Carey. Edgar Allan Poe, who sent Dickens a copy of his *Tales of the Grotesque and Arabesque*, was invited to call at the United States Hotel. The strain in Dickens that gave rise to the eerie delusions of *Barnaby Rudge* and the "Madman's Manuscript" in *Pickwick* was not alien to the lunar, demon-ridden imagination of Poe, and Dickens had that in him too which responded to the melancholy spell of Poe's lost maidens. Impressed and moved by something in this American poet with the brilliant mind and haunted eyes, Dickens undertook to seek an English publisher for Poe on his return to London in July.

Two occurrences in Philadelphia sounded the discordant note that was beginning to reverberate through this American tour. Some gentlemen had written to ask if Dickens would receive their greetings; and on obtaining his assent, their spokesman promptly inserted a notice in the newspapers that Dickens would "shake hands with his friends" for an hour on the Tuesday before he went south. Six hundred people besieged the street in front of the hotel, and Dickens indignantly found he was expected to hold a "levee." There would be a riot, his terrified landlord told him, if he refused. For two mortal hours, therefore, he was forced to let his arm be almost shaken off. As a parting shot of American hospitality, the landlord of the United States Hotel not only charged for the six days' delay before they arrived – which Dickens thought quite right – but also billed him nine dollars a day for the meals he, Kate, and Anne had not eaten.

The train to Washington stopped for a short time in the market place at Baltimore. Instantly the windows were dark with staring heads thrust in and conveniently hooked on to the sills by elbows. A market woman began bawling to a friend, "What's the matter? What is it all about?" "Why," he replied, "they've got Boz here!" "Got Boz?" "Why," said the man, "it's Dickens. They've got him here!" "Well, what has he been doing?" "He ain't been doing nothin'," answered her friend; "he writes books." "Oh!" responded the woman indignantly. "Is that all? What do they make such a row about that for, I'd like to know!"

Dickens found the climate of Washington trying, and was no more impressed by its legislators than by those at Westminster. As he was to remind the readers of *American Notes*, he had never "been moved to tears of joyful pride, at the sight of any legislative body." He had borne the House of Commons "like a man" and "yielded to no weakness but slumber" in the House of Lords; had seen elections without "ever having been impelled (no matter which party won) to damage my hat by throwing it up into the air in triumph."

There were, to be sure, "a great many very remarkable men" in Congress: John Quincy Adams, Clay, Preston, Calhoun. "Adams is a fine old fellow – seventy-six years old, but with the most surprising vigour, memory, readiness, and pluck. Clay is perfectly enchanting; an irresistible man." But what a contrast were some of the others. Daniel Webster feigned "abstraction in the dreadful pressure of affairs of state" and rubbed his forehead wearily in "a sublime caricature of Lord Burleigh." A member of the House of Representatives, who had made a violent speech attacking England, was an evil-visaged man looking "as if he had been suckled, Romulus-like, by a wolf," and "with a great ball of tobacco in his left cheek." Another member, when called to order, replied, "Damn your eyes, Sir, if you presume to call me to order, I'll cut your damnation throat from ear to ear."

Some things Dickens saw he failed to understand the significance of through ignorance of their background. He was shocked, for example, at the hard words that assailed John Quincy Adams for presenting petitions against slavery to Congress. He did not know that the House of Representatives had in 1836 refused to receive any further petitions about slavery, and that Adams, regarding this "gagging" resolution as unconstitutional, was rousing a tremendous storm of public approval by his calculated policy of defiance. Dickens didn't realize that "the old gentleman . . . was deliberately provoking the bad manners of his opponents because of their propaganda value with the electorate at large."

The morning after Dickens's arrival in Washington, he had a private audience with President John Tyler. In the reception hall at the White House and in the blue and silver drawing-room a number of gentlemen – "mostly with their hats on, and their hands in their pockets," Dickens observed – were strolling about; others "lounging on the chairs and sofas; others, yawning and picking their teeth . . . A few were eyeing the movables as if to make quite sure that the President (who is not popular) hadn't made away with any of the furniture, or sold the fixtures for his private benefit." "They all constantly squirted forth upon the carpet a yellow saliva which quite altered its pattern; and even the few who did not indulge in this recreation, expectorated abundantly."

A Negro servant in plain clothes and yellow slippers disappeared to announce Dickens to the President, and returned in five minutes to conduct him into the office. Here, "by the side of a hot stove, though it was a very hot day, sat the President – all alone; and close to him a great spit box . . ." The President rose, and said, "Is *this* Mr Dickens?" "Sir, it is." "I am astonished to see so young a man, Sir," said the President. Dickens thought of returning the compliment, but the President looked so worn and jaded "that it stuck in my throat like Macbeth's amen." "I am happy to join with my fellow citizens, warmly, in welcoming you to this country," said the President. The two men shook hands. Then they sat and looked at each other until Dickens rose, observing that doubtless the President's time was fully occupied and that he had better go.

On Sunday, Dickens and Kate had dinner with ex-President John Quincy Adams, and the courtly old man gave Kate his word to send her a "sentiment" written in his own hand, a promise that he kept three days later:

> *There is a greeting of the heart*
> *Which words cannot reveal –*
> *How, Lady, shall I then impart*
> *The sentiment I feel?*
> *How, in one word combine the spell*
> *Of joy and sorrow too?*
> *And mark the bosom's mingled swell*
> *Of welcome! and Adieu!*

That evening they learned that the long-awaited *Caledonia* had safely arrived, and the following night their letters came. They read exultantly until nearly two in the morning, and decided, Dickens told Forster, "that humorous narrative is your forte, and not statesmen of the commonwealth." And what marvellous tales there were of Charley's precocity at a Twelfth-Night party for children at Macready's, and the governess's dark hints that he had got out of pothooks and hangers and might write a letter any day now, and similar predictions about his sisters, "very gladdening to their mother's heart, and not at all depressing to their father's."

Henry Clay had dissuaded Dickens from his original plan of going on to Charleston. The country, Clay told him, was nothing but dismal swamp, the weather was intensely hot there, and the spring fever was coming on. Dickens had determined, however, that he must see Richmond and some of the tobacco plantations before he turned his face west across the Alleghenies. Washington Irving, who had come to the

Capital to receive his instructions as Minister to Spain, and who did not expect to see Dickens again before setting sail, saw him in a farewell meeting, "and *wept heartily* at parting."

A resolute abolitionist, Dickens had recoiled from having to accept the services of slaves even in Baltimore, where slavery existed, he said, "in its least repulsive and most mitigated form." His flesh crawled with moral revulsion during the entire three days that he spent in Virginia. As they passed deserted plantations with rotting barns and decaying houses, Putnam explained that this barren ground was once "the garden of America." "Great God!" Dickens exclaimed. "Kate, just hear what Mr Putnam says! These lands were once cultivated and have been abandoned because they were worn out by slave labour!"

In the black car on the train that conveyed them from Fredericksburg to Richmond there were a Negro mother and children who were weeping the whole way. "Them damn niggers," said a bluff, well-dressed man; "somebody has bought them and is taking them down to Richmond, and they are making a fuss about it." They were being sold away from the husband and father. No wonder, Dickens felt, that under so hideous and accursed a system Richmond had an atmosphere "of decay and gloom" that the planters themselves admitted to be characteristic of towns in the slave district, "deplorable tenements, fences unrepaired, walls crumbling into ruinous heaps."

He was glad to turn his back on it.

I really don't think I could have borne it any longer [he wrote Forster]. It is all very well to say "be silent on the subject." They won't let you be silent. They *will* ask you what you think of it; and *will* expatiate on slavery as if it were one of the greatest blessings of mankind. "It's not," said a hard, bad-looking fellow to me the other day, "it's not the interest of a man to use his slaves ill. It's damned nonsense you hear in England."

– I told him quietly [Dickens went on – and no doubt he believed that he said it quietly, feeling twelve feet tall –] that it was not a man's interest to get drunk, or to steal, or to game, or to indulge in any other vice, but he did indulge in it for all that. That cruelty, and the abuse of irresponsible power, were two of the bad passions of human nature, with the gratification of which, considerations of interest or of ruin had nothing whatever to do; and that, while every candid man must admit that even a slave might be happy enough with a good master, all human beings knew that bad masters, cruel masters, and masters who disgraced the form they bore, were matters of experience and history, whose existence was as undisputed as that of slaves themselves.

Pausing in Baltimore before proceeding on the western part of his journey, Dickens relieved his mind of all his accumulated disillusion in a long letter to Macready. "This is not the republic I came to see; this is not the republic of my imagination. . . . In everything of which it has made a boast – excepting its education of the people and its care for poor children – it sinks immeasurably below the level I had placed it upon; and England, even England, bad and faulty as the old land is, and miserable as millions of her people are, rises in comparison." Where was freedom of opinion in America?

I see a press more mean, and paltry, and silly, and disgraceful than any country I ever knew. . . . I speak of Bancroft, and am advised to be silent on that subject, for he is "a black sheep – a democrat." I speak of Bryant, and am entreated to be more careful – for the same reason. I speak of international copyright, and am implored not to ruin myself outright. I speak of Miss Martineau, and all parties – Slave Upholders and Abolitionists, Whigs, Tyler Whigs, and Democrats, shower down upon her a perfect cataract of abuse. "But what has she done? Surely she praised America enough!" "Yes, but she told us some of our faults, and Americans can't bear to be told of their faults."

Macready should not think Dickens's observations had been one-sided.

The people are affectionate, generous, open-hearted, hospitable, enthusiastic, good-humoured, polite to women, frank and candid to all strangers, anxious to oblige, far less prejudiced than they have been described to be, frequently polished and refined, very seldom rude or disagreeable. . . . I have seen none of that greediness and indecorum on which travellers have laid so much emphasis. I have . . . not spoken to one man, woman, or child of any degree who has not grown positively affectionate before we parted. In the respects of not being left alone, and of being horribly disgusted by tobacco chewing and tobacco spittle, I have suffered considerably. The sight of slavery in Virginia; the hatred of British feeling on the subject; and the miserable hints of the impotent indignation of the South have pained me very much . . .

Though Dickens had formed a warm attachment, as he gladly admitted, to many Americans, and though he had been given a public progress through the land unequalled even by Lafayette's, he had discovered that he was an Englishman after all with "a yearning after our English customs and English manners." He had bought an accordion to take the place of the one he had borrowed on the *Britannia*, and played "Home, Sweet Home" every night now with a pleasant feeling of sadness. He thought tenderly of Forster and all his kindnesses. "What an unspeakable source of delight" was the pocket Shakespeare his friend had given him in parting at Liverpool!

A small delay in Baltimore enabled Washington Irving to join him for another farewell. The two men dined together in Dickens's rooms at Barnum's Hotel and afterwards they shared "a most enormous mint julep, wreathed with flowers," which had been sent Dickens that day by a Philadelphia admirer. "The julep held out far into the night," and Dickens always remembered Irving "bending over it, with his straw, with an attempted gravity (after some anecdote, involving some wonderfully droll and delicate observation of character) and then as his eye caught mine, melting into that captivating laugh of his, which was the brightest and best that I have ever heard."

Early next morning Dickens and his party were on the train for York. Kate looked forward with mute despair to the rough travelling that lay ahead of them. At York they all transferred into a tremendous rumbling stagecoach drawn by four horses, "a kind of barge on wheels," shaking its sides like a corpulent giant. From Harrisburg they went on to Pittsburgh by canal boat. At night the cabin was separated by a red curtain into a ladies' section and a gentlemen's section. Dickens slept on a shelf sixteen inches wide, with one man below him and another above, twenty-eight of them packed into a tiny room too low to stand upright in with a hat on.

You can never conceive [Dickens wrote Forster] what the hawking and spitting is, the whole night through. *Upon my honour and word* I was obliged, this morning, to lay my fur-coat on the deck, and wipe the half-dried flakes of spittle from it with my handkerchief: and the only surprise seemed to be, that I should consider it necessary to do so.

I am looked upon as highly facetious at night, for I crack jokes with everybody near me until we fall asleep. I am considered very hardy in the morning, for I run up, bare-necked, and plunge my head into the half-frozen water, by half-past five o'clock. I am respected for my activity, inasmuch as I jump from the boat to the towing-path, and walk five or six miles before breakfast; keeping up with the horses all the time. In a word, they are quite astonished to find a sedentary Englishman roughing it so well, and taking so much exercise; and question me very much on that head. The greater part of the men will sit and shiver round the stove all day rather than put one foot before the other. As to having a window open, that's not to be thought of.

The scenery of southern Pennsylvania, Dickens thought, was very grand, with the canal winding through deep and sullen moonlit gorges, though it did not approach the terror of Glencoe. But the forlorn poverty of the new settlements and the detached log houses depressed him. It pained his eye to see the never ending morass and swamp, with rotting stumps and trunks sunk in the unwholesome water, and the great tracts where settlers had burned down the trees, leaving their wounded bodies lying about like murdered creatures, with here and there some charred giant writhing two bare blackened arms aloft.

Pittsburgh, its townsfolk said, was like Birmingham, and it was indeed dark with smoke. At the "levee" to which he and Kate were subjected wherever they went, as if they were royalty, one man with his trousers imperfectly buttoned stood behind the door and another "with one eye and one fixed gooseberry" stood in a corner "like an eight-day clock" and glared throughout the entire reception.

They were going on by river steamer, down the Ohio and thence up the Mississippi to St Louis, and Kate expressed alarm at the danger of a boiler explosion. The steamboats were hardly more than long low barges with paddle-wheels and exposed furnaces glaring and roaring in the midst of a frail jumble of staterooms whose roofs were black with burnt-out sparks falling red-hot from the high chimneys. Dickens, however, was delighted to find that their tiny stateroom opened on a narrow gallery where he could sit undisturbed by the other passengers and gaze upon the landscape.

"The washing department" was a little better than it had been on the canal boat, where there was only dirty water dipped out of the canal by a tin ladle. But even on the steamer, it seemed to Dickens, the ladies were "content with smearing their hands and faces in a very small quantity of water." So were the men, who added to that skimpy mode of washing "a hasty use of the common brush and comb."

Dickens could not spend all his time in his stateroom, and the periods when he had to mingle with his fellow passengers convinced him that there were not on all the rest of the earth "so many intensified bores as in these United States." There was "a horrible New Englander with a droning voice like a gigantic bee" who insisted on sitting by him, droning and snuffling poetry, small philosophy, and metaphysics, and who never would be quiet. There was a weazen-faced, pigeon-breasted old general who was even worse and was "perhaps *the* most horrible bore in this country."

Meanwhile the *Messenger* glided dreamily down the Ohio, past green islands and deep solitudes unbroken by any sign of life except the bright flash of the blue jay. At long intervals a log cabin sent a thread of smoke into the sky. On the river's banks fallen trees bathed their green heads in the stream and put forth new shoots and branches. At night sometimes there would be a place where tall trees were burning, seeming to vegetate in fire against the dark.

Cincinnati was a beautiful place, Dickens said, that had risen out of the forest like an Arabian Nights city, with pretty villas, turf-plots, and well-kept gardens. He liked Judge Timothy Walker, who gave an evening party for him, but the party consisted of "at least one hundred and fifty first-rate bores. . . . I really think my face has acquired a fixed expression of sadness from the constant and unmitigated boring I endure. . . . There is a line in my chin (on the right side of the under-lip) indelibly fixed there by the New Englander . . . A dimple has vanished from my cheek, which I felt myself robbed of at the time by a wise legislator."

The *Messenger* had gone on while Dickens and Kate stayed overnight in Cincinnati. Next morning they took the *Pike* on to Louisville. Here they slept at the Galt House, "a splendid hotel," said Dickens, where they "were as handsomely lodged as though we had been in Paris, rather than hundreds of miles beyond the Alleghanies." Two mornings later they were nearing the junction of the Ohio and the Mississippi. Passing the swampy and fever-plagued hamlet of Cairo – on which Dickens later drew for the creation of "Eden" in *Martin Chuzzlewit* – they came upon the slimy Mississippi eddying its strong current of liquid mud through an enormous tree-choked ditch three miles across. For two days they toiled up this monstrous stream, striking constantly against floating timbers, and stopping repeatedly at night, whenever the lookout rang a bell, to avoid the dangerous snags that might rip a hole in the hull. On the fourth night after leaving Louisville, they reached St Louis, the westernmost point of Dickens's journey.

21

Twenty Feet High

The Planters House, in St Louis, Dickens found as large as London's Middlesex Hospital, with long corridors and plain whitewashed walls, and transoms above the doors to aid in the circulation of air. "They had a famous notion," he wrote Forster, "of sending up at breakfast time large glasses of new milk with blocks of ice in them as clear as crystal. Our table was abundantly supplied indeed at every meal. One day when Kate and I were dining alone together, in our own room, we counted sixteen dishes on the table at the same time."

After a day of sightseeing among the gables, blinking casements, and tumbledown galleries of the French quarter, and the wharves, warehouses, and new buildings in the American sections, Dickens wanted to see the prairie. His hosts accordingly arranged an overnight expedition to Looking Glass Prairie. Starting out at seven in the morning, they ferried across the river into Illinois. All morning their vehicles wallowed through deep mud until around noon they reached the village of Belleville.

This was a flourishing town with brick and stone houses fully 100 feet above the river, whose inhabitants were mightily to resent Dickens's describing it in *American Notes* as "a small collection of wooden houses, huddled in the very heart of the bush and swamp." What Dickens saw as a forest path, with hitching posts for their horses, was the public square; and the hotel that he remembered as a compromise between a cowshed and a kitchen was in fact the Mansion House, a two-storey brick structure only three years old at the time.

At Belleville there was an impromptu reception lasting half an hour while they waited for dinner. The curious citizens were disappointed in the unpretentious appearance Dickens made in a linen blouse and a great straw hat with green ribbons, with his "face and nose profusely ornamented with the stings of mosquitoes and the bites of bugs." He gave only curt and commonplace answers to their remarks, and it was plain that he was bored with them. After a meal of "wheatbread and chicken fixings," the party rode on in time to see the prairie at sunset.

The great plain, Dickens said, was like a sea without water, bare and lonely, with only a few birds wheeling in the empty air. The sun was descending, red and bright, in a glowing sky. As the colours of the twilight mingled richly, they encamped for a picnic dinner: "roast fowls, buffalo's tongue, ham, bread, cheese, butter, biscuits," Dickens wrote Forster, and "sherry, champagne, lemons, and sugar for punch, and abundance of ice."

In St Louis, as the most remote western point of his travels, Dickens made an exception to his rule of not accepting any public entertainment. On the evening of his return from Looking Glass Prairie there was a soirée at the Planters House. "Of course the paper had an account of it. If I were to drop a letter in the street, it would be in the newspaper the next day, and nobody would think its publication an outrage. The editor objected to my hair, as not curling sufficiently. He admitted an eye; but objected again to dress, as being somewhat foppish, 'and indeed perhaps rather flash.' "

In the slave state of Missouri Dickens found himself embroiled in arguments about slavery once more. They wouldn't let him alone about it, he protested. "They say the slaves are fond of their masters," he went on. That, of course, was why the newspapers were full of advertisements for runaway slaves. That was why nine out of ten of these advertisements described the runaway as chained, manacled, mutilated, maimed, or branded. The Negroes worshipped England because of her leadership in emancipation; "and *of course* their attachment to us grows out of their deep devotion to their owners."

On the evening of 14 April, Dickens gladly embarked for his return east, and the next morning even more gladly passed the yellow line where the slimy Mississippi absorbed the clear Ohio. Four nights later, around one o'clock, they reached Cincinnati, where they groped through the darkness among labyrinths of engine machinery and leaking molasses barrels. Stumbling among these obstacles, and making their way over broken pavements, Kate had troubles evidently not unfamiliar to her even in more accustomed surroundings, and multiplied many times by the strange hazards of her American experiences:

"– You recollect her propensity?" Dickens asked Forster. "She falls into, or out of, every coach or boat we enter; scrapes the skin off her legs; brings great sores and swellings on her feet; chips large fragments out of her ankle-bones; and makes herself blue with bruises." But he pays tribute to Kate's endeavours to deal with her difficulties: "She really has, however, since we got over the first trial of being among circumstances so new and so fatiguing, made a *most admirable* traveller in every respect. She has never screamed or expressed alarm under circumstances that would have fully justified her in doing so, even in my eyes;" – this last phrase is significant – "has never given way to despondency or fatigue, though we have now been travelling incessantly, through a very rough country . . . has always accommodated herself, well and cheerfully, to everything; and has pleased me very much, and proved herself perfectly game."

Kate's gameness, however, was soon subjected to more painful trials. All the next day and night they travelled by stagecoach the 120 miles from Cincinnati to Columbus, Kate sitting on the back seat and being showered all night, in spite of Putnam's efforts to screen her, by flying tobacco spittle from a well-dressed man in the middle. As there was no stagecoach next day, Dickens hired for their private use one of the regular four-horse coaches, "an extra," to convey them towards Sandusky. They took a basket lunch of cold meats, fruit, and wine, and set out in high spirits at being by themselves. The road, however, unlike the macadamized highway they had travelled the day before, was a track through swamp and forest, a great portion of it a "corduroy road" of tree trunks left to settle down in the bog.

Dickens tied a handkerchief to the doorpost on each side for Kate to hang on to and brace herself. He and Putnam kept a lookout, giving a warning yell of "Corduroy!" at each yawning hole that they saw. In spite of these precautions the ride was harrowing. "Now the coach flung us in a heap on its floor, and now crushed our heads against its roof. . . . Still, the day was beautiful, the air delicious, and we were *alone*, with no tobacco spittle, or eternal prosy conversation about dollars and politics (the only two subjects they ever converse about, or can converse about) to bore us."

At two o'clock they stopped in the forest to open their hamper. After lunch there was more of the terrific bumping to be endured, but at last they got through the swamp and left the corduroy road behind. Towards eleven o'clock the guard began to sound his horn to arouse the people at the log tavern in Lower Sandusky where they were to spend the night.

The doors of their room, opening on opposite sides to the black wild country, were constantly blowing open. Dickens was concerned because he had £250 in gold in his dressing case, a sum for a small fraction of

which there were "men in the West who would murder their fathers."
Forster should have seen him, he said, in his nightshirt, trying to
blockade the doors with portmanteaus!

Putnam went to bed under the rafters, where another man was
already snoring loudly. He found his mattress swarming with bedbugs
and the night grew piercingly cold. But all the wraps were in Dickens's
barricaded room, so at last he took refuge in the coach. It was not very
warm, and pigs "grunted round it so hideously that he was afraid to
come out again, and lay there shivering, till morning." When Kate
emerged to wash in the tin basin near the door, "Oh, Mr Putnam,"
she exclaimed, "I have been almost devoured by the bugs!" Putnam
then told his own experience. "Charles! Charles! just come here,"
Kate called, "and listen to what Mr Putnam suffered last night!" and
Putnam repeated his story while at the image of him besieged by the
pigs they were torn between sympathy and helpless laughter.

To Dickens, in fact, his solemn New England secretary was a source
of endless amusement. Putnam wore a cloak, "like Hamlet; and a very
tall, big, limp, dusty black hat, which he exchanges on long journeys
for a cap like Harlequin's." He sang, and could often be heard "grunt-
ing bass notes through the keyhole" to attract their attention. He
imitated cows and pigs, and was in the habit of telling "the most
notorious and patriarchal Joe Miller, as something that happened in
his family." He painted, blazing away from an enormous box of oil
colours, and produced a "big-headed, pot-bellied" sketch of Dickens
in his fur coat "which brings the tears into my eyes at this minute."

Nevertheless Dickens also found Putnam indispensably useful. He
took care of all the mass of correspondence from strangers, sifting out
for Dickens's attention only those letters that required a personal reply.
He made advance arrangements for transportation and lodgings,
settled with landlords, and took "such care of the luggage and all
other matters," Dickens wrote, "that I walk into and out of every
coach, car, wagon, boat, and barge, as if I had nothing with me but one
shirt, and that were in my pocket." "I could not by possibility have
lighted on any one who would have suited my purposes so well. I
have raised his ten dollars per month to twenty; and mean to make it
up for six months."

Putnam was quite unaware of these responses to his personality. Mrs
Dickens, with her waving brown hair, her blue eyes melting into violet,
and her small sweet mouth, he thought beautiful, and felt in her a
gentle dignity strikingly different from the "quick, earnest, always

cheerful, but keen and nervous temperament of her husband." He had unbounded admiration for his generous, brilliant, and high-spirited employer, and never ceased to wonder at Dickens's capacity for transforming the vexations of travel into hilarity.

Irritations did not cease, however, up to the very end of their journey. While the boat conveying them from Sandusky to Buffalo stopped overnight at Cleveland, among those streaming on board to see them was "a party of 'gentlemen' " their elbows on the window-sill of the Dickens cabin who stared in "*while I was washing, and Kate lay in bed.*" When the Mayor came on board, Dickens refused to see him.

During the two-hour train ride from Buffalo to Niagara, Dickens was tense with excitement to come within sound and sight of the Falls. "At last, when the train stopped, I saw two great white clouds rising up from the depths of the earth – nothing more. They rose up slowly, gently, majestically, into the air." The travellers clambered down a steep path to the ferry and were soon blinded by the spray and wet to the skin. "I saw the water tearing madly down from some immense height, but could get no idea of shape, or situation, or anything but vague immensity." Only in the very basin did his imagination begin to take in the enormous spectacle. "The broad, deep, mighty stream seems to die in the act of falling; and, from its unfathomable grave, arises that tremendous ghost of spray and mist which is never laid, and has been haunting this place with the same dread solemnity – perhaps from the creation of the world."

With one of his volatile changes from grave to gay, Dickens was amused to note the unimpressed indifference of Kate's maid. Neither Niagara nor, indeed, any scene in all America had excited her in any way. "I don't think Anne has so much as seen an American tree," Dickens wrote. "She objects to Niagara that 'it's nothing but water,' and considers that 'there is too much of that.' " Unmoved by an entire continent, Anne merely maintained her calm level of efficiency, and sustained Kate through all the afflictions of travelling, including the 743 falls that Dickens estimated she had had in going aboard boats and getting in and out of coaches.

At Buffalo Dickens had received from Forster the memorial from a group of English authors in support of his copyright stand. Signed by a dozen distinguished names, including Bulwer, Tennyson, Talfourd, Rogers, Leigh Hunt, and Sydney Smith, it made a dignified appeal for protecting American men of letters from piratical competition, and argued that such a course would ultimately serve in every way the best interests of the American reading public. Carlyle wrote a separate letter emphasizing the commandment, "Thou shalt not steal." Doubtless publishers found it more convenient, he asserted, to take without paying. So had Rob Roy found it more convenient to steal cattle from the glens than to buy beef from the Stirling markets.

Dickens wrote to Felton in Boston, asking his advice on the publication of these documents. Would it be a good idea to send one copy to a Boston newspaper, one to Bryant's New York *Evening Post*, another to the New York *Herald* (because of its large circulation), and a fourth to the *National Intelligencer* in Washington? On 9 May the memorial and its accompanying letters appeared in the New York *Evening Post* and around the same time in other papers.

As Dickens thought of the abuse and intimidations that had sought to prevent his even speaking on the subject, his heart swelled with pugnacious exultation. Was it not "a horrible thing that scoundrel booksellers should grow rich" from books whose authors received not a farthing, and that every "detestable newspaper, so filthy and bestial that no honest man would admit one into his house for a water-closet door-mat," might publish these stolen writings cheek to jowl with its own obscenities? Was it tolerable that they should make him a party to cheating the best men in America out of the just rewards of their writings? His blood so boiled at these enormities that he felt eight feet taller than he had when he previously denounced them, and now seemed "to grow twenty feet high, and to swell out in proportion."

Meanwhile the book-publishing interests had grown alarmed at the agitation Dickens had aroused. At a convention in Boston they appealed to Congress, not only protesting against the passage of any international copyright law, but asking that a duty be imposed on foreign books. Furthermore, they coolly remarked that to give English authors control over the republication of their own books in America would render it impossible "for American editors to *alter and adapt them to American taste*."

Flagrantly dishonest though the booksellers' arguments were, Dickens speedily realized that they were going to win the day. (It was not in fact until he had been twenty-one years in his grave that the United States entered into an international copyright agreement with Great Britain.) Smarting at his defeat and the abuse he had endured, Dickens relieved his feelings in a final angry outburst to Forster. "I'll tell you what the two obstacles to the passing of an international copyright law with England are: firstly, the national love of 'doing' a man

in any bargain or matter of business; secondly the national vanity."
And those who were above such dishonesty were reconciled by the
belief that an author should take pride in the mere fact of being liked in
America. "The Americans read him; the free, enlightened, independent Americans; and what more *would* he have?" "As to telling
them they will have no literature of their own, the universal answer
(out of Boston) is, 'We don't want one. Why should we pay for one
when we can get it for nothing. Our people don't think of poetry, sir.
Dollars, banks, and cotton are our books, sir.' "

For all his disappointment, though, how much there still was that
he could praise about America, and how many noble friends he had
made! Longfellow, Prescott, Sumner, Irving, and dear Felton! "David
Colden is as good a fellow as ever lived," he wrote Macready; "and I
am deeply in love with his wife." To Colden himself, from Niagara,
Dickens sent "all manner of loves to you and yours," and enclosed a
burlesque love letter for Mrs Colden – who was forty-six, a few months
older than her husband and sixteen years older than Dickens – address-
ing her as "My Better Angel."

"If this should meet *HIS* eye, I trust you to throw dust in the same.
HIS suspicions must not be aroused. *HE* says that I have applied
tender epithets to a certain Mrs D. I repel the charge with indignation.
Alas his motive is but too apparent! . . . *HE IS A SERPENT*. You are
the Bride of a Scorpion."

Despite the playful gaiety of these letters to American friends, as
Dickens started for Montreal on the last leg of his tour, he was glad to
find himself on Canadian soil. "English kindness is very different from
American," he wrote. "People send their horses and carriages for your
use, but they don't exact as payment the right of being always under
your nose." "You cannot conceive with what transports of joy, I beheld
an English Sentinel – though he didn't look much like one, I confess,
with his boots outside his trousers, and a great fur cap on his head. I
was taken dreadfully loyal after dinner, and drank the Queen's health
in a bumper . . ."

Nevertheless Dickens did not blind himself to the fact that there
were defects north as well as south of the border. He was shocked to
find that albums carefully preserved at Table Rock, in which visitors
inscribed "remarks and poetical effusions," were scrawled with filthy
ribaldries and obscenity. He was appalled by the rabid toryism in
Toronto, and by political animosities so violent that the successful
candidates in a recent election had been shot at. Unlike the inns in the

United States, so many of which even in the wilderness were surprisingly good, those in Canada were generally vile; indeed, Rasco's Hotel, in Montreal, was "the worst in the whole wide world."

After a trip through the Thousand Islands, shooting the rapids of the river, Dickens and Kate reached Lachine by the afternoon of 11 May, and thence had proceeded by land the last nine miles to Montreal. Here there was a reunion with the Earl of Mulgrave, who on leaving Boston had gone on to Canada. Arrangements had been made for Dickens to join Lord Mulgrave and the officers of the garrison in a theatrical performance for the benefit of a local charity. Dickens promptly became stage manager of the company and started rehearsals with a violence of enthusiasm.

The comedy they were doing was Morton's *A Roland for an Oliver*, followed by Mathews's interlude *Past Two O'Clock in the Morning*, and Poole's farce *Deaf as a Post*. Dickens played in all three, taking successively the parts of Alfred Highflyer, Mr Snobbington, and Gallop. The performance took place on 25 May at the Theatre Royal, renamed for this one night only the Queen's Theatre. The evening was a brilliant success. "The audience, between five and six hundred, were invited as to a party; a regular table with refreshments being spread in the lobby and saloon." "I really do believe that I was very funny," Dickens wrote Forster: "at least I know that I laughed heartily at myself"; and everything "went with a roar." The private performance was followed on Saturday by a public one, before a paying audience, substituting professional actresses for the ladies who had taken part.

One aspect of the evening's triumph occasioned Dickens considerable surprise. "Only think of Kate playing!" he exclaimed in a letter to Forster, "and playing devilish well, I assure you!" In the playbill that he sent Forster, Dickens inscribed the names of the actors opposite those of the roles they played, and when he came to Amy Templeton in *Deaf as a Post* wrote in "Mrs Charles Dickens" and slapped down no fewer than eight exclamation points after it.

Their experiences on the *Britannia* had determined Dickens to return to England by a sailing packet, not a steamship. At night, on the steamers, you saw solid fire two or three feet above the top of the funnel; if it were blown down by a gale the entire boat "must instantly be on fire, from stem to stern." He had consequently engaged passage on the *George Washington*, sailing from New York on 7 June and now gratefully accepted David Colden's offer to see that he had two connecting staterooms on that ship.

Dickens arrived in New York quivering with anticipation. There was a final excursion to the Shaker Village at Lebanon and to West Point, returning through those landmarks that Washington Irving had endeared to Dickens's imagination, the Catskill Mountains, Sleepy Hollow, and the Tappan Zee. On the bright, breezy morning of 7 June, the Coldens gave him and Kate a farewell breakfast. Then, with all their luggage, and a little white Havana spaniel named Timber Doodle, which had been presented to Dickens, they drove to Jersey City, whence they embarked on the steamer that was to take them to the *George Washington*, lying off Sandy Hook. Between decks on this vessel they joined a large company in a cold collation, champagne, and farewell speeches.

From Montreal Dickens had sent a last letter to Forster. "God bless you, my dear friend. As the time draws nearer, we get FEVERED with anxiety for home . . . Kiss our darlings for us. We shall soon meet, please God, and be happier and merrier than ever we were, in all our lives . . . Oh home – home – home – home – home – home – HOME!!!!!!!!!!!"

22

Home Again:
Valedictory on America

During the whole of the voyage home Dickens was uproarious with hilarity. He established with three lively companions a maniacal association called the United Vagabonds, at whose antics their steward lived for the entire three weeks in one broad grin. The captain being ill when they were a few days out, Dickens solemnly produced his medicine chest and "recovered" him. After that Dickens roamed "the wards" every day, accompanied by two Vagabonds, dressed as Ben Allen and Bob Sawyer, "bearing enormous rolls of plaster and huge pairs of scissors." On the twenty-second morning, they were in the harbour of Liverpool, there was a farewell breakfast on shore, and then Dickens was on the railroad tearing through the green fields and leafy hedgerows.

At Devonshire Terrace, brought back from the Macreadys' by Fred, the children were wild with joy. Charley fell into violent convulsions from being, as he told his mother, "too glad," and after he had recovered Dr Elliotson informed the parents he had never seen the like in a child. From these excitements with the children, Dickens hurried off to see Macready in Clarence Terrace. The two friends immediately embraced each other in a transport of delight. Thence Dickens rushed away to see Forster, who was dining out, but who guessed at once who it was when Dickens sent up word that a gentleman wished to speak to him. Forster came flying out of the house, leaped into the carriage, and began to cry, and did not remember until they had driven several miles on their way to see Maclise that he had left his hat behind.

Saturday of the following week there was a festive reunion dinner at Greenwich, with Captain Marryat in the chair and Jerdan as vice-chairman. Talfourd and Macready were unable to be there, but Ainsworth, Forster, Maclise, Stanfield, Cruikshank, and Cattermole gathered together with Procter, Barham, Father Prout, Tom Hood,

Dr Elliotson, and a number of others to welcome Dickens home. Songs and healths followed each other in such numbers that "Cruikshank came home in my phaeton on his head," Dickens reported, "– to the great delight of the loose midnight loungers in Regent Street," and "was last seen, taking Gin with a Waterman."

During the next fortnight Dickens buoyantly renewed relations with scores of friends and acquaintances: Landor, Jeffrey, Rogers, Mrs Norton and her sister Lady Seymour, "both sights for the Gods, as they have always been," Lady Blessington, wearing brilliantly and with "the gloss upon her, yet," Sydney Smith, "in greater force than ever, though waxing gouty." Dickens wrote Lady Holland, sending her a volume of American poetry and an eagle's feather from Niagara Falls, and called on her in the middle of July. Lord Holland was dead now, but the dauntless old creature had fitted up some rooms on the lower floor of Holland House and gave dinners as of yore.

Dickens had learned on his return to London that one of the old Whig newspapers, the *Courier*, had suspended publication. Had he known in time, he wrote Lady Holland, he would have proposed to the leaders of the Liberal Party that they save the paper, "nailing the true colours to the mast, and fighting the battle staunchly," with himself as editor. Would Lady Holland like to ask Lord Melbourne and Lord Lansdowne if the Liberals would give financial backing to such an enterprise? But the statesmen Lady Holland spoke to said no, and Dickens reluctantly agreed that they might be right. Nevertheless, he regretted it when he thought of what a newspaper he might have created, and saw how editorial writers left untouched the very issues that concerned people's "business and bosoms most."

Putting aside these reflections, however, he was soon industriously at work on his *American Notes*. He borrowed from Forster, Maclise, Beard, Mitton, and Fonblanque the letters that he had written them during his journey, to profit from their spontaneity of observation. Rapidly he dashed off an opening chapter and an impressionistic description of that wild January voyage across the Atlantic. Before the end of July the "Boston" chapter was written. It was a wonderful relief to be in his old room, with his books, surrounded by battledores and shuttlecocks, bats and balls, dumb-bells, and little Timber Doodle, looking out with bright eyes from an ambush of white hair.

Nothing could exceed Dickens's delight in his children or their delight in him. When he felt like defying his after-breakfast schedule of work, they played long riotous games in the garden. And before they went to bed Dickens would sit in the American rocking chair he had brought back from the States, singing comic songs to a giggling childish audience: "The Loving Ballad of Lord Bateman" and one about "Guy Fawkes, that prince of sinisters, who once blew up the House of Lords, the King, and all his ministers."

> Crossing over Vauxhall Bridge,
> He that way came to London.
> That is he would have come that way
> To perpetrate his guilt, Sir,
> But a little thing prevented him,
> The bridge it wasn't built, Sir.

His American friends were not forgotten in the joy of homecoming. To Colden, Felton, and others, Dickens sent lively letters. To Mrs Colden, he wrote, "It is more clear to me than ever that Kate is as near being a Donkey as one of that sex whose luminary and sun you are, *can* be." For had she not written about the *Great Western* sailing for England on the fourteenth in a letter that could not possibly reach the Coldens before the sixteenth? Nevertheless, he wished, "sweet Foreigner," that "you would come and live next door; for the best part of my heart is in Laight Street, and I find it difficult to get on without it." "God bless you," he concluded, "– and – yes – and even – *Him*."

During the summer Dickens toiled steadily at *American Notes*. By the middle of August, in Broadstairs, he was blazing away at New York. From the window where he wrote, he could see little Charley "digging up the sand on the shore with a small spade, and compressing it into a perfectly impossible wheelbarrow." The little dog was being taught to leap over a stick, "and jumps, as Mr Kenwigs would say, perpetivally." His name had been changed to Snittle Timbery, and all the children had been fitted out with new nicknames. Charley was Flaster Floby, a corruption of Master Toby; quiet Mamey was Mild Glo'ster; the fiery-tempered Katey Lucifer Box; and baby Walter, from his high cheek-bones, Young Skull.

The seductions of these summer days often made it difficult for Dickens to work. "I have been reading Tennyson all the morning on the seashore," he wrote. "Among other trifling effects, the waters have dried up as they did of old, and shown me all the mermen and mermaids at the bottom of the ocean; together with millions of queer creatures, half-fish and half-fungus, looking down into all manner of coral caves and seaweed conservatories; and staring in with their great dull eyes at every open nook and loophole." And, again, "Today I had not written twenty lines before I rushed out (the weather being gorgeous) to bathe. And when I have done that, it is all up with me in the way of authorship until tomorrow." But by the last week in September he had only the two final chapters to write, and was already receiving proofs.

The bulk of the book was devoted to vivid impressions, in the manner of some of the *Sketches by Boz*, of the scenes through which he had passed. Save, perhaps, in the chapter dealing with slavery, he avoided the sharpness of tone that had crept into his letters, but he painted no idyllic picture of America, and he well knew that that oversensitive country could not bear the faintest whisper of dispraise. He was concerned, however, to assert his freedom of opinion without seeming unappreciative of the enthusiastic reception he had been given. With Forster's aid and advice he therefore worked out a dedication to the two volumes, which finally read: "I dedicate this Book to those friends of mine in America who, giving me a welcome I must ever gratefully and proudly remember, left my judgement free; and who, loving their country, can bear the truth, when it is told good-humouredly, and in a kind spirit."

Among his American friends, nevertheless, there were some who were seriously perturbed at what Dickens might write. He replied that these fears were dictated by an excessive "tenderness for me." Suppose America were a man, he said, instead of a nation; was a friendship worth having that could be retained only by a timid silence, by debating at every turn, "Will he take this? Will he be angry if I say that? Will he find out that I am not a toy for his amusement if I do the other?" Clearly not. He was convinced that there was not in his book "one solitary line" that was not true, and that he had never been betrayed into an unfair expression.

But Dickens was keenly aware of the angry reception the book would have throughout most of the American press. He therefore planned to cut the ground from under some of this resentment by an introductory chapter outlining his position. The book, it explained, was not statistical. It avoided personalities. It was not political. It contained no description of the reception "a most affectionate and generous-hearted people" had given him, because he could not flourish before his readers so much praise of himself. It was simply a day-by-day record of things that had passed under his eye, with some of his reflections upon them.

He knew, he said, that he would be accused of malice and ingratitude by people so delicately made that they could not bear the imperfections of truth. But he did not believe the warm welcome he had received was a vulgar attempt to flatter him into turning a blind eye upon any blemishes in the nation. "From first to last I saw, in those hospitable hands, a home-made wreath of laurel; and not an iron muzzle disguised beneath a flower or two." And consequently he had no more praised the abuses he had observed than he ever had those he saw at home.

Unfortunately, Forster strongly opposed printing this introduction. It might arouse, he thought, the suspicion that Dickens feared hostile judgements and was trying to deprecate them in advance. Dickens disagreed, but at last allowed himself to be won over, so reluctantly, however, that Forster had to promise that the suppressed chapter would be published at some more fitting time in the future. That time did not arrive, in Forster's estimation, until two years after Dickens's death, when he included the chapter in his biography.

Forster's advice was tactically mistaken. Dickens's courteously worded separation of his freedom of utterance from the friendly welcome with which he had been greeted was entirely sound. His statement that he had never softened or glossed over the evils he had found at home was also cogent, and indeed he might have added that on the whole he treated America with a gentler hand than he did England.

The summer weather at Broadstairs had been followed by tremendous northeast gales rolling in heavy seas that drowned the pier in waves twelve feet high. Dickens returned to London eagerly anticipating a promised visit from Longfellow.

How stands it about your visit, do you say? Thus. – Your bed is waiting to be slept in, the door is gaping hospitably to receive you, I am ready to spring towards it at the first indication of a Longfellow knock or ring; and the door, the bed, I, and everybody else who is in the secret, have been expecting you for the last month.

Longfellow reached London on 6 October and came at once to Devonshire Terrace. "I write this from Dickens' study," he told Sumner. "The raven croaks in the garden; and the ceaseless roar of London fills my ears." The very evening of his arrival Dickens took him to see Macready in *As You Like It* and they visited the actor in his dressing-room after the performance. With Cruikshank, Maclise, and Macready there were "mad" dinners in Devonshire Terrace, at which they drank Schloss-Johannisberger and cold punch, and other evenings equally merry beneath Forster's bright dinner lamps in Lincoln's Inn Fields. At Gore House, Longfellow was received by Lady Blessington, and saw Count D'Orsay, who was confined withindoors "by a severe attack of *bum-bailiffs*" and could venture out only on Sundays.

In contrast to London's artistic and fashionable circles, Dickens gave Longfellow a lurid nocturnal glimpse of its criminal slums. Accompanied by Forster and Maclise, they explored the foulest and most sinister thieves' dens of the Borough. Another day Dickens and Forster carried Longfellow down into Kent to show him the Leather Bottle at Cobham, the Bull at Rochester where Mr Pickwick and his friends attended that disastrous charity ball, and the other scenes among which Dickens had passed his childhood.

At the end of two weeks Longfellow set out for Bristol, where he was taking the steamship *Great Western* on the 21st. Forster wanted to give him some port wine to take back to America, but Dickens, remembering the *Britannia* plunging and shuddering through the waves, vetoed the suggestion. "No – no! – the Port will be shaken to the devil before it gets there." Longfellow was entrusted, however, with some Johannisberger and punch for Dickens's friends across the Atlantic. With this he took copies of *American Notes*, which was just off the press, for Felton, Sumner, the elder Dana, Washington Allston, Bancroft, and Prescott.

After you left us [Dickens reported], Charley invented and rehearsed with his sisters a dramatic scene in your honour . . . three small glasses are all raised together, and they look at each other very hard. Then Charley cries "Mr Longfellow! Hoo-ra-a-a-a-a-a-e!" Two other shrill voices repeat the sentiment, and the little glasses are drained to the bottom. The whole concludes with a violent rapping of the table, and hideous barking from the little dog, who wakes up for the purpose.

Hardly was Longfellow gone when Dickens set off, with Forster, Maclise, and Clarkson Stanfield, for a jaunt. "I think of opening my new book" he had written Forster, "on the coast of Cornwall, in some terrible dreary iron-bound spot." To Tintagel, with its legends of King Arthur, they accordingly went, and to St Michael's Mount and Land's End.

Blessed star of morning [Dickens wrote Felton]! Such a trip as we had into Cornwall just after Longfellow went away! . . . Heavens! If you could have seen the necks of bottles, distracting in their immense varieties of shape, peering out of the carriage pockets! If you could have witnessed the deep devotion of the postboys, the wild attachment of the hostlers, the maniac glee of the waiters! If you could have followed us into the earthy old churches we visited, and into the strange caverns on the gloomy sea-shore, and down into the depths of mines, and up to the tops of giddy heights where the unspeakably green water was roaring, I don't know how many hundred feet below!

Into a painting inspired by this holiday, *The Girl at the Waterfall*, Maclise introduced the figure of Kate's young sister Georgina, who was now fifteen years old. She had seen much of the children while their parents were in America and won their hearts to such a degree that they constantly chattered of "Aunt Georgy." Not long after, she was invited to stay at Devonshire Terrace and gradually slid into a place in the household very much like that which Mary had once filled. Dickens traced "a strong resemblance" between her and her dead sister, "so strange a one, at times," he wrote to Mrs Hogarth, "that when she and Kate and I are sitting together, I seem to think that what has happened is a melancholy dream from which I am just awakening."

In London, after the Cornwall holiday, Dickens made a determined onslaught on the opening of his new book. The writing of *American Notes* had delayed its commencement and forced postponing its publication date from November to January. Now, shutting himself up in his own room, he forced himself to the task. During these agonies of plotting and contriving, he wrote Miss Coutts, he walked up and down the house, "smiting my forehead dejectedly," and "so horribly cross . . . that the boldest fly at my approach."

The tale opened, not in Cornwall, but in a little Wiltshire village on a windy autumn evening. Dickens had much trouble finding a name for the book and for his hero. Sweezleden, Sweezlewag, Chuzzletoe, Chuzzleboy, Chubblewig, and Chuzzlewig were among those he tried before he finally settled on Martin Chuzzlewit.

The design of the book was to portray through Pecksniff and the other characters the numerous humours and vices that have their roots in selfishness, and by the third number Dickens had drawn up "old Martin's plot to degrade and punish Pecksniff." That *Martin Chuzzlewit* had a theme as well as a plot is a sign of Dickens's development as a writer. His previous novels, although they have much more structure than some readers find, are still glorious improvisations.

Oliver Twist is not so completely dominated by the campaign against the Poor Law, nor *Nicholas Nickleby* by the attack on the Yorkshire schools, as *Martin Chuzzlewit* is by the revelation of selfishness. Though Dickens deviated widely from parts of his original scheme, he never lost sight of his dominating intent.

The vast gallery of multiple perspectives on selfishness is dazzling – young Martin, thoughtless and self-indulgent; his domineering grandfather seeing selfishness in others everywhere; the tribe of other Chuzzlewits snarling savagely in their greedy hopes for old Martin's fortune; Pecksniff oozing hypocritical eloquence; the brassily glittering swindler Tigg Montague; the fraudulent land speculator Zephaniah Scadder; the mendacious and corrupt New York newspapers; the menacing frontier bully Hannibal Chollop, with his "ripper" and his "tickler"; the mob of rapacious businessmen making "commerce one huge lie and mighty theft."

Towering above all the rest are two marvellous feats of satiric creation, the snuff-stained and fusty Sairey Gamp and the bland and unctuous Pecksniff. Mrs Gamp, with her thick and gurgling flux of speech and its tortured syntax, her weakness for the bottle, and the tributes to her own virtues which she puts into the mouth of the invisible Mrs Harris, is a triumph from beginning to end. Pecksniff, his throat serene and whiskerless, making playful moral reflections "with a sort of saintly waggishness," is magnificent even in defeat as he meekly forgives his unmaskers.

Despite the demands of his own work, Dickens found time to write a verse prologue for Macready's new production at Drury Lane. The first play of a 23-year-old author named Westland Marston, *The Patrician's Daughter*, instead of being staged as costume drama, was courageously presented as a poetic tragedy of current life. Another poetic drama by which Dickens was deeply moved at this time was Browning's *A Blot on the 'Scutcheon*. The poet had confided the manuscript of the play to Forster, and he lent it to Dickens, from whom it compelled "a perfect passion of sorrow."

From Longfellow now came word of his arrival home. Dickens had tried to prevent any copies of *American Notes* reaching the United States before those carried by his friend, but his efforts had failed. While the book was being set up in type a smart American journalist had bribed one of the pressmen at Bradbury and Evans, the printers, and the stolen proof sheets had crossed the Atlantic before Longfellow. By the time he was home three or four publishers were hurriedly pirating

cheap editions that flooded the country at six cents a copy. The New
York *Herald* printed the work in nineteen hours after receiving copy
from England and sold 50,000 in two days. In Philadelphia 3,000
copies went in half an hour.

Among Dickens's friends in America, its reception was favourable.
Longfellow said it was "jovial and good-natured," though "at times
very severe." "He has a grand chapter on Slavery," Longfellow wrote
Sumner. "*Spitting* and *politics* at Washington are the other topics of
censure. Both you and I would censure them with equal severity to
say the least." "Opinions are various," Felton said; "but we agree
pretty well here, in thinking it a capital book; lively, spirited, true and
good humored." Emerson was less laudatory. He thought it lively and
readable, but as an account of American manners "too narrow, too
superficial, and too ignorant, too slight, and too fabulous," full of
exaggeration and caricature.

The American press, of course, let out a howl of superheated rage.
The New York *Herald* said the book was "all leather and prunella,"
not worth any sensible man's perusal, and Dickens, "that famous
penny-a-liner," had "the most coarse, vulgar, impudent, and superficial" mind "that ever had the courage to write about . . . this original
and remarkable country." His view "of the fermentative character of
this land" was that of "a narrow-minded, conceited cockney."

Another newspaper said Dickens was a "flash reporter," with the
feelings of "a low-bred scullion unexpectedly advanced from the
kitchen to the parlour." Still another printed a letter from an angry
citizen of St Louis, saying that Dickens had spent his life "in the stews
of London" and was "fit to associate only with the dancing monkeys
and mulatto girls of Five Points."

Thoughtful readers in England indulged in no such tantrums, but
they did not care much for the book. Macaulay, who had demanded
that it be set aside for him at the *Edinburgh Review*, sent it back. "It is
impossible for me to review it, I cannot praise it, and I will not cut it
up." Captain Marryat, on the other hand, liked the book, and so did
Mrs Trollope. "Let me thank you most cordially," Dickens wrote her,
"for your kind note, in reference to my Notes, which has given me
true pleasure and gratification." Her praise was the more valuable to
him because, he now said, he thought no writer had described America
more entertainingly and truthfully than she had.

More important in practical ways than these disagreements on the
merits of *American Notes* was the fact that the public bought it. Three

thousand copies were sold in the first week, and four large editions before the end of the year. It brought Dickens in a profit of £1,000 which he could readily use after the high expenses of the tour it celebrated.

Most American readers today will find little in *American Notes* to rouse their ire. The tone on the whole is one of courteous moderation. In his desire, indeed, to give no unnecessary offence, Dickens omitted many of those personal observations and all the comments on well-known figures that add spice to his letters. He omitted any account of the copyright irritations that had simmered throughout his journey. He warmly praised many features of American life. He paid generous tribute to the American people. "They are, by nature, frank, brave, cordial, hospitable, and affectionate. Cultivation and refinement seem but to enhance their warmth of heart and ardent enthusiasm . . ."

Surely here was praise enough to satisfy even the most captious. The indignation with which he lashed slavery was applauded even then by many enlightened Americans, and would be resented by none today. But for all his studied moderation, Dickens's disappointment in America gradually emerges as a dislike of the country as a whole which becomes unmistakable before the end of the book.

This dislike is especially clear in his strictures on American "smartness," the excesses of the trading spirit, and the licentiousness of the American press. In surrender to the love of trade, American literature was "to remain for ever unprotected," even though Americans professed to be very proud of their poets. The vicious press was a constant moral poison in the public life of the nation, corrupting politics with its venal hand, smearing every decent opponent with its filthy slanders.

The emotional revulsion behind these criticisms had three intertwining roots: Dickens's own limitations, the distortions inevitable in the only view of America he was given, and the actual character of the nation in the mid-nineteenth century. For all his sharpness and penetration, for all the power of genius, Dickens was still a young man – not yet quite thirty when he stepped ashore in Boston. Beyond a few weeks' holiday in France and Belgium he had had no experience of any country but his own. He had no cosmopolitan standard with which to measure America, no knowledge except knowledge of England to apply. It is significant that he thought Americans a sad rather than a humorous people, taking their straight-faced jests as sober earnest, and reading their wild hyperbole as either mendacity or windy boastfulness. Some of the things Dickens reports as fact suggest a strong suspicion that his leg was being pulled by some melancholy joker; even then the tall tale had long been a favourite sport of the trader, the pioneer, and the flatboatman.

Furthermore, what Dickens saw of America was distorted by the extraordinary furore accompanying his progress. Everywhere he went there were goggling eyes, heads poked in through windows, a raw curiosity mingling with the genuine warmth, that left him less privacy than a sideshow freak. It is remarkable under the circumstances that in the space of less than five months he hit on so much that was shrewd and true.

For of course most of what Dickens said about America, if sometimes exaggerated in detail, was true in essence. That was why it hurt, and why Americans resented it in a way incomprehensible to him. His own youthful intolerance did not understand the gawky adolescence of a country still awkwardly uncertain of its position in the comity of nations. Americans were proud of the conquests they had carved out of a virgin continent in so short a span of generations.

The struggle had made Americans a tissue of contradictions. They deified the dollar, and sowed the land thickly with schools and seats of learning. They adulated the sharp dealer, and gave generously to every noble cause. Their raucous professions of indifference to literature and art contrasted with their loud pride in Washington Irving and Fenimore Cooper, and with the fantastic triumph they gave to Dickens himself. They boasted windily because so many of their foreign visitors were supercilious to the American desire for praise. They talked big, and felt smaller than they could bear to admit. They were oversensitive and bumptious at the same time.

Such a desperate longing to be loved and admired, and the deep-seated diffidence beneath the bluster and swagger, was a paradox incomprehensible to the insular complacence of most Europeans. Although he had imagined he would understand the republican character, he did not see the American character as the product of its world. The New World did not yield its secret to Dickens.

PART SIX

Crescendo of Unrest
1843–1846

[23]

Bay-Salt in the Eyes

During 1843 Dickens worked and worried over *Martin Chuzzlewit*. But the year began gaily with a Twelfth-Night party for Charley. There was a magic lantern, and Dickens had bought the stock in trade of a conjurer, with which he entertained the guests. "O my dear eyes, Felton, if you could see me conjuring the company's watches into impossible tea-caddies, and causing pieces of money to fly, and burning pocket-handkerchiefs without hurting 'em . . . you would never forget it as long as you live."

Since his return from America, Dickens had made no public reference to international copyright, except for a printed letter addressed to the *Athenaeum*, the *Examiner*, and a number of other journals, in which he stated his resolve to continue to forgo all profits from the sale of early proofs to American publishers, and urged others to refuse all correspondence with those engaged in piracy and to deal only with reputable houses. From the Philadelphia publishers Lea and Blanchard, who had pirated *Pickwick* but later paid for advance sheets of *Master Humphrey's Clock*, Dickens now refused offers of £100 for advance sheets of *American Notes* and £440 for *Martin Chuzzlewit*.

In January, the subject came up again. Although not opposed to international copyright, the *Edinburgh Review* repeated the assertion that Dickens had gone to America "as a kind of missionary in the cause of international copyright." He strongly protested the careless acceptance of this falsehood, which portrayed him "as a traveller under false pretences, and a disappointed intriguer." He readily agreed, however, to the offer of a retraction made by the editor. When the London *Times* referred to the same article, he wrote a denial to that paper also.

Three months later, in early April, Dickens presided over a meeting for the establishment of a Society of Authors to protect authors' rights, to work for the enactment of more satisfactory laws, both national and international, and to give legal advice and aid to its members. From it emerged an association whose subscribers included more than a dozen of the leading publishers and printers and listed among its authors the names of Bulwer, Dickens, Forster, Lockhart, Macaulay, and Marryat.

Dickens had hopes that this organization might accomplish some of its purposes, but he was convinced that American piracy would outlast his time. "I quite agree with you," he wrote Longfellow, "that we shall never live to see the passing of an international Law." And to Lewis Gaylord Clark, "What impossible odds shall I set . . . that we shall be in our graves and out of them again in particles of dust impalpable, before those honest men at Washington, in their earthy riots, care one miserable damn for Mind?"

Indignant though he might be about such grievances, however, the injustices from which Dickens suffered himself never absorbed more than a small part of his sympathies. His heart was wrung by the figures Dr Southwood Smith gave him on the hours and wages of labour, although, like many good men, he was baffled to find a solution for the suffering they disclosed. "Want is so general," he wrote, "distress so great, and Poverty so rampant – it is, in a word, so hard for the million to live by any means – that I scarcely know how we can step between them and one weekly farthing. The necessity of a mighty change, I clearly see . . ."

The Government blue book on sanitary conditions among workers which Southwood Smith also sent him left Dickens stricken down with horror. He rose determined that he must strike a great blow against this massacre of the innocents. The fierce polemic of *The Chimes*, published at the end of the following year, was one of the sledgehammer blows animated by this determination.

These feelings of outrage made him wrathful against the selfish complacency that opposes social legislation and extols the good old times.

> Oh Heaven [he wrote Douglas Jerrold], if you could have been with me at a hospital dinner last Monday! There were men there – your City aristocracy – who made such speeches and expressed such sentiments as any moderately intelligent dustman would have blushed through his cindery bloom to have thought of. Sleek, slobbering, bow-paunched, over-fed, apoplectic, snorting cattle, and the auditory leaping up in their delight! I never saw such an illustration of the power of the purse, or felt so degraded and debased by its contemplation . . .

His father's irresponsibility and the careers of his brothers were still giving Dickens personal problems. Even in America he had been vexed by news from Mitton about "that father of mine," and exclaimed, "How long he is, growing up." On his return to England his parents bitterly renewed their complaints about being immured in the doll's house at Alphington. Dickens evidently yielded to their demand to be brought up to London, for he authorized Mitton to offer £70 for "that little house on Blackheath." Not long after, he was writing Miss Coutts to ask if she could help him procure suitable employment for his brother Alfred, who was a civil engineer. And Fred, although his Treasury salary had been increased, was falling into his father's extravagant ways. A creditor at Gray's Inn sent Dickens "*for the second time* a bill which I think is Frederick's."

Under these circumstances, it is no wonder that Dickens sometimes had difficulty in concentrating on his work. "I couldn't write a line yesterday," he told Forster; "not a word, though I really tried hard." At the end of March, in order to immerse himself more completely in his story, he withdrew to Cobley's Farm, a lonely retreat at Finchley, from which he revisited London only at intervals. A companion of Miss Coutts had a serious illness and was under the care of a nurse. From her he derived Mrs Gamp's yellow nightcap, her habit of rubbing her nose along the top of the fender and supping up vinegar with a knife, her addiction to snuff and to tilting the bottle on the "chimley piece" when she felt "so dispoged," although Sairey's legendary friend Mrs Harris seems to have been Dickens's own inspired addition.

Despite the fact, however, that *Martin Chuzzlewit* was indeed, as Dickens himself said, "in a hundred points immeasurably the best" of the novels he had yet written, sales were not going well. *Pickwick* and *Nickleby* had sold 40,000 and 50,000; *The Old Curiosity Shop* had gone as high as 100,000; but the sales of *Chuzzlewit* were reaching only a little over 20,000. Something clearly had to be done, and at the end of the fifth number Dickens had Martin announce that he'd "go to America."

The success of *American Notes* was partly responsible for this decision. It seemed likely that there was an audience for sharp comment on America. And with the uproar still going on in America, that was just what Dickens felt inclined to write. Every post brought him scurrilous letters and marked copies of abusive articles in American periodicals. These challenges aroused the old determination to say all over again what had been objected to, and say it with redoubled violence.

In May, "good old John Black" was retired from the *Chronicle*, where he had served as editor for thirty years. Black was only sixty, but his enforced resignation was one of Sir John Easthope's typically peremptory acts. "I am deeply grieved about Black," Dickens wrote Forster. "Sorry from my heart's core." With Albany Fonblanque Dickens planned a dinner to show their esteem. It took place at Greenwich, where Thackeray, Forster, Southwood Smith, Macready, Maclise, and a group of Black's fellow journalists were among those united to do him honour.

The device of taking Martin across the Atlantic had admirably succeeded in rousing the Americans to fury. "All Yankee-Doodle-dum," wrote Carlyle, blazed "up like one universal soda bottle," and Dickens told Forster "that Martin has made them all stark staring raving mad across the water." On the stage of a New York theatre, to the savage delight of the audience, a copy of the book was destroyed by being thrown into the witches' cauldron in á burlesque of *Macbeth.* "You must settle it with the Americans as you can," Sydney Smith wrote Dickens, "I have only to testify to the humour and power of description."

The enjoyment his American caricatures gave English readers forced up the sales, however, only by another 3,000. And that discouraging fact had serious consequences. The agreement of September 1841, contained a proviso that in the improbable event of the profits being insufficient to repay the advances Chapman and Hall had made Dickens throughout 1842 they might, after the first five numbers, deduct £50 monthly out of the £200 he was being paid. Forster had objected to this detail at the time, but Hall had defended it as mere lawyer's verbiage that would never "be needed." "Mr Dickens need have no concern on that score." And unfortunately Forster had let the matter drop.

One June afternoon Dickens turned up in the Strand to superintend some detail in the number where Mrs Gamp made her first appearance. And, worrying out loud, William Hall remarked in a luckless slip of the tongue, that he hoped they would not have to put the repayment clause into effect. Hall was "a kind well-disposed man," and a shrewd one; he had simply let a half-digested thought escape him. But the effect was disastrous. Flinging out of the office, Dickens fumed home. "Publishers," commented Forster dryly, "are bitter bad judges of an author."

"I am so irritated," Dickens wrote, "so rubbed in the tenderest part of my eyelids with bay-salt, by what I told you yesterday that a wrong kind of fire is burning in my head, and I don't think I *can* write." When he remembered that his writings had transformed them from petty booksellers to one of the richest publishing houses in London, his blood boiled. Before this he had received proposals from Bradbury and Evans urging that he consider them if he ever thought of changing publishers.

He would see what they had to offer. "I am bent upon paying Chapman and Hall *down*. And when I have done that, Mr Hall shall have a piece of my mind."

Forster sympathized but counselled reflection. He prevailed upon Dickens to defer action until after his summer in Broadstairs. Dickens forced himself back to his writing table again and was presently "working like a dragon." But Chapman and Hall soon had some intimation of his temperature; the £50 poor little Hall had only worried about must, Dickens fiercely insisted, be deducted from his monthly payments. This involved a financial pinch, for many expenses were crowding on him all at once, and he did not like to overdraw his bank account at Coutts's when Miss Coutts was "exerting herself in behalf of Alfred."

Before going to Broadstairs, Dickens plunged into the task of raising money to help the children of Edward Elton, an actor drowned when the *Pegasus* went down in the Irish Sea. He arranged a benefit performance of *Hamlet* at the Haymarket, to which Macready and other actors donated their services. From these and other sources well over £1,000 was raised, and subscriptions continued to pour in for a fund of which Dickens became one of the three trustees.

Broadstairs was bright and beautiful as always. This year, though, there was a piano next door, close to the very bay window in which Dickens wrote; and when he took refuge on the other side of the house, that turned out to look into a street "where there are donkeys and drivers out of number" making a noise almost as bad as the piano. But it was not only the donkeys and the piano that disturbed him. The bay-salt of his irritation with Chapman and Hall still stung his eyelids, and he struggled fiercely to subdue these fits of spleen, striding furiously for hours along the cliffs with a seething intensity that disturbed both his work and his rest.

But he regained his spirits as he described the little village and its summer routine to Felton.

> Seven miles out are the Goodwin Sands . . . whence floating lights perpetually wink after dark, as if they were carrying on intrigues with the servants. . . . In a bay-window in a one-pair sits, from 9 o'clock to 1, a gentleman with rather long hair and no neck-cloth, who writes and grins as if he thought he were very funny indeed. . . . At one he disappears, and presently emerges from a bathing-machine, and may be seen – a kind of salmon-coloured porpoise – splashing about in the

ocean. . . . He's as brown as a berry, and they *do* say is a small fortune to the inn-keeper who sells beer and cold punch.

Towards the close of August, Dickens went up to London to attend a farewell to Macready, who was going on a theatrical tour in America. There was a splendid dinner at the Star and Garter at Richmond, and Dickens proposed the only toast, Macready's health, in words so moving that Macready could hardly speak for tears. He had intended to accompany Macready to Liverpool but decided against doing so. "If I were to go on board with him," Dickens wrote to Forster, "I have not the least doubt that the fact would be placarded all over New York before he had shaved himself in Boston." Thousands of men in America "would pick a quarrel with him on the mere statement of his being my friend."

Dickens therefore wrote his decision to Macready:

> If you but knew one hundredth part of the malignity, the monstrous falsehood, the beastly attacks even upon Catherine, which were published all over America, even while I was there, on my mere confession that the country had disappointed me – confessions wrung from me in private society before I had written a word upon the people – you would question all this as little as I do.

In early October Dickens went up to Manchester, where at a meeting of the Athenaeum he sat on the platform with Disraeli and Cobden. It was inspiring to see this institution, he told his audience, with its lectures, its opportunities for exercise and rational enjoyment, and know that amid clanking engines and whirling machinery the mind was not forgotten. He had no patience with the maxim that "a little knowledge is a dangerous thing." A little hanging was once considered a dangerous thing, "with this difference, that, because a little hanging was dangerous, we had a great deal of it; and, because a little knowledge was dangerous, we were to have none at all."

In the course of his wanderings through the slums of London, Dickens had come upon the Ragged Schools conducted in some of them by earnest young workers. These volunteer institutions for giving free instruction to poor children had been slowly spreading throughout the country. In the unsavoury neighbourhood of Field Lane, Holborn, subjected to raids from young hoodlums who pelted the teachers with filth and smashed the furniture, one of these schools was under the guidance of a lawyer's clerk named Samuel Starey. He had appealed to Miss Coutts for support, and in response to her request Dickens had arranged to visit the school. Deeply moved and excited by the experience, he wrote her a long letter praising the work it did.

Located, he said, among the very scenes described in *Oliver Twist*, the school was "an awful sight." It was

held in three most wretched rooms on the first floor of a rotten house: every plank, and timber, and brick, and lath, and piece of plaster in which shakes as you walk. One room is devoted to the girls; two to the boys. The former are much the better-looking – I cannot say better dressed, for there is no such thing as dress among the seventy pupils; certainly not the elements of a whole suit of clothes, among them all . . .

The masters are extremely quiet, honest, good men. You may suppose they are, to be there at all. It is enough to break one's heart to get at the place: to say nothing of getting at the children's minds afterwards. They are well-grounded in the Scotch – the Glasgow – system of elementary instruction, which is an excellent one; and they try to reach the boys by kindness. To gain their attention in any way, is a difficulty, quite gigantic . . .

The school is miserably poor, you may believe, and is almost entirely supported by the teachers themselves. If they could get a better room (the house they are in, is like an ugly dream); above all, if they could provide some convenience for washing; it would be an immense advantage. The moral courage of the teachers is beyond all praise. They are surrounded by every possible adversity, and every disheartening circumstance that can be imagined. Their office is worthy of the apostles . . .

I need not say, I am sure, that I deem it an experiment most worthy of your charitable hand. The reasons I have, for doubting its being generally assisted, all assure me that it will have an interest for you. For I know you to be very, very far-removed from all the Givers in all the Court Guides between this, and China.

Dickens immediately busied himself with plans for improving the institution. He asked Starey to find out how much it would cost to install a large trough or sink, with a good supply of running water, soap, and towels. He had no doubt that Miss Coutts would "do whatever I ask her in the matter. She is a most excellent creature, I protest to God, and I have a most perfect affection and respect for her."

For the *Edinburgh Review*, Dickens offered to write a description of the Ragged Schools. If he did so, he told the editor, he would have "to come out strongly against any system of education based exclusively on the principles of the Established Church." It was an absurd irrelevance for well meaning ladies to ask theological questions about the "Lamb of God" of youngsters who did not know the meaning of honesty. The offer was accepted, but confusions arose about the delivery date of the article. By the time they were straightened out Dickens was too busy in other work to write it.

This dislike of theological dogma was one that had been growing upon him steadily. He had been interested to find that many of his American friends in Cambridge and Boston belonged, as Forster did, to the Unitarian faith. Dickens did not believe in the virgin birth of Christ, and was able to sympathize with the leading features of the Unitarian creed. In November 1842, he had heard the Reverend Edward Tagart preach a funeral service on Dr Channing at the chapel in Little Portland Street, the leading West End place of worship of the Unitarians. Soon after, Dickens took sittings in the chapel and inaugurated a lasting friendship with Tagart.

The undertaking that diverted Dickens from writing on the Ragged Schools was a tale that came to be called *A Christmas Carol*. Something about "the bright eyes and beaming faces" on which he had looked down at the Manchester Athenaeum had given him the inspiration for a glowing, heart-moving story in which he would appeal to people's essential humanity. Its theme was thus closely related to the emphases that would have animated the unwritten *Edinburgh Review* article, an insistence that the sense of brotherhood could be broadened into a deeper and more fruitful concern for the welfare of all men.

With the growing importance of commerce in the eighteenth century, and of industry in the nineteenth, political economists had rationalized the spirit of ruthless greed into a system claiming authority throughout society. Services as well as goods, they said, were subject to the laws of profitable trade. There was no just price; one bought in the cheapest market and sold in the dearest. There was no just wage; employers paid their workers what competition decreed under "the iron law of wage." Scrooge, in the *Christmas Carol*, is nothing less than the personification of "economic man."

Scrooge's entire life is limited to cashboxes and bills of sale. He under-pays and bullies his clerk. All sentiment, kindness, generosity, tender-ness, he dismisses as "humbug." All imagination he regards as a species of mental indigestion. He feels that he has discharged his full duty to so-ciety in contributing the taxes that pay for the prison, the workhouse, and the operation of the treadmill and the Poor Laws. The out-of-work and the indigent sick are merely useless and idle; they had better die and decrease the surplus population.

Against Scrooge and the orthodox economists, Dickens insists that no way of life is sound or rewarding that leaves out men's need of loving and of being loved. *A Christmas Carol* is a serio-comic parable of social redemption, and Scrooge's conversion is the conversion for which Dickens hopes among mankind.

The earnings of the *Carol*, he expected, would help make up for the disappointing returns from *Martin Chuzzlewit*. For although that novel had "forced itself up in people's opinion," it had not forced itself up in sales. And Bradbury and Evans, though they had invited a proposition from Dickens, were rather alarmed when Forster sounded them out. From them emanated only the limited proposal of bringing out a cheap edition of the works already published and establishing a new magazine edited by Dickens.

"I am afraid of a magazine – just now," Dickens wrote Forster. "I don't think the time a good one, or the chances favourable." In addition to this, he feared that a cheap edition of the books was premature. "I am sure if it took place yet awhile, it would damage me and damage the property, *enormously*. . . . I see that this is really your opinion as well; and I don't see what I gain, in such a case, by leaving Chapman and Hall."

What he would really like to do was to "fade away from the public eye for a year, and enlarge my stock of description and observation by seeing countries new to me." If he had made money by *Martin Chuzzlewit*, this is what he would have done. But he thought he could do it anyway. At the close of *Chuzzlewit* eight months hence in July, he would tell Chapman and Hall that he would make no new arrangements for a year. Then he would let Devonshire Terrace, and go abroad to some cheap place in Normandy or Brittany, and later on travel in France and Italy. He could live twice as cheaply as at home, and finance the entire year without binding himself to anyone, simply by giving as security one of his £5,000 insurance policies.

Forster was startled, but Dickens returned to the idea vehemently. This project of foreign travel had got into his head "MONTHS AGO." "What would poor Scott have given to have gone abroad, of his own free will, a young man, instead of creeping there, a driveller, in his miserable decay!" Forster must, consequently, look upon the project "*as a settled thing*," and Chapman and Hall must be told. "If you object to see them, I must write to them."

Forster persuaded Dickens to defer this on tactical grounds. Chapman and Hall were publishing the *Christmas Carol* on commission for Dickens; the announcement that he was quitting them at such a time would foolishly jeopardize the little book's chances. Its profits might help to meet some of those endless financial demands by which his family harassed him. Added to his own domestic expenses, they were a serious drain, which he felt with increasing bitterness. Worried by one of these on a November night, Forster says, Dickens was quite put out of his work, and then blazed away until nine o'clock to make up, stopping only ten minutes for his dinner. And the very next day there was another and worse repetition of precisely the same trouble. Oh, to be abroad beyond the reach of such daily exasperations! "I am quite serious and sober when I say, that I have very grave thoughts of keeping my whole menagerie in Italy, three years."

Nevertheless, in the midst of these irritations, worries, and distractions, and even as "Chuzzlewit agonies" made their unending demands upon him, he felt his power more than ever, and threw himself with such intensity into the writing of his *Christmas Carol* that he completed it in little more than six weeks, before the end of November. Over it, he said, he "wept and laughed, and wept again, and excited himself in a most extraordinary manner in the composition; and thinking whereof he walked about the black streets of London fifteen and twenty miles many a night when all sober folks had gone to bed."

In order to ensure a wide sale of the *Carol*, Dickens had insisted upon its being priced at five shillings. At the same time, the manuscript, scored with corrections and deletions, and with entire redrafts of many pages, to a degree unusual with Dickens at this stage in his career, shows the loving care with which the book was composed. And although Chapman and Hall were publishing it on commission, with Dickens paying all the costs of publication, he insisted on an elaborate and expensive format, with gilt edges, coloured end papers, a title page printed in blue and red, and four hand-coloured plates by John Leech.

When it was finished at last, Dickens said, he "broke out like a madman." During the Christmas season his spirits demanded a release. "Forster is out again," he wrote Felton; "and if he don't go in again, after the manner in which we have been keeping Christmas, he must be very strong indeed. Such dinings, such dancings, such conjurings, such blind-man's-buffings, such theatre-goings, such kissings-out of old years and kissings-in of new ones never took place in these parts before."

Jane Welsh Carlyle bore testimony to the mad hilarity of one of these parties.

Dickens and Forster [she said], above all exerted themselves till the perspiration was pouring down and they seemed *drunk* with their efforts. Only think of that excellent Dickens playing the conjuror for one whole hour – the *best* conjuror I ever saw ... Then the dancing ... the gigantic Thackeray &c &c all capering like Maenades!! ... *after supper* when we were all madder than ever with the pulling of crackers, the drinking of champagne, and the making of speeches; a universal country dance was proposed – and Forster *seizing me round the waist*, whirled me into the thick of it, and *made* me dance – like a person in the tread-mill who must move forward or be crushed to death! Once I cried out, "Oh for the love of Heaven let me go! you are going to dash my brains out against the folding doors!" "Your *brains*!!" he answered. "Who cares about their brains *here*? *Let them go!*"

24

Battles and
Italian Air-Castles

On New Year's morning 1844, Dickens greeted the postman bearing a letter from Felton "with a moist and oystery twinkle" of the eye, a glass of whiskey, and a cheery blessing. His spirits were buoyant with the success of the *Christmas Carol*: 6,000 copies of the first edition sold on the very day of publication, 2,000 of the second and third already taken by the trade, and letters of enthusiastic delight from complete strangers pouring in daily.

Nor was the chorus of praise only a popular one. "Blessings on your kind heart," wrote Jeffrey. "You should be happy yourself, for you may be sure you have done more good by this little publication, fostered more kind feelings, and prompted more positive acts of beneficence, than can be traced to all the pulpits and confessionals in Christendom since Christmas 1842." "Who can listen," exclaimed Thackeray, "to objections regarding such a book as this? It seems to me a national benefit, and to every man or woman who reads it a personal kindness."

The burden of worry under which Dickens had felt weighed down melted into air. He would be able to clear off the nagging debts and family demands, and then for a glorious year of freedom, in France, Italy, perhaps Germany! Bag and baggage, little ones and all, he would leave England at mid-summer and bathe in the luxurious idleness of the southern sun. His genial warmth did not embrace Chapman and Hall, however. For those unhappy booksellers had not even advertised the *Carol* in any of the December magazines except *Blackwood's*. Dickens had been "obliged to write them a most tremendous letter," telling them "not to answer it, or to come near me, but simply to do what I have ordered them." "Do this – Do that – Do the other – Keep away from me – and be damned." The resounding triumph of the *Christmas Carol* was none of their doing; they were summarily directed to submit the accounts as soon after the New Year as possible.

Pending the profits of the Christmas book, however, Dickens found himself hard pressed for cash. His expenses had been high, there would soon be another baby, and in December he had discovered to his horror that he was already overdrawn at Coutts's. But nothing would induce him to accept an advance from his publishers. The only thing was to wait for his *Carol* earnings to come in.

Splendid as these ought to be, the slackness of Chapman and Hall was not the sole reason for thinking they might have been better still. For if Dickens was exasperated by American pirates, he was hardly less plagued at home by plagiarists and imitators. *The Posthumous Notes of the Pickwickian Club*, *Nichelas Nickleberry*, *Oliver Twiss* – there had been an endless series of imitations. Hack dramatists rushed mutilated versions of all his stories to the stage. Unable to prevent these plagiarisms, Dickens had assisted actor friends like Frederick Yates in their productions. But he had never ceased to resent the fact that any hack writer could thus pilfer his work.

And now, in a twopenny weekly called *Parley's Illuminated Library*, appeared a peculiarly flagrant plagiarism of *A Christmas Carol*, with the claim that it was "reoriginated from the original by Charles Dickens, Esq., and analytically condensed expressly for this work." "The story," Dickens exploded, "is practically the same, and the characters the same: and the names the same; with the exception of the name Fezziwig, which is printed Fuzziwig." The incidents were the same, and in the same order. The language was often the same, and where it was not was made "vile, ignorant, and mawkish."

With Talfourd as his counsel, Dickens moved for an injunction to stop publication. Lee and Haddock, the publishers, moved to dissolve the injunction, claiming that they had made great improvements and important additions to the *Carol*, including a song of sixty lines for Tiny Tim. But the Vice-Chancellor, Sir J. Knight Bruce, would have nothing of this defence. He demanded that Lee and Haddock's counsel cite a single passage that was not contracted or expanded from Dickens's book. "And at every successive passage he cried out, 'That is Mr Dickens's case. Find another!'"

"The Pirates are beaten flat," Dickens reported exultantly. "They are bruised, bloody, battered, smashed, squelched, and utterly undone." The way was consequently clear for Dickens to plunge into no fewer than six chancery suits, against the publishers, booksellers, printers, and "author." Talfourd strongly advocated no compromise. The case should be referred to the Court "to ascertain what profits had been made by the piracy," and to order the entire profits paid to Dickens. But Dickens was willing to let the printers off with an apology and their costs, and the booksellers who had merely handled the book might get out with their costs. From the publishers and author, however, he demanded £1,000 damages.

The defendants tried every conceivable dodge. Lee and Haddock took refuge in bankruptcy. Ultimately the four booksellers compounded their cases and paid their costs. But the publishers had proved too wily for Dickens. Instead of the damages and the ample public apology that he might reasonably have expected, Dickens found himself bogged in a legal morass from which he was able to withdraw only with the loss of all the costs of bringing suit. "I have dropped – dropped – the action and the chancery suit against the bankrupt Pirates," he wrote in May.

The blow that was to have annihilated the pirates cost Dickens £700. So little intimidated were publishers who lived by such means that only two years later he was again their victim. But this time he decided to suffer in silence. "I shall not easily forget the expense, and anxiety, and horrible injustice of the Carol case, wherein, asserting the plainest right on earth, I was really treated as if I were the robber instead of the robbed." "It is better to suffer a great wrong than to have recourse to the much greater wrong of the law."

The indignation with which Dickens saw himself left without redress and out of pocket for his pains was not lessened by the fact that the expected baby had arrived on 15 January and that he now had five dependent children. He was a devoted father, but with the four he already had he felt his family, and his expenses, large enough, and he had no enthusiasm for the domestic disruptions following a childbirth. A month later, "Kate is all right again," he wrote; "and so, they tell me, is the Baby. But I decline (on principle) to look at the latter object." Though both comments were intended facetiously, Dickens had made no such jokes about his previous children.

His youngest brother, Augustus, whose nickname "Boses" had suggested the pseudonym of Boz, was now seventeen, and of course it fell upon Dickens to settle him in a means of earning a livelihood. Dickens sought the aid of Thomas Chapman, a wealthy merchant in the City, and Chairman of Lloyd's Registery of Shipping. Augustus, he explained, was quick and clever and "not addicted to authorship, or any bad habits of that nature." Chapman obligingly took Augustus into his office.

On 10 February the eagerly awaited *Christmas Carol* accounts reached

Dickens's hands. He opened them with a pleased anticipation of learning that he had made a clear £1,000. A glance supplied him with the truth. "Such a night as I have passed!" he wrote Forster. ". . . The first six thousand copies show a profit of £230! And the last four will yield as much more." Wondering what he was to do, Dickens fell into a hysteria little short of panic. "My year's bills, unpaid, are so terrific, that all the energy and determination I can possibly exert will be required to clear me before I go abroad; which, if next June come and find me alive, I shall do." As he looked at the disastrous figures, he was "utterly knocked down." But during the night, although he "slept as badly as Macbeth," he recovered his courage. "If I can let the house for this season . . . I am not afraid, if I reduce my expenses; but if I do not, I shall be ruined past all mortal hope of redemption." "What a wonderful thing it is, that such a great success should occasion me such intolerable anxiety and disappointment."

Against Chapman and Hall he felt relentlessly bitter. Nothing could persuade him to return to them now. "I have not the least doubt that they have run the expenses up anyhow purposely to bring me back and disgust me with the charges." Why, the different charges for the plates alone, engraving, printing, colouring, came to more than his profits did!

He would reopen negotiations with Bradbury and Evans at once. They must not be told anything of this quarrel or its causes, "as I think it highly important not to dash the triumph of the book." The printers were more alert this time than they had been when Forster approached them in October. Dickens obtained £500 from them, which relieved his immediate needs. He explained that in addition he wanted to pay off the remainder of the £150 monthly he had received from Chapman and Hall throughout 1842, and to have enough to meet his expenses during his year abroad. To balance these demands there were whatever new books he might produce, the republication of those he had already written, and possibly the new magazine that had been suggested. Whatever the details, it was obvious that Bradbury and Evans would be mad not to secure Dickens.

Chapman and Hall were notified that Dickens intended to have no further dealings with them after the bound volumes of *Chuzzlewit* came out in July. That was a dark day at 186 Strand; and William Hall must have smote his brow and gone in sackcloth and ashes for weeks thereafter. But in truth Dickens's expectations for the *Carol* had been oversanguine. The £1,000 he had expected to clear – and apparently on the first 10,000 copies – was an unreasonably high profit on any book selling to the customer at five shillings. He had himself insisted upon coloured plates and an unusually luxurious format. And when the final accounts came in, the profits on editions totalling 15,000 amounted to £726. It would have been judicious had Chapman and Hall included with their February statement some tentative forecast of this outcome.

But the damage was done, and by the time Dickens went off, near the end of February, to preside at a soirée of the Liverpool Mechanics' Institute, his ties with his old publishers were already severed. When he arrived in Liverpool he found his friend T. J. Thompson awaiting him at Radley's Hotel. Tremendous applause greeted Dickens when he took the chair. In his speech, he praised the city of Liverpool and the founders of the Institute for their noble work in making education and enlightenment available to labouring people. He spoke warmly of the decision to add a girls' school to the institution and extend education to "those who are our best teachers, and whose lessons are oftenest heeded in after life." At the end, the 1,300 people in the audience cheered, clapped, and stamped their feet in a way "thundering and awful."

In the entertainment that followed, Dickens, referring to the programme, said, "I am requested to introduce to you a young lady whom I have some difficulty and tenderness in announcing – Miss Weller, who will play a fantasia on the piano." The whole audience, with happy memories of Mr Pickwick's faithful follower, exploded into laughter; and, looking around, Dickens saw a young girl, painfully embarrassed, frail and ethereally beautiful, looking at him beseechingly. His heart leaped in his breast. Her fragility and loveliness seemed to him too vulnerable for survival in this world; there was "an angel's message in her face . . . that smote me to the heart."

Recovering his self-control, he led her to the piano. Her playing did not dim the shining impression she had made. How she "started out alone from the whole crowd"! Her name was Christiana Weller, he learned, amazed and startled by his feelings. At the end of the evening he asked her to bring her father to lunch with him the next day. Going back to his hotel, he was haunted by that angel face.

The next day obliged him to leave for Birmingham, where he was to speak for the Polytechnic Institution that night. He tore himself away, promising to send her Tennyson's poems, which he learned that she had not read. To Thompson he wrote, "I cannot joke about Miss Weller. . . . Good God, what a madman I should seem, if the incredible feeling I have conceived for that girl could be made plain to anyone!"

The reception at Birmingham was even more elaborate than that at

Liverpool. The entire auditorium of the Town Hall was decorated with artificial flowers. Facing the platform, in front of the gallery, the words "Welcome Boz" appeared in letters of flowers six feet high. At ten minutes to eight he was brought to the Hall, crammed to the roof with 2,000 people. "Tar-nation grand it was," he wrote Thompson, "and rather unbalancing, but Dick with the heart of a lion dashed in bravely and made decidedly the best speech I ever heard him achieve. Sir, he was jocular, pathetic, eloquent, conversational, illustrative, and wise – always wise."

On 11 March, a little more than a week after his return to London, Dickens found in his morning mail a letter from Thompson, who had fallen in love with Christiana Weller. "I felt the blood go from my face to I don't know where," Dickens responded, "and my very lips turn white." Thompson was worried by the fact that he himself was a widower and considerably older than Christiana. What should he do? Dickens's answer came in a rush: "If I had your independent means . . . I would not hesitate . . . But would win her if I could, by God."

To her father, Dickens urged, Thompson should point out that the musical career to which he was bent on devoting her "should not be called her life but Death"; only repose, a mind at rest, a foreign climate, might possibly save her from an end that otherwise was speedy and certain. But even without this hope, Dickens added passionately, "I could bear better her passing from my arms to Heaven than I could endure the thought of coldly passing into the World again to see her no more."

Two days later he was urging Thompson not to tarry, but dash in at once; and then – "Think of Italy!" For of course Thompson must bring her to Italy, where they might all be together "in some delicious nook." "At the father I snap my fingers. I would leap over the head of the tallest father in Europe, if his daughter's heart lay on the other side . . ." "Such Italian Castles, bright in sunny days, and pale in moonlight nights, as I am building in the air!"

Dickens's own plans for departure were shaping up rapidly, and his letter of credit was ready at Coutts's. The house was expeditiously rented. "A most desirable widow (as a tenant I mean) proposed, only last Saturday," Dickens wrote, "to take our house for the whole time of our intended absence abroad – on condition that she had possession of it today." The family therefore went into temporary lodgings at 9 Osnaburgh Terrace from 28 May until they left in early July.

Dickens had asked Lady Blessington what she thought of Nice, but she and Count D'Orsay insisted there was no place to equal Pisa. To Angus

Fletcher, who was in Italy, Dickens wrote suggesting that Fletcher join them in Pisa and asking his help in finding a palazzo for them to rent.

Here is a list of the caravan [he wrote]:

(1) The inimitable Boz.

(2) The other half ditto.

(3) The sister of ditto ditto.

(4) Four babies, ranging from two years and a half to seven and a half.

(5) Three women servants, commanded by Anne of Broadstairs.

The baby, Francis Jeffrey, they would leave in the care of Mrs Hogarth.

About his financial situation Dickens had become less agitated. "The half year's account," he wrote Mitton, "is GOOD. Deducting £50 a month from Chuzzlewit up to the end, the debt is reduced to £1,900 . . . So please God it will have come down bravely by the time I start." Fortunately, Bradbury and Evans had decided that the entire remainder of his debt to Chapman and Hall should be paid before he left, and all matters settled concerning the stock of books in which Dickens had an interest.

Point by point the final details of his arrangement with his new publishers were worked out. From the book sale of *Martin Chuzzlewit* Dickens was able to repay Bradbury and Evans the £500 they had advanced him. He estimated that he would need £1,500 to repay Chapman and Hall and another £1,500 for his year abroad, with perhaps an additional £500 in the spring of next year. The agreements with Chapman and Hall left only *Oliver Twist* and *American Notes* available for immediate republication, but possibly Chapman and Hall would be favourable to a general reissue of the others in volumes, under the auspices of Bradbury and Evans, with new prefaces and notes.

During negotiations Dickens's estimate was decreased a little and on 1 June Bradbury and Evans advanced Dickens £2,800, secured by a fourth share of whatever he might write during the ensuing eight years. No interest was to be paid on this sum, and no obligations imposed about what works were to be written, though it was understood that a successor to the *Carol* would be ready for Christmas 1844. If the magazine that had been discussed were initiated, and Dickens were "only partially editor or author," he was to own two thirds of its copyright and profits, instead of the three quarters that would be his if he were sole contributor.

In the weeks immediately before and after working out this arrangement, Dickens was as busy as ever. He wrote several leading articles for the *Morning Chronicle* which inspired Richard Doyle, Black's successor in the editorial chair of that paper, to ask if he would not send a weekly travel letter from Italy; "for such contributions Easthope would pay anything." But Easthope was "such a damned screw," Dickens told Mitton, that he doubted Easthope's munificence. However, he gave no definite refusal. "I said to Doyle, 'I won't make any bargain with him at all, or haggle like a peddler, but I'll write a leader now and then and leave him in June to send me a cheque for the whole. He shall set his own value on them; and if he sets too little, the shame is his, and not mine.'"

John Overs, the carpenter, was now hopelessly ill, and striving desperately to make some provision for his family before he died. He asked Dickens's aid in getting one of his little boys into Christ's Hospital, the famous Blue Coat School, and Dickens gave him the names of several gentlemen whose influence might help. He also gave Overs a letter to a number of publishers who might bring out a volume of his collected pieces. One of these did accept the little book. When it came out, towards the close of the year, under the title, *Evenings of a Working Man*, it was dedicated to Dr Elliotson and had an introduction that Dickens wrote for it during these last hurried weeks before his departure.

Late in March Thompson sent Dickens a letter announcing his engagement to Miss Weller. "It is a noble prize you have won," Dickens replied. ". . . Good Heavens, what a dream it appears! Shall we ever forget that night when she came up to the piano – that morning when Dick, the energetic Dick, devised the visit!" "The father seems to have acted like a man. I had my fears of that, I confess; for the greater part of my observation of Parents and children had shown selfishness in the first, almost invariably."

Unexpectedly, within the course of the next few days, Thompson's brother-in-law Charles Smithson died. Dickens hurried down to Yorkshire for the funeral. He was surprised to find Thompson again despairing of his courtship. The obstacle to his success, it turned out, had not been the father after all, but "exactly what I predicted," Dickens exclaimed, a prior attachment, "kept secret by her – and the parents *with* Thompson." "She" told Thompson "that there were other footprints in the field – and so forth."

But Dickens counselled Thompson not to give up hope, and on returning to London, he wrote Miss Weller in his friend's behalf. He could not find it in his heart, he said, to remonstrate with Thompson's folly. "Indeed I rather encouraged him in it than otherwise; for I had that amount of sympathy with his condition, which, but that I am beyond the reach – the lawful reach – of the Wings that fanned his fire, would have rendered it the greatest happiness and pleasure of my life to have run him through the body. In no poetical or tender sense, I assure you, but with good sharp Steel."

Meanwhile, preparations for the journey to Italy went forward. Landor had told Dickens that Genoa was preferable to Pisa, and suggested that he try to rent Lord Byron's villa at Albaro, on the sea-coast near the city. It turned out, however, that this house had fallen into ruinous condition and had a cheap wineshop in its ground floor. Dickens had consequently written Fletcher, asking him to find another house, preferably at Albaro. Fletcher wrote back that he had turned up a house named the Villa di Bella Vista. Dickens did not like to bind himself to rent for an entire year a place that he had not seen. "Take the illustrious abiding place for the illustrious man *for three months*," he instructed Fletcher, with the stipulation that he should be able to extend the time to a year if he wished.

It now occurred to Dickens that he might purchase cheaply "some good old shabby devil of a coach" and have the convenience of travelling in his own conveyance. Exactly such a one he found. "As for comfort," he wrote Forster, "– let me see – it is about the size of your library; with night-lamps and day-lamps and pockets and imperials and leathern cellars, and the most extraordinary contrivances." Marked £60, this prodigy was obtained for £45; at the same time Dickens engaged as courier Louis Roche, a beaming and vigorously bustling native of Avignon.

On 4 June, Dickens presided at the London Tavern over a dinner in aid of the Sanatorium at Devonshire Place House established by Dr Southwood Smith as the first nursing home in London. There was also, just before Dickens's departure, a farewell dinner at Greenwich to cele-brate the completion of *Martin Chuzzlewit*. Among the guests came, in the tow of Stanfield, the great painter Turner, enveloping his old throat that sultry day in a huge red belcher-handkerchief, and paying more attention to the changing lights on the river than to the speeches.

At last, on 2 July, Dickens and his entourage started out. With that "vast phantom," the travelling coach, went Dickens and Kate, Georgina, Charley, Mamey, Katey, Walter, and the baby, who was coming after all. With them came Anne, the faithful maid of their American trip, and her domestic staff. With them came Roche, the courier. With them came Timber, leaping and barking excitedly.

Dickens also was excited. He was glad to get away from England, and fed up with the way its social system was dominated by the aristocracy.

I declare I never go into what is called "society" that I am not aweary of it, despise it, hate it, and reject it. The more I see of its extraordinary conceit, and its stupendous ignorance of what is passing out of doors, the more certain I am that it is approaching the period when, being incapable of reforming itself, it will have to submit to be reformed by others off the face of the earth.

All enthusiasm for the "gallant holiday" in Italy, he pictured himself "in a striped shirt, moustache, blouse, red sash, straw hat, and white trousers, sitting astride a mule, and not caring for the clock, the day of the month or the day of the week."

25

From the Bells of Genoa . . .

The Channel crossing was uneventful. In Boulogne, going into the bank for money, Dickens delivered laboriously a rather long address in French to the clerk behind the counter, only to hear the latter ask in English, "How would you like to take it, Sir?" But he took it, as everyone had to, in five-franc pieces, an inconveniently bulky coinage that forced him to carry it in two sacks.

Five days after they left England, on Sunday, 7 July, the party left Paris. The postilion cracked his whip like a madman, shouted "En route! Hi!" and they were off, through the gate of the Hôtel Meurice, rumbling over the cobblestones near the Morgue, across the Pont Neuf and on the road to Marseilles.

For two days the huge coach rolled through dreary plains, past walled towns, châteaux with candle-snuffer towers, wagons loaded with Swiss cheeses, bony women holding cows by ropes. At sunset it would rattle into a market town, and heave under the wooden arch of a rambling inn amid a dementia of excitement. Idlers stared awe-struck at the enormous vehicle, landlord and landlady shouted rapturously over the children, Roche the courier rushed around looking after beds and eating cucumbers, one in each hand. Early next morning, after a fiery dispute over the bill between Roche and the landlord, they were off again, past the lace sellers, and the butter and egg sellers, the fruit sellers swarming in the square.

At Lyons, scorching and chaotic, with garbage rotting in the gutters, the stone pavement in the Cathedral was as dirty as the streets, and the building empty except for some old women and a few dogs engaged in contemplation. The sacristan set in motion the mechanism of the famous clock: hosts of small doors flew open, little figures staggered out and jerked back. From a pigeonhole near the Virgin an evil-looking puppet, Dickens wrote, "made one of the most sudden plunges I ever saw accomplished: instantly flopping back again at the sight of her, and banging his little door after him. . . . I rashly said, 'Aha! The Evil

Spirit. To be sure. He is very soon disposed of.' 'Pardon, Monsieur,' said the Sacristan, with a polite motion of his hand towards the little door, as if introducing somebody – 'The Angel Gabriel!'"

Daybreak of the 11th saw the carriage and the entire party loaded on a grimy vessel and steaming down the arrowy Rhône. The Alps were now close at hand, with ruined castles perched on every eminence and tiny houses white amid the dull green of the olive trees. By afternoon they sighted the bridge of Avignon and all the underdone-piecrust battlements of the city baking in the sun.

The old city of the Popes was cleaner than Lyons, brilliant with oleanders in bloom, but shadowed for Dickens by the ancient palace with its funnel-roofed torture chamber and the dark oubliettes where the prisoners of the Inquisition were lost to the world. As Dickens gazed on the hammers that mashed the victims' limbs, the sharp stake, the irons once heated red-hot, the stone trough of the water torture, and the trap door for disposing of the mangled remains, his heart sickened. "Gurgle, swill, bloat, burst, for the Redeemer's honour! Suck the bloody rag, deep down into your unbelieving body, Heretic, at every breath you draw!" One sight struck him with bitter irony. "Conceive the parable of the Good Samaritan having been painted on the wall of one of these Inquisition chambers!"

Jolting in the unwieldy carriage again, over roads lined with burnt trees and vines powdered white with dust, under a sun that made the noonday air like crisp blue fire, the party passed through Aix and presently reached Marseilles, foul with the stench of its stagnant harbour. Here a gay-awninged little boat took them out to the *Marie Antoinette*, lying near the mouth of the harbour. Their carriage was hoisted on board, bumping into everything amid a Vesuvius of profanity. Under a clear afternoon sky they steamed out into the azure Mediterranean.

Early next morning they were off Nice. Before three, Genoa was in view, and they saw it rise, terrace above terrace, garden above garden, palace above palace, height upon height. Ashore, the bulging carriage was provided with horses for the two-mile drive to Albaro. Dickens was dismayed by his first glimpses of the city. The Strada Nuova and the Strada Balbi, the famous streets of palaces, were a disorderly jumble of dirty houses full of filth and sickening smells, the passages narrower and more squalid than any in the rookeries of St Giles. As they dragged uphill, the way grew still narrower; the carriage had to be measured to see whether it would squeeze through, and was so tight a fit that it scraped holes in the plastered walls on either side. At last they came to a stop before an archway with a rusty and sagging gate opening on a rank, dull, weedy courtyard attached to a building that looked, Dickens reflected, like a pink jail. His heart sank. This "lonely, rusty, stagnant old staggerer of a domain" was the Villa di Bella Vista!

He and Kate did not feel more cheerful as he yanked repeatedly on a bell-pull and no one came. He tried a crumbling old knocker, and at last Roche appeared and opened the gate. They walked through the seedy little garden, into a bleak square hall, up a cracked marble staircase, and through the doors of an enormous conical-vaulted *sala* with whitewashed walls, time-blackened pictures, and monumental furniture in red brocade. On the same floor and upstairs and downstairs were innumerable other gaunt apartments, drawing-room, dining-room, bedchambers, some half dozen small sitting-rooms, and kitchens looking like alchemical laboratories. "A mighty old, wandering, ghostly, echoing, grim, bare house . . . as ever I beheld or thought of."

In a state of lugubrious discouragement, the tired parents saw that the children were given supper and put to bed. How had Angus Fletcher happened to choose a bleak mausoleum like this pink monstrosity? And in fact the kindhearted but inefficient sculptor had made a very poor bargain. M. De la Rue, the Swiss banker in Genoa whom he had consulted, had urged him to take the magnificent Doria Palace, which was to be had at £40 a year. Located only six miles outside Genoa on the seacoast, it was splendidly furnished, and had beautiful gardens and terraces. But Fletcher had been instructed to rent a villa at Albaro, and this pink elephant of a house being the only one available there, he had taken it at four times the price of the Palazzo Doria.

Next morning, though, Dickens felt more cheerful. In a clear blue sky the sun was shining on the deep ultramarine of the Mediterranean. Beyond the Bay of Genoa, the Alps stretched to the far horizon; on the other side were mountains crowned with forts; in between, a dotting of villas, "some green, some red, some yellow, some blue, some (and ours among the number) pink." Below the terrace outside the French windows of the *sala*, the vineyard was bursting with grapes and figs. From the courtyard gate a narrow lane led down to the sea. And "such green, green, green, as flutters in the vineyard down below," Dickens wrote to Maclise, "*that* I never saw; nor yet such lilac and such purple as float between me and the distant hills; nor yet in anything . . . such awful, solemn, impenetrable blue, as in that same sea."

Everything was in extremes. "There is an insect here that chirps all day . . . something like a Brobdingnagian grasshopper. The creature is born to chirp; to progress in chirping; to chirp louder, louder, louder, till it gives one tremendous chirp and bursts itself . . . The summer gets hotter, hotter, hotter, till it explodes. The fruit gets riper, riper, riper, till it falls down and rots." "The day gets brighter, brighter, brighter, till it's night." Suddenly the impatient sun would plunge down head-long, and then "you may behold the broad sea, villas, mountains, houses, forts, strewn with rose leaves . . . For a moment. No more." In one rush there would be the star-sprinkled dark.

In the heat of the day, though, Dickens discovered, the lattice blinds had to be close-shut against the view, "or the sun would drive you mad"; and after sunset the windows had to be shut, "or the mosquitoes would tempt you to commit suicide." The stable was "so full of 'vermin and swarmers,' " he wrote Forster, "that I always expect to see the carriage going out bodily, with legions of industrious fleas harnessed to and drawing it off, on their own account."

In comparison with the fleas, other afflictions were trivial.

As for the flies, you don't mind them. . . . The rats are kept away, quite comfortably, by scores of lean cats, who roam about the garden for that purpose. The lizards, of course, nobody cares for; they play in the sun, and don't bite. The little scorpions are merely curious. The beetles are rather late, and have not appeared yet. The frogs are company. There is a preserve of them in the next villa; and after nightfall, one would think that scores upon scores of women in pattens were going up and down a wet stone pavement without a moment's cessation.

Dickens rapidly set about solving all the problems of adjustment to this strange environment. It was clear that the villa would not do for the winter. Luckily, he had bound himself only for the three summer months, and he could look around for something else meanwhile. The children could play in the garden and the vineyard; and under the terrace there was a stable where three cows lazily chewed vine leaves and supplied milk by the bucketful. Fruit and vegetables were abundant. "Green figs I have already learnt to like. Green almonds (we have them at dessert every day) are the most delicious fruit in the world. And green lemons, combined with some rare hollands that is to be got here, make prodigious punch . . ."

For better ventilation Dickens transformed the dining-room, along-side the *sala*, into a nursery. The corner room, adjoining, which was the best bedroom, he took as his and Kate's, and determined it should also be his writing room. Around the corner were Georgina's room and another nursery. Within a week Dickens had added a piano to the furniture of the *sala*, and they had all settled down to a regular routine. Breakfast was at half-past nine or ten, dinner at four, bedtime at eleven. The servants they had brought with them were soon on cordial terms with the couple of Italian workers who completed the establishment. "To hear one or other of them," Dickens wrote, "talking away to our servants with the utmost violence and volubility in Genoese, and our servants answering with great fluency in English (very loud; as if the others were only deaf, not Italian), is one of the most ridiculous things possible."

Dickens's books and writing equipment had not yet arrived, but meanwhile he engaged "a little patient revolutionary officer," to read and speak Italian with him three times a week, and began Manzoni's *I Promessi Sposi*. Within a month he could ask for whatever he wanted in any shop or coffee-house and read with a fair degree of fluency. "I wish you could see me without my knowing it," he wrote Forster, "walking about alone here. I am now as bold as a lion in the streets. The audacity with which one begins to speak when there is no help for it, is quite astonishing."

A confused and noisy life elbowed the decayed magnificence of Genoa. Gilded sedan chairs plied down tortuous alleys among blind beggars, jingling mules, and naked children. The peasant girls, though not beautiful, carried themselves well; the old women were of an ugliness so stupendous that Dickens seemed to see the witches from *Macbeth* in every doorway. Bare-legged Cappuccini were everywhere in the cramped streets. Palaces with terraces of orange trees had heavy stone balconies and immense public staircases leading to great frescoed halls mouldering and rotting in the oozing corners. Buildings once noble residences were now crammed with miscellaneous occupants. Macaroni and polenta sellers established their stalls under the garbage-strewn arches of ruinous houses. Tumbledown tenements in the narrow byways smelled like cheese kept in hot blankets. Amid the refuse greasy shops sprouted like parasitic fungus.

Only the churches seemed free from the general squalor, although Dickens found much tasteless trash mingled with their rich embellishments and too many "sprawling effigies of maudlin monks." The church of the Annunciata, with its innumerable small chapels and high dome, was so splendidly decorated and set in gold to the utmost height of its cupola that it looked, he said, "like a great enamelled snuff-box."

But every sort of splendour is in perpetual enactment through the means of these churches. Gorgeous processions in the streets, illuminations of windows on feast nights, lighting up of lamps and clusterings of flowers before the shrines of saints; all manner of show and display. The doors of the churches stand wide open, and in this hot weather great red curtains wave in their places . . .

But the "repulsive countenances" of the countless priests and monks seemed to him to bear the legible signs of "sloth, deceit, and intellectual torpor."

By 10 August his paper and inkstand and the knick-knacks he liked to have on his writing table had arrived from England, and he began to think about his Christmas story. Although he had arranged to move to the Palazzo Peschiere in Genoa at the end of September, he felt unsettled until the change was actually made. Not a word, therefore, got on paper during the two and a half months at Albaro.

He had made the acquaintance of the French Consul-General, an enthusiastic admirer who had written about his books in one of the French reviews, and who lived with his English wife in the very next villa. At a dinner there, Dickens met the Marquis di Negri, once the friend of Byron and a prodigious improviser in verse. After dinner the Consul proposed Dickens's health, and the Marquis, giving himself a great rap on the breast, "turns up his fishy eyes, stretches out his arm like the living statue defying the lightning at Astley's and delivers four impromptu verses in my honour, at which everybody is enchanted, and I more than anybody – perhaps with the best reason, for I didn't understand a word of them."

Soon after, the Marquis invited Dickens to a great reception in his splendid residence whose grounds were carved in grottoed walks and lit by many-coloured lamps. Suddenly Dickens remembered in horror that the gates of Genoa closed at midnight and realized that he must make a sudden bolt if he wished to get back to Albaro. He was running as hard as he could, over uneven ground, downhill, when he came to a pole fastened across the street breast-high,

without any light or watchman – quite in the Italian style. I went over it headlong, with such force that I rolled myself completely white in the dust; but although I tore my clothes to shreds, I hardly scratched myself except in one place on the knee. I had no time to think of it then, for I was up directly and off again to save the gate, but when I got outside the wall and saw the state I was in, I wondered I had not broken my neck.

It was not long before he had recovered, and was swimming daily in the "little blue bay just below the house here, like a fish in high spirits." Between plunges he made friends with the coastguard men, amiable fellows, startlingly innocent of maritime knowledge. "One of them asked me only yesterday, if it would take a year to get to England in a ship?"

A delightful discovery was the marionette theatre in Genoa. The puppet that played the comic parts was equipped, Dickens wrote, "with extra joints in his legs: and a practical eye, with which he winks at the pit in a manner that is absolutely insupportable." A miniature ballet brought the entertainment to a delirious climax: "The height to which they spring; the impossible and inhuman extent to which they pirouette; the revelation of their preposterous legs; the coming down with a pause, on the very tips of their toes, when the music requires it; . . . the final passion of a pas-de-deux; and the going off with a bound! – I shall never see a real ballet, with a composed countenance again."

Early in September, Dickens went to Marseilles to meet his brother Fred, who was coming to pass a fortnight's holiday at Genoa. Swimming out the morning after his arrival, Fred was almost drowned in a strong current, and was rescued only by the chance of a fishing boat leaving the harbour at that time. "It was a world of horror and anguish," Dickens wrote Forster, "crowded into four or five minutes of dreadful agitation; and, to complete the terror of it, Georgy, Charlotte [the nurse] and the children were on a rock in full view of it all, crying, as you may suppose, like mad creatures."

On Fred's return to England, near the end of September, Dickens moved from the Pink Jail to the Palazzo Peschiere, the Palace of the Fishponds. He had taken the entire *piano nobile* of this famous building. As the Dickens household reached the stately terraces leading to the Palazzo the sun shone brightly on its urns and sculptured figures, and on the groves of camellias and orange and lemon trees. Goldfish swam in the water of seven fountains, hedges of pink roses blushed in the greenery, vines clambered up the balconies, and beyond the steep descending slope, Genoa stretched its panorama of towers in a bowl of harbour and hills encircled by the blue Mediterranean and the distant mountains sparkling with snow.

Within was "the grand sala, fifty feet high, of an area larger than the dining room of the Academy," Dickens wrote Forster, "and painted, walls and ceiling, with frescoes" designed by Michelangelo, and

as fresh as if the colours had been laid on yesterday. On the same floor as this great hall are a drawing-room and a dining-room, into which we might put your large room – I wish we could! – away in one corner, and dine without knowing it, both covered also with frescoes still bright enough to make them thoroughly cheerful, and both so nicely proportioned as to give their bigness all the effect of snugness. . . .

Adjoining the sala right and left, are the two best bedrooms; in size and shape like those at Windsor Castle but greatly higher; both having altars, a range of three windows with stone balconies, floors tesselated in patterns of black and white stone, and walls painted every inch: on the left, nymphs pursued by satyrs as large as life and as wicked; on the right, Phaeton larger than life, with horses bigger than Meux and Co.'s, tumbling down into the best bed.

The right-hand room Dickens occupied with Kate; of the left he took possession as a study, writing behind a big screen set up before a window whence he could look down into the gardens and out over Genoa to the lighthouse in the harbour.

Dickens was eager to begin his second Christmas story. But in spite of the fact that he had chosen his subject, he still found it difficult to make a start. He missed the London streets that he had paced at night in blazing excitement while the *Christmas Carol* seethed in his imagination. He had no title, and he had never found it possible to make headway in writing until a title was decided on. The bells of Genoa, clanging and clashing the hours from every tower, drove him almost mad with distraction.

Something was wrong. And with the emotional disturbance of his inability to break through the barrier, he dreamed of Mary again in the old heart-rending way. In the dream he was in a vague place of light with a spirit draped in blue like one of Raphael's Madonnas. Although he could not make out the face, he knew that it was Mary's spirit. Weeping with delight, he stretched out his arms, calling it "Dear." In an agony lest the vision leave him, he asked questions: "Give me some token that you have really visited me!" and then, desperate that it might vanish, "What is the True religion?" The spirit hesitated. Dickens suggested that perhaps the forms of religion did not greatly matter, "if we try to do good? – or perhaps," he added, "the Roman Catholic is the best?" "For *you*," it said, with heart-breaking tenderness, "for *you*, it is the best!" Then he awoke with tears streaming down his face.

A week passed by and his work had not progressed an inch. "Never did I so stagger upon a threshold before," he lamented to Forster. Two days later he was longing for his London night walks again. "Put me down at Waterloo Bridge at eight o'clock in the evening, with leave to roam about as long as I like, and I would come home, as you know, panting to go on. I am sadly strange as it is, and can't settle." The sun shone, the water sparkled in the fountains, the bells clamoured with an intolerable resonance that hammered his brain empty. But suddenly the title came, and he announced it to Forster in a letter consisting only of a quotation from Falstaff: "We have heard THE CHIMES at midnight, Master Shallow!"

The bells had evoked some reverberating chord within his imagination. "Let them clash upon me now from all the churches and convents in Genoa, I see nothing but the old London belfry I have set them in. In my mind's eye, Horatio, I like more and more my notion of making, in this little book, a great blow for the poor." And, amid the frescoes of the Palazzo Peschiere, there came to him the image of Trotty Veck, the "sorry old drudge of a London ticket-porter, who in his anxiety not to distrust or think hardly of the rich, has fallen into the opposite extreme of distrusting the poor," fearing them "irredeemably bad," and concluding "that his class and order have no business with a new year, and really are 'intruding.'"

The story was to be a plea for charity no less than justice, an indictment of the hardhearted views that made the alms-house a place of punishment and that condemned the workers to a routine of toil unrelieved by any gleam of genial indulgence. Nineteenth-century political economy denied any outlook to the labouring classes save a dreary hovering on the edge of starvation. The Malthusian doctrine of population hung over England like a dark cloud. "Let the poor live hard lives," it said, "sober, celibate, and unamused, let them eat the plainest food, pinch to save, and save to lower the rates – then 'civilization' might win through. . . . Shut the gin shops, prevent travelling on the only day a workingman can travel, make copulation even in marriage seem a sin . . ." Meanwhile let wages go lower, and "put down" suicide by harsh penalties against any poor creatures who have failed to end their own misery. Such were the harsh doctrines against which Dickens sounded a clarion of resistance.

Soon he was feverishly engrossed in tearing off the story. "I am in a regular, ferocious excitement with the Chimes," he wrote Forster; "I get up at seven; have a cold bath before breakfast; and blaze away, wrathful and red-hot until three o'clock or so: when I usually knock off (unless it rains) for the day. . . . I am fierce to finish off in a spirit bearing some affinity to those of truth and mercy, and to shame the cruel and the canting."

All through October the weather was wild and stormy, "worse than any November English weather I have ever beheld, or any weather I have had experience of anywhere. So horrible today that all power has been rained and gloomed out of me. Yesterday, in pure determination to get the better of it, I walked twelve miles in mountain rain. You never saw it rain. Scotland and America are nothing to it."

Confinement to the house was rendered more trying by the fact that during the entire month Mrs Macready's young sister, Susan Atkins, was staying with the family and proved to be an exasperating guest. Dickens had constantly to curb the irritation that Kate and Georgina were forever inclined to reveal, and to remind them of the sacred duties of hospitality. How could Kate dream of being rude to Susan when she remembered how the Macreadys had taken care of the children when Dickens and Kate were in America?

From these frictions it was even a relief to get back to the toilsome and feverish application of his study. There, despite the rain sweeping in gusts across the terrace and the wind worrying the orange trees, Dickens plunged himself into the emotion of his story until he grew worn and gaunt. "My cheeks, which were beginning to fill out, have sunk again; my hair is very lank; my eyes have grown immensely large; and the head inside the hair is hot and giddy. . . . Since I conceived, at the beginning of the second part, what must happen in the third, I have undergone as much sorrow and agitation as if the thing were real; and have wakened up with it at night." On 3 November, he flung down his pen. "Thank God!" he wrote Forster, "I have finished the Chimes. This moment. I take up my pen again today, to say only that much; and to add that I have had what women call 'a real good cry.'"

Under the efficient direction of Roche, the household was now running smoothly. Carpets were down on the floors, fires burning cheerfully on the autumn nights, curtains at the windows to be drawn cosily against the dark. Charley had a writing master and a French master every day, and he and the little girls were about to learn dancing. Dickens had a box at the opera, with his own key. He had made a number of pleasant acquaintances, among them M. De la Rue, the Swiss banker, who with his pretty little English wife had apartments in the Palazzo Rosso. With *The Chimes* off his hands, Dickens was now free to enjoy himself.

Nevertheless he felt tense, agitated, restless. It had not been easy to keep peace between Susan, Kate, and Georgina; and his nerves were frayed, besides, by the fierceness with which he had felt his story. He was keyed up and overwrought. He missed England. Late in October, he had determined to make the long return journey to England, just to spend a few nights in London and read his story aloud to a group of friends there. "If I come," he told Forster, "I shall put up at Cuttris's" – the Piazza Hotel, in Covent Garden – "that I may be close to you." The unspeakable restlessness that had possession of him, he said, would no more let him remain where he was than a full balloon could be prevented from tugging to go up, and there were no ropes that could hold him down.

He would start off at once, with Roche, on a fortnight's holiday tour that would take in Parma, Modena, Bologna, Venice, Verona, Brescia, and Milan. "Now, you know my punctiwality," Dickens concluded, "Frost, ice, flooded rivers, steamers, horses, passports, and custom-houses may damage it. But my design is, to walk into Cuttris's coffee-room . . . in good time for dinner. I shall look for you at the farther table by the fire – where we generally go."

The day before his departure Dickens had a dinner party of fourteen guests, including the English Consul and his wife, the English banker, and the De la Rues. Roche, as major-domo, delightedly hovered behind Kate with a case of toothpicks in his pocket, looking at Dickens, and whispering to Georgina, whenever he handed her anything, "What does master think of datter 'rangement? Is he cŏntĕnt?" The climax of his joy came with the arrival of the dessert when he triumphantly produced ices frozen in the shapes of fruit.

The next afternoon, 6 November, Dickens and Roche set off for Piacenza in a stagecoach like a travelling caravan. At the end of the journey were England and the longed-for reunion with his friends. Eagerly he drew the picture in his mind, a little circle in Lincoln's Inn Fields on a wet evening, with Forster saying, "My boy, would you give us that little Christmas book (a little Christmas book of Dickens's, Macready, which I'm anxious you should hear); and don't slur it now, or be too fast, Dickens, please!"

26

. . . To the Chimes of London

All next day they drove through a cheerless rain, packed into a small coach with an old priest, a young Jesuit, a provincial lawyer, and a red-nosed gentleman with a very wet brown umbrella. The following day came Parma with its campanile; then Bologna; then Ferrara and Tasso's prison. On the road Dickens had felt it necessary to write Kate warning her again about Mrs Macready's sister. No "natural dislike to her inanities" must be allowed to destroy the memory of their debt to the Macreadys. "You are too easily run away with – and Georgy is too – by the irritation and displeasure of the moment," Dickens wrote. "I should never forgive myself or you, if the smallest drop of coldness or misunderstanding were created between me and Macready, by means so monstrously absurd."

Late in the evening of the 11th, Dickens's coach came to a stop by the waterside, and a black gondola conveyed him five miles over the dark sighing water to a great light lying on the sea. Presently Venice rose like a huge ship, and then he was gliding through the silent canals. Flitting shadows, branching lanes of mysterious water, painted pillars with boats moored to them, torchlit palace entries, bridges, and open spaces of ponderous arches and pillars passed him dreamlike in the night.

Not until the cold, bright, bracing day, when he stood in the Piazza, did the glory of Venice burst around him. "The wildest visions of the Arabian Nights are nothing to the Piazza of Saint Mark, and the first impression of the inside of the church. The gorgeous and wonderful reality of Venice, is beyond the fancy of the wildest dreamer. Opium couldn't build such a place, and enchantment couldn't shadow it forth in vision." Splendid domes and turrets, the majestic palace, the magnificent Cathedral, the campanile, the red granite pillar with the Lion of St Mark, the two bronze giants hammering out the hours, the white houses of the square, all lay floating with incredible buoyance on the bosom of the green sea.

I have never yet seen any praise of Titian's great picture of the Assumption of the Virgin at Venice, which soared half as high as the beautiful and amazing reality. Tintoretto's picture, too, of the Assembly of the Blest, . . . with all the lines in it (it is of immense size and the figures are countless) tending majestically and dutifully to Almighty God in the centre, is grand and noble in the extreme.

But beneath all that iridescent glory there was a nightmare world of "wickedness and gloom – its awful prisons, deep below the water; its judgement chambers, secret doors, deadly nooks, where the torches you carry with you blink as if they couldn't bear the air." With the memory of these horrors, Dickens burst into a passionate denunciation of those witless worshippers of the good old times who always aroused his bitter scorn. That, in the face of these dungeons, there should be "hundreds of parrots," he exclaimed, "who will declaim to you in speech and print, by the hour together, on the degeneracy of the times in which a railroad is building across the water at Venice; instead of going down on their knees, the drivellers, and thanking Heaven that they live in a time when iron makes roads, instead of . . . engines for driving screws into the skulls of innocent men."

From Venice Dickens proceeded rapidly to Milan. The inns were bare and comfortless, but he enjoyed himself thoroughly. The beds were clean, the meals good, and the servants so quick and obliging "that you would be a beast not to look cheerful"; and their light-heartedness was a pleasure. After three days in Milan, seeing Leonardo's *Last Supper* and the jewelled mummy of San Carlo Borromeo, and attending a ballet at the Scala, Dickens left the city at five o'clock on the morning of the 21st.

He crossed the Alps by moonlight, in intense cold; from Strasbourg the fifty-hour ride by diligence to Paris was a sea of mud. Hard frosts made the roads better during the remainder of the journey, the Channel crossing was quickly accomplished, and on the wintry evening of Saturday, 30 November, Dickens strode eagerly into the coffee-room of Cuttris's hotel. In a moment Forster had spied him, and the two men were in each other's arms.

The eight days Dickens spent in London were jammed to overflowing with work and engagements. Forster's letters had objected to some of the satire in *The Chimes*. He thought Filer was a too distorted caricature and the attack on the benevolent feudalism of the Young England movement ineffective. These details Dickens agreed to amend before the book went to press. The revisions occupied Sunday and the completed manuscript was rushed into the hands of the printers on Monday. As Bradbury and Evans had not yet built up any machinery of distribution, they had arranged to use the facilities of Chapman and Hall, under whose imprint the volume appeared. Dickens's heat against his former publishers, however, had cooled, and he was not displeased.

After a busy day at the offices of Bradbury and Evans, he went off to dine at Gore House with Lady Blessington and Count D'Orsay. For the evening of the next day, Tuesday, 3 December, there was scheduled the reading Dickens had so eagerly anticipated.

Forster had assembled a group of some ten friends at Lincoln's Inn Fields. The evening was an overwhelming triumph. Dickens read eloquently, and the guests were so moved and excited that rumours of the wonderful occasion spread over all London. At Richard Barham's urgent persuasion, Dickens repeated the reading on a second evening with a number of new auditors. But *The Chimes* did not require Dickens's talents as a reader to sway the emotions of those who listened to it. "Anybody who has heard it," Dickens reported to Kate, "has been moved in the most extraordinary manner. Forster read it (for dramatic purposes) to A'Beckett" – one of the staff of *Punch*. "He cried so much and so painfully, that Forster didn't know whether to go on or stop; and he called next day to say that any expression of his feelings was beyond his power." "If you had seen Macready last night," Dickens concluded the same letter to his wife, "undisguisedly sobbing, and crying on the sofa as I read, you would have felt, as I did, what a thing it is to have power."

When the little book was published its success was tremendous. Twenty thousand copies were sold almost at once. But among some of its readers its reception was more varied. Thackeray's friend the Reverend W. H. Brookfield told his wife that it was "as utter trash as was ever trodden under foot." "Jeffrey," Dickens wrote Forster, "is most energetic and enthusiastic. Filer sticks in his throat rather, but all the rest is quivering in his heart."

Dickens had in fact delivered a telling thrust against the chill doctrine that the poor had no right to any save the harsh subsistence imposed by the iron law of wages and should resign themselves to a life of unrelieved toil. Filer's horrified condemnation of the wastefulness of a poor man's eating tripe was hardly more fantastic than the economist McCulloch's advice to labouring men that if they wished to improve their economic status they should tighten their belts and have fewer children. The hated Poor Law that confined the indigent in workhouse bastilles where they were fed more sparsely than criminals in jails was not so uncompromising as Malthus, who held that feeding paupers merely increased their numbers. Some passages in *The Chimes* in fact are only a bitter parody of the sentiments of Sir Peter Laurie, a London alderman who had expressed the determination to put suicide down: "There's a certain amount of cant in vogue about Starvation," says the book's Alderman Cute, "and I intend to Put it Down." Through the benevolence of Sir Joseph Bowley, "the Poor Man's Friend," Dickens neatly reveals the other side of the governing class's attitude toward the workers. "You needn't trouble yourself to think of anything. I will think for you, I know what is good for you; I am your perpetual parent."

Only ignorance or blind prejudice could deny the existence of the attitudes Dickens portrays, and *The Chimes* denounces them impartially, whether they spring from selfish complacency or from the credulous and gullible acceptance of an economic dogma that denied the possibility of ameliorating human misery. Poor Trotty Veck, deferring to the judgement of his betters, concludes that the poor are wrong in every way, that they are born bad and have no right to exist. The social plea that Dickens makes is put in the mouth of Will Fern, the rebellious farm labourer: "Give us . . . better homes when we're a-lying in our cradles; give us better food when we're a-working for our lives; give us kinder laws to bring us back when we're a-going wrong; and don't set Jail, Jail, Jail, afore us, everywhere we turn."

The Chimes is evidence of Dickens's growing preoccupation with social problems and of his growing knowledge that they could not be explained in terms of individual villainy. The reports on child labour and on the toil and filth and long hours in the mines and factories had broadened his horizons. He saw that the same forces that made the criminal dens of Saffron Hill and the slums of Bethnal Green were at work in the Black Country, making hard and greedy men harder and greedier, and forcing men who were not naturally cruel or grasping to behave as if they were. Against a callous self-seeking and a cold utilitarianism Dickens asserted the sense of justice, the generosity of the human heart, the virtue of sympathy, the need to extend the helping hand, not merely in relieving individual misfortune but in solving the problems of society.

For the few days Dickens remained in London after the second reading of *The Chimes*, he was almost wholly occupied in one of those private endeavours to help others that for him represented the half of his social philosophy and that no striving for institutional reforms alone could quite replace. John Overs had died, leaving a wife and six young children, one of them a cripple. His *Evenings of a Working Man* had brought in some money, but the family were still left in "great distress and perplexity."

When Dickens left for Italy again on Sunday night, he had a promise from the Governors of the Orphan Workers School that the eldest boy, a youngster of nine, would be admitted to that institution in April. It also occurred to Dickens that Miss Coutts "might have an opportunity of presenting one of the Girls to some other school or charity, and as I know full well that . . . you would rather thank than blame me for making a real and strong case known to you," he sent her the children's names and ages, from Amelia, aged eleven years, to the baby John, four months. "Mrs Overs tells me," Dickens wrote a few months later, "that Miss Coutts has sent her, at different times, sixteen pounds, has sent a doctor to her children, and has got one of the girls into an Orphan School."

On his way back to Italy, Dickens stopped off for a busy three days in Paris with Macready, who was playing *Hamlet, Macbeth, King Lear, Othello,* Sheridan Knowles's *Virginius,* and the most famous of all his roles, *Werner.* He introduced Dickens to his own Parisian friends, Théophile Gautier, Louis Blanc, Victor Hugo, and Alexandre Dumas. At the Salle Ventadour, Dickens saw Grisi in *Il Pirato,* and was carried away by

> the fire and passion of a scene between her, Mario, and Fornasari. They drew on one another, the two men – not like stage-players, but like Macready himself: and she, rushing in between them, now clinging to this one, now to that, now making a sheath for their naked swords with her arms, now tearing her hair in distraction as they broke away from her and plunged again at each other; was prodigious.

The very next day he watched Macready rehearsing the scene in *Othello* before the doge and council. He was also a great deal in the company of Régnier of the Théâtre Français, and of Louis Bertin, editor of the *Journal des Débats,* made friends with the painters Delaroche and Delacroix, and made the acquaintance of the Comte de Vigny, the author of *Cinq-Mars.* It was a wrench to forgo all this stimulation and tear himself away, but Christmas was only twelve days off, and Dickens wished to spend it with his family. On the night of the 13th he left Paris by the *malle-poste,* and took the ship from Marseilles to Genoa, where he rushed into the arms of his expectant family. By the 22nd he had resumed his former Genoa routine, and was looking forward to celebrating his first Christmas season in Italy.

"Miss Coutts had sent Charley, with the best of letters to me," he wrote Forster, "a Twelfth Cake weighing ninety pounds, magnificently decorated." It was exhibited at a Swiss pastry cook's in Genoa, where it was sent to have some of its sugar ornaments repaired after its voyage. No Twelfth-Night confection had ever been seen in Genoa before, and the customers wondered mightily at its bonbons, crackers, and Twelfth-Night characters all wrought in a marvel of confectionery.

27

The Ghost of Old Rome

Dickens had come abroad, six months before, glowing with the dream of writing a novel unharried by the tyranny of monthly deadlines. But the restlessness that perturbed the beginning of *The Chimes* had not been allayed either by his Italian sightseeing or by his impetuous trip to London, and he returned to Genoa with his literary plans no more definite than they had been before.

Back in September, indeed, he had been distracting himself with the thought of further travels in the south of Italy, and from Paris, on his way to England, he had written to Kate suggesting a trip to Naples, where they would climb Vesuvius together. This idea blossomed into an elaborate scheme of going first to Rome, then on to Naples, where they would be joined by Georgina, and then again to Rome for Holy Week, and winding back to Genoa through Perugia, Arezzo, and Florence. By that time it would be April and there would be little more than two months left of Dickens's year abroad.

An indubitable change had come over his habits of determined application. If he was just as energetic as ever, his energies were not being poured into literary channels. Though he had laboured with fierce excitement over *The Chimes*, that little book had occupied him for only a month. Perhaps he was exhausted by the unremitting toil of nine years in which he had written almost two million words, and his imaginative powers needed a rest. Perhaps he felt uprooted in these strange Italian scenes and had not assimilated their crowding exotic impressions. Perhaps, as he himself thought, he felt the loss of his accustomed walks in London streets and rural lanes and missed the stimulus of familiar companionship. Whatever the reasons, nothing is heard of any new book even conceived.

In Genoa, Dickens's friendship with the De la Rues had grown steadily, and he often visited them in their apartment in the Palazzo Rosso. Mme De la Rue was a "most affectionate and excellent little woman" who suffered so distressingly from a nervous tic that Dickens felt sorry for her and suggested to her husband that he might be able to relieve her by means of mesmerism. Possibly her disorder would yield to hypnotic influences, as Kate's headaches had often done. M. De la Rue gladly accepted Dickens's offer.

In the course of the relationship thus established, Mme De la Rue was presently making strange revelations. Her affliction, she told Dickens, was mysteriously rooted in terrifying hallucinations. She constantly found herself on a green hillside with a very blue sky above, in great pain and terror, with stones hurled down upon her by unseen people. But worst of all was a man haunting this place, of whom she was so terrified that she dared not look upon him and trembled when she spoke of him. This phantom figure filled her with an agony of unending fear.

Dickens felt convinced that he could banish the delusions by suggestion during the magnetic sleep. When she was awake, he urged her not to endanger the possibility of a cure by maintaining any reticences with him. The slightest secret withheld might be the clue that would enable him to overcome her malady.

These efforts at exorcism necessitated prolonged meetings at all hours. They often took place, Kate was disturbed to observe, at the most unconventional times. Dickens had explained to her that "poor little Mrs De la Rue" was tortured by phantasms whose faces she could never see, and that he was sure he could help her dispel them, but Kate did not like the situation and began to feel a suppressed antagonism to Mme De la Rue.

While Kate fretted over this undesirable intimacy and Dickens exulted over an improvement he believed he could already discern in his patient, the time of the Roman Carnival drew near. It was a relief to Kate when on Sunday, 19 January, she and Dickens set out on their journey south. The day was gloomy with mist and wind-driven rain. Throughout the long tempestuous drive to Spezzia, Dickens remained silent and distraught. Kate presently learned that he was worrying lest his absence have a harmful effect on Mme De la Rue and was concentrating on giving her absent treatment. At Pisa he heard from the De la Rues that his patient was doing well. He hoped, Dickens replied, that they would be able to join them in Rome and meanwhile would "rely on the idea of her anxious Physician."

In Pisa Dickens hired "a good-tempered Vetturino and his four horses" to drive them to Rome. After they crossed the papal frontier they rolled on until dusk brought them to the melancholy Lake of

Bolsena. Finally they were on the Roman Campagna, and began to strain their eyes for the first glimpse of the Eternal City. When at length it appeared in the distance, "it looked," Dickens recorded, "like – I am half afraid to write the word like LONDON!!! There it lay, under a thick cloud, with innumerable towers and steeples and roofs of houses, rising up into the sky, and high above them all, one Dome."

They entered the city about four o'clock in the afternoon of 30 January. Though the Tiber had seemed "as yellow as it ought," the muddy streets and the commonplace shops were a disappointment. Where were the great ruins, the solemn tokens of antiquity? "It was no more my Rome, degraded and fallen and lying asleep in the sun among a heap of ruins, than Lincoln's Inn Fields is." Dickens went up to bed that night at the Hotel Meloni "in a very indifferent humour."

St Peter's, next day, was also a disappointment. Though it had looked immense in the distance, and though nothing could exaggerate the beauty of the Piazza, with its exquisite columns and gushing fountains, or the first burst of the interior and its glorious dome, the structure looked small on a near approach and the red-and-yellow fripperies swathing the marble pillars, he felt, gave it the frivolous atmosphere of a lavish pantomime. "I had a much greater sense of mystery and wonder in the Cathedral of San Mark at Venice."

The Colosseum, though, in its "solitude, its awful beauty, and its utter desolation," was overwhelming.

To see it crumbling there, an inch a year; its walls and arches overgrown with green; its corridors open to the day; the long grass growing in its porches; young trees of yesterday, springing up on its ragged parapets, and bearing fruits; . . . to climb into its upper halls, and look down on ruin, ruin, ruin, all about it; the triumphal arches of Constantine, Septimius Severus, and Titus; the Roman Forum; the Palace of the Caesars; the temples of the old religion, fallen down and gone; is to see the ghost of old Rome, wicked wonderful old city, haunting the very ground on which its people trod. It is the most impressive, the most stately, the most solemn, grand, majestic, mournful sight, conceivable.

Here was Rome indeed at last; and such a Rome as no one can imagine in its full and awful grandeur! We wandered out upon the Appian Way, and then went on, through miles of ruined tombs and broken walls . . . Broken aqueducts, left in the most picturesque and beautiful clusters of arches; broken temples; broken tombs. A desert of decay, sombre and desolated beyond all expression; and with a history in every stone that strews the ground.

The Carnival Week was a delirium. Throughout the mile length of the Corso draperies of red, green, blue, white, and gold fluttered from innumerable balconies. The open fronts of shops were groves hung with flowers and evergreens; scaffoldings made temples radiant in silver, gold, and crimson. Carriages heaped with confetti, sugarplums, and nosegays crowded the way. Everywhere women's eyes laughed and sparkled; everywhere graceful forms swam in every bewitching madness of dress: "Little preposterous scarlet jackets; quaint old stomachers more wicked than the smartest bodices; Polish pelisses, strained and tight as ripe gooseberries; tiny Greek caps, all awry, and clinging to the dark hair, Heaven knows how; every wild, quaint, bold, shy, pettish, madcap fancy . . ."

Showers of confetti descended from windows and balconies like clouds, making everyone as white as millers. Maskers in carriages pelted each other with bonbons and flowers. "I wish you could have seen me," Dickens wrote Georgina, "catch a swell brigand on the nose with a handful of very large confetti every time we met him. It was the best thing I have ever done." And throughout the entire mad, shouting turmoil the mood mounted to a riotous climax of hilarity, culminating in the horse races and, after nightfall, the bright scenes of blazing torches and multitudes of lanterns and candles.

With the close of the Carnival, Dickens and Kate started south for Naples. Across the undulating Campagna they rolled for miles, always with ruined aqueducts stalking their giant course in the distance. The Pontine Marshes were flat and lonely beneath a shadowed sky. All night from Terracina the road wound under sharp points of rock, with the murmuring sea below. Just at daybreak there came the first glimpse of Naples, and Vesuvius spouting fire. After another day's journey and a night on the road, they had a day's rest at Capua. There, at last, Mount Vesuvius seemed close at hand, its cone white with snow and a dense cloud of smoke hanging in the air.

Georgina joined the travellers at Naples. Dickens was impatient to learn how Mme De la Rue had been faring in his absence. Feverishly he ripped open his mail and was distressed to read that his unhappy patient was sliding back fast. He was relieved, however, by the news that the De la Rues would join them in Rome, where the mesmeric treatments might be resumed during Holy Week.

The famous Bay of Naples Dickens found inferior to that of Genoa and there were no palaces as lovely as the Peschiere. The houses were like pigsties "heaped up storey on storey, and tumbled house on house." He was shocked by the degraded condition of the poor. "What would I give," Dickens wrote Forster, "that you should see the lazzaroni as they really are – mere squalid, abject, miserable animals for vermin to batten on; slouching, slinking, ugly, shabby, scavenging scarecrows!"

The burial place of the poor was

a great paved yard with three hundred and sixty-five pits in it: every one covered by a square stone which is fastened down. One of these pits is opened every night in the year; the bodies of the pauper dead are collected in the city; brought out in a cart . . . and flung in, uncoffined. Some lime is then cast down into the pit, and it is sealed up until a year is past, and its turn again comes round . . . The cart has a red lamp attached, and about ten o'clock at night you see it glaring through the streets of Naples: stopping at the doors of hospitals and prisons, and such places, to increase its freight; and then rattling off again.

The weather had become so atrocious that Dickens gave up going across the sea into Sicily. But he explored all the curving Neapolitan shoreline, with Capri floating across the blue water like a vision of fairyland. He took the railroad along the sea beach to Sorrento, past Torre del Greco to Castellammare with its vineyards, olive trees, and groves of oranges and lemons, and even ranged as far south as Paestum and its temples. And he wandered through the dead streets of Pompeii and Herculaneum, noting that the ashes of the gigantic eruption that had buried the two cities had forced their way even into the earthen vessels in the wine cellars, choking out the wine with dust.

On the afternoon of 21 February, with Kate and Georgina, Dickens undertook the long-anticipated ascent of Vesuvius. They were in a party of six, accompanied by twenty-two guides. The weather, the severest in twenty years, had covered the steep sides of the mountain in deep snow "glazed with one smooth sheet of ice from the top of the cone to the bottom." Halfway up they caught the sunset, lovely in a cloudless sky, and a little later rose a nearly full moon. They rode on saddle horses to where the snow began. Kate and Georgina were then seated in sedan chairs and Dickens was accommodated with a stout stick for "the almost perpendicular ascent."

By prodigious exertions [he wrote], we passed the region of snow and came into that of fire – desolate and awful you may well suppose. It was like working one's way through a dry waterfall, with every mass of stone burnt and charred into enormous cinders, and smoke and sulphur bursting out of every chink and crevice, so that it was difficult to breathe. High before us, bursting out of a hill at the top of the mountain . . . the fire was pouring out, reddening the night with flames, blackening it with smoke, and spotting it with red-hot stones and cinders that fell down again in showers.

At the base of the topmost cone Kate and Georgina, who were now on foot, were obliged to stop. Dickens, the head guide, and another gentleman resolved, however, in spite of the hoarse roaring of the mountain, to climb the hill to the brink and look into the crater.

The sensation of struggling up it, choked with fire and smoke, and feeling at every step as if the crust of ground between one's feet and the gulf of fire would crumble in and swallow one up (which is the real danger), I shall remember for some little time, I think. But we did it. We looked down into the flaming bowels of the mountain and came back again, alight in half a dozen places, and burnt from head to foot.

The solid coating of ice made going down even harder than going up. But they formed a chain of hands, staggering and sliding, and driving sticks into the ice to prevent going sheer down the precipices every time they fell. Two of the guides did fall, and plunged down into the black night 500 feet below, and a boy went shrieking after them. One of the men was rescued, a heap of rags and bruises, and the boy was brought in with his head in a bloody rag. "My clothes are burnt to pieces. My ladies are the wonder of Naples, and everybody is open-mouthed."

A few mornings after this horrendous expedition, the three travellers started on the journey back to Rome. At the Hotel Meloni Dickens found that the De la Rues had also reserved rooms, and as soon as they arrived he began mesmerizing Mme De la Rue. Once Kate wakened to find Dickens striding up and down the bedroom with all the candles lit. He had just come from struggling with Mme De la Rue's terrors and was still violently agitated with the experience. Some nights later M. De la Rue tapped on their door at one o'clock, and begged Dickens to come to his wife's assistance again. Dickens found her, he said, "rolled into an apparently insensible ball, by tic on the brain." Within half an hour he had her peacefully asleep. The fight against her affliction, however, continued to fluctuate desperately; on 19 March she was again very ill in the night and Dickens did not return to his own room until four in the morning.

When Mme de la Rue's health permitted, she and her husband now joined Dickens's party in all their sightseeing. In the Vatican, Dickens assiduously gazed at paintings and sculpture. "There are portraits innumerable by Titian, Rubens, Rembrandt and Vandyke," he wrote Forster; "heads by Guido, and Domenichino, and Carlo Dolci; subjects by Raphael, and Correggio, and Murillo, and Paul Veronese, and Salvator; which it would be difficult indeed to praise too highly, or to praise enough."

The ceremonies of Holy Week, Dickens found merely tedious and wearisome. The scene at the Sistine Chapel on the Wednesday was one of struggling confusion, with the chanting of the Miserere hardly audible through the heavy curtain of the doorway. At the Washing of the Feet, the favoured thirteen all held great bouquets as large as cauliflowers, the Pope moved briskly from one to another, and the Cardinals smiled at each other as if they thought it all "a great farce," a judgement with which Dickens perfectly agreed. The shuffling progress up the Scala Sancta of numerous worshippers making the pious ascent on their knees struck him as ridiculous and unpleasant "in its senseless and unmeaning degradation."

To Dickens, indeed, the entire ancient, magnificent, and solemn ritual was only a painted rigmarole, a humbug for which he could feel little except a contemptuous impatience. He was glad to emerge from its ornate glitter and make his way, as he did again and again, to the desolate grandeur of the Colosseum. It was the ancient Rome of the Republic and the Caesars that burned in his imagination, not the Renaissance pomp of the wicked old city or the ecclesiastical traditions of a Church that seemed to him a mass of degrading superstitions.

On the Tuesday after Easter, the Dickenses left Rome. With them in their carriage travelled the De la Rues, despite the growing tension created by Kate's distrust of the strange relationship between Dickens and Mme De la Rue. It was true that M. De la Rue seemed to entertain no objections, but Kate's doubts were not alleviated by his complaisance. And her disturbance did not diminish with the daily protraction of this unwelcome intimacy.

On 9 April Dickens was once more at home in the Palazzo Peschiere. Kate was miserably unhappy. The later part of the journey had seen such a growth of friction that she was no longer speaking to the De la

Rues. Dickens tried in vain to persuade her that her suspicions had no foundation. She remained hysterically unconvinced. If the intimacy was as innocent as he said, she could not see why he wouldn't give it up. This Dickens rigidly refused to do; he would not surrender the hope of a cure because Kate persisted in monstrous misconceptions. With the De la Rues he endeavoured to excuse her conduct as a nervous break-down, but her behaviour was so undisguised that at last it forced him to make a "painful declaration" of her feelings. M. De la Rue received it with great delicacy, and considerately made no further allusions to it. The confession was humiliating to Dickens's pride, and he did not forget having been obliged to make it.

Fortunately, the date of the departure from Italy was now less than two months away. The children were all well and had flourished ama-zingly. "Charley and his two sisters," he wrote Tom Beard, had learned to dance, and would "rather astonish you, I think, with sundry Polka, Mazurka, and other fine performances." "Master Frank," the baby – nicknamed Chickenstalker – now fourteen months old, was "a pro-digious blade, and more full of queer tricks than any of his predecessors have been at his time of life."

There was good news, too, from Bradbury and Evans. *The Chimes* had made a profit on the first 20,000 of between £1,400 and £1,500. "They were very anxious to know what I thought of their management in general . . . I wrote and told them that I was greatly pleased, and that I was quite certain it couldn't have been better done, as I am." In addition to these profits, Dickens found that his earnings on the books that Chapman and Hall still controlled amounted for the nine months ending in December 1844, to £394 19s. 2d.

There was certainly no longer any need to worry about money. Dickens accordingly sent Mitton directions about having Devonshire Terrace redecorated. The doors and railings in the garden were to be a bright cheerful green, except for the staircases from the windows, which were to remain white. The hall and staircase inside were to be a good green, "not too decided, of course, to spoil the effect of the prints." The street door was to have a letter box constructed in it, with a glass back, "so that John may see when there are letters in the inside."

For more elaborate improvements in the drawing-room Dickens desired an estimate of the expense. These he designed as an affectionate surprise for Kate. The ugly handrail was to be ripped out, and the walls papered in "blue and gold or purple and gold." "I should like the skirting board to be painted in imitation of Satin-wood – the ceiling to have a faint pink blush in it – and a little wreath of flowers to be painted round the lamp." Then, with a final burst of effervescence he added, "Gold moulding around the paper."

The drawing-room estimate, when it came, was "what Mr Swiveller calls a staggerer. I had no idea it would mount so high. It really should be done; for as it is, it is very poor and mean in comparison with the house – and I have been 'going' to do it these five years. But before I quite decide, will you let me know in one line, by return, *about* the cost of the other repairs in the lump." The statement came, and Dickens told Mitton to go ahead immediately so that the smell of paint would evaporate before the family returned.

The last weeks of the Italian sojourn were delightful. The garden, Dickens wrote on 27 April, "is one grove of roses; we have left off fires; and we breakfast and dine again in the great hall, with the windows open." And, by June, "The fireflies at night now are miraculously splendid; making another firmament among the rocks on the sea-shore, and the vines inland. They get into the bed-rooms, and fly about, all night, like beautiful little lamps."

The Peschiere was in a turmoil of packing by 7 June. Dickens himself had "fled the miseries of moving," and was staying at the Palazzo Rosso, with the De la Rues. "They are all at sixes and sevens up at the Peschiere, as you may suppose," he wrote Forster; "and Roche is in a condition of tremendous excitement, engaged in settling the inventory with the house-agent, who has just told me he is the devil himself."

Although Mme De la Rue had been much helped by Dickens's ministrations, and was less haunted by her phantoms, he feared that after his departure she might be troubled by their return. He suggested that M. De la Rue try to acquire the mesmeric technique, and offered to help him. While Kate, Georgina, Roche, and the servants wrestled with the packing, therefore, Dickens was engaged in teaching M. De la Rue how to induce the magnetic sleep.

At last all arrangements for departure were made. Farewells had been said. The travelling coach was loaded to bursting. Once again Kate, Georgina, the children, and the maids were crammed within. Dickens and Roche took their places on the box. With an unwieldy lurch, the vehicle started, heading north for the St Gothard pass.

The road over the Alps had been open only eight days, and curved between massive walls of snow twenty feet high. They reached Lucerne on 14 June.

The cleanliness of the little baby-houses of inns [said Dickens] is wonderful to those who come from Italy. But the beautiful Italian manners, the sweet language, the quick recognition of a pleasant look or cheerful word; the captivating expression of a desire to oblige in everything; these are left behind the Alps. Remembering them, I sigh for the dirt again: the brick floors, bare walls, unplastered ceilings, and broken windows.

Indeed, Dickens had enjoyed Italy much more than he had America. He had relished the grandeur and the spacious leisure of the Peschiere, and even the unflagging energy of his sightseeing had not been the feverish scramble with which he had hastened over thousands of miles in the United States. There were no intrusive mobs, no throngs of damsels snipping fragments off his clothes, no angry snarlings from a noisy press. The upper classes gave him a courteous welcome, but did not intrude; and to the peasants, landlords of inns, shopkeepers, and servants he was merely another travelling English milord.

No doubt, also, Dickens had learned from his American adventures. He had resolved to make no public comments on Italian institutions or the governments of its states. Nor had he expected any such glorious things of Italian society as he had of the republic across the Atlantic. No nineteenth-century liberal entertained utopian pictures of the Papal States, the Venetian territories ruled by Austria, or the Neapolitan kingdom of Ferdinand II.

Dickens went to Italy, therefore, much more in the spirit of a tourist visiting a museum than in that of a social observer. And the beauty of the Italian landscape was a perpetual revelation to him. But he responded no more profoundly than scores of other travellers to Italian art and architecture. His standards in painting were, for the most part, a bluff insistence on the facts of human anatomy and visual perspective, and a feeling of what facial expressions were "natural to certain passions." Rather ostentatiously determined not to be intimidated into insincere raptures, he made facile mockery of the St Sebastians stuck as full of arrows as animated pincushions and the other conventions of religious iconography.

This crude honesty resulted in judgements sometimes shrewd and sometimes merely flippant. Dickens derided brewers' draymen impersonating Evangelists, and grew facetious about "libellous Angels" playing on fiddles "for the delectation of sprawling monks apparently in liquor." Sculpture he hardly mentioned at all, though he was very good on the exaggerated figures of Bernini, those "breezy maniacs, whose every fold of drapery is blown inside-out." Only occasionally, as in Tintoretto's *Assembly of the Blest*, did he note the organizing principle of a picture, "all the lines . . . tending majestically . . . to Almighty God in the centre."

The monuments of ancient Rome and the ruins of Pompeii struck a vibrant chord in his imagination. Romanesque and Gothic churches moved him with emotions like those he had known in English cathedrals. But although he could enjoy the splendour of the Renaissance in palaces and other secular buildings, those styles seemed frivolous and incongruous to him in ecclesiastical structures. Only when their ornate splendour of gold, marble, mosaic, and glowing colour blazed into the Byzantine gorgeousness of St Mark's, like one of the Arabian Nights fantasies of his childhood, could Dickens forget how different was this polychrome glitter from the cool spaces and dim religious light of Rochester or Canterbury.

In addition, of course, he felt still more violently unsympathetic to the Church of Rome than he did to the Church of England. Although he deplored inflicting penalties on any people for their religious affiliations, he thought the influence of the Roman Church almost altogether evil. Everywhere it seemed to him hand in glove with tyranny and oppression. Everywhere he thought it complaisant to privilege and corruption. Everywhere it riveted shackles on the hearts and minds of the poor whom it professed to succour, and wrung its wealth from their toil and misery. Everywhere it did its worst to keep them in degraded ignorance.

Holding such views, Dickens found it hard to believe that its prelates were not cynically pretending to a faith in the rites they solemnly performed. To his impatient scorn it was incredible that any except the victims of superstition could find in such tiresome flimflam a sincere emotional beauty and a deep spiritual truth.

The lower clergy almost uniformly seemed to him sunk in "sloth, deceit, and intellectual torpor." The Cappuccini perhaps did some good among the poor, but the other orders were constantly prying into secrets of families to establish a baleful ascendancy. The Jesuits, above all, Dickens always saw in unfavourable lights, "skulking," "creeping in and out," "slinking noiselessly about, in pairs, like black cats" or ugly birds of prey.

But for the Italian people Dickens felt a warm affection. He liked "the Neapolitans least of all," and "the Romans next, for they are fierce and brutal." "In the mass," though, he told Miss Coutts, "I like the common people of Italy very much." Their cheerfulness, their beautiful manners, their swift response to friendly treatment, their captivating desire to please, brought a glow to his own heart. Saying his farewell to Italy, "with all its miseries and wrongs," he said it with tenderness for "a people naturally well-disposed, and patient, and sweet-tempered."

On the closing page of *Pictures from Italy*, "Years of neglect, oppression, and misrule," he wrote, "have been at work, to change their nature and reduce their spirit . . . but the good that was in them ever, is in them yet, and a noble people may be, one day, raised up from these ashes."

28

Birth Pangs
of the *Daily News*

Since 1842 Dickens's mind had recurred more than once to the idea of founding a great liberal newspaper with himself as editor. Nagged by nervous fears lest his current popularity might wane, he worried about how he could support his large family if the public suddenly stopped buying his books. Now, in 1845, he had five children, and there was another one on the way. A handsome editorial salary would be a comforting provision against future dangers.

Moreover, the time seemed ripe for such an enterprise. During the later years of the Whig administration there had been nothing but deficits, universal stagnation in business, and acute misery in the labouring population; and in 1841 the Tories had been returned to power. Sir Robert Peel's budgets from 1842 to 1845 had reanimated trade by sweeping away duties on exported machinery and imported raw materials, but Peel had done little to help the working classes. Meanwhile the champions of factory reform never ceased agitation, and anti-Corn-Law orators, rubbing in the distress of agricultural labour, "pointed in triumphant pity to the hollow-cheeked serf of the fields, and produced him on platforms in his smock frock to say, 'I be protected, and I be starving.'" During the summer of 1845 the free-trade position was strengthened by the Irish potato blight and a month of rain in England that rotted the corn harvest on the ground.

What a moment for establishing a great new organ to sound the radical doctrines of reform! A daily newspaper could be a very spearhead in the fight against the entrenched forces of privilege. It might do incalculable good in exposing inefficiency and corruption, hammering away at reaction, arousing public sentiment, and advancing the welfare of the masses. Parliament itself feared the voice of the London *Times*, the great "Thunderer," and it was not inconceivable that a brilliantly edited rival might wrest the leadership from the older paper. Memories of his old newspaper days doubtless had a part, too, in rendering the role of editor attractive. What a triumph it would be to show the proprietors of the *Chronicle* the way a newspaper should be run! What trembling there might be even in the great *Times* editorial chambers in Printing House Square!

Before Dickens left for Italy in the spring of 1844 he and Forster had broached the idea to Bradbury and Evans. No decision was then made, but the printing firm agreed to go into its financial aspects and renew their discussions when Dickens returned. Some steps were evidently taken even while Dickens remained abroad, for in Rome he tentatively secured Father Prout (the Reverend Francis Mahony) as Roman correspondent of the projected paper. But that the entire plan was still very shadowy is shown by the fact that a few weeks after settling into Devonshire Terrace again, Dickens was asking Forster's opinion of a quite different sort of periodical.

I have turned it over, the last two days, very much in my mind: and think it positively good. I incline still to weekly; price three half-pence, if possible; partly original, partly select; notices of books, notices of theatres, notices of all good things, notices of all bad ones; Carol philosophy, cheerful views, sharp anatomization of humbug, jolly good temper . . . And I would call it, sir, –

THE CRICKET

A Cheerful creature that chirrups on the Hearth.

Natural History

. . . And I would chirp, chirp, chirp away in every number until I chirped it up to – well, you shall say how many hundred thousand!

Forster, however, poured cold water on this scheme, and it was so swept away as to leave only one trace behind. "What do you think," Dickens wrote in July, "of a notion that has occurred to me in connection with our abandoned little weekly? It would be a delicate and beautiful fancy for a Christmas book, making the Cricket a little household god – silent in the wrong and sorrow of the tale, and loud again when all went well and happy." This grew into *The Cricket on the Hearth*, the Christmas book of 1845.

By August Dickens was busily engaged in calculating the expenses of running a newspaper, and asking his friend Beard in confidence how much the *Herald* spent on its Foreign Department. But meanwhile he had also flung himself headlong into whipping up a private theatrical entertainment to which he had long been looking forward.

He had first suggested the idea to Forster the preceding December. "ARE we to have that play???" he wrote from Genoa in June. "Have I spoken of it, ever since I came home from London, as a settled thing!" Soon after his return from Italy he decided on Ben Jonson's *Every Man in His Humour*, and gaily began assembling a cast.

Each of the players was to be allowed thirty to thirty-five guests. To accommodate this considerable audience, Dickens selected a private theatre in Dean Street, Soho, where the retired actress Frances Kelly conducted a dramatic school. Dickens had cast himself for the braggart Bobadil and Forster for Kitely. Among the other actors were Frederick and Augustus Dickens, T. J. Thompson, the artist Frank Stone, Douglas Jerrold, Mark Lemon (the plump and beaming editor of *Punch*), and the caricaturist John Leech. Stanfield, after two terrified attempts to get through the part of Wellbred, pleaded to be allowed to confine himself to the scenery.

Dickens took charge of everything. Scenery was painted, bright costumes were designed from originals in seventeenth-century pictures. Rehearsals went on while Miss Kelly flitted anxiously about. Still other rehearsals were held in a ground-floor room at 90 Fleet Street, premises belonging to Bradbury and Evans, with whom Dickens was now deep in plans for the proposed newspaper.

As the time for the performance drew near, he lived in a turmoil of property lists, playbills, and rehearsal calls. On the morning of 20 September – the day of the performance – he borrowed a young man from the skeleton office force already in the newspaper premises, and took him along to help out. On the stage, Jerrold prepared a theatrical fire of slacked lime and red tinsel; in the boxes and dress circle Lemon and Dickens, stripping off their coats, numbered the seats.

The curtain was to rise at seven-thirty. By seven carriages crowded Dean Street. Among the guests, Alfred Tennyson had travelled a couple of hundred miles in one direction to be present, and the Duke of Devonshire a couple of hundred in another. Jane Welsh Carlyle, as usual, described the scene acidly. The aristocratic guests, she thought, "looked rather a *rum set*"; adding that the Duke of Devonshire sat opposite her, "with his nose 'looking toward Damascus,' and old Lady

Holland graced it (not the nose but the play) with her hideous presence."

Jane and her husband were equally contemptuous of the acting. Forster, said Carlyle, imitated Macready without ever ceasing to be Forster; and he was grimly patronizing about "poor little Dickens, all painted in black and red, and affecting the voice of a man of six feet." Macready, however, though professionally scornful of the enterprise, admitted that "several of the actors were fine as amateurs" and praised Dickens and Lemon. Most of the other guests lauded Dickens to the skies. He was "glorious in Bobadil," said one of them. "He literally floated in braggadocio. His air of supreme conceit and frothy pomp in the earlier scenes came out with prodigious force in contrast with the subsequent humiliation . . ."

Dickens enjoyed it all hugely. He had had a dresser from one of the large theatres make him up with a peaked black beard and a moustache fiercely curling skyward, which were replaced, after Bobadil was beaten, by a beard all dishevelled and moustache drooping lankly down. And his triumph as director was resounding. "There are whispers of gold snuff-boxes for the indefatigable manager from the performers – Hem!"

The evening ended with a supper for the players and their wives, to which the Macreadys, Count D'Orsay, George Cattermole, and a few others were invited. Public furore about the performance was extravagant. Invitations, applications, petitions, and memorials begged for a repetition. Ultimately Dickens and his colleagues decided on a benefit performance for Dr Southwood Smith's nursing home in Devonshire Place. They took the St James's Theatre to provide more seats. An unexpected event set the date for the middle of November. "Here's a pretty kettle of Fish!" Dickens exclaimed. "Prince Albert has written to say that he dies to see the amateur Performance on behalf of the Sanatorium, and can it be done on the fifteenth! Lord and Lady Lansdowne and the 'Tarnal Smash knows who, have taken boxes . . ."

On the great night the entire theatre glittered with celebrities. There were the Duke of Wellington and Prince George of Cambridge, the Duke of Devonshire again, Lord Melbourne in a box with Mrs Norton, Lady Duff Gordon, and Dwarkanauth Tagore, the last in gorgeous Indian costume, Baron de Rothschild, Macready, and innumerable others. When Prince Albert and his suite arrived, they were given white satin playbills. But the repeat performance did not have the success of the first. "The audience were as cold as ice," wrote Charles Greville; and between the acts Melbourne complained in a stentorian voice, "I knew this play would be dull, but that it would be so damnably dull as this I did not suppose!"

Despite these less than rapturous comments the same amateur company, with a few changes of personnel, gave a benefit performance of Massinger and Fletcher's *The Elder Brother* for Miss Kelly at her theatre on the third day of the new year. One of those who had dropped out of the company was T. J. Thompson, who during the entire preceding year and a half had been engaged to Christiana Weller, the delicate Liverpool beauty by whom Dickens had been so deeply moved. Their marriage took place in mid-October, and Dickens attended it, resplendent in a waistcoat with broad purple stripes copied from one Macready had worn in Bulwer Lytton's *Money*. From England the newly wedded couple were going to Genoa, where Dickens predicted that Christiana would find an affectionate friend in Mme De la Rue.

The distractions of the theatricals had so delayed Dickens's writing, that he did not even begin his Christmas book until after Thompson's wedding. The newspaper scheme was also taking much of his time; it had reached the point where Dickens was constantly making confidential inquiries of Beard and asking him to untangle knots of journalistic procedure.

A new addition to the Dickens family was born on the morning of 28 October. Tennyson and Count D'Orsay stood as godfathers to this sixth child, who was christened Alfred D'Orsay Tennyson Dickens. The extraordinary name aroused a considerable amount of not altogether friendly comment. Edward Fitzgerald took it as evidence that Dickens was a snob. "For what is Snobbishness and Cockneyism," he asked, "but all such pretensions and parade?" Even good-natured Robert Browning joked about it to Elizabeth Barrett: "You observe: Alfred is common to both the godfather and the devil-father."

The end of October also saw the newspaper project rapidly taking shape. Bradbury and Evans were ready to put up a great block of capital. Associated with them was Joseph Paxton, who had begun his career as a gardener and made a fortune in railway shares. "Paxton," Dickens wrote Mitton, "has command of every railway influence in England and abroad except the Great Western, and he is in it heart and purse." Among the prospective backers were Sir William Jackson, the leading champion of liberalism in the north, and Sir Joshua Walmsley, who was closely connected with George Stephenson in railway schemes and was working actively with Cobden and Bright in the Anti-Corn-Law League. He had praised Dickens as "the best friend to progress and reform yet seen in English fiction." Sir Joshua's vigorous endeavours to make the reform movement not a conflict of class interests but a joint concern for the welfare of the entire country became one of the cardinal principles of the new paper.

Although Dickens had not yet absolutely committed himself to assuming the editorship, he began to assemble a formidable staff, striking terror among the older papers by offering salaries well above established rates and wresting away some of their ablest men. He was disturbed, however, by what seemed to him Paxton's "loose, flurried way" of doing business. "It seems to me," Dickens protested, "that Mr Paxton's City man has broken down dead, in the very outset, if the assistance we got this morning be any criterion." With these exasperations, and the struggle of working on his Christmas story at the same time, Dickens felt "sick, bothered and depressed," and was tempted to make off to Brighton.

Forster doubted the wisdom of Dickens's taking the editorship at all. He wrote Dickens, pointing out how little it could enhance his fame and genius, and warning against its party and political involvements. But Dickens made light of these arguments. The times were right for such an effort, he insisted; at worst he could retire unharmed. By 3 November he announced his decision to Bradbury and Evans. "I will take that post of Editor which is marked in the little statement as having a salary of a Thousand Pounds attached to it – for double that salary."

The printers raised no objection to these terms, but overnight came a rude setback. There was a failure of a great broker in the City, "which so affects two of my principal people," Dickens told Beard, "that the Paper *cannot be*, on any proper footing." Bradbury and Evans, after the first shock, desired to proceed despite the loss. Dickens, however, was panicky with the conviction that the enterprise was "a doomed thing." The advertising they had counted on was gone. Some of the men who had been engaged had already asked to be taken back on the *Chronicle*; others had applied to *The Times*, and the *Herald*. If Bradbury and Evans felt committed to going on, Dickens would give them every assistance in his power, but he would not connect himself with it. "Nor can I conceal from you that I believe in my soul it would end in your Ruin."

Meanwhile he was trying desperately to finish *The Cricket on the Hearth* and arranging with no fewer than four artists for its illustrations. But within another week he once again reversed his decision on the newspaper. Bradbury and Evans convinced him that the failure of the brokerage house was not the disaster for them that he had believed, and he agreed to remain as editor. On 17 November an agreement was signed establishing the *Daily News* with a capital of £50,000, of which Bradbury and Evans subscribed £22,500, Paxton £25,000, and a third proprietor named Richard Wright the remaining £2,500. Somewhat later Sir William Jackson and Sir Joshua Walmsley brought the raised or promised capital up to £100,000.

Dickens promptly set about completing his staff. Earlier in the autumn he had chosen William Henry Wills as his personal secretary and administrative assistant. Wills was a sharp-nosed man with a blotched complexion, who was so thin that Douglas Jerrold described him as having spent his life "in training to go up a gas-pipe." He had contributed to *Bentley's Miscellany* in 1837, had been a member of the literary staff of *Punch* at its founding in 1841, and had served since 1842 as assistant editor of *Chambers's Journal* in Edinburgh. Though not a man of great imagination, he was quick, efficient, and thoroughly dependable.

As subeditor, Dickens obtained a journalist named Powell, who had been subeditor of the *Morning Chronicle* and editor of the *Evening Chronicle*. Douglas Jerrold and Mark Lemon also joined the subeditorial staff. Thomas Hodgkinson, of the *Economist*, became assistant subeditor; Scott Russell was railway editor and William Weir wrote railway comments and information; Dudley Costello took charge of foreign news and Frederic Knight Hunt of provincial intelligence. Forster and Albany Fonblanque were among the leader writers, of whom the chief was William Johnson Fox, Unitarian minister and "golden-tongued apostle of untaxed bread." Eyre Evans Crowe, previously the Paris correspondent of the *Chronicle*, took over that post for the *Daily News*. Military and naval news, sports, commerce, and clerical news were all in the hands of the ablest men Dickens could find.

A curious footnote to these major appointments was that Dickens's father-in-law, George Hogarth, was made music critic with "a general liability to Theatres." When Dickens was a youthful reporter Hogarth had been editor of the *Evening Chronicle*. Later he had left Easthope's employ and only recently returned to it. But now he was entirely willing to throw up his post and come to the *Daily News* for five guineas a week, a salary that Dickens had been earning eleven years before. It seems unmistakable that Hogarth had been during the intervening years no great success as a journalist.

The reporting staff included R. H. Horne, Joseph Archer Crowe, Blanchard Jerrold, Laman Blanchard, William Hazlitt, and Thomas Holcroft, the last three sons of the older writers of those names. In charge of them Dickens placed his father, now an obese and bustling man of sixty, still full of fun and energy, and still fond of a glass of grog. John Dickens was a hard-working and efficient organizer. His difficulties had never arisen from lack of professional ability. He proceeded at once to arrange a system for the regular dispatch of copy to the printers, and above all of the pages that would stream in steadily from the men in the Gallery.

The newspaper offices were tucked away in a block of tumbledown rookeries alongside Bradbury and Evans's establishment in Whitefriars. Away from the other offices, high aloft on the third floor, Dickens himself had two rooms with a carpet, a plain office table and armchair, a black horsehair sofa, and a small bookcase containing volumes of Hansard, the *Mirror of Parliament*, some dictionaries and reference books, Shakespeare and the Bible, and a collection of works that the office boy remembered in later years as "a complete set of the Classics."

On 27 December the *Daily News* was publicly announced in *Punch* as an independent newspaper of liberal politics under Dickens's direction. Simultaneously *The Times* printed a savage review of his Christmas book, *The Cricket on the Hearth*, which had just been published. Dickens's confidence, however, in his hold upon the public proved to be justified. As if readers sensed the hostility behind the rival newspaper's onslaught, they only bought the little book in larger numbers. The Keeleys gave a dramatized adaptation at the Lyceum for Christmas, and a fortnight later there were versions playing at six London theatres.

During the three weeks prior to publishing the first number of the *Daily News* Whitefriars was filled with a turmoil of bricklayers, carpenters, painters, and plasterers. On Saturday, 17 January, a party of ladies and gentlemen saw a "christening" ceremony in which a bottle of champagne was dashed against one of the printing machines. Despite these high jinks there were friendly observers who had grave forebodings for the future of the paper.

It came out in a time of tremendous political ferment. Late in November, Lord John Russell had announced his conversion to free trade. Sir Robert Peel also saw the necessity of repealing the Corn Laws. But his party was stormy with dissension and, failing to unite his Cabinet behind him, Peel resigned. Russell was sent for by the Queen. Though the Whigs had pretensions to being the popular party and were the logical ones to carry out the measure, they shrank from the struggle of getting it through the House of Lords. They hoped that Peel would be able to pass the Bill with the least disturbance. Lord John consequently did not complete the formation of a Ministry, and "handed back with courtesy the poisoned chalice to Sir Robert." The entire country was waiting breathlessly for the speech in which Peel would indicate his plans when Parliament reconvened on 20 January.

That night there was pandemonium at the *Daily News* offices. The debate in the House of Commons was a heavy one, and John Dickens had to make great efforts to keep his men moving swiftly and to see that their reports were handled smoothly. During the night Mr Bradbury wandered nervously through the establishment, Joseph Paxton and Douglas Jerrold were in and out of the printing house, and Mr Evans and Mark Lemon were pressed into service as reader and reading boy. Only by superhuman efforts did they get out the first number, Wednesday, 21 January, by three-forty that morning. Dickens had made advance arrangements to have a second edition, containing the speech in which Peel announced his conversion to Cobden's views on the Corn Laws, dispatched "to every town on every line in England." When the paper went on sale in Fleet Street, there was a wild rush and 10,000 copies were sold across the counter.

At first sight of the outer sheet, relief lighted the gloom of the other papers. It was ill-printed on poor paper and "badly made up." There were social rejoicings in editorial chambers that had been long beset by dread. "I need not tell you," Dickens wrote, "how our Printer failed us last night. I hope for better things tonight, and am bent on a fight for it." But the first number of the *Daily News* was by no means as bad as the hostility of its rivals represented it. There was an eloquent leading article by Fox demanding repeal of the Corn Laws, and three others on that subject; nearly an entire page of railway news; two columns on music by Hogarth; the first of Dickens's brilliant *Travelling Letters Written on the Road*, made from his Italian letters of 1844; a total of eight pages, selling for fivepence instead of the established newspaper price of sevenpence.

In an introductory article Dickens outlined the programme of the paper: "The principles advocated by 'The Daily News' will be Principles of Progress and Improvement, of Education, Civil and Religious Liberty, and Equal Legislation – Principles such as its Conductors believe the advancing spirit of the time requires, the Condition of the country demands, and Justice, Reason, and Experience legitimately sanction." Social improvement was so inseparable from the advancement of arts and commerce and the growth of public works, that the true interests of the people were not a class question.

After the first curiosity about the *Daily News*, however, its sales subsided to less than 4,000, and although this did not compare unfavourably with most of the other morning papers, it did not challenge the overwhelming supremacy of *The Times*, with its 25,000. Dickens was often exasperated by slipshod work in his subordinates. In addition, although the members of his editorial staff were all free traders, they differed violently on foreign and colonial policy, and he could not reconcile them to each other or subordinate their views to his own. Worst of all, there developed administrative frictions between him and the proprietors.

Some of these grew out of the paper's railway connections. Though a source of financial advantage, they also limited the independence of its position in ways that Dickens now came to feel dangerous. Perhaps less important but more irritating at the moment were a series of interferences in his powers as editor. Mr Bradbury, a prey to worrisome fidget, was constantly countermanding Dickens's orders. "I consider," Dickens wrote stormily to Evans, "that his interposition between me and almost every act of mine at the newspaper office, was as disrespectful to me as injurious to the enterprise." Bradbury had also been discourteous to Dickens's father, "than whom there is not a more zealous, disinterested, or useful gentleman attached to the paper." Finding greater difficulties and discouragements than he had anticipated, Bradbury seemed to Dickens to have become convinced that everyone on the paper was his natural enemy, to "be suspected and mistrusted accordingly."

These conflicts expanded with startling rapidity. Nine days after the paper began publication Dickens wrote Forster, "I have been revolving plans in my mind this morning for quitting the paper and going abroad again to write a new book in shilling numbers." During the week that followed there was no diminution in the tension. On 9 February Dickens cut the knot. He had been editor of the *Daily News* for just seventeen numbers. His position on the paper he handed over to Forster, in somewhat the same way that he had handed over *Bentley's Miscellany* to Ainsworth. Indeed, in the whole of this brief interlude as a newspaper editor there is a strange, speeded-up resemblance to his prolonged battle with Bentley. But he did not sever his relations with Bradbury and Evans altogether; they were still to remain the publishers of his books.

In the few weeks following his resignation Dickens was explaining to correspondents that his "connection with D. N." was not one of authority that could settle matters, and that he was forwarding their

letters "to the Editor." To personal friends he gave more detailed explanations. "I was not satisfied," he wrote Mme De la Rue, "with the
business managers of the newspaper. In the course of a little more time, I
saw so much reason to believe that they would be the Ruin of what
might otherwise have been made a very fine property . . . that I . . .
walked bodily out of the concern."

Indeed, the paper did almost go by the board. Bradbury proved as
troublesome when Dickens was gone as he had been during Dickens's
editorship. Even when he had long retired from the scene the troubles of
the paper continued. Forster resigned his editorship in October;
Charles Wentworth Dilke became business manager in June 1846;
there was a financial reorganization of the paper in November 1847;
Dilke retired from its management in 1849. During the first ten years of
its struggling life another £100,000 was sunk in it. In the light of these
later facts, Dickens's brief and violent connection with the paper is more
intelligible.

No doubt he was touchy and arbitrary. But no doubt, too, the proprietors did trespass within the realm of his editorial authority. Successful businessmen who own the entire capital of an enterprise are not
likely to defer completely to the demands of any executive, no matter
how important, who has no money invested in its success. Dickens, on
the other hand, was inclined to insist on powers almost as absolute as if
he were the sole proprietor. He did not fail to learn from the experience.
When he next undertook the direction of a publication, he would be
careful to own one half of it outright, and, through Forster and a
subeditor, to control another quarter.

[PART SEVEN]

At Grips with Himself
1846–1851

29

Convulsions of Dombey

Ridding himself of the *Daily News* did not ease Dickens's unsettling anxieties. In the year that followed he was to complain repeatedly about unidentified obstacles to his work and to overcome them only by the most tremendous efforts. A sharp observer might have traced the change from the time of his restless desire to get away from England during the composition of *Martin Chuzzlewit* – almost, indeed, from the time of his return from America. At Genoa and during all his stay in Italy Dickens had written only *The Chimes*. The entire *Daily News* episode had been characterized by caprice of action and touchy irritability.

Although he was now no longer editor, he did not immediately sever all connection with the newspaper. His friend Forster sat in the editorial chair; it had been Dickens's own creation and in the main still represented his reform liberalism. Six more of his brightly coloured Italian travel letters appeared at intervals in its pages. (Near the end of May, with five added chapters, these were published by Bradbury and Evans under the title of *Pictures from Italy*.) Before his resignation Dickens also contributed a letter describing the work of the Ragged Schools; and after it, in March, he wrote three letters on capital punishment.

These letters contain some penetrating observations on the psychology of murder. On crimes of gain, sudden rage, or despairing affection (as when a parent kills a starving child), Dickens insisted that the punishment of death had no restraining influence at all. On those of vengeance or the craving for notoriety, he argued, the death penalty often served as an added stimulus. And over certain morbid imaginations, the publicity of the trial and the tense climax before an assembled multitude exercised a horrible fascination.

Nor could it be claimed that the death penalty diminished crime. Statistics in all countries showed that murders decreased after every period in which the number of death sentences was reduced. Further, the many examples of the death penalty inflicted upon people after-wards proved innocent should make men hesitate to impose it. "I beg to be understood," Dickens concluded, "as advocating the total abolition of the Punishment of Death, as a general principle, for the advantage of society, for the prevention of crime, and without the least reference to, or tenderness for any individual malefactor whatsoever."

Dickens became convinced, however, that the reform was too far in advance of popular feeling to be practicable. Under these circum-stances the major evil was the psychological effect of the horrible drama of hanging before a brutalized and gloating mob. Without changing his personal view, he modified his public position in the next few years to the demand that executions be confined to the interior of the jail.

During the time of these last contributions to the *Daily News* he was apprehensive and uncertain of his future movements. He even dallied with the idea of qualifying as a paid London magistrate and wrote a member of the Government to inquire about his chances of receiving an appointment. But the reply was discouraging; and, besides, the idea for another book was now beginning to simmer in his mind. By April he had arranged with Bradbury and Evans to write a novel in twenty monthly parts. In the end, after some vacillation, he returned to the idea of subletting Devonshire Terrace and going abroad – this time to the Lake of Geneva, possibly at Lausanne.

Meanwhile he continued to receive applications for posts on the *Daily News* – including one from Edgar Allan Poe, who wished to become its American correspondent – to all of which he replied that he was no longer connected with its management. He also presided at the first annual dinner of the General Theatrical Fund, an organization to help aged or invalid actors not eligible for aid under the Drury Lane and Covent Garden funds.

The end of May saw a round of friendly farewell dinners. There was a dinner with Macready on the 28th and with Forster on the 30th. All Dickens's preparations were made for a year abroad: Devonshire Terrace rented to Sir James Duke for £300, Roche hired again as courier. On the last day of the month his menage started on its journey – Dickens himself, Kate, Georgina, the six children, plump beaming Roche, the faithful Anne, two other female servants, and the little white dog Timber. Forster accompanied them as far as Ramsgate, where they embarked for Ostend.

The sunny Rhine journey by river steamboat was picturesque but uneventful. Arriving at Strasbourg on 7 June, the family went on by rail the following day to Basle, and thence in three coaches to Lausanne. Putting up at the Hotel Gibbon, Dickens at once began hunting for a house. On the sloping shore, ten minutes' walk from the hotel, he found Rosemont, a little bandbox of a doll's house, with stone colonnades supporting a balcony, all overwhelmed in a luxuriance of roses. The whole house, Dickens said, might have been put bodily into the *sala* of the Palazzo Peschiere, but there were enough bedrooms to provide one to spare, a hall, dining-room, and two mirrored drawing-rooms with shining inlaid floors. French windows under the balcony looked across the blue waters of Lake Geneva towards the mountain gorges rising to the Simplon Pass.

Rosemont was taken at £10 a month for the first six months with an option at £8 thereafter. A school was promptly found for Charley between Lausanne and Ouchy. Within three days Dickens had settled in a study "something larger than a Plate Warmer," from which he could walk out on the long broad balcony and see the Castle of Chillon glittering in the sunlight. But until his box of books came with the blue ink in which he always wrote and the bronze desk ornaments he had to have before his imagination would flow, he could not get started on his novel. Instead, he devoted himself to clearing away a number of other obligations – correspondence, some material he had promised Lord John Russell about the Ragged Schools, half a simplified story of the New Testament that he was writing for his own children, advice for Miss Coutts upon her charitable activities. The most recent was a home she intended to establish "for the rehabilitation of fallen women."

Before leaving London, Dickens had outlined a plan, and during the summer they corresponded about it. The Governors of the London prisons, he wrote, should be empowered to send any woman who so desired straight to the home when her term expired. Once there, a woman or girl should understand that her purpose was to cease a way of life miserable to *herself*. Never mind society while she is at that pass. Society has used her ill and turned away from her, and she cannot be expected to take much heed of its rights or wrongs. For a number of months she should be placed on probation, receiving stated credits for work and good conduct, and demerits for each outbreak of ill-temper, disrespect, or bad language.

"Her pride, emulation, her sense of shame, her heart, her reason, and her interest, are all appealed to at once, and if she pass through this trial, she *must* . . . rise somewhat in her own self-respect" and advance in forming "habits of firmness and self-restraint." "It is a part of this system, even to put at last, some temptation within their reach, as enabling them to go out, putting them in possession of some money, and the like; for it is clear that unless they are used to some temptation and used to resist it, within the walls, their capacity of resisting it without, cannot be considered as fairly tested."

The institution would emphasize order, punctuality, cleanliness, and the household duties of washing, mending, and cooking. It would be understood, however, by all that its object was not a monotonous round of occupation and self-denial, but the restoration of a way of life and a character that could end in achieving happy homes. The Government was to be sounded on the possibility of helping to send reformed women to the Colonies, where they might be married.

Miss Coutts had doubts about the desirability of suggesting marriage as a goal, and qualms about deliberately subjecting the inmates to temptations. Dickens replied that he did not propose to hold out the hope of marriage as an immediate end, merely as a possible consequence of an altered life. As for temptation, did not all merchants and bankers expose their employees to it daily?

At last, with the arrival of his big box, Dickens settled to his desk. Unpacking, he told Forster, "I took hold of a book, and said to 'Them,' – 'Now, whatever passage my thumb rests on, I shall take as having reference to my work.' It was TRISTRAM SHANDY, and opened at these words, 'What a work it is likely to turn out! Let us begin it!' " Shortly thereafter, on 28 June, he was able to write Forster the exciting announcement –

'BEGAN DOMBEY!

I performed this feat yesterday – only wrote the first slip – but there it is, and it is a plunge straight over head and ears into the story.'

Dickens also had an "odd shadowy undefined idea" of connecting his next Christmas story with a great battlefield. Its title would be *The Battle of Life*. He hoped by the end of November to have finished this book and four numbers of *Dombey*, and then to move to Paris, at "the very point in the story when the life and crowd of that extraordinary place will come vividly to my assistance in writing."

The idea behind *Dombey and Son* Dickens considered "interesting and new." At first, however, he refrained from telling Forster anything about it, for fear of spoiling the effect of the first number for him. He poured out directions to Forster for Browne about the illustrations:

"Great pains will be necessary with Miss Tox. The Toodle family should not be too much caricatured, because of Polly. I should like Browne to think of Susan Nipper, who will not be wanted for the first number. What a brilliant thing to be telling you all these names so familiarly, when you know nothing about 'em! I quite enjoy it."

In a letter dated 25 July he outlined the story and its theme to Forster. Mr Dombey, in the frigid dynastic pride of his great mercantile position, was to repel the love of his daughter and concentrate all his hopes on the frail little boy whom he designed to make his successor. But the tenderness of the child would turn toward the despised sister, and even when he was dying he would cling to her, keeping "the stern affection of his father at a distance." "The death of the boy is a death-blow, of course, to all the father's schemes and cherished hopes; and 'Dombey and Son,' as Miss Tox will say . . . 'is a Daughter after all.' "

> From that time, I purpose changing his feeling of indifference and uneasiness towards his daughter into a positive hatred. For he will always remember how the boy had his arm round her neck when he was dying, and whispered to her, and would take things only from her hand, and never thought of him. . . . So I mean to carry the story on . . . through the decay and downfall of the house, and the bank-ruptcy of Dombey, and all the rest of it; when his only staff and treasure, and his unknown Good Genius always, will be this rejected daughter, who will come out better than any son at last, and whose love for him, when discovered and understood, will be his bitterest reproach.

In Mr Dombey Dickens's changed conception of business and businessmen is given corroding life. Henceforth there are no more Cheerybles and Fezziwigs, benevolent old boys beaming through their spectacles in a warm mist of generosity. Mr Dombey is the spirit of business enterprise, a stark assertion of monetary power. He wants no ties of affection between his infant son and his nurse: "When you go away from here you will have concluded what is a mere matter of bargain and sale, of hiring and letting, and will stay away." It never enters his mind that he cannot purchase the absolute subservience of his business subordinates. He believes he can buy the obedience of an aristocratic wife whose beauty is to reflect lustre on his greatness. The attitudes he displays to those about him are identical with his attitudes towards society as a whole. He is the living symbol of the nineteenth-century theory of business and its social philosophy of *laissez-faire*.

The pleasant distractions of life in Lausanne relaxed Dickens from his work on *Dombey*. A resident English colony mingled in a round of dinner parties and excursions. Dickens dined with William Haldimand, a former member of Parliament who lived nearby with his sister Mrs Marcet, a well-known writer. At their table he met William de Cerjat, a Swiss gentleman, and his English wife, and the Honourable Mr and Mrs Richard Watson of Rockingham Castle in Northamptonshire.

Current political events in England roused Dickens to indignation. Though the Corn Laws had been repealed, an angry rebellion against Peel led by Disraeli and Lord John Manners had driven him out of office. "I little thought," Dickens wrote, "that I should ever live to praise Peel. But d'Israeli and that Dunghill Lord have so disgusted me, that I feel inclined to champion him . . ."

Streams of English visitors passed steadily through Lausanne. In July, Henry Hallam the historian visited Mr Haldimand. "Heavens!" Dickens wrote, "how Hallam did talk yesterday, I don't think I ever saw him so tremendous. Very good-natured and pleasant, in his way, but Good Heavens! how he did talk." Towards the end of August, when Dickens was walking up and down "racking my brain about Dombeys and Battles of Lives," Tennyson turned up, very travel-stained, and Dickens laid aside his work again while he entertained the poet with "Rhine wine, and cigars innumerable."

Among the newcomers settling down in Lausanne were the T. J. Thompsons, who took a house there for eight months. Dickens was now much disappointed in Christiana. "She seems (between ourselves), to have a devil of a whimpering, pouting temper . . ." "She is a mere spoiled child, I think, and doesn't turn out half as well as I expected. Matrimony has improved him, and certainly has not improved her." Dickens's brother Frederick was by this time impatiently eager to marry her younger sister Anna, although his income was insufficient and she was two years too young to be married. Frederick was working himself up to a mood of bitter resentment at Mr Weller's opposition and Dickens was beginning to wish he had never met Christiana and her family.

The interest which he never ceased to feel in public institutions took him shortly after his arrival to those of Lausanne. Mr Haldimand was President of the Blind Institution, and the Director was a brilliant young German named Hertzel, who had taught one of the deaf, dumb, and blind inmates to speak – a feat previously thought impossible. His pupil, a youth of eighteen, was very fond of cigars and Dickens arranged a supply of them for him. "I don't know whether he thinks I grow them, or make them, or produce them by winking or what. But it gives him a notion that the world in general belongs to me."

The jail at Lausanne had been conducted according to the silent system, in which the prisoners were not allowed to speak; but its physician, M. Verdeil, had observed so many cases of terrible fits and madness among them that he had brought about its abolition. His conclusions interestingly substantiated many of those Dickens himself had arrived at in *American Notes*.

In addition to these investigations, there were regattas, children's fetes, and excursions to Chamonix and the Castle of Chillon. What a sight was the ponderous Roche riding through the Col de Balme, "on a very small mule up a road exactly like the broken stairs of Rochester Castle, with a brandy bottle slung over his shoulder, a small pie in his hat, a roast fowl looking out of his pocket, and a mountain staff of six feet long carried crosswise on the saddle"! At the Mer de Glace, when it seemed that they must have reached the top of the world, there suddenly came a cold air blowing, and past a ridge of snow startlingly towered, unseen till then, "the vast range of Mont Blanc, with attendant mountains diminished by its majestic side into mere dwarfs, tapering up into innumerable rude Gothic pinnacles."

Chillon rekindled all Dickens's horror of the Middle Ages.

The insupportable solitude and dreariness of the white walls [he wrote Forster], the sluggish moat and drawbridge, and the lonely ramparts, I never saw the like of. But there is a courtyard inside; surrounded by prisons, oubliettes, and old chambers of torture; so terrifically sad, that death itself is not more sorrowful. . . . Great God, the greatest mystery in all the earth, to me, is how or why the world was tolerated by its creator through the good old times, and wasn't dashed to fragments.

Early in September he took a trip to the monastery of St Bernard. "I wish to God," he exclaimed to Forster, "you could have seen that place. A great hollow on the top of a range of dreadful mountains, fenced in by riven rocks of every shape and colour: and in the midst a black lake, with phantom clouds perpetually stalking over it." Dramatic as was the scene of the monastery Dickens thought the holy fathers were humbugs, "a lazy set of fellows . . . employing servants to clear the road," and growing rich at innkeeping. As for the self-sacrifice of living up there, it was an "infinitely more exciting life than any other convent can offer; with constant change and company through the whole summer."

Throughout all these amusements Dickens continued work on *Dombey and Son*. In the excitement of writing again, he found he had made his first number six pages too long. He wondered if he should not transfer the Wooden Midshipman and its inhabitants to the second number, and substitute a shorter one. Forster, however, thought it would weaken the opening to defer the appearance of Walter Gay and Captain Cuttle, and persuaded Dickens to solve the problem by making cuts instead.

Captain Cuttle and Mr Toots, are among the great portraits of the book, both irresistibly ludicrous and both at the same time possessed of a true dignity shining through all their absurdities. Poor Toots, with his vapid chuckle and his hopeless devotion to Florence, rises to heights of noble selflessness. And even when Captain Cuttle is rambling through chains of association suggestive of Joyce's Molly Bloom and scrambling quotations like a parody of T. S. Eliot, there is a heart of warm sanity in his nonsense.

While Dickens was working at the second number, his enthusiasm was stimulated by the interest of his friends at Lausanne.

> I read them the first number, last night "was a" week, with un-relateable success; and old Mrs Marcet, who is devilish "cute" guessed directly (but I didn't tell her she was right) that Paul would die. They were all so apprehensive that it was a great pleasure to read it, and I shall leave here, if all goes well, in a brilliant shower of sparks struck out of them by the promised reading of the Christmas book.

The enjoyment of his audience gave Dickens a novel idea: "a great deal of money might possibly be made (if it were not infra dig) by one's having Readings of one's own books. It would be an *odd* thing." And half jestingly he suggested that Forster had better step around and engage Miss Kelly's theatre or the St James's. It was the first facetious whisper of a course that would lead to disaster in his later life.

Despite his delight in the story, Dickens found the task of writing uphill work.

> Invention, thank God, seems the easiest thing in the world; and I seem to have such a preposterous sense of the ridiculous, after this long rest, as to be constantly requiring to restrain myself from

launching into extravagances in the height of my enjoyment. But the difficulty of going at what I call a rapid pace is prodigious: it is almost an impossibility. I suppose this is partly the effect of two years' ease, and partly of the absence of streets . . .

Even in Genoa, where he had written only *The Chimes*, he had felt the deprivation of his London rambles; "but Lord! I had two miles of streets at least, lighted at night, to walk about in; and a great theatre to repair to, every night."

The strain of getting *The Battle of Life* under way at the same time also troubled him. It was the first time he had tried to start two stories at once. "I cancelled the beginning of a first scene – which I have never done before – and, with a notion in my head, ran wildly about and about it, and could not get the idea into any natural socket." The difficulty of doing both so put him off that he even considered abandoning the Christmas book. Then, suddenly, the opening came right, and he worked heatedly from nine-thirty to six, and was exultant though exhausted.

A week later, however, he was once more plunged in gloom. "I fear there may be NO CHRISTMAS BOOK!" He had bogged down again, and worried lest he would so wear himself out that he would be unable to resume *Dombey* with the necessary spirit. "If I had nothing but the Christmas book to do, I WOULD do it; but I get horrified and distressed beyond conception at the prospect of being jaded when I come to the other . . ."

Anxiously he tried to understand what was impeding him. Was it purely the effort of beginning two books at the same time? Was it trying to write in such a quiet place, with no stimulating noise and bustle? Was it that constant change was indispensable to him when he was at work? Or was it that there was "something in a Swiss valley" that disagreed with him? And yet he liked Lausanne enormously, and the little society of friends he had made there.

Desperately, he decided in late September on going to Geneva for a week to see if change of scene would stimulate him. He arrived there with a bloodshot eye and a pain across the brow so severe that he thought he must have himself cupped. But within a few days he felt better. "The sight of the rushing Rhone seemed to stir my blood again," he wrote; and "My eye is recovering its old hue of beautiful white, tinged with celestial blue." He got in three good days' work, which encouraged him to hope that he might finish the little book at Lausanne by 20 October. Then he would return to Geneva and have three weeks there to work on *Dombey and Son* before setting out for Paris on 10 November.

Hammering away morning, noon, and night, Dickens actually completed *The Battle of Life* on 17 October. Two days' rest set him up again, and he reported buoyantly to Forster, "I feel in Dombeian spirits already." Meanwhile the first number of *Dombey* had exceeded all his hopes. "The Dombey sale is BRILLIANT! I had put before me thirty thousand as the limit of the most extreme success . . . you will judge how happy I am!"

Despite the difficulty he had had in working at Lausanne, Dickens was sorry to be leaving. Nowhere abroad had he found more congenial friends than Haldimand, the Cerjats, and the Watsons. And for Switzerland and the Swiss, too, he had conceived a warm esteem. Nothing was more unjust, he said, than to call them "the Americans of the Continent."

> They have not the sweetness and grace of the Italians, or the agreeable manners of the better specimens of French peasantry, but they are admirably educated (the schools of this canton are extraordinarily good, in every little village), and always prepared to give a civil and pleasant answer . . . I never saw. . . . people who did their work so truly *with a will*. And in point of cleanliness, order, and punctuality to the moment, they are unrivalled.

The sight of the Swiss intensified Dickens's feelings about what he called "Catholicity Symptoms." In the valley of the Simplon, he told Forster, where

> this Protestant canton ends and a Catholic canton begins, you might separate two perfectly distinct and different conditions of humanity by drawing a line with your stick in the dust on the ground. On the Protestant side, neatness; cheerfulness; industry; education; continual aspiration, at least, after better things. . . . I have a sad misgiving that the religion of Ireland lies as deep at the root of all its sorrows, even as English misgovernment and Tory villany.

When the October revolution occurred in Geneva, Dickens refused to believe "the lies . . . afloat against the radicals" that were circulated by the Sardinian consul and other representatives of the Catholic powers. "Apart from this, you have no conception of the preposterous, insolent little aristocracy of Geneva . . . Really, their talk about 'the people' and 'the masses,' and the necessity they would shortly be under of shooting a few of them as an example for the rest, was the kind of monstrosity one might have heard at Genoa." Consequently, though it was "a horribly ungentlemanly thing to say here," Dickens concluded, "I *do* say it without the least reserve – but my sympathy is all with the radicals."

Less than a fortnight after the revolution, aside from a large smashed mirror at the Hôtel de l'Écu, a few holes made by cannon balls, and two broken bridges, Dickens could see no signs of disorder. "The little streets are rife with every sight and sound of industry; the place is as quiet by ten o'clock as Lincoln's Inn Fields . . ." "Not one halfpenny-worth of property was lost, stolen, or strayed. Not one atom of party malice survived the smoke of the last gun. Nothing is expressed in the government addresses to the citizens but a regard for the general happiness, and injunctions to forget all animosities."

The third number of *Dombey* was duly finished at Geneva. "I hope you will like Mrs Pipchin's establishment," he wrote Forster. "It is from the life, and I was there – I don't suppose I was eight years old; but I . . . certainly understood it as well as I do now. We should be devilish sharp in what we do to children." Mrs Pipchin was in fact a fusion of the old woman who kept the dame school at Chatham and Mrs Roylance of the Bayham Street days. "Mrs Roylance, Mrs Wigchin, Mrs Tipchin, Mrs Alchin, Mrs Somchin, Mrs Pipchin," read Dickens's notes.

Despite this progress, Dickens found writing still a struggle, and his recurrent lamentations throughout his stay in Switzerland are warning signs of a growing inner disquiet. He invented half a dozen reasons to explain his frustration: living in a valley, the dampness of the Lake, too much peace and quiet, a need for the stimulation of London, the lack of streets to walk in. Only on rare occasions in the past had he spent a morning looking at an empty page; no such endless wrestlings to get his ideas on paper had impeded his earlier days, when he could write in a sitting-room filled with chatter or dash off a number of *Barnaby Rudge* at an inn in the Trossachs.

Though he had achieved the opening triumph of *Dombey*, he had done so only through the most desperate contentions with mysterious obstructions. For all the will power that victoriously smashed its way through this block in his accustomed fluency, there was a progressive underlying disturbance at work. But what it was Dickens as yet did not know.

30

The Want of Something

During the three months he spent in Paris his writing went no more easily. The household had left Geneva on 16 November in a train of three carriages, one "a villainous old swing" full of young Dickenses. Arriving with his "tons of luggage, other tons of servants, and other tons of children," Dickens put up at the Hotel Brighton. It was extravagant to stay at a hotel, so the first delay was in finding a residence. "The agonies of house-hunting," he wrote, "were frightfully severe. It was one paroxysm for four mortal days."

The following week, however, saw them all in 48 Rue de Courcelles, Faubourg Saint-Honoré. "The premises are in my belief," Dickens wrote Forster, "the most ridiculous, extraordinary, unparalleled, and preposterous in the whole world; being something between a babyhouse, a 'shades,' a haunted castle, and a mad kind of clock . . . The dining-room is a sort of cavern, painted (ceiling and all) to represent a grove, with unaccountable bits of looking-glass sticking in among the branches of the trees." "There is a gleam of reason in the drawing-room. But it is approached through a series of small chambers, like the joints in a telescope, which are hung with inscrutable drapery."

As soon as he was settled in, Dickens sat down to the fourth number of *Dombey*. Despite his hopes of being inspired by the bustle of Paris, he found himself out of writing sorts, "with a vile touch of biliousness," he said, "that makes my eyes feel as if they were yellow bullets." This time he thought it was the strange surroundings that put him off. He couldn't begin; "took a violent dislike to my study, and came down into the drawing-room; couldn't find a corner that would answer my purpose; fell into a black contemplation of the waning month; sat six hours at a stretch," and wrote only six lines. He tried rearranging all the tables and chairs, then started again, "and went about it and about, and dodged at it, like a bird with a lump of sugar." But in spite of all these efforts, he turned out only five printed pages, and began to fear he should be behindhand.

His observations of the French gave him no such esteem for them as he had formed for the Swiss. "The night after his arrival," Forster reports, "he took a 'colossal' walk about the city, of which the brilliancy and brightness almost frightened him." But he thought it "a wicked and destestable place, though wonderfully attractive."

The Parisian workpeople and smaller shopkeepers are more like (and unlike) Americans than I could have supposed possible. To the American indifference and carelessness, they add a procrastination and want of the least heed about keeping a promise or being exact, which is certainly not surpassed in Naples. They have the American semi-sentimental independence too, and none of the American vigour or purpose. . . . They are fit for nothing but soldiering – and so far, I believe, the successors in the policy of your friend Napoleon have reason on their side.

Agricultural and industrial depression gripped the country, there was diplomatic tension between France and England, the Monarchy was nervously drawing to its inglorious close. Dickens was struck by the sight of King Louis Philippe returning from the country, huddled far back in a carriage dashing hurriedly through the Champs Élysées, closely surrounded by horse guards and preceded by the Préfet de Police, "turning his head incessantly from side to side, like a figure in a Dutch clock, and scrutinizing everybody and everything, as if he suspected all the twigs in all the trees in the long avenue."

Suddenly Dickens found his writing going better, and by the middle of December he was able to dash over to London to settle the form for a new cheap edition of his books and help the Keeleys stage *The Battle of Life* at the Lyceum Theatre. The dramatic version was to open on the 21st, just two days after its publication in book form. The story itself is one of sickly sacrificial sentimentality, in which a younger sister pretends to elope with another man in order to bring about a marriage between her fiancé and her elder sister, whose unspoken love for him the girl has divined. Thackeray thought it "a wretched affair," and Dickens's old foe *The Times* slashed it brutally. Dickens was responsible, *The Times* said, for "the deluge of trash" that glutted the Christmas book market, and this was "*the very worst*" of the lot, without "one spark of originality, of truth, of probability, of nature, of beauty." Nevertheless the book sold well – 23,000 copies on its first day of publication, and by the end of January far more than any of its predecessors.

At the Lyceum Dickens found the "confounded *dramatization* . . . in a state so horrible" that he was almost disheartened about it. All the actors except the Keeleys were so bad that they had no idea of the play. In desperation, he summoned the entire company to Lincoln's Inn Fields and, despite a frightful cold, read the script to them to show how it should go. Forster provided seventy-six ham sandwiches by way of refreshment, and sent the forty-two that remained uneaten to be distributed to the poor. His strict injunction to the servant, Dickens said, "to find out very poor women and institute close enquiry into their life, conduct, and behaviour before leaving any sandwiches for them, was sublime." Soon Dickens whipped the production into shape, and its first-night reception was one of "immense enthusiasm, with uproar and shouting for me."

Christmas saw him back in Paris, ready to start the fifth number, in which Paul would die. Beginning, as usual by now, was hard: he felt "most abominably dull and stupid." But the familiar magic soon flowered, and Dickens half began to think the artfulness of Captain Cuttle and the fading life of little Paul "the only reality . . . and to mistake all the realities for shortlived shadows." On 14 January he wrote Miss Coutts, "– Paul is dead. He died on Friday night about 10 o'clock, and as I had no hope of getting to sleep afterwards, I went out, and walked about Paris until breakfast time next morning."

Paul's death drowned readers in a grief they had not known since the death of Little Nell. "Oh, my dear dear Dickens!" wrote Jeffrey from Edinburgh, "What a No. 5 you have given us! I have so cried and sobbed over it last night, and again this morning; and felt my heart purified by those tears . . ." And Thackeray, whose second number of *Vanity Fair* had just appeared, felt deeply discouraged. Hastening to *Punch*'s printing office, and entering Mark Lemon's room, he dashed a copy of *Dombey* on the table exclaiming, "There's no writing against such power as this – One has no chance! Read that chapter describing young Paul's death: it is unsurpassed – it is stupendous!"

After pacing the Paris streets all night, Dickens went directly to the office of the *malle-poste*, where Forster was arriving at eight o'clock for a fortnight's holiday. Dickens had been delighted to hear in October that Forster was resigning from the *Daily News*, and this visit had been arranged towards the end of November. With "dreadful insatiability" they plunged into a delirium of sightseeing and entertainment: the Louvre, Versailles, Saint-Cloud; prisons, hospitals, and the Morgue; the Bibliothèque Royale, the Opéra, the Conservatoire; all the theatres. At the Gymnase, Rose Chéri expired with heart-rending pathos in

Clarissa Harlowe; a melodrama called *The French Revolution* at the Cirque was spectacular with battles and mob scenes that were "positively awful."

Dickens now spoke French fluently, though with a heavy English accent, and the two friends supped with Dumas and Eugène Sue, met Gautier, and saw a great deal of Scribe. For Dickens the greatest figure of them all, however, was Victor Hugo, at this time just beginning *Les Misérables*, and already a European figure of advanced opinions whose views embraced a league of nations and the reorganization of Europe as a union of republics.

Returning to England at the end of January, Forster took back with him young Charley Dickens, now just turned ten years of age. The boy was to be enrolled at Eton, where Miss Coutts had asked to provide for his schooling. His father immediately set himself to writing the next number of *Dombey*, making his head ache with the difficulties of transferring all the interest of the story now to Florence Dombey. No sooner was this instalment sent to the printer than Dickens discovered to his horror that it was two pages short, and decided that he must hurry to London himself to supply the deficiency.

While he was there he saw Charley, took him to dine at Hampstead, and to Sunday dinner at Gore House. Hardly had Dickens reached Paris again when Charley was taken ill with scarlet fever. Dickens quickly decided to cut short his stay abroad. Devonshire Terrace was still occupied by Sir James Duke, so, leaving the other children with Georgina in Paris, he and Kate went to the Victoria Hotel, Euston Square, while looking for a temporary residence.

When Dickens paid his first visit to Charley the elderly charwoman was much astonished. "Lawk ma'am!" she exclaimed. "Is the young gentleman upstairs the son of the man that put together *Dombey*?" Though she could not read, she attended every month a tea held by subscription at a snuff shop, where the landlord read the month's number aloud. She had not imagined it possible that a single man *could* have put together that work. "Lawk ma'am! I thought that three or four men must have put together *Dombey*!"

Charley's illness and the delays in settling into a house at 1 Chester Place rendered Dickens almost desperate about his next monthly number. It was already 9 March, and "So far from having 'got through my agonies'..." he wrote to Georgina, who was still with the children in Paris, "I have not yet begun them." In consequence, "My wretchedness, just now, is inconceivable."

On 18 April Kate gave birth to their seventh child, who was christened Sydney Smith Haldimand. Kate had such a difficult delivery that the specialist hastily sent for told Dickens he had seen but one such case in his experience. "But thank God she is as well today as ever she has been at such a time," Dickens wrote Macready, "and sends all sorts of love to you."

Somehow or other, nevertheless, Dickens managed to get through that month's "convulsions of Dombey," as he called them. Near the beginning of the next month, his arm was severely mauled by a horse who made a sudden attack on him in the stable – "I believe," Dickens explained, "under the impression that I had gone into his stall to steal his corn, which upon my honour I had no intention of doing." Unstrung by the shock, he felt "hideously queer" each morning and suffered distressingly with "a low dull nervousness." To recover from these symptoms, he took Kate, now "in a brilliant state" again, down to Brighton for the latter half of May. Although he had been too shaken even to start his number before he left town, he picked up heart and went at it so furiously that by the 23rd it was very nearly done.

Returning to London, Dickens found himself involved in a quarrel between Thackeray and Forster. Thackeray had started a series of parodies called *Punch's Prize Novelists*, of which the first, "George de Barnwell," was an annihilating imitation of Bulwer Lytton's pompous literary style. Forster was a friend of Lytton's and he had smarted also at pictorial caricatures of himself that he knew Thackeray had passed around. Talking with a young journalist named Tom Taylor, Forster boiled over and said that Thackeray was "false as hell." Taylor assumed that this outburst was merely a comic pretence, and repeated it to Thackeray. But Thackeray promptly took umbrage. At a large party he publicly refused to shake hands with Forster.

The latter immediately asked Dickens to demand an explanation. Could Thackeray, Forster demanded, deny having given him equal reason for offence both by word and pictorial jibe? Remorsefully Thackeray admitted that he too had been at fault. He understood how Forster, chafed by ridicule, could have exploded as he did. "He consigned me to Hell for making caricatures of him: roasting me as I own & I'm sorry for it, to have done him." Summarizing the whole affair Thackeray wrote, "Forster ought not to have used the words: Taylor ought not to have told them: and I ought not to have taken them up." Forster too expressed his regret, and the quarrel was buried in a reconciliation dinner at Greenwich.

But either Thackeray or Bradbury and Evans (who were the publishers of *Punch*) prudently decided that it might be better not to include Dickens in the series of parodies, as had been originally planned. Thackeray was convinced that people were jealous of his growing reputation. "Jerrold hates me," he wrote, "Ainsworth hates me, Dickens mistrusts me, Forster says I am false as hell, and Bulwer curses me –"

As for Dickens, no writer more warmly and generously praised his contemporaries than he did, or depreciated them so little. But he was disagreeably impressed by what seemed to him a flippant cynicism in Thackeray's work and seldom read him, though he spoke well of his books whenever he mentioned them.

Concerning the parodies, Dickens made a jocose personal complaint. "It is curious, about Punch," he wrote Thackeray, "that I was so strongly impressed by the absurdity and injustice of my being left out of those imitations, that I several times said at home here I would write to you and urge the merits of the case." Nevertheless he felt that literary men lessened their dignity with the public and made enemies among themselves by sneering at each other.

The two men remained on cordial terms with each other. Thackeray dined at Devonshire Terrace and his two little girls were invited to children's parties there. When *Dombey and Son* was finished in March 1848, Dickens gave "a solemn dinner . . . to celebrate the conclusion" of that "immortal book." "It couldn't be done without you," Dickens wrote Thackeray. "Therefore book it, cher citoyen!" But there remained a faint cloud of mutual suspicion between them which cast potential shadows over their future relationship.

Meanwhile the restlessness that fretted Dickens had burst out in another plan for amateur dramatics. The amiable but perennially indigent Leigh Hunt was again in financial straits. The same company that had acted two years previously would present *Every Man in His Humour* and *The Merry Wives of Windsor* in London and then later in Manchester and Liverpool for Hunt's benefit. Dickens was soon deep in gathering together his cast. New members included George H. Lewes and the artist Augustus Egg, as well as Dickens's old friend Cruikshank.

Barely had rehearsals started at Miss Kelly's than, with a concern for unrewarded merit unusual in governments, Lord John Russell's administration granted Hunt a pension of £200. But it took more than such a piece of inconsiderate generosity to frustrate Dickens's desire to give a play. Hunt's debts still remained; and the aging dramatist John

Poole, author of successful farces like *Paul Pry* and *Turning the Tables*, was now desperately poor. Though the London performances were consequently given up and *The Merry Wives* eliminated, the amateurs, under Dickens's leadership, found themselves going ahead with the provincial presentations of *Every Man in His Humour*.

There were the usual managerial problems. One actor was disgruntled at his part having only twelve words; a second couldn't remember his at all; a third, though "hurt by his own sense of not doing well," clutched his part tenaciously; "and three weary times we dragged through it last night." Dickens coaxed, bullied, drilled; taught them expressive movement, proper inflection, natural gesture; wore everybody out and kept everybody in good humour; and resumed operations next day with the energy of a cheerful dynamo.

At the end of June, fairly well satisfied, he went to Broadstairs for a few weeks' vacation. Here there was a dark grey sea with a howling banshee of a wind rattling the windows as if it were late autumn rather than midsummer. All the children proceeded to get whooping cough and wandered about the beach choking incessantly. The only amusement was a wild beast show, in which a young woman in shining scaly armour pretended to fall asleep reclining on the principal lion, while a keeper who spoke through his nose exclaimed: "Beold the abazick power of woobbud!"

Meanwhile Dickens was kept busy writing "100 letters a day, about these plays." He returned to London for rehearsals on 16 July. The performances were scheduled for the 26th and 28th respectively at Manchester and Liverpool, where he made hotel reservations for his entire cast as well as those wives and feminine relations who were accompanying them, and took a large general sitting-room for the use of the company. At the railway station he tore wildly up and down the platform in a perspiration, gloriously excited, and almost got left behind. Both nights were brilliant successes; their receipts were £440 12s. the first night and £463 8s. 6d. the second.

Back in Broadstairs, where the children were almost recovered from their whooping cough, Dickens vigorously settled himself to make up the accounts of the trip, and wrote all the members of the cast to send their share of the expenses to Lemon. No sooner were the last business details tidied up than his restlessness returned again. "I am at a great loss for means of blowing my superfluous steam off, now that the play is over – but that is always my misfortune – and find myself compelled to tear up and down, between this and London, by express trains." In

London he saw *Cymbeline*; in Broadstairs he lamed Frank Stone by walking him seventeen miles, and received a visit from Hans Christian Andersen, whom he had met at Lady Blessington's that June; at Canterbury he bought a copy of Cruikshank's *The Bottle*.

The artist, once a hilarious climber of lamp-posts and wallower in gutters, had now become a fanatical teetotaller and was using his etching needle to depict the horrors of alcoholism. He carried his mania even into social intercourse; dining with Dickens, he snatched a glass of wine from a lady's hand, intending to throw it on the floor. "How dare you," exclaimed Dickens furiously, "touch Mrs Ward's glass?" Cruikshank's plates, however, Dickens thought almost Hogarthian in their power. He objected, nevertheless, that they were wrong in their philosophy: "the drinking should have begun in sorrow, poverty, or ignorance – the three things in which, in its awful aspect, it *does* begin."

But no distractions of fierce walks or racing about in express trains could allay Dickens's sharp unrest, despite the fact that with *Dombey and Son* he had reached a new peak of financial prosperity. In the previous six months his earnings had been £2,000 more than his expenses; and now, after drawing £100 monthly, he had another clear £2,220. This was exhilarating, but he still complained of the difficulty of working: "Deep slowness," he lamented, "in the inimitable's brain."

Although *Dombey* was by this time more than half written and was more successful every day, Dickens groaned again, as he had the preceding year, at the toil of doing a Christmas book at the same time. He felt "seedy"; the longer book took so much out of him that he wondered if it was "wise to go on with the Christmas book." "On the other hand, I am very loath to lose the money. And still more so to leave any gap at Christmas firesides which I ought to fill. In short I am (forgive the expression) BLOWED if I know what to do." In the end, instead of struggling to write it, as he had done at Lausanne and Geneva, he did hold over the little book for a year.

His own difficulties were not the only ones Dickens had to deal with. His brother Fred's love affair with Anna Weller was going badly. Anna's father disliked Fred and would not receive him in his house, but every week-end the young man miserably travelled the 120 miles to Birmingham, where he imposed himself on the grudging hospitality of a son-in-law of Mr Weller's. Anna had violent tempers with her family, and Fred chafed at the injustice of having so little money, spent more than he could afford on each week's journey, and took a high line about how willing he would be to struggle against all difficulties if he were only married.

Dickens sympathized with Fred's unhappiness but pointed out that Mr Weller's position had sense, and tried to establish an understanding about waiting and seeing Anna at reasonable intervals. But by now he had himself deep objections to the match; "breeding, Education, and the weakest parents on this globe" had made Anna's own character one "which can never come right."

Throughout this same period, Dickens was tremendously busied in helping Miss Coutts with her reform home for women, now being inaugurated at Urania Cottage in Shepherd's Bush. He selected the Matron and took great pains to find out all he could about the women admitted, "to give the Matron some useful foreknowledge of them." He insisted that there must be cheerful variety in their lives in the home. He ordered books for them to read, and arranged with his old friend the composer Hullah for them to have lessons in part-singing.

Their religious instruction, he said, should be based on the New Testament, not on the censorious thundering of the more vengeful parts of the Old. All rules framed solely in the abstract should yield to a gentle consideration for the best way of helping these women not to fall back into their old ways. The great point to be remembered always was that they were "to be *Tempted* to virtue."

On 1 December, Dickens had presided at a soirée of the Leeds Mechanics' Institute. Despite a wretched cold, he made an eloquent speech defending education for the masses against those who feared putting the power of knowledge into their hands. The wintry London to which he returned was in a "hideous state of mud and darkness. . . . I am in a dreadful state of mental imbecility myself, and am pursuing Dombey under difficulties." With the icily proud Edith Dombey's desertion of her husband, and the terrified and broken-hearted flight of Florence from her father's house, Dickens had reached one of the crises of the story. As the climax of the novel drew near – Mr Dombey's ruin and his reconciliation with Florence – Dickens's imagination kindled to the ending and he made fewer plaints about his difficulties in writing.

Nevertheless, he was glad after Christmas to take a holiday run to Scotland, where he visited friends in Edinburgh and presided at the first anniversary of the Glasgow Athenaeum. On the railway journey from Edinburgh to Glasgow Kate was taken ill and had a miscarriage.

When the train reached Glasgow, she was hurriedly put to bed, and a famous doctor called in. She recovered sufficiently to return to Edinburgh with Dickens on 30 December, but there she was taken violently ill again and another famous doctor called in. He stated that she would not be fit to travel back to London for another three days.

While Kate was regaining her strength, Dickens passed the time sightseeing, going to Abbotsford, and visiting friends. "I am sorry to report the Scott Monument a failure. It is like the spire of a Gothic church taken off and stuck in the ground." From Jeffrey he learned that the dramatist James Sheridan Knowles, author of *Virginius* and *The Hunchback*, had just declared himself bankrupt. This news rekindled all Dickens's ardour for amateur dramatics, and he returned to London fired with determination to run another benefit.

There was already a project to purchase Shakespeare's house at Stratford-on-Avon for the nation. Why not combine this, Dickens thought, with an endowment for a perpetual curatorship of the house, and make Knowles the first incumbent of the post? The amateur group should be revived to raise money for these purposes. Despite the fact that he had the last three numbers of *Dombey* still to do, Dickens eagerly called the company together again.

Their meetings did not go so smoothly as Dickens had hoped. The company disagreed about the choice of a play; in succession they rehearsed Beaumont and Fletcher's *Beggar's Bush*, Goldsmith's *Good-Natured Man*, Jerrold's *Rent Day*, and Bulwer Lytton's *Money*. Dickens grew disgusted at the bickering of these rehearsals, voiced his annoyance in a sharp note to each member of the cast, and reluctantly abandoned his share in the design.

In the midst of these contentions had come the news of the revolution in France. Dickens was wildly enthusiastic. "Vive la République!" he wrote Forster. "Vive le Peuple! Plus de Royauté!" To M. De la Rue he was less effervescent, but quite as decided: "The aristocratic feeling of England is against it, of course. All the intelligence, and liberality, I should say, are with it, tooth and nail. If the Queen should be marked in her attentions to old Papa Philippe . . . there will be great discontent and dissatisfaction expressed, throughout the country." There were, however, no sharp repercussions of foreign disorders in England. The country was prosperous, the populace showed no disposition to violence, and the middle class was solidly behind the Government.

In March Dickens went to Brighton to finish *Dombey*. After the proofs were returned to Bradbury and Evans, it struck him that he had forgotten to say a final word about Florence's dog, Diogenes. "Will you put him in the last little chapter?" he asked Forster. "After the word 'favourite' in reference to Miss Tox, you can add, 'except with Diogenes, who is growing old and wilful.' Or, on the last page of all, after 'and with them two children: boy and girl' . . . you might say 'and an old dog is generally in their company,' or to that effect."

Shortly after, Forster's *Life of Goldsmith* was published, and Dickens read it with loyal approbation. "I think the Goldsmith very great indeed . . .," he wrote his friend. "As a picture of the time, I think it impossible to give it too much praise." It was a noble achievement in its tracing of Goldsmith's life and its "dignified assertion of him without any sobs, whines, or convulsions of any sort." And above all, it was admirable in its statement of "the case of the literary man."

In some way, probably with no great resistance on Dickens's part, he had been brought back to take charge again of the dramatic amateurs. The town council of Stratford was buying the Shakespeare House, but funds for endowing the curatorship were still to be raised. Soon Dickens was buoyantly arranging all the details for the renewed production.

Another pattern was establishing itself in his life. Increasingly he felt an "unhappy loss or want of something" which he was to lament a few years later. In his youthful days of misery over Maria Beadnell he had discovered that he could dull his heartache by the intensity of his labours. During the most desperate height of his unhappiness he had directed the acting of *Clari* in Bentinck Street. And now, in the course of this last year, when his work itself had grown strangely difficult to him, he had found that by playing at the drama as hard as if it were work he drained off some of his distressing restlessness. More and more often, he was to resort to the same relief. But, like all drugs, it built up ultimately only a more desperate need and afterwards plunged him only into deeper misery.

31

A Haunted Man

The first outline of *Dombey and Son* that Dickens had sent Forster contained no hint of one element in the story that swelled into unforeseen prominence: the friction between Mr Dombey and his wife. It was not altogether chance that what was to have been a study of vainglory became at least in part a delineation of marital unhappiness. To be sure, jealous, plaintive, amenable Kate was no Edith Dombey. But Dickens, though he did not share Mr Dombey's freezing heartlessness, had enough of his rigid self-will. Gradually Dickens had come to feel himself haunted by a spectre of his own unhappiness. Throughout the five months following the completion of *Dombey* he managed to keep up his spirits with the violent stimulations of stage directing and acting. Then, as soon as they were over, he subsided again into outcries of anguish.

He had galvanized himself and his company of amateurs into a frenzy of action. They would not only raise the money for the Shakespeare House curatorship; they would force the Government, as he authoritatively wrote, "to make Knowles the first custodian." This time it was amicably decided to alternate between *Every Man in His Humour* and *The Merry Wives of Windsor*. Dickens willingly accepted a proposal from Mary Cowden Clarke that she should play Mistress Quickly opposite Mark Lemon's Falstaff. It was fitting that the compiler of the great Shakespeare *Concordance* be connected with the enterprise. Soon Dickens was deep in the excitements of production.

Busy though he was, he made a point of asking Forster to arrange an evening at Lincoln's Inn Fields with Ralph Waldo Emerson, who had just returned to England from revolutionary Paris. A fourth member of their party was Thomas Carlyle, whom Forster greeted loudly as "My Prophet!" Carlyle was feeling in one of his savage-Isaiah moods, and fulminated about the lewdness of the London streets and the wickedness of civilization. Chastity in the male sex, he said, was a thing of the past; and Dickens, seeing that their prim-minded American visitor was shocked, mischievously endorsed the judgement. If his own son were "particularly chaste" (Charley was at this time twelve years of age) he would be alarmed about his health. All this Emerson solemnly confided to his journal.

Dickens was now calling rehearsals almost every day for both *The Merry Wives* and *Every Man in His Humour* and the farces to be given with them. He sat to one side near the front of the stage, constantly leaping up to show the performers how some piece of business needed to be done. His own roles he carried off with a fine dash. "In *Love, Law, and Physic*," said Mrs Cowden Clarke, "he used to tuck me under his arm with the free-and-easy familiarity of a lawyer patronizing an actress whom he chances to find his fellow-traveller in a stage coach."

The "protracted agonies of management" kept Dickens, "like Falstaff," he said, " 'in a state of continual dissolution and thaw.' " John Leech was so shaky in his words as the Marquis in *Animal Magnetism* that he put out all the other players. Dickens told him he must either get them perfectly or drop out. Leech obediently bestirred himself: Dickens was soon able to report him positively "limp with being brilliant." The entire company was worked to death. "Beads break out all over Forster's head, and *boil* there, visibly and audibly."

The final rehearsals were held at the Theatre Royal, Haymarket, where the plays were to be performed. As the crucial dates drew near Dickens was swamped in final details – allotting press tickets, checking over how completely the house was sold out, seeing to the numbering of the seats. Even the printing of the tickets he kept under his own eyes, devising a new form with a stub to be returned to the holder, and red pasteboard for the pit, green for the lower boxes, and yellow for the upper.

On 15 May *The Merry Wives of Windsor* and *Animal Magnetism* filled the theatre with a gathering in full evening dress. Two nights later, at *Every Man in His Humour* and *Love, Law, and Physic*, a no less numerous assemblage included the Queen and the Prince Consort. Both performances were brilliantly successful. Carlyle, to be sure, was astringent about Shakespeare's comedy: "A poor play," he said, as the curtain went down, "but *plaudite, plaudite!*" Most of the audience, however, were enraptured. Bulging Mark Lemon was a hilarious Falstaff. Dickens covered himself with glory as Shallow, adopting a senile stoop and feeble step into which he infused "a certain attempted smartness of carriage," and inventing "a kind of impeded sibillation" of utterance, as if through the loss of teeth.

The London performances barely over, demands poured in appearances in Liverpool and Birmingham. Manchester was also fitt in, and saw the first of the provincial performances on Saturday, 3 Jui The theatre echoed to wild enthusiasm, with "the storm of plaudits . loudest when Dickens was recognized."

At railway stations Dickens flashed the free pass the railway aut orities had bestowed upon his entire party. As the train sang along t tracks he entertained them with countless stories. At one stop j leaped out to get food at the refreshment room, and came back with plate of buns, crying "For Heaven's sake, somebody eat some of the buns; I was in hopes I saw Miss Novello eye them with greedy joy."

Every Man in His Humour roused such a furore in Birmingham th: there were insistent pleas for a return engagement to play *The Mer. Wives* as well. As an addition to the bill, Dickens determined on "th screaming afterpiece of *Past Two O'Clock in the Morning*," which he ha originally acted in Montreal. Mrs Cowden Clarke dined at Devonshir Terrace on the evening he and Mark Lemon cut it down to proper siz for this purpose. Sitting out in the garden after dinner while th children played on the lawn, she was amused to see one of the little boy in eager conference with his father, while Dickens looked smiingl down. "The little fellow gave me so many excellent reasons why he should not go to bed so soon," Dickens explained, "that I yielded the point and let him sit up half an hour later."

By this time Edinburgh and Glasgow also were clamorous to have the company come north. Between the second Birmingham engagement, on 27 June, and these Scottish engagements there was an interval of a few weeks during which Dickens tyrannically rehearsed his company in a new farce, *Used Up*, to alternate with the others. In this piece Cruikshank had the part of a blacksmith. Mrs Cruikshank became ill, and he had to give it up. Suddenly Mrs Cruikshank was well again, and he wanted it back. "O questa femina maladetta!" Dickens exclaimed to George Lewes. "O Impressario sfortunato! – ma sempre dolce, tranquilissimo, cristianissimo, exempio di pazienza! – In una parola – Carlo."

On 17 July *The Merry Wives* was played at Edinburgh with *Love, Law, and Physic* and *Past Two O'Clock in the Morning*. The following night, at Glasgow, it was given with *Animal Magnetism*. Two nights later there was a second Glasgow performance, at half prices, announcement of which had been carefully deferred, to prevent its injuring the sale of tickets for the earlier performance. On this occasion *Used Up* was the farce, with Dickens acting Sir Charles Coldstream. The hit of the piece, however, was made by Mark Lemon as one of Sir Charles's fop friends. During rehearsal Lemon startled the company by inventing a ridiculous little laugh, exquisitely inane and disproportioned to the huge bulk of man from which it came, a "squeaking hysterical giggle closing in a suddenly checked gasp." This "incomparably droll new laugh" transformed his small part into an important one and brought down the house every time it was uttered.

The entire series of performances had been highly successful, the gross receipts coming to £2,551 os. 8d. In the end, to be sure, the Government had granted Knowles a pension, so that it proved unnecessary to establish him in the curatorship of the Shakespeare House, and the profits of the theatricals were placed directly in his hands. The enterprise had been no less noteworthy as a source of enjoyment to the performers. "What enthusiastic hurrahs at the rise of the curtain, and as each character in succession made his appearance on the stage!" Mrs Cowden Clarke summarized, "What times those were! What rapturous audiences a-tiptoe with expectation . . ."

Proportional to the exaltation of those glittering nights, however, for Dickens, was the depression that followed. The ghost had returned. How insupportable was Devonshire Terrace "after that canvas farm wherein I was so happy." What was a humdrum dinner at five-thirty "compared with *that* soup, and the hundreds of pairs of eyes that watched its disappearance?" Why did he have seven children, "not engaged at sixpence a-night apiece, and dismissable for ever, if they tumble down, not taken on for an indefinite time at a vast expense, and never – no never, never – wearing lighted candles round their heads" like the fairies in *The Merry Wives*?

As usual, he burlesqued his feelings. Of course he loved his children, but what father of seven would not feel sometimes weighed down by his responsibilities? "I have no energy whatever, I am very miserable. I loathe domestic hearths. I yearn to be a vagabond. Why can't I marry Mary!" Mary was the farmer's daughter in *Used Up*, with whom Sir Charles Coldstream is in love, a fetching little charmer in pink muslin and a ribboned apron: but the name may also have held some nostalgic echo of the Mary of a vanished happy past.

Family troubles also deepened his unhappiness. His sister Fanny in November 1846, had broken down during an attempt to sing at a party in Manchester and was found to be suffering from tuberculosis. Dickens, deeply grieved, insisted on her being brought to London to be looked over by Dr Elliotson. In the course of the following year her illness grew worse. By May of 1848 she coughed incessantly and could obtain rest only by the use of morphine. She was brought to London again, to be examined by Sir James Clark, an authority on pulmonary diseases. From him Dickens learned that she could not possibly live many more weeks. In the purer air of Hornsey, a suburban village north of London, quarters were found for the dying woman and her husband.

Throughout the latter part of July, Dickens visited his sister daily. Then, as she still lingered on, he allowed Kate, who was pregnant once again, to persuade him to join her and the children at Broadstairs, where she might "grumble 'unbeknown' to all, but our hoarse old monster-friend, the sea here." At Broadstairs he continued to feel "used up" and forlorn. Any day might bring the fatal summons to Fanny's deathbed. Walking moodily on the shore, he tried to plan his Christmas book, or, giving that up, stretched out on the sands reading Bulwer Lytton's *Harold*.

On 9 August, he took the boys up to school at the end of their vacation. With the close of the month he received word that Fanny's death was only a matter of days. He hurried back to town and out to Hornsey. He found her in one of the paroxysms now constantly recurrent. "No words," he wrote Kate, "can express the terrible aspect of suffering and suffocation – the appalling noise in her throat – and the agonizing look around," followed repeatedly by a lethargy of exhaustion. "Sleep seems quite gone, until the time arrives for waking no more." On 2 September Fanny was dead, and on the 8th her body was lowered into a grave at Highgate Cemetery.

During these harrowing last days, Fred's engagement to Anna Weller continued to be a source of disturbance. "I must do my duty," Dickens wrote his brother, "by protesting against this connexion as fatal and hopeless." What made it even worse, Dickens learned that Fred, now twenty-eight, was in debt and looked to him for financial aid. "I never supposed it possible that you would contemplate marriage, on your income, with such fetters on your limbs." With all the claims of his own children heavy upon him, he did not feel that he could fling money "into the unfathomable sea of such a marriage with debt upon its breast."

Fred responded angrily. "I shall never justify the mean opinion you have of me," Dickens replied, "when you suppose it possible that such a thing as your letter of Friday, can move me in the least." Nevertheless, in a way that Dickens thought "unworthy of an independent spirit," Fred pressed for the sum of £80 to clear his immediate embarrassments. Dickens demanded a complete accounting of Fred's debts, to whom they were owed and for what, including a statement of what would still remain unpaid, "and how you would propose to clear that off, and exactly what effect these arrangements would have on your intentions as to marriage." In his "present absence of enlightenment on these heads," he refused to "make the least approach to a promise" that he would advance the money. In the end Dickens probably gave Fred some assistance, for not long afterwards we find him confidently asking for further aid.

Dickens had by this time gone back to Devonshire Terrace for the winter. While still at Broadstairs, however, he had been grieved by the serious illness of Roche, "the Brave courier" of his Italian and Swiss sojourns. The stout, bustling, cheerful fellow now had heart disease. During the autumn his condition grew worse. He should have hospital care, Dickens thought, not be left alone in his poor lodgings. Dickens promptly sought Miss Coutts's influence to have Roche admitted to St George's Hospital. "I have the deepest interest in the matter. He is a most faithful, affectionate, and devoted man."

For a time the change and hospital care helped him. "My dear Roche," Dickens wrote him in French, "I am charmed to receive such good news of you, and I hope . . . that you will soon regain your strength, to journey, for the winter, to a milder climate than that of England. Before two years have gone by, we must (the Brave and I) take a trip to Spain." The entire family asked about him continually. "While awaiting that trip to Spain I spoke of, you will have to become excessively robust and ruddy. Courage then, my friend!" But the trip to Spain never took place. Before the end of the following year Roche was dead.

During almost the whole of 1848 Dickens undertook no new work of fiction. It is a far cry from the days when he had exuberantly begun another long novel while its predecessor was still in full career. Between spring and fall his entire literary output amounted to no more than nine short articles – totalling some 14,000 words – all appearing in the *Examiner*. Small enough as the six months' work of any man of letters, for one as copiously productive as Dickens had been in the great period from 1836 to 1844, it represents a striking shrinkage in production. Indeed, save for the great effort of *Dombey and Son* and *The Battle of Life*, these journalistic pieces were his only writings of the past four years.

Several of these articles, however, strongly underline Dickens's

views on social problems. "Ignorance and Crime" uses the Metropolitan Police statistics of 1847 to point out the connection between
illiteracy and crime. Out of 61,000 offenders of all kinds, 22,000 were
totally illiterate and only a few hundred had more "than the mere
ability to blunder over a book like a little child." "Side by side with
Crime, Disease, and Misery in England, Ignorance is always brooding,
and is always certain to be found." Schools of Industry, where useful
knowledge is reinforced by "the sublime lessons of the New Testament
. . . are the only means of removing the scandal and the danger that
beset us in this nineteenth century of our Lord."

In a review of Cruikshank's *The Drunkard's Children*, a sequel to *The
Bottle*, Dickens protests against the notion that alcoholism is caused by
an injudicious nip of gin after dinner starting once decent families on a
downhill rush to destruction. He does not deny that personal faults and
crimes are involved. But drunkenness "as a national horror" grows
from "disgusting habitations, bad workshops and workshop customs,
want of light, air, and water, the absence of all easy means of decency
and health."

Reforming these conditions should come first, not African civilization,
foreign missions, introducing improved agriculture in Fernando Po,
and abolishing the slave trade, praiseworthy as those other goals undoubtedly were. Dickens never falls into the insular complacency of
lauding English ways and occidental civilization generally as free from
those shortcomings and superstitions that afflict other more benighted
parts of the world. Often he seizes upon a foreign delusion to point out
its analogues at home. Visiting a Chinese junk, for example, moored
in the West India Docks, he describes the mimic eye in the vessel's
prow by which she was supposed to find her way, the red rags fastened
on mast, rudder, and cables to ensure her safety at sea, and the eighteen-
armed idol Chin-Tee, with joss-sticks and incense burning before its niche.

It is pleasant, coming back from China by the Blackwall railway
[Dickens then adds ironically], to think that WE trust no red rags
in storms, and burn no joss-sticks before idols; that WE never grope
our way by the aid of conventional eyes which have no sight in
them . . . The ignorant crew of the *Keying* refused to enter on the
ship's books, until "a considerable amount of silvered paper, tinfoil,
and joss-sticks" had been laid in . . . ; but OUR seamen – far less
our bishops, priests, and deacons – never stand out upon points of
silvered paper and tinfoil, or the lighting up of joss-sticks upon altars!

The feelings defined by these articles come to weigh more and more heavily in determining the very choice of dominant themes in almost all the books Dickens later wrote. Even in *David Copperfield*, where their influence is least striking, the cruel, gloomy religion of the Murdstones, the depressing toil in the warehouse, the sardonic passages on aristocracy and blood, and the involved precedents and predatory formulas of the Courts of Doctors' Commons all emphasize society's callousness to human welfare and its worship of blind eyes and brutal idols. From then on, Dickens's attacks became constant and relentless. In *Bleak House* they unify the portrayal of the Courts of Chancery, the slum tenements of Tom-all-Alone's, Mrs Jellyby's neglect of her home for the natives of Borioboola-Gha, and the Parliamentary satire on Coodle and Doodle. They make of *Hard Times* one concentrated onslaught. In *Little Dorrit* they run through the elaborate parallels between the Marshalsea, Mrs Clennam's grim imprisoning theology, Bleeding Heart Yard, and the life of the upper classes, with their reverence for that greasy golden calf, the great financier-swindler Merdle. In *Our Mutual Friend* they dominate the rendition of the Veneerings and Podsnaps, whose only values are in the dust heaps that symbolize their material ambitions. Throughout these novels Dickens develops consistently the social criticism to which his *Examiner* articles bear witness.

Social criticism, however, dwindles to a minor strand in *The Haunted Man*, the Christmas story for 1848, the major theme of which had its roots in Dickens's relation to his own past. Its portrayal of unhappy memories haunting the present may, indeed, have been partly responsible for the fact that he had found himself unable to deal with it the preceding autumn and had been putting it off for an entire year. But now he could delay no longer, and he set himself to write despite those groans of tribulation that had come to afflict his efforts at composition.

The first stage, he wrote Mrs Watson, on 5 October, was "sitting frowning horribly at a quire of paper," and falling into a state of irascibility "which utterly confounds and scares the House. The young family peep at me through the bannisters as I go along the hall; and Kate and Georgina quail (almost) as I stalk by them." "Grinding" away at it, even though he was now in London and could not blame Genoa's lack of crowded streets, or the sluggish waters of Lake Leman, he nevertheless found the story obstinately intractable. "The Haunted Man won't do something I want him to do," he complained to Miss Coutts. "I think of taking him down to Brighton next week for ten days or so, and putting an end to him." Then, just two days before going there, the snarls untangled and the rest of the story was written without too much trouble at the Bedford Hotel. "I finished last night," he reported on 1 December, "having been crying my eyes out over it . . . these last three days."

The Haunted Man was published on 19 December, and sold 18,000 copies before evening of that day. Towards the end of the year a dramatic version by Mark Lemon was produced with considerable success at the Adelphi Theatre. Dickens gave some aid in the writing and rehearsal of the play, though his feelings about the dramatization of a novelist's works remained unaltered. "I have no power to prevent it; and therefore I think it best to have at least one Theatre where it is done in a less Beastly manner than at others, and where I can impress *something* (however little) on the actors."

In its narrative form, however, *The Haunted Man* is a weak performance. Its pallidness is slightly, but not much, relieved by the slap-dash caricature of Little Moloch, the Tetterbys' baby, a fractious blight on the existence of its young brother, who staggers around all day under its weight, never catching more than "meek glimpses of things in general from behind its skirts, or over its limp flapping bonnet." Redlaw, the distinguished chemist, is a dimmer Scrooge, without the latter's almost hilarious misanthropy, a brooding victim of a melancholy lingering on from an unhappy past.

Yet, feeble though the tale is, it is significant because it reflects the inward preoccupations with which Dickens was struggling. Like Redlaw, he himself is a famous and outwardly successful man. In the imaginative laboratory of his art, as in Redlaw's test tubes and retorts, there are hosts of spectral shapes, all subject to his power to uncombine and recombine. But like Redlaw he has known wrongs and sufferings from under the burden of which he cannot escape.

In the first scene with the Spectre, all of Redlaw's feelings about his life are, with slight modifications, what Dickens still felt about his own. "I am he, neglected in my youth, and miserably poor, who strove and suffered, and still strove and suffered, until I hewed out knowledge from the mine where it was buried . . ." "No mother's self-denying love, no father's counsel aided *me*." It was unjust to Dickens's mother, but so he had felt ever since the days when she had been warm for him to return to the blacking warehouse.

Like Dickens too, Redlaw has lost a beloved sister, who lived long enough to see him become famous. He had also had a sweetheart to whom he had given his earliest and deepest devotion. "I was too poor to bind its object to my fortune then, by any thread of promise or entreaty. . . . But, more than ever I had striven in my life, I strove to climb!"

Redlaw's experiences have not made him hardhearted or uncharitable. He hastens to relieve the misfortunes of others. But would not both he and they, he feels, be happier and better if they could lose their unfortunate weight of memories darkening every hour? The Ghost grants his desire to lose his memory of wrong and sorrow, and with it bestows the power to pass on the gift. Then Redlaw discovers that with the memory of unhappiness depart the softening influences on the heart that grief may bring. All those he touches grow callous, surly, bitter, and brutal. The struggling news dealer Tetterby and his devoted wife regret their marriage; Redlaw's servant resents his own aged father; and the old man grows selfish and querulous.

In anguish, Redlaw prays to have the gift reversed. In deeper understanding, he realizes that not oblivion, and not a corrosive brooding, but the purifying and strengthening influences of memory are the sources of self-conquest and peace of mind. Instead of praying for forgetfulness, one should more wisely pray, "Lord, keep my memory green."

Though Dickens knew this in his mind, he was unable to make himself feel it in his heart. Doubtless that is why the story seems so sentimental and overmoralistic. Its artistic deficiencies, however, only underline the sharpness of the inner tensions Dickens was striving to subdue. Neither the intellectual comprehension of a psychological problem nor the attempt to impose its solution by an act of will can produce a successful work of art. It must be felt in the very deepest fibres of its creator's being.

But Dickens, although he tried to feel otherwise, was full of self-justification in his present frustrations and steeped in self-pity for his past sufferings. His only resource was to dash off on a trip or a further bout of theatricals or some other distraction. In his fragment of childhood autobiography, begun shortly before or after *The Haunted Man* was conceived, he had said, "I do not write resentfully or angrily: for I know how all these things have worked together to make me what I am." It was true that he knew that, but it was not true that his bitterness was gone.

It might perhaps be only through committing his entire past and its sorrows to paper and as it were casting it out of himself, that he could lay its unhappy ghost. Some such feeling surely suggested the idea of writing his autobiography, but after struggling with it for a time Dickens found it too painful and gave it up. The part dealing with his childhood, through the blacking warehouse days and up to the time he was a scholar at Wellington House Academy, he did give Forster to read. But as he came to the humiliations of his heartbroken love for Maria Beadnell he found he could not bear to allow anyone else to read, could not bear even to go on. Only in the disguised form of *David Copperfield*, with many changes and omissions which are as significant as what he tells, could he make confessional to the world.

32

Myself into the
Shadowy World

During all the later part of 1848 Dickens's thoughts were turning more and more often to the form his next book should take. About the time Forster was reading the autobiographical fragment, he suggested that the novel be written in the first person. Dickens at once seized eagerly on this idea. The decision to fuse some of his own youthful experiences with those of his hero, and to make the story of David Copperfield at least in part his own story, would enable him, he must have felt, at the same time to reveal and conceal the dark unhealed wounds he could not expose without disguise, to analyse, to assess, to assuage. Surely if in his own heart he confronted it all, the burden would fall from him and leave him free. But how to do it? Shortly after the New Year he took the problem with him on a brief holiday jaunt to Norwich and Yarmouth before settling down to work.

Preceding his departure there had been two festivities at Devonshire Terrace, a dinner on 3 January to celebrate the "christening" of *The Haunted Man* and a Twelfth-Night birthday party for Charley and the children, with a magic lantern and conjuring. For this occasion little Mamey and her sister Katey had taught Dickens the polka. In the middle of the previous night he suddenly found himself afraid he had forgotten the step, and, leaping out of bed in the wintry dark, began practising on the cold floor. On the evening itself, only Captain Marryat and possibly Mrs Macready equalled Dickens in vigour and vivacity. To Macready, who was once again touring in America, Dickens described how they drank his health, "then dashed into a Sir Roger de Coverley – then into a reel –" and "for two mortal hours," he himself and Mrs Macready "danced without ceasing . . . reducing to 'tarnal smash' (as we say in our country) all the other couples one by one."

The following day he started off for Norwich, with Leech and Lemon for companions. Dickens bought a bright Norwich scarf as a gift for Kate, and then with his two friends went on to Yarmouth, whence they took a twenty-three-mile walk down the coast to Lowestoft and back. "Yarmouth, Sir," he wrote Forster, was the success of the trip, "the strangest place in the wide world: one hundred and forty-six miles of hill-less country between it and London. . . . I shall certainly try my hand at it." That spongy and soppy place, with its great dull waste of pebbled beach, was in fact soon to become the home of the Peggottys and Mrs Gummidge and Little Em'ly.

Back in London, Dickens still did not begin his book. Kate was near her time for their eighth child, and she had had great difficulties at the birth of Sydney twenty-one months before. Dickens had learned about the use of chloroform during childbirth, and promised Kate, who was apprehensive, that she should have it.

The baby was born on 15 January. As they had feared, the birth was not an easy one, and Dickens kept his word.

> The doctors were dead against it, but I stood my ground, and (thank God) triumphantly. It spared her all pain . . . and saved the child all mutilation. It enabled the doctors to do, as they afterwards very readily said, in ten minutes, what might otherwise have taken them an hour and a half; the shock to her nervous system was reduced to nothing; and she was, to all intents and purposes, *well* the next day.

A fortnight later Kate was "eating mutton-chops in the drawing room," and the baby – a boy, who was to be christened Henry Fielding Dickens – was so thriving, Dickens said, that he looked like "what the Persian Princes might have called a 'moon-faced' monster."

Three articles Dickens contributed to the *Examiner* show how little the treatment of pauper children had changed since the time of *Oliver Twist*. Cholera had broken out at a baby farm in Tooting where a man named Drouet boarded 1,400 children. Soon the parish churchyard was too small for the piles of infant coffins. Bitterly calling his first article "The Paradise at Tooting," Dickens pointed out that these small cholera victims had been left without medical care, four in a bed, in foul, damp rooms. The potatoes at their table were black and diseased, and their whole diet so inadequate that they had climbed secretly over palings to pick out scraps from the tubs of hogwash. Their bodies were emaciated and covered with boils and sores. The guardians of the poor had paid only the most cursory attention to adverse criticism; one of them recommended that boys who complained should be horsewhipped. In short, the establishment "was brutally conducted, vilely kept, preposterously inspected, dishonestly defended, a disgrace to a Christian community, and a stain upon a civilized land."

There followed, Dickens noted, the usual defensive flourishing of foolscap and red tape. Public indignation nevertheless led to Drouet's being indicted for manslaughter. But the judge before whom the case was tried directed an acquittal. There was no evidence, he said, that the victims had been strong enough, even before they were placed in Drouet's care, to have recovered from the epidemic. "Drouet was 'affected to tears' as he left the dock." Despite this fantastic verdict, however, the publicity, as Dickens hoped, aided in the breaking up of the child-farming system.

By the middle of February, Dickens had taken Kate down to Brighton, where she could enjoy the sea air and he could be thinking out the plan of his novel. At the Bedford Hotel he turned over titles in his mind. At first he thought of *Mag's Diversions*, with various subtitles in which the hero began as "Mr Thomas Mag," then became "David Mag of Copperfield House," and finally "David Copperfield." The title still went through a number of changes, including *The Copperfield Disclosures*, *The Copperfield Records*, *The Copperfield Survey of the World as It Rolled*, and *Copperfield Complete*, before it settled down to the ultimate choice, of which the full form was *The Personal History, Experience, and Observations of David Copperfield the Younger of Blunderstone Rookery, which he never meant to be published on any account*. Dickens was much startled when Forster pointed out to him that the initials were his own reversed, and exclaimed that it was "just in keeping with the fates and chances that were always befalling him. 'Why else,' he said 'should I so obstinately have kept to that name when once it turned up?'"

In London again before the end of February, Dickens wrote the first two chapters. The opening number was to appear in May, but as late as 19 April he was finding it hard to keep the story going. "Though I know what I want to do, I am lumbering on like a stage-waggon." Nevertheless, before the deadline Dickens managed to complete the difficult Yarmouth chapter, with its dewy lyricism and exquisite touches of humour, and its chill transition back to Mr Murdstone ruthlessly petrifying all the tenderness of the Rookery parlour.

The number was an instantaneous success. Thackeray, whose own semi-autobiographic *Pendennis* was already under way in yellow-covered instalments, was warmly generous in his praise. "Get David

Copperfield," he wrote his friend Brookfield; "by Jingo it's beautiful – it beats the yellow chap of this month hollow –" And to Mrs Brookfield: "Have you read Dickens? – O it is charming. Bravo Dickens. It has some of his very prettiest touches – those inimitable Dickens touches which make such a great man of him."

On 12 May, shortly after this initial triumph, Thackeray joined a group of dinner guests at Devonshire Terrace which included Phiz, Jerrold, and the Carlyles. Jane Carlyle, in a letter, was acid about the magnificence of the table, overloaded with "pyramids of figs raisins oranges" and candles rising out of "quantities of *artificial* flowers"; at Lady Ashburton's dinner parties "there were just *four cowslips* in china pots – four silver shells containing sweets, and a silver filigree temple in the middle!" Carlyle was feeling in a more genial mood, and laughingly replied to an inquiry about his health in the words of Mrs Gummidge, "I am a lone lorn creetur' and everythink goes contrairy with me."

David Copperfield now was progressing with rapidity and ease. On 4 May the second chapter of the June number went off to Browne (who illustrated it with pictures of the friendly waiter drinking David's ale for him and of Mr Mell tootling dismally on his flute); the very next afternoon the final chapter of the number was dispatched. At the beginning of July, Dickens fell on his left side, and had to be cupped and blistered. The injury delayed his getting off the first chapter of the following number, but by the 10th it was completed. This was the section in which he used his blacking warehouse experiences. "I really think I have done it ingeniously," he told Forster, "and with a very complicated interweaving of truth and fiction. Vous verrez. I am going on like a house afire in point of health, and ditto ditto in point of number."

Dickens's parents appear as the Micawbers, with all his mother's ineffectual plans for a school in the Gower Street days, and all his father's grandiloquence and financial improvidence. In the story, however, the Micawbers are not embarrassing to David, since they are only a pair of strangers at whose house he lodges. But David's labours at Murdstone and Grinby's are steeped in all the soul-wrenching agony of Dickens's enslavement in the blacking warehouse and all Dickens's feeling of being rejected by his natural parents and cast into a bottomless abyss of despair. In this intermingling of fact and fantasy, in their playful softenings of some humiliations and in their intensified rendering of childhood grief, Dickens made these chapters a profound and tremendous achievement in coming to grips with his own past.

He was now at the Albion Hotel at Broadstairs, which he thought

beat "all watering places into what the Americans call 'sky-blue fits.'"
With Leech, who planned to spend the summer near them, he ran down
to the Isle of Wight, where he rented Winterbourne, "a delightful
and beautiful house" at Bonchurch, and Leech took a neighbouring
cottage. There was, Dickens added in a note to Kate, "a waterfall on
the grounds, which I have arranged with a carpenter to convert into a
perpetual shower-bath." To Beard he wrote that the drop was 150
feet and to Bradbury that it was 500.

At first Dickens found everything there enchanting, although he had
some trouble getting into the swing of his work. "From the tops of the
highest downs there are views which are only to be equalled on the
Genoese shore of the Mediterranean . . ." Forming a club called the
Sea Serpents, whose banner portrayed a curling serpent cut out of
yards of bronze-green calico, he organized picnics to Cook's Castle.
There were merry evenings drinking gin punch, enjoying games, or
watching Dickens give wonderful exhibitions of conjuring as "the unparalleled necromancer Rhia Rhama Rhoos."

A friend much in Dickens's mind at this time was Giuseppe Mazzini,
the Italian revolutionist. He had dined at Devonshire Terrace and taken
Dickens to see the school he had established at Clerkenwell for Italian
organ boys. With the fall of Rome Dickens was anxious until he
learned that Mazzini had escaped back to England. The public appeal
issued that September for the Italian political refugees was of Dickens's
authorship. These exiles, he wrote, were "the good citizens who, when
Rome was abandoned by her Monarch . . . arose to give her law, tran-
quillity and order . . ." Their enforced capitulation "to a foreign army
forty thousand strong" was "an ineffaceable stain upon the honour
and name of France." Now that their noble cause was lost, England
was almost the only free land in which they could be safe; England
should be "worthy of its love of freedom, and its high renown" by
coming to their aid.

In the course of August, Dickens's enthusiasm for Bonchurch gave
way to a note of discomfort. "I have made it a rule," he reported, "that
the Inimitable is invisible, until two every day. I shall have half the
number done, please God, tomorrow. I have not worked quickly here
yet, but I don't know what I *may* do." Then came the feeling that his
health required a different air. He would have to climb daily to the
top of the downs. But he fell prey to an obstinate cough, was "stetho-
scoped" and ordered rubbings for his chest. By the end of the month his
disturbance boiled over to Forster in a long bill of complaints:

Before I think of beginning my next number, I perhaps cannot do better than give you an imperfect description of the results of the climate of Bonchurch after a few weeks' residence. The first salubrious effect of which the Patient becomes conscious is an almost continual feeling of sickness, accompanied with great prostration of strength, so that his legs tremble under him, and his arms quiver when he wants to take hold of any object. An extraordinary disposition to sleep (except at night, when his rest, in the event of his having any, is broken by incessant dreams) is always present . . . Extreme depression of mind, and a disposition to shed tears from morning to night . . . When he brushes his hair in the morning, he is so weak that he is obliged to sit upon a chair to do it. He is incapable of reading, at all times. And his bilious system is so utterly overthrown, that a ball of boiling fat appears to be always behind the top of the bridge of his nose, simmering between his haggard eyes.

His cough was so "constant, deep, and monotonous" that " 'The faithful watch-dog's honest bark' " was nothing in comparison. "Of all the places I ever have been in, I have never been in one so difficult to exist in, pleasantly. . . . I am quite convinced that I should die here, in a year. It's not hot, it's not close, I don't know what it is, but the prostration of it is *awful*."

The hyperbole of this outburst did not mean that Dickens was joking. Something in this climate he did find seriously enervating. By the middle of September he was almost frantic to pull up stakes and get back to the "brisk and bracing" air of Broadstairs. At his old watering place early in October he immediately felt better despite a spell of bad weather. "Such a night and day of rain I should think the oldest inhabitant never saw! and yet, in the old formiliar Broadstairs, I somehow or other don't mind much. The change has done Mamey a world of good, and I have begun to sleep again."

His half-yearly accounts, which Evans had brought him, showed that the first three numbers of *Copperfield* had not done quite so well as *Dombey*, but Dickens was not discouraged. Back numbers continued to go off, and the current numbers were selling a steady 25,000. Nevertheless he began to think again of what he called "the dim design" of a weekly periodical as a regular addition to his novel earnings. Now it seemed clear to him that he must set it going in the spring: "I have already been busy, at odd half-hours, in shadowing forth a name and an idea." Meanwhile he plugged away at his sixth and seventh numbers.

During November work on *David Copperfield* was interrupted and delayed by Dickens witnessing the execution of Mr and Mrs Manning, which he made the occasion of two letters to *The Times* again protesting public hangings. In the first he expressed his horror of "the wickedness and levity of the immense crowd" in Horsemonger Lane – "thieves, low prostitutes, ruffians and vagabonds," – fighting, whistling, joking brutally, letting out cries and howls, showing no touch of pity or awed emotion when "the two miserable creatures who attracted all this ghastly sight about them were turned quivering into the air." In the second he emphasized that such sights had only a hardening and debasing influence on their spectators, and that from the moment a murderer was convicted he should be kept from curious visitors and reporters serving up his sayings and doings in the Sunday papers, and executed privately within the prison walls. These two letters caused an enormous sensation and engulfed Dickens in "a roaring sea of correspondence." It was not, however, until 1868 that the reform he suggested was effected.

Unhappily, the letters also brought about an estrangement between Dickens and Douglas Jerrold, who bitterly resented Dickens's compromising in the slightest degree on the principle of abolishing capital punishment. For a number of months they did not see each other, but then it fell out that each was dining, with his own separate party, at the Garrick Club. "Our chairs were almost back to back," Dickens told Jerrold's son, years later. "I said not a word (I am sorry to remember) and did not look that way." But before long, Jerrold "openly wheeled his chair round, stretched out both his hands . . . and said aloud, with a bright and loving face that I can see as I write to you: 'For God's sake, let us be friends again! Life's not long enough for this!' "

Continuing *David Copperfield*, Dickens brought his hero to the point where he was finishing school and about to enter upon a profession. Rejecting a notion of making him a special pleader, he considered having him enter a banking house, then rejected that too. "Banking business impracticable on account of confinement: which would stop the story, I foresee. I have taken, for the present at all events, the proctor. I am wonderfully in harness, and nothing galls or frets." The 20th of November saw his month's work completed: "Copperfield done after two days very hard work indeed; and I think a smashing number. His first dissipation I hope will be found worthy of attention, as a piece of grotesque truth."

Finishing this number freed Dickens for a long-planned visit to his

Lausanne friends, the Richard Watsons, at their ancestral home of Rockingham Castle in Northamptonshire. He tremendously enjoyed this holiday. He flirted playfully with Miss Mary Boyle, a tiny, blue-eyed niece of Mrs Watson's, two years his senior; she flirted back, and he wrote her a burlesque of Gray's "Elegy." On the last night of his visit there were private theatricals, conjuring by Dickens, and country dances in the great hall lasting until three in the morning. Dickens and Miss Boyle played Sir Peter and Lady Teazle in some scenes from *The School for Scandal*, and the scene of the lunatic on the wall making passionate declarations of love to Mrs Nickleby. "To see all the household," he wrote, "headed by an enormously fat housekeeper, occupying the back benches last night, laughing and applauding without any restraint; and to see a blushing sleek-headed footman produce, for the watch-trick, a silver watch of the most portentous dimensions, amidst the rapturous delight of his brethren and sisterhood; was a very pleasant spectacle . . ."

He signalized his return to London by writing Mrs Watson a letter of mock despair. "Plunged in the deepest gloom," his thoughts were being driven "to madness. On the way here I was a terror to my companions, and I am at present a blight and mildew on my home." Under his elaborate signature he added a postscript: "I am in such an incapable state, that after executing the foregoing usual flourish I swooned, and remained for some time insensible. Ha, Ha, Ha! Why was I ever restored to consciousness!!!" But the first two or three weeks of every month, as he explained to another correspondent, he was "the Slave of the Lamp called Copperfield," and he was soon driving ahead cheerfully enough.

As he neared the end of his number he received a curious and touching communication. This was from a chiropodist and manicurist, Mrs Seymour Hill, a tiny dwarf, whom he had seen trotting around on short legs in the neighbourhood of Devonshire Terrace, and whose grotesque oddity of physique he had used for Miss Mowcher in his story, never imagining it would meet her eyes. But she had seen it, and been bitterly hurt. "I have suffered long and much," she wrote, "from my personal deformities but never before at the hands of a Man so highly gifted as Charles Dickens . . . Now you have made my nights sleepless and my daily work tearfull."

Dickens was moved to remorse. He was unfeignedly sorry, he replied, to have given her a moment's distress. It was true that he had partly had her in mind, but a great portion of the character was based on

someone quite different. "Pray consider all these things and do not
make yourself unhappy." He was so pained by her distress that to
prevent her passing "another of those sleepless nights" he would alter
the entire design of the character from his original intention "and
oblige the Reader to hold it in a pleasant remembrance." This offer
Mrs Hill accepted, and in the later numbers of the novel Dickens faithfully kept his promise.

At the end of December he confronted "the first page of Copperfield
No. 10, now staring at me," he said, "with what I may literally call a
blank aspect," and began mournfully considering little Em'ly's flight
with Steerforth. By February, he was portraying David's infatuation
for Dora. "I begin to have my doubts of being able to join you," he
wrote Forster, "for Copperfield runs high, and must be done to-morrow.
But I'll do it if possible, and strain every nerve. Some beautiful comic
love, I hope, in the number." Although Dora, he knew, was to die, he
had not quite made up his mind when it should happen. "Undecided
about Dora," he wrote Forster in May, "but MUST decide to-day."

Dora is at once the little beauty who had filled Dickens's youthful
heart with delight and longing and the vision of her that has come to
his soberer judgement. But, unlike Maria Beadnell, she is merely silly,
not cruel and flirtatious, and her little heart holds for David all the
affection it can. When she and David are married, without ceasing to
be the childish creature she was, she acquires more and more of a
colouring derived from Dickens's later experience; David learns that
his wife is no mental companion for him and that his love for her was
the "mistaken impulse of an undisciplined heart." And, in the book,
with deep pathos, but unwaveringly, Dickens shapes the story towards
the death of the brainless pretty creature who is both his own youthful
sweetheart and a wife.

The approach of summer saw Dickens so pressed with work that he
looked forward to a visit to the sea. "I hope to go down to that old
image of Eternity that I love so much, and finish . . . to its hoarse
murmur. May it be as good a book as I hope it will be, for your children's children to read." Dickens made a short trip to Paris in June, and
then in August went to Broadstairs, where he expected to remain "until
the end of October, as I don't want to come back to London until I
shall have finished Copperfield."

At Broadstairs the end of the story was written with rising excitement.
"I have been hard at work these three days, and have still Dora to kill.
But with good luck, I may do it to-morrow . . ." He felt a tender

reluctance to kill David's childish bride, but at last it was done, and he moved on to rounding out the rest of his design: "I have been tremendously at work these two days; eight hours at a stretch yesterday, and six hours and a half today. . . . with the Ham and Steerforth chapter, which has completely knocked me over – utterly defeated me!"

The elements of himself and of his own life that were in *David Copperfield* endowed the story for Dickens with meanings unusually deep and personal. "Like many fond parents," he said, "I have a favourite child. And his name is David Copperfield."

At last, on 21 October, he sent word to Forster: "I am within three pages of the shore; and am strangely divided, as usual in such cases, between sorrow and joy." "Oh, my dear Forster, if I were to say half of what Copperfield makes me feel to-night, how strangely, even to you, I should be turned inside out! I seem to be sending some part of myself into the Shadowy World."

33

Household Words

Long before *David Copperfield* had run its course, Dickens had transformed his "dim design" of a periodical into a reality. A weekly miscellany – his old enthusiasm for the *Bee* or *Spectator* type of publication coming out again – it was to be written by various hands and sold for twopence a copy. Innumerable subjects seethed in his mind: a history of piracy, a history of knight-errantry "and the wild old notion of the Sangreal," a history of remarkable characters, a history of savages, showing the ways "in which civilized men, under circumstances of difficulty, soonest become like savages," essays, reviews, fiction, letters, theatrical criticism, "as amusing as possible, but all distinctly and boldly going to what . . . ought to be the spirit of the people and the time."

Binding these together, Dickens imagined "a certain SHADOW, which may go into any place, by sunlight, moonlight, starlight, firelight, candlelight . . . and be supposed to be cognizant of everything . . ." The Shadow would issue "warnings from time to time, that he is going to fall on such and such a subject; or to expose such and such a piece of humbug . . . Now do you make anything of this? which I let off as if I were a bladder full of it, and you had punctured me."

But Forster robustly pooh-poohed this insubstantial Shadow, and Dickens gave it up. With the New Year of 1850 he began bombarding Forster with a fusillade of titles: *The Robin*; *Mankind*; *Charles Dickens: A Weekly journal designed for the instruction and entertainment of all classes of readers: Conducted by Himself*; *The Household Voice*; *The Household Guest*; *The Household Face*; *The Comrade*; *The Microscope*; *The Highway of Life*; *The Lever*; *The Rolling Years*; *The Holly Tree*; and finally *Household Words*. This last was chosen as the name, with a motto adapted from Shakespeare: "Familiar in their mouths as Household Words."

For subeditor Forster suggested William Henry Wills, who had been Dickens's secretary on the *Daily News* and continued with that paper after Dickens resigned. Though not of a lively imagination – he was,

Dickens said, "decidedly of the Nutmeg-Grater, or Fancy-Bread-Rasper School" – his faithfulness and sharp efficiency made him an excellent man to handle the business part of the publication. Dickens offered and Wills accepted a salary of £8 a week and one eighth ownership so long as he retained his post.

Dickens's own salary for what he preferred to call "Conductor" he set at £500 a year. Remembering, no doubt, his contentions with Bentley as well as the frictions between himself and the proprietors of the *Daily News*, he designated himself as half owner. Bradbury and Evans had a quarter share and Forster the remaining eighth, for which he was to contribute occasional literary articles. These arrangements amounted to giving Dickens a clear three-quarters control.

The rest of the editorial staff was not numerous. Richard Henry Horne, a poet and colourful descriptive journalist, was taken on at five guineas a week. George Hogarth also seems to have had editorial duties, as did John Dickens. Dickens wrote personally to literary friends and acquaintances suggesting that they become contributors. Throughout these first few months of getting *Household Words* started, Dickens was also writing *David Copperfield*.

At 16 Wellington Street, just north of the Gaiety Theatre on the Strand, he took a small building for offices. Its three storeys and garret were of brick neatly edged with stone quoins. A small door opened to the left of a round bay window two storeys high, and a single window above opened on a balustraded balcony. Here Dickens arrived at eight on the mornings he spent in the office, and strode up and down the floor thinking and dictating, combing his hair over and over again while he paced.

He knew exactly the kind of magazine he wanted to create. It should be entertaining but at the same time the instrument of serious social purpose. It should portray the "social wonders, good and evil," in "the stirring world around us." It should tell the thousand and one marvellous tales of knowledge, science, and invention, and render vividly both their colour and their meaning. It should range over past and present, and over every nation, with an eye sharp for what was wrong and a heart warm for what was right. It should fight for tolerance and human welfare, and give no quarter to chicanery and oppression.

Many of these aims were identical with those of radical reform, but in one way *Household Words* was to be very different. Animated by "No mere utilitarian spirit, no iron binding of the mind to grim realities," it should "cherish that light of Fancy which is inherent in the human breast" and insist that no class was to be "excluded from the sympathies and graces of imagination." Woe betide that day, said Dickens's Preliminary Word in the first number, when the workers were taught that their lot was to be only a moody, brutal slavery at the "whirling wheel of toil"! "The adventurer in the old fairy story, climbing the steep mountain," the announcement concluded, "was surrounded by a roar of voices, crying to him, from the stones in the way, to turn back. All the voices *we* hear, cry Go on! . . . We echo back the cry, and go on cheerily!"

Dickens did go on. He arranged with his brother-in-law Henry Austin, now Secretary of the Sanitary Commission, to provide the facts for a series of articles on sanitary reform – water supply, lack of light and air in the slums, refuse disposal – on which he intended to hammer away in the magazine. To other possible contributors he wrote that he most needed short stories imbued by "such a general purpose" of calling attention to things wrong in the world.

One of these writers was Elizabeth Cleghorn Gaskell, whose *Mary Barton* had given a sympathetic picture of the sufferings of Manchester factory workers. There was "no living English writer," Dickens told her, whose aid he more desired. Would she write "a short tale, or any number of tales," for his pages? He was gratified to receive from her a gloomy but impressive story entitled *Lizzie Leigh*, centring around a seduced servant girl and her illegitimate child. He suggested a few changes in narrative detail, which Mrs Gaskell accepted, and the tale appeared as a serial in the first three numbers.

Not all those friends Dickens asked became contributors. For he was adhering to the custom, still widespread among magazines, of signing no authors' names to any of the contents, and there were writers who rebelled against this procedure. "But the periodical is anonymous throughout," protested Dickens to Douglas Jerrold. "Yes," replied Jerrold, reading aloud the words that appeared at the top of every page, " 'Conducted by Charles Dickens.' I see it is – *mon*onymous throughout."

And, indeed, some of the younger writers felt that there was an unintentional injustice in this system: everything good in the magazine was credited by readers to Dickens, so that years of successful work might still leave a man unrecognized by the public. But Dickens himself, "the kindliest, the justest, and the most generous of mankind," said one of them, had "no remotest notion that he was putting a bushel over the lights of his staff . . ."

The first number of *Household Words* was dated 30 March 1850. It contained twenty-four double-column pages, roughly something over 20,000 words. After the Preliminary Word and *Lizzie Leigh* came an article, "Valentine's Day at the Post-Office," a brief dramatic parable in verse entitled "Abraham and the Fire-Worshipper" emphasizing religious tolerance, another article, "The Amusements of the People" on the theatres popular among the working class, a biographical "Episode in the Life of Mademoiselle Clairon," a famous eighteenth-century French actress, a short poem, and an article supporting Mrs Caroline Chisholm's society for helping poor people emigrate to Australia, illustrated by a group of emigrants' letters.

Of these, only "The Amusements of the People" was entirely by Dickens. They all, however, illustrate both his point of view and his insistence on colour and imagination. No matter how brilliant, wise, or true something might be, unless it were also readable it might as well be left unsaid. Everything must sparkle with vitality.

"Valentine's Day at the Post-Office," for example, is an informational article dealing with the bulk of mail passing through London's central office. But all the statistical data are presented in a rapid narrative full of descriptive vigour. Glance at the account of the mailing of newspapers. These had to be posted by six o'clock: we begin at quarter to the hour:

> It was then just drizzling newspapers. . . . By degrees it began to rain hard; by fast degrees the storm came on harder and harder, until it blew, rained, hailed, snowed, newspapers. A fountain of newspapers played in at the window. Water-spouts of newspapers broke from enormous sacks, and engulphed the men inside. . . .
>
> Suddenly it struck six. Shut Sesame! Perfectly still weather. Nobody there. Not a trace of the late storm – Not a soul, too late!

Dickens's own article, "The Amusements of the People," describes going with one "Joe Whelks, of the New Cut, Lambeth," to the Victoria Theatre, where prices ranged from one shilling down to three-pence. The gallery was jammed to the roof; the pit crowded with young mechanics and their wives, so many of them accompanied by "the baby" that one looked down on a sea of quiet baby faces fast asleep. In the play, a fantastic melodrama called *May Morning, or The Mystery of 1715 and the Murder!*, the actors ranted through a plot of the wildest improbability. "I ster-ruck him down, and fel-ed in er-orror!" exclaims a repentant assassin, and continues, "I have liveder as a beggar – a roader-sider vaigerant, but no ker-rime since then has stained these hands!"

Dickens has a good deal of fun with these absurdities, but his point is that "Joe Whelks" *must* have entertainment, and that, although such plays might easily be improved, even they are better than if he were to have no training for his imagination and his sympathies at all. Joe Whelks "is not much of a reader, has no great store of books, no very commodious room to read in, no very decided inclination to read, and no power at all of presenting vividly to his mind's eye what he reads about." But in the theatre he follows a story with rapt attention, and its portrayals of good and evil strike home to him. That is why, Dickens insists, the popular theatre is of tremendous importance.

From the start *Household Words* hit the mark it was aimed at; 100,000 copies of the first number are reported to have been sold. Nevertheless, elated though he was, Dickens did not feel quite satisfied as he looked over the plan of the second number. It needed some touch of deeper and gentler emotion. Impelled by this feeling, he wrote "A Child's Dream of a Star," with its memories of Chatham and himself and Fanny when they were small. "The amazing undersigned feels a little uncomfortable at the want of Household tenderness . . . So he puts away Copperfield at which he has been working like a Steam Engine – writes (he thinks) exactly the kind of thing to supply the deficiency – and sends it off, by this post, to Forster! What an amazing man!"

The second and third numbers maintained the level of the first. Horne's "True Story of a Coal-Fire" described the formation of coal from prehistoric forests, its extraction from the mines, and the hideous working conditions of the men, women, and children who worked them. In "The Troubled Water Question" Wills used the facts provided by Henry Austin to attack the excessive charges and the dirty water of the monopolies and the consequent lack of a decent water supply for the poor. "Short Cuts Across the Globe" advocated building canals across Panama and the Isthmus of Suez.

The third number also announced the inauguration of a monthly supplement, *The Household Narrative of Current Events*. Although handled by John Dickens, this publication permitted him no Micawberian flights of eloquence. It presented without editorial comment a skilfully condensed summary of all important news, under the main headings of Parliament and Politics, Law and Crime, Accident and Disaster, Social, Sanitary, and Municipal Progress, Obituaries, Colonies and

Dependencies, Foreign Events, Commercial Record, Stocks and Shares, and Emigration Figures.

Dickens maintained a dictatorial control over every detail in both publications. His hand was everywhere, supplying titles, criticizing stories, eliminating fuzzy or pretentious verbiage, injecting colour, tightening structure, sharpening clarity, cutting out dull patches. "I wonder," he wrote Wills, "you think 'A Night with the Detective Police' would do for a title! After all those nights with Burns and the Industrious Fleas, and Heaven knows what else!! I don't think there could be a worse one within the range of the human understanding." Mrs Gaskell's "The Heart of John Middleton" was very good, but the girl crippled by a stone hitting her in the back would remind readers of the many other victims of accident in her stories, "the girl who fell down the Well, and the child who tumbled down stairs. I wish to Heaven her people would keep a little firmer on their legs!" Harriet Martineau's "The Home of Woodruffe the Gardener" was long-winded. "I have cut Woodruffe as scientifically as I can, and I don't think Miss Martineau would exactly know where." Sometimes, having all these tasks to perform in addition to his own writing almost overwhelmed him. "I really can't *promise* to be comic," he replied to a request from Wills for a humourous piece or two. "As to *two* comic articles, or two any sort of articles out of me, that's the intensest extreme of nogoism."

In May we find Dickens writing to Michael Faraday, the famous scientist, suggesting that articles based on his "lectures on the breakfast-table" and those "addressed last year, to children" would be exceedingly beneficial to the public. "May I ask you whether . . . you would favour me with the loan of your notes of those lectures for perusal." Faraday replied graciously, putting the notes at Dickens's disposal. *Household Words* for 3 August carried an article called "The Chemistry of a Candle," in which a young boy who has attended one of the lectures outlines to his family all that he has learned on the subject. Throughout the whole ten-year course of the publication there is a constant stream of articles on science and invention. "The Planet-Watchers of Greenwich," "A Shilling's Worth of Science," "The Fire-Annihilator" (a new chemical fire-extinguisher), "Ballooning," "India Rubber," "The Stereoscope," "The Power Loom," "Decimal Measures," "Some Account of Chloroform," "Electric Light," and many others.

With the able lieutenancy of Wills, *Household Words* was soon running so efficiently that Dickens felt free in June to run over to Paris for ten days' vacation. In spite of a frightful hot spell, he went to the theatre with Régnier, dined with Sir Joseph Olliffe, physician to the British Embassy, called on Lord Normanby at the Embassy, and visited broken-down old John Poole (to whom Dickens was still regularly doling out money from the benefit performances) in his fifth-floor hovel in the Rue Neuve Luxembourg. Probably thinking of the repressions by which Louis Napoleon was transforming himself into a dictator, Dickens noted: "They made a mighty hullabaloo at the Theatre last night, when Brutus (the play was Lucretia) declaimed about Liberty."

On his return to England, Dickens was shocked by the fatal accident in which Sir Robert Peel was thrown by his horse. Since Peel's display of courage and statesmanship in the abolition of the Corn Laws in 1846, Dickens's respect for him had been steadily rising. "I am in a very despondent state of mind," he wrote Mrs Watson, "over Peel's death. He was a man of merit who could ill be spared from the Great Dust Heap down at Westminster. When I think of the joy of the D'Israelis, Richmonds, and other impostors and Humbugs, I think of flying to Australia and taking to the Bush."

Throughout the effort and excitement of finishing *David Copperfield*, he continued to deal with constant demands from *Household Words*. An article attacking the dirt and cruelty of the Smithfield cattle market had aroused scandalized comment; Dickens planned a return to the attack. He corrected proofs, wrote some half-dozen further pieces used during the next few months, read contributions. "I think the Bank Note *very good indeed*. D⁰. the Hippopotamus. D⁰. Swinging the Ship."

Besides keeping a sharp watch on the contributors, Dickens sometimes had to deal with friction in the office. Wills felt that Horne was not pulling his weight. He estimated that every article Horne wrote cost the publication some £8 out of a weekly budget for contributions averaging £16. Dickens replied that he had always found Horne willing to work and had no intention of terminating his employment. He would, however, pass on Wills's criticisms. Horne professed himself ready to help in any desired way, and remained in his post. In the following year, when Wills returned to the charge, Horne offered to resign. In 1852 he went to Australia, but he continued as a contributor at intervals.

From the middle of August to the end of October Dickens's children were with Georgina at Fort House, Broadstairs, a brick dwelling on the cliff above the bay. Kate, however, who was again in what Dickens called "an anti-Malthusian state," remained in Devonshire Terrace until some weeks after the child was born, and Dickens himself constantly shuttled back and forth between the two places. Signing himself "Wilkins Micawber," he wrote Forster on 15 August, "Mrs Micawber is still, I regret to say, in statu quo." The next day, however, a baby girl was born, whom they named Dora Annie.

From the sea he wrote Kate news of the children and some of the guests at Fort House, although he saw her each time he went up to London. "The Spectre in great glory." (This was three-year-old Sydney, whom Dickens had nicknamed the Ocean Spectre, because of a strange, faraway look in his eyes, as if he saw some phantom out at sea.) "Forster was in tip top state of amiability, but I think I never heard him *half so loud* (!) He really, after the heat of the walk, so disordered me that by no process I could possibly try, could I get to sleep afterwards."

On 6 September Dickens brought Kate down to Broadstairs. From there he continued to supervise *Household Words* with an eagle eye. He approved an article on the "Steam Plough," by Horne, emphasizing the increased productivity that such machines would achieve in agriculture. An entire series, "The Doom of English Wills," written by Dickens in collaboration with Wills, castigated the dirty, dilapidated, and disorderly way in which ecclesiastical records were kept, mouldering away in damp and crowded depositories, almost deliberately inaccessible to the public, while their guardians drew salaries as high as £7,000 for letting them decay.

Frederick Dickens was still trying to extort financial aid from his brother. He had at last married Anna Weller and was tangled deep in debt. Perhaps, if Dickens wouldn't lend him money, he would lend his name. "It gives me extraordinary pain to refuse you anything," Dickens replied, "but I cannot make up my mind to be security for the performance of so extensive a contract." Subsequently, however, he may have weakened: "My dear Fred," we find him writing, "What is the nature of the Security that I should be required to give . . . ?"

With the end of October and the completion of *David Copperfield*, the pressure of Dickens's labours slackened. But he had forestalled any danger of gloomy letdown by arranging another whirl of amateur theatricals, first with Bulwer Lytton at his estate of Knebworth, and second with the Watsons at Rockingham Castle. And of course the endless round of editorial work kept on. "This proof of Morley's . . . will require to be very carefully looked to. I had better go over it myself." This was "Mr Bendigo Buster on Our National Defences

Against Education," an ironical parody of the arguments of those who opposed state support of education out of fear that it would lead to "centralization."

From this time on until the close of his life Dickens's activities as an editor were unceasing. He read, rejected, accepted, rewrote. Though none of the articles were signed, the signature of his style was so obvious that readers often imagined the entire magazine to be written by him. No matter where he was – in Broadstairs, Paris, Boulogne, Italy, America – packets of manuscripts and proofs constantly travelled back and forth between him and the offices at Wellington Street, accompanied by reams of advice. "Keep Household Words imaginative," he reiterated again and again. "Brighten it, brighten it, brighten it!"

He tossed off new ideas for pieces, discovered new writers. The young George Meredith had poems in *Household Words*. Wilkie Collins rode to fame there. A group known as "Dickens's young men" made their start in literature or journalism through his encouragement: George Augustus Sala, Edmund Yates, James Payn, Percy Fitzgerald. Other contributors included Wilkie Collins's gifted brother Charles Allston Collins, Georgiana Craik (Mrs Mulock), William and Mary Howitt, Charles Knight, Elizabeth Lynn, Sheridan Le Fanu, Charles Mackay, Coventry Patmore, and Adelaide Anne Procter. Dickens was among the first to recognize the genius of George Eliot, although he tried in vain to persuade her to write a serial for him. Among the authors of already established reputations who appeared in his pages were Charles Lever, Bulwer Lytton, Charles Reade, and Thomas Adolphus Trollope.

The range of subject matter in the pages of *Household Words* is fascinating and extraordinary. The informational articles alone exhibit the widest variety. Here is an almost random selection: a description of San Francisco during the Gold Rush, the savings to litigants effected by the Small Claims Courts, the work of John Hullah (Dickens's old friend) in providing free classes in choral singing to the poor, the banking rooms, treasure vaults, and banknote engraving at the Bank of England, the hunting of seals and whales, the use of ice for preserving food and making cool drinks and desserts, the industrial exploitations of the great dust heaps formed from the refuse of London, the possibility of crossing the English Channel either by a tunnel or by an enormous bridge arching between a series of artificial islands!

Brief biographical subjects, taken almost equally at random, include Sydney Smith, Angelica Kauffmann the artist, Peter the Great, Fanny Burney, the piano manufacturer Pierre Érard, the two poisoners Mme

Ursinus and the Marquise de Brinvilliers, Héloise and Abelard, William Cobbett, Handel, Napoleon, Robert Burns, Dr Johnson, Philip Sidney and Fulke|Greville, Lesage, and|the philosopher|Pierre Ramus. There were literary articles on Pepys's *Diary*, Margaret Fuller, *Beowulf*, Hazlitt's works, the poems of Caedmon, Leigh Hunt's stories in verse, *Hamlet,* *The|Golden|Ass,*|Robert Herrick, Ebenezer Elliott,| the "Corn-law Rhymer," Edmund Waller, Carlyle's *Frederick the Great*, the plays of Lope de Vega, the Celtic bard Oisin, and a warmly appreciative review of Turgenev's beautiful *Sportsman's Sketches* in its first English translation. Throughout, there is a fusion of freshness and accuracy, neither an archaeological dustiness nor a narrow concentration on the merely contemporary.

The most characteristic feature of *Household Words*, however, is its treatment of current problems. Hardly a week goes by in which it is not attacking some abuse. It consistently opposes racial, national, religious, and class prejudices. It crusades against illiteracy and in favour of Government aid for public education and free elementary and industrial schools. It crusades for proper sewage disposal, cheap and unlimited water supply, and the regulation of industries. It demands the replacement of slums by decent housing, pleads for the establishment of playgrounds for children, and advocates systematic municipal planning. It supports thoughtful prison reform but protests against coddling criminals. Devote half the sums spent on jails, it argues, to improving the surroundings and training the capacities of the innocent, and you won't have to exert so much effort in a largely unsuccessful attempt to rehabilitate the guilty. It insists that industrialists must not be allowed to mutilate and kill their labourers in order to save the cost of preventing accidents. It scandalously affirms that working men have the right to organize into unions, and calls upon the working class to use its power to turn "the Indifferents and Incapables" out of Downing Street and Westminster.

Household Words was especially emphatic on the importance of education. "The Schoolmaster at Home and Abroad" points out that in "the whole of northern Europe" one child "to every $2\frac{1}{2}$ of the population" received "the rudiments of knowledge, while in England there is only one such pupil to every *fourteen* inhabitants." "The Devil's Acre" lauds the work of the Ragged Schools and their more advanced industrial counterparts in the slum districts of London, especially in reforming young criminals and teaching them a trade. "Infant Gardens" praises the work of Froebel and the first English kindergartens.

"New Life and Old Learning" satirically notes that the only concession to the changing times Oxford has made in its curriculum is to permit the study of modern history – but not beyond the year 1790. "Minerva by Gaslight" hails the recent inauguration of evening session classes by the University of London.

Articles on sanitary reform and slum clearance are no less numerous. Statistical analyses demonstrate that the most crowded slums have the highest mortality rates. "Health by Act of Parliament" quotes figures to prove that the monetary loss in the metropolis caused during the year 1848 by typhus alone was £440,000. "This cold-blooded way of putting the really appalling state of the case," it adds, "is, alas! the only successful mode of appealing to . . . John Bull." Typhus is only the most spectacular of many preventable diseases caused by polluted sewers, bad or insufficient water, and crowded, dirty houses.

Until these "epoch-making articles appeared in *Household Words,*" as W. W. Crotch points out in his *Charles Dickens: Social Reformer,* "housing reform had been scarcely heard of." Dickens missed no chance to reinforce his criticisms by constant blasts of all kinds. The state of public health in London, he said in a speech before the Metropolitan Sanitary Association in 1850, was "the tragedy of *Hamlet* with nothing in it but the gravedigger." Such a slum as Jacob's Island could be made decent at a weekly cost of less than two glasses of gin for each inhabitant.

A few nights later Sir Peter Laurie, the London alderman Dickens had satirized in *The Chimes* as Alderman Cute, told a public meeting that Jacob's Island "ONLY existed" in the pages of *Oliver Twist.* Dickens fell upon him savagely. By Sir Peter's logic, he wrote, "When Fielding described Newgate," it "ceased to exist"; "when Smollett took Roderick Random to Bath, that city instantly sank into the earth"; and "an ancient place called Windsor was entirely destroyed in the reign of Queen Elizabeth by two Merry Wives of that town, acting under the direction of a person of the name of Shakespeare." But on reflection was it not equally clear, since Sir Peter Laurie had once been described in a book too, "that there CAN be no such man!"

It would be hard to exaggerate the power of Dickens's aid to the pioneers in sanitation and housing reform. "Lord Shaftesbury, and the Association for Improving the Dwellings of the Poor," Crotch summarizes, "were, like the first Housing Acts, the outward and visible signs of his energies," and the housing developments fostered by these and by other public-spirited foundations erected "not only homes for the people, but monuments to their champion . . ."

Fierce even beyond these attacks on slums and the neglect of public health, however, was the campaign *Household Words* carried on against factory accidents. Since 1844 there had been a law that dangerous machines must be fenced in, but it had been very largely evaded or ignored. "Ground in the Mill" detailed dozens of hideous deaths and mutilations: boys caught in a piece of belting and smashed 120 times a minute against the ceiling, men wedged in a shaft getting battered to pulp, their lungs broken, their heads scalped, their skulls smashed. There were 2,000 of these victims killed or mutilated by machinery in a half-year, "Fencing with Humanity" reported, and told of the formation of a Manufacturers' Association to defy the law and pay the fines of its members if they were convicted. The accidents amounted to fewer than 6 to 10 per cent, argued the factory owners, and the deaths to only 42 a year! "Death's Ciphering-Book" suggested that if percentages had anything to do with the moral issues, one might as well forgo punishing burglary and murder, of which the percentages were far smaller in a population of 21 million.

The viewpoint dominating all these articles, and hundreds of others on scores of additional subjects, represented an uncompromising humanitarian radicalism. Week after week Dickens or his henchmen hammered away, wielding every conceivable weapon: reasoned argument, cajolery, facts and figures, humour, insinuation, irony, parable and allegory, sarcasm, repetition, angry diatribe. In total the contents of *Household Words* are a striking testimony to the enlightenment of Dickens's policy on most of the problems of nineteenth-century society and to the breadth of his interests. But more than that, they are a proof of his editorial skill as well. For unlike the liberal–radical magazines of our own day, *Household Words* was not limited to a small specialized group of intellectuals but had a huge and steadily growing audience ranging in both directions from the middle and upper middle classes.

It was probably this extraordinary achievement that led Lord Northcliffe to declare Dickens the greatest magazine editor either of his own or any other age. Although unmatched, however, the achievement is not mysterious: its secret lies in the pattern of broad appeal to which almost every number of *Household Words* conforms – a pattern that explains how Dickens could persuade his readers to swallow so much radicalism along with their entertainment. For although the magazine fought on every issue its conductor had at heart, it did not limit itself to crusading. Among the six to nine items filling its twenty-four pages, there were never more than two or three devoted to reform causes. The tone might be indignant, but never embittered.

Thus, in the very issue in which one article points out that the workhouse diet is worse than that of the criminal jail, another article gives a dream-vision of all the cruelties that darkened the "good old times." All the rest of the contents was entertainment, colourful information, humour, or sentiment. Great pains were taken to be vivid, great pains were taken to be clear. But at the same time *Household Words* was never patronizing. "Don't think," Dickens warned, "that it is necessary to write *down* to any part of our audience."

With *Household Words*, at last, Dickens had found the instrument towards which he had been groping in the opening, unsuccessful numbers of *Master Humphrey's Clock*. And in the intervening time, he had learned how to work with and control a group of collaborators as he had not been able to do on the *Daily News*. Both in its business and its editorial structure *Household Words* ideally met Dickens's long-felt need for a periodical in which he could say to his readers, without interference from anyone else, everything about all the subjects in the world that he was bursting to say.

34

Splendid Barnstorming

The play, Dickens wrote Bulwer Lytton in July of 1850, "stirs my blood like a trumpet." Lytton had invited the dramatic amateurs to play *Every Man in His Humour* at Knebworth before an audience of his county neighbours. But the combined labours of *Household Words* and *David Copperfield* compelled Dickens to defer the glorious idea until autumn. Before the summer was over, their plans were being made.

Dickens and Bulwer Lytton had been friendly though not intimate for well over a decade. Edward Bulwer – he had not then taken the additional surname of Lytton – was in Parliament when Dickens was in the Gallery. Handsomely aquiline, auburn-curled, beringed and ornate of dress, he had been, together with D'Orsay and Disraeli, one of the glittering dandies emulated by the youthful Boz. Nine years Dickens's senior, and, until the triumph of *Pickwick*, the most popular novelist of the day, he might easily have been resentful, but he greeted his rival only with the heartiest praise. And Dickens knew that he was generous not only in words. The number of literary men he had helped more than justified Macready's tribute to him as the most warm-hearted and high-minded of men.

Nevertheless, even in mid-career, Bulwer continued to be pursued by literary animosity. His birth, his hauteur, his dress, the high circles in which he moved, all aroused bitter sneers. The violent termination of his brief marriage and the half-insane slanders of his estranged wife Rosina were seized upon with snarling joy. And when, on his mother's death, he added her maiden name of Lytton to his own surname, malice could not contain its chortles at the grandiosity of calling oneself Sir Edward George Earle Lytton Bulwer Lytton. But he remained proudly silent, went on writing copiously and successfully, and collected stained glass and medieval armour. Now, at the age of forty-seven, moving through the long library of Knebworth, with his premature slight stoop, grizzled reddish hair, and beaked nose above flaming whiskers, he looked strangely like a refined and elegant Fagin.

Out of Bulwer Lytton's proposal of a "Dramatic Festival" at Knebworth were to grow further plans that would bring him and Dickens into closer association. At the moment, however, all Dickens thought of was the excitement of acting again. The Knebworth performances were scheduled for 18, 19, and 20 November, and those at Rockingham after Twelfth Night in the new year. Rehearsals were held once more in Miss Kelly's theatre in Soho. Almost at the outset, Kate, who had the part of Tib (a character who made four brief appearances and spoke a total of thirty lines), had fallen through a trap door on the stage. Her ankle was so severely sprained that Mrs Lemon took her place.

With the course of years, in fact, the clumsiness Dickens had noted in America seemed to be growing more marked. Richard Horne, who had often dined with the Dickenses at Devonshire Terrace, observed that bracelets would even slide off her arms with a splash into her soup, while Dickens threw himself back in his chair laughing uproariously. Kate's lack of physical control strongly suggests nervous disorder and Dickens's laughter the hilarity with which we hide a secret irritation from ourselves. But in behaviour Dickens was all solicitude, and he arranged that she be taken to Knebworth in a brougham so that she could at least make one of the audience.

The last rehearsal in town took place on 14 November. "Ah, sir," said the master carpenter at Miss Kelly's, to whom Dickens explained some ideas he had about adapting *Used Up* to a small stage, "it's a universal observation in the profession, sir, that it was a great loss to the public when you took to writing books!" – "which," remarked Dickens, "I thought complimentary to Copperfield." The rehearsal was no sooner over than Dickens took the train to Stevenage, the Knebworth railway connection. All week-end he spent seeing to the final details of installing the theatre, testing the oil lamps which they had to use in the absence of gas, and drilling his cast through the very dress rehearsal on Saturday night.

The theatre itself was a portable unit, some twenty feet high, erected at one end of the double-storeyed great hall, leaving the rest of its stone-floored expanse, back to the entrance under the minstrel gallery, for the seats of the guests. Through one of the enormous windows, hoisted over the window seat, had also been brought a huge hybrid instrument called a "choremusicon," clad in "an immense crimson silk waistcoat" and guaranteed to be "better than three musicians."

For three nights the carriages of Bulwer Lytton's county friends

("Dukes, Duchesses, and the like," Dickens said mischievously) rolled
into the great rectangular court with its gargoyle-surmounted walls,
and the guests trooped among his suits of armour, under his stained-
glass windows and the medieval tapestries hung on the dark-panelled
walls, and responded enthusiastically to the dramatic entertainment.

Only one semi-comic rift marred the amenity of the occasion. In
order to allow the curtain to go up at seven-thirty, dinner was at six,
and on the first night after the performance, the host provided only
cake, biscuits, and wine for refreshments. For a group of actors ravenous
from their exertions this was insufficient, and most of the cast went to
bed gnawed by hunger. Next morning they held a council. Forster,
blunt as usual, said they should ask for more to eat. Mark Lemon proposed getting supplies in the village and sneaking up to a surreptitious
supper in Jerrold's room at the top of the tower. This schoolboyish
suggestion carried the day, and that evening there was "a stifled
stampede" of actors smuggling glasses and mugs upstairs under their
costumes. Unhappily, Bulwer Lytton was told and felt solemnly
annoyed until Dickens joked him out of it. On the next night, however,
he served a sumptuous supper.

Contact with Dickens and these three performances crystallized in
Bulwer Lytton's mind a set of ideas that had long been amorphous
there. He had pitied and sent anonymous help to more than one talented
struggling writer. And Dickens and his amateurs had collected large
sums for the benefit of such literary veterans as Leigh Hunt, Sheridan
Knowles, and John Poole. Although Government pensions did exist for
the aid of writers and artists, they were inadequate, often political or
capricious, and even, on occasion, rather humiliating to their bene-
ficiaries. There were able writers who had met with misfortunes,
promising young writers who had not yet made their way, scholarly
writers whose work could not expect a popular audience. What was
needed was something more dignified than the donations of private
charity or of Government pensions and more flexible than a college
lectureship, with its prescribed duties and academic qualifications.

Could they not build, Lytton suggested, an endowment which might
combine these purposes with the bestowing of an honourable distinction? He himself would write a comedy all the earnings of which he
would present to the endowment; Dickens's company would act this
play throughout England for its benefit. With the fame of such a
brilliant beginning, they might then make public appeal for additional
contributions to the fund.

So the Guild of Literature and Art was born. As it matured in their minds it grew more ambitious. Lytton would present the Guild with the use of land on his estate, where a group of neat cottages would be built, and in them would dwell rent-free a little fellowship of artists and men of letters chosen in accordance with the Guild's purposes. Over them would preside a Warden, with a house and £200 a year. Resident Members would receive £170 a year and non-resident Members £200 a year. These were to be men of established names. Finally, there would be a number of Associates, young men of promise, with one-year grants of £100. "I do devoutly believe," exclaimed Dickens, "that this plan carried, will entirely change the status of the literary man in England, and make a revolution in his position, which no Government, no power on earth but his own, could ever effect."

His enthusiasm for the project was fired by efforts in which he was even then engaged to obtain further help for John Poole. The proceeds from his benefit had at last been exhausted, but Poole was so completely shattered in intellect that writing "the most ordinary sentence in a letter" had become "a work of infinite labour to him." "In the sunny time of the day, he puts a melancholy little hat on one side of his head, and, with a little stick under his arm, goes hitching himself about the Boulevards; but for any power he has of earning a livelihood he might as well be dead." Through Lord John Russell, Dickens obtained for him a small sum from the Queen's Bounty, but what he really needed, Dickens explained to Russell, was a pension. On Christmas Eve, he received a reply announcing that Poole had been granted £100 a year, dating "from the end of June last."

Happy in what he had accomplished for Poole, Dickens turned his attention now to the approaching theatricals at Rockingham Castle. The portable theatre used at Knebworth was too lofty for its ancient low-ceilinged rooms. He consequently suggested to Mrs Watson that she rent scenery from Nathan, the "costume-maker" who dressed his company. A special set was assembled under his direction, and adapted to the purpose. After looking this over at Nathan's and finding it new-painted and elegant, Dickens decided he had better make a one-day trip to Northamptonshire to superintend its installation.

Following frenzies of preparation and rehearsal their programme came off on the 15th: *A Day After the Wedding*, *Used Up*, and *Animal Magnetism*. His burlesque love affair with Mary Boyle had reached the point where he was writing her, as he had Mrs Colden years before, incoherent notes of misery and devotion. One of these, dated from

"Loft over Stable," laments that "the call of honour stands between me and my rest – baulks my inclination – beckons me from happiness . . . (do you understand, my angel?)" At Rockingham began the custom, whenever they were together, of Dickens's bestowing a chaste goodnight kiss on Mary's brow.

Kate assumed in the same play the small part of Lady Maria Clutter-buck – by now, of course, her ankle was entirely healed – but we do not hear this time that she "covered herself with glory." No other woman compared with Mary Boyle, enchanting in lemon muslin as Lisette and demure in pink as Mary. Following the three plays, country dances lasted until far into the morning. On his return to London, Dickens relapsed into depression. "I am still feeble, and liable to sudden outbursts of causeless rage and demoniacal gloom, but I shall be better presently."

Unlike his father, young Charley ended the holidays in great spirits. A servant took him to the train for Eton. "Master Charles," he reported, "went off very gay, sir. He found some young gen'lmen as was his friends in the train, sir." "I am glad of that," said Dickens. "How many were there? Two or three?" "Oh dear, sir, there was a matter of forty, sir! All with their heads out o' the coach windows, sir, a-hallowing 'Dickens!' all over the station!"

Bulwer Lytton had sent Dickens the first three acts of his comedy – a costume piece set in the reign of George II. It was "*most admirable,*" Dickens told him, "*and certain to go nobly.*" He himself would take the role of Lord Wilmot. "I think I could touch the gallant, generous, careless pretence, with the real man at the bottom of it, so as to take the audience with him from the first scene."

Dickens in fact almost completely surrendered himself to this project for close to a year. He did not even begin thinking about a new novel until August, when the London engagements of the play were concluded. He did not begin writing it until the end of November. There was always, of course, the unceasing round of supervising *Household Words*, week by week, on which he never relaxed. But that, for his superhuman energy, was almost routine. The writing of his own contributions he wedged into any odd hour or two. His *Child's History of England*, beginning to appear irregularly in the magazine from 25 January on, was a compilation derived from Keightley's *History*, which he dictated to Georgina in spare moments. But all his most earnest efforts, for almost a full year, and much time for another nine months beyond that, were dominated by working for the Guild of Literature and Art.

Bulwer's play, it was agreed, they would try to get off to a great start, by inviting the Queen and Prince Albert to the first performance. This should be, Dickens suggested, about three weeks before the opening on 1 May of the Great Exhibition in Hyde Park, so that it might be "the town talk before the country people and foreigners come." Macready was to read the completed play to the assembled company at Forster's on 19 February.

In the course of the month Dickens made his escape to Paris, where it was frosty but fine, for a five-day holiday. Returning to London, he saw Macready's last stage appearance, in *Macbeth* at Drury Lane, and arranged a farewell dinner at the London Tavern. Macready spoke haltingly, too deeply moved to notice when he said his heart was fuller than his glass that he held an empty glass. Dickens spoke well, but what he felt most profoundly he wrote in a letter: "I have told you sometimes, my much-loved friend, how, when I was a mere boy, I was one of your faithful and devoted adherents in the pit . . . No light portion of my life arose before me when the quiet vision to which I am beholden, in I don't know how great a degree, or for how much – who does? – faded so nobly from my bodily eyes last night."

After further deliberations with Bulwer Lytton about their play, Dickens determined on a bold stroke. He asked the Duke of Devonshire for permission to give its first performance, before Her Majesty and the Court, in Devonshire House, His Grace's palatial residence on Piccadilly. Within two hours the Duke replied: "My services, my house, and my subscription will be at your orders. And I beg you to let me see you before long, not merely to converse upon this subject, but because I have long had the greatest wish to improve our acquaintance, which has, as yet, been only one of crowded rooms."

Dickens was soon in those turmoils of preparation that he loved. Bulwer's comedy, now entitled *Not So Bad As We Seem*, had been read before its prospective cast. Dickens suggested to Augustus Egg that a young writer named Wilkie Collins might take a small part as valet to Lord Wilmot. "He would have an opportunity of dressing your humble servant – frothing some chocolate with an absolute milling-machine that must be revived for the purpose – . . . and dispatching other similar 'business' dear to actors." Shortly after Collins's acceptance, rehearsals were under way at Covent Garden, beginning on 18 March, and continuing every Monday and Tuesday thereafter.

Frank Stone, Dickens complained, was "a Millstone – I shall have to go over that part with him (out of rehearsal) at least fifty times – around my neck." Forster was "going a little wrong" and Lemon was making his part "too farcical." But gradually everyone did better. Told that he was "too loud and violent," Forster "subdued himself with the most admirable pains, and improved the part a thousand per cent." Stone surprised Dickens by playing "inexpressibly better than I should have supposed possible in him." "They are all most heartily anxious and earnest, and, upon the least hitch, will do the same thing twenty times over."

In addition to drilling his company five hours a night two nights a week, Dickens was in a "maze of bewilderment . . . with carpenters, painters, tailors, machinists, and others." David Roberts, Stanfield, and other well-known painters had been asked to donate scenery: the Mall, a distressed poet's garret, a sinister alley called Deadman's Lane, an open space near the Thames. These, and the furniture, were "rapidly advancing towards completion, and will be beautiful. The dresses are a perfect blaze of colour, and there is not a pocket-flap or a scrap of lace that has not been made according to Egg's drawings to the quarter of an inch."

The Queen had replied to Dickens's invitation by appointing the evening of 30 April for the performance, but events in his own family compelled Dickens to postpone it. Early in February the baby daughter, Dora Annie, had been so gravely ill with congestion of the brain that they had hastily had her baptized at once. Then, a month later, Kate became seriously unwell, with "a tendency of blood to the head," "giddiness and dimness of sight," and "an alarming confusion and nervousness."

Southwood Smith advised placing her under medical care at Great Malvern. As Dickens reflected on it now, it seemed to him that he could detect signs of this trouble in Kate as far as three or four years back. He wrote Dr James Wilson, to whom it was recommended that he entrust her, that her case was "a nervous one," and that when they met in person he would "state what Dr Southwood Smith has particularly requested me to mention to you as rendering great caution necessary." Instead of living in Dr Wilson's house, for reasons "founded on my knowledge of her" she would stay in some cheerful cottage in the neighbourhood; she could not possibly form a favourable impression of Malvern if she were in any house but her own. This belief Dickens based on "what I have lately observed when we have been staying in the country houses even of intimate friends." The words clearly refer to their recent visits to Knebworth and Rockingham, and unmistakably hint as much of psychological disturbance as they do of physical illness.

Oscillating between London and Malvern, Dickens received word that his father was mortally ill. His old urinary complaint, mentioned a quarter of a century ago in applying for retirement from the Navy Pay Office, he had ignored and neglected ever since. His family knew nothing of his condition until inflammation of the bladder brought on mortification and delirium. A surgeon "was called in, who instantly performed (without chloroform) the most terrible operation known in surgery, as the only chance of saving him. . . . I saw him directly afterwards – his room, a slaughter house of blood."

In spite of being "wonderfully cheerful and stronghearted," John Dickens grew weaker and weaker. On 31 March, "My poor father died this morning," Dickens wrote Forster, "at five and twenty minutes to six." Dickens had arrived shortly after eleven that night, but by then his father did not know him or anyone. "I remained there until he died – O so quietly." As he looked on his father's dead face, what were the grandiloquence, the improvident borrowings, the irresponsibility, the disappearances to escape the bailiff? He could remember only the hard work, the irrepressible gusto, the old companionship of walks to Gad's Hill, the loving pride in a small boy's singing, the tenderness that throughout many a night had nursed a sick child.

Barely a fortnight later fell another blow. On 14 April Dickens came from seeing Kate at Malvern to preside at the London dinner of the General Theatrical Fund. In the afternoon he had played with little Dora Annie, who had recovered from her illness and was in happy spirits. Shortly before Dickens rose to speak, Forster was summoned out of the room. There was a message that little Dora had suddenly died in convulsions. Returning to the banquet room, Forster heard Dickens saying how often the actor was obliged to come from "scenes of sickness, of suffering, ay, even of death itself," to play his part. At the end of the speech, Forster and Lemon broke the news. Dickens hurried home, arranged with Forster to bring Kate back from Malvern, and spent the rest of the night beside his child's body with Lemon.

In Kate's already upset state, it was necessary to deal with her very thoughtfully. Dickens provided Forster with a letter that did not tell the whole truth, but prepared her for hearing it when she arrived home: "Now observe. You must read this letter, very slowly and carefully," it began. "If you have hurried on thus far without quite understanding (apprehending some bad news), I rely on your turning back, and reading again."

Little Dora, without being in the least pain, is suddenly stricken ill. She awoke out of a sleep, and was seen, in one moment, to be very ill. Mind! I will not deceive you. I think her *very* ill.

There is nothing in her appearance but perfect rest. You would suppose her quietly asleep. . . . I do not – why should I say I do, to you my dear! – I do not think her recovery at all likely.

Kate would not like to be away, the letter continued, and he would not keep her away. But he begged her to remember their other children. Finally, "if – *if* – when you come, I should even have to say to you 'our little baby is dead,' you are to do your duty to the rest, and to shew yourself worthy of the great trust you hold in them."

The shock of this bereavement compelled Dickens to postpone rehearsals and take some days' rest. Consequently he was obliged to ask the Queen to set a later date for the performance of the play, and Her Majesty deferred it to 16 May. Kate was so overwhelmed with grief that she wanted only to get away as soon as possible. Dickens rented Fort House in Broadstairs and decided to sublet Devonshire Terrace until September, when his twelve-year lease would expire. Now he tried to distract Kate by taking her out under various pretences, including that of inspecting houses they might consider. Gradually they resigned themselves to the loss of the child, "our poor little pet," Dickens called her. After a time he was able to write, "I am quite happy again, but I have undergone a great deal."

When rehearsals resumed they took place in Devonshire House, where the Duke had set aside the picture gallery for the audience and the adjacent library for the stage. Behind the theatre, the remainder of the library was screened off as a "green room" for the players. Dickens tyrannically drilled his company all day long three days a week. He went over and over the weak places.

My legs [he said] swell so, with standing on the stage for hours together, that my stockings won't come off. I get so covered with sawdust among the carpenters, that my Infants don't know me. I am so astonishingly familiar with everybody else's part, that I forget my own. I roar to the Troupe in general, to that extent that the excellent Duke (who is deaf) thinks in the remoteness of his own little library that the wind is blowing hard.

377

Finally everything was ready. Dickens had doubtfully asked the Duke if three guineas a ticket would be too much, and on that nobleman's advice had then calmly agreed to demand five. One final precaution he was obliged to take to see that all went smoothly. Rosina Bulwer Lytton sent a frenzied letter to the Duke threatening to make her way in disguised as an orange-girl and create a disturbance. To Dickens she wrote a hysterical outburst, denouncing the actors as "a disreputable set of charlatans," and her estranged husband, "Sir Liar Coward Lytton," as "a ruffian and a scoundrel." Dickens therefore placed on guard in the hall a detective in plain clothes, who was prepared "very respectfully" to "shew our fair correspondent the wrong way to the Theatre, and not say a word until he had her out of hearing . . ." There is no record, however, of Rosina's having tried to force an entrance.

The dress rehearsal took place on 14 May. The Queen's Night followed on the 16th. A large audience crowded the entire picture gallery. After an overture composed for the occasion, played by the Duke's private band, the lights were lowered, the scented oil footlights grew bright, and the curtain rose on Lord Wilmot's lodgings. There were spectators and even fellow actors who did not think Dickens ideally successful in portraying a witty eighteenth-century man of mode, but there can be no doubt that the play triumphed with its audience. At the end the Queen led the hearty applause. There followed a luxurious supper at which Victoria sat in a chair under a Gothic arch elaborately decorated with roses, magnolias, jasmine, and honeysuckle, festooned with orchids, and surmounted by night-flowering cereus, all strewn with opals in simulation of dewdrops.

The Duke was so delighted with the success of the evening that he begged them to play once more in his residence before beginning at the Hanover Square Rooms. There was consequently an additional performance at Devonshire House on 27 May. No farce had been acted the first night: *Not So Bad As We Seem* was long, it did not begin until nine, and "the Queen gets very restless towards 12 o'clock." For an after-piece Dickens collaborated with Lemon on a hilarious absurdity they called *Mr Nightingale's Diary*. The second-night audience now screamed with laughter and were flabbergasted to discover that Dickens in rapid succession had disguised himself to play no fewer than six parts: a lawyer, a Sam Wellerish waiter, a maniacally enthusiastic walker, a hypochondriac, a gabbling Sairey Gamp-like old woman, and a deaf sexton. The Duke rounded off the evening with a sumptuous ball and supper, at which Douglas Jerrold was thrown into such a state of romantic admiration by some of the society beauties present that he moved about with gleaming eyes, "uttering glowing and racy ejaculations."

From Fort House at Broadstairs, where he had joined Kate and the children, Dickens wrote the Duke that he must certainly come to the first Hanover Square performance. "I really believe the actors will go all wrong and want all heart, if they don't see you in your box." Here, too, the production was tumultuously applauded, and the curtain rose and fell repeatedly in a whirlwind of enthusiasm. On 4 August there was a "positively the last" London performance.

The endless editorial activities were continuing as ever. The author of a paper on the treatment of lunatics must be told that it was too didactic and too long. If he would allow Dickens to rewrite and shorten it, well and good; if not, it must be rejected. An unknown young man named George Augustus Sala had written "a very remarkable piece of description" entitled "The Key of the Street," "quite good enough for a first article – but we will not put it first for fear we should spoil him in the beginning." Dickens himself wrote an article called "Whole Hogs" on the uncompromising fanatics who insisted that a teaspoonful of wine in a glass of water was a violation of Temperance, a single sentry before the Queen's palace a denial of Peace, and a bone in a pot of vegetables a fall from the Garden of Eden.

The provincial performances of *Not So Bad As We Seem* began late in the autumn, opening at Bath on 11 November and then going to Clifton for the 12th and 14th. During the following year *Not So Bad As We Seem* went luxuriously barnstorming through the provinces. They had already cleared over £3,000, Dickens told his company, and should keep on till they had £5,000. In February they filled the Free Trade Hall in Manchester and twice played to 3,000 in the Philharmonic Hall at Liverpool. People laughed so hard at *Mr Nightingale's Diary* that half of it was inaudible. "I sincerely believe," Dickens wrote excitedly, "that we have the ball at our feet, and may throw it up to the very Heaven of Heavens."

He left Liverpool almost "blinded by excitement, gas, and waving hats and handkerchiefs." In May came the Music Hall at Shrewsbury on the 10th, and the Birmingham Town Hall on the 12th and 13th. Almost always on these trips Dickens took the two largest sitting-rooms and almost all the beds of the principal hotel; sometimes he took the entire hotel. In addition to the thirty or so members of the acting company and the orchestra conductor, there was "a perfect army of carpenters, gasmen, tailors, barbers, property-men, dressers, and servants." The whole company lunched together, dined lightly before the performance, and then had supper together afterwards, inviting the mayor of the town, the chief civic magnates, and any of their friends as guests. After supper they relaxed in noisy hilarity, sometimes playing leapfrog all around the supper table, with Lemon making so enormous a "high back" as few could surmount.

In August, the tour was whirling to a close. On the 23rd they were at Nottingham. On the 25th, at Derby, the Duke of Devonshire happily turned up at a rehearsal. At Newcastle, on the 27th, they squeezed 600 people at twelve and sixpence "into a space reasonably capable of holding three hundred." On the 28th the deafening cheers from an audience of 1,200 in the just-erected Lyceum at Sunderland filled Dickens with trepidation. There were rumours that the structure was unsafe, and at every round of applause he imagined he "saw the gallery out of the perpendicular, and fancied the lights in the ceiling were not straight." On the 30th, they played at Sheffield. In September the tour ended, with return performances in Manchester on the 1st and Liverpool on the 3rd.

The later course of the Guild of Literature and Art cannot be followed here in detail. Dickens gave it faithful service throughout the rest of his life; the records of the Guild show some thirty-five meetings which he attended, and such minutes, of course, do not show how much additional time he gave to its business. All the funds accumulated for its endowment were invested in Government securities in the names of Dickens and Wills, who were its Chairman and Secretary.

On 2 June 1854, Bulwer Lytton succeeded in getting through Parliament a charter incorporating the Guild. Unfortunately, the charter prohibited any grants under it until seven years from that date. Dickens recommended that the capital and interest be allowed to accumulate over that time, and offered meanwhile rent-free accommodations in the *Household Words* offices. When the excitement of the theatricals was once over, however, general interest in the Guild fell off. By the end of the seven years during which its funds were frozen, the crowds that had laughed and cheered the performances of *Not So Bad As We Seem* had entirely forgotten the Guild.

Nor did the artists and writers for whose benefit it had been inaugurated take to it very kindly. In spite of its laudable aims and its brave words about financial independence, the plan seemed to them to have an unpleasant colouring of patronage; it suggested a slur of pauperism that both writers and artists resented.

And yet the problem to which Dickens and Bulwer Lytton generously addressed themselves was a real one never entirely solved. As we look on it today, the Guild seems a far-sighted anticipation of those modern endowments – for artists, writers, musicians, scientists, philosophers – that enable creative workers to concentrate without other preoccupations on a chosen project.

We are still far short, however, of dealing soundly with great abilities. The learned foundations and the universities are not wealthy enough to endow more than a few of many valuable works of scholarship that cannot command an audience large enough to pay their way. And those who would aid the artist, the seminal thinker, have the even harder task of distinguishing talent from mere oddity or charlatanism. The vision Dickens and Lytton had of the Guild was a noble one that with better fortune might have given priceless aid to learning and genius.

[45] DICKENS, 1850-1852. Photograph by J. Mayall, engraved by Linton

[46] AWFUL APPEARANCE OF A "WOPPS" at a picnic, Shanklin Sands, Isle of Wight. Cartoon by John Leech, in *Punch*, August 25, 1849

[47] MARK LEMON, the Dickens children's "Uncle Porpoise," Editor of *Punch*

[48] WILLIAM HENRY WILLS, Sub-Editor of *Household Words*. A drawing in the possession of *Punch*

[49] ROCKINGHAM CASTLE, home of the Watsons and the original of Chesney Wold in *Bleak House*

[50] THE HONORABLE MRS. RICHARD WATSON. Portrait at Rockingham Castle

[51] THE HONORABLE MR. RICHARD WATSON. Portrait at Rockingham Castle

[52] Edward Lytton Bulwer Lytton, Baron Lytton

[53] Knebworth, Hertfordshire, Garden Front. The home of Lord Lytton

[54] DICKENS, 1856. From the portrait by
Ary Scheffer

[55] MRS. HENRY LOUIS WINTER (Maria
Beadnell)

[56] TAVISTOCK HOUSE, Dickens's home, 1851-1860, where he wrote *Bleak House* and *Little Dorrit*. Photograph by Catherine Weed Barnes Ward

[57] WILKIE COLLINS, favorite companion of Dickens's middle years

[58] CLARKSON STANFIELD, R.A., "Dear Old Stanny," scene-painter of *The Lighthouse* and *The Frozen Deep*

[59] SCENE from the performance of *The Lighthouse* at Campden House, July 10, 1855

[60] WILLIAM MAKEPEACE THACKERAY. Painted by Alonzo Chappell from a drawing by Samuel Laurence

[61] JOHN FORSTER in middle age, his "Podsnap" period. Engraving by C. H. Jeens

[62] CHARLES CULLI-
FORD BOZ DICKENS, age
fifteen. Drawing by
George Richmond

[63] SYDNEY SMITH
HALDIMAND DICKENS.
From a painting by Mar-
cus Stone, R.A.

[64] EDWARD BULWER
LYTTON DICKENS,
"Plorn." From a paint-
ing by Marcus Stone

[65] HENRY FIELDING
and FRANCIS JEFFREY
DICKENS

[66] WALTER LANDOR
DICKENS

[67] MARY DICKENS,
"Mamey."
From a Miniature

[68] KATE MACREADY
DICKENS (Mrs. Peru-
gini). From a portrait
by Marcus Stone, R. A.

A GALLERY OF DICKENS'S CHILDREN

[69] DICKENS, 1859. From the portrait by W. P. Frith, R.A.

[70] FROM WHOM WE HAVE GREAT EXPECTATIONS, 1861. Photographic caricature

[71] DICKENS, 1861. From a pencil drawing by Rudolph Lehmann

[72] GAD'S HILL PLACE, entrance front, Dickens's home, 1857-1870, where he wrote *A Tale of Two Cities, Great Expectations, Our Mutual Friend,* and *Edwin Drood,* and where he died. Photograph by J. Dixon-Scott

[73] DICKENS READING to Mamey and Katey, circa 1865. Photograph by R. H. Mason

[74] GAD's HILL PLACE from the garden. Photograph by Catherine Weed Barnes Ward

[75] THE BRITISH LION IN AMERICA, 1868. From the *Daily Joker*, New York

[76] DICKENS AS PEDESTRIAN, 1868. From the Boston *Daily Advertiser*

CURIOUS EXPERIENCE OF MR. DICKENS AT DELMONICO'S, APRIL 18, 1868.
HE LISTENS TO A DISCOURSE FROM HIS OWN MR. PICKWICK, OR FROM SOMEBODY VERY MUCH LIKE HIM.

[77] DICKENS being introduced by HORACE GREELEY at the New York newspaper dinner

[78] DICKENS, 1868. From the photograph by Ben Gurney

[79] DICKENS IN HIS STUDY at Gad's Hill. From a pen-and-ink sketch by W. Steinhaus

[80] Above, CHARLES DICKENS exhausted after a reading. Pen-and-ink sketch by Harry Furniss

[81] Left, DICKENS, FEBRUARY, 1870. Caricature sketch by Spy (Leslie Ward)

[82] JASPER'S GATE HOUSE, RO-
CHESTER, with the parish church
on the right, used as one of the
settings in *Edwin Drood*

[83] THE SWISS CHALET, in which
the last lines of *Edwin Drood* were
written. Photograph by Catherine
Weed Barnes Ward

[84] "THE EMPTY CHAIR," Gad's Hill, June 7, 1870. Painting by Sir Luke
Fildes on the day of Dickens's death

[85] CHARLES DICKENS AFTER DEATH. Drawing by Sir J. E. Millais, R.A.

[86] WESTMINSTER ABBEY, the Poet's Corner. Dickens's grave at lower right. Pen-and-ink drawing by Arthur Moreland

PART EIGHT

The Darkening Scene
1851–1858

Fog Over England

With the mid-century mark Dickens reached almost exactly the halfway point in his literary career. He was nearing his fortieth year. Though his novels followed one another less swiftly than in his amazing first five years, if there be thrown in the balance his work on *Household Words*, his enormous correspondence, and his acting and play producing, he revealed little if any slackening of energy. And artistically he was at the height of his powers. Firmer in structure, deeper in intellectual grasp, sharper in social criticism, even imaginatively richer, his work assumed new dimensions of profound significance.

In the books that followed *David Copperfield* he was to attempt nothing less than an anatomy of modern society. *Bleak House* articulates its institutions, from government and law to philanthropy and religion – on every level, from Sir Leicester Dedlock's Lincolnshire estates to the rotting tenements of Tom-all-Alone's – as a corrupt and entangled web of vested interests and power. *Hard Times* unmasks the cold-hearted rationalizations of political economy and the industrial greed that uses economic "laws" to justify its callous exploitation of the labouring classes. *Little Dorrit* paints this entire system as a vast jail imprisoning every member of society, from the glittering admirers of Mr Merdle to the rack-rented dwellers in Bleeding Heart Yard.

The grimmer and more comprehensive vision Dickens brought to his enlarged purpose fills these novels with sombre hues. Although his sense of the ludicrous never ceases to be lively, it does not play with the sparkling profusion that once made it a fountain of irrepressible hilarity. Boythorn and the young man named Guppy, delightful as they are, and even the voluble Flora Finching and Mr F's Aunt, are only effervescent flashes in comparison with Dick Swiveller, Mrs Gamp, and Captain Cuttle. The satiric characters – Mr Vholes, the Smallweeds, Mr Bounderby, the Merdles and Tite-Barnacles – are bitten in now with burning acid. But if the old high spirits gleam less frequently, there is in these books a new intensity and integration, rich, dark, sulphurous, that weights every observation and cuts like a sabre.

Dickens began no new novel until the end of November 1851, after the first provincial performances of *Not So Bad As We Seem* at Bath and Bristol. From the early spring on, almost all the attention he could spare from Guild affairs and *Household Words* had been centred upon leaving Devonshire Terrace and finding a larger house. One property at Highgate he lost through insisting that the owners convey to him at their expense the freehold of an adjacent bit of land to which their title was dubious. He then offered £2,700 for Balmoral House, overlooking the Regent's Park. Luckily for him, this was also refused: a few years later a barge of gunpowder passing through the Regent's Canal exploded and wrecked the building. Keeping up his search while the family was at Broadstairs and Devonshire Terrace sublet, he installed iron bedsteads in his Wellington Street offices for use when he had to be in town during the summer.

Coming up from Broadstairs in mid-July 1851, Dickens learned that Frank Stone was moving from Tavistock House next door to Russell House. With the adjoining Bedford House these buildings made a group of three facing Tavistock Square, having an iron-railed front garden and a tree-shaded carriage sweep common to them all. Like its neighbours, Tavistock House had a basement mostly below ground from which it rose three full storeys to a mansard-roofed attic with servants' rooms. A lane on the right connected the front and rear gardens and gave light and air on that side. Wider than Devonshire Terrace, and a full storey higher, Tavistock House would have ample room for Dickens's entire brood of children.

This property could be obtained for a term of forty-five years, the purchaser being responsible during that period for paying the taxes and making his own repairs. "It is decidedly cheap," Dickens wrote Henry Austin, "– most commodious – and might be made very handsome." But it was "in the dirtiest of all possible conditions"; so, before committing himself, Dickens asked Austin to obtain an expert opinion "as to the likelihood of the roof tumbling into the kitchen, or the walls becoming a sort of brick and mortar minced veal." These fears being dissolved, Dickens authorized Stone to offer £1,450 in his behalf.

While the legal details were being settled, Dickens began pondering, with all his usual unhappy symptoms, the subject of his new book: "Violent restlessness, and vague ideas of going I don't know where, I don't know why . . ." "Still the victim of an intolerable restlessness, I shouldn't be at all surprised if I wrote you one of these mornings from under Mont Blanc. I sit down between whiles to think of a new story, and, as it begins to grow, such a torment of a desire to be anywhere but where I am ... takes hold of me, that it is like being *driven away*."

Some of the titles and subtitles he listed reveal the theme as he mulled it over in his mind: *Tom-Alone's: The Ruined House*; *Bleak House Academy*; *The East Wind*; *Tom-all-Alone's: The Solitary House where the Grass Grew*; *Tom-all-Alone's: The Solitary House that was Always Shut Up and Never Lighted*; *Tom-all-Alone's: The Solitary House where the Wind howled*; *Tom all-Alone's: The Ruined House that Got into Chancery and Never Got Out*; *Bleak House and the East Wind: How they Both Got into Chancery and Never Got Out*; *Bleak House*. The name "Tom-all-Alone's" floated up out of his child-hood memories of the lonely house in the waste places outside of Chatham, wrecked by the mines the army had exploded within its walls. But in it fused the image of the desolate London slum with its falling houses and the idea of a social system rotten with forces of its own decay and ultimate self-annihilation.

The key institution of the book is the Court of Chancery, the key image the fog pervading the atmosphere of the entire story with an oppressive heaviness. But both law and fog are fundamentally symbols of all the murky forces that suffocate the creative energies of mankind, the entanglement of vested interests and archaic traditions protecting greed, fettering action, and beclouding men's vision. *Bleak House* is thus an indictment not merely of the law, but of the whole dark muddle of organized society.

Dickens was unable to begin writing the book until the move to Tavistock House was made. He altered the house radically. The entrance hall was carried right through the ground floor to the private garden in the rear. What had been Stone's painting room on the first floor was to be the drawing-room, and the drawing-room transformed into a school-room. A door was cut between the drawing-room and the study.

The equipment and fittings of the house had to be thoroughly modernized. Speaking as the taker of a shower bath every morning, Dickens wrote, he insisted that the water closet be partitioned off from the bath, not allowed to "demonstrate itself obtrusively." "I believe it would affect my bowels." Then there was a new range to be installed in the kitchen, brass ventilators in the dining-room, bookshelves and built-in mirrors in drawing-room and study, and bells in all the bedrooms and connecting the best bedroom, dining-room, and drawing-room with the nursery. "Curtains and carpets, on a scale of awful splendour and magnitude, are already in preparation ..."

The delays and confusions usual to such alterations drove Dickens almost to frenzy. To Austin, who was superintending them, he wrote in large capitals:

NO WORKMEN ON THE PREMISES

. . . I have torn all my hair off, and constantly beat my unoffending family. . . . Then Stone presents himself, with a most exasperatingly mysterious visage, and says that a Rat has appeared in the kitchen, and it's his opinion (Stone's, not the Rat's) that the drains want "compoing"; for the use of which explicit language I could fell him without remorse.

Followed still more lamentations and directions, ending madly:

P.S.–NO WORKMEN ON THE PREMISES!
Ha! ha! ha! (I am laughing demoniacally.)

When the workmen did arrive, the chaos they created was so awful that Dickens escaped back to Broadstairs. But he could not resist fretting and imagining how things were going on in his absence. "I am perpetually wandering (in fancy) up and down the house and tumbling over the workmen. When I feel that they are gone to dinner I become low. When I look forward to their total abstinence on Sunday, I am wretched. The gravy at dinner has a taste of glue in it. I smell paint in the sea. Phantom lime attends me all the day long."

Then he would become distracted, dash back to town, look at the house, and fall into discouragement.

They are continually going up ladders, and never appear to come down again. They roll barrels of lime into the garden, and tap them by the dozen, like a sort of dusty beer. They peck at walls with iron instruments (for no reason that I can discover), and the walls fall down. . . . Yesterday week, I saw a hairy Irishman cultivating mortar with spade-husbandry in the room I am to write in!

But slowly progress was made. When Dickens and Catherine returned from Broadstairs on 20 October and pitched camp in the new house, order was beginning to establish itself. "White lime is to be seen in the kitchens – faint streaks of civilization dawn in the water-closet – the Bath-room is gradually resolving itself into a fact . . ." On the other hand, "The drawing-room encourages no hope whatever. Nor the study. . . . Inimitable hovering gloomily through the premises all day, with an idea that a little more work is done when he flits, bat-like, through the rooms, than when there is no one looking on." Kate was "all over paint, and seems to think that it is somehow being immensely useful to get into that condition."

By the fourth week in November, however, the delays were over and the move into Tavistock House was completed. Dickens was genuinely delighted with the outcome. Every detail about the house was exactly as he – and he only – had determined that it should be. Even the dummy book-backs on the imitation shelves of the door between his study and the drawing-room were so impressively successful as to make them seem part of an unbroken wall of books.

He had derived considerable amusement from inventing titles for these imaginary volumes. Some are purely facetious: *Five Minutes in China*, 3 vols., *Forty Winks at the Pyramids*, 2 vols., *Drowsy's Recollections of Nothing*, and *Heaviside's Conversations with Nobody*. Others are puns: *A Carpenter's Bench of Bishops*, *The Gunpowder Magazine*, *Teazer's Commentaries*. But there is a more satiric bite to *The Quarrelly Review*, *Kant's Eminent Humbugs*, *King Henry the Eighth's Evidences of Christianity*, and *Hansard's Guide to Refreshing Sleep* in "as many volumes as possible." Later Dickens added still more which run the same gamut: *Lady Godiva on the Horse*, *Cockatoo on Perch*, *Socrates on Wedlock* (in which Dickens on Wedlock is inferable), *Strutt's Walk*, *Noah's Arkitecture*, *Shelley's Oysters*, *Cat's Lives* (in 9 vols.), *Malthus's Nursery Songs*, *History of a Short Chancery Suit*, 21 vols., and *The Wisdom of Our Ancestors*, of which the successive volumes were labelled: "I. Ignorance. II. Superstition. III. The Block. IV. The Stake. V. The Rack. VI. Dirt. VII. Disease." Alongside this bulky work was *The Virtues of Our Ancestors*, a single volume so narrow that the title had to be printed sideways.

Sealed away in his study from the rest of the house, he was now ready to begin *Bleak House*. Opposite the two windows a console mirror framed in the mahogany bookcases reflected the trees and sky. His writing table looking out into the garden was neatly decked with all its knick-knacks – the duelling green-bronze frogs, the man with squirming puppies overflowing all his pockets, the ivory knife, and the rest – and equipped with its supply of writing paper, blue ink, and quill pens. Soon his imagination was swirling with the raw mist of Chancery Lane and the dense fog of Jarndyce and Jarndyce. On 7 December he had only a "last short chapter to do, to complete No. 1."

The turn of the year also saw published in *Household Words* the first of Mrs Gaskell's charming village sketches, later collected under the title of *Cranford*, which appeared irregularly for the next year and a half. Mrs Gaskell was irritated when in his own periodical Dickens modestly substituted Hood's *Poems* for her laudatory reference to *Pickwick Papers*, but allowed herself to be mollified by his explanation. His praise of her own work, though, she suspiciously dismissed as "soft sawder."

The first Christmas season in the new house was marked by a burst of festivities. The Dickens children, coached by their father, put on a Twelfth-Night performance of Albert Smith's burletta *Guy Fawkes* in the big schoolroom, transformed into a theatre for the occasion. And it must have been from around this time that Thackeray's daughter Annie remembered a "shining" party that seemed to "go round and round" in an enchanted way. She and her younger sister Minnie, almost the same ages as the two Dickens girls, were lost in a blur of music, streams of children, Miss Hogarth finding dancing partners for them, a vision of Mamey and Katey with white satin slippers and flowing white sashes, more dancing, radiant confusion.

After supper came more dancing and more people arriving, and crowds of little boys shouting and waving arms and legs. And finally, in the hall hung with Christmas greens, as Thackeray arrived to take his daughters home young Charley marshalled the boys on the broad staircase to give three cheers. "That is for you!" Dickens laughingly told Thackeray, who settled his spectacles, surprised and pleased, and nodded gravely at the boys.

Mamey and Katey were now growing up rapidly. Mamey, almost fourteen, was still quiet and docile; Katey, just turned twelve, had the fiery disposition that had given her the nickname Lucifer Box, and revealed enough talent for art so that Dickens enrolled her this year for drawing lessons at Bedford College. The two girls shared a room at the top of the house, which they were allowed to decorate as they pleased, but Dickens insisted that they keep it with military precision. Every morning he inspected their bureau drawers, and left "pincushion notes" to reprimand any untidiness or praise something new and pretty as "quite slap-up." The boys each had pegs for their hats on the hall rack, and woe betide the one who failed to use his! Once, Alfred Tennyson Dickens remembered, "I was busily engaged in brushing my coat in the dining room instead of outside," when his father came in, "and I never by any chance committed that particular offence afterwards." Dickens demanded neatness and he demanded punctuality; but he was "wonderfully good and even-tempered," Alfred said, and even when there had been a flurry of displeasure the next moment would be "like the sun after a shower."

The first number of *Bleak House* came out in March 1852, and was at once a much greater success than *David Copperfield* had been. "Blazing away merrily," it soon sold 35,000 copies every publishing day, and there is no record of how many in back sales or spread out through the month. In spite of its intricate but closely articulated structure, Dickens wrote more easily, or at least with fewer groans of misery and despair, than for years past. He was also able to blow off steam in the whirlwind theatrical trips and footlight excitements that punctuated most of the year. And possibly he was stimulated by a varied and amusing social life and by living in new places – when he was not touring with *Not So Bad As We Seem* – in Dover from the middle of July through September and Boulogne for a few weeks in October.

Now and then, to be sure, there is still one of the familiar outbursts: "Wild ideas ... of going to Paris – Rouen – Switzerland – somewhere – and writing the remaining two-thirds of the next No. aloft in some queer inn room. I have been hanging over it, and have got restless. Want a change I think. Stupid." The plaint anticipates by no more than a week Kate's giving birth, on 13 March 1852, to another child, "a brilliant boy of unheard-of dimensions," who was named Edward Bulwer Lytton Dickens. But although Dickens reported himself happy that both mother and son were in a "blooming condition," he added, "I am not quite clear that I particularly wanted the latter..."

Recovering speedily enough, however, from this mood, he was soon struggling cheerfully with the proofs of the second number of *Bleak House*. In the dilettante parasite Skimpole, in this number, he had imitated Leigh Hunt's playful vivacity of manner and the wilful gaiety of his paradoxes. (Just as in the following number, the gentle but leonine Boythorn was, he wrote confidentially, "a most exact portrait of Walter Savage Landor.") But Skimpole was clearly revealed as, beneath his charm, a selfish cheat; and Forster objected that readers might attribute his moral qualities to Hunt as well. Though Hunt was neither mean nor idle, but a hard-working and warm-hearted man, there was in fact some colour of reason for attributing to him a trace of Skimpole's financial irresponsibility.

Dickens was fond of Hunt and did not wish to give him pain. He therefore toned down the portrayal, introduced traits which were not those of Leigh Hunt, and changed Skimpole's first name from Leonard to Harold. Browne, too, in the illustrations, "helped to make him singularly unlike the great original." The whimsically paraded superiority to financial obligation still remained the same, though, as well as the unmistakable description of Skimpole looking more like "a damaged young man, than a well-preserved elderly one."

During the months that followed Dickens did a dozen different things with all his customary energy. He advised Miss Coutts on a slum clearance and cheap housing project which she was now considering. Small separate houses, he told her, were both more expensive to build and less satisfactory than multiple dwellings. Blocks of flats could have spacious public gardens, soundly constructed walls, good foundations, gas, water, drainage, and a variety of other advantages that would be prohibitively costly in one-family houses. In the course of elaborating these ideas, Dickens outlined an entire plan of schools, savings banks, and public libraries to be established with each group of buildings. From these discussions, in which he was a guiding mind, developed the razing of a slum area in Bethnal Green and the Columbia Square model flats which Miss Coutts built there.

In May the Guild company swooped down upon Shrewsbury and Birmingham, where Dickens kept everything "under the Managerial eye," played Lord Wilmot and Gabblewig, which together were "something longer," he said, "than the whole play of Hamlet – am dressed fourteen times in the course of the night – and go to bed a little tired."

During the month of June a young American girl, a Miss Clarke, visited at Tavistock House, and later recorded her impressions. They talked of *Uncle Tom's Cabin*, published just that spring, which Dickens told her he thought a story of much power, "but scarcely a work of art." "Uncle Tom," she reported "evidently struck him as an impossible piece of ebony perfection . . . and other African characters in the book as too highly seasoned with the virtues . . ." "Mrs Stowe," Dickens said, "hardly gives the Anglo-Saxon fair play. I like what I saw of the coloured people in the States. I found them singularly polite and amiable, and in some instances decidedly clever; but then," he added, with a comical arching of his eyebrows, "I have no prejudice against white people." In the course of the evening Miss Clarke was pleased at seeing that his servants did not wear livery: Dickens replied, "I do not consider that I own enough of any man to hang a badge upon."

July found Dickens in Dover, praising the sea and the country walks to Mary Boyle, but remarking that the place was "too bandy (I mean musical, no reference to its legs) and infinitely too genteel." Once again her Joe was archly tender: "Watson seemed, when I saw him last, to be holding on as by a sheet-anchor to theatricals at Christmas. Then – O rapture! – but be still, my fluttering heart." Insensibly led on from this to voice an undercurrent of deeper emotion, he added, "This is one of what I call my wandering days, before I fall to work. I seem to be always looking at such times for something I have not found in life, but may possibly come to a few thousands of years hence, in some other part of some other system. God knows."

Suddenly his feelings were given more tangible cause by the death of Watson. Only three weeks before, they had dined together merrily in London. "I loved him as my heart," Dickens wrote, "and cannot think of him without tears." Hard upon this came the news that D'Orsay was dead. "Poor d'Orsay! It is a tremendous consideration that friends should fall around us in such awful numbers as we attain middle life. What a field of battle it is!" And within less than another two months Catherine Macready was also no more.

Visiting Macready in his retirement at Sherborne the year before, Dickens had been the last friend to see Mrs Macready, even then sinking in her final illness. "The last flush of pleasure that passed over her face was caused by the sight of him; and as he took her hand to say farewell, she, sinking back exhausted in her chair, said feebly and faintly, 'Charles Dickens, I had almost embraced you – what a friend you have been!' He stooped and kissed her forehead . . ." "Ah me! ah me!" Dickens wrote. "This tremendous sickle certainly does cut deep into the surrounding corn, when one's own small blade has ripened."

In November occurred another death less personal in its meaning, that of the Duke of Wellington. Dickens obtained leave for Charley to come from Eton to see the funeral procession of the great old man, and Alfred recalled being awakened at three in the morning, with Frank and Sydney, to be taken to the offices of *Household Words*, from where they saw the guns and the colours, the troops and the dignitaries, and the Duke's famous charger, Copenhagen, as the dead march moved along Fleet Street to St Paul's. Catherine and Georgina, Mamey and Katey, numbers of friends, and some of the contributors to the magazine also joined them to witness the procession.

Dickens continued writing *Bleak House* steadily throughout the year. From December on the work continued with no interruption except for a trip to Birmingham in January, when the Society of Artists gave him a silver-gilt salver and a diamond ring.

On this occasion Dickens again voiced his scorn for "the coxcombical idea of writing down to the popular intelligence" and his belief in the people. "From the shame of the purchased dedication, from the scurrilous and dirty work of Grub Street, from the dependent seat on sufferance at my Lord Duke's table today, and from the sponging-house or Marshalsea tomorrow . . . the people have set literature free." Many working men were now better versed in Shakespeare and Milton than many fine gentlemen in the days of dear books, and it was the general public that read Macaulay's *History*, Layard's *Researches*, and Tennyson's *Poems*, and applauded the discoveries of Herschel and Faraday.

In March, Dickens spent a fortnight's holiday at Brighton, and May saw the arrival in England of Cornelius Felton, the beaming Pickwickian Greek professor from Harvard of whom Dickens had become so fond when he was in America. "He was one of the jolliest and simplest of men," Dickens said, "and not at all starry, *or* stripey." During the course of the next month, in the time he had free from his work, Dickens piloted Felton around London and introduced him to all his friends, from Forster and Clarkson Stanfield to old Rogers, sitting with a black skullcap on his head and staring out of his drawing-room window on the Green Park.

Despite his steel-coil vitality, by the approach of summer Dickens felt tired and overworked. "The spring does not seem to fly back again directly," he noted, "as it always did when I put my own work aside, and had nothing else to do." He had written more than four fifths of *Bleak House*'s 380,000 words, and during the past two and a half years had dictated over 125,000 words of the *Child's History of England* to Georgina. What with these, he said, "and Household Words . . . and Miss Coutts's Home, and the invitations to feasts and festivals, I really feel as if my head would split like a fired shell . . ."

The novel had achieved from the start an enormous popularity, "exceeding dear old Copperfield," Dickens wrote, "by a round ten thousand or more. I have never had so many readers." The sharpened intensity of its assaults on social institutions, however, had aroused extremes of agreement and dissent. Conservatives were troubled by his tone, and intellectuals felt some aspects of his strictures were unorthodox. The attack on Jarndyce and Jarndyce was so effective that the Vice-Chancellor felt it necessary to defend the Court – at a Mansion House dinner, where his eye rested on Dickens among the guests – by arguing that any slight leisureliness in its legal pace was the fault of a stingy public, which had until recently resisted increasing the number of the judges. "This seemed to me," Dickens commented, "too profound a joke to be inserted in the body of the book, or I should have restored it to Conversation Kenge or Mr Vholes, with whom I think it must have originated."

Some readers as critical of society as Dickens himself misinterpreted his satiric portrayals of Mrs Jellyby and Mrs Pardiggle. John Stuart Mill, for example, the heir of Benthamite radicalism, might well have sympathized with Dickens's smashing indictment of the law and political institutions as instruments for keeping power in the hands of those who had it. Mill saw in these charitable ladies a sneer at the rights of women. But the whole thrust of Dickens's bitter ironies was against those who worried about savages abroad instead of England's exploited and needy, and who made benevolence a device for bullying the poor. It is not remarkable that among his huge body of readers some should have been blind to the tremendous pattern of *Bleak House* and to the immensely broadened outlook with which Dickens had come to look upon this world.

Almost worn out with the labours of ending the book, Dickens had in June a severe recurrence of the kidney trouble that had afflicted him at irregular intervals since childhood, and spent six painful days in bed. Against everybody's advice but Dr Elliotson's, he insisted, however, before he was completely recovered, on setting out for Boulogne, which had pleased him so much the previous October that he had determined to go there for the summer. After a few days at Folkestone during which he still felt aches and pains when he sat up to write, he crossed the Channel with Kate and Georgina on 12 June and settled in the Château des Moulineaux, which had once been occupied by an acquaintance he had made in Switzerland.

Located on a wooded hillside in the midst of a great terraced garden, the villa had all of Boulogne piled and jumbled before it. It was approached by an avenue of hollyhocks and surrounded by thousands of roses and other flowers, with "five great summerhouses, and (I think) fifteen fountains – not one of which (according to the invariable French custom) ever plays," but all stocked with "gasping gold fish." The house had countless little bedrooms and drawing-rooms, a billiard-room, a dining-room looking into a conservatory, a glitter of mirrors everywhere, and a profusion of clocks keeping "correct Australian time – which I think," Dickens explained, "is about ten or twelve hours different from French or English calculation."

The landlord, M. Beaucourt, a portly jolly fellow, was enormously proud of what he always called "the property." All he wanted was that his little estate be admired. "You like the property?" he asked. "M. Beaucourt," Dickens replied, "I am enchanted with it; I am more than satisfied with everything." "And I, sir," said M. Beaucourt, laying his cap upon his breast and kissing his hand, "I equally!"

There was a detailed plan of the property in the hall, looking "about the size of Ireland," whereon every single feature was identified by name.

There are fifty-one such references, including the Cottage of Tom Thumb, the Bridge of Austerlitz, the Bridge of Jena, the Hermitage, the Bower of the Old Guard, the Labyrinth (I have no idea which is which); and there is guidance to every room in the house, as if it were a place on that stupendous scale that without such a clue you must infallibly lose your way, and perhaps perish of starvation between bedroom and bedroom.

As the names of some of these architectural features suggest, M. Beaucourt was a staunch admirer of Napoleon. "Medallions of him, portraits of him, busts of him, pictures of him, are thickly sprinkled all over the property. During the first month of our occupation, it was our affliction constantly to be knocking down Napoleon: if we touched a shelf in a dark corner, he toppled over with a crash; and every door we opened shook him to the soul."

In these Napoleonic surroundings, Dickens was soon able to report himself "brown, well, robust, vigorous, open to fight any man in England of my weight, and growing a moustache." Here, early in July, came the children, "all manner of toad-like colours" from a stormy Channel passage. Here came Frank Stone to a house Dickens found him in the Saint-Omer road, and the Leeches, and Wilkie Collins. Here, in August, came Forster, not at all understanding the customs officers when they asked, "Est-ce que Monsieur ait quelque chose à déclarer?" In consequence of which, said Dickens, he replied, "after a moment's reflection with the sweetness of some choice wind instrument 'Bon jour!' and was immediately seized." And here Dickens continued to keep an iron hand on *Household Words*, bombarding Wills with countless letters in which he was ruthlessly bidden to exclude, rewrite, and rearrange.

"Justice to Bears" wouldn't do as a title. "We have already had Justice to the Hyaena." Change it to "Brother Bruin." As for a garbled sentence like "And the onus of the idea task strangles every newly born smile that struggles for existence" – "strike it out with a pen of iron." "Gore House," by Leigh Hunt, was very poor. The gushing passage in it about the Graces must be deleted: "It is Skimpole, you know – the whole passage."

Amid a burst of stormy weather at the end of August, Dickens wrote the last pages of *Bleak House*. The end of his long effort left him in a state of drowsy lassitude. "I should be lying in the sunshine by the hour together if there were such a thing. In its absence I prowl about in the wind and rain. Last night there was the most tremendous I ever heard for a storm of both."

There is a poetic fitness about this nocturnal violence that marked the close of *Bleak House*, for it is a dark and tempestuous book. The fog choking its opening scene, the rain swirling over the Ghost's Walk at Chesney Wold amid the dripping funeral urns on the balustrade, the black and verminous ruins of Tom-all-Alone's crashing at intervals with a cloud of dust, the besmeared archway and iron-barred gate that lead to the rat-infested graveyard, insinuate their oppressive gloom even amid the genial sunlit scenes. A turbulent and furious hostility to vested evils storms savagely through its pages.

36

The Heaviest Blow in My Power

The tremendous effort and the tremendous creative achievement of *Bleak House*, far from spent, unleashed in Dickens energies that were still seething below the surface. Its structure reflected his sense of society as one monolithic structure dominated by privilege and wealth. His next book, *Hard Times*, would unmask the arid, heartless scheme of values behind these forms and institutions, the dusty, destructive ethics that stunted love, imagination, life itself.

But the struggle to forge the gigantic attainment of *Bleak House* into its huge unity had momentarily exhausted Dickens's powers. He must have rest before he undertook another work of fiction. And so, after his heavy spell of labour, he made ready now in the autumn of 1853 to set out on a two-month holiday in Switzerland and Italy with Augustus Egg and Wilkie Collins.

Since Egg had induced Collins to play the valet in *Not So Bad As We Seem*, a genial association had developed between Dickens and the younger writer. Twenty-six years of age when his first novel, *Antonia*, was published, he was twelve years Dickens's junior. Slight in build, with dainty feet and hands, but with an enormous brow bulging above his spectacles, Collins looked both smug and prim. But his crimson ties and blue-striped shirts insinuated another vein in his character, colourful, Bohemian, running into a taste for rowdy fun. He loved rich food, champagne, and music halls; he was often involved in intricate tangles with several women at once; he was amusing, cynical, good-humoured, unrestrained to the point of vulgarity.

Collins gave only bachelor parties and was regarded askance by nice-minded women. He was lazy, sceptical, slovenly, unpunctual; but he was also gentle, warmhearted, and unpretentious – he was not at all irritated at being told that his books were "read in every back-kitchen." He hated pugnacity, competition, and cruelty, and was interested only in enjoying himself. All these qualities help to explain the appeal he had for Dickens, who was coming himself to feel more and more sceptical of society and many of its conventions, and more and more rebellious against them. He craved colour and variety in his life, of which he found too little in his staid older friends as they grew steadily more respectable and sober – certainly none in Forster, who every day grew more starchified and buttoned up. Collins stood for fun and freedom. With him it was easy for Dickens to be "Albion's Sparkler," as he loved to call himself, seething with champagne gaiety.

In preparation now for the holiday tour, Dickens "cleared the way through Household Words," so that Wills could handle it in his absence. He dictated the remainder of the *Child's History of England* to Georgy, unceremoniously dropping it at the Revolution of 1688 and rounding it off with a hasty list of the reigns from the time of William and Mary to the marriage of Victoria and Albert. Kate, Georgy, and the children were to be sent home from Boulogne, except for Alfred and Frank, who were being left there at a private school.

Before the trip, the Guild of Literature and Art gave a gorgeous dinner for Dickens at the London Tavern, "four immense red scaffolds covered with gold plates – turtle cooked in six ways – astonishing wines – venison – pine[apple]s – all manner of luxuries." The evening "would have been perfect" but that Forster, who realized and jealously resented Dickens's new friendship with Collins, made "a very uncomfortable and restless Chairman." On 10 October, Dickens was off for Paris, whence he, Egg, and Collins started for Strasbourg and Switzerland.

In Lausanne they were guests of Chauncey Hare Townshend, and Dickens met his old friend Cerjat, now thin and very grey, and Haldimand, as loud-laughing and disputatious as ever. In Geneva they stayed at the Écu, and at Chamonix ascended the Mer de Glace. Then they crossed the Simplon and Dickens was delighting in hearing "the delicate Italian once again," and sending greetings home to Catherine and Georgy and all the children, including the baby, now called by the nickname of Plornishghenter.

In imitation of Dickens's moustache and beard, the sad-faced Egg and the wispy Collins were letting their own grow, achieving results, Dickens said, "more straggling, wandering, wiry, stubbly, formless, more given to wandering into strange places and sprouting up noses and dribbling under chins, than anything . . . since the Flood." Suffering from the sight of "these terrific objects," Dickens seized his razor and shaved off his beard as an example; but utterly without effect, "they merely observing with complacency that 'it looks much better so.' " He dragged them across glaciers, hauled them up mountains, raced them along roads, dragooned them into punctuality, and forced them through a fury of sightseeing with a relentless energy that must have worn them down. Nevertheless they all enjoyed each other's company and got on very well together.

The steamer from Genoa to Naples was scandalously overcrowded with passengers who had been sold first-class tickets far in excess of the accommodations, so that ladies were obliged to sleep on deck among heaps of carpetbags, hatboxes, and life buoys. During the second day Dickens "facetiously" led the Captain "such a life" that he found a place for Egg and Collins in the storeroom, "where they slept on little dressers, with the pickles, spices, tea, fruits, and a very large double Glo'ster cheese." Dickens slept in the steward's cabin on a pallet "four feet and a half by one and a quarter," with the engine "under the pillow," an "extremely nervous" wall, "and the whole in a profuse perspiration of warm oil."

At Naples the travellers visited a public bath to rid themselves of the odours of groceries and oil. Dickens was soaped by an old attendant who frothed him all over, rubbed him down, and scrubbed him with a brush, and who "was as much disappointed (apparently) as surprised, not to find me dirty . . . ejaculating under his breath 'O Heaven how clean this Englishman is!' He also remarked that the Englishman was as fair as a beautiful woman – but there, he added, the resemblance ended."

Naples was full of people whom Dickens knew: Sir James Emerson Tennent, who had been on the steamer from Genoa; Austen Henry Layard, the excavator of Nineveh and as uncompromising a radical as Dickens himself, "with whom we ascended Vesuvius in the sunlight and came down in the moonlight, talking merrily." And at nearby Capri, Dickens learned, a son of Mrs Norton, "Young Brinsley Norton, two and twenty years old," had married "a bare-footed girl off the Beach, with whom he had previously fulfilled all matrimonial conditions except the ceremony." The bride had "no idea of a hair brush and is said to be extremely dirty – which her young husband particularly admires, observing that it is 'not conventional.'"

Politically, Dickens soon realized, Italy was in an even more gloomy state of reaction than before the revolutions of 1848. In Naples under "King Bomba" there were 100,000 troops. Dickens asked a Neapolitan Marchese what had happened to a cultivated man he had known there. "In exile," was the reply. "What would you have? He was a remarkable man – full of knowledge, full of spirit, full of generosity. Where should he be but in exile!'"

In Rome the antiquities were smaller than Dickens's imagination in nine years had made them, but the Pantheon he thought "even nobler than of yore" and was fascinated to find the wires of the electric telegraph going "like a sunbeam through the cruel old heart of the Coliseum." Malaria from the Pontine Marshes was gradually "encroaching on the Eternal City as if it were commissioned to swallow it up"; "from the Coliseum through the Street of Tombs to the ruins of the old Appian Way" there was nothing "but ruined houses from which the people have fled, and where it is Death to sleep."

Collins and Egg continued to give Dickens much amusement. "To hear Collins learnedly holding forth to Egg (who has as little of that gammon as an artist *can* have) about reds, and greens, and things 'coming well' with other things, and lines being wrong, and lines being right, is far beyond the bounds of all caricature." Collins was also very learned on music, "and sometimes almost drives me into frenzy by humming and whistling whole overtures – with not one movement correctly remembered from the beginning to the end."

He occasionally expounds a code of morals [Dickens wrote Catherine] taken from modern French novels, which I instantly and with becoming gravity smash. But the best of it is, that he tells us about the enormous quantities of Monte Pulciano and what not, that he used to drink when he was last there, and what distinguished people said to him in the way of taking his opinion, and what advice he gave them and so forth being then exactly thirteen years of age.... All these absurdities are innocent enough. I tell them in default of having anything else to tell. We are all the best of friends, and have never had the least difference.

Before going on to Florence, Dickens sent Wills a little story for the Christmas number of *Household Words*, called "The Schoolboy's Story," and at Venice he succeeded in doing another entitled "Nobody's Story." Under a cold but bright blue winter sky, the fantastic city enchanted Dickens as it had on his first visit. By day the water was a blazing ultramarine, by night a gleaming black, and under the exquisite starlight "the front of the cathedral, overlaid with golden mosaics and beautiful colours, is like a thousand rainbows even in the night." More than ever, though, Dickens felt "that one of the great uses of travelling is to encourage a man to think for himself," and have the boldness to ignore the genteel subserviencies about works of art. "Egg's honest amazement and consternation when he saw some of the most trumpeted things was what the Americans call a 'caution.'"

When he had been at Genoa, Dickens had joyfully visited the De la Rues. Mme De la Rue was still haunted by her phantoms, but otherwise well and in brave spirits. She and her husband both referred warmly and generously to Kate, and Mme De la Rue sent her love. But beyond mentioning the fact that he had seen them, Dickens said nothing about them to Kate until he was in Turin on his way home. Then he reminded her of the time she had constrained him "to make that painful declaration of your state of mind to the De la Rue's," and asked her if what had "looked large in that little place" had not since then "shrunk to its reasonable and natural proportions."

"Now I am perfectly clear," he told her, "that your position beside these people is not a good one, is not an amiable one, not a generous one – is not worthy of you at all." She had the power to set this right by sending Mme De la Rue "a note to say that you have heard . . . of her sufferings and her cheerfulness – that you couldn't receive her messages of remembrance without a desire to respond to them – and that if you should ever be thrown together again . . . you hope it will be for a friendly association without any sort of shadow upon it." Whether or not Catherine now felt persuaded that she had suffered from a mistaken jealousy in those miserable Italian days, she did as he suggested.

Dickens had arranged that at Paris he was to be met by his son Charley, now almost sixteen, who had been spending the past year in Germany. The boy had decided that he did not want to enter any of the learned professions, and on his father's advice had given up an inclination for the army and was planning to become a businessman. He had consequently withdrawn from Eton the preceding Christmas and gone to Leipzig to study German as a serviceable tool for a mercantile career.

From Paris Dickens returned to London. Almost at once on his arrival home he plunged into rehearsing a Twelfth-Night play with the children and preparing three readings he had agreed to give for the benefit of the newly established Birmingham and Midland Institute. These were Dickens's first public readings from his books.

The first night's reading of *A Christmas Carol* on 27 December was attended by 2,000 people, who listened spellbound for three full hours, and repeatedly burst into tumultuous applause. After an almost equally successful reading of *The Cricket on the Hearth*, on the 29th, he gave a second reading of the *Carol* on the 30th, at reduced prices, before 2,500 working people, for whom Dickens had requested that most of the vast auditorium be reserved. These, he thought, were the best audience of the three. "They lost nothing, misinterpreted nothing, followed everything closely, laughed and cried . . . and animated me to that extent that I felt as if we were all bodily going up into the clouds together."

Between £400 and £500 was added to the endowment of the Institute, and the performance made such a furore that Dickens was deluged with invitations to read elsewhere. All these last, however, he refused, and returned to helping the children get up their Twelfth-Night performance of Fielding's *Tom Thumb* in the schoolroom. Little Betty and Lally Lemon trotted over to rehearsals with their father, and Dickens "improvised costumes," one of the childish performers remembered, "painted and corked our innocent cheeks, and suggested all the most effective business of the scenes."

On the night of the performance, Dickens, who played the Ghost of Gaffer Thumb, billed himself under the pseudonym of "the Modern Garrick," and Mark Lemon, who played the Giantess Glumdalca as "the Infant Phenomenon." The little girls were gravely irresistible as Huncamunca and Dollalolla. But the hit of the evening was the small helmeted hero, Tom Thumb, acted with solemn conviction by four-year-old Henry Fielding Dickens.

Caught up in this seasonal turmoil, Dickens had not yet seen two American friends, Mrs David Colden and her brother Dr Wilkes, whom he remembered happily from his New York days, although he had learned of their presence in London on the Sunday night of his own arrival. " 'Good God!' said I, 'I must go and see them directly.' 'You can't,' said Catherine and Georgina both together, 'for they are going to Brighton tomorrow for a few days.' " Then came the Birmingham expedition, and then the children's play. When Dickens did call on 8 January, Mrs Colden, hurt, received him rather frostily. He went home and immediately wrote her a note of explanation.

"Life is not long enough," he pleaded, "for any little misunderstanding among friends who are really friends at heart . . ." He had come as soon as he had cleared away the demands upon his time, and could say, "where shall I go with you, what companionship can we project together . . . Now do dismiss all but that," he concluded, "and let us be as cordial as when I left you a dozen years ago. If there be any blame, I take it all; if there be any slight, you shall have it all. Let it be past in any case." Mrs Colden melted, and agreed that he was not, as he put it at the end of his letter, "a neglectful – And callous – Ruffian – but your old friend – Quite unchanged."

No sooner were the New Year's festivities over than Bradbury and Evans called a business conference to consider plans for the future. The six months' profits of *Household Words* on the preceding 30 September had been only around £528, about half what they had been, and the circulation was still shrinking. After having steadily bettered its initial success, it was now slipping badly. Something drastic would have to be done.

The last instalment of *The Child's History of England* had been published in December, and Bradbury and Evans urged that Dickens spring to the rescue by writing a new serial in weekly numbers especially for the magazine. It had always been understood that he would occasionally contribute a long story, though at the moment he had intended no effort of the kind for a full year. But Bradbury and Evans pressed; Forster and Wills concurred; and Dickens agreed.

Even so, he might have sought other means to swell *Household Words*'s circulation had not the idea for the novel he was to write "laid hold of me," as he put it, "by the throat in a very violent manner." Within him, the conception of the forces shaping society foreshadowed by *Dombey and Son* and darkly, volcanically dominant throughout *Bleak House*, was still fermenting and seething with creative fury. Deeper still, indeed, the roots of the new story went back even further: they were twisted in the flaring gloom of the Black Country and his first horrified vision, sixteen years ago, of mines like underground dungeons and mills filled with clamour and cruelty. He had sworn then "to strike the heaviest blow in my power" for their victims.

In *Nicholas Nickleby* he had hardly been ready to carry out that oath, but, in one sense, all that he had written since had done so. His warm, loving, humorous portrayal of the poor, his sympathy and wrath at their mistreatment, had strengthened the emotions behind every effort for their welfare. Dickens would not stand for any patronizing talk of the labouring class being stupid or lazy or of their not minding dirt and squalor. He utterly rejected the dogma that their earnings must be determined by an iron law of wage, and insisted on their right to a decent livelihood. He demanded that the Government recognize and fulfil a duty to them and their children.

But the cruel and ugly world of mechanized industry had loomed through his stories only in a few nightmare glimpses – from the train windows of Mr Dombey's journey to Leamington or in *The Old Curiosity Shop* as a blur of angry workers silhouetted against the glare of furnaces. Scrooge is not a millowner nor an ironmaster, though he voices their relentless economic creed. And the working people Dickens had so colourfully painted were not the miners, the mill hands, or the pottery workers, but the humble folk already crowded in great cities and coastal towns before the factory wheels began turning. There are no factory machine-minders among them.

Meanwhile, through all the first half of the nineteenth century, the power of the industrial system had been growing until it dominated society. Chimneys smutted the sky and killed grass and trees, chemical waste fouled the streams, bleak miles of tenements spread like a cancerous blight over the countryside. Row upon row of flimsy houses, three quarters of them with no privies, crammed thousands of human beings into damp rooms and cellars. Heaps of ordure and garbage outside drained into ditches which often provided the only water people had to drink. The owners of the factories fought by every evasion against obedience to the Ten Hours Bill, cynically defied sanitary regulations in unventilated workrooms, and recklessly ignored the law requiring that dangerous machinery be fenced in. The philosophy of the industrialists savagely denied that they had any duty to their employees except to pay them the wage established by the law of supply and demand, and insisted that the prosperity of the country depended upon high profits and cheap labour. The industrial system established a tyranny all the deadlier because it professed to be based upon scientific laws inherent in the very structure of society.

This fusion of brutal act and harsh theory was the core of what Dickens had always fought. But he now understood it far more deeply and clearly. And more horrible to him even than the hard reality was the fact that the factory owners confronted it with a clear conscience. Their philosophic principles, so far as they had any, were identical with their practice. For them nothing was real except the statistics of profit and loss; anything else was mere sentimentality, intangible fancy. The degree to which Dickens insisted on this hard materialism as the essential feature of the industrial system is indicated in the bitter list of titles he drew up for the story that became *Hard Times: According to Cocker*; *Prove It*; *Stubborn Things*; *Mr Gradgrind's Facts*; *The Grindstone*; *Hard Times*; *Two and Two are Four*; *Something Tangible*; *Our Hardheaded Friend*; *Rust and Dust*; *Simple Arithmetic*; *A Matter of Calculation*; *A Mere Question of Figures*; *The Gradgrind Philosophy*.

The novel is an analysis and a condemnation of the very ethos of industrialism.

This [says Bernard Shaw] is Karl Marx, Carlyle, Ruskin, Morris, Carpenter, rising up against civilization itself as a disease, and declaring that it is not our disorder but our order that is horrible; that it is not our criminals but our magnates that are robbing and murdering us; and that it is not merely Tom-all-Alone's that must be demolished and abolished, pulled down, rooted up, and made forever impossible, so that nothing shall remain of it but History's record of its infamy, but our entire social system.

With his usual thoroughness Dickens prepared the ground for his story. Though he had so recently passed through the blast furnaces and belching chimneys of Wolverhampton on his way to Birmingham, and looked down from the high railway arches upon the pit mouths and the flaming kilns in the blackened landscape, he decided on a trip to Preston to observe the stubborn and long-drawn-out strike among the workers in its cotton mills. He found Preston a nasty place, but entirely quiet and orderly despite the fact that the strikers were not well fed and had been out of employment for twenty-three weeks. The chimneys were cold and smokeless, and small groups at street corners read placards about the strike, but mostly, he was told, the people sat at home and moped.

In London he was soon wrestling with the problems of writing in weekly instalments which he had not known since the days of *Master Humphrey's Clock*. The task was made still more arduous by the brevity necessary in *Household Words*. "The difficulty of the space," he complained, "is CRUSHING. Nobody can have an idea of it who has not had an experience of patient fiction-writing with some elbow-room always, and open places in perspective."

This conciseness makes *Hard Times* a morality drama, stark, formalized, allegorical, dominated by the mood of piercing through to the underlying *meaning* of the industrial scene rather than describing it in minute detail. In the Gradgrind world there must be no imagination, no fancy, no emotion, only fact and the utilitarian calculus. Its hard-facts philosophy is the aggressive formulation of the inhumane spirit of Victorian materialism.

While Dickens was still engaged on the opening chapters, he was grieved to learn of the death of his old friend Talfourd. He recalled how kind Talfourd had been to him when he was an obscure beginner at his profession. And he remembered a moonlit night at Broadstairs when Talfourd had told of his earnest pleasure at being made a judge and the two of them had playfully disputed at what age he should retire and what he would do at three-score and ten. "So amiable a man," Dickens wrote, "so gentle, so sweet-tempered, of such a noble simplicity, so perfectly unspoiled by his labours and their rewards, is very rare indeed upon this earth."

Hard Times began appearing in *Household Words* on 1 April. The story doubled the circulation in the course of the first ten weeks and before the end the profits multiplied by four or five. But there were readers who were worried by the radical sound of the story. Dickens robustly insisted that its purpose was not to foment discord, but to foster understanding between employers and employed. "The English people," he said, "are . . . the hardest-worked people on whom the sun shines. . . . They are born at the oar, and they live and die at it. Good God, what would we have of them!" And "I often say to Mr Gradgrind that there is reason and good intention in much that he does – but that he overdoes it. Perhaps by dint of his going his way and my going mine, we shall meet at last at some halfway house where there are flowers on the carpets, and a little standing-room for Queen Mab's chariot among the Steam Engines."

In the story Mr Gradgrind does not discover his error until he has blindly ruined the lives of the children he loves. When he is conveying to his daughter Louisa a proposal of marriage from the odious Bounderby, she gazes on the fumes of the factory chimneys and muses aloud that they seem to be nothing but languid and monotonous smoke: "Yet when the night comes, Fire bursts out, father!" But the obtuse, well-meaning father misses all her yearning for sympathy and understanding, even the allusion to those fires of human passion that burst out in the dark night of despair, and Louisa goes to her doom.

Dickens had arranged to begin publishing a serial novel by Mrs Gaskell in September when *Hard Times* should have run its course. Her story was also to have its setting in a mill town and a theme of industrial conflict. She was worried that there might turn out to be too much sameness in their choice of incidents; Dickens wrote her to relieve her fears. "The monstrous claims at domination made by a certain class of manufacturers, and the extent to which the way is made easy for men to slide down into discontent under such hands, are within my scheme"; but she might feel at ease on the point raised, he was not going to have a strike in his tale.

Tired, sometimes "dreary" with his work, Dickens sought distraction whenever it allowed him a little freedom. How about going for the evening, he asked Mark Lemon, to that public house on the Thames where they had the performing dogs: "it will do us good after such a blue-devilous afternoon." He summoned Wilkie Collins for a jaunt to Tunbridge Wells, for a stroll on Hampstead Heath. He took Mrs Colden's brother, Dr Wilkes, on the rounds of "the low and vicious haunts of London." He welcomed Felton back from a tour of the Continent and Scotland, somewhat baffled to understand why Felton should consider Rome "a failure" and Edinburgh so immeasurably "'the drollest' place he had ever seen" that he was unable to speak of it without bursting into fits of laughter.

Another visitor this spring was a young man named Edmund Yates, the son of Frederick Yates, the actor. "God! how like your father!" was Dickens's greeting when Yates was shown into his study. But Yates, who had formed his image of Dickens from the poetic Maclise portrait of 1839, was surprised by his thinning hair, moustache, and "door-knocker" beard, and by his hearty, almost aggressive manner. Sitting with one leg under him and a hand in a pocket, Dickens talked enthusiastically of old days at the Adelphi Theatre and how he had admired Yates's mother. He told Yates he was off to Boulogne for the summer at the end of the coming week, but hoped to see him in the autumn.

Dickens crossed to Boulogne on 18 or 19 June. He had rented the Villa du Camp de Droite, another of M. Beaucourt's houses, a larger cottage with more spacious rooms. "Range of view and air, most free and delightful; hill-side garden, delicious; field, stupendous; speculations in haycocks already effected by the undersigned, with the view to the keeping of a 'Home' at Rounders." A mile away a French military camp was being constructed – the Crimean War had begun at the end of March. With magic speed there were whole streets of mud huts, tents like immense sheets hung out to dry, and soldiers making the roads and bridges red with their trousers.

Promptly on his arrival, Dickens "moved every article of furniture in the house." Three days later came the children, "in every stage and aspect of sea-sickness," a nurse, also prostrate, Mamey's and Katey's governess, and twenty-seven pieces of luggage. With them too came Lally and Betty Lemon, "whose parents had discreetly packed two dozen pairs of brand new stockings in their luggage. Duty on said stockings, 8 francs."

What with making these changes and getting the family and their guests settled in, he wrote only seventy-two words of *Hard Times* during the first five days. But before the middle of July he had made such progress that he was hoping to finish the book and take the last chapters of it to London on the 10th. "Bobbing up corkwise from a sea of *Hard Times*," he suggested that Collins join him in five days "of amiable dissipation, and unbounded licence in the metropolis," and then return with him to Boulogne. He was "stunned with work," he informed Wills. And to Forster he wrote, "I am three parts mad, and the fourth delirious, with perpetual rushing at Hard Times." Of Carlyle he asked permission to dedicate the book to him. "I know it contains nothing in which you do not think with me, for no man knows your books better than I."

He wrote the last lines of *Hard Times* in a wild burst of energy two days earlier than he had expected to, and felt appallingly "used up." He might well feel exhausted, for all its 100,000 words had been written in little over five months. But he took the boat next day, 18 July, and arrived at ten that night in a London intensely close, suffocating, and oppressive. After a busy day at the office, he met Collins at the Garrick for a convivial evening. The next night, with Miss Coutts, he heard Grisi in *Lucrezia Borgia*, and the night after that saw the Spanish dancers at the Haymarket and sat up with Buckstone, the manager, drinking gin slings till daylight. "I have been in a blaze of dissipation altogether, and have succeeded (I think) in knocking the remembrance of my work out."

37

Fire Bursts Out

The unquiet and feverish state of mind in which Dickens finished *Hard Times* was more than the aftermath of an intense effort. True, the strain of writing the novel in less than six months had been overwhelming. But more significant was the mingling of his half-acknowledged feelings about his private life with his deepened realization of how much was fundamentally wrong with England and the world.

For nine years now he had been shouldering enormous burdens of work and adding to them innumerable other distractions. He had founded a newspaper, taken on the editorship of a weekly magazine, devoted days to furthering Miss Coutts's philanthropic projects, dashed about – to Edinburgh, Manchester, Birmingham, Lausanne, Paris, Boulogne, all over Italy – lived in a dozen different places, been restless everywhere, repeatedly organized the most elaborate theatrical benefits, and invariably subsided into cries of misery when they were ended.

The sharpness of his personal unrest was intensified by the feelings with which he looked upon the world. It was not that he believed the cosmos evil. Nor did he believe that human nature was intrinsically bad. But he did believe that the entire machinery of society was evil; it was built upon principles of greed and class interests that systematically frustrated the general welfare.

He saw well enough that this machinery was not operated for the most part with any deliberate and malignant design of producing human suffering. Ralph Nickleby and Squeers were aberrations, but they shaded into the cold indifference of Mr Dombey and Sir Leicester Dedlock's lofty assurance that he and his class were England. But the impersonal workings of the social system were no less brutal than as if those at its controls were an aggregation of villains. And just as Mr Dombey corrected the optimistic distortion of the Cheerybles, the progressive ironmaster, Mr Rouncewell, was replaced by Bounderby and Gradgrind, the one bullying and blustering, the other blind to the imagination and the heart. Land, birth, trade, and industry were all treading the same broad road to destruction.

No wonder that the mechanisms of society, Dickens thought, could not even serve their own masters efficiently, but were always breaking down – symbolic of their final collapse. Privilege could not function without corruption, and corruption undermined itself and the structure of which it was a rotten support. And as he looked about him, he felt the muddle growing ever worse and more desperate. The outbreak of the Crimean War in March 1854, had of course been made the excuse for dropping all attempts at social planning. The Reform Bill that Lord John Russell had introduced in February he had been forced to with-draw in April. And with it, Dickens realized, education, slum clearance, sanitation, hours and wages, factory conditions, every necessary social amelioration would go by the board. "I fear I clearly see," he burst out angrily, "that for years to come domestic reforms are shaken to the root; every miserable red-tapist flourishes war over the head of every pro-testor against his humbug . . ."

Though his judgement remained bitterly unwavering, Dickens's temperament was as mercurial as ever. The emotional effects of *Hard Times* he threw off in that "blaze of dissipation" with Collins for which he had gone to London. But the book had taken a great deal out of him. He was so immeasurably fatigued that on his Boulogne hillside he spent hours in a haystack with a book, falling asleep, and turning a deep coffee colour in the August sun. Through the bright, breezy days he recovered his resiliency.

Mrs Gaskell's story was giving trouble. Dickens had praised the artistry of a first large section of it that she had sent him, and even suggested its title, *North and South*, but as a serial it was slow-moving, the instalments were too long, and not enough happened in each part. In addition she began to be difficult about editorial changes, stipulating that the story was not to be "touched 'even by Mr Dickens.' " Long before the end, the magazine lost some of the additional readers *Hard Times* had gained for it. "I am sorry to hear of the Sale dropping," Dickens said, "but I am not surprised. Mrs Gaskell's story, so divided, is wearisome in the last degree."

The middle of September brought a sudden alarm: an hour and a half after midnight of Sunday, the 17th, Dickens's daughter Mary was taken desperately ill with the cholera. Her nausea and diarrhoea were so acute and she seemed to be sinking so fast that there was not time to wait for a physician. The danger was great in a house full of children.

Dickens had often thought of what would have to be done under such circumstances, and now set himself to applying the remedies recommended. With the morning she seemed better, and the next day it was clear that she had "turned the awful corner."

The other children all remained well. Little Harry, next to the youngest, was between five and six years old, and was called sometimes The Jolly Postboy and sometimes The Comic Countryman. The youngest, now two "and perpetually running about on two mottled legs," had triumphed over Dickens's failure to feel delight at his birth and was a favourite with his father. When Dickens had been in Italy the previous autumn, his letters had been full of "The Plornishghenter," whom he declared "evidently the greatest, noblest, finest, cleverest, brightest, and most brilliant of boys," "an irresistibly attracting, captivating May-Roon-Ti-Goon-Ter."

The villa had entertained the usual lively succession of visitors. Collins had been there until shortly before Mary's illness, writing in a pavilion in the garden. Wills had passed a fortnight there, planning the Christmas number of *Household Words* with Dickens. Then came Beard, in a spell of delicious cool weather during which they lit fires, and then Mitton, and Evans, and Egg. Thackeray had been down the Paris road in June, inhabiting a melancholy old château, "with one milk jug as the entire crockery of the establishment." He came to smoke a farewell cigar with Dickens before going to Scotland.

On 1 October, Dickens saw the military review at which Napoleon III was handed the erroneous telegraphic dispatch announcing the fall of Sebastopol. (The siege did not in fact come to an end until the following September.) Dickens was disturbed to notice that the cheering of the troops at the news was faint and cold, for little as he wished the war to stand in the way of alleviating misery at home, he was convinced "that the future peace of the world" rendered it imperative "that Russia MUST BE stopped."

But it was domestic reform, not Russia, that the war thus far had stopped, and Dickens turned back to England with a resumption of all his old feelings. "I have had dreadful thoughts of getting away somewhere altogether by myself." He considered going to the Pyrenees, starting a new book "in all sorts of inaccessible places," "living in some astonishing convent" "above the snow-line in Switzerland." "*Restlessness*, you will say," he told Forster. "Whatever it is, it is always driving me, and I cannot help it." He had rested nine or ten weeks, and could bear idleness no more.

The cholera had taken its toll in London; throughout England and Wales it had killed 20,000 during the summer. Angrily Dickens wrote for the 7 October 1854 number of *Household Words* a paper of sharper tone than he had taken yet. He told his readers that unless they earnestly set about improving their towns and amending the dwellings of the poor, they were guilty of wholesale murder. He enjoined the working class to insist that they and their children had a "right to every means of life and health that Providence has provided for all."

Any working man of common intelligence, he continued, knew "that one session of parliament" could attain this object if it really wanted to. He charged the workers to make their voices heard, to call on the middle class to join with them, to unite and use the power of their numbers. They could see to it that the men who defied their needs were thrown out of office, and by Christmas there could be "a government in Downing Street and a House of Commons within hail of it, possessing not the faintest family resemblance to the Indifferents and Incapables last heard of in that slumberous neighbourhood."

So fiery an appeal made directly to the workers had a frightening sound to many readers. Most of the working class had no vote. Was the suggestion that they use their numbers to demand their will an invitation to violence? Or, hardly less horrifying, did it mean that Dickens approved of labour unions? (He did; he thought employers had left labour no other alternative, although, as *Hard Times* made clear, he believed labour leaders were often corrupt demagogues.) The article worried even Miss Coutts, who wrote Dickens that she was "in a maze" about it.

He was sorry, he replied. His meaning was simply that the people would never save themselves or their children from disease and death "until they have cheap water in unlimited quantity, wholesome air, constraint upon little landlords like our Westminster friends . . . efficient drainage, and such alterations in building acts" as would preserve open spaces and create new ones. But they would not receive the least attention from "a worthless Government which is afraid of every little interest and trembles before the vote of every dust contractor." Unless such a change were made, he stormily told Miss Coutts, the next return of the cholera might bring "such a shake in this country as never was seen on Earth since Samson pulled the Temple down upon his head."

He poured out the same feelings in letters to other friends. Writing Mrs Watson, he mingled "burning desires to cut the Emperor of Russia's throat" with an even fierier indignation at the wrongs of the people at home. He urged Macready to read in the next number of *Household Words* an article that ranked these problems of health and homes above the vote and the other reforms that had been emphasized in the People's Charter of 1838 and 1848. Let the people demand and by the strength of their union obtain the more substantial reforms in the very conditions under which they lived, said the article, and the political reforms would not fail to come too.

From this theme he turned to making arrangements with Macready for a reading of the *Christmas Carol* that he would be giving on 20 December at Sherborne, his old friend's Dorsetshire retreat, and expressed the pleasure with which he looked forward to their meeting. Dickens read the *Carol* at two other gatherings that December, one at Reading on the 19th, in memory of Talfourd, the other in aid of the Bradford Mechanics' Institute on the 28th.

The children's Twelfth-Night play for 1855 Dickens adapted from Planché's *Fortunio and His Seven Gifted Servants*. Large-lettered announcements heralded the "Reappearance of Mr H." (Henry Fielding Dickens) "who created so powerful an impression last year!" "Return of Mr Charles Dickens Junior from his German engagements!" "Engagement of Miss Kate, who declined the munificent offers of the Management last season!" "First appearance on any stage of Mr Plornishmaroontigoonter (who has been kept out of bed at a vast expense)."

Among the adult actors, a Mr Wilkini Collini played the small part of Gobbler, one of the seven gifted servants, and was "dreadfully greedy" in devouring property loaves. Mark Lemon, under the name of Mr Mudperiod, made a mountainous Dragon for Fortunio to subdue, and that small hero, the six-year-old Harry, watched with sly relish as the sherry with which he had adulterated the monster's drink demoralized his foe into helpless imbecility. As Mr Measly Servile, Dickens was "the Expectant Cousin of the Nobility in General," in which part he "constantly pervaded the stage" with "a fixed and propitiatory smile on his face." As Mr Passé he sang a song presumed to be sung by the Russian Czar:

> *A despot I am of the regular kind;*
> *I'm in a fierce mood and I'm out of my mind*
> *And man was created to swallow the pill*
> *Of my wrong-headed, Bull-headed absolute will.*

But none of these diversions could keep out of Dickens's mind for long his mounting anger at the way England's affairs were managed. The men who saw "figures and averages, and nothing else" were doing all the damage:

the addled heads who would take the average of cold in Crimea during twelve months as a reason for clothing a soldier in nankeens on a night when he would be frozen to death in fur, and comfort a labourer in travelling twelve miles a day to and from his work, by telling him that the average distance of one inhabited place from another in the whole area of England, is not more than four miles. Bah!

Reports were pouring home from the Crimea by this time of the shameful disorganization of supplies, the horrible bungling in the medical arrangements, and the frightful mortality in the military hospital at Scutari. In the House of Commons, Roebuck told in a faltering voice how out of an army of 54,000 men 40,000 had died in the course of a few months, of wounds, of fever, of frostbite, of dysentery and cholera. Men lay crowded in filth amid an intolerable stench in verminous hospitals without enough beds, with only canvas sheets, with no towels, soap, brooms, mops, trays, or plates, with scanty medical supplies, inadequate kitchens, preposterous laundries. Roebuck demanded an inquiry into the conduct of the war, and in the face of an overwhelming vote of censure the Aberdeen ministry resigned.

But for the new Government that was formed under the premiership of Lord Palmerston, Dickens had no more respect than he had felt for its predecessor. He wrote for *Household Words* a satiric parody of *The Arabian Nights*, which he called "The Thousand and One Humbugs," describing how "Abbadeen (or the Addled) . . . had for his misdeeds been strangled with a garter" and succeeded by "Parmarstoon (or Twirling Weathercock)," "the glib Vizier."

So Dickens expressed his distrust of any mere shuffling around of Coodle and Doodle to effect a change for the better. And once again his personal distress sounds in the midst of his political disillusion. He might go to Bordeaux or emigrate

to the mountain-ground between France and Spain. Am altogether in a dishevelled state of mind – notes of new books in the dirty air, miseries of older growth threatening to close upon me. Why is it, that as with poor David, a sense always comes crushing upon me now, when I fall into low spirits, as of one happiness I have missed in life, and one friend and companion I have never made?

On his birthday he dined at Gravesend with a group of friends and afterwards walked the road to Rochester between walls of snow six feet high. Just to get away somewhere, he had desperately determined on a trip to Paris and persuaded Collins to accompany him. They would have a week of indulgence, dining out every night, and throwing themselves "*en garçon* on the festive *diableries de Paris*." On Saturday, 10 February 1855, all his arrangements were made for leaving the following morning. He sat in his study reading by the fire. A handful of letters was brought in and laid on his table. He looked them over carelessly but, recognizing the handwriting of no friend, let them lie there and went back to his book.

But as he sat there he found his mind wandering away through so many years to such early times of his life, that he was perplexed to account for it. At last it came into his head that it must have been something in the look of one of those letters. So he turned them over again – and suddenly did recognize the handwriting of one of them. A riot of heartbreaking memory welled up in him as he remembered the hand of Maria Beadnell! a tumult of pain and ecstasy reborn out of those dead days and alive again in a moment! "Three or four and twenty years vanished like a dream," he wrote her, "and I opened it with the touch of my young friend David Copperfield when he was in love."

It was indeed Maria, writing so pleasantly and affectionately of the past that it all rose magically before him, filled with the fragrance of a "Spring in which I was either much more wise or much more foolish than I am now," but when certainly "the qualities that have done me most good since, were growing in my boyish heart." She was married now, he learned from her letter, to a merchant named Henry Louis Winter, and had two little girls. "In the unsettled state of my thoughts," he replied, "the existence of these dear children appeared such a pro-digious phenomenon, that I was inclined to suspect myself of being out of my mind, until it occurred to me that perhaps I had nine children of my own!"

He was going to Paris the next day, he told her, but when he returned Catherine would call to arrange a day for having her and her husband to a quiet private dinner. Meanwhile if he could discharge any com-mission for her or bring home anything for her little girls she had only to write him there. He ended in an emotion in which he avowed that there was something a little sorrowful. "The associations my memory has with you made your letter more – I want a word – invest it with a more immediate address to me than such a letter could have from anybody else."

In Paris he could think of nothing but Maria, although his letters home did not mention her. But he could not resist talking about her to Lady Olliffe. Was it "really true," she asked, "that I used to love Maria Beadnell so very, very, very much? I told her there was no woman in the world, and there were very few men, who could ever imagine how much."

So he wrote Maria, for she took advantage of his suggestion that he might get something for her children by requesting two brooches. He wondered if she had seen in *David Copperfield*

a faithful reflection of the passion I had for you, and in little bits of "Dora" touches of your old self sometimes and a grace here and there that may be revived in your little girls . . . People used to say to me how pretty all that was, and how fanciful it was, and how elevated it was above the little foolish loves of very young men and women. But they little thought what reason I had to know it was true and nothing more nor less.

All the romance, energy, passion, hope, and determination of his nature, he told her, were inseparable from her. He had never heard anybody addressed by her name without a start.

The sound of it has always filled me with a kind of pity and respect for the deep truth that I had, in my silly hobbledehoyhood, to bestow upon one creature who represented the whole world to me. I have never been so good a man since, as I was when you made me wretchedly happy. I shall never be half so good a fellow any more. . . .
These are things that I have locked up in my own breast and that I never thought to bring out any more. But when I find myself writing to you again "all to yourself," how can I forbear to let as much light upon them as will shew you that they are still there! If the most innocent, the most ardent, and the most disinterested days of my life had you for their Sun – as indeed they had . . . how can I receive a confidence from you, and return it, and make a feint of blotting all this out!

Perhaps, he suggested, she would write him another letter – "all to myself," he quoted her – while he was still in Paris. It arrived after he had left, but followed him immediately to London.

Ah! Though it is so late to read in the old hand what I never read before, I have read it with great emotion, and with the old tenderness softened to a more sorrowful remembrance than I could easily tell

417

you. How it all happened as it did, we shall never know this side of Time; but if you had ever told me then what you tell me now, I know myself well enough to be thoroughly assured that the simple truth and energy which were in my love would have overcome everything.

We can only infer what Maria had written him; from this time, as from their earlier days, none of her letters have been found. But Dickens's words can have no other meaning than that Maria said she had loved him in those days and that they had been separated by misunderstandings. And, on Dickens's part, that he accepted and believed her explanations. But now, she told him, she was "toothless, fat, old and ugly" – "which I don't believe," he answered. Only within the last twelve months he had wandered the streets he used to walk when they were falling apart from each other asking himself "whether any reputation the world can bestow is repayment to a man for the loss of such a vision of his youth as mine. You ask me to treasure what you tell me, in my heart of hearts. O see what I have cherished there, through all this time and all these changes!"

Maria must have suggested that they meet each other alone before the family dinner that Kate was to arrange. Dickens wrote her, "I am a dangerous man to be seen with, for so many people know me. At St Paul's the Dean and the whole chapter know me. In Paternoster Row of all places, the very tiles and chimney pots know me." Still, he too would feel more at ease if they met first before others were by. Would she not like, he suggested, to call at Tavistock House on Sunday, "asking first for Catherine and then for me? It is almost a positive certainty that there will be none here but I, between 3 and 4.... If you think you would not like to come here, make no change. I will come there."

"Remember," he ended passionately, "I accept all with my whole soul, and reciprocate all."

Who knows what rapturous, impossible dreams, what rainbow-hued visions, were swirling deliriously through his mind? Eagerly he believed that they had been separated only by misunderstandings now swept away like a mist. The days that had had her for their sun were almost as if they had never ceased to be. The tremulous notes of a harp long unheard were sounding once more in his ears with an ecstatic music. What would happen after they met – what enchantment melting away the dissonances of his life?

As for Maria, her hopes and intentions are as inscrutable as her true feelings had been in earlier days. Possibly she had no clear purposes at all when she first wrote, and found herself caught up by the intensity of his response in a blurred, breathless excitement. But she was neither shocked nor frightened: she made him an avowal that she asked him "to treasure in his heart of hearts," she proposed a rendezvous at which neither her husband nor his wife should be present. And what could she have told him in her letter that elicited that last earnest outcry: "Remember, I accept all with my whole soul, and reciprocate all"?

Dickens himself was in a feverish beatific haze of blinding emotion. In his letters to Maria he cast all reserve to the winds. Only on the surface was he careful to maintain the proprieties by arranging to have Catherine call on Maria and invite her and her husband to dinner. And in Paris, Lady Olliffe may well have suspected that his love for Maria Beadnell was not all a memory of days gone by. But it is uncertain if he had any aims beyond the tense anticipations of the immediate moment and if his thoughts extended into an envisioned future.

Whether Maria came to Tavistock House or Dickens met her elsewhere, on Sunday 25 February, they did see each other alone. Surely Dickens knew that at forty-four Maria could hardly be the same ethereal vision he remembered. Nevertheless, for all her warning, he was surprised to find her so undeniably fat. But it was not the physical change that was shattering. The gay little laugh had turned into a silly giggle. The delightful little voice, running on in such enchanting nonsense, had become a muddleheaded and disjointed volubility. The prettily pettish flirtatious little ways, the arch glances and tones of voice that suggested a secret understanding, were merely ridiculous affectations in a middle-aged woman. What had happened to the fascinations that had captivated him? Or, still worse, was it possible that Maria had always been this absurd and brainless chatterer, that her angelic charm had been only the radiant hallucination of youth?

Even more terrifying, this stout monster, "tossing her head with a caricature of her girlish manner," throwing him the most distressing imitations of the old glances, behaved as if this private meeting involved them in some intimate agreement. But "this grotesque revival" of what had "once been prettily natural to her" was now like an attempt to resuscitate an old play "when the stage was dusty, when the scenery was faded, when the youthful actors were dead, when the orchestra was empty, when the lights were out."

All these things he wrote, months later, in *Little Dorrit*, where Flora Finching is avowedly suggested by Maria's reappearance in his life. "Flora, whom he had left a lily, had become a peony; but that was not much. Flora, who had seemed enchanting in all she said and thought, was diffuse and silly. That was much. Flora, who had been spoiled and artless long ago, was determined to be spoiled and artless now. That was a fatal blow."

The shock was frightful. With an appalling jolt he came down to earth. The shining dream disappeared like a mirage in a desert. And yet, even in the midst of his disturbance, he could see in the foolish creature traces of something warmhearted that gave her a touch of pathos. And beneath her discursive babble too, he realized, she had in a rush of intuition perceived that he was disappointed. It distressed him, both for the sake of what had been and in sympathy for her now, to give her pain. Gently he endeavoured to conceal his feelings; somehow the meeting ended.

But he could not keep his agitation and distress to himself. Desperate, he confided in Forster, who was incredulous, and thought he must be exaggerating his emotions. Dickens replied,

I don't quite apprehend what you mean by my over-rating the strength of the feeling of twenty-five years ago. . . . Without for a moment sincerely believing that it would have been better if we had never got separated, I cannot see the occasion of so much emotion as I should see anyone else. No one can imagine in the most distant degree what pain the recollection gave me in Copperfield. And, just as I can never open that book as I open any other book, I cannot see the face (even at four-and-forty), or hear the voice, without going wandering away over the ashes of all that youth and hope in the wildest manner.

The family dinner that had been arranged was still to be endured. It took place on 7 March. Mr Winter was a prosy and colourless merchant. Maria was only a silly, kindly, fat woman, not markedly different from his middle-aged, rather red-faced wife. Despite a cold, Maria tittered and chattered at his side, and Dickens caught her cold. "I think," he wrote her, with an effort at playfulness, "I heard somebody sneezing at my desk half the day yesterday, who sounded like the incomparable author." For in spite of her suspicion of his feelings, Maria had not given up, and wrote again, insinuating her hopes of reassurance.

Dickens tried not to sound cruel. But her proposal that she call on Sunday with her little girl he answered evasively. He had promised to participate in "some public literary business," and Sunday might be the day chosen for the meeting. When the day came he did not return home until she was gone. He tried to soften the effect of his absence by sending a few weeks later tickets for a box at the Adelphi and saying that if his work for *Household Words* allowed he would turn up there in the course of the evening. Once again, though, when the evening came he was not there.

Maria tried to see him the next day, and the day after that, but both times he went out. She wrote him a reproachful letter, accusing him of trying to avoid her. Surely he could see her for half an hour? She simply did not understand, he replied,

> the restlessness or waywardness of an author's mind. . . . "It is only half an hour" – "it is only an afternoon" – "it is only an evening" – people say to me over and over again – but they don't know that it is impossible to command one's self sometimes to any stipulated and set disposal of five minutes – or that the mere consciousness of an engagement will sometimes worry a whole day. These are the penalties paid for writing books. Whoever is devoted to an Art must be content to deliver himself wholly up to it, and to find his recompense in it. I am grieved if you suspect me of not wanting to see you; but I can't help it; I must go my way, whether or no. . . .
>
> I am going off, I don't know where or how far, to ponder about I don't know what.

He might go to France, or to the seacoast to walk the shore for four months, or to Switzerland. Last week he had vowed he would go to Spain.

> Two days afterwards Layard and I agreed to go to Constantinople when Parliament rises. Tomorrow I shall probably discuss with somebody else, the idea of going to Greenland or the North Pole. The end of all this, most likely will be that I shall shut myself up in some out of the way place I have never yet thought of, and go desperately to work there.
>
> Once upon a time I didn't do such things, you say. No, but I have done them through a good many years now, and they have become myself and my life.

With these words he went his way for a second time. But this time it was Maria who was dismissed. He wrote her a sympathetic note when her baby died. But she was irrevocably removed from his life.

Nevertheless, the whole experience had shaken him almost unbelievably. He felt, he wrote Leigh Hunt, "as infirm of purpose as Macbeth, as errant as Mad Tom, and as ragged as Timon." He rejected all engagements. "I am in a state of restlessness," he told Miss Coutts, "impossible to be described – impossible to be imagined – wearing and tearing to be experienced."

His emotional strain was in fact heading inexorably towards a crisis. It deepened the bitterness with which he felt the desperate state of the nation.

> A country which is discovered to be in this tremendous condition [he wrote Forster] as to its war affairs; with an enormous black cloud of poverty in every town which is spreading and deepening every hour, and not one man in two thousand knowing anything about, or even believing in, its existence; with a non-working aristocracy, and a silent parliament, and everybody for himself and nobody for the rest; this is the prospect . . .

As his indignation at these evils fermented with his personal agitation they produced an inward disturbance that exploded with more than ordinary violence. He joined fiercely with Austen Layard in a flaming public attack on the incompetence and indifference of the Government. But even the molten vitriol he poured into this denunciation was insufficient to release his pent-up feelings. He simultaneously plunged into all the excitement of producing another play, alternately bullying his cast and blasting the administration. And while he was doing both together, he began wrestling with the conception of his next novel, a story in which existence itself, for rich and for poor, for the imprisoned and the free, is seen as no more than confinement in a variety of jails.

38

Nobody's Fault

With this sense of frustration on every hand, Dickens was possessed more than ever by the need for furious action. The conduct of the war was just one further disgraceful proof of the incompetence and indifference to human suffering that produced a thousand evils at home. Now, as radical member for Aylesbury, Layard was pressing vehemently for administrative reform. Dickens promised staunch cooperation.

He would enlist Mark Lemon's support as editor of *Punch*, and their friend Shirley Brooks would use the *Weekly Chronicle* and the *Illustrated London News* to bring the issues home to their large bodies of readers. He would also speak to Forster, little as that seemed needed. And, "if you ever see any new loophole, cranny, needle's-eye, through which I can present your case in Household Words, I most earnestly entreat you . . . to count upon my being Damascus Steel to the core."

Layard was obstructed in Parliament, of course, with every procedural dodge, and before the public with every device of misrepresentation. When he finally got his motion before the House it was defeated by a vote of 359 to 46. He countered the rejection of his demands with a direct appeal to a discontented public. Miss Coutts, troubled, told Dickens she feared Layard was setting class against class. "The upper class had taken the initiative years ago," Dickens retorted, "and it is *they* who have put *their* class in opposition to the country – not the country which puts itself in opposition to *them*."

The sullen discontent in the country, he was convinced, was "the worse for smouldering, instead of blazing openly"; it was "like the general mind of France before the breaking out of the first Revolution." Any of a thousand accidents – "a bad harvest – the last strain too much of aristocratic insolence or incapacity – a defeat abroad – a mere chance at home" – could precipitate "such a devil of a conflagration as never has been beheld since."

Dickens attended a meeting at which it was decided to organize an Administrative Reform Association, and subscribed £20. He agreed to take the chair at a public meeting to be held at Drury Lane in June. At the annual dinner of the General Theatrical Fund he contrasted the efficiency of dramatic enterprises with governmental blundering in the Crimea. Unlike the War Department, he said, when the Haymarket Theatre staged a battle scene necessary supplies were not "found packed under 500 tons of iron," nor did it prove impossible "to fire a shot because they had all been left somewhere where they were not wanted." Rounds of applause greeted this sardonic hit.

At the same time Dickens was publishing in *Household Words* attacks upon the administration. His "Thousand and One Humbugs" article he followed up with another called "Scarli Tapa and the Forty Thieves," in which the robbers' cave, "with the enchanted letters O.F.F.I.C.E.," is entered by pronouncing the words "Debrett's Peerage. Open Sesame!" and in which Scarli Tapa, instead of slaying the thieves, forms an alliance with their Captain. The following week Dickens satirized Palmerston, the Premier, as the talkative barber, Praymiah, "a frisky speaker, an easy shaver, a touch-and-go joker, a giver of the go-by to all complainers," who never did the work he was hired to do, but instead constantly "danced the dance of Mistapit, and sang the song of Mistafoks, and joked the joke of Jomillah."

Hardly a week went by that Dickens was not hammering away in all manner of forms at the same points. Parliament, "with its feeble jokes, logic-chopping, straw-splitting, tape-tying, tape-untying to tie again, double-shuffling, word-eating," was plainly "the house of Parler and Mentir," the place of wordiness and lies. Why was it that even when a reform was promised it always turned out to consist of dismissing a few clerks at £90 a year and retaining all their incompetent superiors? Was it not obvious "that any half-dozen shopkeepers taken at random from the London Directory and shot into Downing Street out of sacks" could do a better job than these Red-Tapers and Sealing-Wax-Chafers?

Meanwhile Dickens was pushing ahead with the plans for his play. Collins had written "a regular old-style melodrama" called *The Lighthouse* which Dickens intended to put on in the children's theatre. He asked Clarkson Stanfield to paint the one scene, the interior of the lighthouse. "O, what a pity it is not the outside of the Light'us, with the sea a-rowling agin it! . . . So hooroar for the salt sea, Mate, and bowse up!"

Stanfield was soon in the schoolroom "all day long with his coat off," and "up to his eyes in distemper." In addition to the interior he painted a curtain drop showing the Eddystone Light in a raging storm. Dickens dominated rehearsals with his usual relentless determination to obtain perfection. Charley, who operated the "wind-machine" that produced storm effects said later, "I could always tell by the very look of my father's shoulders . . . as he sat on the stage with his back to me that he was ready for the smallest mistake."

Four successive audiences crowded the tiny schoolroom theatre on the nights of 15, 16, 18, and 19 June. Dickens played the role of Aaron Gurnock, the old lighthouse keeper, with wild picturesqueness. All the guests cried plentifully during the melodrama and cheered the farce. Among them, with her son, was Mrs Frederick Yates, who had played Dolly Varden and Sikes's Nancy in the old days at the Adelphi. She wept so profusely that she still had "a large, red circle round each eye," and exclaimed, "O Mr Dickens what a pity it is you can do anything else!"

The production created such a furore that Dickens was asked to present the play again for the benefit of the Bournemouth Sanatorium for Consumptives on 10 July. Campden House, Kensington, which had a private theatre with orchestra, boxes, stage, and footlights, was offered by its owner, Colonel Waugh, to accommodate a larger audience. The charitable performance too came off well.

From this Dickens reverted to the larger drama on the national stage. He was entirely in accord with Layard's accusation that Government blue books revealed "records of inefficiency, records of indifference to suffering, records of ignorance, records of obstinacy," that disgraced the nation. Lord Palmerston, personally, Layard denounced for an attitude of levity towards the sufferings of the people.

Stung by the attack, Palmerston retorted with a sneer about "the private theatricals at Drury Lane." At a second Drury Lane meeting on the 27th, Dickens built the first part of his speech around Palmerston's contemptuous epithet, "I have some slight acquaintance with theatricals, private and public," he said ominously, "and I will accept that figure of the noble lord. I will not say that if I wanted to form a company of her Majesty's servants, I think I should know where to put my hand on 'the comic old gentleman'; nor, that if I wanted to get up a pantomime, I fancy I should know what establishment to go to for the tricks and changes . . ." But he *would* tell the reason for these "private theatricals":

The public theatricals which the noble lord is so condescending as to manage are so intolerably bad, the machinery is so cumbrous, the parts so ill-distributed, the company so full of "walking gentlemen," the managers have such large families, and are so bent upon putting those families into what is theatrically called "first business" – not because of their aptitude for it, but because they *are* their families, that we find ourselves obliged to organize an opposition. We have seen the *Comedy of Errors* played so dismally like a tragedy that we really cannot bear it. We are therefore making bold to get up the *School of Reform*, and we hope, before the play is out, to improve that noble lord by our performance very considerably.

Three objections, Dickens noted, had been made to the Reform Association. First, that it proposed to influence the House of Commons. But the House *was* influenced by interests not at all favourable to the welfare of the people, and needed to be watched and jogged and hustled and pinched into doing its duty. Second, that the Association set class against class. This was mere parrot prattle. Suppose a gentleman to have a crew of incompetent servants, who gave his children stones instead of bread, serpents instead of fish, who consulted "exploded cookery books in the South" when they were ordered to serve "dinner in the North," who wasted and brought everything to ruin. And then, when he says, "I must have servants who will do their duty," his steward cries in pious horror, "Good God, master, you are setting class against class!" The third objection was that the reformers should mind their own business. To which the answer was that this was their business. "Let the hon. gentleman find a day for himself," Lord Palmerston had said scornfully when Mr Layard first asked for a day to present his motion. "Name you the day, First Lord," Dickens warned; "make a day, work for a day beyond your little time . . . and History may then – not otherwise – find a day for you . . ."

The mood that burned in this address was not absent from the new novel he had already started to write. He had experienced more than ordinary difficulty in making a beginning – distraught far beyond anything that getting under way had ever involved before. All his growing personal distress and the excitement and disillusion of seeing Maria again had a part in his feverish state – as did the labours of producing *The Lighthouse* and the blows he was striking for administrative reform. But the immediate source of his difficulty and his tension was the problem of shaping a story that should symbolize the condition of England.

His desire was to portray a vast impersonal system of inefficiency, venality, and evil, baffling all endeavour to fasten responsibility anywhere. No pattern would do which permitted his readers to imagine isolated individual mischiefs as more than small parts of a corrupt social whole. Not until after he had written the first four numbers and the book was on the verge of publication, did he substitute the name *Little Dorrit* for the bitterly ironic title *Nobody's Fault*.

The great structure that he finally evolved integrated his criticism into a whole of remarkable intellectual and artistic power. All the things he wanted to emphasize were there, connected with each other in dozens of ways. There was the rack-renting of the poor for the profit of their exploiters in the benevolent Casby extorting every last farthing from the inhabitants of Bleeding Heart Yard. There was the obstructionism of a bureaucracy that entangled justice and encumbered progress in the convoluted procedures of the Circumlocution Office. There was the sinister alliance between political leadership and the unscrupulous interests that wielded financial power, in the negotiations between Lord Decimus Tite Barnacle and the slinking financial manipulator Merdle. Both literally and symbolically all are linked in the entire political, financial, and social structure of the country.

Even after these major elements in his design were settled, however, the writing remained a struggle. Finally, around 21 May, Dickens got into the first chapter. But throughout the end of that month he made little headway, filling his manuscript with interlineations and erasures. During June and the earlier part of July he was still wrestling with the first number.

He was exasperated beyond bearing by the fact that Layard's reform endeavours were being completely smothered in Parliament. Dining at Lord John Russell's, Dickens "gave them a little bit of truth . . . that was like bringing a Sebastopol battery among the polite company," and Meyerbeer, the composer, said admiringly, "Ah, mon ami illustre! que c'est noble de vous entendre parler d'haute voix morale, à la table d'un ministre!"

From the middle of July, Dickens rented 3 Albion Villas, Folkestone, a pleasant little house overlooking the sea. Here he hoped to write enough of his book to have a comfortable backlog before it began publication in December. At first he found himself utterly unable to concentrate; all the boys were home from school and their feet constantly stamped up and down the wooden stairs. "Why a boy of that age should seem to have on at all times, 150 pairs of double soled boots, and to be always jumping a bottom stair with the whole 150, I don't know." But at the end of the month Walter went back to his school at Wimbledon, and at the end of August, Frank and Alfred returned to their school at Boulogne, taking with them their eight-year-old brother, Sydney, leaving little Harry and Plorn the only small boys remaining with the family.

By the middle of August Dickens had finished the first number and started the second. His superfluous vitality he expended "in swarming up the face of a gigantic and precipitous cliff in a lonely spot overhanging the wild sea-beach." With the completion of the second number he felt steeped in his story, rising and falling by turns into enthusiasm and depression. "There is an enormous outlay in the Father of the Marshalsea chapter, in the way of getting a great lot of matter into a small space." As always, he was coming to live in his tale and feel as if it pervaded all the world around him, "heaving in the sea, flying with the clouds, blowing in the wind." The end of September saw the virtual completion of "No. 3, in which I have relieved my soul," Dickens told Collins, "with a scarifier" – the satiric tenth chapter on the Circumlocution Office, "How Not to Do It," "Containing the Whole Science of Government."

Some details in the portrayal of William Dorrit, "the Father of the Marshalsea" – his insistence on being regarded as a gentleman, his pompous speech, the way his nervous hands wander to his trembling lips – are indubitably derived from Dickens's childhood memories of his father's first imprisonment. But Mr Dorrit is not a deeper attempt to understand John Dickens: Mr Dorrit had not been brought to prison by improvidence, and John Dickens's improvidence was the cause, not the consequence, of his prison experiences. Mr Dorrit's helplessness, his humiliation, his snobbery, and his shame are instead an amazingly brilliant feat of character creation, drawn with wonderful subtlety and psychological penetration.

The Circumlocution Office symbolizes all the forces of petrifaction that obstruct every fruitful and creative endeavour. It is no such limited thing as a single Government department, no single aristocratic bureaucracy, not even all bureaucracies. Instead it is a hardening of the arteries that penetrates all institutions, the imprisonment of habit, custom, established convention, swollen to monstrous power, and confirmed by inertia, profit, selfishness, and privilege. It is rigidity grown supreme.

Shortly before Dickens left for Paris, where he planned to spend the autumn and winter, he was pleased to feel that he had gotten his eldest son started in life. Charley, now eighteen, was back from Leipzig since the previous Christmas – presumably with a sufficient stock of German. Dickens had consulted with Miss Coutts, who held out hopes of a post with a firm trading in Turkey, and he had friends in Birmingham who were willing to recommend the young man to a position there. On the advice of one of the partners in Baring Brothers, Charley was put in a London brokers' office. After he had been there six months, the same gentleman told Dickens there was an opening in Baring's. "I expect the Brokers," Dickens commented, "to have been a device and trial altogether – to get a telescopic view of a youth with a double suspicion on him arising out of his being an author's son and an Eton boy." On 24 September Charley assumed his new duties.

There were still a number of engagements Dickens had to fill before his departure for France. On 4 October he read the *Christmas Carol* for the benefit of an educational institution at Folkestone. And on 11 October he presided over a farewell dinner for Thackeray, who was sailing for America to give a series of lectures on *The Four Georges*. Two days later Thackeray sailed from Liverpool and Dickens crossed the Channel to Boulogne. Georgina had by this time almost completely superseded Catherine in the direction of all domestic matters, and had gone ahead to Paris to take an apartment for the family. Here Dickens joined her, leaving Catherine at Boulogne with the children. Paris was crowded and insanely expensive. Finally an entresol and first floor were found at 49 Avenue des Champs Élysées, near the Barrière de l'Étoile, with six small sunlit rooms looking out on the busy street and lots of others tucked away inside.

The first night there, however, proved the place to be dreadfully dirty. Next morning Dickens routed out the porter, the porter's wife, her sister, various other helpers, and the old lady and little man with a François Premier beard who were owners of the apartment, and demanded that it be cleaned. They were astounded: "It's not the custom," they urged. But gradually they wavered, offered "new carpets (accepted), embraces (not accepted)," and at last responded "like French Bricks." Dickens stalked coatless and dirty-faced through the rooms in a fury of "stage-managerial energies" until by nightfall they were purified to spotlessness.

Soon afterwards, Catherine arrived with Mamey and Katey and the two little boys. Through the six windows facing on the wide avenue the children could watch the constant parading of the regiments marching out to drill in the country and straggling back picturesquely in the afternoon. Sometimes "great storms of drums played, and then the most delicious and skilful bands, Trovatore music, Barber of Seville music," with "all bloused Paris" following "in a sort of hilarious dance."

Again would come striding the Zouaves, sunburnt, with red petticoat trousers and wild beards and moustaches, preceded by their regimental mascot, a little black dog marching "with a profound conviction that he was decorated."

Dickens was now well-known in France through numerous translations. On his arrival he found that daily instalments of *Chuzzlewit* were being published in the *Moniteur,* and it was impossible for him to give his name in a shop without being greeted enthusiastically. "Ah! The famous writer! Monsieur bears a very distinguished name. But! I am honoured and interested to see Monsieur Dick-in." A man who delivered some vases Dickens had bought was ecstatic about Mrs Todgers. "That Madame Tojair . . . Ah! How droll, and exactly like a lady I know at Calais!" In addition to these personal tributes, the *Revue des Deux Mondes* carried in February 1856, a critical article by Hippolyte Taine, "Charles Dickens, son talent et ses oeuvres," proclaiming his European importance and emphasizing his significance as a social critic. To round out the circle of his recognition in France, the publishing house of Hachette arranged with Dickens to bring out a uniform edition of all his novels in a carefully supervised translation.

He now mingled constantly with the most distinguished artists and men of letters in Paris. At the dinner table of Eugène Scribe he met Auber, whose *Manon Lescaut* was having its première at the Opéra Comique. On another evening he dined with Amédée Pichot, director of the *Revue Britannique* and translator of *David Copperfield.* Here he renewed his acquaintance with Lamartine. They talked of the genius of Richardson and Defoe, and Lamartine complimented "ce cher Boz" on his command of French, "whereat your correspondent blushed modestly" and at once "choked himself with the bone of a fowl (which is still in his throat)."

The Scribes were among the guests at dinner, and Dickens was fascinated by Mme Scribe's youthfulness and beauty. Her eldest son, he said, "must be thirty, and she has the figure of five-and-twenty, and is strikingly handsome." And Mme Régnier and Pauline Viardot, the operatic mezzo-soprano – how did these women retain their grace and charm! It was an observation, though, that he could not make about George Sand. The famous novelist was a "chubby, matronly, swarthy, black-eyed" woman, "whom you might suppose to be the Queen's monthly nurse," with "nothing of the bluestocking about her, except a little final way of settling all your opinions with hers."

Nothing in Paris startled Dickens more than the glittering opulence of the Second Empire and the mania for speculation among all classes. Even the writers had made fortunes on the Bourse. Scribe had a delightful apartment in town, a château in the country, and a "sumptuous carriage and magnificent span of horse." Eugène Sue lived surrounded by pictures, statues, and antiquities, in an ornate apartment with hothouses bursting with flowers and fountains playing on gold and silver fish. But most magnificent of all was the press magnate Émile de Girardin, who in addition to owning the great political organ, *La Presse*, ran a whole string of weekly magazines, and had built up stupendous wealth in financial manipulations.

Writing with some slight hyperbole, perhaps, Dickens described a dinner at Girardin's. There were "three gorgeous drawing rooms with ten thousand wax candles in golden sconces," a table piled with mounds of truffles, iced champagne in ground-glass jugs, "Oriental flowers in vases of golden cobweb," "Cigarettes from the Hareem of the Sultan," cool drinks flavoured with lemons just arrived from Algeria and oranges from Lisbon, "a far larger plum pudding than ever was seen in England at Christmas time," and described in a gold-framed menu as "Hommage à l'illustre écrivain d'Angleterre." "That illustrious man staggered out at the last drawing-room door," only to be told by his host, "The dinner we have had, mon cher, is nothing – doesn't count – was quite en famille – we must dine (really dine) soon. Au plaisir! Au revoir! Au dîner!"

On a later occasion, after a banquet terminating with every guest being served "a flower pot out of a ballet . . . piled to the brim with the ruddiest fresh strawberries," Girardin asked Dickens if he would like a cigar. "On my replying yes, he opened, with a key attached to his watch-chain, a species of mahogany cave, which appeared to me to extend under the Champs Élysées, and in which were piled about four hundred thousand inestimable cigars, in bundles or bales of about a thousand each." Among the other diners was a little man "who was blacking shoes 8 years ago, and is now enormously rich – the richest man in Paris – having ascended with rapidity up the usual ladder of the Bourse. By merely observing that perhaps he might come down again, I clouded so many faces as to render it very clear to me that *everybody present* was at the same game for some stake or other!"

The madness of luxury and gambling on the market, in fact, was a fever throughout the city.

If you were to see the steps of the Bourse at about 4 in the

afternoon, and the crowd of blouses and patches among the speculators there assembled, all howling and haggard . . . you would stand
aghast at the consideration of what must be going on. Concierges and
people like that perpetually blow their brains out, or fly into the
Seine, "à cause des pertes sur la Bourse." On the other hand, thor-
oughbred horses without end, and red velvet carriages with white kid
harness on jet black horses, go by here all day long; and the pedestrians who turn to look at them, laugh, and say, "C'est la Bourse!"

These scenes incontestably deepened the hues in which Dickens later
painted the splendour of the Merdle banquets and the widespread ruin
following the crash of the Merdle fortune. But meanwhile the distractions of Paris were making it hard for him even to find time to work on
Little Dorrit. Before he had been there a week Ary Scheffer had expressed
a desire to do his portrait. As Dickens sat to him daily throughout most
of November he was driven almost wild at being kept away from his
desk. Ultimately, as the sittings were prolonged into the following year,
he was privately calling it "the nightmare portrait," and chafing
desperately at his bondage.

Nevertheless, he drove away doggedly at *Little Dorrit*, and managed
to get the first three numbers finished by the time the opening number
was published in December. As it developed, it rendered ever more
darkly his vision of the modern world. Despite its sombre atmosphere,
however, the story from the beginning commanded a greater audience
than Dickens had ever had before.

The day after the first number went on sale, "Little Dorrit has beaten
even Bleak House out of the field," Dickens wrote. "It is a most tremendous start, and I am overjoyed at it." Soon Bradbury and Evans
were proposing that they greatly increase the £200 they paid him each
month, in order to diminish the half-yearly balance, and Dickens made
no objection. "It will be as useful to me in six large portions and a
moderate lump, as in six small portions and a great lump."

He had been in London for a week at the beginning of November,
and in the middle of December he made another brief trip to England
to read the *Christmas Carol* for the benefit of Mechanics' Institutes at
Peterborough and Sheffield. Before the Peterborough reading on the
18th, Dickens spent an evening at Rockingham Castle with Mrs Watson
and saw dear Mary Boyle again, dashed back to London, and then went
to Sheffield for the 22nd.

On the 24th he returned to Paris, and resumed work on *Little Dorrit* with such energy that he finished the fourth number on the very last day of the year. The effort left him feeling depressed and overworked. He was therefore more than usually irritated when the articles on factory accidents which he had been running in *Household Words* were attacked by Harriet Martineau, who had often appeared in its pages. In a violent and one-sided pamphlet published by the National Association of Manufacturers she accused *Household Words* of "unscrupulous statements, insolence, arrogance, and cant."

Dickens had Henry Morley, the author of most of the factory articles, write a reply, which appeared on 18 January under the title of "Our Wicked Misstatements." Impeccably polite, the rejoinder smashed Miss Martineau's every argument. It proved that her statistics on factory accidents were grossly underestimated and based upon sophistical definitions of terms. It showed that the Association of Manufacturers was in purpose and in fact organized to support its members in defying the law. It courteously rebuked the lady's own controversial manners in calling those who wished to see the law enforced "Passionate advocates of meddling legislation" and in dismissing their viewpoint as "philo-operative cant." Miss Martineau tried to claim that the wise and witty Sydney Smith would have taken her position; where he would really have stood was shown by a paper in which he had described the fatalities among the climbing boys as "burning little chimney-sweepers." "What is a toasted child," Smith had asked with grim irony, "compared to the agonies of the mistress of the house with a deranged dinner?"

With the revised proofs of this article Dickens sent back another piece by Morley which he insisted on having drastically rewritten. He would not have *Household Words* say of the strike in Manchester that the men were "*of course* entirely and painfully in the wrong," and he would not be represented as believing that strikes were never justified. He deplored the waste, the angry passions, and the occasional destruction and violence caused by strikes, but what other recourse had those unhappy workers who could not obtain a peaceful hearing? "Nor can I possibly adopt the representation that these men are wrong because, by throwing themselves out of work, they throw other people, possibly without their consent." Such a principle would have meant no resistance to Charles I; "no raising by Hampden of a troop of Horse, to the detriment of Buckinghamshire Agriculture; no self-sacrifice in the political world. And O Good God when Morley treats of the suffering of wife and children," does he suppose the men themselves don't "feel it in the depths of their hearts" and believe devoutly and faithfully "that for those very children when they shall have children, they are bearing all these miseries now!"

In early February Dickens had to make another trip to London on business. He attended a meeting of the Theatrical Fund, checked up on the running of Miss Coutts's Home at Shepherd's Bush, looked into how Charley was getting on at Baring Brothers – learning that his son had done so well that he had been given a bonus of £10 and an increase in salary of £10 a year. He also succeeded in certain efforts he had been making to aid W. H. Wills.

In the previous June, Wills had been offered the editorship of the *Civil Service Gazette*, and asked Dickens if there was any objection to his assuming its duties concurrently with his work as subeditor of *Household Words*. Dickens objected strongly, and Wills dropped the idea. But, aware that his subordinate needed to supplement his income, when Dickens learned from Miss Coutts in November that she desired a confidential secretary to administer her charitable work, he promptly recommended Wills. The duties would not interfere with his work on *Household Words*. Miss Coutts took two months in finally making up her mind, but now decided to offer Wills the position at £200 a year. This offer Wills gladly accepted.

At the same time Forster, who had been feeling that he was not sufficiently consulted about *Household Words* and had come to resent Wills, determined to sever his connection with the magazine. For the last two years he had professed himself too busy to contribute to its pages, but it had been agreed that he should retain his one eighth share on condition of paying his co-proprietors £1,000 by February 1856. But the "Lincolnian Mammoth" was "in bad spirit," Dickens said; perhaps, too, he was annoyed that Dickens was excitedly looking forward to having Wilkie Collins visit him in Paris, but did not press *him* to come. Forster had failed to make the payment, and Dickens immediately bestowed half of the relinquished share on Wills for so long as he should remain subeditor of the magazine.

Forster's step did not mean, of course, that he was terminating his friendship with Dickens, although certainly they were less close than they had been before Wills became Dickens's trusted lieutenant on *Household Words* and Collins took Forster's place as a boon companion. Forster was changed, like everything else in Dickens's life; he had grown burly, broad-faced, authoritative, with a pugnacious jaw, stern features, a booming voice; and dinners at his table were solemn affairs.

On one occasion, after a quarrel with Browning, he gave a reconciliation banquet. When dinner was over, Carlyle lit up his pipe and two young men thereupon ventured to light cigars, only to receive a majestic rebuke: "I never allow smoking in this room, save on this privileged occasion when my old friend Carlyle honours me. But I do not extend that to you Robert Lytton, or to you Percy Fitzgerald." And although Forster took no such tone with Dickens, and their fondness for each other was deeply rooted, the old spontaneous intimacy was gone.

Shortly after Dickens returned to Paris came the formal ending of the Crimean War. It was received with general apathy and Dickens himself felt that it made little difference to any of the social objects he had hoped for. The same forces that had used the war to block progress would go on finding new excuses and erecting new obstacles or merely imposing the ponderous inertia of the Circumlocution Office to wear down the reformers. Although he was never to cease pouring out criticism, Dickens had by now almost entirely lost faith that anything would come of it.

More and more, in fact, he found himself deeply sceptical of the whole system of respectable attitudes and conventional beliefs that cemented all of society into a monolithic structure stubbornly resistant to significant change. He derided the pompous self-assurance of the aristocracy and hated the cold-hearted selfishness of the men of wealth. He despised the subservient snobbery of the middle class. He was contemptuous of the corruption and inefficiency of the Government and bitter over the brutal workings of an economic system that condemned the masses of the people to ignorance, suffering, and squalor.

"As to the suffrage, I have lost hope even in the ballot." Representative institutions were a failure in England because the people were denied the education that was a prerequisite for supporting them. "What with bringing up the soul and body of the land to be a good child, or to go to the beer-shop, to go a-poaching, and go to the devil; . . . what with flunkyism, toadyism," red tape, greed, and apathy, Dickens felt almost hopeless. England was in the hands of Sir Leicester Dedlock, Boodle and Coodle, Mr Dombey, the Tite Barnacles; worse still, of Mr Gradgrind, Mr Bounderby, and Mr Merdle; and, worst of all, England abased itself beneath their feet.

The very values of the imagination and the heart that sustained a healthy culture were deeply undermined. This was why even art and literature were feeble in comparison with what they might be. "Don't think it a part of my despondency about public affairs . . . when I say that mere form and conventionalities usurp, in English art, as in

English government and social relations, the place of living force and truth." The Belgians and the French both did better. Among them, at the international art exposition in Paris that winter, there were "no end of bad pictures," to be sure, "but, Lord! the goodness also – the fearlessness, of them; the bold drawing; the dashing conception; the passion and action in them!"

The same limitations explained the shortcomings of English literature. Mrs Grundy had her grip on everything. What a dishonest state was represented by some smooth gentleman complaining that the hero of an English novel was always "uninteresting – too good – not natural, &c." "But O my smooth friend, what a shining impostor you must think yourself and what an ass you must think me," when both know "that this same unnatural young gentleman . . . whom you meet in those other books and in mine *must be* presented to you in that unnatural aspect by reason of your morality, and is not to have, I will not say any of the indecencies you like, but not even any of the experiences, trials, perplexities, and confusions inseparable from the making or unmaking of all men!"

These emotions, the never-ending toil of his book, and his deep inward unrest, all generated a desperate craving for excitement. Prowling wretchedly about, "tearing my hair, sitting down to write, writing nothing, writing something and tearing it up, going out, coming in," he said, he was "a Monster to my family, a dread Phenomenon to myself." Sometimes as he planned another scathing chapter on officialdom, he had a grim pleasure "that the Circumlocution Office sees the light." Then, his head stinging "with the visions of the book," he would feel the need to plunge "out into some of the strange places I glide into of nights in these latitudes." One night it was the *fête* of the company of the Folies Nouvelles, "which I should think," he told Collins, "could hardly fail to attract all the Lorettes in Paris." Another night it would be a cheap public ball, with "pretty faces, but all of two classes – wicked and coldly calculating, or haggard and wretched in their worn beauty." And with Collins, who was now in Paris, and dining at the Dickens table every day, he would dash off on some "Haroun Alraschid expedition," one of a bachelor "perspective of theatrical and other-lounging evenings."

Back at his writing table again, he allowed his imagination to revel in the portrayal of Flora Finching. With a rather cruel but not entirely unkind comedy, he was modelling her upon the changed Maria Winter who had shattered the gleaming image of Maria Beadnell. "There are some things in Flora in number seven that seem to me to be extraordinarily droll, with something serious at the bottom of them after all. Ah, well! was there *not* something very serious in it once?"

At the end of April Dickens's time in Paris drew to a close. He had arranged in January to take M. Beaucourt's breezy hilltop house in Boulogne again for the summer, but until then, although his family would stay on in Paris, he had to be in London. The Hogarths, however, were in Tavistock House, and were not leaving till 3 May. And in the course of time, except for Georgina, Dickens had come to feel an almost unbearable impatience with his wife's family. They came and remain d in his house for long periods. They cheerfully allowed him to pay their bills for them.

During previous visits, they had been so negligent of the housekeeping and had vacated the place in such a dirty condition that Dickens had felt obliged to remonstrate with them. And even then he returned to find "the dust on the first floor," as he complained to Catherine, "an inch thick," and had to spend hours wallowing in dirt as the study and drawing-room were washed and swept, the windows opened, and the carpets aired. Maddened, he stood in his dismantled study "with the carpet in the corner like an immense roly-poly pudding, and all the chairs upside down as if they had turned over like birds and died with their legs in the air," while the servant put away a disorder of books and papers and tried to get the dreary house neat and comfortable again.

Now, as the time came for returning, Dickens felt that even for a few days he could not "bear the contemplation of their imbecility any more. (I think my constitution is already undermined by the sight of Hogarth at breakfast.)" He therefore determined to stay at the Ship Hotel, in Dover, from Tuesday until the following Saturday, when they would be gone.

But the Hogarths, of course, were only one grey and dusty strand in all the grey fabric that had come to make up the pattern of his life. The English people were "on the downhill road to being conquered," were "content to bear it," and *would* "NOT be saved." And again and again, "as with poor David," when he fell into low spirits, he found himself lamenting "one happiness I have missed in life, and one friend and companion I never made." All he had left was work. "The old days – the old days! Shall I ever, I wonder, get the frame of mind back as it used to be then? Something of it perhaps – but never quite as it used to be. I find that the skeleton in my domestic closet is becoming a pretty big one."

39

Better to Die, Doing

In his distraught state of mind, Dickens longed to be able to drown his unhappiness in the turmoil of producing another play. At his suggestion, Collins started writing a melodrama based on the ill-fated arctic expedition of Sir John Franklin, all of whose members had died of starvation and exposure. But Dickens had already arranged to stay at Boulogne until September, and therefore he could do no more before autumn. Meanwhile, he would have to bear his low spirits as best he could.

While at Dover his landlady at the Ship Hotel pursued him with excited anticipations of the imminent arrival of some Baron Brunow until he snapped, "I don't care a damn about the Baron . . . if he were sunk coming over, it would not make the least difference to me." In London, after four dusty hours clearing the mess the Hogarths had again left in the dining-room and schoolroom, he went to see Miss Coutts and argued hotly with her companion, Mrs Brown, when she talked "nonsense about the French people and their immorality." In England, Dickens said, people hypocritically pretended that social evils and vices did not exist; in France people were honest about them.

The next afternoon Stanfield dropped in at Tavistock House, and on hearing about the play became immensely excited. He upset the schoolroom Dickens had straightened out by dragging chairs to represent the proscenium and outlining the scenery with walking sticks. Surrounded by his old friends, Stanfield, Maclise, Forster, Macready – who turned out to be in town for a few days – Dickens found himself a little more cheerful. He gave a party at the *Household Words* offices, "pigeon pie, collared red partridge, ham, roast fowls, and lobster salad," with "quantities of punch," from which he did not get back to Tavistock House until half past two in the morning. By permission of Dean Milman, he took three companions to the top of St Paul's to see the blazing illuminations with which London on 29 May celebrated the end of the Crimean War.

On 9 June he settled down at the Villa des Moulineaux to work again on *Little Dorrit*. Stranded in M. Beaucourt's other villa were Dickens's old friend Cattermole and his family. The artist was hard up, and the gentle Beaucourt confessed reluctantly that "Monsieur Cattermole 'promises always,'" but does not pay. There was a nurse who refused to leave and refused to work because her wages were in arrears; one of the little boys did the cooking. "I am desolated for them all," said Beaucourt. "And for yourself, Beaucourt, you good fellow," asked Dickens. "Don't you say anything about yourself?" "Ah, Monsieur Dickens, pardon me, it's not worth the trouble; it's nothing, don't let us speak of it!"

The only excitement of the summer was provided by two marauding cats who invaded the house through the open windows to get at the family's canary. They hid themselves behind draperies, hanging "like bats, and tumbling out in the dead of night with frightful caterwaulings." One of the servants borrowed Beaucourt's gun to shoot them. The children kept watch "on their stomachs" in the garden to give the alarm with horrible whistles. "I am afraid to go out," Dickens wrote, "lest I should be shot." Tradesmen cried out as they came up the avenue, "It's me – baker – don't shoot!" For over a week the household was in a state of siege.

The stay in Boulogne was cut short at the end of August by another outbreak of cholera. Dickens sent the children home at once with Catherine while he and Georgy packed up. The 8th of September saw him back in Tavistock House. Collins, now a member of the *Household Words* staff at five guineas a week, was at the same time driving ahead on the second act of his arctic melodrama, and Dickens gave him a stream of eager suggestions. On 2 October, Collins excitedly arrived at Tavistock House with the first two acts finished. Already entitled *The Frozen Deep*, the last act was sufficiently mapped out so that Dickens felt able to set about the production. In its ultimate form, he had suggested so much of the plot and written or revised so many of the lines that it was almost as much his work as it was Collins's – and almost a prophecy of the misery and torment Dickens himself was so soon to feel.

The play takes place during a polar expedition on which Richard Wardour, the rejected suitor to Clara Burnham, rescues amid the perils of the frozen arctic his successful rival, Frank Aldersley. Weakened by hunger, exposure, and the struggle of bringing his rival to safety, Wardour dies, with Clara's tears raining down upon his face.

Georgy, Charley, and the two girls all had parts in the play; Collins and Dickens were to do Aldersley and Wardour, and began growing beards to look their roles. Stanfield was painting the scenery for the second and third acts, William Telbin that for the first act. As early as 16 October Dickens began rehearsing the first two acts. From then on, rehearsals took place every Monday and Friday evening till January. Throughout all this, he was steadily working on his novel: "Calm amidst the wreck," he wrote Macready, "your aged friend glides away on the Dorrit stream, forgetting the uproar for a stretch of hours, refreshing himself with a ten or twelve miles' walk, pitches headforemost into foaming rehearsals, placidly emerges for editorial purposes, smokes over buckets of distemper with Mr Stanfield aforesaid . . ."

The Frozen Deep had its first night on 6 January 1857, Charley's twentieth birthday. There were three repeat performances, on the 8th, 12th, and 14th. Close to a hundred people crowded the little schoolroom theatre each evening, although the ladies' crinolines made it a tight squeeze. A small orchestra rendered an overture and incidental music composed for the play by Francesco Berger, a young musician Charley had met at Leipzig, who presided at the piano. Then, from behind the darkened scene, the voice of Forster intoned the Prologue written by Dickens, comparing the hidden deeps of the heart with the unplumbed depths of the north, and suggesting

> *. . . that the secrets of the vast Profound*
> *Within us, an exploring hand may sound,*
> *Testing the region of the ice-bound soul,*
> *Seeking the passage at its northern pole,*
> *Soft'ning the horrors of its wintry sleep,*
> *Melting the surface of that " Frozen Deep."*

Dickens had devised novel lighting effects, simulating the changing hours of the day, from bright sunshine through crimson sunset to the grey of twilight and the misty blue of night. But the emotional power of the play was derived from the intensity he gave to the character of Wardour, into which he poured all his own repressed desperation. When during the last act Dickens rushed in anguish from the stage, he tossed the other men aside like a charging bull and often left them black and blue. His death scene was so moving that his fellow actors themselves were in tears and members of the audience sobbed audibly.

After an intermission the spectators were restored to cheerfulness by Buckstone's farce of *Uncle John*, in which they found Dickens as sidesplittingly comic as he had been heartrending. The opening night performance was followed by a supper with champagne and oysters. When the curtain descended on the last performance, workmen began "battering and smashing down" the theatre. Soon it was "a mere chaos of scaffolding, ladders, beams, canvases, paint-pots, artificial snow, gas-pipes, and ghastliness." Dickens felt "shipwrecked" and depressed. "The theatre has disappeared," he wrote Macready gloomily, "the house is restored to its usual conditions of order, the family are tranquil and domestic, dove-eyed peace is enthroned in this study, fire-eyed Radicalism in its master's breast." For, as ever in Dickens, among the shadows of his personal dejection always mingled his deep and implacable condemnation of the way the welfare of the public was ignored by England's rulers.

He thought "the political signs of the times to be just about as bad as the spirit of the people will admit of their being." As for the House of Commons, it seemed to him "to be getting worse every day." Privilege had so tainted and perverted all the potentialities of representative government as to make it "a miserable failure among us." The people were far more honest and efficient than Parliament.

In consequence of this "political despondency" and the hollow left by the cessation of the theatricals, Dickens felt a more violent craving than ever for distraction. Collins must take a trip with him – to Brighton, somewhere; he needed a change, was heavy with the galley-slave labour of tugging at his oar. When Collins agreed he was overjoyed. He and Collins were much at the theatres, and in the greenrooms among the actresses, whom they called "little periwinkles." "Any mad proposal you please," he told Collins, would "find a wildly insane response." And, still again, "if the mind can devise anything sufficiently in the style of Sybarite Rome in the days of its culminating voluptuousness, I am your man."

After these frenzied outbursts, Dickens resigned himself to a quiet summer in the country. For at long last, and in a frame of mind that almost destroyed the flavour of the triumph, he had realized the dream of his childhood. A year and a half ago Gad's Hill Place, on the hill two miles outside Rochester, upon which he had so longingly gazed on walks with his father, had come upon the market and he had bought it. Two years before, in the summer of 1855, walking past the old rose-brick dwelling with Wills, Dickens had called his eye to the ancient cedars in front and told him that early fantasy. The very next morning Wills had come to him in great excitement. "It is written," he exclaimed, "that you were to have that house at Gad's Hill."

The previous night at dinner, Wills explained, he had sat beside Mrs Lynn Linton, one of the contributors to *Household Words*, and their conversation had turned on the neighbourhood. "You know it?" he asked. "I know it very well," she replied. "I was a child in the house they call Gad's Hill Place. My father was the rector, and lived there many years. He has just died, has left it to me, and I want to sell it." "So," Wills said to Dickens, "you must buy it. Now or never!"

In August of 1855 Dickens had had Austin estimate how much it would cost to put the house in repair and raise the old slate roof six feet to provide extra rooms in the attic. He had begun by offering £1,500, but his eagerness to own it grew. In the end, he gave £1,700, and then another £90 for the shrubbery across the road which Mrs Linton valued separately. Concluding the purchase on 14 March 1856, Dickens noted that the day fell in with his belief that all the important events of his life took place on Fridays: he was born on a Friday, had been married on a Friday.

Once the place was his own, he felt as proud of "the property" as if he were M. Beaucourt. "It is old fashioned, plain, and comfortable," he said.

On the summit of Gad's Hill, with a noble prospect at the side and behind, looking down into the Valley of the Medway. Lord Darnley's Park at Cobham (a beautiful place with a noble walk through a wood) is close by . . . It is only an hour and a quarter from London by the Railway. To Crown all, the sign of the Sir John Falstaff is over the way, and I used to look at it as a wonderful Mansion (which God knows it is not), when I was a very odd little child with the first faint shadows of all my books in my head – I suppose.

During the negotiations, the house had been occupied by the rector of the parish, and Dickens agreed to let him stay on till the following March. In the course of the year he would decide to occupy it as a permanent residence. By February 1857, he was deep in conferences with Austin about the papering and painting and hiring a builder to overhaul the drainage and raise the roof. His servant John he was constantly sending into furniture stores to buy articles as if for himself (to prevent the shopkeepers from running up the prices) and letting him "bring them away ignobly, in vans, cabs, trucks, and costermonger's trays."

In April, Dickens received word from Hans Christian Andersen that he was coming to England again, and immediately invited him to stay at Gad's Hill when he should arrive in June. And on 17 May there was a housewarming, with a "small and noble army" of guests who ate "cold meat for the first time 'on the premises.' " With 1 June, the family was installed at Gad's Hill for the summer.

Going up to London by train on 9 June, Dickens was shocked to hear a gentleman looking over his newspaper say to another, "Douglas Jerrold is dead." Dickens knew that Jerrold's family would not be left well off. Old affection, generous sympathy, and, no doubt, the burning need for distraction that now gave him no peace, all made a single idea leap into his mind. They must raise a fund; there must be a benefit, a series of performances – T. P. Cooke in revivals of Jerrold's *Black-Eyed Susan* and *Rent Day*, Thackeray giving a lecture, Dickens himself giving a day reading, a night reading, and, of course, subscription revivals of *The Frozen Deep*, all done in a dignified manner, but announced as "In memory of the late Mr Douglas Jerrold."

A committee was speedily formed, rooms were taken for the series in the Gallery of Illustration on Regent Street, the Queen was asked to give her name in support. Her Majesty was intensely eager to see *The Frozen Deep*, but felt that assent would involve either perpetual compliance with other requests or perpetually giving offence. A private performance for the Queen and her own guests was arranged for a week before the subscription night.

Soon Dickens was tearing through rehearsals at all hours, working his company to the highest notch of perfection. In charge of the sale of tickets and other business details he placed Arthur Smith, a brother of Albert Smith, the showman and entertainer. On the two nights before the command performance Dickens drilled his actors until long past midnight.

Meanwhile, Hans Christian Andersen had been welcomed to Gad's Hill, and oscillated happily between there and London. The author of "The Ugly Duckling" was ecstatic over his host and hostess and their home. Dickens was the greatest author in the world, Kate was charming with her "china blue eyes" and "womanly repose," the children delightful to play with in the near-by field of clover.

Although Dickens gave Andersen no sign, he did not take so kindly to his guest. They were "suffering a good deal from Andersen," he wrote. "His unintelligible vocabulary was marvellous. In French or Italian, he was Peter the Wild Boy; in English, the Deaf and Dumb Asylum. My eldest boy swears that the ear of man cannot recognize his German; and his translatress declares to Bentley that he can't speak Danish!" In London "he got into wild entanglements of cabs and Sherry, and never seemed to get out of them again until" he was back at

Gad's Hill cutting "paper into all sorts of patterns" and gathering "the strangest little nosegays in the woods."

Andersen was taken to the private performance of *The Frozen Deep*, and was thrilled to behold the Queen, Prince Albert, and the King of the Belgians. When the curtain fell on the melodrama it was past midnight, but Her Majesty forgot her preference for early hours in her desire to see the farce as well, and gave the word that the evening should go on.

During the interval between the two there took place a curious episode that illustrates Dickens's almost bristling sense of his own dignity.

My gracious Sovereign [Dickens explained to Forster] was so pleased that she sent round begging me to go and see her and accept her thanks. I replied that I was in my Farce dress, and must beg to be excused. Whereupon she sent again, saying that the dress "could not be so ridiculous as that" . . . I sent my duty in reply, but again hoped her Majesty would have the kindness to excuse my presenting myself in a costume and appearance that were not my own. I was mightily glad to think, when I woke this morning, that I had carried the point.

But this private performance was only the beginning of the furore surrounding the Jerrold benefits. The audience for the first public performance on 8 July was positively hysterical. And when Dickens read the *Carol* at St Martin's Hall he reported to Macready, "The two thousand and odd people were like one, and their enthusiasm was something awful." Further performances of *The Frozen Deep* took place on the 18th and 25th, and another reading of the *Carol* on the 24th. And they had played only twice in London when there came a demand that they play in Manchester as well.

In the midst of the London performances, Andersen, who had come for two weeks and remained five, finally took his departure. At Gad's Hill, he had played with the children, making daisy chains, and once, unobserved, slipped a wreath of daisies over the crown of Collins's wide-awake hat, which the latter wore past the Falstaff Inn wondering why the hop pickers laughed at his appearance. Andersen had been innocently unaware that he had outstayed his welcome. But long before he said good-bye Mamey and Katey regarded him as "a bony bore," and when he was gone Dickens stuck a card on his dressing-table mirror, reading "Hans Christian Andersen slept in this room for five weeks which seemed to the family ages."

444

Five days later, Dickens said a farewell that did move him deeply. His second son Walter was now sixteen years of age, a vigorous youngster who had done well at school and even won an occasional prize. Miss Coutts had used her influence to have him nominated for a cadetship, and Dickens had put him to study with a Mr Trimmer at Putney, who prepared boys for Addiscombe and India. But at Addiscombe it seemed unlikely that Walter could attain high distinction in his studies, "least of all in mathematics and fortification," Dickens said, "without which he couldn't get into the Engineers."

In April of 1857 Walter had passed his final examinations. He was to sail from Southampton on 20 July, as a cadet in the East India Company's 26th Native Infantry. The intervening weeks he spent happily learning to swim, ride, fence, and shoot, and studying Hindustani. Dickens bought his outfit, paid his passage, and gave him a generous letter of credit on Calcutta.

It was a mournful thing to realize how Time had "flapped his wings over your head" and that another baby had grown to be a young man. When Walter went on board the *Indus*, waving back cheerfully at his father and his brother Charley, Dickens felt the leave-taking like having "great teeth drawn with a wrench." Walter was "in good spirits, as little cast down as, at 16, one could reasonably hope to be with the world of India before one."

Before the Manchester performances for the Jerrold Fund, Dickens was mostly at Gad's Hill, where he struggled with the problems of a suddenly empty well and clogged drains. The garden had barely begun to look pretty when the drainpipes forced digging up part of it and building two new cesspools. The dug-up garden, the black mud, the drying bath, the delay, and the expense, Dickens lamented, were "changing the undersigned honey-pot into a Mad Bull."

Meanwhile, he had read the *Christmas Carol* for the Jerrold Fund at Manchester on 31 July and arranged the dates for *The Frozen Deep* there on 21 and 22 August. The play was to be given in the Free Trade Hall, an immense auditorium in which only an experienced actress could make her action seen and her voice heard. He would therefore have to find substitutes for Mamey and Katey and most of the other feminine members of the cast. "I am already trying," he wrote Collins, "to get the best who *have been* on the stage." He asked Alfred Wigan, the manager of the Olympic Theatre, for suggestions. Wigan recommended the well-known actress Mrs Ternan and her two daughters, Maria Ternan and Ellen Lawless Ternan.

Dickens assigned Mrs Ternan to the part of Nurse Esther, ~~gave Maria,~~ ~~the more experienced of the sisters,~~ that of Clara Burnham, the heroine, and placed Ellen in the minor one of Lucy Crayford. After "three days' drill of the professional ladies," the entire company set out for Manchester. At the performance Dickens surpassed himself. Although Maria Ternan had seen the play in London and rehearsed it with him, she feared she would not be able to control her emotion on the stage.

> She had to take my head up as I was dying [Dickens explained], and to put it in her lap, and give me her face to hold between my two hands. All of which I showed her elaborately (as Mary had done it before) that morning. When we came to that point at night, her tears fell down my face, down my beard . . . down my ragged dress – poured all over me like rain, so that it was as much as I could do to speak for them. I whispered to her, "My dear child, it will be over in two minutes. Pray compose yourself." – "It's no comfort to me that it will be soon over," she answered. "Oh it is so sad, it is so dreadfully sad. Oh, don't die! Give me time, give me a little time. Don't take leave of me in this terrible way – pray, pray, pray!!" Whereupon Lemon, the softest-hearted of men, began to cry too, and then they all went at it together.

The second night, before an audience of 3,000, Dickens repeated his triumph. "This was, I think," said Wilkie Collins, "the finest of all the representations of *The Frozen Deep*. . . . The trite phrase is the true phrase to describe that magnificent piece of acting. He literally electrified the audience."

The entire enterprise had fully realized Dickens's aspiration of netting £2,000 for the Jerrold family. But barely were the last excitements of those performances over, than Dickens fell back into a deeper wretchedness than ever before. On 29 August – only five days after the final night – in a letter written in "grim despair and restlessness" he implored Collins to come with him "anywhere – take any tour – see anything . . . I want to escape from myself. For when I *do* start up and stare myself seedily in the face, as happens to be my case at present, my lankness is inconceivable – indescribable – my misery, amazing."

In this state of hopelessness Dickens set off with Collins for the fells of Cumberland. They went by rail to Carlisle, thence to Wigton, and on to Allonby. Dickens dragged Collins up Carrick Fell, where they got lost on the mountain in a fog and Collins sprained his ankle leaping down a watercourse. Dickens had to carry him the rest of the way, "Wardour to the life!" For the next three days Collins lay in their sitting-room with "liniment and a horrible dabbling of lotion incessantly in progress" while Dickens feverishly roamed the country.

What the indolent and sybaritic Collins thought of Dickens's frenzied energy is suggested by a dialogue in *The Lazy Tour of Two Idle Apprentices*, a record of their adventures on which the two collaborated for *Household Words*. Dickens doesn't know how to play, says Collins; he makes work of everything. "Where another man would stake a sixpence, you would make for Heaven; and if you were to dive into the depths of the earth, nothing short of the other place would content you."

"A man who can do nothing by halves," he concludes, "appears to me to be a fearful man."

But Dickens was totally unable to be any other kind of man. As soon as Collins could hobble around with two thick canes, Dickens hurried him back to Carlisle, and from there to Lancaster, where they slept in a quaint old house the state bedroom of which contained two enormous red four-posters. The landlord served them an elaborate dinner – salmon trout, sirloin steak, partridges, seven dishes of sweets, and five of dessert, including a bowl of peaches and an enormous bride-cake – at the thought of all which items on their bill Collins turned pale.

Although Dickens hated gambling, in his agitated need of forgetting his own problems somehow, he even visited "the St Leger and its saturnalia" when he and Collins reached Doncaster. In sheer desperation at the track he "bought the card; facetiously wrote down three names for winners of the three chief races" – never in his life having heard of any of them – "and, if you can believe it without your hair standing on end, those three races were won, one after another, by those three horses!!!" But he loathed the place and the crowds he saw there. If a boy with any good in him, Dickens declared, but with a dawning tendency to betting, were brought to Doncaster, it would cure him for life.

Dickens came back from his trip feeling as horribly unsettled as when he had started out. Collins might be the ideal companion for an unrestrained holiday, but he was too young and cynical to give comfort or counsel. Neither age nor experience enabled him to understand the hopeless despair from which Dickens was suffering. For with the final performance of *The Frozen Deep*, the efforts to control his life to an outer decorum at last gave way. He realized that he could not go on forever fleeing his marital unhappiness in violent theatrical dashings from

London to the provinces. His married life was unbearable, yet there seemed nothing he could do except bear it.

In this crisis of his distress, even before going off with Collins, Dickens had turned for understanding to the faithful Forster, staid, heavy, pompous, but always willing to devote his whole heart in sympathy and help to those he loved. In a long letter written either at the end of August or the beginning of September, Dickens now frankly confessed at last what his old friend had long silently known.

> Poor Catherine and I are not made for each other, and there is no help for it. It is not only that she makes me uneasy and unhappy, but that I make her so too – and much more so. She is exactly what you know, in the way of being amiable and complying; but we are strangely ill-assorted for the bond there is between us. God knows she would have been a thousand times happier if she had married another kind of man, and that her avoidance of this destiny would have been at least equally good for us both. I am often cut to the heart by thinking what a pity it is, for her own sake, that I ever fell in her way . . .

If he were sick, Dickens went on,

> I know how sorry she would be . . . But exactly the same incompatibility would arise, the moment I was well again; and nothing on earth could make her understand me, or suit us to each other. . . . What is now befalling me I have seen steadily coming, ever since the days you remember when Mary was born; and I know too well that you cannot, and no one can, help me. Why I have even written I hardly know; but it is a miserable sort of comfort that you should be clearly aware how matters stand. The mere mention of the fact, without any complaint or blame of any sort, is a relief to my present state of spirits – and I can get this only from you, because I can speak of it to no one else.

In the face of this appeal Forster put aside whatever jealousy he may have felt of Dickens's other companions, and responded with a flow of comfort and advice. But with his sturdy common sense he underlined Dickens's confession that the shortcomings were not all on Catherine's side. The disharmonies Dickens mentioned were to be found in many other marriages.

> To the most part of what you say – Amen [Dickens replied]. You are not so tolerant as perhaps you might be of the wayward and unsettled feeling which is part (I suppose) of the tenure on which one

holds an imaginative life, and which I have, as you ought to know well, often only kept down by riding over it like a dragoon – but let that go by. . . . I agree with you as to the very possible incidents, even not less bearable than mine, that might and must often occur to the married condition when it is entered into very young.

Nor did he disguise from himself, he went on,

what might be urged on the other side. I claim no immunity from blame. There is plenty of fault on my side, I daresay, in the way of a thousand uncertainties, caprices, and difficulties of disposition; but only time will alter that, and that is, the end which alters everything. . . . But the years have not made it easier to bear for either of us; and, for her sake as well as mine, the wish will force itself upon me that something might be done. I know too well it is impossible.

He knew, too, that in going off with Collins he had merely run away from his problem, not solved it, and his unappeasable heartache gave him no rest. He could not, as Forster urged, resign himself to the state of affairs in his home. His misery pressed upon him so relentlessly that he could not concentrate his imagination upon the design of another novel or command the discipline to work on it. Forster remonstrated with him in vain.

"Too late to say, put the curb on, and don't rush at hills," Dickens responded wearily, "– the wrong man to say it to. I have now no relief but in action. I am incapable of rest. I am quite confident I should rust, break, and die, if I spared myself. Much better to die, doing."

40

Breaking Point

During the months following the completion of *Little Dorrit*, Dickens's misery was swelling into the anguish of an endless nightmare. Useless to think of sitting down to a new novel; his unhappiness tore through him with the violence of a powerful electric current agitating his very body. There could be no relief but in constant action. "What do you think," he wrote Forster from Gad's Hill, "of my paying for this place, by reviving that old idea of some Readings from my books. I am very strongly tempted. Think of it."

The notion had first come to him, not altogether seriously, years before at Lausanne. But as he had done the *Christmas Carol* for charity, and felt the laughter and tears of his audience course through him, more and more he had asked why not? Forster, of course, obdurately opposed. It was a public exhibition for private gain unworthy of a man of letters and a gentleman. It was true that other writers, including Thackeray, had given lectures for their own profit, but a reading was like descending to the vulgarity of the stage. The fact that Forster himself had acted for charitable causes he considered beside the point. So was the fact that their intimate friend Macready and many other actors were men of the highest character. For a literary artist to become a sort of professional showman was to Forster a lowering of dignity.

But Dickens did not at all agree. He saw no loss of dignity involved. And if charitable causes might legitimately profit from his readings, why should not he? Above all, it would keep him busy, provide an outlet for his nervous tension, bring him and his public into a close contact from which he derived both stimulation and support, and take him away from a domestic association that he found intolerable.

"I believe," he at last brought himself to the point of telling Miss Coutts,

that no two people were ever created, with such an impossibility of interest, sympathy, confidence, sentiment, tender union of any kind between them, as there is between my wife and me. It is an immense misfortune to her – it is an immense misfortune to me – but Nature has put an insurmountable barrier between us, which never in this world can be thrown down.

You know me too well to suppose that I have the faintest thought of influencing you on either side. I merely mention a fact which may induce you to pity us both, when I tell you that she is the only person I have ever known with whom I could not get on somehow or other, and in communicating with whom I could not find some way to come to some kind of interest. You know that I have many impulsive faults which often belong to my impulsive way of life and exercise of fancy; but I am very patient and considerate at heart, and would have beaten out a path to a better journey's end than we have come to, if I could.

The truth was worse than that he had ceased to love Kate. In scores of ways she rasped him beyond bearing. Daily contact with her clumsiness, lassitude, and inefficiency set his teeth on edge. For Dickens, who knew exactly where every article should be in every room in his house, who inspected his children's bedrooms like a drill sergeant every morning, who had a precise place on his desk for every ornament, whose every movement and gesture were made with precision, poor Catherine's mishaps were as irritating as if they were deliberate. In earlier years he had tried to make a joke of these accidents, roaring with laughter when her bracelets fell off her arm with a splash into the soup. But a mounting residue of exasperation remained undischarged.

Related to these shortcomings were her practical incapacities. When they had moved to Tavistock House, Dickens had settled almost every detail of its reconstruction and furnishing himself. Kate's part, he remarked only half jestingly, was limited to wandering about getting herself "all over paint" and seeming to think that "somehow immensely useful." It was common report in London that Dickens did most of the family shopping, "making bargains at butchers and bakers." The internal running of the household was in the hands of Georgina, whether in London, Paris, Boulogne, or any of their English summer residences.

Even the children had been more directly under the supervision of their Aunt Georgy than of their mother. To be sure, there was a nurse, and later a governess, and one by one the little boys had gone to school, but in a family of nine growing children there had still been enough to do. Catherine's role seemed to cease when she had brought them into the world.

Nor, Dickens felt strongly, was there an emotional tie between her and the children. Though she had wept at being separated from them when she went to America,

> she has never attached one of them to herself, never played with them in infancy, never attracted their confidence, as they have grown older, never presented herself before them in the aspect of a mother. I have seen them fall off from her in a natural – not *un*natural – progress of estrangement, and at this moment I believe that Mary and Katey (whose dispositions are of the gentlest and most affectionate conceivable) harden into stone figures of girls when they can be got to go near her, and have their hearts shut in her presence as if they were closed by some horrid spring.

What was true of the girls, Dickens insisted, was true of the boys as well. "She does not – and she never did – care for the children," he told Miss Coutts; "and the children do not – and they never did – care for her."

There is, of course, another side to these observations. Dickens was of a masterful and domineering temperament; it is conceivable that he seized the control even of all domestic details from Kate's unresisting hand. Georgina, too, has sometimes been seen by commentators as a sly and insidious manoeuvrer, gradually drawing into her own grasp the reins of authority that rightfully belonged to Kate. Neither suggestion, however, is entirely plausible. Dickens was not incapable of delegating responsibility. Although on *Household Words* he retained a firm grasp on policy, he left all routine details to Wills. His egoism was not of a kind that needed to assert itself over every roast of meat or scuttle of coal. And when Georgina joined the household she was a girl of fifteen and Kate a young matron of twenty-seven already six years married. There is no evidence for depicting Georgina as a scheming intriguer and Kate as her helpless victim.

It is true that in fifteen years Kate had given birth to ten children and suffered a number of miscarriages. But physically her health was good; she survived her more vigorous husband by nine years. And many Victorian wives had quite as many children as Kate and continued to be lively companions to their husbands.

She sometimes made little effort to control her dislikes and had to be warned against giving way to them. Dickens was obliged to remind her of their obligations to the Macreadys when Mrs Macready's sister was their guest in Genoa. She had never been a great success as the wife of a celebrity. Though Miss Coutts was undeviatingly kind to her, she always spoke of her in terms of gentle sarcasm: the "Poor dear Mrs Dickens" with which Miss Coutts invariably alluded to her was pronounced in a tone of illimitable disparagement.

So little impression did Kate make on Dickens's large circle of friends and acquaintances that during many periods she almost seems to disappear from his life. Aside from formal courtesies, letters between Dickens and his friends seldom mention her. Now and then there is a glimpse of her, giggling and girlish in their early married life, fresh-coloured and elaborately dressed at a ball in America, in tears at an angry scene between Dickens and Forster, stout and red-faced in middle life.

Her inability to deal with the recurrent difficulties of life appears as early as the American voyage of 1842. Journeying across the United States, she stumbled and fell in and out of stagecoaches and river steamers, and got through the ordeal of travel only through the help of an unusually competent maid. In Italy, and later in France, there were the services of a cook, nurse, maids, and other servants, all coming more and more under the direction of Georgina.

Undoubtedly Kate had come to realize her husband's impatience, and nervous apprehension intensified her awkward blunders. As Dickens contrasted her middle-aged dullness and incapacity with the well-preserved youthful charm of Mme Scribe or the grace and ease of Mme Régnier and Mme Viardot, all the qualities he had found in Kate when she was twenty seemed to have disappeared. Now he saw her as sluggish, vague-minded, incompetent, stirring out of self-indulgent idleness only to fall into amorphous self-pity.

Except in one respect. Terrified though she might be of her husband's displeasure, Kate could not believe there was no more than an innocent gallantry in his response to other women or restrain her resentment of the fascination he exercised over them. In Genoa she had had the direst suspicions of his relations with Mme De la Rue; not even the serenity of that lady's husband could convince her there was nothing wrong. What tears, recriminations, hysteria, there had been – even public scenes, for which Dickens had been obliged to invent flimsy excuses. And in the course of the years these frictions had not ceased.

Between ourselves [Dickens wrote to M. De la Rue in October 1857] . . . I don't get on better in these later times with a certain poor lady you know of, than I did in the earlier Peschiere days. Much worse. Much worse! Neither do the childen, elder or younger. Neither can she get on with herself, or be anything but unhappy. (She has been excruciatingly jealous of, and has obtained positive proof of my being on the most intimate terms with, at least fifteen thousand women of various conditions in life since we left Genoa. Please to respect me for this vast experience.) What we should do, or what the girls would be, without Georgy, I cannot imagine.

Over and over again in these later years, Dickens said, Catherine had suggested that they would be happier separated: "it would be better for her to go away and live apart." But the children, he had always insisted, must be "the first consideration," and must bind them "together 'in appearance.' " For the children's sake he and she must bear their misfortune "and fight the fight out to the end." Such was the situation during these months of agitation and misery – but with one new element.

This was Ellen Ternan, the youthful actress who played a minor role in the Manchester performances of *The Frozen Deep*. During the course of rehearsals and the last performances in the north, the impression she had made upon Dickens deepened. While he was buffeting the other characters out of his way and "rending the very heart out of his body" as Richard Wardour, feeling the tears of Maria Ternan showering down upon his face and beard, his heart was weeping its own lamentation over the "one friend and companion" he had never made, the "one happiness he had missed in life."

How his response to the fair young actress wrought upon his impetuous nature is suggested by a letter to Mrs Watson. He found a despairing relief in describing his feelings as if they were merely the restlessness of the artistic temperament:

I am the modern embodiment of the old Enchanters, whose Familiars tore them to pieces. I weary of rest, and have no satisfaction but in fatigue. Realities and idealities are always comparing themselves before me, and I don't like the Realities except when they are unattainable – *then*, I like them of all things. I wish I had been born in the days of Ogres and Dragon-guarded Castles. I wish an Ogre with seven heads (and no particular evidence of brains in the whole of them) had taken the Princess whom I adore – you have no idea how intensely I love her! – to his stronghold on the top of a high series of mountains, and there tied her up by the hair. Nothing would suit me half so well this day, as climbing after her, sword in hand, and either winning her or being killed. – *There's* a frame of mind for you, in 1857.

Sharing the same bedchamber with Kate, with all its domestic intimacies, as he had done these many years, but feeling as he now did, had become intolerable to him. With a sudden determination he wrote to Anne Cornelius, their old servant, who was in charge at Tavistock House, directing her to transform his dressing-room into his bedroom. The doorway between the dressing-room and Kate's room was to be closed by a wooden door and the recess filled with shelves. The closing of that door after twenty-one years of married life was, in the tragedy of Dickens, symbolically as significant as Nora's slamming of the door in *A Doll's House*.

It may have come to the attention of the Hogarths, who were again staying at Tavistock House. Towards the middle or end of October, Dickens had to come from Gad's Hill to London on *Household Words* business, and went home to sleep. Some upset took place, it cannot be said what. Perhaps it grew out of his annoyance with the mere presence of the Hogarths; perhaps there was some question about the change in his sleeping arrangements. Whatever it was, he was "very much put out"; and as he lay afterwards, unable to rest, he thought, "After all, it would be better to be up and doing something, than lying here." So up he rose, and at two o'clock in the morning dressed, and tramped all the thirty miles to Gad's Hill through the dead of night. He did not return to Tavistock House again until the Hogarths were gone forever.

Meanwhile, his outward life continued much as usual. But on their return to town Tavistock House was an unhappy home. There were no children's theatricals on Twelfth Night. Kate wept in her lonely room, Georgina kept the house going, and Dickens debated trying to begin a new book instead of inaugurating the course of readings that Forster opposed. "If I can discipline my thoughts into the channel of a story," he wrote his friend, "I have made up my mind to get to work on one: always supposing that I find myself, on the trial, able to do well. Nothing whatever will do me the least 'good' in the way of shaking off the one strong possession of change impending over us that every day makes stronger . . ."

But he tried in vain to concentrate upon a theme for a story. Everything reminded him of his own frustration. Seeing a performance of a new play by his friend Westland Marston, he protested against the way the hero crushed in his hand a letter from the woman he loved. "Hold it to his heart unconsciously and look about for it the while, he might; or he might do anything with it that expressed a habit of tenderness and affection in association with the idea of her; but he would never crush it under any circumstances. He would as soon crush her heart."

Now he asked once more if he might not find relief in the readings after all.

> The domestic unhappiness remains so strong upon me that I can't write, and (waking) can't rest, one minute. . . . I do suppose there never was a man so seized and rended by one Spirit. In this condition, though nothing can alter or soften it, I have a turning notion that the mere physical effort and change of the Readings would be good, as another means of bearing it.

Forster continued to protest. Dickens felt his resistance to be irrational. He had raised no objection to Dickens's reading for charity; was he not "exhibiting" himself equally when he did that, no matter who got the money? And did not a good part of the public even now suppose him to be paid?

"I must do *something*," he almost implored, "or I shall wear my heart away." And a few days later,

> Quite dismiss from your mind any reference whatever to present circumstances at home. Nothing can put *them* right, until we are all dead and buried and risen. It is not, with me, a matter of will, or trial, or sufferance, or good humour, or making the best of it, or making the worst of it, any longer. It is all despairingly over. Have no lingering hope of, or for, me in this association. A dismal failure has to be borne, and there an end.

What Dickens now decided on was a series of four or six Thursday evening readings in London at St Martin's Hall throughout May and the beginning of June. These would be followed by an autumn tour of "the Eastern Counties, the West, Lancashire, Yorkshire, and Scotland," "extending through August, September, and October," and running to thirty-five or forty all told. Dickens himself would be entirely dissociated from the business management, which would be handled by Arthur Smith, whose efficiency had been proved during the Jerrold benefits. By the following April, Dickens believed, he might gain a very large sum, even without counting Ireland. And there would still remain

America, which he thought (if he could resolve to go there) might be worth £10,000.

On 15 April he had given his reading for the Children's Hospital at St Martin's Hall. On the 20th he inaugurated the series for his own profit. Success was immediate and enormous. "They have let five hundred stalls for the Hospital night," Dickens reported; "and as people come in every day for more, and it is out of the question to make more, they cannot be restrained at St Martin's Hall from taking down names for other Readings." The demand for seats was so strong that the series was expanded from six to sixteen readings extending to 22 July. In addition to *A Christmas Carol*, Dickens read *The Chimes*, although at first he found it hard to maintain his composure during some of its more affecting parts. By the middle of June he had devised two more reading programmes that included the death of little Paul Dombey and some Sairey Gamp scenes from *Martin Chuzzlewit*.

But at home, even as these public triumphs were initiated, the tension between Dickens and Catherine had at last mounted to a crisis. Dickens had purchased a bracelet to give Ellen Ternan, and the jeweller had made the mistake of sending it to Tavistock House, where it fell into Catherine's hands. It was not unusual for Dickens to exchange little gifts and mementos with participants in the theatricals; he had done so with Mary Boyle, and with Mrs Cowden Clarke and her sister Miss Novello. But to Catherine this was different, and she violently resented it.

Grieving over her husband's alienation, it was impossible for her to believe the bracelet a mark of innocent esteem. How could one interpret these personal attentions to a beautiful girl of eighteen, even though Dickens was old enough to be her father? Catherine flared into angry reproaches. Dickens furiously denied any guilt in his relations with Ellen. In the indignant fervour of his emotion he resented the accusation as a slur on Ellen's purity; swirling in a luminous mist, his feelings presented themselves to him as a shining and sanctified devotion and Ellen as the far-off princess on the unscalable mountain. His wife's bitter suspicions enraged him as hideous and degrading.

All his violent will power hardened itself into battering her to surrender. He would not have Catherine, he would not have his daughters believing Ellen was his mistress. Catherine could show her confidence in him, he told her, and her belief in Ellen's innocence, by calling on her and her mother. Going past Catherine's door, eighteen-year-old Katey heard sobs from within. Entering, she found her mother seated at the dressing-table, weeping and putting on her bonnet. When she asked why, Catherine, with streaming eyes, choked, "Your father has asked me to go and see Ellen Ternan." "You shall not go!" exclaimed Katey, stamping her foot. But Catherine Dickens was not strong enough to resist her husband's determination. She went.

Nevertheless, unable to bear her grief, she finally told her story to her father and mother. Mrs Hogarth and her youngest daughter Helen flatly refused to believe Dickens's denials. They had long realized and resented his dislike of them; their own bitterness was no less sharp for the favours they had accepted at his hands. It was Mrs Hogarth who brought matters to an unexpected climax. Catherine, she insisted, must leave Dickens at once and demand a separate maintenance. Catherine, reinforced in her original unhappy suspicions, wept and at last forlornly took her departure.

Georgina, however, took Dickens's side. Her devotion to him was as great as his admiration for her: a half-dozen years earlier she had refused a proposal of marriage from Augustus Egg, and although Dickens had thought it a good match he had admitted that she was far the artist's superior. Her declaration of loyalty to Dickens infuriated her family; their position would be much weakened if the sister who had been a constant member of the household for the past sixteen years supported him before the world. But Georgina refused to be moved.

Georgina's unforeseen and unconventional decision snarled the situation into an even worse tangle. If she had left the house but sought shelter elsewhere than with her parents, that might have forestalled criticism of her conduct and still showed that she believed in Dickens's innocence. But where in nineteenth-century England, except with her family, could a thirty-year-old spinster go, and how would she live? Georgina had been trained to do nothing that would earn a livelihood; the Hogarths themselves had allowed her to become a dependant in Dickens's household. How could she abandon the man for whom she felt admiration and devotion, and join his accusers? Dickens had himself left Tavistock House and taken up quarters in the *Household Words* offices. No imputations against her conduct had been made before the separation crisis, but now, if there were some who were convinced by her remaining in Tavistock Square that the accusations against Dickens were groundless, there were others who spread rumours even more scandalous.

For some time, though, only a few people knew his wife had left his house. And Dickens made desperate endeavours to bring about some compromise short of a public separation. His marriage was an unhappy failure and could never be anything else, but surely they could maintain appearances. Dickens professed no Bohemian indifference to the judgement of society and feared its censures might gravely impair his earning powers. If readers ceased to buy his books, stayed away from his readings, what would happen to his children? He was devoted to them, and all except the two eldest boys were still entirely dependent upon him. Their father's good name was the very foundation of their present welfare and their future prospects.

He therefore asked Forster to try to work out some arrangement that might avoid these dangers. But Catherine distrusted Forster as a partisan. She had long felt that he shared and abetted her husband's contemptuous attitude towards her. She consequently requested that stout, tender-hearted Mark Lemon be brought in to represent her interests. Various suggestions were proposed. One was that Catherine have her own rooms, apart from Dickens's, but still appear as his hostess on social occasions. Another was that she stay at Gad's Hill when he was at Tavistock House, and vice versa. Both these proposals Catherine declined. Although the thought of breaking up her home distressed her terribly, if Charles felt like that about her it would be better for her to go away or to die. She passed days in weeping. But, strengthened by the Hogarths, she held to a complete separation.

Slowly the details were worked out. On 14 May Lemon wrote Forster in Catherine's behalf, accepting the proposed settlement. Catherine was to live in a house of her own and also receive £600 a year. Charley, the eldest son, would go with her and the other children remain with their father, although they might visit her and she them at any time. "Don't suppose," Charley told his father, "that in making my choice, I was actuated by any preference for my mother to you. God knows I love you dearly, and it will be a hard day for me when I have to part from you and the girls." Walter was in India, the next three boys at school; only Harry and Plorn would still be at home with Mamey and Katey and under the care of their Aunt Georgy. Nine and six years old respectively, they were bewildered and confused by the unhappy turmoil of their home, but hardly understood what was going on.

Suddenly all these arrangements were shattered. Dickens learned that Mrs Hogarth and Helen Hogarth were circulating the story that Ellen Ternan was his mistress. The news turned him into a maniac of indignant fury. For these two members of a family upon whom he had heaped favours to be seeking to destroy his good name, to endanger the welfare of his children, was the blackest depth of falsehood and ingratitude. Fiercely Dickens refused to make any agreement, any settlement whatsoever. They must retract their wicked accusations, formally and in writing, for themselves and for Catherine, or he would do nothing, pay not a penny.

The Hogarths refused to put their names to the document he demanded that they sign and he refused to give way an inch. His home was in a turmoil with the hysteria of his anger. "My father," Katey said later, "was like a madman . . ." Catherine asked Miss Coutts to serve as an intermediary between them. Miss Coutts tried, but Dickens rejected her endeavours. "I think I know what you want me for," he wrote. "How I value your friendship and how I love and honour you, you know in part, though you never can fully know. But nothing on earth – no, not even you – no consideration, human or Divine, can move me from the resolution I have taken."

For almost two weeks the Hogarths held out. Dickens, however, was still more obdurate. Finally Mrs Hogarth and Helen gave way, and on 29 May signed the retraction he was bent on forcing from them:

> It having been stated to us that in reference to the differences which have resulted in the separation of Mr and Mrs Charles Dickens, certain statements have been circulated that such differences are occasioned by circumstances deeply affecting the moral character of Mr Dickens and compromising the reputation and good name of others, we solemnly declare that we now disbelieve such statements. We know that they are not believed by Mrs Dickens, and we pledge ourselves on all occasions to contradict them, as entirely destitute of foundation.

Meanwhile, all clubland and literary London had been humming with rumour. Going into the Garrick Club, Thackeray was told that the separation was caused by a love affair between Dickens and Georgina. "No such thing," said he with his usual clumsiness; "it's with an actress." His intention was only to scotch the more scandalous story, but the remark came back to Dickens, who angrily wrote him denying all charges against Ellen Ternan and himself.

Dickens was filled with bitterness against Catherine. "O my dear Miss Coutts," he wrote, "do I not know that the weak hand that could never help or serve my name in the least, has struck at it – in conjunc-

tion with the wickedest people, whom I have loaded with benefits!"
To his seething imagination it seemed that the whole world must be
clamouring with the hideous story. Filled with this delusion, he rushed
into more feverish action. He would send out a public statement explaining the truth, and this would set the minds of his admirers at rest
and silence the tongue of scandal. Forster advised against it, Lemon advised against it, even young Edmund Yates, to whom Dickens chanced
to show the statement in proof, added his voice. But Dickens was set on
his own course. The utmost he would concede was that he would consult
John Delane, the editor of the London *Times*, and abide by his opinion.

Forster himself advised with Delane for an hour and a half. Unhappily, Delane was for publication. Thereupon Dickens took the
maddest step he had yet made in his unhappy and hysterical state.
Catherine docilely agreed to the statement's publication, and under the
heading PERSONAL it appeared on the front page of *Household Words*
for 12 June 1858.

"Some domestic trouble of mine, of long-standing," Dickens told the
public, had "lately been brought to an arrangement" involving "no
anger or ill-will," and all the details of which were known to his
children.

> By some means, arising out of wickedness, or out of folly, or out of
> inconceivable wild chance, or out of all three, this trouble has been
> made the occasion of misrepresentations, most grossly false, most
> monstrous, and most cruel – involving, not only me, but innocent
> persons dear to my heart . . . I most solemnly declare, then – and this
> I do both in my own name and in my wife's name – that all the lately
> whispered rumours touching the trouble at which I have glanced,
> are abominably false. And that whosoever repeats one of them after
> this denial, will lie as wilfully and as foully as it is possible for any
> false witness to lie, before Heaven and earth.

This statement he not only published himself, but sent to the newspapers. He quarrelled furiously with Mark Lemon and with Bradbury
and Evans for feeling that it was not appropriate for inclusion in the
pages of a comic magazine and for consequently refusing to print it in
Punch. Newspapers did print it, often with unfavourable comments, and
bewildered readers, who knew nothing of Dickens's domestic affairs,
asked each other what it was about. His friends were embarrassed, although they loyally rallied to his defence, and wrote him notes of

sympathy. Dickens, growing constantly more rigid and unyielding throughout the furore, was determined to face it down.

But there remained a still worse ordeal. In his agitation, Dickens gave Arthur Smith, his manager, a much more explicit letter, to which he attached a copy of the Hogarths' retraction of their accusations. This he empowered Smith to show "to anyone who wishes to do me right, or to anyone who may have been misled into doing me wrong." In an excess of zeal, Smith allowed a newspaperman to see it. Presently it appeared in the New York *Tribune*, from which later in the summer it was copied by English newspapers. "Nothing has, on many occasions, stood between us and a separation," Dickens said in this statement,

> but Mrs Dickens's sister, Georgina Hogarth. From the age of fifteen, she has devoted herself to our home and our children. . . . In the manly consideration towards Mrs Dickens which I owe to my wife, I will merely remark of her that some peculiarity of her character has thrown all the children on someone else. I do not know – I cannot by any stretch of fancy imagine – what would have become of them but for this aunt, who has grown up with them, to whom they are devoted, and who has sacrificed the best part of her youth and life to them. . . .
>
> For some years past Mrs Dickens has been in the habit of representing to me that it would be better for her to go away and live apart; that her always increasing estrangement made a mental disorder under which she sometimes labours – more, that she felt herself unfit for the life she had to lead as my wife and that she would be better away . . .
>
> Two wicked persons who should have spoken very differently of me, in consideration of earned respect and gratitude, have (as I am told, and indeed to my personal knowledge) coupled with this separation the name of a young lady for whom I have a great attachment and regard. I will not repeat her name – I honour it too much. Upon my soul and honour, there is not on this earth a more virtuous and spotless creature than this young lady. I know her to be as innocent and pure, and as good as my own dear daughters. Further, I am quite sure that Mrs Dickens, having received this assurance from me, must now believe it, in the respect I know her to have for me, and in the perfect confidence I know her, in her better moments, to repose in my truthfulness.

The publication of this statement provoked even more severe

comment in the press than its predecessor had. *John Bull* noted dryly, "Qui s'excuse, s'accuse," and said Dickens had "committed a grave mistake in telling his readers how little after all, he thinks of the marriage tie." The Liverpool *Mercury* struck a still sharper note: "This favourite of the public informs some hundreds of thousands of readers that the wife whom he has vowed to love and cherish has utterly failed to discharge the duties of a mother; and he further hints that her mind is disordered. . . . If this is 'manly consideration,' we should like to be favoured with a definition of unmanly selfishness and heartlessness."

On the assumption, which it was natural for the newspapers to make, that Dickens had authorized the publication of this statement no less than of the one he had sent out to the press himself, the rebuke was well merited; and, indeed, considering the vagueness of the instructions Dickens had given Smith, it is difficult to see how he could have expected that the letter would not sooner or later get into print. But Dickens always referred to it as the "violated letter," and was much upset at its publication.

With horrible and needless publicity – and largely of his own making – Dickens had at last become freed from his wife. Through all the cruel pillorying she suffered she had remained meekly silent. But Dickens too had undergone emotional turmoil and dreadful abrasions of the spirit.

If, deep within him, he had longed to be rid of Catherine, he had considered it hopeless, and had not wanted an open break nor willed any of the circumstances that had been forced upon him with this separation. It had come only through the public separation he had sought to avoid and amid a noise of slander that his very efforts to silence had made even more clamorous.

Nor, though he could not admit it even in his own heart, had his own behaviour been stainless. He had seized with ruthless intensity upon the advantage the venom of the Hogarths gave him. He had been far from chivalrous to poor Kate – much less generous than she in her silence had been to him. No sooner had her family assailed his good name than he hastened to proclaim her deficiencies in ways that were bound to be published to all the world. And although he had not precipitated the final breach, secretly he knew he was not without reproach, technically innocent though he might be of the Hogarths' accusations.

He felt that he had been hideously wronged at the hands of those from whom he might justly have expected gratitude. Contending with his indignation, however, and suppressed by it, were a dark frustration and an unavowed sense of guilt. During the entire struggle he was half deranged with hysteria and anguish. "Nothing," said Katey, "could surpass the misery and unhappiness of our home." But Catherine was gone now, and Dickens could take his way through life unimpeded by having to drag her in his wake. It remained to be seen how happy he would be.

PART NINE

The Last Assay
1858–1865

41

The Track of a Storm

On a Thursday evening in the middle of June 1858, Dickens stepped out onto the brightly lighted platform of St Martin's Hall. It was his first reading after the publication of his "personal" statement in *Household Words*; London was buzzing with scandal. His friends were worried lest he be greeted by an outburst of antagonism. His manager, Arthur Smith, was tremulous with fears of his being hooted from the stage. Dickens kept his own counsel and maintained a demeanour of absolute calm. Walking rather stiffly, right shoulder aggressively forward, flower in button hole and gloves in hand, he strode across the stage and confronted the audience.

The applause that roared through the hall might have been heard half a mile away at Charing Cross. Although the newspapers and even Dickens's friends might disapprove of his personal statement, it had not alienated the great body of his readers. His devoted admirers had not deserted him; their cheers were a tumultuous testimony of loyalty and support. Dickens showed no emotion. Taking his place at his reading desk, he opened his book and began with as much composure as if he were in his own study. Throughout the remaining six weeks of his London season there were enthusiastic crowds at every reading.

But he was keeping an iron restraint upon himself. Wild rumour linked him infamously with Georgina, with Ellen, with various other actresses. The storm raging through his heart left it "jagged and rent and out of shape" under the sense of wrong and strain. In his bitterness he broke off relations with everyone he associated with the Hogarth accusations. Although Mark Lemon withdrew from representing Catherine when these charges became a part of the negotiations, and declined to forward any communications dealing with them, Dickens could not forgive the refusal to insert his statement in *Punch*. He angrily read the decision as the treacherous act of a false friend denying him a means of self-defence.

There is no telling whether it occurred to Dickens that Bradbury and

Evans rather than Lemon might have been responsible for the *Punch* veto, but he was vehement in his resentment of them as well. He was so strongly convinced that Evans above all was aligned with his detractors that he forbade his family even to remain in the same company with the publisher.

> I have had stern occasion to impress upon my children [he wrote Evans], that their father's name is their best possession and that it would indeed be trifled with and wasted by him, if either through himself or through them, he held any terms with those who have been false to it, in the only great need and under the only great wrong it has ever known. You know very well, why (with hard distress of mind and bitter disappointment), I have been forced to include you in this class.

With Thackeray too the separation troubles brought about an enduring breach. The two men had never really been congenial, and several times their relationship had been strained. The difference that now developed between them brought out all that each most disliked in the other. Its immediate cause, however, lay not in Dickens's marital discords or even in Thackeray's luckless remark about his having a liaison with an actress, but in an article written by Edmund Yates.

For some time the young son of Dickens's old friend Frederick Yates had been supplementing his income as a Post Office employee by literary journalism, and had recently taken a place on the staff of a little weekly called *Town Talk*. Coming into the office one warm June evening to make up the paper, Yates discovered that one of the contributors had not sent in his copy. Stripping off his coat, he cudgelled his brains for something to fill in the gap. Only the previous week he had written a brief pen-portrait of Dickens; the best he could think of on the spur of the moment was a gossipy column about Thackeray. Dashing this off hastily, he rushed it to the printer and forgot all about it.

But Thackeray, more sensitive than he thought it reasonable for others to be, no sooner saw this article than he fell into a raging fury. There was, indeed, cause for offence in Yates's hurried improvisation. Yates had written,

> No one meeting him could fail to recognize in him a gentleman; his bearing is cold and uninviting, his style of conversation either openly cynical, or affectedly good-natured and benevolent; his

468

bonhomie is forced, his wit biting, his pride easily touched . . . No one succeeds better than MR THACKERAY in cutting his coat according to his cloth: here he flattered the aristocracy, but when he crossed the Atlantic, GEORGE WASHINGTON became the idol of his worship, the "Four Georges" the objects of his bitterest attacks. . . . Our own opinion is that his success is on the wane . . . there is a want of heart in all he writes, which is not to be balanced by the most brilliant sarcasm and the most perfect knowledge of the workings of the human heart.

Some of these remarks were silly, some of them were false, and all of them were wounding to Thackeray's pride. The savage portraits of the Crawley family and the Marquis of Steyne in *Vanity Fair* did not flatter the aristocracy, and Thackeray's lectures on the four Georges had been delivered in both England and America. Tenderly affectionate with his friends, he was often in scrapes through a sense of humour that, without meaning any more harm than an awkward puppy, managed to sound rude and cutting. To his already shaky friend Forster, who was born the day after April Fool's, the same day of the year as that on which Dickens was married, Thackeray wrote, "I wish you many happy returns of your birthday, Dickens of his marriage-day, & both of you of the day previous." Beneath these gaucheries Thackeray was really a shy sentimentalist who disguised his diffidence with hauteur and his soft-heartedness with cynicism. His pride and his modesty combined to make him assume the uneasy tone of depreciating both "society" and art and behaving as if he thought more of being a gentleman than of being a genius.

One other aspect of Yates's strictures stabbed a tender nerve in Thackeray. Despite the humiliating inferiority of his sales to those of Dickens, he knew that there were people who regarded him as a better writer, and he had never ceased to be humbly grateful for his own success. But he also knew that he was beginning to repeat himself and feared that his creative vein was running dry. He felt hardly less wounded by the suggestion that his popularity was on the wane than he did by the imputations against his integrity. In his anger he wrote Yates a stinging letter.

As I understand your phrases, you impute insincerity to me for sentiments which I have delivered in public, and charge me with advancing statements which I have never delivered at all. . . . We meet at a club, where, before you were born I believe, I and other gentlemen have been in the habit of talking without any idea that our conversation would supply paragraphs for professional vendors of "Literary Talk"; and I don't remember that out of that Club I have ever exchanged six words with you. Allow me to inform you that the talk which you have heard there is not intended for newspaper remark; and to beg – as I have a right to do – that you will refrain from printing comments on my private conversations; that you will forego discussions, however blundering, upon my private affairs; and that you will henceforth please to consider any question of my personal truth and sincerity as quite out of the province of your criticism.

Infuriated in turn by this castigation, Yates drafted an insolent reply, pointing out how often Thackeray had caricatured their fellow members in the Garrick Club: Captain Shindy, for example, in the *Book of Snobs*, and Foker, in *Pendennis*, who were recognizable parodies of the phrases, gestures, and appearance of well-known members. In *Punch's Prize Novelists*, moreover, Thackeray had ridiculed Ainsworth, Disraeli, Lever, and Bulwer Lytton in a way holding them up to contempt; his pursuit of Lytton, indeed, "Mistaw Edwad Lyttn Bulwig," had verged upon persecution. This sharp *tu quoque*, Yates thought, would make Thackeray draw in his horns.

Before sending it, however, Yates sought the advice of Dickens, in whose behalf he had just published a warm defence. Dickens was in a state of emotional agitation, he was grateful for Yates's support, he had not forgotten Thackeray's blundering reference to the rumours about himself and Ellen Ternan. Had Dickens been under less strain he might have told Yates to apologize. As it was, he advised Yates that the sketch was indefensible and his reply too violent, but he agreed that Thackeray's tone made an apology impossible. After further consultation, Yates sent an answer concluding, "If your letter to me were not both 'slanderous and untrue,' I should readily have discussed its subject with you, and avowed my earnest and frank desire to set right anything I have left wrong. Your letter being what it is, I have nothing to add to my present reply."

Thackeray promptly appealed "to the Committee of the Garrick Club to decide whether the complaints I have against Mr Yates are not well founded, and whether the practice of publishing such articles . . . is not intolerable in a society of gentlemen." The Committee notified Yates that they would consider the complaint at a special meeting.

Yates, surprised, replied that he felt they had no jurisdiction: his article did not mention the Club and referred to no conversation that had taken place there.

The Committee ordered Yates "to make an ample apology to Mr Thackeray, or to retire from the Club." Yates refused to withdraw from the Club and appealed to a General Meeting of its members. Meanwhile, in the ninth number of *The Virginians*, which had just made its appearance, Thackeray alluded to Yates as "young Grubstreet, who corresponds with three penny papers and describes the persons and conversation of gentlemen whom he meets at his 'clubs.'" Not long afterwards, he returned to the attack with some sneering remarks about "Tom Garbage," "an esteemed contributor to the *Kennel Miscellany*."

Dickens voiced his feelings about Thackeray's course by summarizing this stage of the controversy: "Committee thereupon call a General Meeting, yet pending. Thackeray *thereupon*, by way of showing what an ill thing it is for writers to attack one another in print, denounces E. Y. (in Virginians) as 'Young Grub Street.' Frightful mess, muddle, complication, and botheration ensue. Which witch's broth is now in full boil."

Neither Thackeray nor Yates attended the General Meeting on 10 July. A letter from Yates was read, offering to apologize to the Club, but not to Thackeray. Dickens supported Yates, saying he had been on good terms with Thackeray many years and was sorry to be opposed to him. The Meeting sustained the Committee by a vote of seventy to forty-six, giving Yates a period of grace in which to apologize to Thackeray or be expelled from the Club. On his refusal to yield, his name was erased from the list of members. Following Dickens's advice, Yates took Counsel's opinion on the legality of his expulsion and was told that if he were forcibly refused admission to the Club he could bring suit. He consequently made a formal attempt, in the presence of witnesses, to enter its premises, and had himself ejected by the Secretary. These moves in the wrangle had protracted themselves throughout the whole summer and autumn. On 24 November Dickens appealed to Thackeray for a peaceful settlement.

Could there not be a conference, he asked, "between me, as representing Mr Yates, and an appointed friend of yours, as representing you, with the hope and purpose of some quiet accommodation of this deplorable matter, which will satisfy the feelings of all concerned?" Yates had consulted him from the first, he admitted, and he had told him the article in *Town Talk* could not be defended but confirmed his feelings that the strong language of Thackeray's letter made an apology impossible. He would be glad to mediate between them, Dickens concluded – "and God knows in no hostile spirit towards any one, least of all to you. If it cannot take place, the thing is at least no worse than it was; and you will burn this letter, and I will burn your answer."

But Thackeray read Dickens's words as a confession that he had been a secret enemy guiding all Yates's moves. "I grieve to gather from your letter that you were Mr Yates's adviser in the dispute between him and me. His letter was the cause of my appeal to the Garrick Club from insults against which I had no other remedy." Since Thackeray had submitted the case to the Club it was out of his hands. "Yours, &c., W. M. Thackeray." Forster had a burst of rage when Dickens showed him this letter. "He be damned with his 'Yours, &c.' "

Thackeray was annoyed to hear from an acquaintance that even his admirers blamed him for "condescending to quarrel with so young and unimportant a person as Mr Yates." "You may not think, young 'un," he exclaimed, "that I am quarrelling with Mr Yates. *I am hitting the man behind him.*" But to the Committee of the Garrick Club he addressed a letter quoting Dickens's offer and saying that if they could devise any peaceful means of ending the affair no one would be better pleased than he. The Committee, however, were in no mood for compromise, and Yates learned that he could pursue the matter only by bringing a Chancery suit that would cost him £200 to £300 if he lost.

The affair ended any semblance of cordiality between the two novelists. Thackeray imagined Dickens jealous of him as a dangerous rival. Dickens blamed Thackeray for an undignified stooping to public resentment and for using his prestige to punish so cruelly a younger and weaker man. He was exasperated too by the violation of his confidence in quoting to the Committee any part of a letter that he had suggested should be burned if Thackeray refused his offer of mediation. All visiting ceased between Dickens and Thackeray, although their daughters continued to be friends. Not until a few days before Thackeray's death in 1863 did he and Dickens ever speak to each other again.

The country reading tour from which Dickens had returned in mid-November had been as spectacularly triumphant as his London readings. Everywhere, in England, Ireland, and Scotland, he was greeted with tumultuous applause. Standing coolly behind his desk, Dickens always waited for absolute hush. Then the amazing performance began. It was more than a reading; it was an extraordinary exhibition of acting that seized upon its auditors with a mesmeric possession. Without moving from the centre of the stage, solely by changes of voice, by gesture, by facial expression, Dickens peopled his stage with a throng of characters.

He had countless voices and countless faces. His Mrs Gamp was snuffy, husky, and unctuous, his Paul Dombey the weary alto of a tired child, his Justice Stareleigh a series of sudden snorts and convulsive starts, his Bob Cratchit a frightened gasp in the meckest of tones. He could be a cockney medical student, a country yokel, an overbearing London alderman, the plump sister at the Christmas party crying out, "It's your uncle Scro-o-o-oge!" His face could flash from the pinched, avaricious countenance of Scrooge to the browbeaten and bewildered Mr Winkle. Simply by drumming on his desk top he suggested all the dash and gaiety of Mr Fezziwig's ball, and by a humbly placatory bob Trotty Veck's respect for Alderman Cute. Spectators noted how monstrous he looked as Squeers, how murderous as Jonas Chuzzlewit, and in their enthusiasm even insisted that in the scene between Fanny Squeers and Nicholas one side of Dickens's face looked like Fanny and the other like Nicholas.

When Dickens had first read the *Christmas Carol* for charity, it had taken him three hours. Gradually he subjected it to increasingly drastic cuts until it could be performed in two hours. Descriptive passages he ruthlessly pruned or entirely omitted. He speeded up the narrative, tightened the dialogue and made it more sharply typical of each speaker. In his reading copy, whole areas of text were blocked out in red ink and changed wordings written between the lines or bulging out in encircling balloons. In the margins there were stage directions to himself in blue, such as "Snap your fingers," "Rising action," "Scrooge melted," and "Soften very much."

He prepared similar reading versions of *The Chimes, The Cricket on the Hearth*, "The Story of Little Dombey," and a group consisting of "Mrs Gamp," "The Poor Travellers," and "The Boots at the Holly Tree," the last two of which were shorter Christmas stories from *Household Words*. A little later he added from *Pickwick* the "Trial Scene" and "Bob Sawyer's Party." All these he practised hundreds of times, striving for perfection in every intonation, achieving absolute mastery over every episode. The time came when he knew each reading by heart, keeping the book before him only for safety, "gagging" on sudden inspiration, magnetizing his hearers to follow him at will.

His first provincial reading was at Clifton on 2 August 1858. In the large room there "the people were perfectly taken off their legs by

473

The Chimes." The following night, at Exeter, "was a prodigious cram"; then, during the same week, came Plymouth, and Clifton again. On the closing night there, "a torrent of five hundred shillings bore Arthur away, pounded him against the wall, flowed on to the seats over his body, scratched him, and damaged his best dress suit." The week's receipts were nearly £400.

At Liverpool on one of the three nights of the readings 2,300 people crowded the hall and the receipts were 200 guineas. From there, Dickens crossed over to Ireland, where he read at Dublin, Belfast, Cork, and Limerick. The Irish audiences were highly excited, and of the quickness of their response to humour Dickens had no question, but he did not feel at first that they were as sensitive to pathos. He soon revised this impression. "I have never seen *men* go in to cry so undisguisedly as they did at that reading yesterday afternoon. They made no attempt whatever to hide it, and certainly cried more than the women."

Everywhere he was received with a warmth of personal affection almost overwhelming. People stopped him on the street, saying, "Do me the honour to shake hands, Misther Dickens, and God bless you, sir; not ounly for the light you've been to me this night, but for the light you've been in mee house, sir (and God love your face!) this many a year." Every night ladies begged John, his personal servant, for the flower from his coat. One morning, when the petals from his geranium showered on the platform while he was reading "Little Dombey," the women swarmed up on the platform after he was gone, and picked *them* up as keepsakes.

These blossoms for his buttonhole Dickens found himself receiving everywhere he travelled, by order of Mary Boyle.

> Dearest Meery [he wrote her], First let me tell you that all the magicians and spirits in your employ have fulfilled the instructions of their wondrous mistress, to admiration. Flowers have fallen in my path wherever I have trod. . . . Touching that other matter on which you write me tenderly and with a delicacy of regard and interest that I deeply feel, I hope I may report that I am calming down again. I have been exquisitely distressed. . . . I had one of these fits yesterday, and was utterly desolate and lost. But it is gone, thank God, and the sky has brightened before me once more.

During all this time Ellen Ternan was living in London at her family lodgings, 31 Berners Street, Oxford Street, with her sister Maria.

Dickens had taken all the Ternans under his protection. The eldest sister, Frances Eleanor, he had sent to Italy with her mother to complete her musical education. There, a few years later, she became the second wife of Thomas Adolphus Trollope. Dickens also tried to advance the theatrical career of Maria. "She is accomplished and attractive," he wrote Benjamin Webster, "well used to the stage, sings prettily, and is favourably known to London audiences."

Returning to London for a week-end in October, Dickens angrily learned that the two sisters, living alone, had been subjected to indecent persecution from a policeman. Wills must go at once to Scotland Yard and demand an investigation. "My suspicion is, that the Policeman in question has been suborned to find out all about their domesticity by some 'Swell.' If so, there can be no doubt that the man ought to be dismissed." The outcome of the episode is unknown, but the personal and protective outrage in Dickens's tone is unmistakable.

Meanwhile, his reading tour had moved on through the Midlands and the north of England. His reception everywhere continued to be an ovation. At the Harrogate reading one man "found something so very ludicrous in Toots, that he *could not* compose himself at all, but laughed until he sat wiping his eyes with his handkerchief. And whenever he felt Toots coming again he began to laugh and wipe his eyes afresh, and when he came he gave a kind of cry, as if it were too much for him."

At Newcastle upon Tyne, Dickens was joined by Katey and Mamey, who went on with him into Scotland. Edinburgh the readings took by storm: "The Chimes shook it; Little Dombey blew it up." The readings in Dundee, Aberdeen, Perth, and Glasgow were also a triumph. With the middle of October he was starting on the last part of his tour. Bradford, Manchester, Birmingham, Nottingham, Derby, Leamington, Wolverhampton, and Southampton were all crowded into a single month. He wound up in Brighton on 13 November. In less than three and a half months he had given eighty-seven readings. After deducting all expenses he found that he had cleared over 1,000 guineas a month.

More than the money, though, was the comfort and reassurance of the loving faces and grateful words with which he was greeted everywhere. The continuing newspaper castigations of his "violated" letter made him wince with a pain all the more severe because his conscience must have whispered that it was not entirely undeserved. For all these distresses the warmth of his audiences was a balm. "The manner in which the people have everywhere delighted to express that they have a personal affection for me," he wrote Miss Coutts, "and the interest of tender friends in me, is (especially at this time) high and far above all considerations."

During the Irish part of Dickens's journeyings, in Belfast, he had been astonished to receive a visit from his brother Frederick. It had been more than a year and a half since Dickens had firmly declined to incur further financial responsibilities for his undependable brother. Thereupon Fred had managed to obtain money from both Wills and Henry Austin, failed to repay it, and then, unabashed, asked Dickens for a loan of £30. Dickens refused any further aid:

> Firstly, because I cannot trust you, and because your bad faith with Wills and Austin makes the word "lend" an absurdity.
>
> Secondly, because if this were otherwise it would do you no real good and would not in the least save you against the creditors who have already the power of taking you in execution.

Now, however, at the sight of the wastrel for whom he had tried to do so much, Dickens's heart melted. "I was dreadfully hard with him at first," he wrote Georgina, "but relented." The warmer relationship did not last long. Barely had Dickens ended his tour than he learned from his old friend Thompson, Fred's brother-in-law, that Fred was in deeper trouble. The marriage that the Wellers and Dickens had both opposed had turned out badly, Fred and Anna quarrelled furiously, and Fred left her, bitterly refusing to make her any allowance.

At Thompson's request Dickens tried, but fruitlessly, to work out some kind of agreement. This was the end, at last, of Dickens's efforts to help Frederick in any way. There are only scattered references to him in Dickens's later correspondence. And no more is heard of him until Fred's death in 1868.

On Dickens's return to London from his tour, he took up his quarrel with Bradbury and Evans. He was determined to break off all relations with them. For the publication of his books he would go back to Chapman and Hall. William Hall was dead, Edward Chapman was thinking of retirement. His cousin Frederic, now a partner, was a bluff, cheery businessman bent on giving Dickens anything he wanted. The only thing Dickens wanted was that his publishers should do exactly what he wanted, and that was the way it was henceforth to be.

But Bradbury and Evans must be ousted from having any connection with the production of *Household Words* as well. They had always printed the periodical, and Evans claimed that the other proprietors had no control over its manufacture. Dickens insisted that as the largest proprietor he could change the printer and publisher at will. Evans tried in vain to make conciliatory advances; Dickens refused to see him. Forster rode over the unfortunate printers like a majestic human steamroller. It would be best for Bradbury and Evans, he told them, to sell their share of *Household Words* to Dickens. When they refused to do this, Forster threatened that Dickens would destroy the value of the magazine by announcing that he was withdrawing from it and starting another of exactly the same kind.

No agreement with Bradbury and Evans proved possible, and Dickens promptly set about putting the threat into effect. He flabbergasted Forster by suggesting for the new magazine a title drawn from Shakespeare's *Henry VI*: *Household Harmony*. When Forster pointed out what derisive capital could be made out of the recent lack of harmony in his own household Dickens was irritated but he knew Forster was right, and threw out a cluster of other ideas: *Once a Week, The Hearth, The Forge, The Crucible, The Anvil of the Time, Charles Dickens's Own, Seasonable Leaves, Evergreen Leaves, Home, Home Music, Change, Time and Tide, Twopence, English Bells, Weekly Bells, The Rocket, Good Humour.*

None of these chimed, however, with his desire to use with his title a quotation from Shakespeare. A few days later he found one in *Othello*, which he slightly altered for his purpose:

"The story of our lives, from year to year." – *Shakespeare*.
ALL THE YEAR ROUND.
A weekly journal conducted by Charles Dickens.

With his usual energy Dickens made all the business arrangements. The new editorial headquarters were at 11 Wellington Street, only a few doors from those of *Household Words*. Dickens owned three quarters of the venture and Wills the remaining quarter. Dickens was editor at a salary of £504 a year, and Wills subeditor and general manager at £420. If Wills retired, his share was to be reduced to one eighth, and the name *All the Year Round* was Dickens's exclusive property.

Bradbury and Evans brought suit to restrain Dickens from "injuring their joint property." Dickens received the news with deadly and self-assured calm, Forster with rage. "The dear fellow was here yesterday morning," Dickens wrote, "smoking all over his head, and fuming himself like a steamboat ready to start." But it was obvious that Dickens could not be forced to continue editing *Household Words* or prevented from starting another periodical. Nor could Bradbury and Evans, who owned only a one quarter share in *Household Words*, appoint another editor without Dickens's consent. The Master of the Rolls therefore decided on 26 March 1859, that the magazine should be sold at auction. Meanwhile, Dickens had advertised that the last number of *Household Words* would be published on 28 May and that the first number of *All the Year Round* would appear on 30 April.

When the auction took place on 16 May, Dickens had arranged that Arthur Smith should bid for him. Dickens acquired the property, including its stock and stereotype plates, for £3,550. Inasmuch as he valued the stock and plates at £1,600 and paid only one quarter of the purchase price to Bradbury and Evans, he estimated that he had acquired the name and prestige of *Household Words* for less than £500.

In the 28 May number of *All the Year Round* he consequently added to its title the words "with which is incorporated *Household Words*," and published a triumphant valedictory in the final number of the magazine he had killed. Bradbury and Evans struck back by establishing a rival magazine called *Once a Week*, one of the titles, as it chanced, that Dickens had considered and rejected. They tried slavishly and blindly to imitate Dickens's editorial policies. "What fools they are!" he exclaimed contemptuously. "As if a mole couldn't see that their only chance was in a careful separation of themselves from the faintest approach or assimilation to All the Year Round!"

All the Year Round, from the very first, was a phenomenal success. Its only striking innovation was that its first pages were always reserved for a serial story by a well-known writer, who was no longer left anonymous but advertised with the magazine. To start off with a bang, Dickens began with his own new novel, *A Tale of Two Cities*. This was followed in November by Wilkie Collins's *The Woman in White*. For the right to publish an American edition of the magazine one day after it appeared in England, Dickens received £1,000 a year. Its circulation at home rose with hardly a break. By its fifth number it had trebled that of *Household Words*, which during its very best years had sold perhaps some 40,000 copies a week. Within ten years *All the Year Round* reached 300,000.

The idea for his new novel had come to Dickens more than a year before, in the midst of the turmoil and anguish of his disintegrating marriage. "I have so far verified what is done and suffered in these pages," Dickens wrote in the Preface, "as that I have certainly done and suffered it all myself."

The statement was true. While he was tearing himself apart as Richard Wardour in *The Frozen Deep* he had conceived Dr Manette's long imprisonment and Sidney Carton's death amid the flames of the Terror. He had thought of his own life with Catherine as an iron-bound and stone-walled misery weighed down by adamantine chains. It is not strange that in the fantasy from which imagination is born he should dream of a prisoner bitterly immured for years and at last set free, and of a despairing love rising to a noble height of sacrifice. The story as a whole reflected Dickens's anguished sense of the grandeur of renunciation, his longing, and his rebellion against the imprisoning codes of a society that inflicted the most hideous sufferings on mankind.

At first he thought of calling the novel *One of These Days*. Then, "What do you think," he asked Forster, "of *this* name for my story – BURIED ALIVE? Does it seem too grim? Or THE THREAD OF GOLD? Or, THE DOCTOR OF BEAUVAIS?" But at the time, and for months thereafter, he was too agitated to compose himself for any protracted work of creation. In February 1859, when it became necessary for him to make a start if the tale was to begin in the first number of *All the Year Round*, he still had trouble getting under way.

To aid him in the writing of the book, with its background of eighteenth-century England and France, Dickens appealed to Carlyle, whose *French Revolution* he deeply admired, to suggest some source materials that he might consult. He was grateful but staggered when Carlyle sardonically chose two cartloads of books at the London Library and had them all sent to him. The more Dickens waded through them, however, the more he felt with amazed admiration that Carlyle had torn out their vitals and fused them into his fuliginous masterpiece, "which was aflame with the very essence of the conflagration."

By March Dickens's difficulties in writing had smoothed themselves out. "I have got exactly the name for the story that is wanted," he reported exultantly; "exactly what will fit the opening to a T. A TALE OF TWO CITIES. Also . . . I have struck out a rather original and bold idea. That is, at the end of each month to publish the monthly part in the green cover, with two illustrations at the old shilling." With his usual business astuteness he thus simultaneously appealed to a weekly and a monthly audience.

When Edmund Yates was considering taking legal action against the Garrick Club, Dickens had accompanied him to a consultation in the chambers of Edwin James, a pushing and unscrupulous barrister who was later disbarred for malpractice. Dickens quietly observed his florid, hard-faced bluster; in the sixth and seventh numbers of *A*

Tale of Two Cities he brought in the character of Mr Stryver, for whom Sydney Carton serves as legal "jackal." "Stryver is a good likeness," Yates observed. Dickens smiled. "Not bad, I think," he agreed, "especially after only one sitting."

Meanwhile Dickens had begun sitting for his own portrait to W. P. Frith. His expression, Frith thought, was that of a man "who had reached the topmost rung of a very high ladder and was perfectly aware of his position." The portrait, Dickens jokingly observed, was "a little too much (to my thinking) as if my next-door neighbour were my deadly foe, uninsured, and I had just received tidings of his house being afire . . ."

With the coming of June, Dickens settled down in Gad's Hill to working on his story. Mamey and Katey were away visiting friends and Dickens and Georgina were alone in the house with Plorn, the servants, and the two dogs, Turk, a bloodhound, and Linda, a St Bernard. He was still suffering from the remains of a cold contracted in the late spring.

> I have been getting on in health very slowly [he wrote Forster in July], and through irksome botheration enough. But I think I am round the corner. This cause – and the heat – has tended to my doing no more than hold my ground, my old month's advance, with the Tale of Two Cities. The small portions thereof drive me frantic; but I think the tale must have taken a strong hold. The run upon our monthly parts is surprising, and last month we sold 35,000 back numbers.

Dickens had by this time reached Book Three, "The Track of a Storm," in which his pen caught fire portraying those wild tumults of the Revolution that he understood with a deeper sympathy through the bitterness and turmoil, the intolerable sense of wrong, that had agitated his nights and days. The boiling cauldron of the Terror was a macrocosm filled with huge and flaming projections of his own raging emotions.

And again, as when he described the Gordon Riots in *Barnaby Rudge,* his emotions are divided. He pities the victims, but his deepest understanding is with a people driven mad. Though he sickens at the cruelty of mass murder, in his heart there is also a sympathy for these frenzied mobs, turned wolfish by oppression, that rises to a fierce exultation. As the dreadful scenes poured out of him, he achieved a kind of relief.

If he still did not feel happy, he was calmer in mind. Like an aroused people punishing its rulers, or an angry lion attacking its tormentors, he had lashed out and severely mauled his publishers for daring to disobey his mandates. He had established a new periodical even more profitable than the one he had destroyed. Caught up in the excitement of his new story, he had already proved that he had not lost his hold upon his public. In his paid readings he had struck into an enormously remunerative course that at the same time relieved his need of distraction, satisfied his appetite for theatrical excitement, and gratified his love of establishing a close personal contact with an audience.

The affection with which he was received everywhere was grateful to his torn feelings amid the upheaval of his life. Some of the emotions still with him the following spring are touched on in a letter to Miss Coutts: "I do not suppose myself blameless, but in this thing as in all others know . . . how much I stand in need of the highest of all charity and mercy. All I claim for myself, is, that when I was very young, I made a miserable mistake . . ."

And yet the storm through which he had passed, the relentless spirit he had displayed, had not left him unscarred. The look of exultant enmity Dickens had felt in Frith's portrait of him was a true echo of the passions to which he had given rein during these fifteen months that followed his separation from Catherine. Though he humbly confessed himself in need of charity and mercy, he believed that all his sufferings had resulted from the mistake of a marriage contracted in his youth. He had never shown the least sign of deviating from the conviction that his every step during and after the dissolution of that marriage had been moderate and just. He even professed to believe that he was altogether gentle and mild. "You surprise me," he wrote Mrs Watson, "by supposing that there is ever latent a defiant and roused expression in the undersigned lamb!"

42

Surface Serene

All the summer of 1859, save for business trips to London, Dickens remained at Gad's Hill. The girls had returned, and now and then there were visitors: Wilkie Collins in July, Tom Beard in August, and a young Irish writer named Percy Fitzgerald, who had contributed to *Household Words*. In September Dickens spent a few days at Broadstairs, where he hoped the sea air and sea water would enable him to get rid of his still lingering cold. During the autumn he directed his attention chiefly to three aims: planning for the futures of his sons, finishing *A Tale of Two Cities*, and lining up further serial stories to succeed Collins's *The Woman in White* when it was concluded the following summer.

Upon the prospects of the boys Dickens looked with various degrees of solicitude. Charley seemed to be doing well; he had spent several years with Baring Brothers, where he was highly praised, and since 1858 had been looking forward to setting up in business for himself. In the spring of 1860 he went to Hong Kong, "strongly backed up by Barings, to buy tea on his own account . . ." Walter, too, had distinguished himself in India during the Mutiny and been made a lieutenant before his eighteenth birthday.

But Frank presented more difficult problems. Afflicted with a painful stammer, he also suffered on occasion from deafness. All agog to be a doctor, he had been sent to Germany to learn the language. But there Frank became convinced that he would never get over his stammering and that consequently all professions were barred to him; the only thing he would like to be was a gentleman-farmer, at the Cape, in Canada, or Australia. Back in England, he again veered towards medicine, but Dickens was not convinced that he had any steadiness of purpose.

Alfred, a dependable and self-reliant boy of fourteen, was studying at Wimbledon to qualify for an Army commission in the Artillery or the Engineers. Sydney, now twelve, was mad about the sea and wished to enter the Navy. In May Dickens placed him in a preparatory school at

Southsea and later obtained his nomination as a Naval Cadet. The following year, after passing his examination, Sydney went on board his training ship at Chatham.

For the two youngest boys, Harry, aged ten, and Plorn, only seven, it was too early to make plans. Plorn was still so much the baby of the family that his eldest sister did not want him sent to Boulogne, where most of the other boys had started school. Harry was consequently brought back from Boulogne to join Plorn in attending the near-by Rochester Grammar School.

Meanwhile Dickens had been applying himself doggedly to *A Tale of Two Cities*. By mid-October it was completed. "Carlyle says 'It's wonderful'" (although he complained of having to read it by "teaspoonfuls") "and Forster turns white with admiring approval."

Then came a crowded two weeks of reading in the Midlands, a new place almost every night. "Cambridge beyond everything," Dickens wrote; at Oxford in spite of persistent rain the University came out brilliantly. On the concluding night at Cheltenham the profits for that single occasion were £70.

Promptly on his return to London in November, Dickens flung himself into obtaining the next serial for *All the Year Round*. The first person to whom he wrote was George Eliot, whose *Scenes of Clerical Life* he had tremendously admired when she sent him a copy in 1858. Although at that time he had no idea of who the author was, he shrewdly suspected her sex. If the tale were not by a woman, he wrote her, "I believe that no man ever before had the art of making himself, mentally, so like a woman, since the world began."

Later, in sending him a copy of *Adam Bede*, George Eliot revealed her identity. The new novel intensified Dickens's admiration of her genius:

> Every high quality that was in the former book, is in that, with a World of Power added thereunto. The conception of Hetty's character is so extraordinarily subtle and true, that I laid the book down fifty times, to shut my eyes and think about it. . . . The whole country life that the story is set in, is so real, so droll and genuine, and yet so select and polished by art, that I cannot praise it enough to you.

Now, on 14 November, he wrote to her companion, George Lewes, specifically proposing that she write a story for *All the Year Round* to begin publication some eight months hence. She should retain the copyright of the book, and be free on its completion as a serial to bring it out in book form with any publisher she chose. At first George Eliot demurred merely that she felt this arrangement would not give her enough time, and Dickens suggested eagerly that he extend it by having in the meanwhile a shorter story by Mrs Gaskell. Not until the following February did he learn that "Adam Bede" felt the serial form of publication sacrificed too much "to terseness and closeness of construction" and must disappoint him by refusing to undertake it.

During these negotiations he asked Mrs Gaskell to write a story to run twenty-two weeks, for which he offered her 200 guineas. While this was under discussion he joyfully concluded an arrangement with Charles Lever, the author of *Harry Lorrequer*, to publish a novel by him, either at the conclusion of *The Woman in White* or that of its successor. When neither Mrs Gaskell nor George Eliot proved able to oblige, Lever's novel, now called *A Day's Ride: A Life's Romance*, was definitely scheduled for the following July.

On reading the first instalments of Lever's story in June Dickens was delighted, although he thought a little condensation was needed. "I think the rising of invention in the drunken young man, extraordinarily humourous; it made me laugh to such an extent and with a heartiness that I should like you to have seen and heard. Go on and prosper!" He did not foresee anything ominous in the slight prolixity he had noticed.

Another book Dickens had read with loyal admiration only a few weeks before was Forster's *The Arrest of the Five Members*, a continuation of his extended treatment of the history of the Great Rebellion against Charles I. "I admired it all, went with it all, and was proud of my friend's having written it all. I felt it to be all square and sound and right, and to be of enormous importance in these times."

That spring Dickens had been heartily glad to hear that Macready at the age of sixty-seven was going to remarry and leave his gloomy Sherborne retreat for a handsome new home at Cheltenham, only four or five hours from London. But all the news of Dickens's friends was not so cheerful. Leigh Hunt had died the preceding August, and in November Frank Stone, his old companion of the splendid barnstorming days. In *All the Year Round* Dickens published an article regretting that he had imitated Hunt's "gay and ostentatious wilfulness" in the portrayal of Harold Skimpole, and denying again that Skimpole was intended to be like Hunt in any except these whimsical and airy qualities.

There were troubles and bereavements in Dickens's family as well. His youngest brother, Augustus, the pet "Boses" of twenty years ago, proved even more of a disappointment than Frederick. Augustus's wife had gone blind and he had finally deserted her, running away to America with another woman and leaving Dickens with still one more dependent relative to be provided for. Even under these circumstances Augustus continued to clamour for help. "I have been painfully restrained from communicating with Augustus," Dickens wrote his brother Alfred's wife, "by the knowledge (gained from a stern experience), that the least communication with him would be turned to some account, and that some suddenly virtuously indignant person would proclaim that but for me he would never have been drawn . . . to that advance of money, or to that recommendation, or what not."

On 27 July 1860, Alfred Dickens died of pleurisy. He had always been a hard-working engineer, employed in railway construction, but never managed to do more than earn a living. He

> left a widow and five children – you may suppose to whom . . . My mother, who was also left to me when my father died (I never had anything left to me but relations), is in the strangest state of mind from senile decay; and the impossibility of getting her to understand what is the matter, combined with her desire to be got up in sables like a female Hamlet, illumines the dreary scene with a ghastly absurdity that is the chief relief I can find in it.

Later in the autumn Elizabeth Dickens was established with Alfred's widow, Helen, in a house Dickens found for them on Haverstock Hill, a little south of Hampstead Heath. Here he visited them one day in November. His mother "was not in bed, but down-stairs. Helen and Letitia were poulticing her poor head, and, the instant she saw me, she plucked up a spirit, and asked me for 'a pound.' "

But these distresses and responsibilities do not altogether explain the restless uneasiness that still lay heavily upon Dickens's spirits. His freedom from the old domestic unhappiness had not brought him the peace of heart he had dreamed of. Even when he had imaged Ellen Ternan as an unattainable princess prisoned from him by the ogres of law and convention, he had despairingly exclaimed that "never was a man so seized and rended by one Spirit." But there is no evidence that his emotions had yet found any happy response; only that agonized outcry of horror at policemen prowling around Berners Street and serving as panders to some lustful "swell." The distractions of toil at his desk or the feverish thrill of moving enthralled audiences to laughter, excitement, and tears were still all he had.

Beneath a surface of serenity Gad's Hill was filled with under-currents of unhappiness. Mary adored her father and sided with him in the separation, but during this last year she had been in love and refused her suitor because Dickens did not approve. Her submission left her low-spirited and dejected. Katey sided with her mother and felt a vague suspicion that Aunt Georgy had played some devious role in the separation. Mary never saw her mother again until after Dickens's death, but Katey defiantly paid her visits to which Dickens had agreed, but which he felt were meant as a reproach to him. Katey was so miserable at home that when Wilkie Collins's brother Charles proposed she accepted him, although she did not love him.

Charles Allston Collins was thirty-one years of age, very tall, with a white face and flaming, floating orange hair. He had been a member of the Pre-Raphaelite Brotherhood with Rossetti, Burne-Jones, and Hol-man Hunt. He also had talents as a writer that Dickens respected sufficiently to publish a series of his sketches in *All the Year Round*; and wrote two small books of delicate humour, *A New Sentimental Journey* and *A Cruise on Wheels*. But he was almost twelve years older than Katey and often in ill health. Dickens sensed, moreover, that he had not won Katey's heart, and advised against the match. But fiery Katey was not her mild and malleable sister. She loved yet resented her father, chafed against him, and shared much of his obstinate self-will.

Dickens was obliged to yield, and the marriage was set for 17 July. At the wedding one person was conspicuously absent. It was Catherine Dickens.

Gad's Hill neighbours crowded the little church, "the people of the village strewed flowers in the churchyard," "and the energetic black-smith of the village had erected a triumphal arch in the court, and fired guns *all night* beforehand – to our great amazement: we not having the slightest idea what they meant."

At last, rustling and billowing in her crinoline, Katey was off for Dover, to spend her honeymoon in France. The red-faced infant, the small child Dickens had taken to Holborn every Christmas for toys, the little girl with scratched knees, the fiery-tempered "Tinderbox," the young girl dancing at Tavistock House in satin shoes and flowing white sash, the talented youthful artist, had grown up, changed to a woman, married, and gone. When the house was quiet and empty, Mary found her father in Katey's bedroom alone. He was on his knees, sobbing, with his head buried in her wedding gown. "But for me," he wept brokenly, "Katie would not have left home."

For some time Dickens had been desirous of selling Tavistock House and living entirely at Gad's Hill. He had come to dislike London, with its evil-smelling river and the heavy canopy of smoke forever lowering over its housetops. And his home there of the past nine years was over-shadowed with memories of misery and desperation poisoning even the glow of Christmas festivities and the feverish glitter of Twelfth-Night theatricals. He now determined that he would spend a large part of his time at Gad's Hill and rent a furnished house in London during the winter season. Most of the furniture of Tavistock House could be moved to the country, and there was enough to furnish a sitting-room and two bedrooms at the *All the Year Round* office that could be used whenever any of the family wanted to come into town.

When Tavistock House was put up for sale, a banker named J. P. Davis presented himself as a purchaser. "I must say," Dickens told Wills, "that in all things the purchaser has behaved thoroughly well, and that I can-not call to mind any occasion when I have had money-dealings with any one that have been so satisfactory, considerate, and trusting."

Clarkson Stanfield's scenes for *The Frozen Deep*, which Dickens had transformed into wall decorations, were accordingly taken down and rolled for transportation, together with all the other household effects that were to be moved. At Gad's Hill Dickens turned the downstairs bedroom to the right of the little entrance porch into his study. Here the books from the Tavistock House library and the door with the dummy bookbacks were installed. From its bow window he was able to look out across the lawn with its beds of scarlet geraniums to where a brick tunnel under the Dover Road gave access to his shrubbery on the other side. All morning long as he sat at his writing table he could raise his eyes and rest them on the blue sky between the green of two ancient cedars.

During this time of breaking up Tavistock House, Dickens seemed torn by a mania for breaking with the past. In the field behind Gad's Hill he burned all the accumulated letters and papers of twenty years. For the rest of his life he destroyed every personal letter he received as soon as he had answered it. So, innumerable letters from Ainsworth, Talfourd, Lady Blessington, Landor, Lady Holland, Miss Coutts, Leigh Hunt, Jeffrey, Sydney Smith, Rogers, Maclise, Cruikshank, Thackeray, Carlyle, Macready, Tennyson, Browning, Forster, Bulwer Lytton, Wilkie Collins, George Eliot, and many others all went up in the flames. When the last sheets had been consumed he said, "Would to God every letter I had ever written was on that pile!"

While Gad's Hill was still unsettled by painters and carpenters Dickens began writing in the best spare room. Since the conclusion of *A Tale of Two Cities*, his only contributions to *All the Year Round* had been a series of personal essays, under the title of *the Uncommercial Traveller*. "Nurses' Stories," "Travelling Abroad," "Birthday Celebrations," and "Chatham Dockyard" all contain fragments of autobiography. The little sketch on which he now started, however, developed so surprisingly that he decided to cancel it and reserve the idea for a new book. At first Dickens intended that it should become one of his long stories in twenty monthly numbers. The needs of *All the Year Round* forced him to reconsider this decision.

The Woman in White had been a sensation, but Lever's story, *A Day's Ride*, was not taking with the public, and for the first and only time the circulation of *All the Year Round* began to fall off. After its comic opening, Dickens complained, the story became too discursive and had no vitality.

Early in October "I called a council of war . . . It was perfectly clear that the one thing to be done was, for me to strike in. I have therefore decided to begin a story, the length of the Tale of Two Cities, on the First of December – begin publishing, that is. I must make the most I can out of the book . . . The name is, GREAT EXPECTATIONS. I think a good name?"

Although it was a sacrifice to turn the story into a weekly serial, it was a sacrifice for his own welfare. He could no longer, as in earlier days, write two novels simultaneously; if he made *Great Expectations* a story of twenty monthly parts he would be unable for almost two years to write a serial for *All the Year Round*, and that magazine was far too valuable to be endangered.

On the other hand, by dashing in now, I come in when most wanted; and if Reade and Collins follow me, our course will be shaped out handsomely and hopefully for between two and three years. A thousand pounds are to be paid for early proofs of the story to America.

The book will be written in the first person throughout, and during these first three weekly numbers you will find the hero to be a boy-child, like David. Then he will be an apprentice. You will not have to complain of the want of humour as in the Tale of Two Cities. I have made the opening, I hope, in its general effect exceedingly droll.

Though the story is told as autobiography, Pip, its hero, is much less literally a portrayal of Dickens than David Copperfield was, and the outward events of his life have no resemblance to those in the career of his creator. But, with an emblematic significance, they are so shaped as to enable Dickens to plumb those youthful humiliations and griefs that even in maturity he buried from all the world. Subtly disguised, but now seen in a new light, those shames recur as central themes in *Great Expectations*.

Fundamentally, the novel is a reassessment of Dickens's own former subservience to false values. The blacksmith and "the taint of prison and crime" which so mortify Pip, and which he comes to feel a remorseful humiliation at ever having been ashamed of, are both more humbling to genteel thought than the blacking warehouse and the debtors' prison. "The reappearance of Mr Dickens in the character of a blacksmith's boy," as Shaw remarks, "may be regarded as an apology to Mealy Potatoes."

There is a layer of criticism, however, in *Great Expectations* still deeper than this personal triumph over false social values. It pierces to the very core of the leisure-class ideal that lurks in the heart of a pecuniary society. This is symbolized in Pip's dream of becoming a gentleman living in grandeur on money he has done nothing to earn, supported entirely on the labour of others. Pip's "great expectations" are the great expectations of Victorian society. And Dickens's analysis of the emptiness and falseness that the acceptance of that ideal imposed on Pip is a measure of the corruption he now found in the society it dominates.

It was decided to start publication in *All the Year Round* before Lever's novel could inflict any further damage. Dickens set himself at once to soften the blow to Lever's self-esteem. He tried to break the news gently. "The best thing I can say in the beginning," he wrote Lever, "is, that it is not otherwise disagreeable to *me* than as it imposes this note upon me. It causes me no other uneasiness or regret." Their stories would have to go on side by side, however, for as long as Lever's continued. "Now do, pray, I entreat you," Dickens pleaded, "lay it well to heart that this might have happened with any writer." "Some of the best books ever written would not bear" the serial "mode of publication."

Lever felt deeply mortified. In his humiliation he spoke of bringing his own story to a speedy conclusion. "As to winding up," Dickens replied, "– you are to consider your own reputation, your own knowledge of the book as a whole, your own desire what it shall be, and your own opinion what it ought to be . . . Now, do take heart of grace and cheer up." *A Day's Ride* consequently limped along beside *Great Expectations* from the beginning of December, when the latter began, until almost the end of March 1861.

Dickens paid Lever £750 for the unsuccessful serial, and went to great pains to persuade Chapman and Hall to publish both it and its successor, *Barrington*. He continued to publish articles by Lever in *All the Year Round*, paying for them on acceptance. And Lever inscribed *Barrington* to Dickens: "Among the thousands who read and re-read your writings, you have not one who more warmly admires your genius than myself; and to say this in confidence to the world, I dedicate to you this story."

On 1 November, Dickens and Wilkie Collins went into North Devon together, to gather material for "A Message from the Sea," a story they had arranged to write in collaboration for the Christmas number of *All the Year Round*. At "a beastly hotel" in Bideford, "We had stinking fish for dinner, and have been able to drink nothing, though we have ordered wine, beer, and brandy-and-water." Back in London, Collins wrestled with the difficulties of his part of the story, "getting up spasmodically all day, and looking, in high-shouldered desperation out at window." Then things came right and he shot ahead. Dickens wrote the final part, which was sent to the printer at the end of the month.

At the turn of the year Dickens felt in better health than he had for some time. He took a furnished house at 3 Hanover Terrace, Regent's Park, until midsummer. Charley was now back from China, looking for his business partnership, and Dickens believed that he had solved the problem of what to do with Frank by taking him into the office of *All the Year Round*. "If I am not mistaken," Dickens said hopefully, "he has a natural literary taste and capacity, and may do very well with a chance so congenial to his mind, and being also entered at the Bar."

The move into London made it easier for Dickens to see Ellen Ternan, who was now established with her mother in a house at No. 2 Houghton Place, Ampthill Square. Here he was able to visit her, coming up from Wellington Street, and perhaps trudging home, in the late hours, through the Regent's Park. Francesco Berger, the young composer who had written the music for *The Frozen Deep*, tells of card games there on Sunday evenings and playing the piano part while Dickens and Ellen sang duets together.

It is inevitable that we should associate Pip's helpless enslavement to Estella with Dickens's passion for Ellen Ternan. Never before had he portrayed a man's love for a woman with such depth or revealed its desperation of compulsive suffering. David Copperfield's heartache for Dora is an iridescent dream-grief compared with Pip's agonized nightmare-reality. Pip's love is without illusion, all self-absorbed need; his desire for Estella is as self-centred as his desire to be a gentleman. It is the culminating symbol and the crowning indictment of a society dedicated to selfish ends. But Pip is not all selfish; he is capable of generosity and love. Indeed, by the close of the novel, he has learned from his experience, learned to work, learned to think for others, learned to love.

During the spring Dickens made such headway with *Great Expectations* that he felt able to undertake a series of six readings in London between 14 March and 18 April. They were given in St James's Hall, Piccadilly, St Martin's Hall having burned down. "The result of the six was, that, after paying a large staff of men and all other charges, and Arthur Smith's ten per cent. on the receipts, and replacing everything destroyed in the fire at St Martin's Hall (including all our tickets, country-baggage, cheque-boxes, books, and a quantity of gas-fittings and what not), I got upwards of £500."

He was now well into the last third of *Great Expectations*. As he had originally conceived it, in the end Pip was to lose Estella, to realize that his love for her had always been mad and hopeless, and know that they could never have been happy together. Thus, like his belief that he was Miss Havisham's chosen heir and like the wealth Magwitch really intended for him, the passion of Pip's life was to melt away, and all of his "great expectations" to come to naught. But such an ending distressed Bulwer Lytton, who read it in proofs while Dickens was staying with him for a few days at Knebworth. He urged Dickens to change it for one closing on a happier note. Could not Estella's heart be softened by sorrow and she and Pip brought together after all?

Lytton "supported his views with such good reasons" that Dickens determined to take his advice. It may be, too, that the changed ending reflected a desperate hope that Dickens could not banish from within his own heart. That hope had crept almost from the beginning into the delineation of Estella. Though Miss Havisham has brought her up to break men's hearts, she always makes a difference between Pip and the lovers she scorns and torments. Deep within him Dickens wanted to believe Estella might melt. And there could be no doubt that such an ending would be more agreeable to many of his readers than the twilight melancholy he had envisioned. "I have put in a very pretty piece of writing," he told Forster, "and I have no doubt the story will be more acceptable through the alteration."

With the conclusion of *Great Expectations* Dickens went down to Gad's Hill to relax during the summer and get ready to resume another series of his provincial readings in the autumn. He added a reading made from the Dotheboys Hall scenes of *Nicholas Nickleby*, and another embodying the Peggotty, Steerforth, and Dora parts of *David Copperfield* and including the great storm at Yarmouth in which Steerforth was drowned.

He was looking forward, he wrote Macready, to reading at Cheltenham in November and seeing his old friend there. Carlyle, he reported with derisive irony, had so "intensified his aversion to Jews" that he represented King John as an enlightened sovereign for drawing their teeth to extract money from them. The tone of the remark suggests that Dickens had at last lost his awe of Carlyle.

But indeed the whole pattern of Dickens's life had changed. The great old men whom he had known in his startling youth were almost all gone: Rogers dead, Hunt dead, Jeffrey dead, Sydney Smith dead, Landor far off in Italy, Carlyle growing ever more atrabilious and prophetically intolerant. Many of Dickens's closer associates were gone or scattered, too. Talfourd dead, Frank Stone dead, Stanfield enfeebled and ailing, Maclise isolated in an eccentric valetudinarianism, Cruikshank withdrawn to his fanatical teetotalism, Lemon estranged. Ainsworth, the close companion who introduced him to his first publisher, vanished into obscurity. Phiz was soon to disappear, too; when *Great Expectations* appeared in book form, Dickens's old illustrator was dropped and the volume came out with designs by young Marcus Stone. Only three of Dickens's old intimates remained: Macready rusticating down at Cheltenham, Lytton amid the gargoyles and medieval trappings of Knebworth, Forster tightly buttoned up and armoured in dogmatic complacency.

The companions who surrounded Dickens now were mostly younger men, many of them literary dependants: Wilkie Collins, Edmund Yates, Percy Fitzgerald, Francesco Berger, the actor Charles Fechter. Although Dickens was only forty-nine, his health was failing under the strain of the labours to which he subjected himself and the maniacal swift-paced walks in which he still indulged, but he touched up his grizzling hair, dressed as gaily as ever, and continued to act like a young man. In Ampthill Square there was Ellen Ternan, "Nelly," as he now called her, glamorous in all her fair young beauty.

But the separation from Catherine, which had forced so much distress and bitterness upon Dickens, had not worked out at all as he had hoped. He was still a prey to restlessness and emptiness. Labour and the fever of his readings were only anodynes. His imagination, his demoniacal creative power alone remained, but that was deeper, more vibrant, more penetrating than ever, exploring his world with an insight constantly more profound, ascending in *Great Expectations* to new triumphs even as the beating wings began to falter.

43

Intimations of Mortality

Gold now poured itself out for Dickens in an endless stream. Advance sheets of his novels brought him handsome sums from Harper and Brothers in New York. Whenever he wished he could obtain £1,000 for a short story. The sales of *All the Year Round*, already risen with the publication of *Great Expectations* to several thousands higher than the London *Times*, continued rising when Lytton's *A Strange Story* began coming out. *Great Expectations* went into a fourth edition within a few weeks of its appearance in book form.

But Dickens struggled with personal distresses that weighed upon him ever more heavily. Frank was proving of little use in the office. Alfred, who had been destined for the Royal Military Academy, was not a good enough student to meet the competition. Plorn, now at Wimbledon with Harry, was shy, lonely, and ill-adjusted. Deaths among old friends and associates gave Dickens the feeling that he was part of a forlorn charge steadily mown down upon the field. Deaths in his family loaded him with more griefs and responsibilities. He chafed bitterly at the troubles of society and the state of the world. His health was gradually breaking, but his will refused to recognize any warnings and relentlessly laid upon his body the most wearing exertions.

He had arranged that *Great Expectations* should be immediately followed in *All the Year Round* by Lytton's *A Strange Story*. " I would gladly pay you £1,500," he had written in the preceding December; and he promised that in addition he could obtain Lytton £1,200 "for the right of re-publication in collected form for two years," as well as £300 for the transmission of weekly proofs to America. Reading advance sheets of the first third in his bedroom at night, "I COULD NOT lay them aside," he wrote his friend, but "got into a very ghostly state indeed."

Despite neuralgic pains in his face, Dickens practised assiduously on the readings for the autumn, adding to them "the Bastille prisoner from the Tale of Two Cities" and "Mr Chops the Dwarf," from the Christmas story of 1858. Arthur Smith, his manager, was seriously ill, but so desperately unwilling to relinquish his post that Dickens hesitated to replace him. Finally, however, he engaged Thomas Headland, an assistant of Smith's, to take over all the heavy part of his duties. "Of course I pay him," Smith said faintly, "and not you."

In the first few days of October, Arthur Smith died; "it is as if," said Dickens, "my right arm were gone." Hard upon this Henry Austin died, and Dickens found that his sister Letitia, Austin's widow, would be left in straitened circumstances. In virtue of Austin's services as Secretary to the Board of Health it seemed that Letitia might be given a Government pension, but it was not until almost three years later that the slow-moving processes of the Circumlocution Office at last approved a grant of £60 a year. Meanwhile Dickens as trustee took charge of Letitia's affairs. Even here he was pursued with unjustifiable demands. "I can only pay Mr Henry Austin's own lawful debts," he wearily told one creditor. "His father's I have nothing to do with."

November saw the marriage of Charley Dickens to Bessie Evans, the daughter of Frederick Evans. Dickens did not approve the match and feared it would be disastrous. His antagonism to Frederick Evans had not diminished. "Of course," he wrote to Beard, Charley's godfather, "I understand your responding to any request on the part of Charley, . . . to attend the dear fellow's marriage. But I must add the expression of my earnest hope that it is not your intention to enter Mr Evans's house on that occasion." And, just as Catherine had not been present at Katey's wedding, Dickens was absent from Charley's. But a year later, when Bessie had borne her first child, she and Charley and Dickens's baby granddaughter were at Gad's Hill for Christmas. "Think of the unmitigated nonsense," Dickens exclaimed, "of an inimitable grandfather!"

The readings got off to a poor start with *Copperfield* on 28 October at Norwich. Headland had mismanaged things; Dickens missed Arthur, and felt that he himself was reading badly. Headland did his best, Dickens said, but "the look of him is very different from the poor lost fellow in his evening dress."

Mistakes continued to be made. At Newcastle all the billposters announcing the readings were lost and finally turned out to have been sent by Johnson, the printer, to the reading hall. "Johnson's mistake," said Headland. Somehow *Little Dombey* was announced for an evening when Dickens had decided on *Copperfield*; "Johnson's mistake," said Headland again. From Edinburgh came frantic complaints that no posters and no tickets had arrived. "'Johnson's mistake,' says the unlucky

Headland. Of course, I know that the man who never made a mistake in poor Arthur's time is not likely to be always making mistakes now."

On the first night at Edinburgh countless tickets had been sold for which there were no seats. "There was a tearing mad crowd in all the passages and in the streets, . . . forcing a great turbid stream of people into the already crammed hall." When Dickens appeared, a hundred frantic men mounted upon ledges and cornices shouted objections. He offered to adjourn to the Music Hall or to cancel this engagement "and come back later and read to all Edinburgh." There were cheers and a cry, "Go on Mr Dickens. Everybody will be quiet now." But uproarious spirits clamoured, "We *won't* be quiet." Calmly closing his book, Dickens assured them the reading would not be given until they were all agreed.

When quiet was restored and Dickens was about to begin, a gentleman cried out a suggestion that some of the ladies, at least, might be accommodated on the platform. "Most certainly," Dickens agreed. "In a minute the platform was crowded. Everybody who came up, laughed, and said it was nothing when I told them in a low voice how sorry I was; but the moment they were there, the sides began to roar, because they couldn't see." Dickens proposed that those on the platform sit down. "Instantly they all dropped into recumbent groups, with Respected Chief standing up in the centre . . . So I read Nickleby and the Trial. From the beginning to the end they didn't lose one point, and they ended with a great burst of cheering."

Despite Headland's incompetent management, the readings themselves were a prolonged series of triumphs. The *Copperfield* was "without precedent in the reading chronicles." When Dickens got to Cheltenham in January, Macready, "with tears running down his face," was rendered utterly incoherent.

And when I said something light about it, he returned: "No – er – Dickens! I swear to Heaven that, as a piece of passion and playfulness – er – indescribably mixed up together, it does – er – No, really, Dickens! – amaze me as profoundly as it moves me. But as a piece of Art – and you know – er – that I – No, Dickens! By God! – have seen the best Art in a great time – it is incomprehensible to me. How it is got at – er – how it is done – er – how one man can – well! It lays me on my – er – back, and it is of no use talking about it."

The readings were temporarily interrupted at Liverpool on 14 December by the death of the Prince Consort, but then were resumed at the end of the month and brought to their planned conclusion on 30 January 1862. The endless national lamentations struck Dickens as exaggerated: "the Jackasses that people are at present making of themselves on that subject!" In the course of later years the legend of the Prince's marmoreal perfections filled him with impatience. Seeing the words "Prince Albert Pudding" on the dinner menu at Gad's Hill, he crossed them out and substituted "Flunkey Pudding," although later still he allowed that dessert to be called "The Great and Good Pudding."

With the end of February Dickens exchanged Gad's Hill for a house at 16 Hyde Park Gate South for a few months, and in March began his London readings. He was enthusiastic about Collins's *No Name*, which was soon to begin in *All the Year Round*, but he disliked the London residence and complained that "this odious little house seems to have stifled and darkened my invention." He was saddened by the death of Cornelius Felton. "Poor dear Felton! It is 20 years since I told you of the delight my first knowledge of him gave me," he wrote Forster.

Dickens was anxious about Georgina, too, who had developed "degeneration of the heart" and who was "very low about herself." He planned, therefore, to take her and Mary to Paris in the autumn, hoping the rest and change would do her good. With this worry and "with my own old load (of which you know something)," he confessed to Collins, "I am become so restless that I cannot answer for anything." The desperate infatuation mirrored in Pip's obsession with Estella was gnawing with ever sharper fangs into his heart. Though he could speak of it only to Collins and Forster, his mood was one of repressed misery.

He had by now hit upon an idea for another twenty-number serial. The setting of the book was London; but, when Dickens came to write it, it would prove to be a London darkly changed from the days when Mr Pickwick had leaped out of bed "like another sun" to see the dawn irradiating Goswell Street. The great city has become for Dickens a barren and stony desert, "a hopeless city with no rent in the leaden canopy of its sky." The structure of its society is one in which dominance has passed from the aristocracy to the middle class, capitalism, and the stock exchange. Money now seemed its only aim, pecuniary respectability its only standard.

The central symbol of its worship is the dust-heap, that profitable mountain of soot, refuse, garbage, and human faeces that represent the

497

essence of what society regards as valuable. The image of wealth as filth, the sovereign goal of the nineteenth-century world as dust and ordure, gave a savage irony to Dickens's hatred of its governing values. Ultimately he magnifies the dust-heaps into an all-embracing metaphor of mistaken endeavours piling up rubbish, mounds marking the dust and ashes of human aspiration.

For the novel Dickens had even found a title, *Our Mutual Friend*; "but whether, with all this unsettled fluctuating distress in my mind, I could force an original book out of it, is another question." And yet his consciousness of all those dependent upon him made him feel that he ought to do something to spur his earnings. The American Civil War rendered impossible the reading tour in that country which he had considered a few years earlier, but earnest invitations were now coming from Australia. Only that June an Australian in London had offered him £10,000 outright for an eight months' tour; still others considered £12,000 a low estimate for the profits of a six months' absence.

But the more Dickens reflected upon the long separation from all that was dear to him, the more his heart sickened at the exile. "I know perfectly well before-hand how unspeakably wretched I should be." "The domestic life of the Readings is all but intolerable to me when I am away for a few weeks at a time merely, and what it would be –" "If I were to go it would be a penance and a misery, and I dread the thought of it more than I can possibly express." In the end, he found the idea unbearable, and rejected it.

On 16 October Dickens started for Paris, where he took a pretty apartment in the Rue du Faubourg Saint-Honoré. Settled as was his "animosity towards the French Usurper," Napoleon III, he thought the Emperor right in proposing to England and Russia that they join with France in making an earnest "appeal to America to stop the brutal war." Dickens had no sympathy with either side, and was surprised when an American friend told him that the North would win. Slavery he believed had nothing to do with the quarrel, save insofar as the industrial and more powerful North found it convenient to lay down a line beyond which slavery should not be permitted to extend lest the South be able to recover its old political power.

During Dickens's stay in Paris he wrote his last known letter to Maria Winter. Four years earlier, in 1858, her husband had failed in business and after a fruitless appeal to her father, she had turned to Dickens for aid.

I wish to Heaven [he had replied] it were in my power to help Mr Winter to any new opening in life. But you can hardly imagine how powerless I am in such a case . . . I really think that your Father who could do so much . . . without drawing at all heavily upon his purse, might be induced to do what – I may say to you, Maria – it is no great stretch of sentiment to call his duty. . . . But what you tell me about George seems so strange, so hard, and so ill balanced, that I cannot avoid the subject.

Now, in November 1862, George Beadnell died, leaving an estate of £40,000. "Of course I could not be surprised, knowing his great age, by the wearing out of his vitality," Dickens wrote Maria; "but – almost equally of course – it was a shock too, for the old Past comes out of its grave when I think of him, and the Ghosts of a good many years stand about his memory."

The stay in Paris improved Georgina's health, and she and Mary returned to Gad's Hill with Dickens for Christmas with the boys, Katey and her husband, and Charley, his wife, and "his preposterous child." "Somebody's Luggage," the Christmas story of that year, had sold 185,000 copies by 22 December. In the middle of January, leaving Georgina and Mary at Gad's Hill, Dickens returned to Paris, where he now took a suite of rooms at the Hôtel du Helder. On the 17th and again, by clamorous demand, on the 29th and 30th, he read for charity at the British Embassy. "The Reading so stuns and oversets the Parisians," he reported to Wills, "that I shall have to do it again. Blazes of Triumph!"

They are so extraordinarily quick to understand a face and gesture, going together, . . . that people who don't understand English, positively understand the Readings! . . . When Little Emily's letter was read, a low murmur of irrepressible emotion went about like a sort of sea. When Steerforth made a pause in shaking hands with Ham, they all lighted up as if the notion fired an electric chain. When David proposed to Dora, gorgeous beauties all radiant with diamonds, clasped their fans between their two hands, and rolled about in ecstasy . . . As to the Trial, their perception of the Witnesses, and particularly of Mr Winkle, was quite extraordinary. And whenever they saw the old Judge coming in, they tapped one another and laughed with that amazing relish that I could hardly help laughing as much myself.

Although Dickens could not resist the infection of their hilarity, his own emotional state was far different. There is no undeniable evidence pointing at this time to the development of his connection with Ellen Ternan, but it seems not unlikely that either now or perhaps during the previous period of almost a month in England, Ellen had at last given way. If so, her surrender brought him little of that shining ecstasy with which throbbing imagination conceives the world will be transfigured by triumphant love. The fatal confluence of his old unhappy passion for Maria Beadnell with his ideal vision of Mary Hogarth, the deepening misery of his life with Catherine, and the heartrending evaporation of a dream with Maria's reappearance, all led almost inevitably to his longing for the solace of a beautiful and youthful tenderness, and to his desiring to know, before it was too late, the enchantment that had always eluded him. But the dream did not die; it still haunted him.

Despite the fact that Collins had been able to draw him in the desperation of his later married years into nocturnal adventures beginning in the greenrooms of London theatres or mingling with the *lorettes* of Paris, Dickens could never really share those dissipations so easy to the younger man. All his heart yearned for loyalty, devotion, and ideal love. The domestic serenity and romance he had not found with Catherine, and that his separation from her rendered forever impossible, was the very essence of his need.

Whether or no this was the period when the relationship between Dickens and Ellen deepened into a liaison, their intimacy, though as much hidden from the world as possible, was known to numbers of those surrounding him. Though even when Dickens was dead they were guarded in referring to their knowledge, they reinforce the conclusive evidence in Dickens's own hand that emerged later still. ". . . There are circumstances connected with the later years of the illustrious novelist," wrote George Augustus Sala in 1893, "which should not and must not be revealed for fifty years to come at the very least." And Edmund Yates, in 1884, said: "My intimacy with Dickens, his kindness to me, my devotion to him, were such that my lips are sealed and my tongue is paralysed as regards circumstances which, if I felt less responsibility and delicacy, I might be at liberty to state."

It was legally impossible for Dickens and Ellen to marry, but from the middle sixties she often stayed at Gad's Hill, Georgina called her "dearest Ellen," and Dickens provided her with "an establishment of her own at Peckham." In 1865 Ellen was with Dickens when he was returning from a short vacation in Paris, and travelled in the same compartment of the boat train from Folkestone to London. Planning his American reading tour two years later in 1867, he longed desperately to be able to have Ellen join him, and settled with her that, after he had arrived there and decided whether her presence could be arranged without scandal, he would send Wills a cablegram in code for transmission to her. In his diary, opposite the calendar for November of that year, he entered the memorandum:

> IN ANY CASE. TEL:
> Tel: all well means
> *You come*
> Tel: safe and well, means
> *You don't come.*

And on a sheet of instructions to Wills he included two items concerning Ellen:

NELLY

If she wants any help will come to you, or, if she changes her address will immediately let you know the change. Until then, it will be Villa Trollope, a Ricorboli, Firenze, Italy . . .

On the day after my arrival out, I will send you a short Telegram at the office. Please copy its exact words (as they will have a special meaning for her) and post them to her by the very next post after receipt of Telegram . . .

FORSTER

has an ample power of attorney from me, in case you should want any legal authority to act in my name. He knows Nelly as you do, and will do anything for her if you want anything done.

There is no word of what Dickens's daughter Mary thought of this relation between her father and a young woman born a year later than herself. Katey, however, was less restrained, and bitterly resented Ellen. "My poor, poor mother!" Katey exclaimed. And coming down to Gad's Hill for a visit once, and learning that Ellen had taken a hand at cricket, Katey observed tartly, "I am afraid she did not play the game."

But as Katey looked back on the tangled and unhappy story in after years, her judgement softened. "She flattered him," Katey said, "– he was ever appreciative of praise – and though she was not a good actress she had brains, which she used to educate herself, to bring her mind more on a level with his own. Who could blame her? He had the world at his feet. She was a young girl of eighteen, elated and proud to be noticed by him."

About her father, Katey's feelings were ambiguous and confused, a mingling of antagonism and fascination. Though she fought him, she feared and loved him at the same time. He stormed her heart with tenderness and overwhelmed it with awe. "What could you expect from such an uncanny genius?" she exclaimed. The life of Dickens that she began writing in her old age, she burned: "I told only half the truth about my father, and a half-truth is worse than a lie . . ." "I knew things about my father's character that no one else ever knew; he was not a good man, but he was not a fast man . . . he was wonderful."

The relationship between her father and Ellen Ternan, Katey declared, was "more tragic . . . than that of Nelson and Lady Hamilton." It was not happy. There is reason for believing that Dickens had won Ellen against her will, wearing down her resistance by sheer force of desperate determination. In later years, according to Thomas Wright, she confided the story and her remorse to a clergyman. " 'I had it,' said Canon Benham, 'from her own lips, that she loathed the very thought of the intimacy.' "

There are overtones in Dickens's later novels which suggest that he too was troubled by the feeling that this was a guilty love. Even now in 1863, something of his distress is hinted by the emotion with which he heard *Faust* at the Paris Opera on 31 January. Mephistopheles, he observed, was "surrounded by an infernal red atmosphere of his own" and

Marguerite by a pale blue mournful light. The two never blending. After Marguerite has taken the jewels placed in her way in the garden, a weird evening draws on, and the bloom fades from the flowers, and the leaves of the trees droop and lose their fresh green, and mournful shadows overhang her chamber window, which was innocent and gay at first. I couldn't bear it, and gave in completely.

And in another letter, to Georgina, he repeats, "I could hardly bear the thing; it affected me so, and sounded in my ears so like a mournful echo of things that lie in my own heart."

What were the mournful things that echoed in his being to that story and that music? What analogies did he feel to the infernal red atmosphere surrounding Mephistopheles and the innocent brightness of Marguerite's window? What intimate meaning was there for him in the acceptance of those jewels which shows that Marguerite has already yielded to Faust in her heart and that the ultimate surrender will soon take place? What symbolic identification between himself and Faust, who wields magical powers? What foreshadowing of the future in those fading leaves and flowers and in that fading light?

Not until the middle of February did Dickens return to London. There, however, in March he began another series of readings, this time at the Hanover Square Rooms, which lasted until the end of May. Carlyle came to the "Trial from Pickwick" on Dickens's invitation. "I thought Carlyle would split," said one spectator, "and Dickens was not much better. Carlyle sat on the front bench and he haw-hawed right out over and over till he fairly exhausted himself. Dickens would read and then he would stop in order to give Carlyle a chance to stop."

During the intermission Dickens came and took Carlyle backstage, and over a glass of brandy and water Carlyle, nodding again, said, "Charley, you carry a whole company under your own hat." Next day he praised the performance to his youngest sister, but with that mingling of depreciation he customarily brought to everything: "Dickens does it capitally, such as *it* is, acts better than any Macready in the world; a whole tragic comic heroic *theatre* visible, performing under one *hat*, and keeping us laughing – in a sorry sort of way some of us thought – the whole night."

By the end of the summer Dickens's thoughts were turning more and more purposefully to his new serial, *Our Mutual Friend*. Late in September he signed an agreement with Chapman and Hall giving them a half share of the profits in return for a payment of £6,000. He wanted to start publication in the spring, but was determined not to begin with fewer than five numbers finished.

Only a short time earlier there had come to him a communication that curiously influenced the design of his story. Mr Davis, who had purchased Tavistock House, was a Jew. His wife, Mrs Eliza Davis, now wrote Dickens a letter telling him that Jews regarded his portrayal of Fagin in *Oliver Twist* as "a great wrong" to their people. If Jews thought him unjust to them, he replied, they were "a far less sensible, a far less just, and a far less good-tempered people than I have always supposed them to be." Fagin, he pointed out, was the only Jew in the story (he had forgotten the insignificant character of Barney) and "all the rest of the wicked *dramatis personae* are Christians." Fagin had been described as a Jew, he explained, "because it unfortunately was true of the time to which that story refers, that that class of criminal almost invariably was a Jew. . . . I have no feeling towards the Jews but a friendly one," Dickens concluded his letter.

Nevertheless he was troubled at being so seriously misinterpreted. In *Our Mutual Friend* he therefore included a group of Jews, of whom the most important is Mr Riah, a gentle old man caught in the toils of a *Christian* money-lender. Lizzie Hexam, one of the two heroines, takes refuge among a community of Jews, who treat her with the most generous tenderness. To a clergyman worried about her remaining with them, she defends her Jewish employers: "The gentleman certainly is a Jew," she says, "and the lady, his wife, is a Jewess, and I was brought to their notice by a Jew. But I think there cannot be kinder people in the world."

Near the end of the book there is a passage showing that Dickens had continued to be troubled by Mrs Davis's reproach, even though it imputed to him an injustice he had never intended. "For it is not in Christian countries with the Jews as with other peoples," Mr Riah reflects. "Men say, 'This is a bad Greek, but there are good Greeks. This is a bad Turk, but there are good Turks.' Not so with the Jews. Men find the bad among us easily enough – among what peoples are the bad not easily found? – but they take the worst of us as samples of the best; they take the lowest of us as presentations of the highest; and they say 'All Jews are alike.' "

Mrs Davis saw the meaning of this group of Jewish characters. During the course of the novel's publication she wrote Dickens in terms that can be inferred from his reply: "I have received your letter with great pleasure, and hope to be (as I have always been in my heart) the best of friends with the Jewish people." Some years later she gave him a copy of Benisch's Hebrew and English Bible, inscribed: "Presented to Charles Dickens, in grateful and admiring recognition of his having exercised the noblest quality men can possess – that of atoning for an injury as soon as conscious of having inflicted it." These words, Dickens told her, assured him "that there is nothing but good will left between you and me and a people for whom I have a real regard, and to whom I would not wilfully have given an offence or done an injustice for any worldly consideration."

During this summer of 1863 Dickens did not cease to be worried about his sons. At Wimbledon, Plorn was confused and homesick, and felt that he would do better in a smaller school. At the new year Dickens confided him to the Reverend W. C. Sawyer, at Tunbridge Wells. "He is a shy boy of good average abilities, and an amiable disposition," Dickens told his new master. "But he has not yet been quite happy away from home, through having lived – as the youngest of my children

– a little too long at home with grown people. He has never been a spoiled child, however, for we are too fond of children here to make them disagreeable."

Frank had adapted himself poorly to his duties at the *All the Year Round* office. Now, at twenty, he expressed a strong desire to enter the Bengal Mounted Police, and Dickens obtained a nomination for him. Near the end of January he went out to India, where he expected to see his brother Walter. But before he arrived, Dickens received word that Walter had died on the last day of the old year. He had been only twenty-two. "My poor boy was on his way home from an up-country station, on sick leave. . . . He was talking to some brother-officers in the Calcutta hospital about his preparations for home, when he suddenly became excited, had a rush of blood from the mouth, and was dead."

Death, indeed, was striking on every hand. The preceding April of 1863 Augustus Egg had died. On 13 September died Dickens's mother, who had long been sunk in hopeless senility. And a week before the death of Walter, Thackeray died on Christmas Eve in his home at Palace Green. There had been a reconciliation between him and Dickens only a few days earlier.

Calling on Katey at her London house, Thackeray had voiced his regret at the disagreement with her father, and she had urged him to "say a few words –" "You know," Thackeray interrupted, "he is more in the wrong than I am." But, "he is more shy of speaking than you are," she returned, "and perhaps he mightn't know you would be nice to him." "In that case," Thackeray said, with a glare of his spectacles, "there will be no reconciliation." Then, after a long pause, "And how do I know he would be nice to me?" "Oh," exclaimed Katey joyfully, "I can answer for that. There is no need for me even to tell him what has passed between us, I shall not say a word; try him, dear Mr Thackeray, only try him, and you will see."

Not long afterwards, Thackeray was talking with Sir Theodore Martin in the great pillared hall of the Athenaeum Club. Dickens came out of the morning room on his way to the staircase, passing close to them with no sign of recognition. Suddenly Thackeray broke away, and reached Dickens just as he had his foot on the stair. "It is time this foolish estrangement should cease," he exclaimed, "and that we should be to each other what we used to be. Come; shake hands." Dickens held out his hand, and some friendly words were exchanged. Returning to his companion, Thackeray said, "I love the man, and I could not resist the impulse."

Thackeray reported to Katey with radiant face. "How did it happen?" she asked. "Oh," he said gaily, "Your father knew he was wrong and was full of apologies –" "You know you are not telling me the truth, you wicked man. Please let me hear immediately what really did happen." Thackeray's eyes were gentle as he told how he had held out his hand: "your father grasped it very cordially – and – and we are friends again, thank God!"

Dickens heard of Thackeray's death on his way to Gad's Hill on Christmas Eve. Young Marcus Stone was meeting him at the station; as soon as he saw Dickens he knew something had distressed him. "What is it?" Stone asked. In a breaking voice, Dickens said, "Thackeray is dead." "I know you must feel it very deeply, because you and he were not on friendly terms." Dickens put his hand on Stone's arm. "Thank God, my boy, we were!" he said earnestly; and then told about the meeting at the Athenaeum.

On 29 December Dickens stood beside Thackeray's grave in Kensal Green. There was "a look of bereavement in his face which was indescribable. When all the others had turned aside from the grave he still stood there, as if rooted to the spot, watching with almost haggard eyes every spadeful of dust that was thrown upon it."

The Christmas number of *All the Year Round*, a story called "Mrs Lirriper's Lodgings," had shot far ahead of even the story of the previous year, selling about 220,000 copies. With that work out of the way, Dickens settled down seriously to *Our Mutual Friend*. Marcus Stone was doing the illustrations, and Dickens bombarded him with a series of instructions. "Note, that the dustman's face should be droll, and not horrible." "Mrs Boffin, as I judge of her from the sketch, 'very good indeed,' I want Boffin's oddity, without being at all blinked, to be an oddity of a very honest kind, that people will like." "The doll's dressmaker is immensely better than she was. I think she should now come extremely well. A weird sharpness not without beauty is the thing I want."

Labouring away thus, in the house at 57 Gloucester Place which he had taken from February to June, Dickens got *Our Mutual Friend* in train for publication. The first number came out at the beginning of May, and sold 30,000 copies in three days. A fortnight before it appeared, Catherine wrote to Frederick Chapman at Chapman and Hall's, and asked to have a copy of each month's number sent her as it came out.

Near the end of June, Dickens was off on a short trip in France and

Belgium, and then returned to Gad's Hill for the summer and autumn. Gradually he had transformed his little freehold, which he had "added to and stuck bits upon in all manner of ways." The outside, with its rosy brick and little entrance porch and bell turret, he had left almost untouched. But under the gambrel roof on the third floor he had built in two bedrooms facing the garden, and he had enlarged the drawing-room, first by building an additional one and then by throwing the two together into one large and handsome room. In what had been part of the orchard he made a walled croquet ground. He rounded out the property by obtaining an eight-acre meadow at the back of the house, through an exchange of land with the trustees of the Rochester Free School.

But he was not in good health and his writing went slowly. He had already fallen behind one number from the advance with which he had started. Hot weather slowed him still further in August, and Wills became ill, so that Dickens had to take over the duties on *All the Year Round* that his subeditor ordinarily performed.

Although Dickens thought little of Wills's imaginative powers, he had a high regard for his efficiency and loyalty. When he put Wills up for membership in the Garrick Club in the autumn of 1864 and his nominee was blackballed, Dickens was infuriated. To mark his feeling he resigned.

Matters within the public realm outraged him as well. The contentions among the Christian churches and their common endeavours to oppose the advance of scientific knowledge infuriated him. The excited controversy about Bishop Colenso's commentary on the Pentateuch and the Book of Joshua seemed to him so much obscurantist superstition. "Joshua might command the sun to stand still, under the impression that it moved round the earth; but he could not possibly have inverted the relations of the earth and sun, whatever his impressions were." The "science of geology is quite as much a revelation to man as books of an immense age and of (at the best) doubtful origin." It was unintelligent of the Church to "shock and lose the more thoughtful and logical of human minds," and assume revelation "to be finished and done with."

Hardly less revolting were "the indecent squabbles of the priests of most denominations" among themselves.

And the idea of the Protestant establishment, in the face of its own history, seeking to trample out discussion and private judgement, is an enormity so cool, that I wonder the Right Reverends, Very Reverends, and all other Reverends, who commit it, can look in one another's faces without laughing . . . How our sublime and so-different Christian religion is to be administered in the future I cannot pretend to say, but that the Church's hand is at its own throat I am fully convinced.

On the heels of this outburst comes another cry of personal lamentation. John Leech had just died. "I have not done my number," Dickens says. "This death of poor Leech . . . has put me out woefully. Yesterday and the day before I could do nothing; seemed for the time to have quite lost the power; and am only by slow degrees getting back into the track today."

And more and more his body was giving him trouble. Christmas 1864, went by, and during a protracted winter at Gad's Hill his left foot swelled with excruciating pains and had to be treated with poppy fomentations. But he would not have it that he had gout. "I got frost-bitten by walking continually in the snow," he insisted to Forster, "and getting wet in the feet daily." At the end of April he was still calling it his "frost-bitten foot," but claimed that he could again walk his ten miles in the morning without inconvenience. "I am working like a dragon at my book," he wrote Macready from London, "and am a terror to the household, likewise to all the organs and brass bands in this quarter."

After his son Alfred had given up his medical ambitions and his desire to be a farmer, Dickens had used the help of friends to get him a position in a City mercantile house, hoping that he might ultimately go out to some firm in Ceylon or China. Alfred had taken hopefully to the idea too, but after two years in London felt that he would like to go to Australia. This also Dickens aided him to do; on 29 May 1865, Alfred sailed for Melbourne.

At the end of May, Dickens went to Paris for a week's vacation. It is probable that Ellen Ternan was with him on this brief holiday; it is certain that she returned with him. While there Dickens picked up rapidly. "Before I went away," he wrote Mary, "I had certainly worked myself into a damaged state. But the moment I got away, *I* began, thank God, to get well."

The 9th of June, the day of their return, was clear and beautiful. Steamers could enter Folkestone Harbour only at high tide, which that day was a little after two. Dickens and Ellen boarded the "tidal" train, and a little later they were spinning along the rails at fifty miles an hour.

At eleven minutes past three the train entered on a straight stretch of track between Headcorn and Staplehurst. One third of the way there came a slight dip in the level country to a stream bed crossed by a railway bridge of girders. Suddenly the driver clamped on the brakes, reversed his engine, and whistled for the guards to apply their hand brakes. He had seen a flagman with a red flag and a gap of ripped-up rails.

A crew of repairmen were carrying on a routine replacement of worn timbers, but their foreman had looked at the time-table for the next day and imagined the train would not be along for another two hours. The flagman was supposed to be 1,000 yards beyond the gap and to have laid down fog signals, but that day he had neglected the signals and was only 550 yards from the bridge. When the engineer saw him it was too late. As he reached the bridge the train was still going almost thirty miles an hour.

The engine leaped the 42-foot gap in the rails and ran to the farther bank of the river bed. The guard's van that followed was flung to the parallel track, dragging the next coach with it. The coach immediately behind was that in which Dickens and Ellen were seated. It jolted partly over the side of the bridge, ten feet above the stream, with its rear end on the field below. The other coaches ran down the bank, turning upside down in the marshy ground, where four of them were smashed to matchwood. Only the very rear of the train remained on the rails.

"Suddenly," Dickens said, "we were off the rail, and beating the ground as the car of a half-emptied balloon might do." Dickens clambered out the window to obtain help in opening the door. Standing on the step, he saw the timbers of the bridge gone and the river ten feet below. Two guards were running wildly up and down. Dickens called authoritatively to one of them and demanded the key that would open the carriage doors. With the aid of a labourer and a few planks, he brought Ellen to safety and freed the occupants of the other compartments.

Then he went back for his brandy flask, filled his hat with water, and began trying to help the injured and dying. Remains of the shattered carriages were projecting wheels-upwards from the water. The screams of the sufferers were appalling. A staggering man covered with blood had "such a frightful cut across the skull," Dickens said, "that I

couldn't bear to look at him. I poured some water over his face, gave
him some drink, then gave him some brandy, and laid him down in the
grass . . ." One lady who had been crushed to death was laid on the
bank just as her husband, screaming "My wife! my wife!" rushed up
and found her a mangled corpse. Dickens was everywhere, helping
everyone.

When he had done everything he could, he remembered that he had
had the manuscript of the next number of *Our Mutual Friend* with him,
and coolly climbed into the carriage to retrieve it. Only when he was
back at Gad's Hill did he realize how shaken he was. His hand was so
unsteady that to most of the inquiries that poured in about his health
he dictated his replies. But he nerved himself to write the Station
Master at Charing Cross on Ellen's behalf:

> A lady who was in the carriage with me in the terrible accident on
> Friday, lost, in the struggle of being got out of the carriage, a gold
> watch-chain with a smaller gold watch-chain attached, a bundle of
> charms, a gold watch-key, and a gold seal engraved "Ellen."
>
> I promised the lady to make her loss known at headquarters, in
> case these trinkets should be found.

Throughout the month Dickens was unable to throw off the effects
of the accident. "I am curiously weak – weak as if I were recovering
from a long illness," he told Forster. And a little later, "I begin to
feel it more in my head. I sleep well and eat well; but I write half a
dozen notes, and turn faint and sick." "I am getting right, though still
low in pulse and very nervous. Driving into Rochester yesterday I felt
more shaken than I have since the accident."

In his weakness and shock he did not forget about Ellen. Solicitously
he sent her little delicacies by John, his personal servant. "Take Miss
Ellen tomorrow morning, a little basket of fresh fruit, a jar of clotted
cream from Tuckers, and a chicken, a pair of pigeons, or some nice
little bird. Also on Wednesday morning, and on Friday morning, take
her some other things of the same sort – making a little variety each
day."

At the end of June, "I cannot bear railway travelling yet," Dickens
wrote Forster. Indeed, he never fully recovered. "To this hour," he
wrote over three years later, "I have sudden vague rushes of terror,
even when riding in a hansom cab . . ." For a while he could bear
railway travel only by slow trains, but long journeys and boredom were
worse than the tension of the express. It became his invariable habit,

however, to carry a flask of brandy with him. "My reading secretary and companion knows so well when one of these odd momentary seizures comes upon me in a railway carriage, that he instantly produces a dram of brandy, which rallies the blood to the heart and generally prevails." Even so, when the train jolted over intersections, he often clutched the arms of his chair, his face whitened, and his brow broke out in perspiration.

44

Pilgrim of Gad's Hill

"The fifty-eight boxes have come, sir," said Dickens's groom, meeting him one day at Higham Station. "What?" said Dickens. "The fifty-eight boxes have come, sir." "I know nothing of fifty-eight boxes." "Well, sir," replied the man, "they are all piled up outside the gate and we shall soon see, sir."

When they were opened, the astonishing consignment turned out to be the parts of a small Swiss chalet, made to fit together like the joints of a puzzle. A gift from the actor Charles Fechter, the little building was two storeys high, with an outside staircase leading to an airy room above. A brick foundation was soon laid for it across the road deep among the leafy trees of the shrubbery. "It will really be a very pretty thing," Dickens wrote, "and in the summer (supposing it not be blown away in the spring), the upper room will make a charming study."

For the donor of the chalet Dickens had conceived an almost extravagant admiration. Strolling one night into a Parisian theatre where Fechter was playing the lover in *La Dame aux Camélias*, Dickens found himself carried away by his romantic tenderness. " 'By heavens!' I said to myself; 'a man who can do this can do anything.' " The performance took Paris by storm. Meeting the actor and discovering that he spoke English musically and fluently, Dickens pressed him to act in England.

Fechter's passionate Hamlet startled London by its fiery logic of conception; his Iago convincingly deceived his victims instead of giving himself away by sneers and diabolic grins. Dickens thought his performance in *Ruy Blas* very fine, and in 1863 hailed his production of *The Duke's Motto* as "a brilliant success." In 1864 Dickens aided Fechter by adapting Bellew's *The King's Butterfly* to more effective stage production. Later he was generous with advice and assistance in putting on *The Master of Ravenswood*, a dramatization of Scott's *The Bride of Lammermoor*, and in staging a revival of Lytton's *Lady of Lyons*.

Many of Dickens's other protégés thought it an unaccountable attraction. Marcus Stone insisted that Fechter was no gentleman, and Percy Fitzgerald did not like him. But Dickens "became his helper in disputes, adviser on literary points, referee in matters of management, and . . . no face was more familiar than the French actor's at Gad's Hill or in the offices of his journal." "I shall be heartily pleased to see you again, my dear Fechter, and to share your triumphs with the real earnestness of a real friend," Dickens wrote; and, again, "Count always on my fidelity and true attachment."

Fechter completed his gift of the chalet "by furnishing it in a very handsome manner." Inviting Lytton to Gad's Hill, Dickens suggested his using it to write in. The two had just spent a pleasant day together during the ceremonies of dedicating the Guild of Literature and Art houses at Stevenage. The seven years' delay provided by the Act of Parliament was at last over, and its founders celebrated with a formal banquet in the dining hall of Lytton's Knebworth estate.

Dickens came up from Gad's Hill for the dedication with Percy Fitzgerald, Mary, and Georgina, stopping off at Wellington Street to pick up Wills. Thence they drove in great spirits through Seven Dials to the station, where they met some of Lytton's other guests. Soon they were in the green countryside of Hertfordshire, with Dickens joking and telling stories about Adah Isaacs Menken, who was to be seen at Astley's Circus in *Mazeppa*, bound to a horse, "ascending the fearful precipice not as hitherto done by a dummy."

"Grand old Knebworth," Fitzgerald thought, was like an Elizabethan palace, with its vases, statues, and high green hedges. Lytton was reported too delicate in health to act as host, and John Forster, gloriously majestic, served as his vizier and displayed the three Gothic houses of the Guild partly enclosing their pretty garden-quadrangle. Dickens strode around in high spirits, a flower in his buttonhole and his hat a little on one side. Forster was so grandiose that Fitzgerald half complained to Dickens about his intolerable condescension. Dickens shook with laughter. "Lord bless you, why he *didn't see* ME! . . . He was in the clouds like Malvolio."

Lytton appeared at dinner, hawk-nosed and surprisingly keen of eye, and the two famous authors indulged in reminiscence about the old days when they had been youthful unknowns beginning their careers. But after dinner the baronial pomp of Lytton's hospitality proved too overpowering for some of the other literary guests, who gradually drifted away to the tavern across the road from the Guild houses. At nine, Dickens's party took the train back to London, where they dropped in at the office for *pâté de foie gras*, cold game, and wine. Their trained reached Gravesend at midnight, and from there Dickens drove them home by moonlight along the white high road.

Although Dickens and Forster maintained their old affection for each other, they were less often together than in earlier years. More and more Dickens found himself amused by Forster's swelling Johnsonian dignity. Sometimes he rolled on a sofa in agonies of enjoyment at some new story grotesquely revealing his friend "impregnably *mailed* in self-complacency." Forster had shouldered his way from his post as Secretary to the Lunacy Commission to an even more lucrative appointment as one of the Commissioners. "I never let old Brougham go," he told Fitzgerald. "I came back again and again, until I wore him out. I forced 'em to give me this."

Since his marriage a few years before Forster had given up his chambers at Lincoln's Inn, and now lived in ostentatious magnificence in a large mansion at Palace Gate. At his dinner table his guests were astounded, his wife terrified, and only his butler unmoved by his roars of indignation at an incompetent page-boy. "Biscuits," he murmured to the page; then, more loudly, "Biscuits!" and when this went unheeded, with a bellow, "BIScuits!" On the guests, Robert Browning said, he would "wipe his shoes," giving his "rhinoceros laugh," bullying and shouting them down with a rolling "In-*tol*-er-able," "Don't tell me!" "Incredible!" "Monstrous!"

With Dickens's faithful henchman, Wills, he got on as badly as ever. Seldom did Forster turn up in the *All the Year Round* offices without the two "growling at each other like angry dogs." On one occasion, "I had at last," Dickens told Fitzgerald, "to say to Wills, 'Please to withdraw.'" Glaring hostility, Wills did withdraw, but muttered, "Never mind, a time will come – all right," while Forster snorted, "That Wills is neither more nor less than a stock-jobber . . ."

All his acquaintances saw embedded in Podsnap some of Forster's mannerisms and even some of his attitudes – the indignant flush, the sweeping gesture of dismissal, the concern for conventional respectability – but nobody who knew him doubted his entire inability to see himself there. It is not impossible, however, that they were wrong; just around the time that the earliest chapter on Podsnap appeared in *Our Mutual Friend*, near the end of July 1864, "Forster fluttered about in the Athenaeum," Dickens wrote Georgina, "as I conversed in the hall with all sorts and conditions of men – and pretended not to see me – but I saw in every hair of his whisker (left hand one) that he saw Nothing Else."

If Forster perceived himself in Podsnap he might well have felt resentment. For in that pompous upholder of convention Dickens embodied all the forces he had spent a lifetime in fighting. Podsnap is the smug complacence that refuses to be told of any short-comings in society. Podsnap is the Mrs Grundyism that seeks to smother thought beneath heavy layers of propriety. He is Philistinism secretly mistrustful of the arts and despising the artist as a mountebank. He is British insularity contemptuous of everything "Not English." Pod-snappery is the dominant attitude of respectable society, a vast, meretricious, and vulgar materialism.

Much of Podsnap, of course, was wildly untrue of Forster, but there is just enough of him in its grotesquerie to make its fusion with his unmistakable peculiarities wounding; and Dickens cannot be acquitted of a certain cruelty in painting the portrait. But if Forster recognized and took offence at it, he soon became mollified and forgave; before the end of August he and his wife spent a long week-end at Gad's Hill.

During the summer the house was filled with guests; sometimes there was even an overflow into the Sir John Falstaff across the road beyond the shrubbery. In Gad's Hill itself, each bedroom had the most comfortable of beds, a sofa, an easy chair, a large writing table with paper, envelopes, and an almost daily change of quill pens. There was also a small library of books, a fire in winter, and a shining copper kettle, with cups, saucers, tea caddy, teapot, sugar and milk on a side table.

Life at Gad's Hill reflected a routine of strenuous hospitality. Breakfast was between nine and ten-thirty. Descending the staircase with its Hogarth prints, the visitor saw on the first-floor landing an illuminated plaque:

This House, GAD'S HILL PLACE, stands on the summit of Shakespeare's Gad's Hill, ever memorable for its association with Sir John Falstaff in his noble fancy. *But, my lads, my lads, tomorrow morning, by four o'clock, early at Gad's Hill! there are pilgrims going to Canterbury with rich offerings and traders riding to London with fat purses; I have vizards for you all; you have horses for yourselves.*

Beyond the square entrance hall a wide passage, with Stanfield's scenes from *The Frozen Deep* decorating the walls, opened on the rear lawn, separated from the meadow by a stone wall and massive iron gates.

In the dining-room, bright with mirrors, Dickens gave a morning greeting and recommended some savoury dish from the sideboard, perhaps kidneys with an appetizing dressing, although he was an abstemious eater himself, and seldom took more than a rasher of bacon, an egg, and a cup of tea. After breakfast, Dickens wrote all morning, while his guests pleased themselves, smoking cigars, reading the papers, strolling in the garden among its clambering honeysuckle, red geraniums, nasturtiums, and mignonette.

At one o'clock Dickens emerged for lunch, a substantial meal, though again he himself ate little, usually bread and cheese and a glass of ale. The dinner menu was always on the sideboard at lunchtime, and Dickens would discuss the items. "Cock-a-leekie? Good, decidedly good; fried soles with shrimp sauce? Good again; croquettes of chicken? Weak, very weak; decided want of imagination here." For the rest of the day he devoted himself to his guests.

First there might be a trip to the stables to see the horses: Toby, a good sturdy animal, Mary's riding horse Boy, Trotty Veck, and the sober Newman Noggs, a Norwegian pony who drew the basket cart in a jingling harness of musical bells. Romping along came the dogs Turk and Linda tumbling over each other, and, frisking along with them, Mrs Bouncer, Mary's Pomeranian, for whom Dickens had a special voice and who amused him with her airs because "she looks so preposterously small."

The vagrants who tramped the Dover Road made dogs a desirable protection, and one was usually chained on each side of the entrance gate. In September 1865, Fitzgerald delighted Dickens with the gift of an Irish bloodhound named Sultan, who turned out to be gentle with his master but so ferocious with everyone else that he had to be kept muzzled. "He has only swallowed Bouncer once, and temporarily," Dickens wrote Fitzgerald. A little later came Don, a black Newfoundland sent by a friend from America. Sultan proved fiercely unmanageable. He hated other dogs; he hated policemen; he hated soldiers. When he attacked a little girl, sister of one of the servants, Dickens decided he would have to be shot.

"You heard," he wrote Fitzgerald, "of his going to execution, evidently supposing the procession to be a party detached in pursuit of something to kill or eat? It was very affecting. And also of his bolting a blue-eyed kitten, and making me acquainted with the circumstance by his agonies of remorse (or indigestion)?" "A stone deftly thrown across him by the village blacksmith (chief mourner) caused him to look round for an instant, and then he fell dead, shot through the heart."

When his guests had been shown around the little estate, Dickens suggested a walk, but of those who had walked with him before only the bravest dared face the ordeal again. He maintained a relentless pace of four miles an hour, swinging his blackthorn stick and talking cheerfully all the while. Sometimes his perspiring companions gave way to blisters and breathlessness. "I have now in my mind's eye," wrote Edmund Yates, "a portly American gentleman in varnished boots, who started with us full of courage, but whom we left panting by the wayside, and for whom the basket-carriage had to be sent." On their return, tired and dripping, Dickens saluted the energetic survivors: "Well done! Twelve miles in three hours."

No sooner had they returned to Gad's Hill than Dickens plunged into games. He was an expert at rounders, relentless at battledore and bagatelle, and loved bowling and quoits. Even when the tall maid in her spotless cap came out to the green turf to announce five o'clock tea, Dickens still "played longer and harder than any of the company, scorning the idea of going in to tea at that hour, and beating his ball instead, quite the youngest of the company up to the last moment!"

In the summer he allowed a local working-men's club to hold cricket matches in his meadow, and got up a day of foot races and rustic sports each Christmas season. As he had never yet had a case of drunkenness, he explained, he allowed

the landlord of the Falstaff to have a drinking-booth on the ground. Not to seem to dictate or distrust, I gave all the prizes (about ten pounds in the aggregate) in money. The great mass of the crowd were labouring men of all kinds, soldiers, sailors, and navvies. They did not, between half-past-ten, when we began, and sunset, displace a rope or a stake; and they left every barrier and flag as neat as they found it. There was not a dispute, and there was no drunkenness whatever.

After taking a shower bath, Dickens would be as fresh at dinner as any of his guests. Though he was not a glittering conversationalist, he sparkled with the pleasure of companionship. He was sometimes so comical that he convulsed the servants and left them quite unable to keep a straight face. But, better than a brilliant talker, he was a brilliant listener, filling each one with the conviction that he delighted in his special company. In those glowing eyes, Fitzgerald said, you could see the first gleam of laughter, "twinkling there" and then spreading downwards while "the mobile muscles of the cheek began to quiver," and finally reaching "the expressive mouth" under its grizzled moustache, where it broke into "*crimpled* wrinkles of enjoyment."

Following dinner, there would be dancing and games. Dickens was not a very good dancer, his daughter Mary said, but he could do a lively sailor's hornpipe, and was best at Sir Roger de Coverleys and other country dances. Card games he did not care for, but he loved charades, "Dumb Crambo," pantomimes, and guessing games. Even years later Marcus Stone was convulsed whenever he tried to imitate Dickens's dumb show of "frog." An American visitor remembered a pantomime of the beheading of Charles I: Dickens with a black handkerchief on his head and a fire shovel as an axe, with Collins brought in as the victim, and the company's desperate attempt, despite Collins's trousers, to identify him as Mary Queen of Scots.

Dickens was always one of the survivors in memory games, where each player added a phrase until one after another forgot something and dropped out. Sometimes his fellow players were puzzled by the oddity of his additions, as when with a curious twinkle in his eye he supplied the words, "Warren's Blacking, 30, Strand." He was swift and intuitive in "Twenty Questions," bombarding the other players with such a rapid stream of queries that he positively extorted the solution. On one occasion, he failed to guess "The powder in the Gunpowder Plot," although he succeeded in reaching Guy Fawkes; but on the same evening he ferreted out what Fitzgerald had believed impossible, "the left leg of a postilion's boots."

The steaming brandy punch or gin with lemon that Dickens delighted to brew was a ritual, with a devout attention to the blending of the ingredients and whimsical auguries of the staggering impact the beverage might be expected to have. But for him the enjoyment lay almost entirely in the associations of clinking cannikins and warm conviviality. He himself seldom took more than a glass or two: "Never was there a more abstemious bibber." Later in the evening the men had whiskeys and soda in the billiard and smoking-room. Bending over the billiard table, with his red but worn cheeks, his thinning greyish hair, the sharp wrinkles around his eyes magnified by the large double-glasses he now wore for reading or playing, he looked unexpectedly middle-aged. At midnight he would retire, but his guests sometimes played until dawn.

Although Dickens still took a house in London for the spring, he spent most of the year now at Gad's Hill. Occasionally, however, he liked to get away by himself. For this purpose he had rooms at the

Five Bells Inn, a few miles south-east of London, at the corner of New Cross Road and Hatcham Park Road. Less than a mile south was Linden Grove, Nunhead, where from 1867 on Ellen Ternan was living at Windsor Lodge, a villa with a large garden that Dickens had taken for her. In the ratebooks at Peckham Town Hall between 1867 and 1870 the name of the occupant appears at first as Turnham and later as Tringham. A woman who worked at the Lodge knew Dickens only as Mr Tringham, although she was aware of the fact that he was a writer.

Numbers of Dickens's friends knew about Ellen, although he kept her as closely guarded a secret as possible. To Frances Dickinson, an old friend who had acted with him in *The Frozen Deep*, he wrote:

> The "magic circle" consists of but one member . . . I feel your affectionate letter truly and deeply, but it would be inexpressibly painful to N to think that you knew her history. She has no suspicion that your assertion of your friend against the opposite powers ever brought you to the knowledge of it. She would not believe that you could see her with my eyes, or know her with my mind. Such a presentation is impossible. It would distress her for the rest of her life. I thank you none the less, but it is quite out of the question. If she could hear that, she could not have the pride and self reliance which (mingled with the gentlest nature) has borne her, alone, through so much.

Dickens's description in *Our Mutual Friend* of the neighbourhood in which Bradley Headstone's school was located tallies exactly with what New Cross and Hatcham were like in the sixties. Near by in Lewisham High Street was a private school where a pretty daughter of his Barrow relations was learning French, music, and dancing. Emily Barrow learned that her famous kinsman had rooms at the Five Bells and called on him there with her best friend, Charlotte Elizabeth Lane. Dickens loved pretty faces and girlish chatter, and gave them apples from the pyramid he always had piled on his table, and invited them to Gad's Hill. During visits there, the two girls noticed that he was often pensive and silent at the table. Suddenly he would push back his chair, leave in the middle of a meal, and hurry off to his writing. Later the family stole peeps at his manuscript, and came away laughing at what they read.

Throughout all this time, Dickens's health remained a cause for concern. During the winter, changes in weather from mugginess to frost and back brought recurrences of the trouble with his foot, and early in 1866 his pulse was so bad that his doctor Frank Beard, brother of his old friend Thomas Beard, told him "an examination of the heart was absolutely necessary."

Nevertheless, despite his realization that these symptoms were sharpened by the strain of his readings, Dickens now resolved to undertake another series of thirty readings "in England, Ireland, Scotland, or Paris," as it might be decided. Messrs Chappell, of New Bond Street, offered him £50 a night plus all expenses, and Dickens accepted the offer. He insisted, however, that there be good shilling seats. "I have been the champion and friend of the working man all through my career, and it would be inconsistent, if not unjust, to put any difficulty in the way of his attending my Readings." Chappell's was to handle all business details. "All I have to do is, to take in my book and read, at the appointed place and hour, and come out again."

His opening night at St James's Hall, London, on 10 April 1866, was devoted to "Doctor Marigold," adapted from his Christmas story of that year, which had sold over 250,000 copies. The excitement in the audience was tremendous. The very next day Dickens went on to Liverpool and Manchester. As manager Chappell's had appointed George Dolby, a brother of the well-known singer Mme Sainton Dolby. Dolby was a tall, bulky, bald-headed man with a stammer and a bluff manner, whom Mark Twain described as "a gladsome gorilla." At the train Dolby met the scrawny Wills, who was to be Dickens's travelling companion, and Dickens himself, in a pea jacket, a Count D'Orsay cloak, and a soft felt hat worn on one side, which gave his lined and bronzed face the look of a "modernized gentlemanly pirate."

Wills began by putting Dolby through a severe cross-examination about how he handled his work. Dickens was agitated by the railway journey and, until they reached Bletchley, forty miles from London, wore an expression of anxiety and nervousness. But then the flask of brandy was brought out and they fell into conversation over their cigars. On later journeys, Dolby provided a cold collation of anchovy and hard-boiled egg sandwiches, salmon mayonnaise, pressed beef, cold fowl and tongue, Roquefort cheese, and cherry tart, with wine and gin punch iced in the washstand, and coffee made with a spirit lamp.

The provincial tour went with a rush everywhere. There were enormous "lets" in Glasgow and Edinburgh, and even in Aberdeen, where the local agent told Dolby, "I'm no prapared t' state positively what yewr actiel receats'll be, *for ye see, sir, amangst ma ain freends there are vairy few wha ha' iver haird o' Charles Dickens.*" Everywhere the demand for shilling seats was a tidal wave. In Birmingham, Dickens read "Nickleby" instead of the "Trial," which was announced on the programme. Discovering his error, he came out on the platform again at ten o'clock "and said that if they liked I would give them the Trial. They *did* like, and I had another half hour of it in that enormous place."

In Portsmouth, where the tour ended near the close of May, Dickens wandered around with Wills and Dolby and found himself in Landport Terrace. "By Jove!" he exclaimed, "here is the place where I was born"; and began trying to identify the house. One house he thought must be it, because "it looked so like his father"; another "because it looked like the birthplace of a man who had deserted it; a third was very like the cradle of a puny, weak youngster . . . and so on through the row." One open square in the town, with red brick houses dotted by white window frames, so resembled the scene for a comic pantomime that Dickens was unable to resist a temptation to imitate the clowning of Grimaldi. Mounting the steps to a brass-plated green door, he gave three raps, and lay down on the top step, when a stout woman suddenly opened the door, and all three men beat a hasty retreat, with Dickens in the rear pretending to be chased by an imaginary policeman.

Despite all these high jinks, Dickens was not well. He was unable to sleep at night, and between halves of his performance had to take some oysters and a little champagne as a restorative. He developed a severe pain in his left eye. Early in May he caught a cold that refused to leave him. For weeks, even months, he was troubled by distention and flatulency, with pains in the pit of the stomach and chest.

But the demoniac possession that drove him would not let him rest. The readings closed with three London engagements ending on 12 June. Their total receipts turned out to be £4,672. Several weeks before the end, Chappell's tempted him with an offer for fifty more nights to begin at Christmas. Dickens at first thought of demanding £70 a night, but ultimately agreed to give forty-two readings for £2,500. The stimulus and excitement that he had come to need, the constant nagging sense of family demands that would still exist even when he was dead, were inexorably driving him on a disastrous course.

In July 1863, fourteen-year-old Harry, aided by his younger brother, had started a domestic paper, printed by hand, called *The Gad's Hill Gazette*. The two boys continued to turn it out in the winter and summer holidays, and in 1865 Wills gave them a small printing press for the purpose. The paper chronicled arrivals and departures, billiard matches, excursions, and evening amusements, told anecdotes of the guests, and ran a sprinkling of acrostics and conundrums. Dickens made joking contributions to it and read it with interest, but he did not feel that its authors had any literary talent.

Harry was hard-working and quick-minded. But over Plorn, so long his favourite child, Dickens was beginning to feel almost discouraged. The boy seemed to have no intellectual talents and small powers of industry. "His want of application and continuity of purpose," Dickens felt, were part of an "impracticable torpor . . . in his natural character," and therefore a misfortune rather than a fault. His best course, Dickens decided, would be to look towards becoming a farmer in Australia, to drop Latin, and learn some practical chemistry, carpentry, and smith's work, such as would be of use to him "in a rough wild life" there. But Dickens's belief in the boy died hard. As "he is fond of animals, and of being on horseback, and of moving rapidly through the air, I hope he may take better to the Bush than to Books."

The lassitude Dickens observed in his youngest son troubled him all the more because he had earlier noted the same failing in Charley, and feared it was a quality both had inherited from their mother. Charley, after having tried so many other things, was now engaged in a paper-mill business established on capital found by Miss Coutts, but like his brother Walter, who had died deep in debt, Charley was finding it difficult to handle money with prudence and understanding.

With all the doubts aroused by the other boys, Dickens felt uncertain even about Harry, though he now seemed to be doing well at Wimbledon. Harry had declared he "did not wish to enter the Indian Civil Service"; Dickens replied "that many of us have many duties to discharge in life which we do not wish to undertake," and "that I could by no means afford to send a son to College who went there for any other purpose than to work hard, and to gain distinction."

Dickens finally agreed, however, to ask the Reverend William Brackenbury, the head of the school, if he believed Harry really "worth sending to Cambridge," and really possessed of "the qualities and habits essential to marked success there." If Mr Brackenbury so advised, "he should study accordingly." If not, "he should decidedly go up for the Indian Civil Service Examination."

Around this time, Catherine asked Dickens to come and counsel her about some household problem. He refused. Catherine must "decide the question out of her own daily experience . . . I will never go to her house," he declared obdurately, "and . . . it is my fixed purpose (without any abatement of kindness otherwise) to hold as little personal communication with her as I possibly can."

Mary was now in her late twenties, and it began to look as if she would never marry. Dickens had tried without success to interest her in Percy Fitzgerald. "I am grievously disappointed that Mary can by no means be induced to think as highly of him as I do – what a wonderful instance of the general inanity of Kings, that the Kings in the Fairy Tales should have been always wishing for children! If they had but known when they were well off, having none!"

About the world, too, Dickens felt discouraged. The year before, Governor Eyre had suppressed a Negro uprising in Jamaica with a severity that was sharply criticized by such leaders of liberal opinion as Mill, Spencer, and Huxley. Judgements on the matter were divided, however, by memories of the bloody Indian Mutiny of 1857–8. Ruskin, Tennyson, and Carlyle justified Eyre's stern measures as just and necessary preventatives of further violence. Dickens joined Eyre's defenders, but regarded the episode, like the Mutiny, as mainly significant for showing how the Government had been blind to the most appalling dangers.

Everywhere he looked he saw equal reason for disillusion. The railroads were a muddle, with "no general public supervision, enormous waste of money, no fixable responsibility." In France there was dangerous unrest; and the Emperor's secret police were "making discoveries that render him desperately uneasy." In England "the great masses were deeply dissatisfied with the state of representation," while the middle and upper classes continued to oppose any reform in the franchise with "the old insolent resource of assailing" the poor as ignorant and politically indifferent. "I have such a very small opinion of what the great genteel have done for us," Dickens wearily commented, "that I am very philosophical indeed concerning what the great vulgar may do, having a decided opinion that they can't do worse."

In January Dickens turned again to the profitable anodyne of his readings. His old servant John had been found out in a long series of pilferings from the cashbox of *All the Year Round* and discharged. But Dickens could not bear to cast him off altogether after twenty years, and tried to find him a place in which he would not have the opportunity or temptation to steal. It was even more distressing that John seemed to feel very little "the enormity of his offence, except as it inconveniences himself. Wills telling him today that he might be able to get him made a waiter at the Reform Club, he replied, 'Oh I couldn't do that Sir.'" At last Dickens set him up in a small business, saying, "Poor fellow, he has lost his character, and will not be able to get another situation."

His new man, Scott, proved splendidly satisfactory.

As a dresser he is perfect. In a quarter of an hour after I go into the retiring room, where all my clothes are airing and everything is set out neatly in its own allotted space, I am ready . . . He has his needles and thread, buttons, and so forth, always at hand; and in travelling he is very systematic with the luggage. What with Dolby, and what with this skilful valet, everything is made as easy to me as it possibly *can* be.

Indeed, Chappell's arrangements were in every way unexceptionable. "Not the faintest trace of the tradesman spirit ever peeps out," Dickens said; and Dolby was "an agreeable companion, an excellent manager, and a good fellow." But the strain of travelling and reading was harder than ever. Dickens was unable to sleep at night, and after his first Liverpool reading was taken so faint that he had to lie on a sofa at St George's Hall for half an hour. At Chester his hotel was freezing cold; at Wolverhampton it rained bitterly and after the reading he felt heavily beaten. During the forty-minute ride to Birmingham it was all he could do to hold out on the journey. To Georgina he wrote that he believed it an effect of the railway jolting. "There is no doubt of the fact that, after the Staplehurst experience, it tells more and more, instead of (as one might have expected) less and less."

Back at Gad's Hill, Dickens received word from Wilkie Collins of old companions in Paris. "Glad to hear of our friend Régnier," he replied; and with a burst of his old fun: "As Carlyle would put it: 'A deft and shifty little man, brisk and sudden, of a most ingenious carpentering faculty, and not without constructive qualities of a higher than the Beaver sort. Withal an actor, though of a somewhat hard tone. Think pleasantly of him, O ye children of men!'"

Then, in spite of the Fenian troubles in Ireland, Dickens was off to Dublin and Belfast for readings. Friends in Tipperary wrote him that they were living fortified in a state of "acute rebellion." Kingstown was full of armed policemen. Servants in Dublin were reported to be all Fenians. It was feared that in an uprising they might set fire to all the houses. Dublin, however, seemed perfectly calm. "The streets are gay all day . . . and singularly quiet and deserted at night. But the whole place is secretly girt in with a military force."

Within a few weeks more the tour was over. In a day's interval Dickens visited the deathbed of his old friend Clarkson Stanfield, and, on Stanfield's plea, was reconciled with Mark Lemon. Before the very last reading Dickens came again, and still again, but when he saw upon the door the symbol of what had taken place he could not bring himself to ring.

In May the readings were ended. At night Dickens found himself so tired he could hardly undress for bed. But already he was thinking of another and even more toilsome engagement. Every mail brought him proposals that he read in America. A committee of private gentlemen in Boston was ready to deposit a guarantee of £10,000 in advance at Coutts's bank. "Every American speculator who comes to London repairs straight to Dolby, with similar proposals."

"I am in a tempest-tossed condition, and can hardly believe that I stand at bay at last on the American question. The difficulty of determining amid the variety of statements made to me is enormous, and you have no idea how heavily the anxiety of it sits upon my soul." "I begin to feel myself drawn towards America," he told Georgina and Mary, "as Darnay in the Tale of Two Cities was attracted to the Loadstone Rock, Paris . . ."

PART TEN

The Bottom of the Cup
1865–1870

45

To the Loadstone Rock

But despite the golden lure of America, Dickens wavered. How could he bear the parting from his friends, from Georgina and the children? Ellen had been ill throughout part of April and recurrently to almost the end of May, but was better with the return of summer. In his distress at so long a separation, Dickens thought of having her join him in America.

Wills and Forster, who so often disagreed, united in trying to dissuade him from making the journey at all. Both feared his health would break down under the strain of foreign travel. Dickens tried in vain to shake Forster's objections. Wills's arguments he vigorously answered in a letter. Even in England he would never rest; he had that within which would be "rusting and corroding" him unless he were active.

Battering down all resistance, Dickens decided to send Dolby over to investigate the lay of the land. On 3 August Dolby sailed, taking with him the manuscripts of two brief stories, "George Silverman's Explanation" and "A Holiday Romance," for each of which Dickens was to receive £1,000. Both had been commissioned that spring, the first by State Senator Benjamin Wood, a New York newspaper publisher, the second by Ticknor and Fields for appearance in *Our Young Folks*, a children's magazine.

"George Silverman" has a strange and suggestive psychological theme. The narrator of the story, rescued from a slum childhood and brought up as a clergyman, seems to himself always to be acting with the most nobly disinterested of motives, but is constantly striking others as selfish and disingenuous. Opinion, however, is divided, some thinking him proud, others a sneak, still others generous and unselfish. Believing himself cruelly misjudged, Silverman at the same time has a lurking suspicion of his own guilt. These ambiguities, in fact, represent the very point of the story, and one feels as if it were haunted by Dickens's troubled consciousness of ambiguities within himself. But he could not grapple successfully with the theme; it wavers half-heartedly between apologia and accusation, an unresolved conflict.

The other manuscript was a group of four light and whimsical stories supposedly written by children. "I hope the Americans will see the joke of Holiday Romance," he said. "The writing seems to me so like children's, that dull folks (on *any* side of *any* water) might perhaps rate it accordingly! . . . It made me laugh to that extent that my people here thought I was out of my wits, until I gave it to them to read, when they did likewise."

In Boston, Dolby hastened to turn over "A Holiday Romance" to Ticknor and Fields. Everyone there was sure the readings would be a success, and Dolby tentatively chose for the purpose the Tremont Temple, a building holding around 2,000 people. In New York, Horace Greeley, Editor of the *Tribune*, and William Cullen Bryant, Editor of the *Post*, agreed that Dickens's triumph would "eclipse that of Jenny Lind." James Gordon Bennett, of the *Herald*, insisted that Dickens must "first apologize" for *American Notes* and *Martin Chuzzlewit*, but believed that he might then charge ten dollars a ticket.

The next morning, by way of helping out, Bennett published the offensive *Notes* in a "'special,' *free of cost*" supplement to the paper. Unlike the public of 1842, however, the current generation proved untroubled by the book, and Ticknor and Fields subsequently sold large numbers in a 25-cent reprint. "Whatever sensitiveness there once was to sneering criticism," said the New York *Times*, "the lapse of a quarter of a century, and the profound significance of a great war, have modified or removed."

From Senator Wood there had been no reply to messages that he could claim the manuscript of "George Silverman." Suddenly, at the very moment Dolby was leaving New York, Wood appeared and flung "a bag – *supposed* to contain a thousand sovereigns – on the table." But Dolby had been warned that, like Joey Bagstock, the senator was "de-vil-ish sly." He told Wood he no longer had time to count the money, but would leave the manuscript with Ticknor and Fields, who would conclude the business. No more was heard from Wood, and in 1868 the story was published in the *Atlantic Monthly*.

While Dolby was in America, Dickens worked at *No Thoroughfare*, the next Christmas story on which he was collaborating with Collins, and helped with a dramatic version for Fechter. "Welcome back, old boy!" he telegraphed on Dolby's return. "Do not trouble about me, but go home to Ross first and see your wife and family, and come to me at Gad's at your convenience." Dolby's report, when they met, enthusiastically supported an American tour, with plans of all the halls in which Dickens would speak and estimates of the profits at various prices of admission. For presentation to Wills and Forster, Dickens boiled it down to a statement which he entitled "The Case in a Nutshell." The statement concluded that on a series of eighty readings the clear profit would be £15,500.

Far from being persuasive to Forster, this argument was like a red flag to a bull. "He had made up *his* mind, and there was an end of the matter." Since the Staplehurst accident, he told Dolby, Dickens had been in a bad state of health; a sea voyage was the worst thing in the world for him. If he went, there would be a recurrence of riots like the Forrest–Macready riots. There was no money in America; if there were, Dickens wouldn't get any of it; if he did, it would be stolen from his hotel; and if he put it in a bank, the bank would fail. There "was no reason why the interview should be prolonged," he concluded testily; he had "fully made up *his* mind that Dickens should *never go to America again.*"

For Forster's worry there was reason enough. Ever since Dickens had seen Dolby off, six weeks before, he had again been having trouble with his left foot. "I cannot get a boot on," he wrote Georgina; and to Forster, "I am laid up with another attack . . . and was on the sofa all last night in tortures." Nevertheless, "I make out so many reasons against supposing it to be gouty, that I really do not think it is." He even managed to hypnotize the surgeon who looked at it into diagnosing it as "erysipelas" supervening "on an enlargement in the nature of a bunion." All through August the foot continued inflamed, and by the middle of September Dickens was still lame and unable to wear a shoe.

Exaggerated rumours of his ill health spread through all the newspapers. Dickens felt obliged to send their editors letters of denial. He suggested to one that "critical state of health" was a misprint for "cricketing." "This is to certify," he facetiously wrote his friend Finlay, of the *Northern Whig*,

that the undersigned innocent victim of a periodical paragraph disease which usually breaks out once in every seven years (proceeding from England by the Overland route to India, and per Cunard line to America where it strikes the base of the Rocky Mountains and rebounding to Europe, perishes on the Steppes of Russia), is NOT in *a critical state of health*, and has NOT consulted *eminent surgeons*, and never was better in his life, and is NOT recommended to proceed to the United States for *cessation from literary labour*, and has not had so much as a headache for twenty years.

On 30 September a cablegram was sent to Ticknor and Fields: "Yes. Go ahead." Almost immediately the American press broke out with the old controversies and accusations. Dickens indignantly countered them. For twenty years, he said, his only allusion to the republication of his books in America had been "the good-humoured remark, 'that if there had been international copyright between England and the States, I should have been a man of very large fortune, instead of a man of moderate savings, always supporting a very expensive public position.'"

On 2 November, Dickens was given a farewell dinner at the Freemason's Hall. Almost all the notables of the literary, dramatic, and artistic world were among an assembly numbering close to 450. Charley was seated with these, but Mary and Georgina joined the 100 feminine guests in the ladies' gallery. Just two days before, Dickens's sailor son, Sydney, had managed to come up from Portsmouth, where his ship was in harbour, and was squeezed in at the last moment.

White statuary gleamed among green plants in lobbies, corridors, and reception rooms. British and American flags decked the dining hall, bright against walls whose twenty arched panels were decorated with golden laurels on a deep red ground. The chairman was Lord Lytton, created a baron in 1866, now sixty-four years old, gaunt, bent, black-clad, and keen of eye.

Wild enthusiasm greeted the arrival of the two most famous living novelists as Dickens entered on Lytton's arm. Following in procession were Lord Chief Justice Cockburn, the Lord Mayor of London, Lord Houghton, Sir Charles Russell, and an assemblage of Royal Academicians. Lytton spoke with stately fervour. They were there, he said, to do honour to the conquests of art.

Happy is the man who makes clear his title-deeds to the royalty of genius while he yet lives . . . Though it is by conquest that he achieves his throne, he at least is a conqueror whom the conquered bless. . . . Seldom, I say, has that kind of royalty been quietly conceded to any man of genius until his tomb becomes his throne, and yet there is not one of us now present who thinks it strange that it is granted without a murmur to the guest whom we receive tonight.

A score of times Lytton was interrupted by cheers, but when Dickens rose shouts stormed upon him. Men leaped on chairs, tossed up napkins, waved glasses and decanters above their heads. The ladies' gallery was a flag of waving fans and handkerchiefs. Colour and pallor followed each other in Dickens's face, and "those wonderful eyes," said one guest, "flamed around like a searchlight"; tears streamed down his cheeks and as he tried to speak his voice faltered. Even when he found speech, although his words were eloquent, there were those who "felt the real eloquence of the evening had reached its climax in the silent tears of Dickens."

In the next few days good-byes were said, including farewells to Charley's children. Dickens disliked the name "Grandfather," and little Mekitty, as his granddaughter Mary Angela was called, and her tinier brother Charles were jestingly taught to know him as " 'Went-ables,' which they sincerely believe to be my name," Dickens said, "and a kind of title that I have received from a grateful country."

Ellen was going to Italy to stay with her sister Frances Eleanor and her brother-in-law Thomas Adolphus Trollope. But Dickens could not bear to surrender his hope that she might be able presently to join him in America. Carefully he arranged with Wills to forward the code telegram that would tell her what to do. Would he write "all well" or the words "safe and well" that meant she was to remain in Europe? Meanwhile, Wills was always to have her address, to help her in any unforeseen difficulty, and to invoke Forster's aid for her in case of need.

Dolby had already sailed for America again, and Dickens had been given "the Second Officer's cabin on deck" in the *Cuba*, leaving Liverpool on 9 November. With a window and a door open, it gave him plenty of fresh air – always a prime requirement with him – but he found the cabin "of such vast proportions that it is almost large enough to sneeze in." They ran into a head wind halfway across, and rolled and pitched, but Dickens felt wonderfully well except for his foot, which continued painful.

The staid city of Boston was in a state of frenzy. "No sooner was the news flashed along the cable, that he was coming," reported the New York *Tribune* facetiously, "than everything was immediately put in apple-pie order. The streets were all swept from one end of the city to the other for the second time in twenty-four hours. The State House and the Old South Church were painted, offhand, a delicate rose pink." There were "Little Nell Cigars," "Mr Squeers Fine Cut," the "Mantalini Plug," and the genuine "Pickwick Snuff." There was even a "Dickens Collar," ornamented with two rosebuds and a likeness of the author.

On the customs steamer *Hamblin*, Dolby set out at midday on

19 November, in a choppy and freezing sea, to meet the *Cuba*. He and his companions, Howard Ticknor and James Fields, and their junior partner James Osgood, were joined by a large staff of reporters. It was not until after dark that the *Cuba* appeared. Ignoring a perfect shower of rockets, it tore straight on, portholes alight, making the harbour hideous with the shrieks of its whistle. Within fifty yards of the wharf, however, the vessel ran on a mudbank, and while it was snorting and backing, Dolby heard his Chief calling his name. Soon everyone was shaking hands, and they were off to the Parker House, where Dolby had taken a third-floor corner suite.

After the excitement of greetings, Dickens felt fatigued and depressed. At supper the waiters left the door of his sitting room ajar, and from the corridor eyes peered in at him through the crack. "These people," he said irritably, "have not in the least changed during the last five and twenty years – they are doing now exactly what they were doing then." But he was cheered by the sale of tickets for the first four readings. The night before the sale, a line had begun forming, and by eight the next morning it was almost half a mile long. Every ticket had been disposed of and $14,000 taken in. The box-office price was two dollars, but speculators were already getting as much as twenty-six dollars for a ticket.

To give his Chief time to rest from the voyage Dolby had not scheduled the first reading until a fortnight hence, 2 December, and Dickens chafed at the delay. Meanwhile, however, there were old friendships to be renewed. Longfellow called, looking benign and handsome with his white hair and long white beard, and later brought Holmes, Agassiz, and Emerson. Longfellow found Dickens as "elastic and quick" as ever, "with the same sweetness and flavour as of old, and only greater ripeness." Within the next two days Dr Samuel Gridley Howe and Richard Henry Dana, Jr, also called.

On the 21st, Dickens dined at the Fields home on Charles Street. One of the enraptured young men who had cheered Dickens in 1842, Fields was now a brown-bearded man of almost fifty. He and his wife made an adoring cult of Dickens, proudly displaying the Francis Alexander portrait of him in their drawing-room. Besides Longfellow, Agassiz, Emerson, and Holmes, the other guests included Judge Hoar and Charles Eliot Norton. Dickens was gay and entertaining and often had them in tempests of laughter, although Mrs Fields fancied Holmes "bored him a little by talking at him." At one of his own lectures, Holmes said, his landlady's face "was the only one which relaxed its grimness"; "probably," Dickens rejoined, "because she saw money enough in the house to pay your expenses."

Dickens's fears that he would be troubled by intrusive strangers proved unfounded. "The Bostonians having been duly informed that I wish to be quiet, really leave me as much so as I should be in Manchester or Liverpool." He walked his seven to ten miles a day without being stopped or followed, but if he looked in a shop window a score of passers-by stopped too. Though there was certainly more tact and consideration than there had been twenty-five years ago, it was clear that Ellen could not be with him. The cablegram that Wills received on 22 November therefore resignedly opened with the words, "Safe and well," but went on more cheerfully, "expect good letter full of hope."

On Thanksgiving Day Dickens dined at Longfellow's home in Cambridge. Longfellow now owned the house in which he had roomed twenty-five years ago, and they dined in the square, white-wainscoted dining-room. In the bookshelves Dickens saw his own works and said with a wink that delighted Longfellow's children, "Ah-h-! I see you read the best authors." But through all the enjoyment of the day Dickens could not blot from his imagination the dreadful picture of Longfellow's beautiful wife who had burned to death in that home six years before. "She was in a blaze in an instant, rushed into his arms with a wild cry, and never spoke afterwards."

Among Dickens's callers was his old secretary Putnam. "Grey, and with several front teeth out, but I would have known him anywhere." "It was quite affecting to see his delight in meeting his old master again. And when I told him that . . . I had (unacknowledged) grandchildren, he laughed and cried together." He rose "into the seventh heaven" when Dickens gave him tickets to a reading, for himself and his wife and daughter.

Anticipation was now at fever heat. All Cambridge was booked for the first night, and 500 undergraduates unable to get tickets begged Longfellow to intercede in their behalf. Dickens was in despair about what could be done. In the packed audience to hear the *Christmas Carol* that night was Longfellow, "looking like the very spirit of Christmas," Holmes, "crisp and fine, like a tight little grape-skin full of wit instead of wine," Lowell, "with his poet's heart smiling sadly through his poet's eyes," even the elder Dana, a man of eighty, "with long grey hair falling round a face bright with shrewd intelligence." The end of the *Carol* was greeted with cheers and calls.

After the intermission, Dickens read the "Trial." Throughout and at the close there were screams of delight. "The old Judge," said Longfellow, "was equal to Dogberry." John Greenleaf Whittier was even more enthusiastic. "Those marvellous characters of his come forth, one by one, real personages, as if their original creator had breathed new life into them. . . . But it is idle to talk about it: you must beg, borrow, or steal a ticket & hear him. Another such star-shower is not to be expected in one's lifetime."

In his dressing-room before the reading, Dickens felt a "glow of pleasure and amazement" to find his usual buttonhole from Mary Boyle. The Boston *Post* reported that he returned a bouquet to a lady who had sent it on his opening night, thanking her, but saying "that a lady of London supplied him with flowers for his button-hole, not only in England, but America." "Oh, Charles," carolled the paper, "at your age and with that bald head and that grey goatee!"

Such journalistic familiarities Dickens attributed to "the public's love of smartness," but he was pleased to observe that in his personal meetings with reporters they treated him with perfect courtesy. Indeed, all America was greatly changed "for the better." Newspapers, to be sure, still expressed "the popular amazement at 'Mr Dickens's extraordinary composure.' They seem to take it ill that I don't stagger on the platform overpowered by the spectacle before me, and the national greatness." "My eyes are blue, red, grey, white, green, brown, black, hazel, violet, and rainbow-coloured. I am like 'a well-to-do American gentleman' and the Emperor of the French, with an occasional touch of the Emperor of China, and a deterioration from the attributes of our famous townsman, Rufus W. B. D. Dodge Grumsher Pickville."

The hotel expenses were enormous – £10 a day for the three rooms he and Dolby had together – but the accommodations were excellent. The Parker House had "all manner of white marble public passages and public rooms," there were hot and cold baths, and the dinners provided by Sanizan, its chef, were unsurpassed. The only trouble was that the place was so overheated that Dickens felt faint and sick, and had to leave all his windows wide open. "The air is like that of a pre-Adamite ironing-day in full blast."

From an opening week in Boston that brought in clear profits of over $9,000 Dickens moved on to New York. It was the first of a series of back-and-forth journeys, with a week in one city and then a week in the other, that continued until early January. New York was no less delirious than Boston. The night before tickets went on sale, lines of people with blankets and mattresses began forming in front of Steinway

Hall, shivering in the bitter cold, singing, dancing breakdowns, making night hideous with fighting; by morning there were at least 5,000, with waiters from neighbouring restaurants serving breakfasts in the frosty air.

Dolby tried to prevent tickets falling into the hands of speculators, but his efforts gave universal dissatisfaction. If he decreed that no more than six tickets a performance would be sold to any one purchaser, the speculators put fifty dummy buyers at the head of a line; if, noticing that most of these wore caps, he suddenly announced that he would sell only to those wearing hats, all manner of battered hats miraculously appeared. Special precautions had to be taken against bogus tickets. People would not refrain from paying speculators three times the established price, and then reviled Dolby bitterly. The New York *World* exploded, "Surely it is time that the pudding-headed Dolby retired into the native gloom from which he has emerged"; in consequence of which, Dickens explained, "We always call him P. H. Dolby now."

In New York Dickens stayed at the Westminster Hotel, in Irving Place, which he said was "quieter than Mivart's in Brook Street" and its "French cuisine immensely better." He drove out in a carriage and pair and admired all the new Central Park from a jingling red sleigh. At Niblo's he saw *The Black Crook*, a preposterous musical comedy that had been running sixteen months. "The people who act in it have not the slightest idea what it is about"; but Dickens fancied that he had "discovered Black Crook to be a malignant hunchback leagued with the Powers of Darkness to separate two lovers; and that the Powers of Lightness coming (in no skirts whatever) to the rescue, he is defeated."

The New York readings went even more wildly than those in Boston. "Mr Digguns," said the German janitor at Steinway Hall, "you are gread, meinherr. There is no ent to you." Then, reopening the door and sticking his head out, "Bedder and bedder," he added; "Wot negst!" One entire family came over from Brooklyn by ferry in a blinding snowstorm. On such a night, some astonished friends said, they wouldn't have come from Brooklyn to hear the Apostle Paul. "No, neither would we," was the reply, "but we came to hear Dickens." At the end of the first week there, Dickens sent £3,000 to England.

On Saturday, 21 December, he went back to Boston, where he found that Mrs Fields had decorated his hotel rooms with flowers and red-berried holly, while another admirer had imported a branch of English mistletoe. In the Fields home there was a dinner with a blazing plum pudding, and on Christmas Eve, suffering from a dismal cold, Dickens gave another reading of the *Carol*. Christmas Day, doleful with his "American catarrh," he made the return journey to New York.

The railway travelling he found even more distressing than in England. The cars were bumped and banged on and off the East River ferries; they were overheated by a great stove, with the closed windows making the atmosphere detestable. Sometimes, Dickens found that the only way he could bear it was to go out on the platform, where "it snows and blows, and the train bumps, and the steam flies at me, until I am driven in again."

With his heavy cold returned that "low action of the heart" from which he had suffered the preceding spring. After the Christmas night's reading, he "was laid upon a bed, in a very faint and shady state"; next day he did not get up till afternoon. That night he felt unfit to read, but forced himself to do so, and the following morning had to send for Dr Fordyce Barker. He wanted to "stop the readings altogether for some few days," but Dickens insisted that he must go on. Despite his New York landlord's prescription of a "Rocky Mountain Sneezer" of brandy, rum, bitters, lemon, sugar, and snow, the "true American catarrh" refused to budge.

Back in Boston, he often could not sleep till morning. Longfellow's twelve-year-old daughter "Allegra" later recalled her joy in the nightly readings:

> Sam Weller and Mr Pickwick, Nicholas Nickleby and the old gentleman and the vegetable marrows over the garden wall. *How* he did make Aunt Betsy Trotwood snap out, "Janet, donkeys" – and David Copperfield yearn over the handsome sleeping Steerforth. How the audience loved best of all the Christmas Carol and how they laughed as Dickens fairly smacked his lips as there came the "smell like an eating house and a pastry cook's next door to each other, with a laundress's next door to that," as Mrs Cratchit bore in the Christmas pudding and how they nearly wept as Tiny Tim cried "God bless us every one!"

Before heading south for Philadelphia, Baltimore, and Washington, Dickens had another week of readings in New York, including Brooklyn. The usual riotous scenes attended the sale of tickets, with "the noble army of speculators" building bonfires, fighting, and greeting Dolby with roars of "Hallo! Dolby! So Charley has let you have the carriage, has he Dolby? How is he, Dolby? Don't drop the tickets, Dolby! Look alive, Dolby!"

Dickens's cold still would not stir an inch. "I have tried allopathy, homoeopathy, cold things, warm things, sweet things, bitter things, stimulants, narcotics, all with the same result. Nothing will touch it." He was hardly able to eat.

I rarely take any breakfast but an egg and a cup of tea, not even toast or bread-and-butter. My dinner at three, and a little quail or some such light thing when I come home at night, is my daily fare. At the Hall I have established the custom of taking an egg beaten up in sherry before going in, and another between the parts. I think that pulls me up; at all events, I have since had no return of faintness.

He had determined by now to confine the readings to the east, in spite of anguished outcries from St Louis, Cincinnati, and Chicago. "Good heavens, sir!" exclaimed George W. Childs, the publisher of the Philadelphia *Public Ledger*, "if you don't read in Chicago the people will go into fits!" Chicago in fact led a violent assault upon Dickens, with bitter imputations against his reasons for avoiding that city. His brother Augustus, who had deserted his wife in 1858, had died there in 1866, leaving a "widow" and three children. Dickens refused to explain that he had long supported the only legitimate Mrs Augustus Dickens or that since his brother's death he had been sending £50 a year to Chicago. The newspapers painted lugubrious pictures of his "brother's wife and her helpless children."

Amid these accusations of penurious cruelty, Dickens was telling his daughter Mary to take care of their old servant Anne Cornelius, whose husband was ill and very poor. "The question . . . is not one of so much or so little money on my side, but how *most efficiently* to ease her mind and help *her*." And on 3 February the Boston *Transcript* recorded that Dickens had "sent $1,000 to Mrs Clemm, Poe's mother-in-law," who had been in needy circumstances since Poe's death. Dickens also arranged with Dr Samuel Gridley Howe to print 250 copies of *The Old Curiosity Shop* in Braille, to be distributed as a gift to the asylums for the blind, and later sent Dr Howe $1,700 for that purpose.

Baltimore, Dickens felt, was haunted by "the ghost of slavery" and still wore "a look of sullen remembrance." It was here that "the ladies used to spit when they passed a Northern soldier." For the first reading in Washington, President Andrew Johnson, the chief members of the Cabinet, the Supreme Court, ambassadors, naval and military officers in full uniform, leading Government officials and political figures came almost in a body. The President had a whole row for every reading of the week.

On 5 February the President invited Dickens to call at the White House. He found the Executive quiet and composed in spite of the political storms that were gathering about him (he was impeached on 24 February). "A man not to be turned or trifled with," Dickens judged. He also dined with his old friend Charles Sumner, and met Secretary of War Stanton, whose dismissal by the President had set the nation on fire.

For Dickens's birthday in Washington flowers bombarded his room, garlands, bouquets, and green baskets, together with other gifts and "letters radiant with good wishes." But his cold was so bad that when Sumner came in at five and found him voiceless and covered with mustard poultices, he said, "Surely, Mr Dolby, it is impossible that he can read tonight." "Sir, I have told the dear Chief so four times today, and I have been very anxious." But by some mysterious act of will Dickens always managed to overcome his affliction so that "after five minutes of the little table" he was not even hoarse.

Immediately after his birthday, Dickens turned north again on the second half of his tour. He gave farewell readings in Baltimore and Philadelphia, and then made a week's swing through New Haven, Hartford, Worcester, and Providence. Going on ahead, Dolby discovered that his advance ticket-agent, a man named Kelly, had been speculating in tickets and taking bribes from speculators. Kelly was peremptorily dismissed. After a few days, however, Dickens relented and allowed him to remain, although in disgrace and "within very reduced limits." Employees about Steinway Hall swore to give him a beating when he returned to New York.

On 24 February Dickens was back in Boston for another fortnight's readings there. The impeachment of the President, however, cut so drastically the audiences for all entertainments that for the first time there were empty seats. Dickens decided to cancel the second week and see if his cold would yield to rest. Dolby and Osgood, who were always doing ridiculous things to keep him in spirits, had decided to hold a walking match on the 29th. "Beginning this design in joke, they have become tremendously in earnest, and Dolby has actually sent home (much to his opponent's terror) for a pair of seamless socks to walk in."

In Baltimore, Dickens had given them "a breather" of five miles in the snow, at a pace of four and a half miles an hour, from which the two returned "smoking like factories." "They have the absurdest ideas," he wrote, "of what are tests of walking power, and continually get up in the maddest manner and see *how high they can kick* the wall! . . . To see them doing this – Dolby, a big man, and Osgood, a very little one, is ridiculous beyond description."

Back in Boston, Dickens drew up burlesque articles of agreement for this "Great International Walking Match," in which Dolby was given the sporting nickname of the "Man of Ross" and Osgood was the "Boston Bantam." The umpires were Fields, "Massachusetts Jemmy," and Dickens, "whose surprising performances (without the least variation) on that truly national instrument, the American catarrh, have won for him the well-merited title of the Gad's Hill Gasper." Going at a tremendous pace, Dickens and Fields laid out the course: six and a half miles along the Mill Dam Road to Newton Center and then back. It was covered with snow and sheets and blocks of ice.

Despite his cold, Dickens turned up for the race. There was a biting wind and furious snow. "It was so cold, too, that our hair, beards, eyelashes, eyebrows, were frozen hard, and hung with icicles." After the turning the Bantam forged ahead and "pegged away with his little drum-sticks as if he saw his wives and a peck of barley waiting for him at the family perch." "We are not quite decided whether Mrs Fields did not desert our colours, by coming on the ground in a carriage, and having *bread soaked in brandy* put into the winning man's mouth as he steamed along. She pleaded that she would have done as much for Dolby, if *he* had been ahead, so we are inclined to forgive her."

Afterwards Dickens gave an elaborate dinner in the Crystal Room at the Parker House. Among the guests were Fields, James Russell Lowell, Holmes, Charles Eliot Norton, Ticknor, Aldrich, and their wives, "and an obscure poet named Longfellow (if discoverable), and Miss Longfellow." Later, Dickens went upstairs to his room with Dolby and Osgood, in joking high spirits. Water had been drawn for his bath and he entertained his companions by imitating Grimaldi on the rolling edge of the tub. In the midst of the complicated feat, he lost his balance and, with a tidal wave of a splash, fell in, evening dress, boutonnière, gold chains, brilliantined earlocks, and all.

At a bachelor dinner a few nights later Dickens was in his wildest form. John Bigelow, the ex-Minister to France, was one of the guests, and they enacted a burlesque of an English election, with Bigelow as Fields's candidate and Dolby as Dickens's. Dickens made a campaign speech pretending that Dolby's superiority lay in his lack of hair. "We roared and writhed," said Fields, "in agonies of laughter, and the candidates themselves were literally choking and crying . . ." When Fields tried to speak for his man, Dickens interrupted "with imitative jeers," in a variety of voices, including "a pretended husky old man bawling out at intervals, 'Three cheers for the bald 'un!' 'Down with the hairy aristocracy!' 'Up with the little shiny chap on top!' "

With the exposure and exertion of the walking match, the true American had taken "a fresh start, as if it were quite a novelty," and was "on the whole rather worse than ever." Nevertheless, Dickens began a ten days' circuit of one-night stands in upstate New York, Syracuse, Rochester, Buffalo, ending with two nights in Albany. At Syracuse he began to have trouble walking; this time it was something that he called an eruption on his right leg. The hotel there fascinated him with a menu which listed "chicken de pullet," "Turpin Soup," "Rolard mutton," and "Paettie de Shay." The last of these, the Irish waiter said with a broad grin, was "The Frinch name the steward giv' to oyster pattie."

In spite of these diversions, Dickens was tired and depressed and homesick. He was saddened to hear of the death of his old friend Chauncey Townshend. Between Rochester and Albany floods stranded the train overnight at Utica. Next day they continued slowly through "drowned farms, barns adrift like Noah's arks, deserted villages," with 100 booted men pushing blocks of ice out of the way with long poles. At half-past ten that night Dickens arrived at his hotel in Albany "pretty well knocked up."

On 20 March he entered the last stage of his journeyings. There were still to be ten days of moving through Springfield, Worcester, New Haven, Hartford, and New Bedford, up to Portland, Maine. Then there would remain only the farewell readings in Boston and New York. But he reached Portland sick and exhausted. "With the return of snow, nine days ago, the 'true American' (which had lulled) came back as bad as ever. I have coughed from two or three in the morning until five or six, and have been absolutely sleepless. . . . Last night I took some laudanum, and it is the only thing that has done me good." To Forster he admitted, "I am nearly used up. Climate, distance, catarrh, travelling, and hard work have begun to tell heavily upon me." If he had engaged to go on into May, he thought he must have broken down.

But the killing odyssey was nearly over. On the train back to Boston, Dickens felt more cheerful and talked briskly with Osgood. From the rear of the car, near the water cooler and the trainboy with his popcorn balls and molasses candy, he was watched by an adoring little girl later known as Kate Douglas Wiggin. When Osgood got up to go to the smoking car, she speeded up the aisle and planted herself timorously "in the seat of honour."

"God bless my soul," Dickens exclaimed, "where did you come from?" "I came from Hollis, Maine," she answered, "and I'm going to Charlestown to visit my uncle. My mother and her cousin went to your reading last night, but, of course, three couldn't go from the same family, so I stayed at home. . . . There was a lady there who had never heard of Betsey Trotwood, and had only read two of your books." "Well, upon my word! you do not mean to say that *you* have read them!" "Of course I have," she replied; "every one of them but the two that we are going to buy in Boston, and some of them six times."

Under pressing she admitted that she skipped "some of the very dull parts," and Dickens laughed heartily. Taking out a notebook and pencil, he examined her elaborately on the books in which the dull parts predominated. "He chuckled so constantly during this operation that I could hardly help believing myself extraordinarily agreeable, so I continued dealing these infant blows, under the delusion that I was flinging him bouquets. It was not long before one of my hands was in his, and his arm around my waist . . ."

"Did you want to go to my reading very much?" asked Dickens. This was a question that stirred the depths of her disappointment and sorrow. Her lips trembled as she faltered, "*Yes; more than tongue can tell.*" Only when she was sure the tears in her eyes were not going to fall did she look up, and then she saw that there were tears in his eyes too. "Do you cry when you read out loud?" she asked. "We all do in our family. And we never read about Tiny Tim, or about Steerforth when his body is washed up on the beach, on Saturday nights, or our eyes are too swollen to go to Sunday School." "Yes, I cry when I read about Steerforth," Dickens answered quietly.

They were now fast approaching Boston. Several times Osgood had come back, but had been waved away by Dickens. "You are not travelling alone?" he now asked. "Oh, no, I had a mother, but I forgot all about her." "You are a passed-mistress of the art of flattery!" Dickens said.

He reached Boston none too soon. Dickens thought his lungs might have been done a lasting injury; he coughed constantly and was sunk in gloom. He petulantly refused to see two of Osgood's friends from

New Bedford: "No, I'll be damned if I will!" "I think, too," said Mrs Fields, "only $1,300 in the house was bad for his spirits!" But although Longfellow and all his Cambridge friends urged him to give in, he astonished them and even himself by his rendering of the last Boston readings.

He could hardly eat now, and had established a fixed system:

At seven in the morning, in bed, a tumbler of cream and two tablespoonsful of rum. At twelve, a sherry cobbler and a biscuit. At three (dinner time), a pint of champagne. At five minutes to eight, an egg beaten up with a glass of sherry. Between the parts, the strongest beef tea that can be made, drunk hot. At a quarter past ten, soup, and anything to drink that I can fancy. I don't eat more than half a pound of solid food in the whole twenty-four hours, if so much.

The final New York readings were all that remained. Only the daily attention of Dr Fordyce Barker and the devoted care of Dolby brought Dickens through the ordeal. In the excitement and exertion of the readings, the blood rushed into his hands until they became almost black, and his face turned red and white and red again without his knowing it. After one of the last readings, Mrs Fields found him prostrated, "his head thrown back without support on the couch, the blood suffusing his throat and temples again where he had been very white a few minutes before."

There was still a great press banquet at Delmonico's on 18 April which Dickens had promised to attend. Two hundred and four tickets were sold at fifteen dollars a plate. But at five o'clock Dickens felt so unwell that it was not certain he could leave the hotel. Messengers ran back and forth with inquiries and bulletins, Dickens was determined to make the effort, and by the application of lotions and a careful bandaging of his foot and leg Dr Barker enabled him to get out. He was an hour late when he limped into the restaurant leaning heavily on the arm of Horace Greeley.

The staggering affair progressed through course after course in which the diners had choices of at least three dozen elaborate dishes, including such items as "*Crème d'asperges à la Dumas*," "*Timbales à la Dickens*," "*Filets de boeuf à la Lucullus*," "*Coutelettes à la Fenimore Cooper*," "*Aspic de foie gras historiés*," and "*Soupirs à la Mantalini*." The confectionery triumphs of the pastry cooks included a "*temple de la Littérature*; *trophées à l'auteur*; *Stars and Stripes*; *pavilion internationale*; *armes Bri-*

544

tanniques; la loi du Destin; monument de Washington; and *colonne triomphale.*"
"Sairey Gamp and Betsy Prig, and Poor Joe and Captain Cuttle
blossomed out of charlotte russe, and Tiny Tim was discovered in
paté de foie gras."

Unaware of how severe was Dickens's pain, Greeley was "one vast,
substantial smile." In response to his welcoming speech, Dickens rose.
He was henceforth charged with a duty, he said,

> on every suitable occasion . . . to express my high and grateful sense
> of my second reception in America, and to bear my honest testimony
> to the national generosity and magnanimity. Also, to declare how
> astounded I have been by the amazing changes I have seen around
> me on every side – changes moral, changes physical . . . changes in
> the graces and amenities of life, changes in the press, without whose
> advancement no advancement can be made anywhere. Nor am I,
> believe me, so arrogant as to suppose that in twenty-five years there
> have been no changes in me, and that I had nothing to learn and no
> extreme impressions to correct when I was here first.

Though he had no intention of writing any other book on America,
he wished

> to record that . . . I have been received with unsurpassable polite-
> ness, delicacy, sweet temper, hospitality, consideration, and with
> unsurpassable respect for the privacy daily enforced upon me by the
> nature of my avocation here, and the state of my health. This
> testimony, so long as I live, and so long as my descendants have any
> legal right in my books, I shall cause to be republished as an appendix
> to those two books of mine in which I have referred to America.

His feelings he believed representative of those of the majority of the
English people. Essentially the two peoples were one, with a common
heritage of great achievement. In conclusion,

> I do believe that from the great majority of honest minds on both
> sides, there cannot be absent the conviction that it would be better
> for this globe to be riven by an earthquake, fired by a comet, overrun
> by an iceberg, and abandoned to the Arctic fox and bear, than that it
> should present the spectacle of these two great nations, each of which
> has, in its own way and hour, striven so hard and so successfully for
> freedom, ever again being arrayed the one against the other.

So severe was Dickens's pain by the end of this speech that he was forced to beg to be excused. The mechanism of the body, indeed, was disastrously weakened, but the steel-coiled will that dominated it would not surrender. Two nights later, on 20 April, he forced himself to the final reading and bade his American listeners farewell forever. But though in some miraculous way the vessel had not been dashed to pieces against the Loadstone Rock, all its fabric was twisted and broken with the dreadful strain. Could it attempt another such voyage and not go down? Yet it was precisely such a course that Dickens even now was charting.

46

Last Rally

The night before Dickens was to sail, Fields told him he felt like erecting a statue to him for heroism in doing his duty. "No, don't," Dickens gasped, laughing at the same time, "take down one of the old ones instead!" The next day, 22 April, dawned with a bright blue sky. His bandaged foot swathed in black silk, Dickens limped among heaped boxes filled with parting gifts of vintage wines, choice cigars, pictures, books, and photographs. In Irving Place a carriage waited to take him to a private tug that would put him on board the *Russia*, instead of exposing him to the enormous crowd waiting at the Cunard pier.

In front of the Westminster Hotel, too, a huge crowd was assembled. As he came out, there was a ringing cheer and flowers showered from the windows. A swift drive brought him and Dolby to the foot of Spring Street, where they were joined by Fields and the other friends who were seeing them on board. When Dickens saw the sparkling water, he exclaimed, "That's *home!*" After a pleasant half-hour sail down the North River and the Bay, they were alongside the *Russia*. The Cunard Company provided a magnificent lunch; Dickens's stateroom – the Chief Steward's, on deck – bloomed with floral tributes. After lunch the passenger tender arrived with the bulk of the voyagers and a group of others coming to say good-bye: du Chaillu, the African explorer; George W. Childs, the Philadelphia publisher, bearing a splendid basket of flowers from his wife; and Anthony Trollope, who had arrived that very day on the *Scotia* and hastened out to Dickens.

The tug screamed a note of warning. Dickens's lame foot came down from the rail and he and Fields were locked in an embrace. Then Fields scrambled down the side. A cheer went up for Dolby, another cheer for Dickens. The tug was now steaming away. Dickens put his soft hat on his cane and waved it. "Goodbye," he called, "God bless you every one." Even then, a police boat, private tugs, and steam launches followed the *Russia* down the Bay, firing salutes from miniature cannon.

Financially, the American tour had been successful beyond all expectations. The total receipts had been $228,000, and the expenses not quite $39,000, including hotels, travelling, rent of halls, and a 5 per cent commission to Ticknor and Fields on the receipts in Boston. The preliminary expenses in England had been £614, Dolby's commission close to £3,000. The three years that had elapsed since the close of the Civil War had not yet restored American currency to its normal exchange value; if Dickens had invested in American securities and waited for the dollar to go back to par, his profits would have been nearly £38,000. Even paying a discount of almost 40 per cent for conversion to gold, "my profit," Dickens wrote Forster, "was within a hundred or so of £20,000."

But it had been bought at a shattering cost of pain and exhaustion. Perhaps if he had given up all further public readings his extraordinary vitality might even now have restored his strength. But he had always forced his body to do exactly what he determined; at fifty-six he was not going to change. He would neither give up the prospect of placing his entire large family forever beyond the fear of want, nor strangle those emotional needs the readings relieved with a drugged excitement. On his way out to America, he had already begun negotiations with Chappell's for another English series, to start in the autumn of 1868. Before the first week of Boston readings closed he had settled the terms.

They were glittering but ominous. He was to read a hundred times and receive £8,000. On the American tour an original schedule of around eighty had been reduced by a few cancellations to seventy-six; and under their strain Dickens had been brought to the verge of prostration. Nevertheless he refused now to alter his plans. The only concession he made was to announce that this would be his farewell tour. For one more series – 100 more times – he would be "cooked before those lights" and exult in that intoxication. On the dangers of this determination he closed his eyes.

In part he was deceived by the almost unbelievable resilience with which a little rest reanimated his vigour. Four days out at sea the "true American" turned faithless at last, and for the first time he was able to cram his right foot into a shoe. His spirits and his appetite returned: he "made a Gad's Hill breakfast" and watched Dolby eating his way through "A large dish of porridge into which he casts slices of butter and a quantity of sugar. Two cups of tea. A steak, Irish stew, Chutnee and marmalade." Dickens reached England bronzed and well-looking.

"My doctor was quite broken down in spirits when he saw me . . . 'Good Lord!' he said, recoiling, 'seven years younger!' "

At Gad's Hill, Mary and Georgina had got wind of a plan among the villagers to meet Dickens at Higham Station, take his horse out of the shafts, and draw him home in triumph. To prevent this, Dickens had himself met by the basket phaeton at Gravesend. Even so, the houses along the road were all decorated with flags and the local farmers turned out in their market chaises, calling "Welcome home, sir!" The servants at Gad's Hill "had asked Mamie's permission to 'ring the alarm-bell' (!) when master drove up, but Mamie, having some slight idea that that compliment might awaken master's sense of the ludicrous, had recommended bell-abstinence."

When Dickens drove into the stable yard, "Linda (the St Bernard) was greatly excited; weeping profusely, and throwing herself on her back that she might caress my foot with her great forepaws. . . . Mrs Bouncer barked in the greatest agitation on being called down and asked by Mamie, 'Who is this?' and tore round and round me." On Sunday, the village choir at the little church made amends for the servants' disappointment at the silence of the bell on Dickens's return. "After some unusually brief pious reflections in the crowns of their hats at the end of the sermon, the ringers bolted out, and rang like mad until I got home."

Dolby, at his home in Ross, found his small daughter less excited by the birth of a baby brother than by the arrival of a Shetland pony that Dickens had sent as a present while in America. "The little girl winds up her prayers every night," Dickens reported to Mrs Fields, "with a special commendation to Heaven of me and the pony – as if I must mount him to get there!"

Return to England brought Dickens no rest but a resumption of labour. During his absence Wills had had an accident on the hunting field, which led to concussion of the brain. Even when he had partly recovered he was unable to do the slightest work. His retirement from the subeditorship of *All the Year Round* forced Dickens to take over its financial supervision, which had always been in Wills's hands, and learn it from A to Z.

Townshend's will had appointed Dickens his friend's literary executor, with the request that he publish "without alteration as much of my notes and reflections as may make known my opinions on religious matters." When the notes arrived, they proved so bulky, repetitious, and chaotic that publishing them "without alteration" was impossible:

the volume would fall stillborn from the press. Dickens privately gave it the title *Religious Hiccoughs*, but he faithfully arranged, collated, selected, and saw it published the following year.

No Thoroughfare, the Christmas story on which he had collaborated with Collins, had proved highly successful in their dramatized version at the Adelphi with Fechter. But Dickens thought it dragged; a drugging and attempted robbery in a Swiss inn should be done with the sound of a waterfall in the background – it would enhance enormously "the mystery and gloom." No sooner were these changes made than Dickens took a flying trip to Paris to give a few pointers to the French production before it opened there. Entitled *L'Abîme*, and presented at the Vaudeville, the play promised to be a success in Paris as well.

In June, Longfellow and his daughters came to England. Dickens hurried to the Langham Hotel, where they were staying, and invited them to spend the "Fourth of July" week-end at Gad's Hill. On the morning of the 4th, a Saturday, Longfellow was to see the Queen at Windsor, and Monday evening he had to be back in London, but into the brief visit Dickens crowded a breathless hospitality. "I turned out a couple of postilions in the old red jacket of the old red royal Dover road for our ride; and it was," he wrote Fields, "like a holiday ride of fifty years ago. Of course we went to look at the old houses in Rochester, and the old cathedral, and the old castle . . ."

Dickens's neighbours, Lord and Lady Darnley, had given him keys to the gates of Cobham Park; and Alice, Longfellow's eldest daughter, was delighted by the drive over its undulating turf, with the splendid great trees standing up to their knees in ferns and little rabbits dashing in and out. The Gad's Hill meals were wonderful, "with more cold dishes on the sideboard than we ever dreamed of. In the evening the great tray on wheels was brought into the drawing-room, full of bottles and glasses. Punch, hot or cold, lemons, hot water, and every drinkable imaginable."

In the midst of these convivialities Dickens's responsibilities were weighing upon him as heavily as ever. Among his sons, only Harry gave him no trouble. He had risen to be Head Censor at Wimbledon, was highly praised by the head of the school, and was preparing for Cambridge. But Charley's paper business had gone bankrupt, and although the fault seemed to be more his partner's than his own, Charley was personally in debt for £1,000. At the age of thirty-one he still had no settled profession or income. In the end, Dickens took him on *All the Year Round* to assume some of Wills's routine duties. Plorn, who was now almost seventeen, was being sent out to join his brother Alfred in Australia. The expenses of buying his outfit and of getting Harry ready for Cambridge were staggering. "I can't get my hat on in consequence of the extent to which my hair stands on end at the costs and charges of these boys."

On 26 September Plorn was to sail on the *Sussex*. His father gave him a cheque for £200.

> I need not tell you [Dickens wrote in a farewell letter], that I love you dearly, and am very, very sorry in my heart to part with you. But this life is half made up of partings, and these pains must be born. . . . I put a New Testament among your books, for the very same reasons, and with the very same hopes that made me write an easy account of it for you, when you were a little child . . . I hope you will always be able to say . . . that you had a kind father.

Both father and son were greatly distressed at parting. "Just before the train started," Dickens wrote Mary, "he cried a good deal, but not painfully. (Tell dear Georgy that I bought him his cigars.) These are hard, hard things, but they might have to be done without means or influence, and then they would be far harder." As the boy went off, Dickens looked after him sadly. "He seemed to me to become once more my youngest and favourite child . . . and I did not think I could have been so shaken."

In October, Harry went to Cambridge, where, Dickens was gratified to hear, he had won a scholarship of £50 a year. So well did Harry work that later he won the best mathematical scholarship at Trinity. Excitedly he broke the news to his father, who met him at Higham. "Capital! capital!" exclaimed Dickens, but no more. Deeply self-restrained in whatever moved him deeply, after all his disappointments with the other boys he could not trust himself to speak. Harry felt bitterly hurt. The two started to walk home in silence. Suddenly, his father turned to him with tears in his eyes, and clasped his hand in a painful grip. "God bless you, my boy," he said brokenly, "God bless you!"

Even before the farewell readings began there were renewed signs that Dickens's strength was impaired. Although he could call upon a deceptive vivacity, Forster never saw him during that summer without sensing a loss in his elasticity of bearing. Once, as they walked from Dickens's office to dine together in Forster's house at Palace Gate, Dickens alarmed his old friend by confessing that he could read only the right-hand sides of the signs over the shop doors.

He got through his opening night at St James's Hall on 6 October without penalty, but soon painful symptoms appeared. He wrote Mary and Georgina three days later from Manchester, admitting that he was hoarse and croaking. He confessed to Frank Beard that he felt such nausea after his nightly exertions that the next morning he could not even bear the taste of the tincture he used for cleaning his teeth. "I have not been well," he wrote Forster on 25 October, "and have been heavily tired. However, I have little to complain of – nothing, nothing; though, like Mariana, I am aweary." With the end of the month he was worse. "I cannot get right internally," he told Georgina, "and have begun to be as sleepless as sick."

He had just learned, too, of the death of his brother Frederick, whom he had not seen in seven years. "I am glad to remember that it never involved on my side, the slightest feeling of anger. He lost opportunities that I had put in his way, poor dear fellow, but there were unhappy circumstances in his life which demanded great allowances." "It was a wasted life, but God forbid that one should be hard upon it . . ."

During November there were no provincial readings, and those Dickens gave in London were no great strain. But meanwhile he had decided that his listeners needed a new sensation. From *Oliver Twist* he carved a reading culminating in the murder of Nancy and Sikes's haunted flight and death, and then felt afraid to use it. "I have no doubt I could perfectly petrify an audience . . .," he explained. "But whether the impression would not be so horrible as to keep them away another time, is what I cannot satisfy myself upon."

He had indeed made something appalling. One warm afternoon Charley was working in the library when he heard a sound of violent wrangling from outside. At first he dismissed it as some tramp brawling with his wife, but as the noise swelled into an alternation of brutal yells and dreadful screams Charley leaped to his feet, convinced that he must intervene. He dashed out. There was his father – murdering an imaginary Nancy with ferocious gestures. After dinner Charley mentioned what he had seen and Dickens acted it for him again. What did he think of it?

"The finest thing I have ever heard," Charley replied, "but don't do it." But he knew his father could not bear any suggestion that his health was failing, and therefore steadily refused to give any explanation of his verdict. Forster also opposed, but would give no reason except that "such a subject was out of the province of reading." Dolby also tried dissuasion, and, when Dickens persisted, proposed that he ask the Chappells for their opinion. They suggested that he canvass the judgements of a private audience of invited friends at St James's Hall.

Around 100 people were present on 14 November. Beside his usual violet screen, Dickens had two flanking screens and curtains beyond them, narrowing the stage to the space surrounding his own figure. Into the reading he threw all his genius as an actor, bringing to life the comic, oily, crafty Fagin, the cowardly and stupid Noah Claypole, the brutal Sikes, and Nancy's terrifying shrieks. The audience stared with blanched and horror-stricken faces.

Directly Dickens had done, the screens were whisked aside, revealing a long banquet table and a staff of waiters "ready to open oysters and set champagne-corks flying." Soon the wine restored the colour to people's cheeks. Dickens was triumphantly excited. The actresses, Mme Celeste and Mrs Keeley, were rapturous. Should he do it or not? Dickens asked. " 'Why, of course do it,' " Mrs Keeley replied. " 'Having got at such an effect as that, it must be done . . . the public have been looking for a sensation these last fifty years or so, and by Heaven they have got it!' With which words, and a long breath and a long stare, she became speechless."

Dickens turned to his son. "Well, Charley, and what do you think of it now?" "It is finer even than I expected," was the reply, "but I still say, don't do it." As Dickens looked at him, puzzled, Edmund Yates came up. "What do you think of this, Edmund?" Dickens asked. "Here is Charley saying it is the finest thing he has ever heard, but persists in telling me, without giving any reason, not to do it." Yates gave a quick look at Charley, and said gravely, to Dickens's intense amazement, "I agree with Charley, Sir."

But of course Dickens ignored the verdict he did not want to hear. The ominous warnings had been repeated over and over. That inability to read the street signs on his left side was a plain foreshadowing of paralysis, and his sleeplessness, nausea, and lameness were little less threatening. The danger was clear to all who knew him intimately. Nevertheless, he chose to close his eyes on what they saw, and on what his letters telling his symptoms reveal that he himself saw. No matter what the consequences, he would go on doing what he loved. In deciding to add the murder of Nancy to his repertory, he was sentencing himself to death.

Perhaps Dickens would have felt shocked had he been accused of a deliberate effort at suicide. Since 1866 he had been reckless in expending his waning energies. But he had ceased to care. All his fame had not brought him the things he most deeply wanted. The long frustration of his marriage had ended in a failure that left him ruthless and embittered towards Catherine. There is no direct evidence of what part Ellen played in his unhappiness, but there can be no doubt that in some way she, too, failed his need. Did he suspect her, like Bella Wilfer, the heroine of *Our Mutual Friend*, of being calculating and mercenary, and, unlike Bella, of having remained so? Was his tenderness for her, too, shot through with the bitterness of disillusion?

Even his children whom he loved were one after another worrying and disappointing him. And when he looked from his home to the affairs of the world, the gleaming hopes of his earlier career were largely unrealized. Though he had seen the domination of the country pass from a landed aristocracy to the commercial and industrial middle class, inefficiency, cruelty, corruption, and privilege were still entrenched. As he gazed into the future it seemed to him that he could discern no prospects but the decline of England and ever renewed international conflicts. Only in the people did he still have faith.

But every perspective left him weary of his own struggle. Though he could still relish the comic and still whip himself up at intervals to his old gusty enjoyment of life, more and more these efforts broke down and the darkness and emptiness came crowding back. What was there then but the fearful stimulus of the readings, and returning to them as Jasper in *The Mystery of Edwin Drood* would return to the dangerous excitement of his drugged visions?

In December the provincial grind began again. Going to Edinburgh on the "Flying Scotsman," he calculated that travelling such a distance involved "more than thirty thousand shocks to the nerves." The weather was diabolical, and again he had wretched nights.

After the first public reading of the "Murder" in London on 5 January, he was utterly prostrated the next morning. A few days later there were final readings to be given in Dublin and Belfast. Dickens took Georgina and Mary with him. On the return train from Belfast, their carriage was directly behind the engine. Suddenly they heard a crash overhead and there was a shock that threw them all forward. An enormous fragment of iron went tearing along the line, knocking down the telegraph poles. The windows were bombarded with flying stones, mud, and gravel. Aghast, they all threw themselves to the floor. With a grinding and hissing the train jolted to a standstill.

Controlling his agitation, Dickens climbed out and began talking to the engineer. In a moment they were surrounded by a crowd of terrified passengers. The engineer excitedly explained that the metal tyre of the great driving wheel had been fractured and shot into the air. It was one of these pieces that had struck the roof of Dickens's carriage. A little more force and it might have crashed down upon their heads. The experience did not lessen the nervousness Dickens felt during his almost daily railway journeyings.

He had arranged his schedule to take in Cheltenham especially so that Macready might hear the "Murder." The famous old Macbeth, seventy-five now, and very infirm, sat in the front row, grimly staring. Afterwards, he went to Dickens's dressing-room, and scowlingly took a glass of champagne from Dolby. He glared speechlessly at Dickens. Dickens tried to laugh away his emotion, but Macready would not have it.

"No, Dickens – er – er – I will NOT," with sudden emphasis, – "er – have it – er – put aside. In my – er – best times – er – you remember them, my dear boy – er – gone, gone! – no," – with great emphasis again, – "it comes to this – er – TWO MACBETHS!" with extraordinary energy. After which he stood (with his glass in his hand and his old square jaw of its old fierce form) looking defiantly at Dolby as if Dolby had contradicted him; and then trailed off into a weak pale likeness of himself as if his whole appearance had been some clever optical illusion.

At Clifton the "Murder" brought about "a contagion of fainting. And yet the place was not hot. I should think we had from a dozen to twenty ladies borne out, stiff and rigid, at various times." In Bath, Dickens felt as if he were haunted by the ghost of Landor going along the silent streets before him. "The place looks to me like a cemetery which the Dead have succeeded in rising and taking. Having built streets of their old gravestones, they wander about scantily trying to 'look alive.' A dead failure."

Two weeks later Dickens's foot went lame again. Sir Henry Thompson, the renowned physician, refused to let him read that night, and forbade his going to Scotland the following day. "Heavens knows what engagements this may involve in April!" Dickens exclaimed. "It throws us all back, and will cost me some five hundred pounds." But in a few days he felt so much better that, resisting all the entreaties of family and friends, he set out for Edinburgh on 20 February. Once more, two days later he collapsed and had to consult another doctor. This one prescribed a special kind of boot which gave Dickens some relief, but fell in with his theory that the trouble originated in walking in the snow.

Dickens professed to feel gratified that the last readings were being disposed of one by one. With an ominous quotation he anticipated the end: " 'Like lights in a theatre, they are being snuffed out fast,' as Carlyle says of the guillotined in his Revolution. I suppose I shall be glad when they are all snuffed out. Anyhow, I think so *now*."

But he enjoyed the readings. Above all he enjoyed shocking his audiences with the murder and liked to joke about his "murderous instincts." "There was a fixed expression of horror of me, all over the theatre, which could not have been surpassed if I had been going to be hanged. . . . It is quite a new sensation to be execrated with that unanimity; and I hope it will remain so!" He consequently put the "Murder" on his programme again and again. By this time he had given up drinking champagne during the readings, and took only some weak iced brandy and water.

Following the last Edinburgh reading he was obliged to lie on the sofa some time before he could utter a word. After supper, he handed Dolby the list of readings for the remainder of the tour. "Look carefully through the towns you have given me," Dolby said, "and see if you note anything peculiar about them." "No. What is it?" "Well, out of four Readings a week you have put down three Murders." "What of that?" Dickens asked. "Simply this," Dolby replied; "the success of this farewell tour is assured in every way, so far as human probability is concerned. It therefore does not make a bit of difference which of the works you read . . ."

Dolby went on to say that Dickens should refrain from tearing himself to pieces and suffering the tortures he endured. He should reserve the "Murder" for the larger towns – "Have you finished?" Dickens angrily interrupted. "I have said all I feel on the matter." Dickens bounded up from his chair and threw his knife and fork violently on his plate, smashing it to pieces. "Dolby!" he shouted, "your infernal caution will be your ruin one of these days." It was the only time Dolby had ever heard him address an angry word to anyone. "Perhaps so, sir," Dolby replied. "In this case, though, I hope you will do me the justice to say it is exercised in your interest."

Turning aside, he left the table. Then he saw that his Chief was crying. "Forgive me, Dolby!" Dickens exclaimed between sobs, embracing him affectionately. "I really didn't mean it; and I know you are right. We will talk the matter over calmly in the morning."

But the few concessions he made were too little and too late. Through deepening exhaustion he struggled on. In March he learned of the death of Sir James Emerson Tennent, with whom he had passed delightful days during the Italian visit of 1853 and to whom he had dedicated *Our Mutual Friend*. The news shook him with grief; and by cutting out his intermissions at a York reading he barely managed to make the London train and attend the funeral. To Forster he appeared dazed and worn.

On 20 April, at St George's Hall in Liverpool, "the Mayor, Corporation, and citizens" gave a dinner in Dickens's honour which he found as exhausting as the reading. He had effusions of blood from his bowels now, and his foot was so bad that Scott, his valet, carried a supply of flannel and of poppyheads to make fomentations at a moment's notice. His giddiness had returned, he was uncertain of his footing, and felt "extremely indisposed to raise" his hands to his head. "My weakness and deadness," he told Georgina, "are all *on the left side*, and if I don't look at anything I try to touch with my hand, I don't know where it is."

He wrote to Francis Beard suggesting that these symptoms were the results of his medicine. But Beard at once emphasized what they really meant. "The medicine cannot possibly have caused them," he replied firmly. Hastening the 200 miles to Dickens's side, he examined him, and insisted that the readings must stop at once. If he took the platform that night, Beard said, "I will not guarantee but that he goes through life dragging a foot after him." Great tears rolled down Dickens's cheeks, and he threw himself on Dolby's neck. Then, turning to Beard, he pleaded, "Let me try it tonight. It will save so much trouble." Beard refused to take the responsibility. "But how will Dolby get through?" "Never mind me," Dolby struck in, "I'll get through somehow, if you and Beard will only leave town at once."

Beard took his patient back to London that very night, and the following day, 23 April, arranged a consultation with the distinguished physician Sir Thomas Watson. The latter confirmed Beard's judgement. Dickens's giddiness, the feeling of insecurity about his left leg, the strangeness in his left hand and arm, his inability to lay his hand on a spot unless he looked at it carefully, the unreadiness to raise his hands, and especially his left hand, towards his head, all showed unmistakably that he "had been on the brink of an attack of paralysis of his left side, and possibly of apoplexy."

With relentless determination Dickens had managed to force himself through seventy-four of the hundred planned readings – two less than the number which in America had brought him so near collapse. Within a few weeks, as soon as he felt himself recovered, he began urging Sir Thomas Watson to authorize his resuming the readings.

Sir Thomas reiterated the need for caution, but finally Dickens got his way. The resumed readings were to number no more than twelve, they were to involve no railway travel, and they would be deferred at least eight months until early in 1870. Dickens believed that the joy with which he looked forward to them was only a relief that the Chappells would more nearly realize the profits they had anticipated. He told Forster,

> I do believe that such people as the Chappells are very rarely to be found in human affairs. To say nothing of their noble and munificent manner of sweeping into space all the charges incurred uselessly . . . comes a note this morning from the senior partner, to the effect that they feel that my overwork has been "indirectly caused by them, and by my great and kind exertions to make their venture successful to the extreme."

Sustained by the assurance that he might still slay Nancy a few more times, Dickens gave himself over to the routine of running *All the Year Round*. But in his heart he knew that he had deferred death by a narrower margin than he would admit; early in May he proceeded to make his will. His first bequest was "the sum of £1,000 free of legacy duty to Miss Ellen Lawless Ternan, late of Houghton Place, Ampthill Square," a strange legacy which he could hardly have believed would fail to arouse scandalized comment after he was dead. It was almost as if he desired to defy convention from his grave. And in view of his passionate concern for Ellen's reputation at the time of his separation from Catherine, it reveals an odd blindness, carelessness, or indifference – surely one of the three – to the certainty that her name would be coupled with his when the contents of the will became known. As a provision for Ellen's welfare it seems insufficient, but there is no indication that he made any other and no known reason for his not having done so without naming her in the will at all.

He bequeathed to Georgina Hogarth £8,000 free of legacy duty, and the interest upon an equal sum to Catherine, after which the principal was to descend to his children. Mary was to receive £1,000 and an annuity of £300 if she remained single, but if she married her income was to be divided equally among his surviving children, and she was then to share equally with them in the rest of his estate. Georgina was also given most of his personal jewellery and his private papers, Charley his library, engravings, and prints, and some articles of jewellery and silver, Forster the gold watch presented to Dickens at Coventry and the manuscripts of his books. Forster and Georgina were made his executors.

After these provisions there was a tribute to Georgina: "I solemnly enjoin my children always to remember how much they owe to the said Georgina Hogarth, and never to be wanting in a grateful and natural attachment to her . . ." The only further mention of Catherine was cold: "I desire here simply to record the fact that my wife, since our separation by consent, has been in the receipt from me of an annual income of £600, while all the great charges of a numerous and expensive family have devolved wholly upon myself." He concluded by directing that he be buried privately, "that those who attend my funeral wear no scarf, cloak, black bow, long hatband, or other such revolting absurdity," and that his name on his tomb be "in plain English letters" with no "Mr" or "Esquire."

Charley was developing into a useful helper on *All the Year Round*. "He is a very good man of business," Dickens told Macready, "and evinces considerable aptitude in sub-editing work." But two of the other boys worried Dickens more than ever. For the last year Sydney had been drifting into the same courses of extravagance that Walter had been following before he died. As Dickens recalled the strange faraway look in the enormous eyes of the small child he had called "the Ocean Spectre," and his pride in the brightness and popularity of the little "Admiral," he was bitterly distressed. He gave a sharp reproof, but not long afterwards the young man was again squandering money and leading a life headed towards *"certain misery."* Severely, Dickens forbade him to appear at Gad's Hill when he should return to England.

In Australia Plorn, too, was failing to settle down, though Dickens still hoped that he might take better to colonial life. But, "He will not fail," Dickens prophesied forebodingly, "to report himself unfit for his surroundings, if he should find that he is so." A year later, in May 1870, Plorn was so "persistently ignoring the possibility of his holding any other position in Australia" than the temporary one he filled, that Dickens "inferred from it a homeward tendency. He has always been the most difficult of the boys to deal with, away from home. There is not the least harm in him . . . But he seems to have been born without a groove. It cannot be helped. If he cannot, or will not find one, I must try again, and die trying."

Dickens's troubled concern over Plorn mingled with his darkening fears for the state of the world. The American press was displaying a blustering violence about the Alabama claims and the Northwest Boundary dispute that might "at last set the patient British back up" and bring "into existence an exasperating war-party on both sides." In France the régime of Napoleon III was on the verge of collapse. But of the results of the Reform Bill of 1867, which seemed threatening to so many others, Dickens felt calmly confident; "the greater part of the new voters will in the main be wiser as to their electoral responsibilities and more seriously desirous to discharge them for the common good than the bumptious singers of 'Rule Britannia,' 'Our dear old Church of England,' and all the rest of it."

Feeling more cheerful in May, Dickens prepared to welcome Mr and Mrs Fields to England. With these two Boston friends arrived the Charles Eliot Nortons and James Russell Lowell's daughter Mabel, as well as Dr Fordyce Barker and Sol Eytinge, the illustrator of the American "Diamond Back" edition of Dickens's works. To be with them in London, Dickens took a suite at the St James's Hotel for himself, Georgina, and Mary. On one evening, protected by detective police, he took Fields, Eytinge, and Dolby through the lowest criminal dives of the Ratcliffe Highway. Another time he showed Fields over Windsor and took him to dinner at the Star and Garter in Richmond.

Of course all the glories of Gad's Hill and Rochester were also displayed for his guests. Once again, too, Dickens revived the red jackets of the old red royal Dover Road, and they dashed merrily to Canterbury. The ancient cathedral was glorious with stained glass and groined vaulting, and in the streets they tried to decide just which bulging old house with twinkling windows was Agnes Wickfield's home. They drove back in the twilight, fireflies shining in the orchards, the red coats of the postilions gleaming under an occasional roadside lamp, and returned a little after nine to the welcome lantern and open gates of Gad's Hill Place.

With the end of his provincial readings, Dickens started revolving in his mind the conception of another novel. "What should you think," he asked Forster in July, "of the idea of a story beginning in this way? – Two people, boy and girl, or very young, going apart from one another, pledged to be married after many years – at the end of the book." It was an idea that partly shaped the relation of Edwin Drood and Rosa Bud in the story. But early in August, "I have laid aside the fancy I told you of," Dickens wrote Forster, "and have a very curious and new idea for my new story. Not a communicable idea (or the interest of the book would be gone), but a very strong one, though difficult to work."

An agreement with Frederic Chapman was soon drawn. It provided that Dickens was to receive £7,500 against the profits on the first 25,000 copies, and that all profits beyond that were to be shared equally. There was one clause that had never been in a Dickens contract before. It was included by Dickens's own desire: if he should die or be unable to finish the story, Forster was to serve as an arbitrator to decide what amount should in fairness be repaid to Chapman and Hall.

On a Sunday in October one of the Gad's Hill servants knocked on Fields's chamber door with a note: "Mr Charles Dickens presents his respectful compliments to the Hon. James T. Fields (of Boston, Mass., U. S.) and will be happy to receive a visit from the Hon. J. T. F. in the small library as above, at the Hon. J. T. F.'s leisure." Hastening down, Fields heard from Dickens's own lips the opening chapters of *The Mystery of Edwin Drood*. With absorbed attention Fields listened to Jasper's awakening from his opium visions in that Ratcliffe Highway dive he and Dickens had so recently visited, and he recognized in the description of Cloisterham the grey and ancient city of Rochester. But the story of which he listened to the beginning that day was destined to have a more disastrous ending than any conceived by its creator.

47

The Dying and Undying Voice

Edwin Drood is Dickens's swan song. In its very heart there is a core of death. The Cloisterham of the story is no longer the spring-drenched Rochester of his *Pickwick* days, but a city where darkness already dims the bright colours and frost sprinkles the ground. Christmas there is no season of glowing cheer; it is a time when murder lurks to immure its victim within a hollow tomb.

John Jasper, tormented soul, drug addict, dark enigma, is the central figure in its web. His mad jealousy of the nephew whom he also loves is only one facet of the deep division in his soul. His outwardly staid life as a sober choirmaster is darkened by an inward rebellion, in which he sinks down into the filth of the opium den and ascends to the skies in the musical aspiration of his art. Is he now Dickens's vision of the artist as a secret misfit in the world? Is the artist a traitor in society's midst, a subverter of its standards, or is he a heroic rebel fighting its corruptions and its charnel decay?

Certainly it is a dead world that lies heavy and brooding over *Edwin Drood*. The social criticism that had grown more biting in all Dickens's later books is perhaps less obvious, but is deeply implicit. Beneath Cloisterham's somnolent air of peace lurk all the inhumanities Dickens had felt so bitterly, grown more monstrous as they have spread to engulf the world. Mr Sapsea, the Mayor of Cloisterham, represents both the outlook of its businessmen and the pompous conceit of officialdom. The time-serving timidity of the Dean of the Cathedral has rejected the merciful teachings of his Church for a cautious conformity. The bellowing philanthropist Honeythunder is Dickens's final thrust at all the would-be legislators of public virtue. The three form a striking secular trinity: the regnant jackass enthroned between the spiritual trimmer and the bigot of reform.

There is no hope for society in the forces exemplified by these three. But, as always, Dickens's trust is not in the official or self-appointed powers of Church and state; it is in the health of human nature itself.

This hope emerges from many other characters in the book, from the honesty of Mr Crisparkle, the athletic Minor Canon; from the impulsive warmth of Rosa Bud, the heroine; from the awkward rectitude of the attorney, Mr Grewgious; from the fiery courage of the second heroine, Helena Landless. Here, for the last time, Dickens projected the fundamental antagonisms and the fundamental problems of his world. And here for the last time he reaffirmed his fundamental creed: his belief in the generous loyalties and affections of the human spirit.

Dickens's whole career and achievement, indeed, were singularly consistent. While he grew in understanding and vision, he never lost the living sympathies that lie at the heart of his greatness. Those sympathies were rooted in an almost endless relish for the richness and variety of life, a love of experience that exulted in the pure vividness with which things are themselves. Dickens liked and disliked people; he was never merely indifferent. He loved and laughed and derided and despised and hated; he never patronized or sniffed. He had no fastidious shrinkings, no snobberies, no dogmatic rejections.

These are the qualities that give his world such intensity. He was as fascinated by the decaying cabbage-stalks of Covent Garden, or by the fishy smell of Mr Peggotty's outhouse as he was by the Cratchits' goose in its hissing hot gravy. The foul gutters of Saffron Hill held him as much as the clowns and spangle-skirted bareback riders of Astley's Circus, the tangled masts of Limehouse Hole, the shadowy rafters of Westminster Hall, the salt reaches of Cooling Marsh, the dripping urns of Chesney Wold, Boffin's dust heaps, and the polluted air of the Old Bailey. He was not repelled by a lively scoundrel like Mr Jingle or revolted by Jo's verminous body; he felt no scorn for chuckleheaded Mr Toots or the shabby and bibulous Newman Noggs; even for the merry and blackhearted Fagin Dickens had a gleam of sympathy.

In his comprehensive delight in all experience Dickens resembles Walt Whitman, but he was innocent of that nebulous transcendentalism that blurred Whitman's universe into vast misty panoramas and left him, for all his huge democratic vistas, unable to tell a story or paint a single concrete human being. Dickens saw the brilliant individual quality of each person and experience in its comic or pathetic or dramatic essence, and in so doing he surprisingly realized Walter Pater's aspiration towards "a life of constant and eager observation." Though he burned with a warm and tender, rather than a "hard, gem-like flame," Dickens vibrated with the very pulsations "of a variegated, dramatic life." It is the welter of existence that he embraced.

But for all the enthusiasm with which he welcomed the multiplicity of experience, Dickens did not fail in moral discrimination. His very sympathy with life's thronging variety made him stern to whatever impoverished and destroyed. From the hypocritical Stiggins in *Pickwick* to the bullying Honeythunder in *Edwin Drood*, he abominated those who sought to reduce life to a dispirited grey or to subordinate people to their desire for power. He hated the gloomy and ferocious self-righteousness of the Murdstones. He derided the woolly-mindedness of Mrs Jellyby, neglecting London's poor and her own family while she worried about the natives of Borioboola-Gha; he detested the domineering presumption of Mrs Pardiggle, pushing her way into labourers' cottages with useless and arrogant advice. He saw England plundered by Boodle and Coodle, controlled by the landed aristocracy of Sir Leicester Dedlock, the selfish commercialism of Mr Dombey, the industrial greed of Mr Bounderby, and the slippery financial machinations of Mr Merdle. He saw England helplessly obstructed by the Circumlocution Office, while Mr Gradgrind sifted the ashes of the national dust heap and formulated the dogmas of political economy. Meanwhile, he beheld with loathing how this dreadful structure of iniquity and suffering spawned a host of lesser parasites and beasts of prey, the Fagins, Bumbles, Squeerses, Tiggs, Pecksniffs, Scrooges, Smallweeds, Vholeses, Casbys, Barnacles, Weggs, Lammles, and Fledgebys, all sucking or bludgeoning their victims.

Not primarily a systematic thinker, but a man of feeling, intuitive and emotional, Dickens had nevertheless a sharp intelligence which pierced through the complexities of the social scene to a comprehension of its shocking realities. His instinctive sympathy with the fruitful and creative enabled him to see how the generous potentialities of human nature were crippled, and he felt his way to a comprehension of the forces that blighted men's health and happiness. As a young reporter he watched the landowners resisting the abolition of the rotten boroughs. As a mature man he saw the slum landlords rack-renting their tenants and breeding cholera by their determination not to spend a penny on sanitary improvement, observed the factory owners mutilating their workers with unfenced machinery, heard them screaming that they would be ruined by a ten-hour day and a living wage. He could put two and two together, and he did. By the time he had reached the middle of his career he understood capitalist industrialism at least as well as most nineteenth-century political economists.

He understood it with unwavering hostility. Every book he produced was not only a celebration of the true wealth of life; it was an attack on the forces of cruelty and selfishness. His heart seized the sword of a sharp and witty logic that slashed through innumerable varieties of logical humbug and rationalist special pleading. He had no patience with statistical abstractions and economic theories that ignored the welfare of flesh-and-blood human beings. Unlike so many lovers of humanity who are bitterly unable to love human beings, it was not an abstract humanity that Dickens loved, but men, women, and children, with all their frailties and follies. His hatreds sprang full-armed out of that love.

His weapons were those of caricature and burlesque, of melodrama and unrestrained sentiment. But whether he poured out operatic harmonies of tears or wielded a slapstick landing with a loud whack, his exaggerations focus the brilliant light of truth upon squirming absurdity or vice plausibly disguised as virtue, and magnify the disease until its corruption is glaringly revealed. Bernard Shaw explained that his own method was to find the right things to say and then say them with the utmost exaggeration and levity. That is almost precisely the procedure of Dickens. He fought foolishness and evil by exaggerating their excesses. He painted monomania and sophistry in colours of lurid absurdity. He belaboured dogmatism and bigotry with fantastic ridicule. Every form of fanatical extremism he attacked with the wildest hyperbole. In a passion of glorious violence he defended the golden mean.

If his moderation seems a paradox it is only because of the gigantic extravagance with which it is presented. Pecksniff is grotesque, but there is nothing immoderate about the judgement on hypocrisy he symbolizes. Bounderby is grotesque, but he might easily be a spokesman for any number of businessmen. Dickens nowhere suggests abolishing private enterprise or individual wealth, but he saw with indignation how incessantly they abused their power. Therefore, though he was well aware of the inefficiency of Government agencies, no fear of "centralization" prevented him from demanding that the Government regulate industry and protect the public from private greed.

Two such different commentators as Chesterton and Shaw have paid tribute to the insight with which Dickens portrayed the modern world. The Circumlocution Office, said Chesterton, "is a complete picture of the way England is actually governed at this moment." And Shaw notes:

... his day as a social prophet and social critic is only dawning. ... Thackeray's England is gone, Trollope's England is gone; and even Thackeray and Trollope mixed with their truth a considerable alloy of what the governing classes liked to imagine they were, and yet never quite succeeded in being. But Dickens's England, the England of Barnacle and Stiltstalking and Hamlet's Aunt, invaded and overwhelmed by Merdle and Veneering and Fledgeby, with Mr Gradgrind theorizing and Mr Bounderby bullying in the provinces, is revealing itself in every day's news, as the real England we live in.

All this Dickens saw and despised as bitterly as Carlyle, but unlike Carlyle he did not call upon an aristocratic elite or a dictator hero to step in. Instead, he called upon the people to assert and save themselves. He saw red at the snobberies that, after making education a class monopoly, then sneered at the masses as ignorant and brutish. "My faith in the people governing," he said in 1869, "is, on the whole, infinitesimal; my faith in the People governed is, on the whole, illimitable."

Even at that time there were those who tried to twist this declaration into the belief not in the people governing themselves but in their being governed by others. Dickens himself clearly demolished that interpretation. Quoting Buckle's *History of Civilization in England*, he restated his meaning:

Lawgivers are nearly always the obstructors of society instead of its helpers ... in the extremely few cases where their measures have turned out well, their success has been owing to the fact that, contrary to their usual custom, they have implicitly obeyed the spirit of their time, and have been – as they always should be – the mere servants of the people, to whose wishes they are bound to give a public and legal sanction.

The people were Dickens's only real hope for the world. He had no panacea to solve all problems. In his own day he worked within limited areas for particular improvements that seemed to him attainable. Though he understood how external circumstances could twist men's lives, and hoped to make the opportunities for human fulfilment available on the widest scale, he was not an economic determinist and did not believe that people were only the products of environment. Nor, though he saw that Government agencies were corrupted by powerful influences, did he believe that it was because of an intrinsic defect in the potentiality of government. He never ceased to demand that government remake itself into the instrument of human welfare. Instead of trying to elaborate an entire machinery for the improvement of the world, he sought to portray its human goals, and spoke for the hopes of mankind.

Those hopes are implicit in the hosts of living people crowding the great panorama of his pages. What writer except Shakespeare has created a larger and more various world or one more rich with the pulsing truth of actuality? If there are novelists whose characters are more subtly realized than those of Dickens, whose creations have a more intricate psychological complexity, there are none whose characters have more vitality or are truer to humanity at its core. His method, to be sure, is neither the enormous and elaborate complexity of Shakespeare and Tolstoy nor the psychological analysis so differently exemplified by Stendhal and Dostoevsky. The contrast between Dickens and such writers is essentially the same as that painted by Lytton Strachey in a brilliant antithesis of Shakespeare and Molière:

> The English dramatist shows his persons to us in the round; innumerable facets flash out quality after quality; the subtlest and most elusive shades of temperament are indicated; until at last the whole being takes shape before us, endowed with what seems to be the very complexity and mystery of life itself. Entirely different is the great Frenchman's way. Instead of expanding, he deliberately narrows his view; he seizes upon two or three salient qualities in a character and then uses all his art to impress them indelibly upon our minds.

Tartuffe, Strachey points out,

> displays three qualities, and three only – religious hypocrisy, lasciviousness, and the love of power . . . Beside the vast elaboration of a Falstaff, he seems, at first sight, hardly more solid than some astounding silhouette; yet – such was the power and intensity of Molière's art – the more we look, the more difficult we shall find it to be certain that Tartuffe is a less tremendous creation even than Falstaff himself.

Molière's method was Dickens's method, too, and in Fagin and Pecksniff, in Uriah Heep and Squeers, it achieves its own astounding triumphs. But with that English exuberance Dickens has in common with Jonson and the comic dramatists of the Restoration, he does not restrict himself to Molière's stripped classical structure. With inordinate gusto, he returns to Micawber again and again, perpetually renewing our joy in recognizing a character that under countless variations of the same quality is always richly itself. Like the recurrent themes in a symphony, Dickens's people appear and reappear, David's Dora always pattering her childish-pathetic tinkle of keys, Mr Bounderby sounding his bombastic brass, Miss Flite or Gridley or Captain Cuttle or Mr Toots being themselves. But Mr Dorrit and Pip are there too, reminding us that these figures are not always simple, that they are capable of psychological complexity, that they even change and develop.

To certain readers, however, they seem unreal, vivid perhaps, enormously entertaining, but mere caricatures rather than people. E. M. Forster is vaguely worried by the feeling that in consequence they ought to be merely mechanical and Dickens's vision of humanity shallow. At the same time, he uneasily recognizes their "wonderful feeling of human depth" and admits Dickens's greatness. It may be argued that no character in literature is ever more than a selection of representative qualities from among the infinite number that constitute the whole of any actual human being, hence that all literary portraits are really a kind of caricature, with omission and exaggeration a part of their very nature, and their appearance of "reality" a victory of their art. There is no need, however, of resorting to any such mere defence. Santayana hits the very heart of the issue in a direct attack:

> When people say that Dickens exaggerates [he writes], it seems to me they can have no eyes and no ears. They probably have only *notions* of what things and people are; they accept them conventionally, at their diplomatic value. Their minds run on in the region of discourse, where there are masks only and no faces, ideas and no facts; they have little sense for those living grimaces that play from moment to moment upon the countenance of the world.

When Dickens slashes through the convention, Santayana continues, the human ego protests.

> "What a bad mirror," it exclaims; "it must be concave or convex; for surely I never looked like that. Mere caricature, farce, and horse play. Dickens exaggerates; *I* never was so sentimental as that; *I* never saw anything so dreadful; *I* don't believe there were ever any people like Quilp, or Squeers, or Serjeant Buzfuz." But the polite world is lying; there *are* such people; we are such people ourselves in our

568

true moments, in our veritable impulses; but we are careful to stifle and hide those moments from ourselves and from the world; to purse and pucker ourselves into the mask of our conventional personality; and so simpering, we profess that it is very coarse and inartistic of Dickens to undo our life's work for us in an instant, and remind us of what we are.

The courage that gave Dickens this "true vision of the world" and the generosity of spirit that made it predominantly a comic one, also account, Santayana points out, for his gusto in piling up reiterative detail to mountainous heights that distress shrinking delicacy as over-emphatic;

he mimics things to the full; he dilates and exhausts and repeats; he wallows . . . This faculty, which renders him a consummate comedian, is just what alienated him from a later generation in which people of taste were aesthetes and virtuous people were higher snobs; they wanted a mincing art, and he gave them copious improvisation, they wanted analysis and development, and he gave them absolute comedy.

Only in Dickens's earlier days, however, was his art one of improvisation; he became a conscientious literary craftsman, painstaking to the minutest detail of style and structure. He strove to perfect a narrative technique that should never call attention to the devices whereby the reader was prepared for each development in the story, but was unobtrusively put in possession of all that he needed to know in order to make every sequence both spontaneous and inevitable. Only on the surface does Dickens have affinities with naturalism; deep below, he is vibrant with poetic undertones, pregnant with the weighted symbols of allegory, dwelling often within the obscure and mysterious region of myth. At his best he is dazzling in verbal brilliance, coruscating in comedy, and even exorbitant in his ingenuity of plotting. *Bleak House*, *Little Dorrit*, and *Our Mutual Friend*, all masterpieces of his maturity, are dark and tremendous symphonic structures reaching almost epic magnitude. But amid the torrential plenty of Dickens's creation it is almost invidious to single out individual novels. "He is, by the pure force of genius," Shaw summarized it, "one of the greatest writers of the world. . . . There is no 'greatest book' of Dickens: all his books form one great life-work: a Bible in fact . . . all are magnificent."

Few of the world's great novelists surpass him in vitality and scope. In the thousands of pages of his works he paints the thronging complexity of nineteenth-century society with a range, solidity, and panoramic inclusiveness equalled only by Balzac. He was Dostoevsky's master, as Edmund Wilson points out: *Crime and Punishment* and *The Brothers Karamazov* are tremendously indebted to Dickens's studies of murderers and rebels against society. And with John Jasper, in 1870, Dickens was approaching those dark and tangled labyrinths of alienation that Dostoevsky was to explore in Raskolnikov. Although there is a kind of twisted comedy in Dostoevsky, he cannot come within measurable distance of Dickens's high-spirited and irresistible vivacity. There, indeed, even the great humourists, even Rabelais, Voltaire, and Fielding, must bow to him. "We must go back," Santayana proclaims, "for anything like it to the very greatest comic poets, to Shakespeare or to Aristophanes."

Charles Dickens, said his adoring friend James T. Fields, was "the *cheerfullest* man of his age." But Fields did not see beneath the surface and did not realize that the cheerful demeanour, the courage were as much achievements as they were the sparkling gifts of temperament. The *Pickwick* sun had risen out of the darkness of the prison and the blacking warehouse, not out of the radiance of a cloudless childhood. The resolute belief in life and in humanity that Dickens maintained was a banner he held high despite all the evils he saw in society, and despite the gathering clouds of personal misery that shadowed his later years.

Dickens himself refused to remain in the darkness. Over and over again, though with increasing weariness and difficulty, he beat back the shadows. Out of his sympathy and indignation at men's sufferings, he built up a picture of society and its failures, of the obstacles to the harmonious fulfilment of human needs, that is unsurpassed for clarity and understanding. Out of his own life of struggle and frustration, he wrought a philosophy of generous valour that could laugh while it fought and struck its mighty blows for mankind. He was one of the heroes of art, not merely battling the unpastured dragons of life's waste, but enriching and creating a world. When Keats was near the point of death, "Perhaps," he was heard to say, "I may be among the English poets after my death." Matthew Arnold gave the world's reply: "He is; he is with Shakespeare." Of what English novelist can that be said except Charles Dickens?

48

The Narrow Bed

The mild autumn days following Dickens's breakdown were the Indian summer of his life. Mornings he worked in the chalet on the book his hand would leave unfinished. In the sunny afternoons he strolled among the trees and rhododendrons of Cobham Park, or ruminated in straw hat and velvet jacket along Rochester High Street, through the old gatehouse into the green Cathedral close.

His health was still uncertain, but his spirits were cheerful. Teasing Fields's mania for antiques, he pretended to have found for him a decrepit chair without a bottom, "very ugly and wormy," of which it was claimed that "Washington declined to sit down on it." He felt buoyant with the further improvements at Gad's Hill, a new staircase with a parquet floor on the first landing, and in October the beginning of a conservatory, "glass and iron," opening from both the drawing-room and the dining-room. "You are not expected to admire," he wrote Macready, "but there *is* a conservatory building at this moment – be still my soul!"

Recently, Percy Fitzgerald had married a little charmer whose pretty face and engaging prattle everyone declared to be delightfully like David Copperfield's Dora. Dickens was enchanted. Forster too proclaimed himself captivated, and was her most obstreperous slave. Prevented by illness from attending one of her little dinner parties, he sent Dickens a note of mock warning: "I can't join you today. But mark you this, sir! No tampering, no poaching on *my* grounds; for I won't have it. Recollect *Codlin's the friend not Short!*" With a twinkling eye Dickens read this note aloud to his host and hostess. "What can he mean? What do you make of it?" Fitzgerald knew quite well, as did his wife, who stood there smiling and fluttered, but both felt it awkward to admit; they could only agree "that Forster at times was perfectly 'amazing.'"

Christmas Dickens spent at Gad's Hill. His left foot was again pain-ful, and he sat in the library all day having it poulticed; at dinner it rested bandaged on a chair. But he was feeling pleased: Harry had done so well at Cambridge that the family confidently expected him to win a fellowship. Shortly after the new year, Dickens entered him at the Temple. Dickens was also looking forward excitedly to the last twelve readings, which would partly make up for the twenty-six cancelled by his breakdown the previous spring. Partly to cut out railway travelling and partly for Mary's sake, he rented the Milner Gibson house at 5 Hyde Park Place, just opposite the Marble Arch, from January to 1 June. New Year's Eve he spent at Forster's, where his old friend was troubled by observing that Dickens's left foot and left hand both gave him pain. Dickens, however, made light of his uncertainties of touch and tread, and read the second instalment of *Edwin Drood* with such overflowing humour that Forster enthusiastically pronounced the number "a clincher."

On 6 January 1870, as President of the Birmingham and Midland Institute, Dickens awarded the prizes and certificates. He seized the occasion to reaffirm his declaration of the preceding autumn that he had "very little faith in the people who govern us," but that he had "great confidence in the People whom they govern."

The last twelve readings began at St James's Hall on the evening of 11 January. Throughout most of that month he read twice a week, on Tuesdays and Fridays, and thereafter once a week. Two performances were scheduled for afternoons, and there was a morning one given at the request of actors and actresses, who could not come later in the day. Dickens's family and friends feared he might break down again under the strain. Dr Frank Beard came to every reading, and he privately bespoke Charley's attendance as well. "I have had some steps put up at the side of the platform," he told him. "You must be there every night, and if you see your father falter in the least, you must run and catch him and bring him off to me, or, by Heaven, he'll die before them all."

David Copperfield and the "Trial," on the opening night, went "with the greatest brilliancy." But Beard found that Dickens's pulse had gone from its normal 72 to 95. From that night on, it rose ominously. Even before the first "Murder" reading, on the morning of the 21st, his fermenting anticipation raised it to 90; at the end it was 112. Dickens was so prostrated that he could not get back his breath for some time, but the pretty actresses in his audience delighted him with their rapture. As he went on, his pulse rose to 114 – to 118 – to 124. During intermissions he had to be laid on a sofa; fully ten minutes would pass before he could speak a consecutive sentence. Then he would swallow a wineglassful of weak brandy and water and rush back on the platform. Throughout February his hand never ceased to be swollen and painful. As he wiped out the readings, his feverish excitement and bodily pain grew ever greater.

His audiences, however, were almost hysterical with enthusiasm. A boy whose father was a friend of Dickens brought him to one of the *Pickwick* readings, and the youngster laughed, roared, wept, and howled; "I must have been a terrible nuisance to Dickens," he said in later years, "for I was at his feet, and at least twice I remember very distinctly he looked at me, I am sure with the idea of having me removed." At the end, stepping down to speak to the father, Dickens looked quizzically at the boy, "but he gave me a friendly tap or pat of forgiveness on the head."

As the ordeals drew to their close, Dickens's energies were nearing exhaustion. During one of the last three readings Charley noticed that he was unable to articulate "Pickwick" correctly, "calling it 'Pickswick,' 'Picnic,' 'Peckwicks,' " and "all sorts of names except the right one, with a comical glance of surprise" at friends in the front row. On the last evening of all, 15 March, he read the *Christmas Carol* and the "Trial." An audience of over 2,000 gave him a tumultuous ovation. Dickens's granddaughter, little Mekitty, had been brought for the first time that night to hear him read, and she was frightened by the apparition of her "Wenerables" as a terrible and unfamiliar figure a long way off "speaking in unknown voices." And, worst of all, came "the dreadful moment when he *cried*."

He had been called back to the platform at the end by thunders of applause, and looked tremulously at his audience while tears rolled down his cheeks. It was the end. These clamours that had meant so much to him were sounding in his ears for the last time; this ferment of excitement which for twelve years had often been almost all his life, would soon be over. With effort he restrained himself sufficiently to say the words of appreciation and love on which he had determined. "From these garish lights," he concluded, "I now vanish forevermore, with a heartfelt, grateful, respectful, affectionate farewell." Mournfully he limped from the stage, only to be recalled by repeated demonstrations. His cheeks still wet, he kissed his hand, and then walked off for the last time.

All told, the paid readings had numbered almost 450, including around 135 given under the management of Arthur Smith, 70 under

Thomas Headland, and 242 under Dolby. Dickens had no exact record of his profits under Smith and Headland, but he always estimated them at about £12,000. Under Dolby he cleared nearly £33,000. The impressive total of £45,000 amounted to almost half of the £93,000 that proved to be the value of his estate when he died.

But the great sum was bought at more than a sacrifice of health. In melancholy inversion of one of those legendary bards at whose singing palaces rose in the enchanted air, Dickens's voice had been sinking his grave. His reckless energy hardly more than veiled a weariness almost indistinguishable from that which Macaulay expressed in his journal shortly before he died: "A month more of such days as I have been passing of late would make me impatient to get to my narrow little crib, like a weary factory child." Despite the sparkling face Dickens still turned on the world, the warehouse child that time had so transformed was hastening to his rest.

Though the readings were almost over, his impetuosity continued, working, walking, hurrying excitedly. There were invitations to dinners, invitations to speak at public functions, an invitation to Buckingham Palace from the Queen. Not long since, Dickens had shown some American Civil War photographs to Arthur Helps, the Clerk of the Privy Council, who had mentioned them to the Queen. At her request, Dickens had sent them for her to look at, and presently Helps brought a message that the Queen would like to thank him in person. Formally responding that he would be "proud and happy to wait upon Her Majesty," Dickens also sent Helps a facetious little note pretending to believe that he was about to be made a baronet. "We will have 'Of Gad's Hill Place' attached to the title of the Baronetcy, please – on account of the divine William and Falstaff," he wrote jestingly.

The meeting took place on 9 March. Court etiquette did not allow Dickens to sit down, but Victoria herself remained standing throughout the entire hour and a half of their interview, leaning over the back of a sofa. Gracious though the gesture was, she could do so with less strain than if she had been an ailing man with a swollen foot. Under like circumstances the preceding year, Carlyle had bluntly announced that he was a feeble old man and helped himself to a chair. But Dickens's pride would have driven him to collapse before he would have yielded to an infirmity.

The fifty-year-old widow was as changed from the breathless girl who had delighted in dancing all night as Dickens was from the wildly spirited young writer who vowed himself madly in love with her. She regretted, the Queen said, that she had never heard one of the readings. He too was sorry, Dickens replied, but they were now finally over. The Queen agreed that it would be inconsistent for him to alter his decision, adding that she knew him to be the most consistent of men. Perhaps she was remembering his firm refusal to wait upon her in his farce dress, after the performance of *The Frozen Deep*. She then made some complimentary references to her pleasure in seeing that play; and after some further conversation the Queen presented him with an autographed copy of her *Journal of Our Life in the Highlands* and asked for a set of his works. She would like, if possible, she added, to have them that afternoon. Dickens begged for time to have the books suitably bound, and later sent her a set in red morocco and gold.

Little more than a week later Dickens was bidden to Her Majesty's next levee. Soon after, Mary was presented to the Queen; later still, in May, Dickens was invited to dinner at Lord Houghton's to meet the Prince of Wales and the King of the Belgians. All these events, and possibly a circulation of his little joke about a baronetcy, gave rise to rumours that he was to be made a member of the Privy Council, even offered a peerage. "If my authority be worth anything," he wrote a correspondent, "believe on it that I am going to be nothing but what I am, and that includes my being as long as I live, – Your faithful and heartily obliged, Charles Dickens."

Shortly after the last reading, he confessed to Forster that once more, walking along Oxford Street, he was unable to read more than the right-hand halves of the shop signs. "My uneasiness and haemorrhage, after having quite left me, as I supposed, has come back with an aggravated irritability that it has not yet displayed."

Nevertheless, Dickens went his way undeterred. On Forster's birthday he dined with his old friend, and three nights later presided at the dinner of the Newsvendors' Institution. On 7 April he gave a reception at Hyde Park Place. Joachim played the violin, and there were songs by Cummings, the eminent tenor, and Santley, the famous baritone. Dickens was everywhere, his face a little strained and worn, but genial and smiling. Towards suppertime, Fitzgerald's wife stopped him, saying, "Mr Dickens, you have passed me constantly during the night and have never *once* stopped to speak to me." He threw up his hands in horror. "Good gracious! N-n-o? You *don't* tell me so? Then let us make up for it at once, and go downstairs together to supper!" At the table he chatted vivaciously, pulling paper crackers, and exclaiming over one of the favours, a green fan of tissue paper, which she carried away as a souvenir.

For all these light dissipations, Dickens went on toiling as hard as ever. The first number of *Edwin Drood* had "*very, very far outstripped every one of its predecessors*," and he laboured to make the numbers that should follow no less successful. "For the last week," he reported, as he drew near the completion of the fifth number, "I have been most perseveringly and ding-dong-doggedly at work . . ." As he limped to the office of *All the Year Round* one morning, oaken staff in hand, he was seen by a son of Douglas Jerrold, who hardly recognized him, so deep were the lines in his face and so much more nearly white was his grizzled hair.

Luckily, Charley had taken good hold of his work on the magazine, and was able to relieve Dickens of all the routine duties Wills had once discharged. At the end of April, his father officially installed him as subeditor. It seemed to Dickens that his eldest son had at last found something for which he was fitted. A month and a half later, by a codicil to his will, Dickens left Charley all his share and interest in the publication.

On 27 April Dickens heard with sorrow of the death of Daniel Maclise. The painter's solitary ways had kept them apart for long years, but Dickens had never ceased to be fond of him. At the Royal Academy dinner on 2 May, Dickens paid tribute to his friend's memory. "The gentlest and most modest of men, the freshest as to his generous appreciation of young aspirants, and the frankest and largest-hearted as to his peers," no artist, Dickens said, "ever went to his rest leaving a golden memory more pure from dross, or having devoted himself with a truer chivalry to the art goddess whom he worshipped." Only a few weeks later, stout, good-hearted Mark Lemon died, and Dickens was at once grieved and gladdened to remember that he and Lemon had been reconciled affectionately at Stanfield's deathbed.

Dickens's foot was by now a source of pain that would "yield to nothing but days of fomentation and horizontal rest." "Last night," he wrote Georgina on 11 May, "I got a good night's rest under the influence of Laudanum but it hangs about me very heavily today. I have had the poultices constantly changed, hot and hot, day and night . . ." On the 16th the foot was "a mere bag of pain." The following evening, despite having "viciously bubbled and blistered it in all directions," he was unable to go with Mary to the Queen's Ball, to which they had both been invited.

Deep within, he must have known the end was near. Receiving a young girl with literary aspirations whom Lord Lytton had sent to him, he spoke of his habits of publication while his work was still in progress. "But suppose," she said diffidently, "suppose you died before all the book was written?" "Ah-h!" he said, and paused. "That has occurred to me at times." His gaze seemed to her to be penetrating golden veils. Then, looking at her kindly, he said cheerfully, "One can only work on, you know – work while it is day."

Forster saw him for the last time on 22 May. Not long before, an admirer had written Dickens from Liverpool, describing himself as a self-raised man, attributing his prosperous career to what he had learned of kindness and sympathy from Dickens's writings, and asking that Dickens accept an enclosed cheque for £500. Dickens refused the gift, but replied that he would be glad to accept any small memorial in some other form. Presently there arrived a silver basket, and a silver centrepiece designed to portray Spring, Summer, and Autumn. The giver explained that he desired to connect Dickens "with none save the brighter and milder days." "I never look at it," Dickens told Forster, "that I don't think most of the Winter." The gift, Forster mournfully wrote, foreshadowed that season which Dickens was never again to see.

Throughout all the month of May the pace of his engagements never slackened. Gladstone, the Prime Minister, invited him to breakfast; he dined with John Lothrop Motley and Disraeli at Lord Stanhope's. He met Arthur Stanley, the Dean of Westminster, at Frederick Locker-Lampson's, and a little later dined at Stanley's with the Russells, the Clarendons, and Connop Thirlwall, the Bishop of St David's. He attended the theatre with Lady Molesworth and Lord Redesdale, and was so full of droll thoughts that he kept himself and his companions "laughing at the majesty of his own absurdities"; his talk, Lord Redesdale said, "had all the sparkle of champagne."

It was almost the last flare of that delight in the theatre that had burned brightly throughout Dickens's life. Walking with a friend only a short time before, Dickens had paused in the shadow of Westminster Abbey and asked, "What do you think would be the realization of one of my most cherished day-dreams?" It would be to "hold supreme authority" in the direction of a great theatre, with "a skilled and noble company." "The pieces acted should be dealt with according to my pleasure, and touched up here and there in obedience to my own judgement; the players as well as the plays being absolutely under my command. That," he ended, laughing, and glowing at the fancy. "*that's* my day-dream!"

Towards the end of May he took charge of some private theatricals at the home of his London neighbours, Mr and Mrs Freake. Mary and Katey were among the cast, and Millais painted the scenery. Dickens rehearsed the company daily, brilliantly demonstrating how to do all the parts, from the "old man" to the "young lover." He had intended to take a role himself but was prevented by his lameness. Though 2 June, the night of the production, was a stifling one, he acted as stage manager, ringing all the bells, working all the lights, and between these activities sitting in the prompter's corner.

Dolby had been with him at the office that very afternoon. Rising to leave, Dolby was shocked by the pain mirrored in his Chief's face, and noticed that his eyes were suffused with tears. Throwing off his emotion, Dickens also rose. Grasping Dolby's hand, and looking him full in the face, instead of using the words "Good day" or "Good night," as he usually did, Dickens earnestly said, "Goodbye, Dolby, old man."

On Friday, 3 June, he was back at Gad's Hill. The country was delicious with the foliage and flowers of early summer. Dickens rejoiced in his escape from London and "the preposterous endeavour to dine at preposterous hours and preposterous places." He had sent off for a "Voltaic Band" which he hoped might give some relief to his foot, He was looking forward to uninterrupted morning hours among the leaves and mirrors and fresh scents of the chalet. But Katey, coming down on Saturday for the week-end, felt heavyhearted to see him looking so worn. Dickens, however, was talkative and cheerful. The new conservatory had been completed, and he delighted in its perfumed brightness of massed blossoms. "Well, Katey," he exclaimed gaily, "you now see POSITIVELY the last improvement at Gad's Hill"; and they all laughed at the joke against himself.

On Sunday Dickens seemed refreshed on returning from a quiet afternoon walk. When dinner was over, he and Katey remained sitting in the dining-room to be near the flowers in the conservatory, while they listened to Mary singing in the drawing-room. At eleven o'clock Mary and Georgina retired, but Dickens and Katey sat on enjoying the warm perfumed night air. He and his daughter talked long and affectionately. He wished, Dickens told her, that he had been "a better father, and a better man." Later he spoke of his hopes that he might make a success of *Edwin Drood*, "if, please God, I live to finish it." Katey looked startled: "I say *if*," Dickens told her, "because you know, my dear child, I have not been strong lately." It was three o'clock, and the summer dawn was creeping into the conservatory before they went upstairs.

When Katey arose late in the morning, he was already writing in the chalet. She had to go up to London, and would be unable to return to Gad's Hill until the following Saturday. But she felt uneasy about her father, and drew a promise from Georgina to write the next day with news of how he was. Knowing his dislike of partings, she was going only to leave her dear love for him without any farewell. As she waited for the carriage, however, she felt an uncontrollable impulse, and went down the tunnel, through the shrubbery to the chalet.

"His head was bent low down over his work, and he turned an eager and rather flushed face towards me as I entered." Usually, Dickens merely raised his cheek for a kiss, "saying a few words, perhaps, in 'the little language' " he had used when his daughters were children, "but on this morning, when he saw me," Katey remembered, "he pushed his chair back from the writing table, opened his arms, and took me into them." She hurried back to the house, saying to herself, without knowing why, "I am so glad I went – I am so glad."

In the afternoon Dickens walked with the dogs to mail some letters in Rochester. Tuesday morning, Mary left for a visit to Katey in London. Dickens felt tired, and only drove in the carriage to Cobham Wood with Georgina, where he strolled about under the trees. That evening he strung some Chinese lanterns in the conservatory, and sat with Georgina enjoying their shimmering illumination. He was happy, he told her, at having finally abandoned London for Gad's Hill. Only a few days before, he had repeated a hope he had often expressed that he might lie in the little Cathedral graveyard at the foot of the Castle wall when he died.

On Wednesday, 8 June, in violation of his usual habits, he wrote all day, returning to the house only for lunch, and then going back to the chalet to work again on the novel he was never to finish. The last page he wrote there pictures a brilliant morning in Rochester: "Changes of glorious light from moving boughs, songs of birds, scents from gardens, woods, and fields – or, rather, from the one great garden of the whole cultivated island in its yielding time – penetrate the Cathedral, subdue its earthy odour, and preach of the Resurrection and the Life. The cold stone tombs of centuries ago grow warm; and flecks of brightness dart into the sternest marble corners of the building, fluttering there like wings." The words, so serene and still elegiac, are a fitting valedictory to the exalted, laughing, despairing, tormented, and triumphant career.

He was late leaving the chalet, but in the study before dinner he wrote a few letters. In one of them he quoted Friar Laurence's warning to Romeo: "These violent delights have violent ends." It was true. Looking at him across the table, Georgina was alarmed by the expression of pain on his face. Nevertheless he desired dinner to go on. He made a few random and disconnected remarks. Suddenly he said he had to go to London at once. Pushing back his crimson-damasked chair, he rose, but would have fallen where he stood if Georgina had not hurried around the table to support him. She tried to help him to a sofa. His body was too heavy for her strength, however, and she was obliged to lower him to the floor. "On the ground," he murmured faintly.

With the aid of the servants Georgina placed him on the sofa. She at once summoned a local surgeon, and dispatched telegrams to Mary and Katey and Dr Beard. Charley also received a telegram instructing him to bring a London physician for consultation. Mary and Katey arrived late that night with Frank Beard. It was judged safer not to move him, and all night he remained unconscious on the dining-room sofa. Early next morning Charley brought the London doctor. But nothing could be done. It was a paralytic stroke; an effusion of blood on the brain left no gleam of hope. Katey was sent back to London to break the news to her mother, and returned that afternoon, when Ellen Ternan also came. All day Dickens lay, breathing heavily, in the bright dining-room opening on the scarlet geraniums, musk, and blue lobelias in the conservatory. The day was mild and the windows were wide. Katey and Charley sat outside on the steps, where the scent of syringa was heavy in the air.

Just before six in the evening – Thursday, 9 June – Dickens's breathing grew fainter. At ten minutes past, he gave a deep sigh. His eyes were closed, but a tear welled from under his right eye and trickled down his cheek. Then he was gone. "Like a weary factory child," he had sunk to his narrow bed.

Charley went to the porch, where Mary Boyle had been sitting outside all afternoon, and brought her in to gaze on her adored friend. Harry arrived from Cambridge too late to see his father alive. The following day, 10 June, came John Everett Millais, who made a sketch of Dickens's bandaged head. With him he brought Thomas Woolner, the sculptor, for whom Dickens had promised to pose. Woolner took a death mask from which he later modelled a bust. The deep wrinkles, he said, had nearly faded from the face; Dickens looked calm.

The news of Dickens's death flashed over the world, overwhelming men and women everywhere, in India, in Australia, in America, with incredulous sorrow. "I never knew an author's death," Longfellow wrote Forster, "to cause such general mourning. It is no exaggeration to say that this whole country is stricken with grief." "My pen trembles between my fingers," said a writer in the *Moniteur des Arts*, "at the thought of all we – his family – have just lost in Charles Dickens." In Genoa, Mary Cowden Clarke read the telegraphed four words in an Italian newspaper " '*Carlo Dickens è morto*,' and the sun seemed suddenly blotted out." "The well of kindness" in him, exclaimed Blanchard Jerrold, "was open to mankind, and from it generations will drink: but it was never fathomed."

"It is an event world-wide," Carlyle wrote Forster: "a *unique* of talents suddenly extinct, and has 'eclipsed' (we too may say) 'the harmless gaiety of nations.' No death since 1866" – the year his own wife died – "has fallen on me with such a stroke, no Literary Man's hitherto ever did. The good, the gentle, ever friendly noble Dickens – every inch of him an Honest Man!" And as Carlyle reflected longer, he attained an insight more profound than he had ever voiced before. Beneath Dickens's "sparkling, clear, and sunny utterance," beneath his "bright and joyful sympathy with everything around him," Carlyle perceived, there were, "deeper than all, if one has the eye to see deep enough, dark, fateful silent elements, tragical to look upon, and hidden amid dazzling radiances as of the sun, the elements of death itself."

The London *Times* took the lead in demanding that Dickens's body be buried in Westminster Abbey. "Statesmen, men of science, philanthropists, the acknowledged benefactors of their race," it said editorially,

> might pass away, and yet not leave the void which will be caused by the death of Dickens. . . . Westminster Abbey is the peculiar resting place of English literary genius, and among those whose sacred dust lies there, or whose names are recorded on the walls, very few are more worthy than Charles Dickens of such a home. Fewer still, we believe, will be regarded with more honour as time passes, and his greatness grows upon us.

The Dean of Westminster sent a message that he was "prepared to receive any communication from the family respecting the burial." They had already learned that the little graveyard at the foot of the Castle was closed to further burials. So were the churches of Cobham and Shorne, where Dickens had sometimes thought he would like to lie. But the family had accepted an offer from the Dean and Chapter of Rochester to lay him to rest within the Cathedral itself, and a grave had been prepared in St Mary's Chapel when Dean Stanley's letter came into their hands. Forster and Charley went up to London to tell the Dean that the terms of Dickens's will bound them to an absolutely private and unannounced funeral. These instructions made impossible any ceremony of public homage. Dean Stanley, however, assured them that Dickens's wishes should be obeyed, and they yielded to the desire of the nation.

At six o'clock on the morning of 14 June a plain coffin left Gad's Hill and was brought in a special train to Charing Cross. There it was removed to a hearse without funeral trappings. Three coaches followed it to the Abbey. The first held those four of Dickens's children who were in England, Charley, Mary, Katey, and Harry. In the second were Georgina, Dickens's sister Letitia, Charley's wife, and John Forster. In the third were Frank Beard, Charles and Wilkie Collins, and Dickens's solicitor, Frederic Ouvry.

The bell of St Stephen's was just sounding the half-hour after nine when the procession reached the entrance to the Dean's Yard. All was still as the little cortège swept round the Broad Sanctuary and drove under the archway. Then, a moment later, the great bell began tolling. Through the western cloister door the body was conveyed along the nave into the South Transept, the Poets' Corner. In the peacefulness and silence of the shadowy arches the words of the burial service were said. There were no choristers, but at the end the organ sounded a Dead March. Last to turn away, when all was over, was a burly man tightly buttoned up in a black frock coat, who could not trust himself to speak.

Outside, the day grew sultry, but it was cool and dim beneath the vast stone vaulting. Already the public had somehow come to know, and a great crowd was gathered in the transept. Gazing down into the grave they saw the polished oak coffin, with the plain inscription, CHARLES DICKENS. "There was a wreath of white roses lying on the flags at his feet, a great bank of ferns at his head, rows of white and red roses down the sides."

"He sleeps as he should sleep," said an elegy in *Punch* –

> *He sleeps as he should sleep – among the great*
> *In the old Abbey: sleeps amid the few*
> *Of England's famous thousands whose high state*
> *Is to lie with her monarchs – monarchs too.*

Dean Stanley had given permission for the grave to be left open a few days, and even on that first day, before the afternoon papers bore the news, word continued to spread throughout the metropolis. Thousands came to pay the tribute of their hearts. Flowers were cast upon the coffin until the enclosure was heaped to overflowing. At six o'clock, when the Abbey closed, there were still 1,000 outside who had not yet obtained admittance. For two days more, while the grave remained open, the endless processions filed past, with tears and flowers innumerable. For many months after it was closed no day passed without still other mourners coming and leaving the Abbey floor around the great block of stone that bore Dickens's name a mound of fragrant colour.

At dusk on 16 June, the Abbey was closed to the public. From Dean Stanley Lord Houghton heard that the grave would not be closed until near midnight. With a lantern for his only light, he came and looked upon the coffin. It lay at the foot of the grave of Handel, with that of Macaulay by its side. A few feet away lay Johnson, and not far on each side in the solemn darkness were the busts of Milton and Spenser and the monuments of Dryden, Chaucer, and Shakespeare.

More than a hundred years have passed since Charles Dickens died. His passionate heart has long crumbled to dust. But the world he created shines with undying life, and the hearts of men still vibrate to his indignant anger, his love, his tears, his glorious laughter, and his triumphant faith in the dignity of man.

Index

Shorter writings by Dickens that appeared in *All the Year Round* and *Household Words* are all identified in the index by the abbreviations *A.Y.R.* or *H.W.* in parentheses after the title. Characters in his novels and stories are identified by indicating in parentheses the following abbreviations for the titles of the works in which they appear:

B.H.	*Bleak House*	*L.D.*	*Little Dorrit*
B.R.	*Barnaby Rudge*	*M.C.*	*Martin Chuzzlewit*
C.C.	*A Christmas Carol*	*N.N.*	*Nicholas Nickleby*
Chimes	*The Chimes*	*O.C.S.*	*The Old Curiosity Shop*
C. on H.	*The Cricket on the Hearth*	*O.M.F.*	*Our Mutual Friend*
D.C.	*David Copperfield*	*O.T.*	*Oliver Twist*
D. and S.	*Dombey and Son*	*P. from I.*	*Pictures from Italy*
E.D.	*The Mystery of Edwin Drood*	*P.P.*	*Pickwick Papers*
G.E.	*Great Expectations*	*S. by. B.*	*Sketches by Boz*
H.M.	*The Haunted Man*	*T.T.C.*	*A Tale of Two Cities*
H.T.	*Hard Times*	*U.T.*	*The Uncommercial Traveller*